D0022888

Bloom's Major Literary Characters

King Arthur

Nick Adams

George F. Babbitt

Elizabeth Bennet

Leopold Bloom

Holden Caulfield

Sir John Falstaff

Huck Finn

Frankenstein

Jay Gatsby

Hamlet

Willy Loman

Macbeth

Hester Prynne

Raskolnikov and Svidrigailov

Satan

Bloom's Major Literary Characters

Satan

Edited and with an introduction by
Harold Bloom
Sterling Professor of the Humanities
Yale University

CHELSEA HOUSE
PUBLISHERS
A Haights Cross Communications Company
Philadelphia

HOUSTON PUBLIC LIBRARY

RO1304 71090

©2005 by Chelsea House Publishers, a subsidiary of
Haights Cross Communications.

A Haights Cross Communications Company ®

www.chelseahouse.com

Introduction © 2005 by Harold Bloom.

All rights reserved. No part of this publication may be
reproduced or transmitted in any form or by any means
without the written permission of the publisher.

Printed and bound in the United States of America.

10   9   8   7   6   5   4   3   2   1

Library of Congress Cataloging-in-Publication Data

Satan / edited by Harold Bloom.
        p. cm. — (Major literary characters)
    Includes bibliographical references and index.
    ISBN 0-7910-8177-X (alk. paper)   0-7910-8386-1 (pb)
    1. Devil in literature. I. Bloom, Harold. II. Series.
    PN57.D4S28 2004
    809'.9333547—dc22

                            2004025649

Contributing editor: Camille-Yvette Welsch

Cover design by Keith Trego

Cover: © Chris Hellier/CORBIS

Layout by EJB Publishing Services

All links and web addresses were checked and verified to be correct at the time of
publication. Because of the dynamic nature of the web, some addresses and links may
have changed since publication and may no longer be valid.

Every effort has been made to trace the owners of copyrighted material and secure
copyright permission. Articles appearing in this volume generally appear much as they did
in their original publication with little to no editorial changes. Those interested in
locating the original source will find bibliographic information on the first page of each
article as well as in the bibliography and acknowledgments sections of this volume.

Contents

HAROLD BLOOM

The Analysis of Character

"Character," according to our dictionaries, still has as a primary meaning a graphic symbol, such as a letter of the alphabet. This meaning reflects the word's apparent origin in the ancient Greek character, a sharp stylus. *Charactēr* also meant the mark of the stylus' incisions. Recent fashions in literary criticism have reduced "character" in literature to a matter of marks upon a page. But our word "character" also has a very different meaning, matching that of the ancient Greek *ēthos*, "habitual way of life." Shall we say then that literary character is an imitation of human character, or is it just a grouping of marks? The issue is between a critic like Dr. Samuel Johnson, for whom words were as much like people as like things, and a critic like the late Roland Barthes, who told us that "the fact can only exist linguistically, as a term of discourse." Who is closer to our experience of reading literature, Johnson or Barthes? What difference does it make, if we side with one critic rather than the other?

Barthes is famous, like Foucault and other recent French theorists, for having added to Nietzsche's proclamation of the death of God a subsidiary demise, that of the literary author. If there are no authors, then there are no fictional personages, presumably because literature does not refer to a world outside language. Words indeed necessarily refer to other words in the first place, but the impact of words ultimately is drawn from a universe of fact. Stories, poems, and plays are recognizable as such because they are human utterances within traditions of utterances, and traditions, by achieving authority, become a kind of fact, or at least the sense of a fact. Our sense that literary characters, within the context of a fictive cosmos, indeed are fictional

personages is also a kind of fact. The meaning and value of every character
in a successful work of literary representation depend upon our ideas of
persons in the factual reality of our lives.

Literary character is always an invention, and inventions generally are
indebted to prior inventions. Shakespeare is the inventor of literary character
as we know it; he reformed the universal human expectations for the verbal
imitation of personality, and the reformation appears now to be permanent
and uncannily inevitable. Remarkable as the Bible and Homer are at
representing personages, their characters are relatively unchanging. They
age within their stories, but their habitual modes of being do not develop.
Jacob and Achilles unfold before us, but without metamorphoses. Lear and
Macbeth, Hamlet and Othello severely modify themselves not only by their
actions, but by their utterances, and most of all through *overhearing
themselves*, whether they speak to themselves or to others. Pondering what
they themselves have said, they will to change, and actually do change,
sometimes extravagantly yet always persuasively. Or else they suffer change,
without willing it, but in reaction not so much to their language as to their
relation to that language.

 I do not think it useful to say that Shakespeare successfully imitated
elements in our characters. Rather, it could be argued that he compelled
aspects of character to appear that previously were concealed, or not
available to representation. This is not to say that Shakespeare is God, but to
remind us that language is not God either. The mimesis of character in
Shakespeare's dramas now seems to us normative, and indeed became the
accepted mode almost immediately, as Ben Jonson shrewdly and somewhat
grudgingly implied. And yet, Shakespearean representation has surprisingly
little in common with the imitation of reality in Jonson or in Christopher
Marlowe. The origins of Shakespeare's originality in the portrayal of men
and women are to be found in the *Canterbury Tales* of Geoffrey Chaucer,
insofar as they can be located anywhere before Shakespeare himself,
Chaucer's savage and superb Pardoner overhears his own tale-telling, as well
as his mocking rehearsal of his own spiel, and through this overhearing he is
emboldened to forget himself, and enthusiastically urges all his fellow-
pilgrims to come forward to be fleeced by him. His self-awareness, and
apocalyptically rancid sense of spiritual fall, are preludes to the even grander
abysses of the perverted will in Iago and in Edmund. What might be called
the character trait of a negative charisma may be Chaucer's invention, but
came to its perfection in Shakespearean mimesis.

 The analysis of character is as much Shakespeare's invention as the
representation of character is, since Iago and Edmund are adepts at analyzing

both themselves and their victims. Hamlet, whose overwhelming charisma has many negative components, is certainly the most comprehensive of all literary characters, and so necessarily prophesies the labyrinthine complexities of the will in Iago and Edmund. Charisma, according to Max Weber, its first codifier, is primarily a natural endowment, and implies a primordial and idiosyncratic power over nature, and so finally over death. Hamlet's uncanniness is at its most suggestive in the scene of his long dying, where the audience, through the mediation of Horatio, itself is compelled to meditate upon suicide, if only because outliving the prince of Denmark scarcely seems an option.

Shakespearean representation has usurped not only our sense of literary character, but our sense of ourselves as characters, with Hamlet playing the part of the largest of these usurpations. Insofar as we have an idea of human disinterestedness, we tend to derive it from the Hamlet of Act V, whose quietism has about it a ghostly authority. Oscar Wilde, in his profound and profoundly witty dialogue, "The Decay of Lying," expressed a permanent insight when he insisted that art shaped every era, far more than any age formed art. Life imitates art, we imitate Shakespeare, because without Shakespeare we would perish for lack of images. Wilde's grandest audacity demystifies Shakespearean mimesis with a Shakespearean vivaciousness: "This unfortunate aphorism about art holding the mirror up to Nature is deliberately said by Hamlet in order to convince the bystanders of his absolute insanity in all art-matters." Of *Hamlet*'s influence upon the ages Wilde remarked that: "The world has grown sad because a puppet was once melancholy." "Puppet" is Wilde's own deconstruction, a brilliant reminder that Shakespeare's artistry of illusion has so mastered reality as to have changed reality, evidently forever.

The analysis of character, as a critical pursuit, seems to me as much a Shakespearean invention as literary character was, since much of what we know about how to analyze character necessarily follows Shakespearean procedures. His hero-villains, from Richard III through Iago, Edmund, and Macbeth, are shrewd and endless questers into their own self-motivations. If we could bear to see Hamlet, in his unwearied negations, as another hero-villain, then we would judge him the supreme analyst of the darker recalcitrances in the selfhood. Freud followed the pre-Socratic Empedocles, in arguing that character is fate, a frightening doctrine that maintains the fear that there are no accidents, that overdetermination rules us all of our lives. Hamlet assumes the same, yet adds to this argument the terrible passivity he manifests in Act V. Throughout Shakespeare's tragedies, the most interesting personages seem doom-eager, reminding us again that a Shakespearean reading of Freud would be more illuminating than a Freudian exegesis of

Shakespeare. We learn more when we discover Hamlet in the Freudian Death Drive, than when we read *Beyond the Pleasure Principle* into *Hamlet*.

In Shakespearean comedy, character achieves its true literary apotheosis, which is the representation of the inner freedom that can be created by great wit alone. Rosalind and Falstaff, perhaps alone among Shakespeare's personages, match Hamlet in wit, though hardly in the metaphysics of consciousness. Whether in the comic or the modern mode, Shakespeare has set the standard of measurement in the balance between character and passion.

In Shakespeare the self is more dramatized than theatricalized, which is why a Shakespearean reading of Freud works out so well. Character-formation after the passing of the Oedipal stage takes the place of fetishistic fragmentings of the self. Critics who now call literary character into question, and who proclaim also the death of the author, invariably also regard all notions, literary and human, of a stable character as being mere reductions of deeper pre-Oedipal desires. It becomes clear that the fortunes of literary character rise and fall with the prestige of normative conceptions of the ego. Shakespeare's Iago, who wars against being, may be the first deconstructionist of the self, with his proclamation of "I am not what I am." This constitutes the necessary prologue to any view that would regard a fixed ego as a virtual abnormality. But deconstructions of the self are no more modern than Modernism is. Like literary modernism, the decentered ego came out of the Hellenistic culture of ancient Alexandria. The Gnostic heretics believed that the psyche, like the body, was a fallen entity, mechanically fashioned by the Demiurge or false creator. They held however that each of us possessed also a spark or pneuma, which was a fragment of the original Abyss or true, alien God. The soul or psyche within every one of us was thus at war with the self or pneuma, and only that sparklike self could be saved.

Shakespeare, following after Chaucer in this respect, was the first and remains still the greatest master of representing character both as a stable soul and a wavering self. There is a substance that endures in Shakespeare's figures, and there is also a quicksilver rendition of the unsettling sparks. Racine and Tolstoy, Balzac and Dickens, follow in Shakespeare's wake by giving us some sense of pre-Oedipal sparks or drives, and considerably more sense of post-Oedipal character and personality, stabilizations or sublimations of the fetish-seeking drives. Critics like Leo Bersani and René Girard argue eloquently against our taking this mimesis as the only proper work of literature. I would suggest that strong fictions of the self, from the Bible through Samuel Beckett, necessarily participate in both modes, the sublimation of desire, and the persistence of a primordial desire. The mystery of Hamlet or of Lear is intimately invested in the tangled mixture of the two modes of representation.

Psychic mobility is proposed by Bersani as the ideal to which deconstructions of the literary self may yet guide us. The ideal has its pathos, but the realities of literary representation seem to me very different, perhaps destructively so. When a novelist like D.H. Lawrence sought to reduce his characters to Eros and the Death Drive, he still had to persuade us of his authority at mimesis by lavishing upon the figures of *The Rainbow* and *Women in Love* all of the vivid stigmata of normative personality. Birkin and Ursula may represent antithetical and uncanny drives, but they develop and change as characters pondering their own pronouncements and reactions to self and others. The cost of a non-Shakespearean representation is enormous. Pynchon, in *The Crying of Lot 49* and *Gravity's Rainbow*, evades the burden of the normative by resorting to something like Christopher Marlowe's art of caricature in *The Jew of Malta*. Marlowe's Barabas is a marvelous rhetorician, yet he is a cartoon alongside the troublingly equivocal Shylock. Pynchon's personages are deliberate cartoons also, as flat as comic strips. Marlowe's achievement, and Pynchon's, are beyond dispute, yet they are like the prelude and the postlude to Shakespearean reality. They do not wish to engage with our hunger for the empirical world and so they enter the problematic cosmos of literary fantasy.

No writer, not even Shakespeare or Proust, alters the available stock that we agree to call reality, but Shakespeare, more than any other, does show us how much of reality we could encounter if only we retained adequate desire. The strong literary representation of character is already an analysis of character, and is part of the healing work of a literary culture, which implicitly seeks to cure violence through a normative mimesis of ego, *as if it were stable*, whether in actuality it is or is not. I do not believe that this is a social quest taken on by literary culture, but rather that we confront here the aesthetic essence of what makes a culture *literary*, rather than metaphysical or ethical or religious. A culture becomes literary when its conceptual modes have failed it, which means when religion, philosophy, and science have begun to lose their authority. If they cannot heal violence, then literature attempts to do so, which may be only a turning inside out of the critical arguments of Girard and Bersani.

I conclude by offering a particular instance or special case as a paradigm for the healing enterprise that is at once the representation and the analysis of literary character. Let us call it the aesthetics of being outraged, or rather of successfully representing the state of being outraged. W.C. Fields was one modern master of such representation, and Nathanael West was another, as was Faulkner before him. Here also the greatest master remains Shakespeare, whose Macbeth, himself a bloody outrage, yet retains our imaginative sympathy precisely because he grows increasingly outraged as he experiences the equivocation of the fiend that lies like truth. The double-natured promises and the prophecies of the weird sisters finally induce in Macbeth an apocalyptic version of the stage actor's anxiety at missing cues, the horror of a phantasmagoric stage fright of missing one's time, of always reacting too late. Macbeth, a veritable monster of solipsistic inwardness but no intellectual, counters his dilemma by fresh murders, that prolong him in time yet provoke him only to a perpetually freshened sense of being outraged, as all his expectations become still worse confounded. We are moved by Macbeth, however estrangedly, because his terrible inwardness is a paradigm for our own solipsism, but also because none of us can resist a strong and successful representation of the human in a state of being outraged.

The ultimate outrage is the necessity of dying, an outrage concealed in a multitude of masks, including the tyrannical ambitions of Macbeth. I suspect that our outrage at being outraged is the most difficult of all our affects for us to represent to ourselves, which is why we are so inclined to imaginative sympathy for a character who strongly conveys that affect to us. The Shrike of West's *Miss Lonelyhearts* or Faulkner's Joe Christmas of *Light in August* are crucial modern instances, but such figures can be located in many other works, since the ability to represent this extreme emotion is one of the tests that strong writers are driven to set for themselves.

However a reader seeks to reduce literary character to a question of marks on a page, she will come at last to the impasse constituted by the thought of death, her death, and before that to all the stations of being outraged that memorialize her own drive towards death. In reading, she quests for evidences that are strong representations, whether of her desire or her despair. Such questings constitute the necessary basis for the analysis of literary character, an enterprise that always will survive every vagary of critical fashion.

Editor's Note

My Introduction moves from the Mephistophilus of Marlowe's *Doctor Faustus* to Milton's heroic Satan in *Paradise Lost* and then on to Satan-as-tempter in *Paradise Regained*.

William Bysshe Stein studies the Faustian Satan of Hawthorne's "The Haunted Mind," while C.S. Lewis, an eminent Angel (in William Blake's sense), travesties the Miltonic Satan as a foolish monomaniac.

Mark Twain, no Angel, is analyzed by Stanley Brodwin as a Satanic theologian in *The Mysterious Stranger*, after which Frank Kastor traces different versions of the literary Satan before Milton.

J.W. Smeed chronicles the Devil's decline in various Faustian works, while Stella Purce Revard shrewdly compares the Miltonic Satan's debasement to the stalwart glory of the great rebel in the Dutch post Vondel and other celebrants.

A Satanic authority, Jeffrey Burton Russell, considers Lucifer in two essays, one on the medieval Devil and the other in the High Romantic Satan.

A major scholar of Gnosticism and early Christianity, Elaine Pagels, exposes the vast conflation of Satan in the Gospels as compared to the Hebrew Bible, after which Laura Lunger Knoppers concludes this book with Milton's Protestant vision of a Papist Satan in *Paradise Regained*.

HAROLD BLOOM

Introduction

I

Doctor Faustus is now regarded by most critics as Marlowe's greatest play. Marlowe had a collaborator (perhaps two) in *Doctor Faustus*, and we do not seem to have an authentic text of the play. Many of the comic scenes are scarcely readable, and no other Elizabethan play mixes superb and dreadful writing to the extent that this one does.

Marlowe, whose learning was curious and extensive, presumably knew that Faustus (Latin for "the favored one") was the cognomen taken by Simon Magus, founder of the Gnostic heresy, when he went to Rome. Doctor Faustus is a Hermetic drama in its range and implications, but it has few Gnostic overtones. It scarcely matters whether its overt theology is Catholic, Lutheran, or Calvinist, since the theology is there as a good, boisterous mythology that the hyperbolist Marlowe is happy to exploit. As many critics have recognized, Marlowe maintains his distance from Faustus and expresses himself fairly directly through the splendidly bitter Mephostophilis, who walks about in the likeness of a friar and who suffers a profound nostalgia for the loss of heaven. Marlowe is not representing himself in or as Mephostophilis and yet clearly Mephostophilis, not Faustus, is the play's intellectual, its advanced, or modern, thinker. He cannot exactly be called disinterested and yet he is remarkably detached, while carefully always knowing both his limits and his allegiances. Though a loyal follower of Lucifer, his rhetoric indicates a personal and poignant distance from his own camp and conveys a more formidable pathos than Faustus himself will evoke until his final speech. The opening dialogue between Faustus and his personal devil (as it were) provides a remarkable dramatic contrast between the two, a contrast in which we find we prefer Mephostophilis to the human magus who thinks he has summoned this spirit:

> MEPHOSTOPHILIS: I am a servant to great Lucifer,
>   And may not follow thee without his leave;
>   No more than he commands must we perform.
> FAUSTUS: Did not he charge thee to appear to me?
> MEPHOSTOPHILIS: No, I came now hither of mine own accord.
> FAUSTUS: Did not my conjuring speeches raise thee? Speak.
> MEPHOSTOPHILIS: That was the cause, but yet *per accidens*;
>   For when we hear one rack the name of God,
>   Abjure the scriptures and his saviour Christ,
>   We fly in hope to get his glorious soul;
>   Nor will we come unless he use such means
>   Whereby he is in danger to be damned.
>   Therefore the shortest cut for conjuring
>   Is stoutly to abjure the Trinity
>   And pray devoutly to the prince of hell.
> FAUSTUS: So Faustus hath already done, and holds this principle:
>   There is no chief but only Belzebub,
>   To whom Faustus doth dedicate himself.
>   This word "damnation" terrifies not him,
>   For he confounds hell in Elysium.
>   His ghost be with the old philosophers.
>   But leaving these vain trifles of men's souls,
>   Tell me, what is that Lucifer, thy lord?
> MEPHOSTOPHILIS: Arch-regent and commander of all spirits.
> FAUSTUS: Was not that Lucifer an angel once?
> MEPHOSTOPHILIS: Yes Faustus, and most dearly loved of God.
> FAUSTUS: How come it then that he is prince of devils?
> MEPHOSTOPHILIS: O, by aspiring pride and insolence,
>   For which God threw him from the face of heaven.
> FAUSTUS: And what are you that live with Lucifer?
> MEPHOSTOPHILIS: Unhappy spirits that fell with Lucifer,
>   Conspired against our God with Lucifer,
>   And are for ever damned with Lucifer.

FAUSTUS: Where are you damned?
MEPHOSTOPHILIS: In hell.
FAUSTUS: How comes it then that thou art out of hell?
MEPHOSTOPHILIS: Why, this is hell, nor am I out of it.
    Think'st thou that I who saw the face of God
    And tasted the eternal joys of heaven,
    Am not tormented with ten thousand hells
    In being deprived of everlasting bliss?
    O Faustus, leave these frivolous demands,
    Which strikes a terror to my fainting soul.
                                        (3.40–82)

Lucifer would not be pleased by the language of his loyal but elaborately wistful follower, we must suspect. The hints that Milton took from Marlowe are plain enough, but even the sublimity of the Miltonic Satan of the early books of *Paradise Lost* does not allow for anything quite like the epigrammatic snap of the justly famous "Why, this is hell, nor am I out of it," the most Gnostic statement in the drama. Harry Levin rather strangely compared Mephostophilis to Dostoevsky's Porfiry, the examining magistrate in Crime and Punishment. But Porfiry is a good man; Mephostophilis, I venture, is Marlowe's version of the Accuser, the Satan who appears at the opening of the Book of Job. Blake, in a Gnostic insight, called the Accuser the God of this world. Mephostophilis has no such pretensions and is closer to the biblical Book of Job's Accuser because he functions as what Saul Bellow rather nastily calls a Reality Instructor. Mephostophilis has uncanny insight into Faustus, indeed he seems to be the Daemon or Genius of Faustus, perhaps the spiritual form that Faustus will take on in Hell.

Mephostophilis has a horror of marriage. Not merely because it is a sacrament but because this "ceremonial toy" might threaten his curious intimacy with Faustus. This aversion to connubial bliss is mild compared to the exalted view of man held by this surprising spirit, who seems both more of a Hermeticist and more of a Humanist than either Marlowe or Faustus:

FAUSTUS: When I behold the heavens then I repent,
    And Curse thee, wicked Mephostophilis,
    Because thou hast deprived me of those joys.
MEPHOSTOPHILIS: 'Twas thine own seeking, Faustus, thank
    thyself.
    But think'st thou heaven is such a glorious thing?
    I tell thee, Faustus, it is not half so fair
    As thou or any man that breathes on earth.

> FAUSTUS: How prov'st thou that?
> MEPHOSTOPHILIS: 'Twas made for man; then he's more
>   excellent.
> FAUSTUS: If heaven was made for man, 'twas made for me.
>   I will renounce this magic and repent.
>   (6.1–11)

Mephostophilis evidently desires Faustus, at least aesthetically, and we remember his initial insistence that he first came to Faustus not because he was conjured, but of his own accord. Forbidden by Lucifer to love the creator, Mephostophilis loves the creature and refuses to discuss origins:

> FAUSTUS: Well, I am answered. Now tell me, who made the
>   world?
> MEPHOSTOPHILIS: I will not.
> FAUSTUS: Sweet Mephostophilis, tell me.
> MEPHOSTOPHILIS: Move me not, Faustus.
> FAUSTUS: Villain, have not I bound thee to tell me anything?
> MEPHOSTOPHILIS: Ay, that is not against our kingdom:
>   This is. Thou art damned, think thou of hell.
> FAUSTUS: Think, Faustus, upon God, that made the world.
> MEPHOSTOPHILIS: Remember this—
> FAUSTUS: Ay, go, accursèd spirit to ugly hell.
>   'Tis thou hast damned distressèd Faustus' soul.
>   Is't not too late?
>   (6.67–78)

It is definitely too late, and I wonder at the exegetes who debate the supposedly relevant theologies—Catholic, Calvinist, Lutheran—and their presumed effect upon whether Faustus either will not or cannot repent. Marlowe is no more interested in letting Faustus escape than in giving the wretched Edward II a good death. The play's glory is in the last speech of Faustus, an extraordinary rhapsody whose sixty lines form one of the great dramatic poems in the language. All of it is magnificent and subtle, but the final line almost transcends Faustus and his situation:

> I'll burn my books!—Ah, Mephostophilis!

To burn his books of magic or Hermetic knowledge would be to burn himself, for he has become what he desired to become, his daemonic books. That "Ah, Mephostophilis!" spoken to the spirit who leads him off the stage is a sigh of surrender, a realization that, like Mephostophilis, he goes, after all, of his own accord and not just because he is summoned. We are not much moved by this damnation, any more than Marlowe could be much moved. Barabas has an extraordinary personality, and so in very different ways do Tamburlaine and Edward II. Doctor Faustus is scarcely a person and so hardly a personality at all. He is Marlowe's Victim or scapegoat, sacrificed in Marlowe's own Black Mass, so as to utter a gorgeous, broken music in his demise. Simon Magus, the original Faustus, was a sublime charlatan; the nihilistic genius of Marlowe was content at the end with a merely eloquent charlatan.

II

By 1652, before his forty-fourth birthday and with his long-projected major poem unwritten, Milton was completely blind. In 1660, with arrangements for the Stuart Restoration well under way, the blind poet identified himself with the prophet Jeremiah, as if he would "tell the very soil itself what her perverse inhabitants are deaf to," vainly warning a divinely chosen people "now choosing them a captain back for Egypt, to bethink themselves a little, and consider whither they are rushing." These words are quoted from the second edition of *The Ready and Easy Way*, a work which marks the end of Milton's temporal prophecy and the beginning of his greater work, the impassioned meditations upon divine providence and human nature. In these [meditations] Milton abandons the field of his defeat, and leaves behind him also the songs of triumph he might have sung in praise of a reformed society and its imaginatively integrated citizens. He changes those notes to tragic, and praises, when he praises at all, what he calls the better fortitude of patience, the hitherto unsung theme of Heroic Martyrdom. Adam, Christ, and Samson manifest an internal mode of heroism that Satan can neither understand nor overcome, a heroism that the blind Puritan prophet himself is called upon to exemplify in the England of the Restoration.

Milton had planned a major poem since he was a young man, and he had associated his composition of the poem with the hope that it would be a celebration of a Puritan reformation of all England. He had prophesied of the coming time that "amidst the hymns and hallelujahs of the saints some one may perhaps be heard offering at high strains in new and lofty measures to sing and celebrate thy divine mercies and marvellous judgements in the land throughout all ages." This vision clearly concerns a national epic, very probably on a British rather than a Biblical theme. That poem, had it been written, would have rivaled the great poem of Milton's master, Spenser, who in a profound sense was Milton's "Original," to cite Dryden's testimony.

Paradise Lost is not the poem that Milton had prophesied in the exuberance of his youth, but we may guess it to be a greater work than the one we lost, for the unwritten poem would not have had the Satan who is at once the aesthetic glory and the moral puzzle of Milton's epic of loss and disillusion.

The form of *Paradise Lost* is based on Milton's modification of Virgil's attempt to rival Homer's *Iliad*, but the content of Milton's epic has a largely negative relation to the content of the *Iliad* or the *Aeneid*. Milton's "one greater Man," Christ, is a hero who necessarily surpasses all the sons of Adam, including Achilles and Aeneas, just as he surpasses Adam or archetypal Man himself. Milton delights to speak of himself as soaring above the sacred places of the classical muses and as seeking instead "thee *Sion* and the flow'ry brooks beneath," Siloam, by whose side the Hebrew prophets walked. For *Paradise Lost*, despite C.S. Lewis's persuasive assertions to the contrary, is specifically a Protestant and Puritan poem, created by a man who finally became a Protestant church of one, a sect unto himself. The poem's true muse is "that eternal Spirit who can enrich with all utterance and knowledge, and sends out his seraphim, with the hallowed fire of his altar, to touch and purify the lips of whom he pleases." This Spirit is one that prefers for its shrine, in preference to all Temples of organized faith, the upright and pure heart of the isolated Protestant poet, who carries within himself the extreme Christian individualism of the Puritan Left Wing. Consequently, the poem's doctrine is not "the great central tradition" that Lewis finds it to be, but an imaginative variation on that tradition. Milton believed in the doctrines of the Fall, natural corruption, regeneration through grace, an aristocracy of the elect, and Christian Liberty, all of them fundamental to Calvinist belief, and yet Milton was no orthodox Calvinist, as Arthur Barker has demonstrated. The poet refused to make a sharp distinction between the natural and the spiritual in man, and broke from Calvin in his theory of regeneration. Milton's doctrine of predestination, as seen in *Paradise Lost*, is both general and conditional; the Spirit does not make particular and absolute choices. When regeneration comes, it heals not only man's spirit but his nature as well, for Milton could not abide in dualism. Barker makes the fine contrast between Milton and Calvin that in Calvin even good men are altogether dependent upon God's will, and not on their own restored faculties, but in Milton the will is made free again, and man is restored to his former liberty. The hope for man in *Paradise Lost* is that Adam's descendants will find their salvation in the fallen world, once they have accepted Christ's sacrifice and its human consequences, by taking a middle way between those who would deny the existence of sin altogether, in a wild freedom founded upon a misunderstanding of election, and those who would repress man's nature that spirit might be more free. The regenerated descendants of Adam are evidence that God's grace need not provide for the abolition of the natural man.

To know and remember this as Milton's ideal is to be properly prepared to encounter the dangerous greatness of Satan in the early books of *Paradise Lost*. The poem is a theodicy, and like *Job* seeks to justify the ways of Jehovah to man, but unlike the poet of *Job* Milton insisted that reason could comprehend God's justice, for Milton's God is perfectly reasonable and the perfection of man in Christ would raise human reason to a power different only in degree from its fallen status. The poet of *Job* has an aesthetic advantage over Milton, for most readers rightly prefer a Voice out of a Whirlwind, fiercely asking rhetorical questions, to Milton's sophistical Schoolmaster of Souls in Book III of *Paradise Lost*. But Milton's God is out of balance because Satan is so magnificently flawed in presentation, and to account for the failure of God as a dramatic character the reader is compelled to enter upon the most famous and vexing of critical problems concerning *Paradise Lost*, the Satanic controversy itself. Is Satan in some sense heroic, or is he merely a fool?

The anti-Satanist school of critics has its great ancestor in Addison, who found Satan's sentiments to be "suitable to a created being of the most exalted and most depraved nature.... Amid those impieties which this enraged spirit utters ... the author has taken care to introduce none that is not big with absurdity, and incapable of shocking a religious reader." Dr. Johnson followed Addison with more eloquence: "The malignity of Satan foams in haughtiness and obstinacy; but his expressions are commonly general, and no otherwise offensive than as they are wicked." The leading modern anti-Satanists are the late Charles Williams and C.S. Lewis, for whom Milton's Satan is to some extent an absurd egoist, not altogether unlike Meredith's Sir Willoughby Patterne. So Lewis states "it is a mistake to demand that Satan, any more than Sir Willoughby, should be able to rant and posture through the whole universe without, sooner or later, awaking the comic spirit." Satan is thus an apostle of Nonsense, and his progressive degeneration in the poem is only the inevitable working-out of his truly absurd choice when he first denied his status as another of God's creatures.

The Satanist school of critics finds its romantic origins in two very great poets profoundly and complexly affected by Milton, Blake and Shelley. This tradition of romantic Satanism needs to be distinguished from the posturings of its Byronic-Napoleonic cousin, with which anti-Satanists have loved to confound it. The greatest of anti-Satanists (because the most attracted to Satan), Coleridge, was himself guilty of this confusion. But though he insisted upon reading into Milton's Satan the lineaments of

Bonaparte, Coleridge's reading of the Satanic character has never been equaled by any modern anti-Satanist:

> But in its utmost abstraction and consequent state of reprobation, the will becomes Satanic pride and rebellious self-idolatry in the relations of the spirit to itself, and remorseless despotism relatively to others; the more hopeless as the more obdurate by its subjugation of sensual impulses, by its superiority to toil and pain and pleasure; in short, by the fearful resolve to find in itself alone the one absolute motive of action, under which all other motives from within and from without must be either subordinated or crushed.

Against this reading of the Satanic predicament we can set the dialectical ironies of Blake in *The Marriage of Heaven and Hell* and the imaginative passion of Shelley in his Preface to *Prometheus Unbound* and *A Defence of Poetry*. For Blake the Satan of Books I and II supremely embodies human desire, the energy that alone can create. But desire restrained becomes passive, until it is only a shadow of desire. God and Christ in *Paradise Lost* embody reason and restraint, and their restriction of Satan causes him to forget his own passionate desires, and to accept a categorical morality that he can only seek to invert. But a poet is by necessity of the party of energy and desire; reason and restraint cannot furnish the stuff of creativity. So Milton, as a true poet, wrote at liberty when he portrayed Devils and Hell, and in fetters when he described Angels and God. For Hell is the active life springing from energy, and Heaven only the passive existence that obeys reason.

Blake was too subtle to portray Satan as being even the unconscious hero of the poem. Rather, he implied that the poem can have no hero because it too strongly features Milton's self-abnegation in assigning human creative power to its diabolical side. Shelley went further, and claimed Satan as a semi-Promethean or flawed hero, whose character engenders in the reader's mind a pernicious casuistry of humanist argument against theological injustice. Shelley more directly fathered the Satanist school by his forceful statement of its aesthetic case: "Nothing can exceed the energy and magnificence of Satan as expressed in *Paradise Lost*." Whatever else, Shelley concluded, might be said for the Christian basis of the poem, it was clear that Milton's Satan as a moral being was far superior to Milton's God.

Each reader of *Paradise Lost* must find for himself the proper reading of Satan, whose appeal is clearly all but universal. Amid so much magnificence it is difficult to choose a single passage from *Paradise Lost* as surpassing all others, but I incline to the superlative speech of Satan on top of Mount Niphates (Book IV, ll.32–113), which is the text upon which the anti-Satanist, Satanist, or some compromise attitude must finally rest. Here Satan makes his last choice, and ceases to be what he was in the early books of the poem. All that the anti-Satanists say about him is true *after* this point; all or almost all claimed for him by the Satanists is true *before* it. When this speech is concluded, Satan has become Blake's "shadow of desire," and he is on the downward path that will make him "as big with absurdity" as ever Addison and Lewis claimed him to be. Nothing that can be regenerated remains in Satan, and the rift between his self-ruined spirit and his radically corrupted nature widens until he is the hissing serpent of popular tradition, plucking greedily at the Dead Sea fruit of Hell in a fearful parody of Eve's Fall.

It is on Mount Niphates again that Satan, now a mere (but very subtle) tempter, stands when he shows Christ the kingdoms of this world in the brief epic, *Paradise Regained*. "Brief epic" is the traditional description of this poem (published in 1671, four years after *Paradise Lost*), but the description has been usefully challenged by several modern critics. E.M.W. Tillyard has warned against judging the poem by any kind of epic standard and has suggested instead that it ought to be read as a kind of Morality play, while Arnold Stein has termed it an internal drama, set in the Son of God's mind. Louis L. Martz has argued, following Tillyard, that the poem is an attempt to convert Virgil's *Georgics* into a mode for religious poetry, and ought therefore to be read as both a didactic work and a formal meditation on the Gospel. *Paradise Regained* is so subdued a poem when compared to *Paradise Lost* that we find real difficulty in reading it as epic. Yet it does resemble *Job*, which Milton gave as the possible model for a brief epic, for like *Job* it is essentially a structure of gathering self-awareness, of the protagonist and hero recognizing himself in his relation to God. Milton's Son of Man is obedient where Milton's Adam was disobedient; Job was not quite either until God spoke to him and demonstrated the radical incompatibility involved in any mortal's questionings of divine purpose. Job, until his poem's climax, is an epic hero because he has an unresolved conflict within himself, between his own conviction of righteousness and his moral outrage at the calamities that have come upon him despite his righteousness. Job needs to overcome the temptations afforded him by this conflict, including those offered by his comforters (to deny his own righteousness) and by his finely laconic wife (to curse God and die). The temptations of Milton's Son of God (the poet's fondness for this name of Christ is another testimony to his Hebraic preference for the Father over the Son) are not easy for us to sympathize with in any very dramatic way, unlike the temptations of Job, who is a man like ourselves. But again Milton is repeating the life-long quest of his poetry; to see man as an integrated unity of distinct natures, body and soul harmonized. In Christ these natures are perfectly unified, and so the self-realization of Christ is an image of the possibility of human integration. Job learns not to tempt God's patience too far; Christ learns who he is, and in that moment of self-revelation Satan is smitten with amazement and falls as by the blow of a Hercules. Milton had seen himself in *Paradise Lost* as Abdiel, the faithful Angel who will not follow Satan in rebellion against God, defying thus the scorn of his fellows. Less consciously, something crucial in Milton had found its way into the Satan of the opening books, sounding a stoic defiance of adversity. In *Paradise Regained* Milton, with genuine humility, is exploring the Jobean problem within himself. Has he, as a Son of God also, tried God's patience too far, and can he at length overcome the internal temptations that beset a proud spirit reduced to being a voice in the wilderness? The poet's conquest over himself is figured in the greater Son of God's triumphant endurance, and in the quiet close of *Paradise Regained*, where the Savior returns to his mother's house to lead again, for a while, the private life of contemplation and patience while waiting upon God's will, not the public life forever closed to Milton.

WILLIAM BYSSHE STEIN

The Devils of Hawthorne's Faust Myth

With renewed sincerity Hawthorne declares in *Twice-Told Tales* that the archetypal covenant with the devil most persuasively symbolizes the enigma of human destiny.[1] This statement occurs in "The Haunted Mind," a narrative that defines the creative patterns of Hawthorne's imagination. In a few words he unbosoms the secret inspiration to which he rarely alludes directly: "there is no name for him unless it be Fatality, an emblem of the evil influence that rules your fortunes; a demon to whom you subjected yourself by some error at the outset of life, and were bound his slave forever, by once obeying him. See! those fiendish lineaments graven on the darkness, the writhed lip of scorn, the mockery of the living eye, the pointed finger, touching the sore place in your heart!" As Hawthorne speculates on the different literary forms that the idea might wear, he stumbles upon an experiential equivalent in the spiritual state of the mind represented by remorse, where riotously cavort "the devils of a guilty heart, that holds its hell within itself."[2] And here presented clearly, for the first time, is the hypothesis of universal moral truth: ordeal by sin. This mythic conception, as he develops the ramifications of his Faust myth, will activate the plots of such tales as "John Inglefield's Thanksgiving" and "The Minister's Black Veil." When at times he feels that his preoccupation with diabolic symbolism reflects his own disturbed consciousness, he reassures himself by fixing his

From *Hawthorne's Faust: A Study of the Devil Archetype.* © 1953 by the University of Florida.

attention upon the realities of life to discover that "the fiends [are] anywhere but in [his] haunted mind."[3] In the parallel between human life and the inspiration which he cultivates, he observes: "In both you emerge from mystery, pass through a vicissitude that you can but imperfectly control, and are borne on to another mystery." The point of view is singularly rewarding: the imagination "strays, like a free citizen, among the people of a shadowy world, beholding strange sights, yet without wonder or dismay."[4]

The prerequisite to a consuming interest in the lives of other individuals is a Faustian curiosity about oneself. Hawthorne discloses this attitude in "Monsieur du Miroir." His image in a mirror taunts him with the ontological mystery of existence. The confused inconsistencies of man's spiritual life, he confesses, must ever remain insoluble unless he can unravel the secret motivations of his own being: "I will be self-contemplative, as Nature bids me, and make him [the other self] the picture or visible type of what I muse upon, that my mind may not wander so vaguely as heretofore, chasing its own shadow through a chaos and catching only the monsters that abide there. Then will we turn our thoughts to the spiritual world ..."[5] If the sphinx in the mirror should deign to commit himself, then Hawthorne may legitimately probe into the multifarious expressions of human nature. He is not content to accept passively the limitations imposed upon his knowledge by God. Some uncontrollable impulse of his soul urges him to lift the veil that divine intelligence has dropped before his eyes: "A few words, perhaps, might satisfy the feverish yearning of my soul for some master thought that should guide me through this labyrinth of life, teaching wherefore I was born, and how to do my task on earth, and what is death."[6] Thus Hawthorne submits the thesis that man's spiritual unrest derives from his Faustian desire to apprehend the eternal truths of the universe. Though they forever elude the grasp of his intelligence, nevertheless they retain the ambiguous reality of the fleeting reflections that haunt the face of a mirror. But the Faustian soul will have no peace until it has realized its destiny, however vague its promptings, however illicit its quest. In "The Ambitious Guest" and "The Threefold Destiny," Hawthorne deals with the ironic configurations of this compulsive yearning; in "The Great Carbuncle" and "The Prophetic Pictures," he warns of the moral perversions that attend desperate Faustian enterprises.

It is necessary to remember that Hawthorne was not morbidly serious, for in evolving his Faust myth he also investigated its potential of humor. He recognized that not all the foibles of mankind were worthy of moral consideration; yet, as he pondered them, he could not resist attempting their solution with the Faustian equation. In the lighter variations of diabolic myth, as represented in the didactic folk tale, he found his prototype of the puckish demon. This incomparable artificer, who was not at all interested in immortal souls, tempted his victims into laughably gigantic follies. Hawthorne first mentions the comic devil in "The Seven Vagabonds." The association is aroused by his meeting with a wandering fortune-teller and conjurer who "pretended to familiarity with the Devil...." But so far as Hawthorne is able to judge, the scheming old man is only a shallow counterpart of the evil spirit with whom he professes intimacy. His mental and moral traits resemble those of a down-at-the-heel Mephistopheles: "Among them might be reckoned a love of deception for its own sake, a shrewd eye and keen relish for human weakness and ridiculous infirmity, and the talent of petty fraud. Thus to this old man there would be pleasure even in the consciousness so insupportable to some minds, that his whole life was a cheat upon the world...."[7] This undignified disciple of the mighty Lucifer appears in "Peter Goldthwaite's Treasure" and "Mrs. Bullfrog."

Though Washington Irving's "The Devil and Tom Walker" is usually called the "comic New England *Faust*," on the basis of sheer humor Hawthorne's "Peter Goldthwaite's Treasure" perhaps has a more legitimate claim to the title. Peter is a crackbrained schemer, impatient of ordinary business methods. He trades only in bubbles and wishful dreams, the vast fortunes of legendary El Doradoes. He is at last compelled to pin his hope for riches on the tradition that his great grand-uncle once hid a fabulous treasure in the ancestral mansion, the last of Peter's possessions. Rumor had it that the uncle had acquired this vast wealth through a deal with "Old Scratch," but ultimately the devil had tricked the elder Peter by "some secret impediment ... [which] debarred him from the enjoyment of his riches."[8] The heir chooses to ignore this part of the old wives' tale, and begins to disembowel the house, confident of uncovering untold wealth; symbolically he is emptying himself of all desire to live within ordinary society.

Throughout the remainder of the story Hawthorne uses the symbol of the roguish devil of the popular Faustian folk tale to amplify Peter's stupendous folly. Tabitha, Peter's witch-like housekeeper, tells her master that he ought to take cognizance of his uncle's bad luck, for, as the latter "went to unlock the chest, the Old Scratch came behind and caught his arm. The money, they say, was paid Peter out of his purse; and he wanted Peter to give him a deed of this house and land, which Peter swore he would not do."[9] In the process of the wrecking operation, Peter finds a charcoal sketch on the wall of a room which momentarily disconcerts him, for it is a pictorial embodiment of Tabitha's yarn: "It represented a ragged man, partly supporting himself on a spade, and bending his lean body over a hole in the earth, with one hand extended to grasp something he had found. But close behind him, with a fiendish laugh on his features, appeared a figure with horns, a tufted tail, and a cloven hoof." With an "Avaunt Satan!"[10] Peter puts an axe to "Old Scratch," convinced that he has lifted the evil spell held by the demon over his uncle's treasure. Not until Peter has demolished everything in the house except the kitchen does he find a large chest which holds the reward of his labors. But as Tabitha hinted, the devil was not to be tricked. Peter finds a useless fortune in old provincial currency—the emblem of his status in the community.

Hawthorne once again uses the symbol of the jesting demon to give "Mrs. Bullfrog" the moral that fraud begets fraud. Mr. Bullfrog, a fastidious bachelor, marries a woman who epitomizes his quest for perfection. She possesses charm, good breeding, and virginal innocence, besides a considerable sum of money. The bride is intelligent enough to reason that her assets constitute about ninety-five per cent of her attraction for Mr. Bullfrog. Immediately after the ceremony the couple sets off in a stagecoach for a distant town. As they are riding along, the vehicle capsizes. Mr. Bullfrog, who is slightly stunned, rises from the side of the road to go to the assistance of his lovely wife. But the person in his wife's garb has metamorphosed into a monster. Gone are the glossy curls, the elegance, and the gentility. Blaming the driver for her ruin, this strange creature, bald, hollow-cheeked, and toothless, belabors the unfortunate man with an umbrella to the accompaniment of blistering imprecations. Mr. Bullfrog is terrified. He fears that the mocking fiend is at the bottom of the troubled situation: "In my terror and turmoil of mind I could imagine nothing less than that the Old Nick, at the moment of our overturn, had annihilated my wife and jumped into her petticoats. The idea seemed the more probable, since I could nowhere perceive Mrs. Bullfrog alive, nor, though I looked very sharply about the coach, could I detect any traces of the beloved woman's dead body."[11] Shortly thereafter, Mr. Bullfrog is confronted with the unhappy truth that he has married an impostor; instead of a treasure he has picked up a bundle of artificiality which, according to the standards of innocent beauty, is almost as worthless as Peter Goldthwaite's outmoded currency. Mr. Bullfrog's spontaneous conviction that "Old Nick" was the key to the duplicity is figuratively confirmed. His wife is indeed an old witch with as much guile as the folk-tale demon. When her husband indignantly protests the imposture, she merely remarks that she still has her fortune. Hearing this, Mr. Bullfrog, somewhat abashedly, recants the ideal of perfection, and the devil of greed wins again.

But as skillfully as Hawthorne managed the less meaningful symbol of the folk-tale Mephistopheles, it was no more than an experiment in technique. Perfect control over his mythic imagery presupposed a knowledge of the ideas that it could embrace on every level of human experience. The

follies of a Peter Goldthwaite or the duplicities of a Mrs. Bullfrog illustrated
only the proverbial truths of the practical world; they could not preoccupy
Hawthorne long. In the melancholy expression of the young Faust of "The
Ambitious Guest" there was more to learn of the tormented human soul than
in a thousand recitals of the petty aspirations of an empty-headed speculator
of Goldthwaite's stature. The ambitions of the youth who is a chance guest
in the cottage situated in the notch of the sublimely beautiful White
Mountains are for Hawthorne an exemplification of life's bitter irony. Rising
above the shallow desires of the masses, the ambitious guest cries: "But I
cannot die till I have achieved my destiny. Then, let Death come!"[12] Not
achievement for achievement's sake is his ideal, but an abstract ambition to
leave "a glorious memory in the universal heart of man."[13] For this reason
"he had travelled far and alone; his whole life, indeed, had been a solitary
path; for, with the lofty caution of his nature, he had kept himself apart from
those who might otherwise have been his companions."[14] The death that
overtakes this proud, reserved Faust is as anonymous as his vague, high-
souled ambitions. A sudden landslide sweeps down from the heights to bury
him with the humble family of the cottage. Only he among the group dies
unnoticed: an unheralded stranger, an uninvited guest. So Hawthorne
depicts the illicit character of an overruling desire for fame that left its
aspirant stranded on an untraveled highway of life. Without depending upon
the dynamic archetypal symbolism, he pronounces isolation from humanity
the inevitable doom of the eccentric Faustian soul. The author does not
condemn the actions of the ambitious guest; as in "Monsieur du Miroir," he
views them as a quest for the "master-thought," human nature in rebellion
against the limitations imposed upon it by unknown forces.

 "The Threefold Destiny" serves as a companion piece to "The
Ambitious Guest." But Hawthorne in this story allows his mythic symbolism
to operate overtly. Ralph Cranfield, who believes "himself marked out for a
high destiny," imbibes the idea through supernatural means: it is "revealed to
him by witchcraft, or in a dream of prophecy...."[15] Three signs are to confirm
the approach of these marvelous attainments: a heart-shaped jewel on the
bosom of a maiden is to proclaim the discovery of the only woman who can
make him happy; a hand, visible only to him, is to point out a mighty treasure
hidden in the ground; and an extensive influence and sway over his fellow-
creatures is to be a harbinger of great leadership. Ralph becomes a world-
wanderer, but nowhere does he encounter the fateful signs. When he returns
to his native village, he finds the illusive tokens; but they augur more modest
achievements than he had hoped. He accepts his prophetic destiny, adjusting
his wild Faustian dreams to the commonplace duties of those precincts in
which he had been born.

In neither of these tales of high-destined individuals does Hawthorne extend the outline of his myth. Though aware of the spiritual tensions generated by overweening ambition, he loses dramatic impact by his failure to give them expression. The conflict with conventional mores prevails only by implication, or is given a romantic solution, as in *Fanshawe*. The symbolic pursuits excite moral platitudes, not philosophical truths. But as he writes in "The Threefold Destiny," he is still experimenting with "the spirit and mechanism" of legend or myth, searching for the incidents, "the characters [and] manners of familiar life" to embody in the form.[16]

When symbol and idea perfectly balance, as in "The Prophetic Pictures," Hawthorne assumes the role of a moral philosopher. The mysterious painter of this tale is the counterpart of Leonardo da Vinci, the Italian Faust, who "chose rather to know than to be, and that curiosity led him within forbidden portals."[17] Not only does Hawthorne's painter excel in his peculiar art, but he "possesses vast acquirements in all other learning and science."[18] His most astounding gift, deriving from his prodigious knowledge, is the awful power to delineate in a picture not merely his subject's features but his mind and heart. Hawthorne, in this instance mentally attuned to the harmonies of his Faustian imagery, ascribes this talent to intercourse with the devil. Pious New Englanders inveigh against this rare pictorial skill: "Some deemed it an offense against the Mosaic law, and even a presumptuous mockery of the Creator.... Others, frightened at the art which could raise phantoms at will, and keep the forms of the dead among the living, were inclined to consider the painter as a magician, or perhaps the famous Black Man, of old witch times, plotting mischief in a new guise."[19] Yet the painter is indifferent to public opinion. What his art reveals he accepts dispassionately. He displays no more interest in a sitter than a scientist does in a specimen to be dissected. Each flaw of character that he is able to portray adds but another objective fact to his knowledge of human nature. This intellectualization of emotion is severely criticized by Hawthorne. Aloofness from the ordinary feelings of mankind is a patent evil: "Like all other men around whom an engrossing purpose wreathes itself, he was insulated from the mass of human kind. He had no aim—no pleasure— no sympathies—but what were ultimately connected with his art.... he did not possess kindly feelings; his heart was cold; no living creature could be brought near enough to keep him warm."[20] In this fatal inadequacy, Hawthorne discovers the fallacy of the Faustian superman. Deliberate isolation from the common aspirations of the human heart he considers a breach of universal morality. When knowledge becomes an end in itself, divorced from the public good, it takes on the function of evil. It ceases to seek a verification of its ethics in the external world, being a law unto itself:

"It is not good for man to cherish a solitary ambition. Unless there be those around him by whose example he may regulate himself, his thoughts, desires, and hopes will become extravagant, and he the semblance, perhaps the reality, of a madman. Reading other bosoms with an acuteness almost preternatural, the painter failed to see the disorder of his own."[21] Translated into the values of the devil-image, the diabolic portraiture of the artist, in its failure to direct his spiritual government, merely corroborates the thesis that the evil of the ego-consciousness is the inability of this presumptuous faculty to think itself capable of wrong.

In "The Prophetic Pictures" Hawthorne realizes the full ethical potential of Faustian mythmaking. The supernatural endowments of the painter, attributed to intercourse with the devil, bring the hero into contact with the inherent capacity for evil which every individual possesses. In transmitting these secrets to the canvas, literally the lineaments of a devil-image, the painter himself fails to heed the counsel with self which they urge. He is oblivious to his own evil instincts because his ego overrules all responsibility to the community; for the image which he surveys is, after all, a communal symbol whose ethical purpose eludes him. He has divorced himself, emotionally, from his human heritage. On another level of the story, Hawthorne focuses on still another inadequacy of Puritan morality. He condemns his forefathers' intolerance of art, their fear that it encroached upon God's prerogatives; and indirectly he deplores their suspicion of the beautiful in painting, the only ideal that momentarily exalts man to the status of a god. And in equating the beautiful with infernal conjuration, they were exposing to public gaze the deserts of their souls over which the hot breath of the devil blew in fiendish glee. They, too, were blind to their devil-thoughts.

The fabulous jewel of "The Great Carbuncle" embraces the idea of a quest as infamous as the painter's pursuit of dispassionate knowledge. But the search for the carbuncle enables Hawthorne to broaden the canvas of his narrative picture. With the possible exception of the young couple, each individual participating in the adventure is motivated by a desire that reflects a specific phase of universal human conduct. Hawthorne is therefore allowed to pass moral judgment on their actions. Because "the quest for the Great Carbuncle is deemed little better than a traffic with the Evil One," doing "grievous wrong to [the] soul [and] body, ..."[22] Hawthorne's symbol acquires its necessary mythic connotations.

The story, in relation to Hawthorne's development of his Faust myth, shows him widening the periphery of meaning of his conceptual pattern. The motives inciting the different adventurers gain his strong disapprobation. He censures mere romantic pursuit, vain and directionless ambition; the pride of the scientist who sees the carbuncle as a "prize ... reserved to crown [his] scientific reputation ..."; the selfishness of a merchant who thinks only of "the marketable value of the true gem"; the egotism of the poet who believes its radiance will be diffused through his works, establishing "the splendor" of his "intellectual powers"; the haughtiness of the nobleman who deems the carbuncle the only fitting "ornament for the great hall of [his] ancestral castle"; the cynicism of the disbeliever who wishes to prove that the legend of the great carbuncle "is all a humbug."[23] At the end only the couple prove themselves "so simply wise as to reject [the] jewel" because it "would have dimmed all earthly things" by its splendor.[24] Thus Hawthorne contemptuously dismisses all forms of human activity actuated by vanity, selfishness, or pride. In the process he casts the net of his Faust myth into the deeper waters of mankind's experiences.

The two historical tales "Edward Randolph's Portrait" and "Lady Eleanore's Mantle" present another variant of the Faust myth. Hawthorne this time utilizes the symbolic pact with the devil to magnify political tyranny in the American colonies. In the first story the portrait of Randolph, who obtained the repeal of the first provincial charter, is the symbol of the people's curse on all irresponsible rulers. The action begins with the provincial governor meditating an oppression against the inhabitants of old Boston. As he sits at his desk, momentarily reluctant to add his signature to the document that will implement the offense, his eyes scrutinize Randolph's portrait. A military aide, noticing the governor's curiosity, volunteers to relate the history of the dark canvas. His recital introduces the connection between the devil and political injustice: "One of the wildest, and at the same time the best accredited, accounts, stated it to be an original and authentic portrait of the Evil One, taken at a witch meeting near Salem; and that its strong and terrible resemblance had been confirmed by several of the confessing wizards and witches, at their trial, in open court. It was likewise affirmed that a familiar spirit or demon abode behind the blackness of the picture, and had shown himself, at seasons of public calamity, to more than one of the royal governors."[25] The governor ridicules the story as a fantasy. And when his niece chides his skepticism, he harshly announces his intention of putting the city under martial law. One of the representatives of the people urges him to rescind the order, warning, "If you meddle with the devil, take care of his claws!"[26]

Angered by these threats against royal authority, the governor seizes the pen, resolved to sign his name to the paper that will put his orders into execution. A provincial captain calls his attention to Randolph's portrait, and he lifts his eyes to scan it. The governor stares at it aghast. His aide's tale begins to materialize: "The expression of the face ... was that of a wretch detected in some hideous guilt, and exposed to the bitter hatred and laughter and withering scorn of a vast surrounding multitude. There was the struggle of defiance, beaten down and overwhelmed by the crushing weight of ignominy. The torture of the soul had come forth upon the countenance. It seemed as if the picture ... threw its evil omen over the present hour."[27] The governor, however, stubbornly persists in enforcing his will. Casting a second glance of defiance at the picture, he affixes his signature. The rumors flowing from this crucial meeting relate that his name was scrawled in "characters that betokened it a deed of desperation.... Then, it is said, he shuddered, as if that signature had granted away his salvation."[28] With ineffable ingenuity, Hawthorne deepens the significance of a historic moment in New England culture, giving it an unforgettable emphasis by equating political dictatorship with the loss of salvation: the signing away of one's soul to the devil. And again the mythic image is evoked to direct and guide individual human behavior, but aristocratic pride prohibits its lesson to prevail. The governor refuses to take counsel with the evil that divides his heart.

The pride of Lady Eleanore Rochcliffe in the second of the stories symbolizes the hell-inspired harshness of the British agents ruling the American colonies. By retelling history with this pardonable democratic bias, Hawthorne succeeds in representing the courage that went into the founding of the republic. Haughtily conscious of her heredity and personal advantages as a relative of the royal governor of Massachusetts, Lady Eleanore places herself above the sympathies of the common nature which binds together human souls. This scornful attitude, coupled with an extraordinary loveliness, is ascribed to supernatural influences by the ladies of the province. The article that sets off her irresistible charms is an embroidered mantle "which had been wrought by the most skillful artist in London, and possessed even magical properties of adornment."[29]

To re-enforce the impression of Lady Eleanore's Luciferian pride, Hawthorne foreordains the dark fate that will smite her soul. One of her rejected lovers, a colonial youth of unimportant birth and no fortune, insanely importunes her to drink consecrated wine to prove her human ties: "... in requital of that harm, if such there be, and for your own earthly and heavenly welfare, I pray you to take one sip of this holy wine, and then to pass the goblet round among the guests. And this shall be a symbol that you have not sought to withdraw yourself from the chain of human sympathies—which whoso would shake off must keep company with fallen angels." When she refuses to do his bidding, the youth presents another strange petition to the arrogant woman: "It was no other than that she should throw off the mantle, which, while he pressed the silver cup of wine upon her, she had drawn more closely around her form, so as almost to shroud herself within it."[30] But still she will not relinquish this other talisman of her superiority.

When shortly thereafter a small-pox epidemic breaks out in the colony, the source of the dreadful plague is traced back to Lady Eleanore's mantle. Now the residents of the region find confirmation of their belief that the diseased mantle was the devil's banner: "The people raved against the Lady Eleanore, and cried out that her pride and scorn had evoked a fiend, and that, between them both, this monstrous evil had been born."[31] And soon the pride which brought the downfall of the mighty Lucifer and his most ardent disciple, Faust, also reduces Lady Eleanore to shame and to ruin. Her lovely face is blasted by the horrible scourge. Her lunatic suitor, whose very name Helwyse apparently provides a foreknowledge of her doom, insanely pronounces her elegy: "All have been her victims! Who so worthy to be the final victim as herself?"[32] And with this homonymic symbol Hawthorne concludes another historical tale whose macabre tension derives from the fire and brimstone of his devil-image. The poetic liberties that he takes with historical data are equally determined by art and by personal democratic conviction. The pride evinced by Lady Eleanore, with its immovable cruelty and heartless indifference, was for Hawthorne the emotional and intellectual index of British imperialism and, in historical perspective, of all conquering powers. In the light of his artistic method, nothing could project abuse of authority more clearly than the functional imagery of his plastic Faust myth. He had used it to ferret out the evils of Puritanism in "The Maypole of Merry Mount" and other tales, in one way; now, in another manner, he applied it to enhance the heroic courage of the founding fathers in their struggle with the evils of monarchical persecutions.

"The devils of the guilty heart," upon whom Hawthorne mused in "The Haunted Mind," are his subject in "John Inglefield's Thanksgiving." Here he studies the war between good and evil raging continually in the guilty conscience, and he focuses once more on the educative image of the devil, in this instance on a negative reaction. The dilemma in which Prudence Inglefield finds herself has its parallel in the Faust chapbook and in Marlowe's *Faustus*. The chapbook Faust, though he wants to repent, will not repent: "In this perplexity lay this miserable Doctor Faustus, having quite forgot his faith in Christ, never falling to repentance truly, thereby to attain the grace and holy spirit of God again, the which would have been able to have resisted the strong assaults of Satan; for although he had made him a promise, yet he might have remembered through true repentance sinners come again into the favour of God."[33] Hawthorne does not merely report Prudence's fleeting impulse toward repentance. He presents it as a concrete action, having reality in time and place. In the theatre of her conscience occurs her struggle with the devil, actually the attempt to school herself to a genuine understanding of the mythic image which her conscience invokes to warn her of evil. On the evening of Thanksgiving Day, in the midst of dissolute revelry, Prudence suddenly remembers the pious celebrations of her innocent youth. She re-creates in her imagination what would take place if she were now to visit the fireside circle. She envisions a cool welcome, with family affection growing in warmth the longer she stays. When her mind turns to the hour of domestic worship, her heart suddenly yearns for this solace. For a moment she is on the verge of repentance. But in this crisis she is intimidated by the demonic image of the devil which rises to her consciousness: "But her face was so changed that they hardly recognized it. Sin and evil passions glowed through its comeliness, and wrought a horrible deformity; a smile gleamed in her eyes, as of triumphant mockery, at their surprise and grief."[34] At the sight of their unhappiness, Prudence dares to challenge the negative power of the devil-image: "... her countenance wore almost the expression as if she were struggling with a fiend, who had power to seize his victim within the hallowed precincts of her father's hearth."[35] But, as with Faustus, she lacked the conviction of faith in God, and her volition was strangled by the overpowering challenge to her spirit. In this narrative Hawthorne, by recourse to the oneiric symbols of myth and by constructing an other-worldly domain of myth, succeeds in achieving the dramatic persuasion of similar scenes in Marlowe's *Faustus*. By conceding the reality of the invisible world of the conscience, he presents good and evil as the chief actors in the kaleidoscope of individual human experience.

The sharp-toothed devils of remorse that gnaw at Mr. Hooper's conscience in "The Minister's Black Veil" are symbolized in the black veil, which is the physical emblem of his secret sin. As Hawthorne develops the meaning of the veil, he denotes it the sign of the parson's bondage to the devil: "... catching a glimpse of his figure in the looking-glass, the black veil involved his own spirit in the horror with which it overwhelmed all others. His frame shuddered, his lips grew white, he spilt the untasted wine upon the carpet, and rushed forth into the darkness."[36] Here Hawthorne merely gives tangible embodiment to the general idea of the devils of the guilty conscience which he discussed in "The Haunted Mind," transforming the mythic devil-image into the shape the plot of his tale demands. On another occasion he confirms this transmutation, for he remarks that behind the crepe veil "ghost and fiend consorted" with Mr. Hooper. To enforce this impression further, he notes that "among all its bad influences" it had only one good result: "By the aid of his mysterious emblem ... he became a man of awful power over souls that were in agony for sin."[37]

In this extremely subtle fashion Hawthorne repeats the moral import of "Young Goodman Brown." The over-emphasis on sin obscures the possibilities of good in the human soul. Mr. Hooper's claim that every individual "loathsomely treasur[es] up the secret of his sin ..."[38] is an indictment of no one but himself. In effect, Hawthorne states that a minister, as a human agent of God, is not supposed to flaunt the power of Lucifer. His mission is to guide both the pure and the sinful along the path to righteousness. He must demonstrate the capacity of good which is inherent in any individual who dares confront evil, triumphing over its negations and reading the sphinx-like mystery of the devil-symbol. The very veil which ought to have guided Mr. Hooper to a new understanding of spiritual truth distorts his mind as a similar experience had affected Goodman Brown.

That Hawthorne's attitude toward evil was going through a stage of ethical refinement, consistent with the principle advanced in "The Minister's Black Veil," is clearly indicated in "Fancy's Show-Box." He grants that man is tempted into evil "by many devilish sophistries," since the fiend has "a wondrous power, and terrible acquaintance with the secret soul...."[39] Nevertheless Hawthorne insists that man's capacity for evil is overestimated: "In truth, there is no such thing in man's nature as a settled and full resolve, either for good or evil, except at the very moment of execution."[40] In other words, neither human depravity nor original sin but rather the pressure of circumstances and the confusion of purpose operate to promote the commission of sin. Such an outlook on evil is obviously in direct opposition to the Calvinistic exposition of the idea. This stand verifies the fact that Hawthorne approached the problem philosophically, not theologically. In terms of the Faust myth this philosophical curiosity is of even greater importance. It suggests that Hawthorne's ethical analyses are rapidly assuming the direction of those in Goethe's *Faust*. Since both men were interested in evil only in the narrow sense that experience with it awakened spiritual conflict, they could determine the enduring validity of man's ethical ideals by taking man's reaction to participation in sin as a positive test of his moral integrity. If sin functions to distort completely man's prospects of the good, then he is indeed damned; if, however, he consciously admits his errors and thereby resolves to transcend them, he is admitting his responsibility to the unwritten laws of universal truth. In the specific sense of Hawthorne's art, the mythic image of the devil functions in exactly this way: it is the oneiric projection of the great racial memory that has endlessly mediated the problem of good and evil for man.

"Dr. Heidegger's Experiment" lays open to view another of Hawthorne's attempts to examine the individual's ability to profit morally as the result of a previous experience with evil. The elixir of life motif, as in Goethe's *Faust*, is the device Hawthorne employs to elucidate his problem.

But unlike the playwright, he is compelled to resolve the consequences of temptation to further evil within the limits of a short narrative. All the magic paraphernalia of the play are reproduced in Hawthorne's setting. Faust's enchanted mirror is converted into a fitting ornament for Dr. Heidegger's study: "Between two of the bookcases hung a looking-glass, presenting its high and dusty plate within a tarnished gilt frame. Among many wonderful stories related of this mirror, it was fabled that the spirits of all the doctor's deceased patients dwelt within its verge, and would stare him in the face whenever he looked thitherward."[41] The witches' apes and the steaming cauldron that attend the preparation of the rejuvenating liquor are symbolically expressed by the doctor's black book: "The greatest curiosity of the study remains to be mentioned; it was a ponderous folio volume, bound in black leather, with massive silver clasps ... and nobody could tell the title of the book. But it was well known to be a book of magic; and once, when a chambermaid had lifted it, merely to brush away the dust, the skeleton had rattled in its closet, the picture of the young lady had stepped one foot upon the floor, and several ghastly faces had peeped forth from the mirror...."[42] Five venerable friends of Dr. Heidegger are invited to share in the experiment of rejuvenation. They, like Faust, have long since expended the vitality of youth. Before the scientist offers them the potion, he urges them to use their past experience in the event that the elixir produces the desired effects: "... it would be well that, with the experience of a lifetime to direct you, you should draw up a few general rules for your guidance, in passing a second time through the perils of youth. Think what a sin and shame it would be, if, with your peculiar advantages, you should not become patterns of virtue and wisdom to all the young people of the age!"[43] But once they have sipped the magical draught, they immediately revert to the conduct of youth. And in the exuberance of their revived energies, they topple over the container of precious fluid. The effects of the preliminary samplings wear off, and the five return to their dotage. In the spontaneous lapse of these aged people to the sinful behavior of the past, Hawthorne isolates the ethical problem broached in "Fancy's Show-Box." Even if the individual engages in evil once, he nevertheless can attain the good life. All he needs to do is to become conscious of his moral lapse. Dr. Heidegger's friends, instead of perceiving their errors, resolve to search for the fountain of youth. They fail to reap the truth that is implicit in evil. Only the old doctor, who does not bemoan the loss of the elixir, reads the lesson so vividly illustrated by their' actions. In this way Hawthorne transforms the elixir of life motif of the Faust myth into an instrument of ethical clarification.

Hawthorne's two stories of the Shaker community in New Hampshire tentatively explore the fringes of contemporary life within the confines of his mythic imagery. This act betokens his confidence in his operative conception, and anticipates its later extension into the more critical problems of his times. The Shakers, whose religious principles forbade the practice of sexual intercourse, allow him to speculate on the type of moral rigorism that he associated with dogmatic Puritanism: in a word, with the spiritual pride which reflects the negative aspect of evil embodied in the devil-archetypes. In "The Canterbury Pilgrims" two lovers fleeing from the Shaker village are accosted by a group of pilgrims who, conversely, are seeking refuge with the sect. The pilgrims attempt to persuade the lovers to renounce their plan, pointing out that the outside world breeds only disillusionment. The young couple, however, are not to be shaken in their mutual faith. They are willing to accept "mortal hope and fear" as a substitute for a "cold and passionless security."[44] The truth that emerges from this story is simply explained: a religion intolerant of human nature is a worse evil than any its practices may seemingly thwart. In a Faustian context, the philosophy which subsumes this belief recognizes the sources of moral perversion in the denial of the natural man and in a complete surrender to evil. The inversion of emotions which Hawthorne condemns is what each individual's personal Mephistopheles fosters if there is no attempt made to circumvent his trickery.

The principle of moral cowardice is re-examined in "The Shaker Bridal." Hawthorne describes the evil wrought in family relations by an unthinking submission to abnormal dogmas: "One, when he joined the Society, had brought with him his wife and children, but never, from that hour, had spoken a fond word to the former, or taken his best-beloved child upon his knee. Another, whose family refused to follow him, had been enabled ... to leave them to the mercy of the world."[45] But it is in the marriage of Martha and Adam that Hawthorne sees a travesty on natural morality. The couple, who are in the prime of life, are about to be ordained the temporal spiritual leaders of the movement. A mock marriage is to symbolize their consecration to the ascetic ideal. The despair which originally drove Adam to forsake normal existence has crystallized into a hard core of selfishness in the new environment. He has disciplined his emotions to the extent that they are now brutally impersonal. Martha, who joined the community upon the urging of Adam, has sustained herself on the hope that Adam, once rehabilitated, would return to the world of men and consummate their long-delayed marriage. But now that Adam has risen to leadership among the Shakers, his pride in the specious success has entirely divorced him from thoughts of Martha. As a consequence, when Adam signifies his intention to remain celibate, Martha dies, being unable to endure a desolate agony. Thus Hawthorne, in his first attempt to study contemporary life, castigates the diabolic negations of a current religious sect. In relation to his myth, he has progressively expanded its definition until now he is at a point in modern life identical with the one he had assumed in his examination of Puritan history. His moral objection to the negative aspects of Puritanism was the creative origin of his mythic conception; his first effort to adapt its motivations to the life that surrounded him is characterized by this coincidence of approach.

In summary it may be said that, with the statement in "The Haunted Mind" reaffirming his belief that all the evils of life could be balanced with the infernal pact of the Faustian equation, Hawthorne declared his intention to extend the outlines of his Faust myth. In "Monsieur du Miroir" he indicated that the peculiarity of individual destiny would engage his attention. And since human ambition is usually the most powerful influence in shaping destiny, Hawthorne, beginning with the rather vague and romantic motivations of "The Ambitious Guest" and "The Threefold Destiny," moved toward a moral clarification of the compulsive desires dominating man's nature in "The Prophetic Pictures" and "The Great Carbuncle." The humorous possibilities of the devil-inspired folk tale momentarily diverted him in "Peter Goldthwaite's Treasure" and "Mrs. Bullfrog." The dramatic value of the mythic imagery in enforcing the lessons of American history was skillfully realized in "Edward Randolph's Portrait" and "Lady Eleanore's Mantle." His concern with the insidious effects of evil upon moral volition in "John Inglefield's Thanksgiving" and "The Minister's Black Veil" reflected an attitude toward evil that was a necessary prelude to the dogmatic standpoint of "Fancy's Show-Box." No Faust myth, in the sense of the greatness of Marlowe's *Faustus* or Goethe's *Faust*, is possible unless the author holds to a definite opinion on the function of evil in the universe. In this latter sketch he adopted a Pelagian position: man, hampered by no deterministic principle of natural depravity, has the power within himself to overcome evil and attain moral truth. "Dr. Heidegger's Experiment" isolated the negative aspect of this issue, suggesting that the individual is prone to be overwhelmed by evil only when he refuses to profit by the counsel with self which it urges. The last stage of this particular development in Hawthorne's Faust myth found him tentatively exploring its practicability in appraising the moral values at stake in contemporary life. The Shaker stories, though they are tangential to the real problems of the age, anticipate the direction of his thinking in the next evolution of his myth.

NOTES

1. The tales and sketches considered in this chapter were written between 1830 and 1842; most of them were included in the two editions of *Twice-Told Tales* (1837, 1842).

2. *Complete Works*, I, 346.

3. *Ibid.*, I, 347.

4. *Ibid.*, I, 348.

5. *Ibid.*, II, 194.

6. *Ibid.*, II, 195.

7. *Ibid.*, I, 405.

8. *Ibid.*, I, 433.

9. *Ibid.*, I, 440.

10. *Ibid.*, I, 442.

11. *Ibid.*, II, 153.

12. *Ibid.*, I, 368.

13. *Ibid.*, I, 369.

14. *Ibid.*, I, 367.

15. *Ibid.*, I, 528.

16. *Ibid.*, I, 527.

17. Edward McCurdy, *Leonardo da Vinci's Notebooks* (New York: Empire State Book Company, 1923), p. 8.

18. *Complete Works*, I, 192.

19. *Ibid.*, I, 195.

20. *Ibid.*, I, 206.

21. *Ibid.*, I, 207.

22. *Ibid.*, I, 179.

23. *Ibid.*, I, 178–182.

24. *Ibid.*, I, 191.

25. *Ibid.*, I, 295.

26. *Ibid.*, I, 301.

27. *Ibid.*, I, 303.

28. *Ibid.*, I, 304.

29. *Ibid.*, I, 310–311.

30. *Ibid.*, I, 316–317.

31. *Ibid.*, I, 321–322.

32. *Ibid.*, I, 325.

33. Rose, *The Famous History of Dr. Faustus*, pp. 89–90.

34. *Complete Works*, III, 589.

35. *Ibid.*, III, 590.

36. *Ibid.*, I, 59.

37. *Ibid.*, I, 65.

38. *Ibid.*, I, 69.

39. *Ibid.*, I, 255.

40. *Ibid.*, I, 257.

41. *Ibid.*, I, 259.

42. *Ibid.*, I, 260.

43. *Ibid.*, I, 263.

44. *Ibid.*, III, 530.

45. *Ibid.*, I, 474.

C.S. LEWIS

Satan

le genti dolorosi
C'hanno perduto il ben de l'intelletto

—DANTE

Before considering the character of Milton's Satan it may be desirable to remove an ambiguity by noticing that Jane Austen's Miss Bates could be described either as a very entertaining or a very tedious person. If we said the first, we should mean that the author's portrait of her entertains us while we read; if we said the second, we should mean that it does so by being the portrait of a person whom the other people in *Emma* find tedious and whose like we also should find tedious in real life. For it is a very old critical discovery that the imitation in art of unpleasing objects may be a pleasing imitation. In the same way, the proposition that Milton's Satan is a magnificent character may bear two senses. It may mean that Milton's presentation of him is a magnificent poetical achievement which engages the attention and excites the admiration of the reader. On the other hand, it may mean that the real being (if any) whom Milton is depicting, or any real being like Satan if there were one, or a real human being in so far as he resembles Milton's Satan, is or ought to be an object of admiration and sympathy, conscious or unconscious, on the part of the poet or his readers or both. The

From *A Preface to Paradise Lost*. © 1961 by Oxford University Press.

first, so far as I know, has never till modern times been denied; the second, never affirmed before the times of Blake and Shelley—for when Dryden said that Satan was Milton's 'hero' he meant something quite different. It is, in my opinion, wholly erroneous. In saying this I have, however, trespassed beyond the bounds of purely literary criticism. In what follows, therefore, I shall not labour directly to convert those who admire Satan, but only to make a little clearer what it is they are admiring. That Milton could not have shared their admiration will then, I hope, need no argument.

The main difficulty is that any real exposition of the Satanic character and the Satanic predicament is likely to provoke the question 'Do you, then, regard *Paradise Lost* as a comic poem?' To this I answer, no; but only those will fully understand it who see that it might have been a comic poem. Milton has chosen to treat the Satanic predicament in the epic form and has therefore subordinated the absurdity of Satan to the misery which he suffers and inflicts. Another author, Meredith, has treated it as comedy with consequent subordination of its tragic elements. But *The Egoist* remains, none the less, a pendant to *Paradise Lost*, and just as Meredith cannot exclude all pathos from Sir Willoughby, so Milton cannot exclude all absurdity from Satan, and does not even wish to do so. That is the explanation of the Divine laughter in *Paradise Lost* which has offended some readers. There is a real offence in it because Milton has imprudently made his Divine Persons so anthropomorphic that their laughter arouses legitimately hostile reactions in us—as though we were dealing with an ordinary conflict of wills in which the winner ought not to ridicule the loser. But it is a mistake to demand that Satan, any more than Sir Willoughby, should be able to rant and posture through the whole universe without, sooner or later, awaking the comic spirit. The whole nature of reality would have to be altered in order to give him such immunity, and it is not alterable. At that precise point where Satan or Sir Willoughby meets something real, laughter *must* arise, just as steam must when water meets fire. And no one was less likely than Milton to be ignorant of this necessity. We know from his prose works that he believed everything detestable to be, in the long run, also ridiculous; and mere Christianity commits every Christian to believing that 'the Devil is (in the long run) an ass.'

What the Satanic predicament consists in is made clear, as Mr. Williams points out, by Satan himself. On his own showing he is suffering from a 'sense of injur'd merit' (I, 98). This is a well known state of mind which we can all study in domestic animals, children, film-stars, politicians, or minor poets; and perhaps nearer home. Many critics have a curious partiality for it in literature, but I do not know that anyone admires it in life. When it appears, unable to hurt, in a jealous dog or a spoiled child, it is usually laughed at. When it appears armed with the force of millions on the political stage, it escapes ridicule only by being more mischievous. And the cause from which the Sense of Injured Merit arose in Satan's mind—once more I follow Mr. William—is also clear. 'He thought himself impaired' (V, 662). He thought himself impaired because Messiah had been pronounced Head of the Angels. These are the 'wrongs' which Shelley described as 'beyond measure.' A being superior to himself in kind, by whom he himself had been created—a being far above him in the natural hierarchy—had been preferred to him in honour by an authority whose right to do so was not disputable, and in a fashion which, as Abdiel points out, constituted a compliment to the angels rather than a slight (V, 823–843). No one had in fact done anything to Satan; he was not hungry, nor overtasked, nor removed from his place, nor shunned, nor hated—he only thought himself impaired. In the midst of a world of light and love, of song and feast and dance, he could find nothing to think of more interesting than his own prestige. And his own prestige, it must be noted, had and could have no other grounds than those which he refused to admit for the superior prestige of Messiah. Superiority in kind, or Divine appointment, or both—on what else could his own exalted position depend? Hence his revolt is entangled in contradictions from the very outset, and he cannot even raise the banner of liberty and equality without admitting in a tell-tale parenthesis that 'Orders and Degrees Jarr not with liberty' (V, 789). He wants hierarchy and does not want hierarchy. Throughout the poem he is engaged in sawing off the branch he is sitting on, not only in the quasi-political sense already indicated, but in a deeper sense still, since a creature revolting against a creator is revolting against the source of his own powers—including even his power to revolt. Hence the strife is most accurately described as 'Heav'n ruining from Heav'n' (VI, 868), for only in so far as he also is 'Heaven'—diseased, perverted, twisted, but still a native of Heaven—does Satan exist at all. It is like the scent of a flower trying to destroy the flower. As a consequence the same rebellion which means misery for the feelings and corruption for the will, means Nonsense for the intellect.

Mr. Williams has reminded us in unforgettable words that 'Hell is inaccurate,' and has drawn attention to the fact that Satan lies about every subject he mentions in *Paradise Lost*. But I do not know whether we can distinguish his conscious lies from the blindness which he has almost willingly imposed on himself. When, at the very beginning of his insurrection, he tells Beelzebub that Messiah is going to make a tour 'through all the Hierarchies ... and give Laws' (V, 688–690) I suppose he may still know that he is lying; and similarly when he tells his followers that 'all this haste of midnight march' (V, 774) had been ordered in honour of their new 'Head.' But when in Book I he claims that the 'terror of his arm' had put God in doubt of 'his empire,' I am not quite certain. It is, of course, mere folly. There never had been any war between Satan and God, only between Satan and Michael; but it is possible that he now believes his own propaganda. When in Book X he makes to his peers the useless boast that Chaos had attempted to oppose his journey 'protesting Fate supreame' (480) he may really, by then, have persuaded himself that this was true; for far earlier in his career he has become more a Lie than a Liar, a personified self-contradiction.

This doom of Nonsense—almost, in Pope's sense, of Dulness—is brought out in two scenes. The first is his debate with Abdiel in Book V. Here Satan attempts to maintain the heresy which is at the root of his whole predicament—the doctrine that he is a self-existent being, not a derived being, a creature. Now, of course, the property of a self-existent being is that it can understand its own existence; it is *causa sui*. The quality of a created being is that it just finds itself existing, it knows not how nor why. Yet at the same time, if a creature is silly enough to try to prove that it was not created, what is more natural than for it to say, 'Well, I wasn't there to see it being done?' Yet what more futile, since in thus admitting ignorance of its own beginnings it proves that those beginnings lay outside itself? Satan falls instantly into this trap (850 et seq.)—as indeed he cannot help doing—and produces as proof of his self-existence what is really its disproof. But even this is not Nonsense enough. Uneasily shifting on the bed of Nonsense which he has made for himself, he then throws out the happy idea that 'fatal course' really produced him, and finally, with a triumphant air, the theory that he sprouted from the soil like a vegetable. Thus, in twenty lines, the being too proud to admit derivation from God, has come to rejoice in believing that he 'just grew' like Topsy or a turnip. The second passage is his speech from the throne in Book II. The blindness here displayed reminds one of Napoleon's utterance after his fall, 'I wonder what Wellington will do now?—he will never be content to become a private citizen again.' Just as Napoleon was incapable of conceiving, I do not say the virtues, but even the temptations, of an ordinarily honest man in a tolerably stable commonwealth, so Satan in this speech shows complete inability to conceive any state of mind but the infernal. His argument assumes as axiomatic that in any world where there is any good to be envied, subjects will envy their sovereign. The only exception is Hell, for there, since there is no good to be had, the sovereign cannot have more of it, and therefore cannot be envied. Hence he concludes that the infernal monarchy has a stability which the celestial lacks. That the obedient angels might love to obey is an idea which cannot cross his mind even as a hypothesis. But even within this invincible ignorance contradiction breaks out; for Satan makes this ludicrous proposition a reason for hoping ultimate victory. He does not, apparently, notice that every approach to victory must take away the grounds on which victory is hoped. A stability based on perfect misery, and therefore diminishing with each alleviation of that misery, is held out as something likely to assist in removing the misery altogether (II, 11–43).

What we see in Satan is the horrible co-existence of a subtle and incessant intellectual activity with an incapacity to understand anything. This doom he has brought upon himself; in order to avoid seeing one thing he has, almost voluntarily, incapacitated himself from seeing at all. And thus, throughout the poem, all his torments come, in a sense, at his own bidding, and the Divine judgement might have been expressed in the words '*thy* will be done.' He says 'Evil be thou my good' (which includes 'Nonsense be thou my sense') and his prayer is granted. It is by his own will that he revolts; but not by his own will that Revolt itself tears its way in agony out of his head and becomes a being separable from himself, capable of enchanting him (II, 749–766) and bearing him unexpected and unwelcome progeny. By his own will he becomes a serpent in Book IX; in Book X he is a serpent whether he will or no. This progressive degradation, of which he himself is vividly aware, is carefully marked in the poem. He begins by fighting for 'liberty,' however misconceived; but almost at once sinks to fighting for 'Honour, Dominion, glorie, and renoune' (VI, 422). Defeated in this, he sinks to that great design which makes the main subject of the poem—the design of ruining two creatures who had never done him any harm, no longer in the serious hope of victory, but only to annoy the Enemy whom he cannot directly attack. (The coward in Beaumont and Fletcher's play, not daring to fight a duel, decided to go home and beat his servants.) This brings him as a spy into the universe, and soon not even a political spy, but a mere peeping Tom leering and writhing in prurience as he overlooks the privacy of two lovers, and there described, almost for the first time in the poem, not as the fallen Archangel or Hell's dread Emperor, but simply as 'the Devil' (IV, 502)—the salacious grotesque, half bogey and half buffoon, of popular tradition. From hero to general, from general to politician, from politician to secret service agent, and thence to a thing that peers in at bedroom or bathroom windows, and thence to a toad, and finally to a snake—such is the progress of Satan. This progress, misunderstood, has given rise to the belief that Milton began by making Satan more glorious than he intended and then, too late, attempted to rectify the error. But such an unerring picture of the 'sense of injured merit' in its actual operations upon character cannot have come about by blundering and accident. We need not doubt that it was the poet's intention to be fair to evil, to give it a run for its money—to show it *first* at the height, with all its rants and melodrama and 'Godlike imitated state' about it, and *then* to trace what actually becomes of such self-intoxication when it encounters reality. Fortunately we happen to know that the terrible soliloquy in Book IV (32–113) was conceived and in part composed before the first two books. It was from this conception that Milton started and when he put the most specious aspects of Satan at the very beginning of his poem he was relying on two predispositions in the minds of his readers, which in that age, would have guarded them from our later misunderstanding. Men still believed that there really was such a person as Satan, and that he was a liar. The poet did not foresee that his work would one day meet the disarming simplicity of critics who take for gospel things said by the father of falsehood in public speeches to his troops.

It remains, of course, true that Satan is the best drawn of Milton's characters. The reason is not hard to find. Of the major characters whom Milton attempted he is incomparably the easiest to draw. Set a hundred poets to tell the same story and in ninety of the resulting poems Satan will be the best character. In all but a few writers the 'good' characters are the least successful, and every one who has ever tried to make even the humblest story ought to know why. To make a character worse than oneself it is only necessary to release imaginatively from control some of the bad passions which, in real life, are always straining at the leash; the Satan, the Iago, the Becky Sharp, within each of us, is always there and only too ready, the moment the leash is slipped, to come out and have in our books that holiday we try to deny them in our lives. But if you try to draw a character better than yourself, all you can do is to take the best moments you have had and to imagine them prolonged and more consistently embodied in action. But the real high virtues which we do not possess at all, we cannot depict except in a purely external fashion. We do not really know what it feels like to be a man much better than ourselves. His whole inner landscape is one we have never seen, and when we guess it we blunder. It is in their 'good' characters that novelists make, unawares, the most shocking self-revelations. Heaven understands Hell and Hell does not understand Heaven, and all of us, in our measure, share the Satanic, or at least the Napoleonic, blindness. To project ourselves into a wicked character, we have only to stop doing something, and something that we are already tired of doing; to project ourselves into a good one we have to do what we cannot and become what we are not. Hence all that is said about Milton's 'sympathy' with Satan, his expression in Satan of his own pride, malice, folly, misery, and lust, is true in a sense, but not in a sense peculiar to Milton. The Satan in Milton enables him to draw the character well just as the Satan in us enables us to receive it. Not as Milton, but as man, he has trodden the burning marl, pursued vain war with heaven, and turned aside with leer malign. A fallen man *is* very like a fallen angel. That, indeed, is one of the things which prevents the Satanic predicament from becoming comic. It is too near us; and doubtless Milton expected all readers to perceive that in the long run either the Satanic predicament or else the delighted obedience of Messiah, of Abdiel, of Adam, and of Eve, must be their own. It is therefore right to say that Milton has put much of himself into Satan; but it is unwarrantable to conclude that he was pleased with that part of himself or expected us to be pleased. Because he was, like the rest of us, damnable, it does not follow that he was, like Satan, damned.

Yet even the 'good' characters in *Paradise Lost* are not so unsuccessful that a man who takes the poem seriously will doubt whether, in real life, Adam or Satan would be the better company. Observe their conversation. Adam talks about God, the Forbidden Tree, sleep, the difference between beast and man, his plans for the morrow, the stars, and the angels. He discusses dreams and clouds, the sun, the moon, and the planets, the winds, and the birds. He relates his own creation and celebrates the beauty and majesty of Eve. Now listen to Satan: in Book I at line 83 he starts to address Beelzebub; by line 94 he is stating his own position and telling Beelzebub about his 'fixt mind' and 'injured merit.' At line 241 he starts off again, this time to give his impressions of Hell: by line 252 he is stating his own position and assuring us (untruly) that he is 'still the same.' At line 622 he begins to harangue his followers; by line 635 he is drawing attention to the excellence of his public conduct. Book II opens with his speech from the throne; before we have had eight lines he is lecturing the assembly on his right to leadership. He meets Sin—and states his position. He sees the Sun; it makes him think of his own position. He spies on the human lovers; and states his position. In Book IX he journeys round the whole earth; it reminds him of his own position. The point need not be laboured. Adam, though locally confined to a small park on a small planet, has interests that embrace 'all the choir of heaven and all the furniture of earth.' Satan has been in the Heaven of Heavens and in the abyss of Hell, and surveyed all that lies between them, and in that whole immensity has found only one thing that interests Satan. It may be said that Adam's situation made it easier for him, than for Satan, to let his mind roam. But that is just the point. Satan's monomaniac concern with himself and his supposed rights and wrongs is a necessity of the Satanic predicament. Certainly, he has no choice. He has chosen to have no choice. He has wished to 'be himself', and to be in himself and for himself, and his wish has been granted. The Hell he carries with him is, in one sense, a Hell of infinite boredom. Satan, like Miss Bates, is interesting to read about; but Milton makes plain the blank uninterestingness of *being* Satan.

To admire Satan, then, is to give one's vote not only for a world of misery, but also for a world of lies and propaganda, of wishful thinking, of incessant autobiography. Yet the choice is possible. Hardly a day passes without some slight movement towards it in each one of us. That is what makes *Paradise Lost* so serious a poem. The thing is possible, and the exposure of it is resented. Where *Paradise Lost* is not loved, it is deeply hated. As Keats said more rightly than he knew, 'there is death' in Milton. We have all skirted the Satanic island closely enough to have motives for wishing to evade the full impact of the poem. For, I repeat, the thing is possible; and after a certain point it is prized. Sir Willoughby may be unhappy, but he *wants* to go on being Sir Willoughby. Satan *wants* to go on being Satan. That is the real meaning of his choice 'Better to reign in Hell, than serve in Heav'n.' Some, to the very end, will think this a fine thing to say; others will think that it fails to be roaring farce only because it spells agony. On the level of literary criticism the matter cannot be argued further. Each to his taste.

STANLEY BRODWIN

Mark Twain's Masks of Satan: The Final Phase

Perhaps there is no more intriguing—or perplexing—phase in Mark Twain's life and art than the final one, the 1890's and early 1900's. During these years, according to Bernard DeVoto, Twain threshed out his "symbols of despair" from a wide variety of material much of which was left incomplete, though virtually all of it saturated with a bitter or "black" satiric mood.[1] And DeVoto's hypothesis that Twain sought to free himself from an intolerable burden of guilt through the dream-philosophy of Philip Traum, the mysterious stranger, remains one that still must be considered fruitful, though it has set off some impressive countertheories.[2] Yet there is no easily perceived, clearly defined artistic direction in this phase of Mark Twain's work as a whole. What we do see is that Twain's mind and art were coiled around a number of stakes driven into the heart of a dominant symbolic and thematic complex: fallen man with all his attendant personal, social and political evils; an "absurd" universe grotesquely deterministic and dream-like at the same time; the problem of personal (psychic) identity; and a Satan-figure, who, ironically, very likely developed out of a persistent Mark Twain character-type, the sometimes "innocent," sometimes devious stranger striving either to "con" or to "reform" the people and society around him. The Satan-figure has received serious critical attention, since it is he who is at the center of the "Mysterious Stranger" manuscripts—the uncompleted

From *American Literature* 19, no. 2 (May 1973): 206–227. © 1973 Duke University Press.

"last testament" of Mark Twain.[3] But there were several Satans for Mark Twain, each one a mask or persona embodying a different aspect of his thought in a particular work, as well as his satiric or comic voice and style. To study Mark Twain's protean Satan is to study the trajectory of a great writer's intellectual and artistic attempts to find "salvation" in an apparently unsalvageable world.

Mark Twain cast Satan into four basic roles,[4] each requiring a separate characterization so that the created mask could express the proper tone and philosophic stance for the immediate story or sketch at hand. Interestingly, there seems to be no strict chronological development which would indicate that Twain had a clear "plan" when to employ one Satan mask or another. The creative ferment of these decades, producing so many reworked and unfinished projects, very likely made it impossible for Twain to formulate a consistent strategy in his uses of Satan. But the figure haunted his imagination which was fueled by his reading of *Paradise Lost*, Voltaire's *Zadig*, Goethe's *Faust*, the Apocrypha and other works. Nevertheless, the following Satan figures stand out in the wide range of his work.

First, there is the conventional tempter and "Father of Lies," in "The Man that Corrupted Hadleyburg" (1899).[5]

Second, in "That Day in Eden (A Passage from Satan's Diary)" and "Eve Speaks" (ca. 1900), Satan is a sympathetic commentator on the tragedy of man's fall, but one who fails to make Adam and Eve understand the concepts which would have saved them. The idea of Satan-as-failure crops up again in a number of unpublished pieces and in "Sold to Satan" (1904), all of which contain burlesque and serio-comic portraits of and attitudes toward the Tempter. "Sold to Satan," in particular, comically establishes the "ancestral" relationship between Twain and the Devil.

Third, in *Letters from the Earth* (1962),[6] Satan becomes a mischievous, sarcastic questioner of God's ways, writing secret letters to St. Gabriel and St. Michael about the absurdity of man, God's experiment.

Fourth, in "The Mysterious Stranger" stories (1897–1908), Satan is presented (with some variations) as a force of spiritual though amoral "innocence" charged with divine-like creative power. Though man, himself, is consistently viewed as a base creature in each of the three main versions, it is clear that Mark Twain's imagination was gripped by the relationships among the universe, Satan, and man.

I

"The Man that Corrupted Hadleyburg" embodies Twain's cynicism concerning the damned human race in the character of the vengeful stranger.

In this Western version of the fall, the lines of action are determined, both artistically and philosophically, by Satan—or Howard L. Stephenson, as he is called.

Stephenson, a "ruined gambler" (XXIII, 4),[7] begins the action of the story by translating his anger at Hadleyburg into a plan for corrupting it. "Bitter" and "revengeful" (XXIII, 2), he is actually as guilty of spiritual pride as his victims. In the mythical ramification of the biblical story, Satan also falls through pride and is thereby able to recognize and penetrate to the pride in Adam and Eve. Stephenson does indeed expose an inherently sinful Hadleyburg. His last "gamble" pays off. Critics have therefore read the tale as Mark Twain's "affirmation"[8] of his belief in man's ability to learn and accept the truth about himself. From that point of view, Satan's role is easily interpreted as that of a "savior."[9] But the many complex ironies in the story suggest another interpretation. Satan-Stephenson, as in the traditional Christian view, wins only to lose, since at the end he is duped into thinking Richards was in fact incorruptible. At the same time, the ending of the story in which we find the citizens of Hadleyburg willing to confront temptation and not be caught "napping" (XXIII, 69), again, does not necessarily suggest any real *moral* change in them that would justify reading the conclusion as a genuine version of the *felix culpa*. We can see this by examining the complex and ironic relationships Stephenson triggers, but which entrap him, too.

One of the most piercing ironies in the story derives from the relationship between Edward Richards and Burgess, a relationship Stephenson exploits after Mary and Edward discover the sack of "gold" (actually lead discs) left by Stephenson. Their initial response is to keep it and to burn the note which orders the money to go to the man who gave advice to Stephenson, whose exact words are recorded in a sealed envelope. Mary and Edward momentarily control themselves and assume that the advice was given by Barclay Goodson, the good samaritan, now dead. Of course, Goodson had not been brought up in Hadleyburg. They then wonder why the stranger made the hated Burgess the one to deliver the wealth, and they discuss the fact that Edward was guilty of not clearing Burgess from some (unnamed) accusation which destroyed his reputation. The implication, as the story progresses, is that Stephenson somehow knows this, but counts on Burgess's repaying Edward with kindness. This Burgess does, for in the grand revelation scene in which he reveals the letters of eighteen of the town's "incorruptible" families, he holds back Edward's note containing the secret advice: "You are far from being a bad man: Go, and reform" (XXIII, 22). By preventing the Richardses' disgrace, Burgess unwittingly exposes them to a second temptation. They accept the proceeds from the sack the town had auctioned off. But our elderly Adam and Eve are destroyed by guilt, for they become obsessed with the idea that Burgess was kind only to expose them later in revenge for Richards's earlier failure to help him. Although Richards had warned Burgess to leave town so as to avoid being tarred and feathered, he did not clear him. The dying Richards therefore convinces himself that Burgess "repented of the saving kindness which he had done me, and he *exposed* me" (XXIII, 68). But Burgess had not exposed the Richardses, and is ironically hurt by them again. He will be more hated than ever now. Stephenson's plan succeeds because he has insight into both the weaknesses and the strengths of his victims. He is, so to speak, a *psychological* determinist, capable of creating a situation in which people can be emotionally manipulated toward his desired end: mutual physical or spiritual destruction. This Satan has insight into *guilt*, just as, in "The Mysterious Stranger" fables, "44" can read minds. Stephenson emerges, in part, as a demonic mask for Mark Twain's own obsession with guilt, turned here to destructive rather than creative purposes. One of the consequences of such power, however, is to risk exile, a frequent condition for many of Twain's characters other than Satan. In "Hadleyburg," Twain gives us Burgess and Halliday, perhaps as pointed contrasts to Stephenson, for they are both good men who have grown embittered in their social exile.

Halliday is described as "the loafing, good-natured, no-account, irreverent fisherman, hunter, boys' friend, stray-dogs' friend, typical 'Sam Lawson' of the town" (XXIII, 18). He also becomes, in part, the author's satiric voice, a grown-up Huck Finn. The change in the people is not noticed "except by Jack Halliday, who always noticed everything; and always made fun of it, too, no matter what it was" (XXIII, 19). Here we see an Adamic figure developing a "Satanic" characteristic, that inability to believe in the essential goodness of others. If he exists at all, the "good" man is pushed towards exile, with its embitterment and estrangement. However unwilling, man may come to share a common vision with his ArchEnemy. "The Mysterious Stranger" stories may be read as a demonstration of this idea, as well.

It is given to the Richardses to recognize the larger tragic dimension of the situation Stephenson created. Confronting his lie-filled life, Edward realizes that the money "came from Satan. I saw the hell-brand on them, and I knew they were sent to betray me to sin" (XXIII, 67). And again: "like the rest I fell when temptation came" (XXIII, 68). Still, this confession, however "realistic" and "affirmative" it may be, serves only to create yet another lie: that Burgess had exposed him. To the end, Richards is trapped in lies, whether motivated by greed or by what he felt was the truth of man's nature.

Mary, too, has her insight. When Edward rationalizes that it "was so ordered" (XXIII, 15) that the money be sent to them, she replies:

Ordered! Oh, everything's *ordered*, when a person has to find some way out when he has been stupid. Just the same, it was *ordered* that the money should come to us in this special way, and it was you that must take it on yourself to go meddling with the designs of Providence—and who gave you the right? It was wicked, that is what it was—just blasphemous presumption. (XXIII, 15)

Her point is clear, and reflects Mark Twain's own view of the matter. Man invokes Destiny or a form of determinism to bolster his own selfish rationalizations. The next step is to meddle with Providence. For what *is* ordered is man's pride which leads him to destined ends in spite of himself. The revised motto of Hadleyburg, "Lead Us Into Temptation" (XXIII, 69), is not merely a recognition that morality must be continually tested by experience, though of course that is an important theme in the fable. The deeper meaning seems to be that the only way to confront destiny is to surrender to it. At least man will not be caught "napping" when he falls, but fall he must. But the grand irony is that Satan will not see the proof of this. He, too, is a victim of the lie, and writes to Richards that he is "*a disappointed man. Your honesty is beyond the reach of temptation*" (XXIII, 62). This appears so only because, as the reader knows, Burgess did not tell the truth at the court. Satan is justified in thinking that all men will fall when tempted, but the reality of it eludes him. Also eluding him will be the consolation that Hadleyburg has not really changed. Certainly, Hadleyburg will be shrewder, more careful, more alert, in the future. The citizens welcome temptation, not because any profound moral change has taken place in them, but because they are now "experienced." Twain's implication, I believe, is that expediency will still be the basis of morality, a conviction he often expressed throughout his writings. To be sure, a morality based on "enlightened" expediency is better than the sham, self-righteous attitudes of the Hadleyburgians before the fall, and must not be despised. But it is not authentic moral reform. One thinks of an early Twain quip: "the serene confidence which a Christian feels with four aces."[10] No doubt Stephenson, the ruined gambler, would have bitterly recognized the truth of that description.

II

The Satan we meet in *Letters from the Earth* is quite different from Stephenson. Where the latter was a portrait of a quietly sinister, embittered manipulator of human souls, the Satan of *Letters* is drawn as a questioning, intellectual Archangel, unafraid to voice his opinions about God. Predictably, he is sarcastic about God's experiment, man, and vicious in describing God's Laws of Nature which compel creatures to be dominated by certain characteristics that define their being. God banishes him on account of "his too flexible tongue" (*LE*, p. 6), but he is used to this. Satan flies into space and eternal night, and then finally decides to observe man. In this description it is possible to see Mark Twain defining himself and his role in life. He had no trouble in identifying himself with this kind of Satan, who is but a fuller extension of the type of spiritual exile developed in the figures of Pudd'nhead Wilson and Halliday. What follows is eleven letters written to Michael and Gabriel, embodying the most explicit condemnation of God, the Bible and man of which Mark Twain was capable.

As is to be expected, God creates Adam and Eve insufficient to stand, and, when they fall, He carries out the sentence of death against them. Satan's comment is sharply ironical: "As you perceive, the only person responsible for the couple's offense escaped; and not only escaped but became the executioner of the innocent" (*LE*, p. 20).[11] This is the essence of Mark Twain's case against God. God is the devil, while Satan is the bitterly ironic sympathizer of man. God sends forth Adam and Eve "under a curse— a permanent one" (*LE*, p. 20). And it was of the consequences of this curse that Mark Twain wrote and over which he agonized much of his creative life. It is significant, too, that Satan is not involved in this fall. There is only the traditional serpent, as in the biblical account, to tempt man. Moreover, this serpent offers man what he naturally (according to God's laws) must have: knowledge. By contrast, Mark Twain tells us, "the priest, like God, whose imitator and representative he is, has made it his business from the beginning to keep him *from* knowing any useful thing" (*LE*, p. 17). Even the serpent emerges sympathetically.

Yet the full force of Twain's attack centers on the New Testament. The gift of the God of the Old Testament was death, and death to a life that is only a "fever-dream ... embittered by sorrows.... a nightmare-confusion of spasmodic and fleeting delights ... interspersed with long-drawn miseries," was "sweet," "gentle," and "kind" (*LE*, p. 44). What the New Testament and the figure of Jesus do is to create hell, so that man cannot claim "the blessed refuge of the grave" (*LE*, p. 44). In Mark Twain's embittered mind and personal theology, "The palm for malignity must be granted to Jesus, the inventor of hell ..." (*LE*, p. 45).[12] The Sermon on the Mount becomes a collection of "immense sarcasms" (*LE*, p. 54), in the light of the fact that man cannot by temperament and the permanent curse upon him turn the other cheek or be meek and humble. Above all, it is a God who cannot fulfill these moral precepts and who makes a mockery of man's life by demanding that humanity must. Such is the view of Satan-Mark Twain concerning these key aspects of traditional Western theology. The rather obvious Satan mask here functions only to voice a polemic. Hell, for this Satan, is having to watch the workings of a cruelly absurd Divine Plan. Satan shifts from a demonic glee to an almost tragic indignation as he observes the victimization of man and the cosmic insanity of his Judge.

III

The next Satan-mask is curiously two-sided, though the two sides are joined by a single motif: Satan-as-failure. In "That Day in Eden" and "Eve Speaks," Satan becomes a tragic failure whose predicament enlists our sympathies, and in a group of unpublished short works he emerges as a vulgar—even grotesque—fool. He may appear quite polished in "Sold to Satan," but nevertheless admits to his past silly blunders. One of the story's main concerns, however, is to demonstrate the "ancestral" relationship between the narrator (Twain) and himself.

Satan's failure in the Adamic pieces comes about not as a result of any flaw in Satan, himself, but as a consequence of an insoluble situation created by the Deity: Adam and Eve can in no way understand God's prohibitions. Nothing Satan can do will make them grasp the meanings of words whose substance they have never experienced. Satan must watch helplessly as they eat of the Tree of Knowledge and acquire the "disaster" (XXIX, 344) that is the Moral Sense. Therefore Twain invests Satan's narrative with a pathetic tenderness:

> Poor ignorant things, the command of refrain had meant nothing to them, they were but children, and could not understand untried things and verbal abstractions which stood ... outside of their ... narrow experience. Eve reached for an apple!—oh, farewell, Eden and your sinless joys, come poverty and pain, ... envy, strife, malice and dishonor, age, weariness, remorse; then desperation and the prayer for the release of death, indifferent that the gates of hell yawn beyond it! (XXIX, 345)

After the fall, Satan simply comments that the change in Eve "was pitiful" (XXIX, 345), and then describes in a quietly lyrical way, the onrush of old age in the First Couple. And, at the end of "Eve Speaks" when Eve discovers the death of Abel, Satan returns as the Consoler: "Death has entered the world, the creatures are perishing; one of The Family is fallen; the product of the Moral Sense is complete. The Family think ill of death—they will change their minds" (XXIX, 350). By using Satan as his compassionate mask, and keeping the Deity narratively detached from the account of the fall and primal murder, Twain is able to "humanize" Satan, contrasting his sympathy—even compassion—for man, with the Deity's distantness and absurd prohibition.

A wholly different emphasis on Satan's failures emerges from a group of unpublished fragments in the Mark Twain Papers and the short novel "The Refuge of the Derelicts" (1905–1906). In this novel, Admiral Stormfield sympathizes with Satan over his failure to tempt Christ and his inability to prevent bishops from breaking their contracts with him. In these matters, Satan comes off somewhat as an incompetent. More ironically, the Admiral, complaining that Satan "only" converted "nine tenths of the human race," ponders the question: "Is he one of life's failures? ... *One* of them? why, he's It!"[13] In another piece (untitled, ca. 1909), "little Sammy" mocks Satan's reputation for "commercial" ability, using again the example of Christ in the Wilderness. How could a place no more than "a hundred miles in diameter"[14] tempt God? This subject seems to have gripped Twain as early as the 1880's when he wrote "Bible Citations in proof [of?] a real devil," nine pages of short, exegetical notes on over twenty-three New Testament references to a real or substantive devil. Matthew 4 is again the central illustration. The note on Matthew 4:8 contains a biting remark on America:

> They ... go to the mountains—an *exceedingly* high mountain from whose top all the vast Roman Empire was easily visible ... also America. [This is the *real* discovery of America, & the devil ought to have credit of it, not Columbus.] The D offers to give all ... these to C to worship him. He is now both ... dishonest & foolish, since he owns ... no part of this territory, yet offers it to a personage whom he suspects owns it all.[15]

Twain could never quite free himself from reading the Bible with fundamentalist passion even as he ridiculed it in the name of reason. But neither could he escape seeing irony in all things. In these fragments he characterizes Satan indirectly by discussing his actions rather than by dramatizing them. Satan appears stupid in dealing with God and priests, but effective with man, becoming, as Twain wrote in "Concerning the Jews" (1899), "spiritual head of four fifths of the human race and political head of the whole of it ..." (XXII, 265); he could be compassionate or destructive; and Twain's own relationship to him could oscillate between ironic "respect" or contempt or horror. If Satan occasionally fails to teach man the true nature of reality, he nearly always awakens and reveals some inner corruption or lie within him. As with Adam, Twain assumed the spiritual "kinship" between Satan and himself.[16] "Sold to Satan" dramatizes this relationship perfectly.

"Sold to Satan" is a clever burlesque exploiting the discovery of radium by the Curies. Twain inserts in it a comic temptation scene built around the themes of science, American big business tactics, and the spiritual consanguinity between himself and Satan. Here is a courteous, apparently successful Tempter who is made of radium worth millions on the market. Only Satan's polonium shield—still undiscovered by science—prevents him from blowing up the world. Indeed, Satan is an eerie forecast of The Ultimate Bomb. But it is the economic temptation that first works on the narrator, who sees what an "original" idea it would be to "kidnap Satan, and stock him, and incorporate him, and water the stock up to ten billions—just three times its actual value—and blanket the world with it!" (XXIX, 328). Satan tells him:

> "Do you know I have been trading with your poor pathetic race for ages, and you are the first person who has ever been intelligent enough to divine the large commercial value of my make-up."
>
> . . . .
>
> "Yes, you are the first," he continued. "All through the Middle Ages I used to buy Christian souls at fancy rates, building bridges and cathedrals in a single night in return, and getting swindled out of my Christian nearly every time that I dealt with a priest— as history will concede—but making it up on the lay square- dealer now and then, as *I* admit; but none of those people ever guessed where the *real* big money lay. You are the first." (XXIX, 328–329)

The interesting conceit here is that, instead of Satan tempting man with some external precious thing, it is Satan himself—pure power which can run all the world's "machines and railways a hundred million years" (XXIX, 331)—who is the overwhelming temptation to economic and technological man. The narrator cries: "Quick—my soul is yours dear Ancestor; take it— we'll start a company!" (XXIX, 331). The narrator then gets a lesson in "modern" physics while Satan demonstrates his power by lighting cigars with his fingertips and his wit by casting backhanded compliments at Madame Curie for having discovered his (and Hell's) natural element. Only when Madame Curie isolates polonium, will the narrator be able to clothe himself in it and take possession of the radium located in a firefly cemetery. The story concludes: "Stock is for sale. Apply to Mark Twain" (XXIX, 338).

Clearly, then, Mark Twain sees himself in this tale as a mirror-image of Satan (or *vice versa*), since both have an immediate, intuitive sense of what the other wants and the knowledge of how to get it. In getting the power that is radium, the narrator fulfills the Gilded Age dream that so many of Mark Twain's characters dreamed—to make the biggest "killing" and the grandest "effect" ever. The burlesque is as much a satire and exposure of Twain's own character as it is of man's crude exploitation of scientific discoveries. The witty and business-like attitudes of both the narrator and Satan sharpen the disparity between their "styles" and moral natures. "Sold to Satan" gives us a single mask whose transparency allows the reader to see that the separate entities—the Tempter and the Tempted—are one and the same.

IV

Perhaps the most significant role of Satan for Mark Twain is to be found in "The Mysterious Stranger" complex. It is in this group of stories that Twain reached an identification of himself as a creative artist with the divine-like creative powers of an unfallen Satan. It is here that we receive his final condemnation of the damned human race and attempt to describe the nature of the universe. And, as DeVoto originally suggested, these works reflect Twain's striving for some salvational ideal. By contrast, the other masks of Satan we have observed are constructions whose function is to voice the tragicomic relationship between man and God, sometimes compassionately, more often cynically or satirically. But these Satan-masks did not escape Twain's criticism, either, as the failure theme attests. That is why, in all likelihood, these Satans do not offer "solutions" to the massive moral and theological problems inherent in the "human condition." This may also be the reason why Twain was never able to achieve an esthetically and intellectually complete version of "The Mysterious Stranger" idea. Dream psychology, determinism, the myth of the fall—all these explanatory "solutions" to universal problems were deeply ingrained in Twain's mind. On an intellectual level, "The Mysterious Stranger" stories represent Twain's attempts to make these conflicting "philosophies" seem harmonious and persuasive. To do this, Twain employed a version of one of his most profound patterns—the contrast and relationship between a putative Huck Finn-Tom Sawyer narrator who has not yet dreamed of "lighting out" for the territory, and an "Adamic" Satan who utterly transcends the human condition. It is this pattern that creates whatever unity the stories possess and into which dreams, determinism, and the fall are woven. And lurking in almost every line, there exists an emotional force which derives from Mark Twain's confronting himself in an inner dialogue between the "earthly" man and the "divine" artist.

Insofar as the stories represent projections of this inner dialogue going on within Mark Twain, himself, their real meanings and tensions can be located in his need to "liberate," psychically and philosophically, his creative Self from the noncreative claims of what he called in a letter to Howells, his "mud image." The letter, dated February 23, 1897, the period during which the Satan figure was to emerge dominantly, deals with Twain's mood after the death of Susy. He writes that he is "Indifferent to nearly everything but work." Yet he must persist:

> This mood will pass, some day—there is history for it. But it cannot pass until my wife comes up out of the submergence. She was always so quick to recover herself before, but now there is no rebound, & we are dead people who go through the motions of life. Indeed I am a mud image, & it puzzles me to know what it is in me that writes, & that has comedy-fancies & finds pleasure in phrasing them. It is a law of our nature, of course, or it wouldn't happen; the thing in me forgets the presence of the mud image & goes its own way wholly unconscious of it & apparently of no kinship with it.[17]

The "thing" in him—clearly his creative power that in some way "forgets" (is *indifferent* to?) his mud image—is the salvation here, ultimately finding expression in the Satan of "The Mysterious Stranger" stories. In "real" life, these two aspects of being are mysteriously embodied, to use Theodore Dreiser's phrase, in "Mark the Double Twain." In "The Mysterious Stranger" stories they confront one another as separate entities, characterized by a kind of love–hate or love–fear relationship. And in the first of the stories, "The Chronicle of Young Satan," Philip Traum says that

> Man *is* made of dirt—I *saw* him made. I am not made of dirt. Man *is* a museum of disgusting diseases, a home of impurities; he comes to-day and is gone to-morrow, he begins as dirt and departs as a stench; I am of the aristocracy of the Imperishables. And man has the *Moral Sense*. (p. 55)

Adamic man *is* what his name means: earth. His evil-creating Moral Sense is an inextricable part of this dirt origin. The need to be liberated from this condition is touched upon in "No. 44, The Mysterious Stranger," when Emil Schwarz, August Feldner's Dream-Self, cries out against his being an embodiment of man:

> oh, free me from *them*; these bonds of flesh—this decaying vile matter, this foul weight, and clog, and burden, this loathsome

sack of corruption in which my spirit is imprisoned, her white wings bruised and soiled—oh, be merciful and set her free! (p. 369)

He goes on to bemoan the fact that he is a "servant!—I who never served before; here I am a slave—slave among little mean kings and emperors made of clothes, the kings and emperors slaves themselves, to mud-built carrion that are *their* slaves!" (p. 369)

Mud, dirt, "earth-shod,"—these terms are at the center of Mark Twain's metaphor for fallen man. To be "free," "Imperishable," without the Moral Sense, describes unfallen creative Satan. The tension and relationship between the two provides, as I have suggested, the unifying pattern in all three versions. Seen from this perspective, the other key themes in the stories find significant, but supportive roles. The kind of determinism that characterizes fallen man or the mud image is a fixed, mechanical process well suited to man's nature. Mechanical determinism becomes, in effect, a covering definition for fallen man. It becomes a way of *knowing* him. Yet, as we shall see, that determinism is itself, when examined, intrinsically absurd in its workings and results. The determinism that characterizes unfallen Satan is really a species of idealism, that is, it describes the nature of the universe and its manifestations as dream—as unreal ontologically speaking, though "real" enough in appearance. Satan's mission is to teach man this "truth." The creative powers of Satan become a vital way by which this truth is to be conveyed. This is a fascinating inversion of the Gospels in which Jesus uses his divine powers to heal, teach, and create faith and preparedness for the Kingdom to come. For Mark Twain-Satan the Kingdom to come ends in nothing but an escape into solipsistic idealism, a consequence of a metaphysical irreconcilability in a universe in which the primal drama has always been strife between Flesh and Spirit. The earth-bound narrators of "The Mysterious Stranger" stories find themselves in the very center of this struggle which began historically and theologically in the Garden of Eden.

The "Paradise" of Eseldorf is the final fictional *locus* of this drama for Mark Twain. And it is in the "Schoolhouse Hill" version that the problem of the fall is treated most explicitly. This is significant especially in the light of the fact that the other two versions mainly stress the problems of dreams and determinism. It is true that all three versions portray the creative powers of Satan, although the young "44" of "Schoolhouse Hill" is made remarkable (at least at the outset) by his learning abilities rather than his cosmic gifts. Toward the end of this unfinished story "44" does indeed perform the miracle of saving people who are trapped in a mysterious snowstorm from death. The other two versions play considerably more on his ability to create and destroy life, and to manipulate and reveal the past and the future. Similarly, "44"'s indifference to human suffering is lightly touched upon in "Schoolhouse Hill" but intensified in the other two. In all three versions man is presented as small-minded and corrupt. In all three the Satan-figure tries to teach "truths" to ignorant man. What, then, is the "truth" in "Schoolhouse Hill"? It is simply that man's entrapment in flesh and human history with all its moral perversities is nothing but an absurd, primal error. This is what "44" tells Mr. Hotchkiss in their discussion of biblical events. He says: "There was no tempter until my father ate of the fruit himself and became one. Then he tempted other angels and they ate of it also; then Adam and the woman." The elder Satan is very upset for "he could do nothing but grieve and lament" (p. 215). According to "44," Satan gave no warning to Adam because he had an "erroneous" idea of what the fruit could do once eaten: "His error was in supposing that a knowledge of the difference between good & evil was *all* that the fruit could confer" (p. 216). Young Satan elaborates:

> "Consider the passage which says *man is prone to evil as the sparks to fly upward*. Is that true? ...."
> "Indeed it is—nothing could be truer."
> "It is not true of the men of any other planet. It explains the mystery. My father's error stands revealed in all its nakedness. The fruit's office was not confined to conferring the mere knowledge of good and evil, it conferred also the passionate ... eager and hungry *disposition to* DO *evil*. Prone as sparks to fly upward; in other words, prone as water to run down hill—a powerful figure, and means that man's disposition *is* wholly evil, ... inveterately evil, and that he is as undisposed to do good as water is undisposed to run *up* hill. Ah, my father's error brought a colossal disaster upon the men of this planet. It *poisoned* the men of this planet—poisoned them in mind and body...."
> "It brought death, too."
> "Yes—whatever that may be...." (p. 216)

"44" then goes on to say that he will try to lift part of the "burden of evil consequences" (p. 217) from man, although the evil is now "permanent." At that point the discussion breaks off and is not referred to again. But its implications for the entire "Mysterious Stranger" complex seem to me to be considerable. First, the passage is another remarkable instance of Mark Twain's intellectual struggle with the idea of the fall.[18] Some new elements present themselves here that are not to be found in his earlier treatment of the myth, but fit into the general pattern of Mark Twain's thinking on the subject. The idea that the fall was an "error" on the part of a guilt-struck Satan is a new perspective, though it serves once again to reinforce Twain's picture of a tragically victimized Adam and his descendants. For not only is Adam an innocent victim, but the whole "temptation" situation is a lamentable mistake. Adam *and* Satan have been fooled by God, and are therefore natural objects of sympathy for Mark Twain. Satan had only wished to give man moral discrimination; instead he gave him a permanent disposition to evil. To underscore this, Twain plays with biting wit on the passage in Job 5:7: "Man is born unto trouble, as the sparks fly upward." The substitution of "prone to evil" for "born unto trouble" reveals one of Twain's habitual responses to the problem of human suffering.

Secondly, the idea of the fall as an "error" reinforces—even provides the grounds for—the metaphysics of dreams and determinism which permeate the other two versions of "The Mysterious Stranger." It is the fall which *creates* the conditions of a world characterized by imprisonment in flesh and the ironbound consequences flowing from this state. The fact that the fall was an "error" only provides more "proof" for an absurd universe. It therefore is reasonable to assume that the philosophic "positions" presented in "The Chronicle of Young Satan" and "No. 44, The Mysterious Stranger," are organically tied to the Adamic myth and spring from it as final descriptions of man's fate.

The first "position" made explicit in "The Chronicle" may be termed "deterministic nihilism," a description that covers all the mechanistic, but purposeless aspects of existence."[19] By changing the life-events of Nikolaus, Lisa, and Fischer, the weaver, Satan only teaches the narrator, Theodor, the futility of knowing one's history in advance. Theodor says, "Satan had shown me other people's lives and I saw that in nearly all cases there would be little or no advantage in altering them" (p. 147). Not only do Satan's lessons "prove" man's life to be contemptible and miserable, but also that there is no redemption from this misery. One "determined" life turns out to be no better than any other "determined" life. It is clear that life has no meaning. Though Satan does say that "Some few will profit in various ways by change" (p. 132), this does not really offer any consolation to Theodor or qualify the meaninglessness significantly. The very Heaven mortals yearn for and may receive is ruled over by a God who has no "compassion" in "His hard heart" (p. 129). This is said by the embittered Frau Brandt whose prayers to God went unheeded. The irony is that she should have prayed for the death of her child. Theodor sees into mankind's dilemma: "Ah! that poor woman! It is as Satan said, we do not know good fortune from bad, and always mistaking the one for the other. Many a time, since then, I have heard people pray to God to spare the life of sick persons, but I have never done it" (p. 129). All that could possibly be called "redemptive" is death. And yet one of Satan's prime demonstrations even undercuts the dubious consolation of death. For early in the story, in explaining to Nikolaus that the "Fall did not affect me nor the rest of the relationship" (p. 49), Satan casually squashed two little workmen he had created and then "wiped the red from his fingers ... and went on talking ..." (p. 49). Their lives were meaningless—an illusion—and so were their deaths. Finally, Satan teaches the boys that mankind "duped itself from cradle to grave with shams and delusions which it mistook for realities, and this made its entire life a sham" (p. 164). There is no way, then, for man to reach any kind of "truth" or positive meaning in existence. There is only the negative meaning that all is sham or meaninglessness precisely because man cannot distinguish appearance from reality, good fortune from bad, and the value of one deterministically shaped life from another. Such are the true consequences of the fall.

If this is true, it explains Mark Twain's mask or portrait of Satan. He must be completely freed from any mortal element in order to dramatize unequivocally man's fate. His indifference to human suffering can then be made to function as an artistic device which would make his teachings "believable." The excitement the boys feel in Satan's company is based on not only his tricks and effects, but also, more importantly, on his irreverence and aura of transcendence emanating through his cosmic power. These elements make possible, at best, the grounds for a condescending relationship between the Immortal and the Mortal. Mark Twain has provided us with no middle ground, as it were, for both to inhabit meaningfully. This radical polarization in character only underscores what little hope Twain had that a redemptive ideal could be found in a world ultimately "empty and soundless" (p. 403). Knowing this, Satan says that "No sane man can be happy, for to him life is real, and he sees what a fearful thing it is. Only the mad can be happy, and not many of those" (p. 164).

The second position developed in "No. 44, The Mysterious Stranger," is that of the much-discussed solipsism presented in the famous dream-ending Twain wrote in 1904. This passage was written four years after Twain had stopped work on "The Chronicle" and six years after "Schoolhouse Hill." Yet it was written four years *before* the scene of the historical pageant "44" shows August and then dissolves, leaving an "empty & soundless world." This surely indicates that both positions maintained their hold on Twain's mind, and that he could not separate, intellectually, the two. William M. Gibson suggests that the pageant-ending might have been intended as an alternate to the dream-passage.[20] If so, it does not seem to reflect any real philosophic confusion in Twain's mind, though it certainly presented him with an artistic choice to make. Twain's philosophic task was to integrate or harmonize his view that existence is essentially meaningless and determined at the same time, with his view that reality is a dream dreamed by a "vagrant Thought" (p. 405)—the isolated Self. However artistically unfinished "No. 44, The Mysterious Stranger" is, Mark Twain did work out a meaningful, though not totally logical, pattern of ideas. The key to the pattern lies in the final mask of Satan and his dream-philosophy.

This mask embodies the marriage of two major preoccupations and themes in Twain's work: the Adamic myth and the problem of identity in its relationship to a dreamed and/or deterministic world. Thus, "44" is a Satanic Dreamer, a version of the Superintendent of Dreams in the fragment "The Great Dark."[21] The Superintendent is a "trickster" who uses and manifests the basic absurdity of dreams, in themselves. What makes most dreams absurd is that they always reflect the horror of reality and man's fate as they are archetypically dramatized in the Adamic myth. This thematic marriage becomes strikingly clear in the long fragment called "Which Was It?" (1902). George Harrison, a major character, reflects on his father's crime of paying off debts with counterfeit money and the excuse he constructs for himself:

> He [the father] argued with Rev. Mr. Bailey about temptations, and said a character that hadn't been exposed to them and solidified by fighting them and *losing* the fight was a flabby poor thing and couldn't be depended upon in an emergency. He said a temptation successfully resisted was good, but a fall was better. He said he wouldn't go so far as to put temptations in the way of a child of his, but had always been willing to see them come; and said a person wouldn't ever be safe until he had tried and *fallen*.[22]

Later in the story, after the son has experienced a long series of calamities as a result of a murder he commits to save his family from debt, he analyzes his predicament by drawing a tree entitled the "genealogy of a lapse." The root of the tree is called "False Pride," the trunk, "Disaster," and on the limbs are eleven fruits or crimes (p. 241). For George, each crime was a consequence of a preceding crime revealing a deterministic pattern. But Twain had planned to have George awaken to find that all was a nightmare, anyway. The awakening from the nightmare of the fall was no doubt a desperate wish-fulfillment for Mark Twain. Actually, his sense of a fallen world went so deep that he ironically could not believe in the forms of salvation offered by the "Judeo-Christian" tradition. Moreover, it was a belief that found dubious consolation in philosophic determinism, since genuine moral and spiritual reform seemed illusory. The picture is that of a fallen world that cannot be redeemed, deterministically structured yet at the same time chaotic and a "sham" through which man wanders in a kind of schizoid dream-state, never knowing quite who and what he is. The solipsistic view of Satan-Mark Twain can be seen now as a direct emotional and intellectual spin-off from the idea or perception that there is a Cosmic Contradiction at the heart of things.[23] That is why Satan, after describing these contradictions to August in terms of a God who "mouths justice, and invented hell—mouths mercy, and invented hell" (p. 405), says: "You perceive, now, that these things are all impossible, *except* in a dream" (p. 405, "except" in my italics). This seems to me to be the crucial line in the argument of the dream-passage. Because the world is fallen, trapped in flesh and mud, and beset by insoluble moral and metaphysical contradictions, it must be a dream. This is the inverse of Tertullian's "*certum est, quia impossible.*" For Twain, reality has no inner logic to make it believable as an objective-existent structure with a meaningful *telos*. The universe, therefore, comes closest to the nature of a dream-nightmare. "44" wonders why August did not see the analogy before: "Strange, indeed, that you should not have suspected that your universe and its contents were only dreams, visions, fictions! Strange, because they are so frankly and hysterically insane—like all dreams" (p. 404). Then, "44" proceeds to list his examples of cosmic contradictions. But he has made the key analogy: "insane—like all dreams." His next step—though a *non sequitur*, yet emotionally, existentially, true—is to say that this insane reality is a dream. He moves from analogy to identification, from simile to metaphor. Nevertheless, "44" cannot escape the fact that some one mind must be making or perceiving the identification. He tells August that "Nothing exists but You. And you are but a Thought ... wandering forlorn among the empty eternities!" (p. 405). And "Thought" had been defined as "inextinguishable, indestructible" (p. 404). The exhortation by "44" to "Dream other dreams, and better!" is not the consolation it seems.[24] It may be possible to dream less insane dreams than man is now dreaming, but little else. Every dream will end by revealing the Self's forlorn state amid empty eternities. True, there is the consolation of being "set ... free" (p. 404) as "44" says. August is indeed set free, at least intellectually, from being a mud image. Not only is he set free from the "nightmare of history" *qua* history, but also from the nightmare implicit in the conditions of the Adamic myth. Still, what good would it be for August to dream other dreams in a human context? To be truly "saved," August's thought-reality would have to be precisely the same as "44"'s. August would have to dream himself—actually be—a god. Earlier in the story, "44" had told him that "a man's mind cannot *create*—a god's can, and my race can. That is the difference. *We* need no contributed materials, we *create* them—out of thought. All things that exist were made out of thought—and out of nothing else" (p. 333).

A god can create out of a thought-stuff which is pure essence; man can only create by associating external realities received through the senses into set forms as a machine does. Man does not enjoy *true* creativity. Only unfallen Satan can experience this. Ultimate salvation is to be set free from the consequences of the fall and to become a god. Mark Twain's remarkable irony is that the cardinal sin of pride is salvation itself. Unlike Howard L. Stephenson and the other Satan-masks, this Tempter is translated through a new dream into a genuine Savior. The concept is best understood as a revelation of Mark Twain's spiritual and philosophic anguish in his final years, rather than as serious metaphysics. But as a metaphorical description or radical theological concept it resonates forcefully with the truth of man's existential confrontation of a reality that he can make little sense of and that always throws him back on himself to find truth. As such, it is a serious theological statement, replete with symbols and paradox and the striving for transcendence. In turning the theology of the Adamic myth upside down, Mark Twain created his most outrageous protest against God's world and mediated it through a Satan no longer angry, only free and detached. Though tentatively and incompletely worked out in "The Mysterious Stranger" stories, Mark Twain had come to the "position" that salvation lay outside of man, in the inevitable triumph of Satan.

NOTES

Copyright © 1972 by Mark Twain Company—all previously unpublished works of Mark Twain. I wish to thank Mr. Thomas G. Chamberlain and the Trustees of the Mark Twain Company for permission to use unpublished material.

1. See Bernard DeVoto, *Mark Twain at Work* (Cambridge, Mass., 1942), pp. 105–130.

2. A good sampling of the criticism on *The Mysterious Stranger* is in *Mark Twain's The Mysterious Stranger and the Critics*, ed. John S. Tuckey (Belmont, Calif., 1968). See particularly Part Four, the essays by Coleman O. Parsons, Glades C. Bellamy, Roger B. Salomon, Albert E. Stone, H.N. Smith, and James M. Cox.

3. We now have these manuscripts in a definitive edition: *Mark Twain's Mysterious Stranger Manuscripts*, ed. with an Introduction by William M. Gibson (Berkeley, Calif., 1969), whose texts I will use in this paper unless otherwise indicated. Indispensable, too, is John S. Tuckey's *Mark Twain and Little Satan: The Writing of "The Mysterious Stranger"* (Lafayette, Ind., 1963).

4. See Gibson's "Introduction," pp. 14–16. Professor Gibson sees Satan as forming a "Square Deific." He is a "rebel," and "the truth-speaker ... banished from heaven"; the "Father of the Old Testament and Missouri Presbyterianism"; and the "supernal Power not so much indifferent to men as wholly unaware of them" (p. 15). Gibson is here expanding the formulation presented by Coleman O. Parsons in "The Devil and Samuel Clemens," *Virginia Quarterly Review*, XXIII (Autumn, 1947), 582–606. I am clearly

indebted to the formulations of both scholars. However, my emphasis is on the separate characterizations of Satan Twain gives us, especially as they relate to particular variations of mood and theme. I am also concerned with the relationships of comedy, satire, and tragedy as they are reflected in these Satan-masks. I feel that my category, "Satan-as-failure," has not been delineated by critics, despite its strong thematic presence in Twain's treatment of the figure. Of course, I am not attempting in this article to give a comprehensive listing and analysis of all of Mark Twain's references to Satan, but only those that suggest meaningful patterns and ideas.

5. Though most critics have seen the "stranger" as Satan in this story, the most complete demonstration is by Henry B. Rule, "The Role of Satan in 'The Man that Corrupted Hadleyburg,'" *Studies in Short Fiction*, VI (Fall, 1969), 619–629.

6. Edited by Bernard DeVoto (New York, 1962). Hereafter referred to in my text as *LE*. For a brief background to these letters from Satan, see Albert B. Paine, *Mark Twain: A Biography* (New York, 1912), III, 1531–1532. The pieces were written in 1909.

7. *The Writings of Mark Twain*, ed. A.B. Paine, 37 vols. (New York, 1923). Unless otherwise noted, all references will be to this Stormfield Edition.

8. See Clinton S. Burhans, "The Sober Affirmation of Mark Twain's Hadleyburg," *American Literature*, XXXIV (Nov., 1962), 375–384.

9. Rule, "The Role of Satan in 'The Man that Corrupted Hadleyburg,'" p. 620. Like Burhans, Rule sees the story as Twain's version of the *felix culpa*. I agree, but as I try to demonstrate, the fall was not all that fortunate or affirmative.

10. From a "Letter to a Young Gentleman in Missouri Who Wanted Information on the Nevada Territory," *Territorial Enterprise*, 1863. Quoted in *Mark Twain's Frontier*, ed. James E. Camp and X. J. Kennedy (New York, 1963), pp. 30–31. I am quoting "out of context," of course, but the amusing description applies.

11. See also Mark Twain, "Reflections on Religion," ed. Charles Neider, *Hudson Review*, XVI (Autumn, 1963), 352: "God alone is responsible for every act and word of a human being's life between cradle and grave."

12. In his *Notebook*, ed. A.B. Paine (New York, 1935), p. 290, Twain wrote: "There seems to be nothing connected with the atonement scheme that is rational. If Christ were God, He is in the attitude of One whose anger against Adam has grown so uncontrollable ... that nothing but a sacrifice of life can appease it, & so without noticing how illogical the act is going to be, God condemns Himself to death ... and wipes off that old score."

13. In *Mark Twain's Fables of Man*, ed. with an Introduction by John S. Tuckey (Berkeley, Calif., 1972), p. 195. References to this volume in the present section will appear in the text, cited by page.

14. In the Mark Twain Papers, Berkeley, California: DV#30, p. 9 of the holograph.

15. In the Mark Twain Papers, Berkeley, California: DV#81, Typescript, p. 2.

16. For a good compilation and discussion of Twain's references and allusions to this kinship, see Allison Ensor, *Mark Twain and the Bible* (Lexington, Ky., 1969), pp. 24, 40–61 passim.

17. *Mark Twain–Howells Letters*, ed. Henry Nash Smith and William M. Gibson (Cambridge, Mass., 1960), II, 664–665.

18. Many critics of Twain have commented on his concern with Adam but very few in-depth studies have been made on the subject. See my article "The Humor of the Absurd: Mark Twain's Adamic Diaries," *Criticism*, XIV (Winter, 1972), 49–64; and Thomas Werge, "Mark Twain and the Fall of Adam," *Mark Twain Journal*, XV (Summer, 1970), 5–13. Also see Ensor for an overall account of Twain's Adamic references. See too, my unpublished dissertation, "Mark Twain and the Fall of Man," Columbia University, 1967.

19. Many excellent insights into Twain's determinism are developed by Ellwood Johnson, "Mark Twain's Dream Self in the Nightmare of History," *Mark Twain Journal*, XV (Winter, 1970), 6–12. Johnson argues persuasively that "The two thematic developments [in *The Mysterious Stranger*] may be termed ideational determinism (thesis) and mechanistic determinism (antithesis); these are brought together and resolved in solipsistic determinism" (p. 7).

20. Gibson, "Introduction" to *Mark Twain's Mysterious Stranger Manuscripts*, p. 11. Also see pp. 26–33, on the ideas and problems involved with the ending.

21. In *Letters from the Earth*, DeVoto's notes on the story contain the idea that the Superintendent of Dreams is "clearly an unconscious anticipation of Satan in *The Mysterious Stranger*" (p. 299).

22. "Which Was it?" in *Mark Twain's Which Was the Dream? and Other Symbolic Writings of the Later Years*, ed. with an Introduction by John S. Tuckey (Berkeley, Calif., 1967), p. 195.

23. John S. Tuckey in his *Mark Twain and Little Satan*, p. 64, describes some notes written by Twain at Florence at the same time the dream-ending was written. The notes tell of a man whose "foible" it was to believe that life was a dream and himself a foolish thought in it. This does not, it seems to me, qualify the essential seriousness and pessimism inherent in the solipsistic conclusion. But for another approach to the idea of the "Absurd" in Twain's work, see Richard Boyd Hauck, *A Cheerful Nihilism: Confidence and "The Absurd" in American Humorous Fiction* (Bloomington, Ind., 1971), chapter 5.

24. But see John S. Tuckey's "Mark Twain's Later Dialogue: The 'Me' and the Machine," *American Literature*, XLI (Jan., 1970), 532–542. Tuckey gives some evidence for the view that Twain was struggling against his deterministic philosophy of *What is Man?* Thus, the "dream self" might suggest man's essentially spiritual nature and the final chapter of *The Mysterious Stranger* evidence that Satan is a reflection of man's own creative powers. For Tuckey, Mark Twain was not totally pessimistic. One can easily agree that Twain sought release from his despair and that that was in itself an affirmative search. But his "dialogue" was never resolved. And Twain still asserts that, though all reality is the product of a single, creative dream self, it is still *nothing but a dream*, with no ultimate meaning.

FRANK S. KASTOR

The Satanic Pattern

Study of the character of Satan through a large number of literary versions
of The Christian Story of Divine History reveals a definite pattern of
characterization—one not found in the general historical character of Satan.
The pattern is distinct, albeit complex. The nucleus of the pattern is Satan's
roles. In the story he participates in three main events: the war or apostasy in
heaven, the council and subsequent scenes in hell, and the temptation in the
garden. Each involves a different role: Archangel, Prince of Hell, and
Tempter. Not only is each role established in a very different world (Heaven,
Hell, Earth), but each involves very different functions and types of actions
and, ultimately, characterization. Put simply, Satan is a trimorph, or three
related but distinguishable personages: a highly placed Archangel, the grisly
Prince of Hell, and the deceitful, serpentine Tempter. Viewed another way,
he is a kind of unholy trinity: one adversary—three persons. Usually the roles
are unified by a single consciousness, but it is by no means uncommon to find
the roles separated into distinctly separate characters.

The body of literature which incorporates the myth and comprises the
tradition is clearly heterogeneous.[1] As previously noted, it varies in genre,
treatment, scope, emphasis, purpose, length, and so forth. Consequently,
the degree of characterization of the Satanic figure, as well as the
distinctiveness of his roles and tripartite separation, varies from account to

From *Milton and the Literary Satan*. © 1974 by Editions Rodopi N.V.

account. In some works no attempt at characterization is made. Other versions are too short and sketchy for either clear characterization or the tripartite separation (e.g., Spenser's "An Hymne of Heavenly Love"). Still others, by omitting some of the three major events in which the Satanic figure appears or by concentrating upon one (e.g., *Bellum Angelicum* [1604] or *Parlamentum of Feendis* [c. 1430]) omit major roles in the Satanic trimorph, or concentrate upon one role. Still, the overall pattern remains consistent in the tradition.

The methods of differentiating (and subsequently characterizing) the roles vary. One finds, for example, overt statements about changed roles (such as Satan becoming the Prince of Hell or the Tempter). Descriptions of the figure which may show pronounced differences in size, shape, stature, or appearance in each of the three roles are commonplace. Changes in motivation and differences in characteristic actions by role are regular differentiaters. Different names are used for the figure in different roles: most commonly, Lucifer (Archangel), Satan (Prince of Hell), and the Devil (Tempter). Differences in an author's attitude toward each of the three roles often distinguish them too. Finally, each of these roles is acted out against a very different setting or background and in different circumstances; the conceptual and descriptive differences in the worlds of Heaven, Hell, and the Garden on Earth profoundly affect the corresponding role and its characterization.

With drama, however, the means reflect the special circumstances of stage presentation. Distinctions in the roles are often made absolute and unmistakable when three separate parts are written into a play to cover the three roles and are so specified in the *Dramatis Personae*; when, say, Lucifer, Satan, and the Serpent have separate parts in the same play. However, the dramatist is clearly more restricted in presenting differences in size and shape or in terms of cast, settings, and actions than the narrative writer, who can summon up a cast of thousands of angels as large and resplendent as suns with a few strokes of his pen.

Furthermore, the trimorphic pattern seems to be endemic to the tradition and basically pan-historic. At least it appears as distinctly in early as late versions. Both period and place of composition appear to be less significant factors affecting the pattern than such purely literary matters as length, degree of literary development, fullness of episode, and especially the degree of attention to characterization in a given work. Of course extraliterary matters also weigh upon the literary phenomenon of the Satanic trimorph. For example, for many centuries a distinction was made between the Archangel in Heaven and the fallen apostate angel.

THE ARCHANGEL

From the third century A.D. onward, the name Lucifer was given to the leader of the rebel angels in Heaven. Lucifer (Latin: "light-bearer") in classical mythology was the name of the planet Venus when it shone in the morning sky. The early church fathers arrived at this name for the Archangel by coupling two passages from scripture: Luke 10:18, "I saw Satan like lightning falling from heaven," and Isaiah 14:12–14, "How art thou fallen from Heaven, O Lucifer...." That Lucifer was Satan's name before his fall became an accepted fact in the Christian tradition. Arnold Williams, for example, notes that the Renaissance commentators on Genesis "all follow the Christian tradition that Satan is the fallen Lucifer, who led a third (or a tenth) of the angels into revolt against God."[2] Indeed, most of the church fathers assigned him in a position in the highest order of angels, and St. Thomas thought that he was probably the supreme Archangel.[3] Furthermore, the name Lucifer was used regularly to describe the Archangel before his fall and the name Satan to describe the fallen figure or the Prince of Hell. Chaucer reflects this distinction in "The Monk's Tale":

Lucifer

At Lucifer, though he an angel were,
And nat a man, at hym wol I bigynne.
For though Fortune may noon angel dere,
From heigh degree yet fel he for his synne
Doun into helle, where he yet is inne.
O Lucifer, brightest of angels alle,
Now artow Sathanas, that mayst nat twynne
Out of miserie, in which that thou art falle.

But the distinction between Lucifer and Satan is more substantial than name difference. Many Christians accepted the idea that, because of their fall, the apostate angels became devils or demons. John M. Steadman writes that "the convention of demonic disfigurement was an old one, and the belief that Lucifer and his companions forfeited their beauty with their allegiance—that their transition from angels to fiends entailed a corresponding debasement in form—had been a recurrent theme in medieval and Renaissance art and literature."[4] Furthermore, the idea of disfigurement or alteration had a sound basis in accepted church teaching. The Master of Oxford's Catechism (early fifteenth century) includes the following question: "C. Where be the anjelles that God put out of heven, and bycam devilles?[5] Calvin indicated that the fallen angels had become devils; by revolting they had "ruined themselves." Both the Augsburg and Westminster Confessions made the same distinction. The Catholic Church from the Fourth Lateran Council's "sed ipsi per se facti sunt mali" has thought that when the angels became devils they lost their "supernatural grace," although not their "natural gifts." Martin Luther even rejected the idea that the Devil's original "natural" properties had remained intact: "Thus they state that the natural endowments have remained unimpaired not only in the nature of man but also in the devil. But this is obviously false."[6] Theological speculation and literary embodiment of course took the doctrine much further.

In literary versions of the story, the principal recurrent characteristic of Lucifer, the Archangel, is probably his lofty stature and position. Avitus (*Poematum*, [c. 507]) speaks of "he, who had shone the foremost in the ranks / Of all created things." He stands usually pre-eminent among angels, often second only to God, Himself, as in the *Cursor Mundi* account (c. 1300):

> He [God] zaf oon moost to knowe & fele
> If þat he coupe haue born him wele
> And sett him beste in his halle
> As prynce & sire of oþere alle
> And for he was so wondir lizt
> Lucifer to name he hizt.[7]

Furthermore, Lucifer is regularly described in images of brilliant, blazing light; this relates both to his name (light bearer) and to his proximity to God, the even more blinding "Light." Sir William Alexander, *Doomes-Day or the Great Day of the Lords Judgement* (1614), gives a characteristic description:

> That glorious angell bearer of the light,
> The mornings eye, the messinger of day,
> Of all the bands above esteem'd most bright.
> He is amongst the rest the month of May.[8]

Usually, he is also beautiful and resplendent as in Salandra's *Adamo Caduto* (1647): "Sublime in worth, immortal in ... form / Bright flames and flashing stars." And also, as in *Adamo Caduto*, the size and stature of the Archangel are regularly conveyed by analogy with the largest bodies: stars, suns, planets.[9]

He is, in short, an impressive and admirable figure—at least until his characteristic pride, vanity, envy, or conceit overcome him. Then he becomes depicted as morally culpable, sometimes foolish, and finally as the Apostate, rebel against God.

Few works deal exclusively with the Archangel and the war in Heaven or apostasy (many accounts have no actual war). Among those that do, Erasmo Valvasone's epic, *L'Angeleida* (1590), and Joost Van Den Vondel's tragedy, *Lucifer* (1654), are probably the longest and fullest. The two bear certain similarities in respect to the Archangel. In both, he is the principal Archangel in Heaven, a beautiful resplendent figure, after whom followers troop with admiration. So great is his power and determination that Heaven itself is threatened by his army. Pride, however, perverts his loftiness and results in down-fall. Since both accounts are peopled with immense figures in a cosmic setting and describe the war in epic fashion, the Archangel takes on particularly massive dimensions.

Valvasone's presentation of Lucifer differs most markedly from Vondel's by its commencement of the demonic disfigurement during the course of the war in Heaven, rather than after his fall. The Valvasone Lucifer becomes as grotesque and hideous as the dragon in *Revelation* after whom it was undoubtedly modelled; he has seven heads, serpents for hair and eyebrows, a hundred arms and wings, and a long monstrous tail; he is awesome:

> He stood above them like an Alpine peak
> With countless shapes of horror on its back,—
> Tall oaks and hollow caves and summits bleak,
> Harsh torrents, and the glacier's icy track,
> Gaunt rocky passes, twisted paths oblique,
> Terrors and toilsome hazards, deep and black,
> Fierce beasts, and, where the pathway sinks or soars,
> A silence broken by appalling roars.[10]

With the fall from Heaven, the transformation from Archangel to Prince of Hell is complete: "With scorn he marvels in himself to scan / No mark of what he was when he began" (p. 83).

The immense dimension and stature of the Archangel in these two works, his awesomeness and loftiness, are features which regularly separate his role from that of the Prince of Hell in literary versions of The Christian Story of Divine History.

THE PRINCE OF HELL

The role of Prince of Hell, on the other hand, is regularly distinguished from that of Archangel, as well as characterized, by demonic disfigurement. Demonic disfigurement not only entails alterations (diminishment) in shape, stature, and dimension, but also a change (diminishment) in state—angel to devil—which in turn results in different motivation, behavior, and characteristics. In short, the full implications of demonic disfigurement are far-reaching. Generally, the longer the account, the fuller are the manifestations of demonic disfigurement, and, consequently, the greater is the separation between the roles of Archangel and Prince of Hell.

In short accounts, the contrast in terms of demonic disfigurement may often be the sole way in which the two roles are distinguished. For example, in *The Story of Genesis and Exodus* (c. 1250; 412 lines) both the slight characterization and the differentiation of the two roles rest upon a few statements of disfigurement like the following:

Tho wurth he *drake* that ear was knigt,	dragon
This wurth he *mirc* that ear was ligt.	dark
And *euerile* on that helden wid him	everyone
Tho wurthen mirc, and *swart*, and dim,	black
And fellen ut of heuones ligt,	
In to this middil *walknes* nigt.[11]	welkin's (?)

But even in long, detailed accounts, as we shall see, disfigurement plays an important part in the trimorphic separation; and in accounts which center upon the role of Prince of Hell, disfigurement is stressed almost inevitably. The Archangel serves, in these cases, principally as a minor foil to the Prince to show what he had been.

Playwrights often center their attention upon the Prince of Hell, apparently to simplify the staging. They set the stage in Hell or Paradise and have one of the characters relate the past events in Heaven. The Archangel appears only indirectly and in foil contrast to the fallen Prince of Hell, helping to define him. This is the case in Dryden's opera, *The State of Innocence and Fall of Man* (1674), a stage adaptation of several of the scenes in *Paradise Lost*. The Prince of Hell, "Lucifer," lying on the burning lake (I, i), comments upon his demonic disfigurement to Asmoday:

> ... how chang'd from him
> Companion of my Arms! how wan! how dim!
> How faded al thy Glories are! I see
> My self too well, and my own Change, in thee.[12]

Later, alone, he strikes the same note:

> Am I become so monstrous? so disfigur'd
> That Nature cannot suffer my Approach
> Or look me in the Face? but stands aghast. (II, i)

That the fallen angels have become devils is indicated by a stage direction (I, i): "The rest of the Devils rise up, and fly to the Land" (p. 31), and verified by the Prince of Hell: "I must forget, / Awhile, I am a Devil ..." (II, i).

Likewise, in Hugo Grotius' *Adamus Exul* (1601) the role of Prince of Hell is so pervasive that the subtle transformation into that of Tempter could easily pass unnoticed. "Sathan" is the only Satanic figure in the play; the scene is the garden of Eden. As the play opens, Sathan delivers the prologue "standing alone on an eminence commanding a wide prospect of The Garden of Eden."[13] The vast difference between his present state and his former state as Archangel is made quite clear:

> Ah, how different is that lot of theirs
> From my harsh lot! We who were stars, coeval make
> With all the wheeling sky, unharm'd by the fervent flame
> Of white sidereal fire or by the fluid chill
> Of clammy air or water or the numbing clod
> Of heavy earth,—we, without bond of bodies made,
> The spiritual peers of Him, the most high God,
> Now scarcely live as slaves; our life is less than life. (p. 105)

He is now the Prince of Hell:

> The savage Thunderer's foe, exiled from heaven, my home
> I hither come in flight from Tartarus' grim cave
> And the black wilderness of everlasting Night.
> Hatred has drawn me forth from that unblest abode,
> Planning in wicked mind dire plots against the good.
>   ... just as a cruel lion seeks
> Through wandering ways, with formidable open jaws,
> Some hapless flock that he may rend with greedy fangs. (p. 99)

Sathan's two images for his two roles reflect the comparison of their respective dimensions: the Prince of Hell is to the former Archangel as a "lion" is to the "stars." The contrasts of light and darkness, Heaven and Tartarus' grim cave, peers and slaves, further emphasize the difference.

Grotius' Prince of Hell is a full, round character, motivated not only by cruelty but also by "Envy and grief and care, sorrow and fear and hate" (p.

149). Yet he is more like the Satan of early Book IV of *Paradise Lost* than like that of Books I and II. The play has only one stage set—the garden—yet speeches like "the savage thunderer's foe ..." above and the following, which is delivered in Act V after the fall of man, delineate and add dimension to his role as Prince of Hell:

> Now I possess Earth's rule, the sceptre of the Sea,
> And I have placed the realms of Air beneath my yoke.
> Now punishment delights me, evil pleases me:
> Now let all Acheron rejoice, and all the phalanx
> Of damn'd Avernus! Know Thy avenging Nemesis,
> Thou King of Kings! (p. 189)

In Acts III and IV the Satanic role becomes that of the Tempter. In Act III, he approaches Adam with "pretended love ... for double dealing guile!" He becomes "the wolf," who "silently afar / Examines signs of footprints ... / ... gives no sound ... pausing," corners "his prey" (p. 147). When Adam, "his prey," escapes, he becomes the serpent and approaches Eve. However, the gradual reduction of his stature from lion to wolf to serpent occurs slowly over three acts. The Tempter's serpentine qualities—his "slantwise path" and "winding ways," his "scaly head ... hissing mouth," his "slippery," "sinuous" manner—elicit a different reaction and attitude from Grotius, and from many other writers, than do the Prince of Hell's lionish qualities.

However, the role of the Prince of Hell is the main one in the play, and the gradual and subtle change in attitude toward the Tempter could be missed; whereas in other plays the two roles are assigned to two actors, and the distinction is unmistakable.

THE TEMPTER

By far the most popular single episode in the story as reflected both by extended treatment and by the number of separate treatment, was the Temptation in the Garden. The role and character of the Tempter seems to have become both more popular and diverse than the other two.

The use of disguise is of course one of the principal characteristics of the Tempter generally. In the story his major, although not exclusive disguise is the serpent—his major scene, the Garden. In fact, in dramatic versions of the story, "The Serpent" is regularly a separate character, a distinct role which is included as such in the *Dramatis Personae*. For example, in Hans Sachs' *Tragedia von schöpfung, fal und austreibung Ade aus dem paradeyss* (c. 1530), Jacob Ruff's *Adam and Heva* (1550), and Giambattista Andreini's

L'Adamo (1613), the *Dramatis Personae* include among the fallen angels Lucifer, Satan, and the Serpent as separate characters. The latter is the Tempter and appears alone with Eve on stage. The stage directions of Sachs' play reflect concisely the separation: "Die schlang steht auff ihr füss. Die drey teuffel [Lucifer, Satan, and another] gehen ab. Eva kumpt. Die schlang spricht."[14] In both the Ruff and Andreini plays, Satan says he will use the serpent ("die schlang wil ich reitzen an,"), but as almost always in such plays only "die schlang," or the "Worm" as he is called in the York mystery cycle, does the tempting.[15] The appearance of the Tempter as an actual serpent on stage dramatically reflects a major aspect of the separation of that role. Regardless of genre, it is always and only the Tempter who is associated with the serpent. That very old and repeated association clearly accounts for the notable snakelike qualities of his character.

Another factor which often distinguishes the Tempter is appellation. Although the satanic names and epithets vary among the versions, the appellation most often used for the Tempter alone is "the Devil." For example, *The Fall of Lucifer* (from the Chester mystery plays) presents "Lucifer" as an archangel characterized chiefly by pride in his own beauty and loftiness. After his fall he is disfigured; his title becomes "Devil Lucifer" and his characteristic feature is enmity to God and man. In the temptation scene with Eve, however, his title is "the Devil" and he is a serpent throughout the scene.[16] The *Norwich Play* (14th C.), for example, deals only with the garden episode. It is very short and has only four characters—Pater, Adam, Eve, and Serpens. There is little characterization. "Serpens," the Tempter, is characterized only by the fact that throughout the play he is a serpent. However, the audience is told in the prologue that Serpens, the Tempter, is the Devil. "And of the deavilles temptation, diseaivinge with a lye / The woman...."[17] When used specially for the "Tempter, "the Devil" is more than a name; almost always it has the force of a dyslogistic term, an opprobrious epithet, and reveals a special attitude toward that role alone.

This is especially apparent in Thomas Peyton's *The Glass of Time, in the First Age* (1620). Peyton devotes less than half of his epic poem to The Story, and concentrates upon the scene in Paradise. Although other satanic roles are manifest, the Tempter's is dominant. And although other satanic names appear once or twice each, the name "the Devil" appears over fourteen times, and applies only to the Tempter. It occurs always in connection with the serpent, temptation, disguise, or fraud: "that dismal day / ... the woman did the Devil obey," "by the envy of a *viperous* tongue / Hatched by the Devil."[18] The fact that Peyton occasionally calls the Devil "a Devil" does not alter the essential point. The name is associated with a type of behavior or action. It is a derogatory term as well as a proper name for the role of Tempter. Its use

indicates an emotional response and an attitude of contempt and loathing for
that role:

> In these and such like shapes thou liest in waight,
> To gull the world as with a poisoned baight,
> That being tane man's vitall life straight baines,
> Infects his blood, and runs through all his vaines,
> And as thou art, dost cozen, lie and lurch,
> Transformed sometimes into a man in th' church,
> Under that holy habit, maske and guise,
> Thou setst abroad thy cancred venom'd lies.
> And thus thou camst unto our Grandam Eve,
> And as a Devill into her thoughts doth live,
> Seeming a serpent crawling on thy breast,
> Much like a simple foul mishapen beast.... (stanza 71, p. 63)

It is this attitude toward the Tempter as serpent and loathsome devil which
distinguishes the Devil from Satan for many writers and which so often
makes the Tempter in the garden different from the Leader of the Infernal
Council.[19]

As the quotation from Peyton reflects also, the Tempter through the
course of history has appeared habitually as a man among men. In versions of
the story too, a regular feature of the role is that it is man-sized and manlike.
Furthermore, the implications of this feature far exceed the simple matter of
disguise. A widespread practice is exemplified by Joseph Fletcher's *The Perfect-
Cursed-Blessed-Man* (1629). The brief version of The Story, and particularly of
the Temptation and Fall, serves primarily as material for a sermon or treatise
on "Man's Miserie by his Degeneration."[20] Fletcher graphically depicts at
length the physical, moral, and spiritual decay which man has undergone as a
result of original sin. The Tempter is the Devil and becomes the major
example and even metaphor of degenerate man. The cause of man's fall was
that he was "Proud, Lucifer-like, greedy to arise." But, as a result of man's fall,
"he shook hands with the devill" and engaged in "ev'ry kinde of evill."

> For all man's powers and pers'nall faculties
> Were pois'ned all; chang'd their abilities.
> In doing well; he once did well resemble
> The Glorious God: but now— ...
> He rightly represents the devill in
> Pravitie of perverse disposition.

The conclusion of Fletcher's exemplum-sermon continues the analogy: "Such is this monster-cripple, devill-man." For Fletcher and many another writer, the Devil-Tempter and man bear a close, profound, and ugly family resemblance.

In fact, in those works in which the Tempter is characterized other than as simply a serpent or devil, it is his very human qualities which mark the role. These qualities do vary of course; however, several stereotypes are also readily apparent in the tradition. A major one is the comic Tempter.

In D'Arnould Greban's *Le Mystère de la Passion* (1452), the comic Tempter is absolutely separate from all other satanic roles. The leader of the fallen angels is "Lucifer;" the Tempter is "Sathan," one of the fallen crew: "*Icy s'en va Sathan a quatre piez comme un serpent entortiller autour de l'arbre.*"[21] Following the fall of Adam and Eve, he says, "J'ay bien joué mon parsonnage." Indeed, he has played his role well. As Greban develops it, Sathan is a comic buffoon, an idiotic and light-hearted punster, or "roy de la feve," the king of laughter, as Lucifer calls him. The sharp contrast between the two characters and their different roles emerges clearly in the following dialogue:

Sathan:	Fronssez de vostre orde narine,
	Lucifer, dragon ferieux,
	gettez souppirs sulphurieux,
	brandonnez de flamme terrible,
	cornez prise a voix tres horrible;
	nous avons eu cruelz vacarmes.
Lucifer:	Comment va nostre herault d'armes?
	Es tu venu, roy de la feve?
Sathan:	J'ay admené Adam et Eve,
	qui sont ja du siecle transsis;
	ilz sont la en ce limbe assis,
	si tres piteus qu'il n'y fault rien.
Lucifer:	Laissez les moy la, ilz sont bien;
	ilz y ont, je croy, beau poser.
	Deables, ne vueillez repposer,
	randissez moy, grans et petis,
	courez moy tous nos appatis,
	tout le monde est a moy donné.
Sathan:	Grand mercy a moy, *Domine*:
	j'en ay este l'embassateur.

(p. 24, ll. 1698–1717)

Lucifer is an angry, taciturn figure, a "dragon furieux ... [to whom] tout le monde est ... donné." The Tempter is a "roy de la feve", "l'embassateur," a clown ("Grand mercy a moy, *Domine*"), a comic subordinate to the Prince of Hell for whom "les piez et le' corps serpentin" were a fitting garb.

In Gil Vicent's *Breve Sumário da História de Deos* (1526), "Lucifer, o maioral do inferno" (prince, captain or leader of hell) and "Satanas, fidalgo de seu conselho" (nobleman of his council) who becomes the "tentador" (Tempter) are also separate characters.[22] The comedy of the work resides largely in the Tempter. He is a boorish country nobleman with ambitions at the court of Lucifer; a comic rustic mainly, with an uncomic love of deceit, whom a suave and calculating Lucifer manipulates to accomplish the fall of man. Lucifer tells Satanas, "Faze-te cobra, por dissimular" (p. 44), but the Temptation occurs off stage, and the Tempter never appears as a serpent. The character is developed along strictly human and comic lines.[23]

The Tempter of Andreini's *L'Adamo* exemplifies a different stereotype as well as a sub-portrait of a single satanic figure. Andreini's Lucifer is a consistent character through four of the five acts. Like the figure in Books I and II of Milton's epic, he is the proud, unrelenting adversary of God and Man. Dynamism characterizes his words and deeds, whether as the "hot, reckless rebel" or the warrior-general torn from heroic mold and rousing his troops to action. In Act III as the Tempter, he is transformed. Not only his shape (now half-woman, half-serpent), but his whole character is utterly changed by the new role, which is developed at some length. Like his appearance, he is first of all seductive. As Eve says,

> For arms and hands it has, a human bosom,
> And all the rest appears but trailing serpent.
> How the sun, gilding with his rays those scales,
> Flashing with fair hues, dazzles both my eyes!
> I wish to draw more near ...
>
> The nearer I approach, the greater charm
> He shows to view, sapphire and emerald
> And ruby now and amethyst and now
> All jasper, pearl and jacinth is each fold.[24]

In contrast to the rest of the portrait, the Tempter is a poetic character, sensitive to beauty, "courteous" and "wise," as Eve says (p. 245), and honey-tongued—a courtier with feminine traits who makes a fine art of flattery:

You vanquisher of eyes, charmer of souls,
Darling of hearts, fair maiden, pray approach me!
Lo, I disclose myself. Behold me here,
Yea, all of me, and sate your eyes with gazing:
You the chief ornament of all the world,
You Nature's show-piece, micro-paradise,
To whom all things on earth bow down in praise.

His job in Paradise, as he tells Eve, is gardening. How appropriate to his character,

To wreathe the lilies or weave rose with rose;
Here giving contour to a fragrant hedge,
Or causing there a crystal rill to flow
In flowers' bosoms and by tiny herbs,

for he is a half-womanish embroiderer of words and flowers into "sweet displays." The difference between the Tempter and the rest of the satanic portrait is nearly absolute: aside from the sharp contrasts of appearance, shape, action, and temperament, the whole tone of the Tempter's scenes are strikingly dissimilar to the rest.[25]

Another major type is the Machiavellian Tempter, the very human villain. This type is well exemplified in Vondel's Adam in *Ballingschap* (1664), a lengthy discussion of which will be found in the next chapter.[26] And in many ways the role and character of the Tempter are more varied than the other two. However, all three of the roles and their characterizations are distinctive and separable enough, both in practice and as quintessential *typos*, to be considered separate portraits—or perhaps three sub-portraits of a Satanic triptych.

NOTES

1. Watson Kirkconnell, *The Celestial Cycle* (Toronto, 1952), provides one of the best descriptions of the tradition; it has proved invaluable for this study. Helpful also with the phenomenon and tradition are J.M. Evans, *Paradise Lost and the Genesis Tradition* (Oxford, 1968), E.M.W. Tillyards, *The Elizabethan World Picture* (New York, 1959), p. 18; C.A. Patrides, *The Phoenix and the Ladder: The Rise and Decline of the Christian View of History* (Berkeley and Los Angeles, 1964) and *Milton and the Christian Tradition* (Oxford, 1966), Chapter 8; R.S.P. Milburn, *Early Christian Interpretations of History* (1954); C.H. Dodd, *History and the Gospel* (1938); Roland M. Frye, *God, Man, and Satan: Patterns of Christian Thought and Life in Paradise Lost, Pilgrim's Progress, and the Great Theologians* (Princeton, N.J., 1960); L. Ginzberg, *The Legends of the Jews*, trans. H. Szold (Philadelphia, 1909–25); N.P. Williams, *The Ideas of the Fall and of Original Sin* (1927).

2. *The Common Expositor: An Account of the Commentaries on Genesis, 1572–1633* (Chapel Hill, 1948), p. 117. For background on these and related matters which follow see Edward Langton, *Satan: A Portrait. A Study of the Character of Satan through all the Ages* (London, 1945); *The Encyclopedia of Religion and Ethics*, ed. James Hastings et al. (New York, 1920), IV, pp. 565–636, 568–571; *The New Schaff-Herzog Encyclopedia of Religions*, ed. S.M. Jackson et al. (New York and London, 1908–12), III, 399 et passim; *The Oxford Dictionary of the Christian Church*, ed. F.L. Cross (London, 1957). *The Catholic Encyclopedia*, ed. C.G. Herbermann et al. (New York), IV, 746, 964; IX, 410. Joseph Turmel, *The Life of the Devil, by Father Louis Coulange [pseud.]*, trans. from Fr. by Stephen Haden Guest (London, 1929); E.H. Jewett, *Diabology: The Person and Kingdom of Satan* (New York, 1890); Giovanni Papini, *The Devil*, trans. from Italian by Adrienne Foulke (New York, 1954); Maximilian Rudwin, *The Devil in Legend and Literature* (Chicago, London, 1931).

3. *Summa Theologica*, I, 63, 7. See also Turmel, p. 4.

4. John M. Steadman, "Archangel to Devil: The Background of Satan's Metamorphosis," *MLQ*, XXI (1960), 321. In somewhat different form in *Milton's Epic Characters* (Chapel Hill, 1968), Ch. 18. The importance of "demonic disfigurement" in separating the Archangel and the Prince of Hell in the Satanic trimorph of the celestial cycle will become apparent in this chapter.

5. *Included in Reliquias Antiquae*, vol. I, p. 231. See also *Early English Homilies*, ed. Morris (1868), p. 219, for a popular rendition of the idea; and James Durham, *A Commentarie Upon the Book of the Revelation* (Edinburgh, 1658), p. 527: "... *what was casting from heaven, is* here *casting down* or degrading."

6. *Lectures on Genesis 1–5*, in *Luther's Works*, ed. Jaroslav Pelikan (St. Louis, 1958), I, p. 142. *Institutes of the Christian Religion*, trans. Henry Beveridge, 3 Vol. (Edinburgh, 1846), I, ch. 14, sec. 16, p. 152. *The Book of Concord: the Confessions of the Evangelical Church*, trans. and ed. Theodore G. Tappert (Philadelphia, 1959) contains the *Augsburg Confession: The Confession of Faith; The Larger and Shorter Catechism* ... (Philadelphia, 1838) and the *Westminster Confessional* (see Head I, III, p. 446). See also the famous catechism for school and church of David Pareus and Zacharias Ursinus, *The Summe of Christian Religion*, "first Englished by D. Henry Parry" (London, 1633), p. 191. *Library of Anglo-Catholic Theology* (Oxford, 1841); H. Denzinger, *Enchiridion Symbolorum*, tr. R.J. Deferrari, *The Sources of Catholic Dogma* (St. Louis, 1957); *Summa Theologica*, I, 63, 2; note above.

7. *Cursor Mundi*, ed. Rev. Richard Morris, *EETS* #57 (London, 1874–93), p. 33. ll. 437–42. "Z" stands for "3 throughout. On his position see also e.g., Spenser, "A Hymne on Heavenly Love," ll.81ff. *Genesis B*, Kirkconnell, p. 27. *Le Mistère Du Vieil Testament* (Paris, 1878), "La Creation des Anges," pp. 3–4.

8. *The Poetical Works of Sir William Alexander* (Glasgow, 1872), III, 18. On his brightness and light see, e.g., T. Heywood, *The Hierarchie of the Blessed Angells, the Fall of Lucifer with his Angels* (London, 1635), p. 412. H. Grotius, *Adamus Exul* (1601), Chorus, 1, ll. 250–60. Spenser, loc. cit. D. Greban, *Le Mystère de la Passion* (Paris, 1874), p. 7.

9. On size see, e.g., Grotius, *Adamus Exul*, I, ll. 95–100. Caedmon, *Genesis B, The Celestial Cycle*, pp. 26, 28; *Le Mistère Du Vieil Testament*, p. 4.

10. Trans. Watson Kirkconnell, *The Celestial Cycle*, pp. 81–2. Canto II, stanza 29.

11. *The Story of Genesis and Exodus, An Early English Song*, ed. Richard Morris, *EETS* #7 (London, 1865); c. 1250; MS. 1300; ll. 283–8. See also *Caedmons Metrical Paraphrase*, tr. and ed. B. Thorpe (London, 1832), pp. 269–272, 287 et passim. Dryden, *State of Innocence, and Fall of Man* (London, 1735), pp. 30–1; and almost all examples.

12. (London, 1735), p. 30. See also Grotius, *Adamus Exul*.

13. A five act play. Trans. Watson Kirkconnell, *The Celestial Cycle*, p. 99.

14. [Complete Works of] *Hans Sachs*, ed. Adelbert Von Keller (Tübingen, 1870), I, pp. 34, 37.

15. Jacob Ruff, *Adam and Heva*, ed. Herman M. Kottinger (Leipzig, 1848), p. 35; *The York Cycle of Mystery Plays*, ed. J.S. Purvis (London, 1957), Pageant No. 5, p. 18. See also, e.g., Amoldus Immessen, *Der Sündenfall* (ca. 1475), ed. Otto Schönemann (Hanover, 1855); Troilo Lancetta, *La scena tragica d'Adamo ed Eva* (Venice, 1644); Serafino della Salandra, *Adamo caduto* (Cosenza, 1647).

16. *The Chester Mystery Plays*, ed. Maurice Hussey (London, 1957), pp. 1 ("Characters"), 8, 16, 20. Another variation appears in the *Ludus Coventriae*. Three of the characters listed are "Lucifere," an angel who debates in Heaven with God; "Serpens," who tempts Eve; and "Diabolus," who operates with "Serpens" in the Temptation scene and claims responsibility for the act ("I dede hem att pis velony"); ed. K.S. Block (London, 1922), p. 26. For further evidence of this distinction, see, e.g., *Norwich Play* (14th cent.) in *The Nonc-Cycle Mystery Plays*, ed. Osborn Waterhouse, *Ser. 2*, #104 (London, 1909, p. 12; *Le mystère d'Adam*, Tours MS., new trans. by Henri Chamard (Paris, 1925), Act II; Charles Perrault, *Adam, ou la création de l'homme, sa chute, et sa réparation* (Paris, 1697), Bk. II; Sir William Alexander, *Doomes-Day*, in *The Poetical Works of Sir William Alexander* (Glasgow, 1872), III, "First Hour," pp. 10–27.

17. In *The Nonc-Cycle Mystery Plays*, ed. Osborn Waterhouse, *EETS*, series 2, #104 (London, 1909), p. 12. The "A" version is 90 lines; the "B" version is 163 lines.

18. Reprint (New York, 1886), p. 86, sts. 131, 132; also pp. 62, 82, et passim.

19. The difference in attitude toward this role is manifest in one way or another in almost every version I have examined; only the degree and type vary. Also, it seems that the separation of roles in the story accounts for the fact that the distinction in names appears more markedly in versions of the story than in general practice. Sometimes the shift from "Satan" to "the Devil" seems to occur almost unconsciously in connection with temptation, disguise, or the serpent; see, e.g., Du Bartas' *Semaine* in *Du Bartas: His Poems* (London, 1621); "The Imposture," Pt. 2, day i, week 2, pp. 186–200, and particularly Sylvester's marginal notes (pp. 14, 15, 191).

20. The title of Ch. ii, in which the story occurs; see *The Poems of Joseph Fletcher*, ed. Rev. A.B. Grosart (private printing, 1869), pp. 65ff.

21. Paris, 1878, p. 692f, a stage direction.

22. Ed. Joao de Almeida Lucas (Lisbon, 1943), pp. 42, 44.

23. Mystery plays are particularly rich in comic Tempters: e.g., in *Le mystère d'Adam* (Paris, 1925), Act II, "La Seduction"; *Le mystère du Vieil Testament*, publ. by baron James de Rothschild (Paris, 1878). In both, the Tempter is also a separate character.

24. See trans. Watson Kirkconnell in *The Celestial Cycle*, pp. 244–245, for this and the following quotations.

25. Another good example of this type of Tempter is in Della Salandra, *Adamo caduto*.

26. For other villainous Tempters, see, e.g., *Cursor mundi*, ed. Rev. Richard Morris, *EETS*, #57 (London, 1874–93), pp. 30ff et passim; Caedmon's "Christ and Satan" and "Genesis B" in Thorpe (n. 10) or in *The Junius Manuscript*, ed. George P. Krapp (New York, 1931); John Bunyan, *The Holy War*, ed. M. Peacock (Oxford, 1892), pp. 14–17.

J.W. SMEED

The Devil

It is obviously beyond the scope of this chapter to give a 'history of the Devil'. The reader can find this in Roskoff and Graf (see Bibliography, xiv). Here it is sufficient to recall Roskoff's demonstration of how a picture of the Devil gradually emerged from study of the Old and New Testaments, how the Church Fathers, and medieval theologians after them, elaborated and systematized, how Neoplatonic, Talmudic, and Cabbalistic concepts were taken up at different times, both enriching and confusing the picture, how in the later Middle Ages and the century of the Reformation there grew up a pathological obsession with the Devil, so that learned and ignorant alike saw him, his legions and his works everywhere. Learned *and* ignorant: it is worth stressing this fact, for it is a very unhistorical point of view that distinguishes all too sharply between 'learned' and 'popular' elements in the early chapbooks of Dr. Faust.

For Luther, the Devil is 'Lord of the world': cunning and arrogant, envious of God and archenemy to mankind. He afflicts men with all manner of diseases and misfortunes, tempts them to sin, deceives and deludes them through false promises, lies, visions, and dreams. He is hostile to marriage, encourages men to break the Commandments and uses the Papacy to further his ends. (All of this, except the last point, is traditional and can be found in the Bible, the Church Fathers and/or the medieval theologians.) Clearly the

From *Faust in Literature*. © 1975 University of Durham.

anonymous author of the 1587 Faustbook was largely influenced by this Lutheran Devil in depicting his Mephostophiles [*sic*]. He adds, of course, traits from the devils of comic literature and legend, laughable and fairly harmless workers of magical tricks, stewards of a magical *Schlaraffenland*-pantry. But it would be idle to try to distil any sort of logical and unified characterization of Mephisto from this chapbook, or indeed from any of the popular treatments of the Faust-theme. The characterization has taken second place to the author's didactic intentions. When Mephisto tells Faust of Lucifer's fall, of Hell, of what he would have done in Faust's place, and so on (Chapters 11–17), he is not really addressing Faust at all; he is talking to the readers, exhorting them to shun pride and rebelliousness. (Most critical accounts of the Mephisto of this earliest chapbook have tacitly admitted this by tending to trace Mephisto's ancestry rather than to characterize him.) In fact, it is Mephostophiles' fondness for sermonizing rather than any other character trait that influenced the Devils of succeeding popular Faust-works. In the Faustbook of the 'Christlich Meynender', Mephisto at one point steps right out of character and warns Faust against the course he is taking. The author's comment on this episode is that it demonstrates God's indescribable mercy, 'daß alle Kreaturen, ja der Teufel selbst wider seinen Willen die abtrünnigen Sünder zur Buße vermahnen müssen'.[1] This seems an anticipation (although in very limited and naïve form) of Goethe's view of a Devil who wills the bad, yet conduces to the good.

The popular Faust-pieces often follow the chapbooks in the naïvete of their presentation of Mephisto. In the Ulm puppet play Mephisto assures Faust that, in his place, he would have been virtuous in order to gain Heaven (ii, 6). Usually Mephisto affirms that he would be prepared to climb to Heaven on a ladder with sharp knives as rungs.[2] In one Austrian puppet play, he would be prepared to put up with still more: 'Glaube mir, wenn die ganze Welt mit glühenden Nägeln beschlagen wäre, so ginge ich bis zum jüngsten Tag barfüßig darauf herum, wenn ich die Himmelsseligkeit noch erlangen könnte.'[3]

None of this is surprising. One would expect to find a preaching Mephisto in didactic works, or in naïve works of entertainment. What *is* surprising is to encounter these out-of-character utterances in the Devil of more sophisticated, 'literary' *Fausts*. Thus, in Klinger's *Faust*, when countless demonstrations of the evil effects of civilization have driven Faust to despair of ever finding goodness in his fellow men, it is Leviathan who points the Rousseauesque moral: Faust has been looking in the wrong places—he should have sought out simple people in humble spheres. It is interesting that Leviathan abandons his 'devilish' tone as soon as he embarks on this idyll; his manner of evoking it is exactly like that of any sentimental eighteenth-century writer turning against the artificial civilization of his day: '... nicht den [hast du gesehen,] der unter dem schweren Joche seufzt, des Lebens Last geduldig trägt und sich mit Hoffnung der Zukunft trostet. Stolz bist du die Hütte des Armen und Bescheidnen vorubergegangen, der ... im Schweiß seines Angesichts sein Brot erwirbt, es mit Weib und Kindern treulich teilt und sich in der letzten Stunde des Lebens freut, sein mühsames Tagwerk geendet zu haben' (v, 6).

In J.F. Schink's pact-scene ('Doktor Fausts Bund mit der Hölle', 1796) Mephisto again mounts the pulpit:

> MEPH.: Du vertraust dich bösen Geistern an, das endliche Geschöpf wagt das gefährliche Spiel mit dem unendlichen; ist das nicht Raserei?
> FAUST: Ich glaube gar, du predigst?
> MEPH.: Und Besserung. Aber dein Ohr ist taub für Warnung; sie mag von guten oder bösen Geistern kommen ... (p. 82)

So, as already in the *Faust* of the 'Christlich Meynender', devils can warn men just as well as can good spirits. It should be added, however, that the rest of Schink's scene up to the point where Faust signs the pact is so confusing that it is difficult to form any clear idea of what sort of a Devil this is supposed to be. What is interesting in this connection is that Schink obviously sees no reason why the Devil should not help to drive the moral point home in the most explicit terms.

C.C.L. Schöne (*Faust*, 1809) copies Klinger and, like Klinger, allows Leviathan to point the moral at the end. But he goes much further than Klinger:

> Wo dir zu glauben auferlegt, war'st [*sic*] du
> Vermessen, stolzer Faust! Du wolltest gar
> Auf Kosten deiner Ruhe ein Geheimniß lösen,
> Was hier dem Sterblichen verborgen ist.
> Die Hoffnung und der Glaube sind's, die hier
> Das Herz des Guten im Gewirr der Welt
> Erhalten, und zum schanen Ziele leiten.
> Dein kühner Geist verwarf Geduld and Glauben,
> Du wolltest Wahrheit und dir wurde Wahn! (v, 13)

It is above all Schöne's choice of words that gives this speech its false tone. That Leviathan should crow over Faust for taking the wrong turn: this is well and good. That he should use 'vermessen' and 'kühn' as terms of disapprobation much as the author of the Spies Faustbook had done is just acceptable. But his reference to 'das Herz des Guten' and 'das schöne Ziel' are all wrong for this evil and malicious character.[4] The falsity again comes from a desire to make the message of the work explicit.

One last example of these moralizing Devils (tuppence-coloured, where Schink and Schöne had been penny-plain) is to be found in C.E. Mölling's tragedy *Fausts Tod* (1864), where Mephisto soliloquizes on the enigma of man:

> Teufel in der Leidenschaft,
> Mensch in seiner schwachen Kraft,
> Engel oft in seiner Güte,
> Göttlich in des Schaffens Blüthe
> Ist's ein Räthsel unauflöslich!
> Er ist ewig und verweslich!
> Er ist Tag und er ist Nacht! (ii, 1)

The notion that Satan commanded a legion of devils, who were allotted quite specific tasks of temptation, has complex and ancient origins. The Old Testament speaks of the spirit of jealousy, a lying spirit, the spirit of whoredom, and so on.[5] (These spirits are often represented as instruments of the Lord's purpose, a point which is obviously important for any consideration of the role of Mephisto in the various Faust versions.) Once the view that spirits embodied particular vices and tempted men to practise these became joined to the New Testament idea of a legion of devils,[6] the way was open to the notion of a whole infernal army, with various devils concerned with particular vices or weaknesses. A satanic hierarchy was set off against the heavenly hierarchy, the devils having their precisely defined spheres of influence just as the good angels were thought to have specified duties or territories, or particular classes of people to protect. Systematized first by the Church Fathers, later by medieval theologians, the idea became common in morality plays and other works, where we often find 'specialized' devils tempting men by means of a particular sin (vanity, lechery, gluttony, etc.).[7] In the fifteenth chapter of the 1587 Faustbook ('... von Gewalt deß Teuffels'), there is some account of particular spirits sent out on particular tasks. Widmann gives us, as might be expected of him, a good deal more

> Denn gleich wie zu einem Reich viel Personen und ungleiche
> Empter gehören, also sindt ungleiche Empter unter den Teuffeln.
> Dann etliche sindt geringe Teuffel, die mit Hurerey, Ehrgeitz

und dergleichen Sünden anfechten, andere aber sindt höhere Geistere, die da anfechten mit unglauben, mit verzweiflung und mit Ketzerey, wie die rottengeister und der Babst solche teuffel haben, etliche teuffel sind verordnet zu dieser sünd, andere zu andern Sünden, als etliche böse Geistere sindt, abgöttische Teuffel, Tyranneyteuffel, Zäuberteuffel, Fluchteuffel, Sauffteuffel, Eheteuffel, Hurenteuffel, ... und ziergleichen mehr, die die Menschen zu sölchen Sünden reitzen und blenden ...[8]

Now, in some lists there appears a *Klugheitsteufel*—a devil who tempts men through their intellectual curiosity and arrogance. The account we have from the pen of Georg Schröder of a Faust play performed in Danzig in 1669 mentions this 'Klugheit-Teüffel', and seems to equate him with the devil sent to serve Faustus. This is the only such identification in any Faust version known to me, but it is clear that, by implication, the Mephisto of early Faustbooks and plays is the *Klugheitsteufel* of the popular imagination. If the lecher, the glutton, the quarreller—later even the smoker!—had devils to play on their weaknesses, why should not Dr. Faust have one too? The identification of Faust's tempter with the *Klugheitsteufel* of tradition is apparent in Lessing's Faust-plan and (arguably, at least) lives on in Thomas Mann's Devil, projection of Leverkühn's self-tormenting and self-destroying intellect. But in all too many *Fausts*, as the author turned aside from metaphysical debate to concentrate on the less demanding theme of Faust's love life, Mephisto is demoted from *Klugheitsteufel* to *Hurenteufel*. The wittiest example of this occurs in Heine's Faust-ballet, where Faust is tempted by a vision of beauty and the Devil is a ballet-dancer. In Heine's notes (*Erläuterungen*), he justifies this by mentioning the agreeable old anecdote that the Devil invented the galliard to tempt the faithful and annoy the puritanical. The first stage in the development which is to transform Faust from retiring scholar into man of the world takes the form of a dancing lesson from Mephistophela and her companions. In Lenau too we have the spectacle of a Devil who uses music to awaken slumbering lascivious desires in Faust ('Der Tanz'). For a much more sombre treatment of a Faust led astray by a 'Hurenteufel', see the account of W. Nürnberger's *Josephus Faust* (below).

It is with Marlowe that one first notices the tendency of the Devil to steal the show. Marlowe's Devil is there to tempt Faustus, yes, and to bargain with him and to serve him; to do all those things which he is represented as doing in the chapbook. (And it may be added that Marlowe's Devil still has the inconsistency of the chapbook Devil: he moralizes *and* tempts, warns *and* eggs Faustus on.) But what chiefly seems to concern Marlowe is to depict the Devil as a fallen angel, brooding on the Hell that he carries about with him. After his famous speech locating Hell wherever God is not (i, 3), it seems of little consequence whether he is entirely consistent in his attitude towards Faustus.[9] To find this Mephisto presently providing out-of-season fruit and magic means of transport seems tolerable only if he is represented as performing these feats in a spirit of bored indulgence, underlining the irony of the fact that this is the sort of thing for which Faustus signed away his soul.

But for nearly two centuries after Marlowe the Faust theme lived on only in popular and trivialized versions, and Mephisto became trivial with all the rest, part naïvely wicked and treacherous spirit, part provider of magical court entertainments and exotic feasts, often permitting himself a little moralizing and occasionally acting as pander. Not until Goethe does he again come to dominate the scene.

Goethe did not read Marlowe's *Doctor Faustus* until long after the completion of his own Part 1, and manifestly the popular Faust versions known to him in his youth had little to offer by way of hints concerning the characterization of the Devil. He had to create his own Mephisto just as he had to 'look into his own heart' (*in meinen eigenen Busen greifen*) for Faust. I do not wish to add unduly to the enormous amount that has been written on this subject, only to say enough to present Goethe's characterization of Mephisto as an important stage in the history of the Devil in the Faust legend.

The Mephisto of the *Urfaust* is linked with that strange cosmogony which Goethe constructed for himself as a young man under the influence of Pietistic, mystical, alchemical, and Cabbalistic writings. From such sources, Goethe tells us, he had come to conceive of a godhead which reproduced itself from all eternity, giving rise to a trinity (rather a Neoplatonic than a Christian one) and, in due course, to a fourth member, Lucifer, from whom material creation emerged

> ... alles das, was wir unter der Gestalt der Materie gewahr werden, was wir uns als schwer, fest und finster vorstellen, welches aber, indem es, wenn auch nicht unmittelbar, doch durch Filiation vom göttlichen Wesen herstammt, eben so unbedingt mächtig und so ewig ist, als der Väter....[10]

So, this material world was imperfect but never, as it were, quite forgetful of its divine origin, so that individual souls had the opportunity of sinking further down (into the realm of the material) or of rising towards perfection. In this world too dwelt various spirits capable of communicating with and influencing mankind in sundry ways. It is easy to see how these views led

Goethe to the conception of his *Erdgeist*, a spirit which dominates the natural life of our planet, is the living and visible garment of the divinity and represents both the dynamism and the constant death and rebirth which characterize the world of nature. That Mephisto was originally thought of as a spirit subordinate to, or as an emissary of the *Erdgeist* is tolerably clear from *Urfaust* 159f ('Du gleichst dem Geist den du begreiffst, / Nicht mir!'), and from the passage in the prose-scene where Faust implies that Mephisto first appeared to him in the form of a dog and at the bidding of the *Erdgeist* ('Wandle ihn du unendlicher Geist ...'). This linking of Mephisto with the *Erdgeist* was later to receive confirmation in the words addressed by Faust to the *Erdgeist* in the scene 'Wald und Höhle'.

But, say some critics, when we reach Part 1, with its Prologue in Heaven, an ambiguity has arisen. For the passages from the *Urfaust* and the *Fragment* which link Mephisto with the *Erdgeist* remain, while the Prologue introduces a new framework of references and one which is apparently, from its clear echoes of the Book of Job, a more Christian one. In the most strictly literal terms (who dispatched Mephisto to Faust in the first place?) there may indeed be an ambiguity or at least an untidiness here, but I think that the more general difficulties with regard to Mephisto's role have been exaggerated. If we turn to the famous speech of the *Erdgeist* (*Urfaust*, 148ff; Part 1, 501ff), we find terrestrial existence described in all its imperfection—but also as a reflection of the divine. It is easy to see how a servant of this spirit could carry out the ambivalent role allotted to Mephisto by the Lord and later defined by Mephisto himself (Part 1, 1335f). Mephisto's nihilism corresponds to the constant dying and destruction in the realm of nature (the *Grab* of the Earth Spirit's speech). But since this dying constantly leads to rebirth, Mephisto's nihilism must always be vain (Part 1, 1371f). And if the law of terrestrial life is constant change and activity, and if it is only through striving and activity that man develops towards higher things, the spirit who goads men on *must* unwillingly help to carry out God's purpose. Here again, the words of the Lord in the Prologue and those of the Earth Spirit carry similar implications.

Goethe took over (from what sources is impossible to establish exactly, and is anyway not important) a good deal of traditional material concerning the Devil. There is the 'crazy hocuspocus' (*das tolle Zauberwesen*) of the 'Hexenküche' and the 'Walpurgisnacht', treated ironically and grotesquely, as if to say: these are all traditional trappings of Western witch and Devil belief, and I suppose they must go in somewhere. But there are much more serious links with tradition. Goethe's Mephisto, who knows much but not everything (line 1582), is wholly in accord with the theologians' Devil, who was commonly represented as knowing more than man, but less than the

good angels.[11] The discordant note introduced into the angels' hymn of
praise by the 'spirit who denies' recalls the Devil's traditional role as accuser,
as denier of man's moral worth. (The explicit link here is with the Book of
Job, but there is also an echo, deliberate or accidental, of the old 'Trials of
Satan', in which the Devil accused mankind of wickedness, with the Virgin
as defender and, usually, Christ as judge—cf. Graf, pp. 225ff.) Goethe's view
of the usefulness of the Devil as a goad has also theological sanction,
although Goethe's position is clearly very unorthodox and rests on an
altogether less cut-and-dried notion of what is a 'good' and what an 'evil' act.
The orthodox view has been that God permitted a certain freedom of action
to Satan, so that he might tempt and plague men. Thus men would remain
alert, would not sink into slothfulness or moral complacency and would
achieve greater moral deserts by resisting the Devil than would be possible if
there were no tempter to resist.[12] Since the possible ultimate salvation of this
highly useful Devil is faintly hinted at in Goethe ('Grablegung'), and since it
was to become an issue in some later works,[13] it deserves a word here.

Origen had argued that not even devils were incapable of good, and
that in the end Satan's hostile will would be destroyed in a return to harmony
with God.[14] This view was taken over by St. Gregory of Nyssa, to be sternly
denounced by St. Augustine as 'a pitiful error'.[15] But, as with most heresies,
it pops up from time to time through the centuries. Luther finds it necessary
to oppose the idea, by the way (xxii, 34), and it was still a subject of serious
discussion in the eighteenth century. William Law, after some hesitation,
became convinced that Satan, as the negation of the principle of love, would
ultimately be saved when Divine love triumphed over evil and darkness.[16]
Goethe himself will assuredly have come across the idea in Georg von
Welling's *Opus mago-cabbalisticum* (Homburg, 1735). Welling deals with
Lucifer's rebellion in terms of the breaking-away of the earthly realm from
the Divine whole, terms which curiously combine Neoplatonic, cabbalistic
and Christian notions (i, 4–5). Given this theory of the Devil's origins,
Welling can go on to argue that, after a period of purification, Lucifer too
will participate in the general redemption:

> ... diese Reinigung wird ... fortfahren, biß alle Kreyse, ja selbst der
> Mittel-Punct und Ursprung oder Ursach aller Verdammnuß und
> Verderbens, der Lucifer, gantz entblösset, nach der ewigen
> Erlösung seuffzen, und also auch er, als der letzte Feind,
> aufgehoben, wiederum in seine erstere herrliche Lichts-Gestalt
> verwandelt worden, und also das gantze Geschöpff wiederum in
> seinem ersten Principio erscheinen wird. (p. 467)

Thus, from Welling, Goethe derived not only hints for the cosmogony of the *Urfaust* and the linking of Mephisto with the Earth Spirit, but also perhaps the idea of the Devil's possible salvation.

But to treat Goethe's Mephisto as if he were the personification of some principle or cosmic force and to note the links with the evil spirits of Christianity and other traditions is, although interesting, very partial. For, once introduced, Mephisto takes on a life of his own, begins to display individual characteristics, and adopts a mode of speech peculiar to himself. Hence he must be approached like any other character in a play, or else we are left, like Faust at the beginning of Goethe's drama, with 'Tiergeripp' and 'Totenbein', dry bones instead of living nature. For some of Goethe's readers, in fact, Mephisto became not only a vital, living character, but the hero

> Le diable est le héros de cette piece; l'auteur ne l'a point conçu comme un fantôme hideux ... Goethe a voulu montrér dans ce personnage ... la plus amère plaisanterie que le dédain puisse inspirer, et néanmoins une audace de gâité qui amuse. Il y a dans les discours de Méphistophélès une ironie infernale qui porte sur la création toute entière, et juge l'univers comme un mauvais livre dont le diable se fait le censeur.[17]

D.L. Sayers, in the preface to her own Faust play, *The Devil to Pay*, has the same point to make:

> ... as ... Goethe, and every other writer who has meddled with the devil has discovered, the chief difficulty is to prevent this sympathetic character from becoming the hero of the story.

'Hero' is obviously too much (Gretchen? Philemon and Baucis?), but it is clear that there is always some likelihood that Goethe's Mephisto will be the dominant figure. Here a subjective element enters, but most people would probably agree that it is Mephisto who dominates most scenes in Part 1 where he and Faust appear together, and that, even in Part 2, where he has less to do and certainly calls the tune far less, his presence is still felt far more than his effective role would lead one to expect. It is noteworthy how often he is given the last word—sometimes in scenes where he has played comparatively little part, as if to suggest that 'devilish' mockery and denial are the most appropriate reactions to human greed and folly, and that he is the ruler here, the stage-manager of these antics, even if they seem to be played out wholly or largely without his help.[18]

It is in Part 2 particularly that Mephisto's role becomes so complex that it is altogether pointless to try to define it by any sort of formula. He is in turn Faust's helper and adversary (continuing the ambivalent role suggested by lines 340–3 and 1335f). He appears as court jester, as personification of envy, as Phorkyas, as stage-manager both of a financial crisis and of a military campaign, and as overseer. Yet he remains recognizable under all his disguises:[19] less as an evil and sinister spirit (except in the Philemon and Baucis episode) than as the 'spirit that denies'. But from the moment when he declares himself unable to procure Helen for Faust (6209f), he either withdraws from the scene to leave Faust to act independently, or actively helps him! The Devil who unwillingly 'works the good' is now much more apparent than in Part 1. In fact, Mephisto's dilemma, hinted at in the Prologue, becomes acute in Part 2: to damn Faust, Mephisto must keep him alive (cf. 318–22). But life, in Faust's case, means action, and action conduces towards salvation. Moreover, as Faust grows older, his impulses become maturer, less hedonistic and subjective, so that Mephisto, in serving him, cannot but appear as unwilling altruist.

But this does not exhaust his role in Part 2. He also provides light relief and has an important part to play in the *Klassische Walpurgisnacht*. Here the exile from the Harz Mountains is made to stand for northern incomprehension of the classical ideal. Hence his bewilderment at all the creatures he encounters, hence is nostalgia for the familiar German mountain peaks (7678–82), and hence Homunculus' scorn (6923–7, 6945–7). The contrast between Faust and Mephisto is pushed to the point of farce when Mephisto is shown wooing the Phorcides at a moment when Faust is absent in search of Helen.

In the most general terms, Goethe's Mephisto is the adversary of all faith and optimism, the personification of mockery. Few escape his sardonic glance. Wherever characters take themselves too seriously (Faust), or fall into arrogance (Baccalaureus) or ignore the obvious (Wagner), Mephisto is there to underline the fact. Even at the last, when Faust is filled with noble aspirations, Mephisto is the realist who cuts him down to size. And Mephisto is a *witty* Devil, with a wit that can at times make Faust seem solemn and self-important. Perhaps it is this factor which, above all others, has made it possible for some readers to see the 'hero' in him and has blinded them to the objective (evil) consequences of his actions.

An account of some of the more successful attempts to copy Goethe's Mephisto will be found in Chapter 7. There has also been a witty musical comment on Goethe's 'spirit that denies'. Liszt's *Faust-Symphony* (1854–7) has, as its first three movements, orchestral portraits of Faust, Gretchen and Mephisto. But whereas Faust and Gretchen are given characteristic themes and motifs, Mephisto has no themes of his own; his movement is built up out of parodies of the Faust-themes from the first movement, as if to suggest that he is a spirit opposed to everything positive and creative, merely mocking what others have willed. Significantly the Mephisto-movement dies away into nothingness, for 'alles, was entsteht, / Ist wert, daß es zu Grunde geht.'

Klinger's Leviathan is an intriguing figure. He is clearly based on Milton's tragic Devil and has a few (accidental) similarities to Marlowe's. Here he is on his first appearance before Faust, grandiose, bitter, obsessed with a sense of his deprivation:

> in erhabner, kühner und kraftvoller Gestalt.... Feurige, gebietrische Augen, leuchteten unter zwo schwarzen Braunen hervor, zwischen welchen Bitterkeit, Haß, Groll, Schmerz und Hohn dicke Falten zusammengerollt hatters ... Er hatte die Miene der gefallnen Engel, deren Angesichter einst von der Gottheit beleuchtet wurden, und die nun ein düstrer Schleier deckt. (i, 8)

He has adopted human form because this exterior best corresponds to the evil within him, and appeals to Faust because of his power to see through human pretensions. He has the nihilism and the devilish laughter of all the best Devils of Faust literature (ii, 11). It could be argued that, like others that have been mentioned in this chapter, he steals the show. Or does he? It seems to me that, if one looks more closely at him, one can already see traces of that decline of the Devil which was to become one of the characteristics of Faust literature in the nineteenth and twentieth centuries. In one way this is simply a natural result of treating this magical theme in a sceptical age. Leviathan himself makes merry over Faust for expecting him to appear with horns and cloven hoofs (i, 8); thus too Klinger's treatment of magic is ironic (cf. ii, 4: more of this later). But there is a deeper reason. The deal with Leviathan, after all, has very little to do with the traditional pacts according to which the Devil was to serve Faust, shower him with gifts and procure him power and fame; it is a bet in which Faust will try to convince Leviathan of the moral nobility of mankind and Leviathan will try to confound Faust's faith in his fellow-men. So, although there is occasional recourse to magic, Leviathan's main weapon is his cynical insight into human weaknesses. He hardly needs to corrupt men or tempt them; he merely uncovers, explains and interprets. Indeed, he comes near to declaring himself redundant!—

> Brauchen Die des Teufels, die ihn durch ihr Thun beschämen? (iii, 3)

The gradual decline of the Devil will form the theme of the last part of this chapter. But before this happened, he was to live through a sort of Indian summer in the works of the German Romantics.

Lenau's sombre and malevolent Devil is a combination of the exiled fallen angel of Milton and Marlowe and Goethe's nihilistic Devil. The work of damnation is explicitly stated to be an act of revenge on the creator:

So will Verstoßner ich mein Leiden kühlen,
Verderbend mich als Gegenschöpfer fühlen. (p. 28)

This is a treacherous Mephisto who saves Faust from accidental death at the beginning ('Der Morgengang'), only to destroy him at leisure. (Goethe's image of the cat playing with the mouse is, in fact, much more applicable to Lenau's Mephisto than to his own.) The pact itself is full of double-edged and misleading promises, and Mephisto's final treachery is, of course, his betrayal of Faust to Hubert. Mephisto's tactics are gradually to isolate Faust and to bring him to despair. He easily turns him against God, the 'despot' who fills a man with infinite desire and curiosity but gives him only a limited capacity to know and to experience. (One can see plainly the appeal that the Faust theme had for the Romantics.) Then he draws him away from his friends and his past life and involves him in a web of guilt culminating in a murder which estranges him from nature. (The argument is that the law of nature is to preserve and propagate life, so that Faust's murder has alienated him from nature.) And so Faust, alone, is driven back within himself—but finds only cause for disgust. Remorse is combined with a feeling of futility—for he has done all this and is just as much a mortal with mortal limitations as at the outset.[20]

There are clear traces of Lenau's Devil in the Mephisto of Adalbert Lenburg (*Faust*, 1860)—another treacherous character, who is not merely content with winning Faust's soul, but also wishes to cause him as much suffering and disgust as possible in the process. But the most striking successor to Lenau's Mephisto and one who makes him seem almost amiable by contrast is the Devil in Woldemar Nürnberger's dramatic poem *Josephus Faust* (1842). The author was admired by Storm, who vainly tried to persuade Heyse to include something of his in the *Novellenschatz*. The Faust poem remained neglected until E.M. Butler gave a glowing account of it in *The Fortunes of Faust* (pp. 294–300). This account conveys the atmosphere of the work well, but does not analyse it closely enough to do justice to its subtleties. As the work opens, Faust is seen turning away from a hopeless quest for truth, longing for experience of life instead of futile studies. (This beginning obviously derives from Goethe and Lenau, but the tone is more turbulent and desolate than in either.) He is visited in the night by Mephisto:

Mephisto beugt sich traulich zu ihm vor,
Und um den Hals er seinen Arm ihm legt,
Dann flüstert er gar leis' ihm in das Ohr
So rasch, so rasch, daß kaum den Mund er regt. (p. 15)

This seductive whispering in Faust's ear will recur twice in the work. Since it is unheard by the reader, he has to guess what is said. But this is not difficult; the course of the poem shows Faust embarking on a career of wild and destructive Donjuanism. Mephisto is cast as the *Hurenteufel* of tradition. As in Lenau, Faust is cut off from his old life, to find nothing but bitterness in the new. This is underlined by an extraordinary variation on a motif from Lenau. It will be recalled that Lenau's Faust at the dissecting-table rails against the futility of asking the dead for the secrets of life. But Nürnberger's Faust returns nostalgically to the anatomical theatre, and regards the corpse awaiting dissection almost lovingly—for this body can at least make no demands on him:

An dieser Leiche ruh ich heute aus,
Von dem bewegten, teuflisch wilden Leben,
Von meines Neigens, meines Hassens Graus. (p. 95)

—But he is soon fetched away by Mephisto, to resume his course as Don Juan.

Mephisto is not only adept at temptation; he takes a sinister delight in it:

Er hinkt und taumelt auf und ab im Sande,
Von seinen Frevelplänen still ergötzet. (p. 102)

He is no fallen angel, still tormented by thoughts of what he has lost. He has never seen God; God goes his way, and the Devil his (p. 136). Nürnberger's Mephisto is shown to be 'God of this world' in a much more literal way than in any other Faust version known to me. Nature too is his 'whore' (p. 136: for more on this, see Chapter 3). But often he is bored with his role, obsessed with the pointlessness of it, longing to annihilate the whole universe (himself and God included). The devilish boredom, which we have already encountered in Goethe and Klinger, and the Devil's nihilism, which would give up even his own power over the material world in favour of nothingness (cf. Goethe, 11595ff) returns here in a more radical and even blasphemous form. You can say of me what you will, says Nürnberger's Mephisto, but at least I have never committed the most frightful of all crimes

> —Nennt mich 'nen Hurensohn, nennt mich 'nen schlechten Affen,
> Ich sei nun, wer ich will, *ich habe nicht geschaffen*! (137f)

It is a measure of Nürnberger's nihilistic pessimism that Mephisto is not the real villain of this dark work; the true Devil is the creator. The hint for a nihilistic Devil may well have come from Goethe, but the mood is that of Büchner's *Dantons Tod*.

The malevolence of Nürnberger's Mephisto seems to be reinforced at all points by the settings and the tone of the work. There is, for instance, a wild scene in a ruined convent, where Mephisto, with a band of demons, apes the Crucifixion:

> Die mittelste von den drei Trümmersäulen
> Steigt er hinan; wie er sich äffisch schmiegt
> Um das Gestein, gleich einem Jesus, eilen
> Flugs zu den beiden seitlichen Basalten
> Noch zween andre nächtige Gestalten.[21]

Even Mephisto's magic tricks have an authentic Gothic horror about them, as when he frightens a company of diners by the apparition of a murdered youth's head in a dish of food.[22] Nature herself is wild and sinister in this poem, and the style is mysterious and fragmented, full of lacunae, hints and rumours, so that the work seems like some dire folk-ballad, whose very textual mysteries and corruptions seem to make the horrible more horrible. For this is not a question of a Faust damned in a context which suggests that goodness, order and salvation are possible; the whole world of this poem is made over to the Devil. Mephisto, witnessing a frenzied scene of drinking and gambling, says to Faust

> Du glaubst es nicht, wie sehr es mir geneigt,
> Das Völkchen, das da drinnen wogt und reigt.
> Was wetten wir, Doctoren nicht allein,
> Verschreiben sich den ew'gen Teufelein.
> Was wetten wir, in einer halben Stunde
> Sind insgesammt die drin mit mir im Bunde! (146)

The surrealist imagery of this scene suggests, as so often in Jean Paul's visions of Hell, a verbal equivalent to the fantastic Hell-paintings of Bosch:

Mit diesen Kuben die man Würfel nennt,
Die ganze Schaar mir in den Rachen rennt.
Sie saugen fest und tief sich in mein Bein,
Als hielt ich's Egeln in den Teich hinein. (ibid.)

—but Nürnberger's Hell is this world, and the existence of Heaven is nowhere hinted at.

It will be recalled that Klinger's Devil makes a mocking reference to the old popular belief in a Devil with a cloven foot, horns and the rest. This mockery is, of course, in tune with the attitudes of, at least, educated men of the Enlightenment.[23] But even if the Devil had been banished, the wickedness that he had seemed to personify and encourage remained:

Er [Satan] ist schon lang ins Fabelbuch geschrieben:
Allein die Menschen sind nichts besser dran,
Den Bösen sind sie los, die Bösen sind geblieben.[24]

And so inevitably the Devil of the Faust plays, no longer the stage representation of a spirit in whose objective existence people really believed, became more and more a mere symbol for the 'darker' side of man. Even in the naïve popular treatments one can occasionally catch a hint, perhaps barely conscious, of this. It will be remembered that Faust traditionally subjects the various spirits of Hell to a speed test and that he finally chooses Mephisto, who boasts that he is swift as men's thought. Swift as thought? Must this not mean that he will be there at Faust's side as soon as Faust thinks of him? And, if so, is he not something resembling the making-material of a certain mood of Faust's? The point is made more explicitly in the puppet play which Heine saw in Hamburg in the mid-1820s and of which he gives an account in the *Erläuterungen* to his Faust ballet. The devils had appeared veiled and shrouded ('tief vermummt in grauen Laken') and, when Faust had asked them what they really looked like, had replied: 'Wir haben keine Gestalt, die uns eigen wäre, wir entlehnen nach deinem Belieben jede Gestalt, worin du uns zu erblicken wünschest: wir werden immer aussehen wie deine Gedanken' (pp. 67f in the original edition). This could mean that the devils really exist and that only their appearance when they make themselves manifest to humans is determined by men's thoughts, but for the less naïve members of the audience the exchange must have sounded very like an admission that the devils exist only in the mind.

In the literary treatments of the theme, the tendency to turn the Devil into a symbol is more conscious and more marked. (Given the pessimism of men like Lenau and Nürnberger, it is plainly no contradiction to have a powerful, malevolent and dominating fiend who is, at the same time, little more than a symbol for certain aspects of human nature.) Some people would argue that this development away from an 'objective' Devil towards a 'subjective' one can already be seen in Goethe's *Faust* or, indeed, in Marlowe's. But it seems to me that Lenau is the real starting-point. By this I do not of course mean to suggest that the Mephisto in Lenau's *Faust* is 'in the mind' like Ivan Karamazov's or Leverkühn's Devils. Lenau's Mephisto is a superbly drawn dramatic character, and the progress of the work depends on the tragic conflict between him and Faust. Nevertheless, there are points where Mephisto seems, for brief moments at least, to be the projection of one side of Faust. He appears when Faust is ripe for him, and there are passages in their conversations which almost give the impression that Faust is arguing with his *alter ego*:

> FAUST: Warum doch muß in meiner Seele brennen
>   Die unlöschbare Sehnsucht nach Erkennen! ...
> MEPH.:   Dein Schöpfer ist dein Feind, gesteh dirs keck,
>   Weil grausam er in diese Nacht dich schuf. (p. 8)

The deduction seems so logical in this context that it hardly needs anyone outside Faust to draw it. And when, later, Faust turns on Mephisto in disgust ('Der See'), he is in fact only feeling disgust at himself. Later still ('Das Waldgespräch'), Mephisto's temptation of Faust—that to assert himself truly and independently as an individual he must cut himself loose from God and nature—is again almost a case of Faust's tempting himself, for the arrogant subjectivity was there from the outset, and what follows in this scene is only the logical outcome of it. Mephisto's temptation can be summed up as 'dare to be yourself' and it hardly needs the Devil to whisper that to Faust.

The author of the other major late Romantic *Faust*, Nürnberger, takes the process further still. This may sound odd, after what has been said about Nürnberger's Mephisto. Unchallenged lord of this world, despoiler of mankind with no sly and seductive angels to rob him of his prey—surely this is the apogee of the Devil in Faust literature? And yet the question of this Mephisto's objective existence seems open to doubt. For, towards the end, in a strange anticipation of Dostoievsky and Thomas Mann, as Faust curses Mephisto, his adversary isn't there at all—Faust is ranting against the empty air. But the most significant instance comes in the final scene. Here a wretched, crippled, beggared Faust calls on Mephisto, as if longing for his traditional 'grewliches und erschreckliches Ende'. But no Devil comes to carry off this Faust; he is left to wander out the rest of his life in loneliness.

This really seems to suggest that there is no Devil except the one within Faust that first drags him into guilt and then condemns him to a lifetime of remorse.

That the Devil, if he exists, is within man, is stated quite positively in Spielhagen's novella *Faustulus* (1898). This is a Faust story within a Faust story, since the hero, Arno, is both the author of a Faust tragedy and a man who feels some affinity with the Faust figure, a man whose fate, moreover, bears a slight resemblance to that of Goethe's *Faust*. Although this synthesis is not very well achieved, Faustulus is one of the few late-nineteenth-century Faust versions which deserve respect and serious consideration. Our immediate concern here is with Spielhagen's conception of the Devil: 'Bei ihm [= Arno, in his Faust play] spielte sich der Kampf des Guten mit dem Bösen in der Seele seines Helden ab und nirgends sonst' (p. 73). When asked whether he believes in the Devil (a fair question to put to the author of a Faust tragedy), Arno replies: 'An den in uns: sehr' (p. 147).

As I have already said, some had seen this demotion of Mephisto to a principle within man as already implied by Goethe. Fr. Th. Vischer had argued something of the sort from the link of Mephisto with the Earth Spirit. If Mephisto is the servant and emissary of this spirit, then he is to be associated with the 'earthy' parts of human nature too, with the passions and impulses.[25] This view, which obviously gains support from what Goethe has to tell us of his youthful philosophy (see above, p. 40), can easily degenerate into a trivial and oversimplified equation according to which Faust embodies the good and positive, Mephisto the bad and negative parts of man. In fact, the banishment of Mephisto to a point within man had entered Goethe-criticism as early as 1845, when Julius Mosen had described Faust and Mephisto as 'ein in zwei Hälften zerrissener Mensch', and Mephisto as 'das gegen den Geist und seine Überschwänglichkeit gerichtete Menschentier in der Brust Faust's....'[26] Such an interpretation would obviously commend itself to many who were both unable to believe in a 'real' Devil, and indisposed to pursue the complex question of exactly who or what Goethe's Mephisto was. And in fact several treatments of the Faust theme confront us with a Mephisto who is no more than spokesman for a pessimistic or cynically realistic view which opposes itself to Faust's idealism. This is the case with Geibel's scene of dialogue between Faust and Mephisto in 'Historische Studien' (1865), and there is a similar case in Turgenev's *Faust* of 1856. The process is taken a stage further in Julius Sturm's poem 'Faust und Mephistopheles', 1883. Here Faust himself has been demoted to an Everyman-figure, so that Mephisto is no more than the voice of doubt within each man's heart:

Faust—Mephistopheles—es sind die Beiden
Im Herzen jedes Menschen eingeschlossen.

Der gefesselte Faust by Johannes Gaulke (1910) is a sceptical and
astringent twentieth-century variation on Klinger's *Faust*, in which Mephisto
destroys Faust's faith in morality and progress much as Leviathan had done
in Klinger. But here God and the Devil are one, and they *both* lodge in the
human breast. 'Himmel und Hölle sind eins; ein jeder trägt den Himmel,
aber auch die Hölle in seiner Brust' (p. 80). And presently Faust asks:

> Mephisto, ... gib mir Antwort: Bist du der Gute und Böse in einer
> Person? ...
>   Er lächelte ablehnend, aber aus dem Lächeln sprach etwas, das
> mich mit Grauen erfüllte: Gott und der Teufel eins! ...
> Entsetzlicher Gedanke! (p. 81)

But Gaulke goes yet further; for his Faust, his faith in humanity destroyed,
awakens to find that he has dreamt the whole thing! So Mephisto is but a
figure in Faust's dream. 'Der Verneiner' in Gstöttner's Faust play (*Der
Wanderer*, 1933: see Chapter 7) is similarly placed inside Faust, so that Faust's
debates with the Devil are arguments between the forces of affirmation and
denial *within man*:

> WANDERER: So lüstern hundsgemein
>   Kann wirklich nur der Satan sein.
>
> VERNEINER: (ironisch) Bin ja nur ein Teil von Eurem Ich! ...
>   Bin nur Gestaltung Eurer eigenen Gedanken!
>   (124f)

All this prepares us for the death-blows dealt, in their different ways by
Valéry and Thomas Mann. If the Devil *is* in the mind, he reflects men's views
and feelings at any particular time, will change as men change, can be
reduced to insignificance or even annihilated. By making his characters
aware of the literary tradition of which they are part, Valéry makes it possible
for Faust: to comment to Mephisto on his waning influence: 'tu ne tiens plus
dans le monde la grande situation que tu occupais jadis ... tes méthodes sont
surannées ...' (294f). Man's intellectual development and his scientific
conquests have gradually made Mephisto out of date, small-time, almost a
joke.[27] But at least Valéry's Devil is 'there' in the sense that he is permitted
to appear as a character. With Thomas Mann, we reach the end of the road.

His Devil, like Ivan Karamazov's, is a hallucination. To characterize him would be merely to characterize part of Leverkühn himself; his Devil's insights are things dimly realized by Leverkühn, his Devil's gifts are symbolical of the artistic genius already latent in Leverkühn. And even when we take into account the wider meaning of Mann's *Faustus*—that Germany is Faust and that the most fateful of all Faust's pacts with the Devil took place in 1933—the Devil is no more than a convenient symbol for the evil in men. As an earlier Devil had said: 'Den Bösen Sind sie los, die Bösen Bind geblieben.' Again, here is the Devil ('the Stranger') in Albert Lepage's *Faust et Don Juan* (1960) bowing out, as Faust finally comes to face the fact that the Devil has only ever been the invention of man and an alibi for the evil done by man:

FAUST:	Je ne veux plus de cette lâcheté! Je suis la seule source
	du mal que je fais ...
ÉTRANGER:	Donc, je meurs!
DON JUAN:	La mort d'un mythe! (p. 116)

In short then: the Devil lost much of his importance in this type of work, as men ceased to believe in him except as a symbol and as the magic which he was previously represented as working came to appear increasingly trivial compared with what science could achieve by perfectly natural means (see too Chapter 9). But it is arguable that there is another major factor which contributed towards his decline, that Mephisto was bound to become ineffective with the increasing tendency to save Faust. The two things are, of course, linked. Mephisto becomes the symbol for an evil which is bound to be vanquished. The defeat of the Devil need not *in itself* mean that he is represented as harmless (witness the accounts of the battles between the saints and their tempters). For example, Mampell (1962) manages to save Faust without reducing Mephisto to a nonentity. But as soon as the conviction that Faust can be made to symbolize the forces in man which deserve 'salvation' rather than 'damnation' coexists with disbelief as to the actual existence of Hell and the Devil, then the Devil (where he survives at all, as a convenient fiction or symbol) is doomed to ineffectiveness. The process begins for all practical purposes with Goethe. For all Mephisto's cynical wit and eloquence, he is beaten from the outset. The reference to Faust's 'confused' service to God (line 308) marks him for salvation and condemns Mephisto to unwilling collaboration. But what is acceptable in Goethe as a symbolic representation of a world-view involving a very complex interaction of 'good' and 'evil' becomes trivial in later writers, in whom we find a conflict in which Faust cannot lose and the forces of evil are unrealistically inept. In Müffling's *Faust* (see Chapter 7), for instance, Mephisto sends a chorus of spirits to sing seductively to Clementine—but she resists temptation effortlessly. Again, he sends his emissary, the *Zeitgeist*, to stir up unrest, but the people quickly return to order as soon as they see Faust and the Duke together. It would be depressing to give details of the witless devices adopted by successive Devils. They make cynical and disillusioned remarks intended to shake Faust's optimism, they break out into devilish laughter, they disguise themselves, hatch plots, stir up anarchy, preach hedonism and try to lure Faust away from virtue with the aid of Helen and other seductive creatures, but they cannot win; the heavenly choir is too patently waiting in the wings.[28]

Perhaps even worse is the situation in which Mephisto is relatively *successful* in his wiles, but is still robbed of his prize in the end. In Mölling's *Fausts Tod* (see Chapter 7), Mephisto does in fact quite easily win Faust over to all sorts of dastardly exercises, but still loses him—*has* to lose him. It is all rather like those old films in which the villain binds and gags the heroine and places her on the railway line. Who, even among the rawest novices in cinema-going, ever thought that the train would hit her?

A. Großmann's *Faust* of 1934 provides the most fitting conclusion to this chapter. As so often, Faust is manifestly predestined for salvation, so that Mephisto is a non-starter. But here he is also very halfhearted as a tempter and gradually loses all zest in his hellish enterprises until—in an exact reversal of the traditional situation—he is ripe for seduction into goodness by Faust! But who is this Mephisto anyway? Only one half of man's soul again:

> Faust und Mephisto
> Sind des Menschen Seele ... (p. 197)

So his 'salvation' is no more than the overcoming of the spirit of doubt within man. The final union of Faust and Mephisto, all doubt and discord now resolved at the foot of the Cross, heralds the worst play on words in Faust literature: 'Mephaustus' (p. 247).

Poor Mephisto! Once the arch-enemy of mankind, now Faust's Siamese twin, co-redeemable with him. Perhaps 'decline' is too weak a word.[29]

NOTES

1. Scheible, ii, 84. A similar exchange is already present in Widmann (i, 22), although the point concerning the usefulness of the Devil is not made explicit.

2. For example, in the version edited by Hamm, 1850, iv, 3.

3. *Der Schutzgeist* ... , 1885, p. 187. There is a moralizing Mephisto, too, in F. Brutschin's modern version of the puppet play (*Faust*, Lucerne, 1948). Here Mephisto has the traditional passages about the red-hot nails and the sharp knives, and a long moralizing speech in addition, in which he condemns Faust's desire to be an *Übermensch* (pp. 62f, 72f). Widmann's Devil sermonizes too.

4. The danger is already present in Klinger—cf. 'die himmlische Angelika', v, 6. But Klinger sees the trap and tries to avoid it by making Leviathan periodically stress the joy which he derives from seeing the innocent suffer.

5. Num. 5:14; I Kings 72:21–3; Hos. 4:12.

6. Mat. 2–5:41; Rev. 12:7–9.

7. Cf. Roskoff, i, pp. 189, 219, 7.52, 381.

8. Widmann's note to i, 21 ('Von der Ordnung der Teuffel'). In a shortened version in Pfitzer too. Some later writers take up the tradition, drawing on the puppet plays. Examples: Maler Müller, Holtei.

9. Contrast 'O *Faustus* leaue these friuolous demandes' (i, 5) with 'What will not I do to obtaine his soule?' (ii, i).

10. *Dichtung und Wahrheit*, Book 8.

11. Cf. Roskoff, i, pp. 234 and 272; Luther, lx, 14.

12. Roskoff, i, 277–9. See also St. Chrysostom, *Works*, vol. i (= *Library of the Nicene and Post-Nicene Fathers*, ed. Schaff, vol. ix), pp. 189 and 192; St. Augustine, *City of God*, xx, 8.

13. See Chapter 7; also in Bailey's *Festus*. Schink too, in his *Johann Faust* of 1804, had hinted at Mephisto's ultimate salvation (ii, 329f).

14. *De Principiis*, i, 8 and iii, 6.

15. *City of God*, xxi, 17.

16. *Address to the Clergy*, London, 1761, pp. 172ff.

17. Mme. de Staël, *De l'Allemagne*, ii, 23.

18. Cf. 5061–4, 6172, 6360, 6564f, 6815ff.

19. Cf. 7134–7 and 8992f.

20. 'Der Ritter' in Grabbe's *Don Juan und Faust* is to some extent an anticipation of Lenau's Devil, although not so witty.

21. P. 26. This scene was probably suggested by a motif in the Faust ballads and some of the puppet plays, where Faust demands of Mephisto to be shown Christ on the Cross.

22. P. 85. A similar motif in Klinger, iii, 1.

23. For further examples, see Pfeiffer, *Klinger's Faust*, Würzburg, 1890, pp. 65f.

24. Goethe, lines 2507–9. See too Lenz, *Hofmeister*, v, 9.

25. *Goethes Faust*, 1875, p. 14.

26. *Über Goethe's Faust*, Oldenburg, 1845, pp. 9f.

27. For more on this, see Chapter 9. This patronizing attitude towards a pre-technological Devil can be seen in more than one of the Science Fiction stories in the collection *The Devil his Due*, ed. Douglas Hill, London, 1967. See especially 'Return Visit' by E.C. Tubb.

28. Examples of such feeble Devils in Schink, 1804; Braun von Braunthal, 1835; W.S. Gilbert, 1879; F. Keim, 1890; H. Schilf, 1891; P. Degen, 1924; and W. Webels, 1951.

29. Mephisto is saved too in Rudolf Pannwitz's postscript to Goethe, 'Mechristopheles Himmelfahrt' (1940). Faust: 'Fehltest du wär ein riss / Durch Gottes Wahrheit ...'.

TRANSLATIONS OF PASSAGES QUOTED IN THE TEXT

72   .... that all creatures, even the Devil himself against his will, must try to bring
        rebellious sinners to repentance.

72   Believe me, if the whole world were covered with red-hot nails, I would walk
        around barefoot until the Day of judgement, if I could then come to heavenly
        bliss.

73   You have not seen the man who sighs under a heavy yoke, carries life's burden
        with patience and comforts himself with hopes of the future. In your pride you
        passed by the but of the poor and humble man who earns his bread in the sweat
        of his brow, faithfully shares it with his wife and children and, in the last hour of
        his life, rejoices that his hard toil is ended.

73   MEPH.:   You are putting yourself into the hands of evil spirits;
                 the finite being is playing a dangerous game with the
                 infinite. Is that not madness?

        FAUST: I do think you're preaching.

        MEPH.:   Yes: reform. But your ear is deaf to warnings,
                 whether they come from good or evil spirits.

73   Where you were enjoined to believe, you became presumptuous, proud Faust!
        At the cost of your peace [of mind] you wished to solve a secret which is hidden
        from the mortal here below. It is hope and faith which sustain the good man's
        heart in the maze of this world and lead him on to his fair goal. Your bold spirit
        rejected patience and faith; you wanted truth but your reward was delusion!

74   Devil in his passion, mortal in his weakness, often an angel in his goodness,
        divine in the flowering of creativity: he is an insoluble riddle! He is eternal and
        subject to decay, he is day and he is night!

74–75   Just as many persons and many offices of differing degrees go to make up a
        kingdom, so there are offices of differing degrees among the devils. For some
        are lesser devils who tempt men to whoring, ambition and such sins, but some
        are higher spirits who tempt men to doubt, despair and heresy, such devils as
        possess the rebellious mobs and the Pope. Certain devils are bidden to concern
        themselves with this sin, others with other sins. These wicked spirits include
        idolatrous devils, tyranny-devils, sorcery-devils, curse-devils, drink-devils,
        marriage-devils, whore-devils and many others who incite and delude men to
        commit such sins.

76   ... everything which we perceive in the form of matter, which we picture to
        ourselves as heavy, solid and dark but which, stemming—if only indirectly,
        through affiliation from the Divine Being, is just as absolutely powerful and
        eternal as the Father.

78   This purification will ... continue until all classes of beings, even the mid-point
        and source or cause of all damnation and ruin, Lucifer, will be laid bare and will
        long for eternal deliverance, and so he too, as the last enemy, will be lifted up
        and changed back into his previous glorious figure of light, and so the whole of
        creation will again appear in its original form.

79   The Devil is the hero of this play; the author did not conceive him as a hideous
        phantom ... Goethe wished to show in this character ... the most bitter wit that
        disdain could inspire, but together with this an audacious gaiety which can

amuse us. In Mephisto's speeches there is a devilish irony which is directed at the whole of creation and which judges the universe like a bad book of which the Devil has made himself the critic.

81 ... everything which comes into being deserves to perish.

81 ... in a lofty, bold and powerful form ... Fiery commanding eyes shone out from beneath black eyebrows, between which bitterness, hatred, rancour, pain and scorn had etched deep lines ... He had the aspect of the fallen angels, whose faces, once illuminated by the Divinity, are now covered by a sombre veil.

81 Do those people need the Devil whose actions shame him?

82 Thus I in banishment will cool my suffering and feel myself an anti-creator in my destructive work.

83 Mephisto bends down confidentially to him and puts his arm round his neck. Then he whispers very quietly into his ear, so quickly, quickly, that his mouth hardly moves.

83 I will rest today in the company of this corpse and find relief from my agitated, wild and devilish life, from the horror of my loves and hates.

83 He hobbles and reels about in the sand, quietly delighted with his wicked plans.

84 Call me the son of a whore, call me a wicked ape; whatever I am, *I have never created anything*!

84 He climbs up the middle one of the three ruined columns. As he clings apelike to the stone, like a Christ, two other dark shapes hurry quickly to the basalt columns on either side of him.

84 You wouldn't believe how they are drawn to me, that surging and dancing crowd in there. What shall we bet: not only doctors sign away their souls to devils. What shall we bet: in half an hour all of them in there will be in league with me.

85 With these cubes that they call dice the whole crowd will run into my jaws. They are sucking themselves firm and deep into my leg as if I were putting it into a pond for leeches.

85 Satan has long since passed into fable but men are no better off. They have got rid of the Evil One; the evil ones remain.

85 We have no form of our own; according to your pleasure, we take on any form in which you desire to see us. We shall always appear as in your thoughts.

86 FAUST: Why must an unquenchable yearning for knowledge burn in my soul?

MEPH.: Be bold enough to admit that your creator is your enemy because he cruelly placed you in this world of night.

87 For him the battle between good and evil was played out in the soul of his hero and nowhere else.... 'The Devil in us: very much so.'

87 A man torn in two halves ... the human animal in Faust's breast, opposed to the spirit and its boundless exuberance.

88 'Mephisto, answer me: are you the Good and the Evil Beings in one person?' He smiled dismissingly, but out of his smile spoke something which filled me with horror: God and the Devil one and the same I ... ghastly thought!

88 WANDERER: Truly only Satan could be so lewdly contemptible.

DENIER (ironically): I am only a part of your self! ... I am only
                              the embodiment of your own thoughts!

89   FAUST: I will have no more of this cowardliness. I am the sole
                                  source of the evil which I do.

                       STRANGER: Well then, I die.

                       DON JUAN: The death of a myth!

STELLA PURCE REVARD

Satan as Epic Hero

On the rough edge of battle ere it join'd
Satan with vast and haughty strides advanc'd,
Came tow'ring, arm'd in Adamant and Gold....

[6.108–110]

Satan, proud but magnificent, unyieldingly resolute in battle, emerges in the Renaissance poems wearing the full splendor of epic trappings. To these poems we owe in large measure the hero Satan as he is developed in *Paradise Lost*. Renaissance poets drew on two traditions to depict Satan or Lucifer: the hexaemeral and the epic. Hexaemera described Lucifer as a prince, glorious and unsurpassed, whose ambition caused him to strive above his sphere; epics described their heroes as superhuman in battle and accorded them, whatever their arrogance or mistakes in judgment, "grace" to offend, even as they are called to account for their offenses. The Lucifer of the Renaissance thus combines Isaiah's Lucifer with Homer's Agamemnon, Virgil's Turnus, and Tasso's Rinaldo. Milton's Satan, in turn, follows the Renaissance Lucifer and is both the prince depicted in hexaemera and the classical battle hero.

As he had been in hexaemera, the Renaissance Lucifer is the first and most beautiful of the angels. So he is described by Taubmann, Acevedo, Valvasone, Alfano, and Vondel. Heywood calls him the first in creation and

From *The War in Heaven: Paradise Lost and the Tradition of Satan's Rebellion*. © 1980 by Cornell University.

the first in virtue.[1] Murtola remarks that Lucifer outshone all the angels in beauty as the sun outshines everything else in the sky.

Fra quanti furo in Cielo Angeli Amori
Semplici, luminosi, e fiammeggianti,
Lucifero più chiari almi splendori
Più bello aprì fra tanti spiriti, e tanti,
E come il Sol più viui aurei folgori
Spande, e più vaga è l'Alba al Sole auanti.[2]
[Stanza 56]

Among so many angels as were in Heaven, Loves,
Pure, shining, and blazing,
The most clear splendid souls,
Lucifer appeared most beautiful among so many spirits, and by so much,
As the Sun scatters the most brilliant golden splendors,
Even so the Dawn seems most beautiful when the Sun has advanced.

Lucifer's power, moreover, is celebrated along with his beauty. Medieval poets had related that Lucifer held high position in Heaven; Renaissance poets, however, assign him specific political powers. For them his position in Heaven is not merely ornamental or ceremonial, a complement, so to speak, to the splendor he possessed as the loveliest of the angels. Lucifer is a regent or viceroy or governor. Valmarana tells us that as he is the angel closest to God and partakes of the fountain of light; he is the "magister" in Heaven.[3] Vondel makes him viceroy and allows his readers to infer from the manner in which he is treated by Gabriel and Raphael that he was principal governor of Heaven. Valvasone and Taubmann and Alfano make him a great prince with angels to administer. Heywood makes him head of all the principalities of Heaven.

Milton, like his Renaissance predecessors, places strong emphasis on Satan's position in Heaven before his fall: "Great in Power, / In favor and preeminence" (5.660–661). Unlike them, he glances only obliquely at his prelapsarian beauty. Only after his fall does Raphael accord him his former name *Lucifer* or describe him as "brighter once amidst the Host / Of Angels, than that Star the Stars among" (7.132–133). Only in Hell do we see a beauty now eclipsed or in Eden a splendor vaunted but no longer recognizable to others (1.591–600; 4.835–840). In Heaven Milton first and foremost shows us Satan not as the most beautiful, but as the most powerful of the angels. He describes him as a potentate with great name and high degree, whose angels obey his superior voice without demur. He is the one whose power easily conveys one-third of God's angels away from their God. It is not unlikely that he has taken his cue for this portrait of power from his Renaissance predecessors. For in their poems Lucifer is designated, as was the great king Agamemnon in the *Iliad*, as the leader of multitudes, the *anax andron* (lord of men). Lucifer as general and epic leader is a creation of the Renaissance.

We may discern this clearly as we study his genesis and development in the Renaissance poems. In them pride and ambition, long identified as Lucifer's sins, acquire specific political ramifications. They are more than the personal or private sins medieval tradition had sometimes made them. Medieval poets tended to look at Lucifer's ambition simply. Lucifer yearned to aggrandize himself personally and to be worshiped like God. In the mysteries, his pride takes the form of an absurd and blasphemous desire to sit in God's seat. In the Lucifer play from the Coventry cycle, for example, Lucifer, hearing the angels sing a song of praise to God, decides that he is worthy to sit in God's seat and be so praised.

> To whos wurchipe synge ȝe songe
> to wurchip god or reverens me?
> but ȝe me wurchipe ȝe do me wronge
> ffor I am þe wurthyest þat evyr may be.[4]

Intoxicated by his own vaunted excellence, he attempts to sit in God's seat when God's absence affords him the occasion. In the York and Towneley cycles, he feels himself falling the moment he ascends to God's place; in the Coventry and Chester cycles, God returns and, finding Lucifer in his place, orders him to Hell.[5] What the mysteries have done, of course, is to take quite literally Isaiah's account of Lucifer's vaunt: "I will exalt my throne above the stars of God: I will sit also upon the mount of the congregation" (Isa. 14:13). In so doing they succeed in dramatizing his personal ambition to be like God, but they sometimes create grotesque and comic effects. Lucifer becomes a strutting braggart who attempts to take his master's seat and falls from it.

Of course, some biblical dramas treat Lucifer's rebellion simply and seriously. In *Adam and Heva*, performed in Zurich in 1550, Jacob Ruff creates a Lucifer whose ambitions can be easily presented and easily controlled. His Lucifer has wished to be like God. God, recognizing this wish, has dispatched Michael with a group of angels to throw Lucifer from Heaven. Michael, confronting the apostate angel, accuses him of having thought in his heart to place his seat above the stars and be like the most high. For this sin—and clearly it is a mental sin or transgression—Lucifer must be punished with pains of Hell. And so the angels literally carry out their commission.[6]

For the Renaissance, however, Lucifer's pride is not portrayed merely as a forbidden wish or a breaking of a taboo (sitting in God's seat). Wish is rendered not only into action, but into military action. So it is that the Lucifer of Mollerus's poem, *De creatione et angelorum lapsu carmen*, may begin with longings not unlike those of the Lucifers in the English mysteries or in Ruff's play. He longs—Mollerus permits us to eavesdrop—for praise comparable to that God receives. He wishes that his state not be inferior to God's. But as he reflects upon honors of higher estate, he becomes not so much the blaspheming angel as the epic opponent. He declares that as leader of legions of angels he deserves greater recognition. Thus he determines to seek the counsel of his allies and, gaining that, to challenge God's empire.[7] For most of the Renaissance poets Lucifer's vaunt to sit in God's seat and be like the most high is no empty blasphemy. It is a challenge to war. Like the medieval poets before them, many render Isaiah's words exactly, translating them into the language of the poem. But they restore them to their metaphorical rather than their literal sense. Their Lucifer is no simple egoist admiring his own beauty and desiring praise. Nor is his projected act so baldly absurd that its attempt can only move us to laughter. The poets not only treat Lucifer's attempt seriously; they glamorize it by according it the trappings of an epic enterprise. They permit Lucifer, like Achilles, to dream of glory or, like Tamerlane or Alexander, to attempt to realize it through conquest. If the sheer fact of his ambition is unattractive (and the poets do deplore his ingratitude to God and his greediness for power), its expression as military ambition places it in a human category that epic poets had long rendered acceptable and understandable.

But besides rationalizing Lucifer's ambition, many poets provide him with yet stronger motives for his revolt. As it was not merely rivalry with Agamemnon that stirred Achilles in his quarrel, but a loss of place, a sense of honor forfeited or merit injured, so is it with the epic Lucifer. He is first moved not because he desires a higher place, but because he feels the place he already occupies is dishonored. New Honors given to the Son or to man make Lucifer feel he lacks sufficient honor. Of course Valmarana and Taubmann, who record Lucifer's resentment of the Son, and Peri and Vondel, who tell how he felt threatened by man's creation and exaltation, do not invent these motives for their Lucifers. The tradition that Lucifer was rival to the Son, though little used in literary works, goes as far back as the church father Lactantius. More popular in literature, however, was the tradition of Lucifer's rivalry with man; dating back to the church father Irenaeus and passed down by the Books of Adam and Eve, it had found place in medieval poems.[8] Both the Auchinleck and the Trinity manuscripts contain poems, for example, that recount how Satan refused to bow down and worship man as God's image and for his sin was excluded from Heaven.[9] The Renaissance poets take these motives and reshape them. They make Lucifer's resentment of the Son or of man the occasion for his rising in arms against God and attempting to rival the Almighty in power.

Thus both motives, as interpreted by Renaissance poets, gain a certain political thrust. In *Bellum angelicum*, it is not just that Lucifer resents the splendor and majesty of the Son (this was often, as we saw in chapter 2, the theologian's emphasis), but that he resented the power the Son wielded. Lucifer begins, as Taubmann tells us, with the euphoria of pure pride. He reflects that since he is the highest and the most beautiful of the angels, he is able as prince of Heaven to sway the kingdom alone. Full of himself, so to speak, and swelling with pride, he sends a messenger to God proclaiming that he will no longer abide beneath the yoke of God and the Son. The Son, he observes, rules earth like a demigod and men and angels are required to bow the knee to him. He, declares Lucifer, and not the Son is better qualified to rule.

> Huic ego sim supplex? ego? quo praestantior alter
> Non agit in superis, mihi jus dabit ille, suumque
> Dat caput alterius sub jus & vincula legum?
> [p. 79]

> To him should I be subordinate? I? Than whom no other holds sway more illustriously in the upper world? To me will he give law? Does he put another's rights under authority and the bonds of law?

Lucifer in *Daemonomachiae* has like ambitions. He asks God to place the world under his authority and is indignant at God's reply that the world belongs to the Son to rule. He is further incensed when God goes on to explain that all things are to be placed under the yoke of the Son and all must bow before him. Displeased that he is to be second in Heaven and oppressed by the yoke of the *Verbum Dei*, Lucifer utters his famous vaunt that he will place his seat in the North and be like the most high. Valmarana in this sequence makes Lucifer's revolt the direct result of the thwarting of his political ambitions.

Lucifer in Peri's and Vondel's plays is likewise thwarted by circumstances and placed in a position of being second in God's favor. Man, however, and not the Son supersedes him. As Heywood's use of this story in his *Hierarchie of the blessed Angells* testifies, it had attained some currency in the Renaissance to supplement the accounts of pride—which Heywood also quotes—that Isaiah and Ezekiel narrated. At man's creation, so Heywood says, God intended some singular honor for him, either because man was made in God's own image or because in future time Christ was to be incarnated as man. Thus God ordains that the angels bow before man or serve him. Heywood offers the following rationalization: the angels were superior to man in all but one respect, that being:

> God from all eternitie decreed,
> That his owne Sonne, the euerlasting *Word*
> (Who to all Creatures *Being* doth afford,
> By which they first were made) should Heav'n forsake,
> And in his Mercy, humane Nature take.
> [p. 339]

Lucifer, hearing God's decree, swells with pride and envy, resenting that man, "being but Terrene" should receive such favors and not he and the angels, by nature "much more excellent." Drawing his angels to his side, he determines to raise seditious war in order to "hinder this irrevocable Deed" (pp. 338–340).[10]

Like Heywood, Peri and Vondel make the war in Heaven spring directly from Lucifer's resentment of man's elevation. Peri devotes two scenes to the dramatization of this motive. The first is a political council in which Lucifer's allegorical advisors, Invidia and Superbia, spur him to action. Lucifer first explains to them that God has so blessed man in his creation that he has given him angel servitors. That he who was created first by the divine mind should be required to serve man seems insupportable. He contrasts his own incorruptible and immortal essence, his beauty and presence sublime, with man's vile substance and low origin. His high estate as head of angelic squadrons further supports his conviction that he should not bow before man. Superbia assures him of the justice of his case, reiterating the very arguments Lucifer had first introduced. She calls Lucifer the highest hero in Heaven and urges that it is man who should serve him, not he man. Lucifer now orders his two *fidei consorti* to gather his brothers to him while he himself erects his throne in the North. In act 2 Lucifer is permitted once more to argue the justice of his revolt. In the intervening time, still more faithful cohorts have risen to support Lucifer, among them his daughters Discordia and Ingratitudine, who, like Sin in *Paradise Lost*, are born spontaneously of his revolt. They endeavor to persuade the angels to Lucifer's cause. A strong opposition led by the angel Michael likewise has arisen. Therefore Lucifer must now argue the justice of his revolt not to Superbia and Invidia, the shadows of his desire, but to Pace, who is disturbed that war has sprung up in Heaven. What is interesting in this second justification is that Peri permits Lucifer even greater latitude in his arguments. Did not God deceive him, asks Lucifer, for he created him noble and beautiful but ordained that his nobility and beauty be obscured by vileness. What vileness could God do, questions Pace. Do you not think it vile to create from earth a man and make me serve him, counters Lucifer. Pace of course, tries to reason with Lucifer, arguing that God intended the angels as custodians rather than servants of man. Besides, she says, it is foolish and vain to oppose God the Creator, who after all was the one who created all things—not Lucifer. Lucifer, however, will not be moved, and as the scene mounts to a climax he vows that man will not boast that he had him as a servant.[11]

The Lucifer of Vondel's play is likewise eloquent in arguing his prerogatives to higher station than man. Act 1 compellingly lays the foundation. The angel Apollyon returns from Eden, having been dispatched there by Lucifer himself, to report on the pleasures Adam and Eve enjoy as lords of Paradise. Lucifer's closest angels—Belial and Beelzebub—express their wonder and also their envy at man's blessings. At this moment Gabriel arrives to announce that man's state is to be raised still higher. God has ordained that the everlasting Word is to become man, and in recognition of this future honor to man the angels are bidden to serve Adam and bow before him. A chorus of angels glorify this decree and pledge their obedience. As this chorus dies away, Lucifer enters for the first time and announces to Beelzebub that the "morning star" is past its zenith.

> Embroider no more crowns upon my robes!
> Gild not my forehead with the light of dawn's
> Bright star to which Archangels bow the head!
> Another radiance now rises, lit
> With glory from the Deity Himself
> That dulls our light.... Go hence, rejoice and serve
> And honour this new race in mean subjection.
> Man has been made for God, but we for man;
> And now his feet shall tread on Angels' necks,
> Yea, we must guard him, draw him by the hand,
> Or bear him on our wings to thrones on high.
> Our birthright goes to him, the favorite son,
> Who violates our primogeniture.
> The youngest son, in face so like the Father,
> Obtains the crown, and there is given him
> The sceptre before which the first-born bow
> And tremble greatly.
>   [2.2, p. 372]

Borduurt geen kroonen meer in Lucifers geweat;
Vergult zijn voorhooft niet met eenen dageraet
Van morgenstarre en strael, waer voor d'Aertsenglen nijgen;
Een andre klaerheit komt in 't light der Godtheit stijgen,
En schijnt ons glanses doot;
. . . .
                              gaet heene, viert, en dient,
En eert dit nieuw geslacht, als onderdane knapen:
De menschen zijn om Godt, en wy om hen geschapen.
't Is tijt dat's Engles neck hun voeten onderschraegh',
Dat ieder op hun passe, en op de handen draegh',
Of op de vleugels voere, in d'allerhooghste troonen:
Onze erfnis komt hun, als uitverkore zoonen.
Onze eerstgeboorte leit nu achter, in dit Rijck.
De zoon des zesten daghs, den Vader zoo gelijck
Gaschapen, strijckt de kroon.[12]

Like Superbia and Invidia in Peri's play, Beelzebub seconds his lord's dissatisfaction. (He had himself registered distress at Gabriel's decree: "That man will be exalted, we abased? / That we are born to serve, and man to rule?") But it is Lucifer who first plans revolt and "seduces" Beelzebub to his plans. Now, Vondel shows that there is pride in Lucifer's plans for revolt. He is hungry for first place in Heaven, and Vondel puts sentiments in his mouth not too unlike the Satanic boast of *Paradise Lost* 1.263: "Better to reign in Hell, than serve in Heav'n."

> Better it were by far
> To be the first Prince in a lower Court
> Than second, or still less, in heaven's light.[13]
>   [p. 374]

> En liever d'eerste Vorst in eenigh laeger hof,
> Dan in 't gezalight licht de tweede, of noch een minder.
>   [p. 14]

But there are other emotions and motives that Vondel also exploits. There is anger at alleged power or tyranny used to crush him: "Submit who will: I shall not yield a foot" (p. 374). There is the anxious desire to preserve his own: "I am a Son of Light, a ruler too, / In realms of Light, and shall defend my own" (p. 373). The crux of the matter is the same reluctance that Lucifer in Peri's play evinced: the reluctance of the angel as a superior creature to bow before an inferior. Lucifer openly admits to Gabriel how distasteful it is for him who has never bowed except before God now to bow to man. God's own honor, he argues, is abased when the angelic nature, until now closest to God's own, is abased. Gabriel in response does no more than advise obedience and caution Lucifer about the results of disobedience.

It is hardly surprising that dramatists like Peri and Vondel or epic poets like Valmarana and Vondel felt the need for motivation stronger than spontaneous pride. Lucifer does not wake up one morning and decide to displace the Father. Only when his own place is threatened does he move to usurp God's. Pride clearly impels him, true, but fear first stirs him—fear that he might lose his own vicegerent power. As a motive, this fear of lost power, this sense of injured merit, is more dramatically and psychologically complex than the spontaneous pride patristic writers had ascribed to Lucifer. C.S. Lewis, even as he berated the absurdity of Satan's claim to "injured" merit, recognized its force.[14] It is a motive that makes Satan as a character more humanly understandable. We can sympathize with his fear; we can understand his disappointments; we can even feel his sense of injured merit. These emotions, of course, do not excuse his actions, but they show how his actions have come about. Dame Helen Gardner was certainly right in recognizing that the villain-hero of Jacobean drama with his "reasonable" motives for action was an ancestor of Milton's Satan.[15] But the Lucifer of the Renaissance poem with his deep sense of humiliation at the Son's or Adam's advancement is an ancestor as well. The force that chagrin or political disappointment exerts upon him is not to be minimized. Dramatically, a villain with a motive makes better sense than a motiveless malignancy (which patristic tradition gives us) or a strutting egotist (which the medieval mysteries pose). And Milton's Satan is that: a character with a motive. Of the two motives available to him, Milton chose the one less current in the Renaissance. He chose to make Satan rebellious at the advancement of a superior rather than an inferior. Accordingly, he strikes a kind of mean. Milton's Satan evokes less sympathy from the reader with his refusal to bow the knee to *the Son* (newly appointed king) than does Peri's or Vondel's with the parallel refusal to bow to Adam. (Adam's advancement—whatever its reasons—had at least the advantage of "appearing" arbitrary.) Clearly, in providing Satan a motive Milton wants that motive to be one both reasonably understood and also reasonably answered. The answer, moreover, that Abdiel voices in book 5 is more incisive than the answer Pace or Gabriel had provided to Lucifer in the plays. Abdiel, like them, on the one hand argues that God may do as he likes, but on the other hand points out with superb logic that the Son was, even before his appointment as king, Satan's superior. No such case can Pace or Gabriel make for Adam; they can merely

urge Lucifer to find a benevolent purpose in God's designs. Milton thus
shows Satan suffering from deep chagrin at the disappointment of his
political ambitions, but he denies him a fully acceptable motive for that
chagrin.

If Renaissance poets work hard to show that Lucifer's motives for
rebellion were compelling, if not excusable, they work even harder to accord
him a kind of magnificence as he plans and carries out his revolt. There is the
princely flourish with which Lucifer dispatches the messenger to God in
Bellum angelicum and the impetuous anger with which he hears God's
negative reply. His eyes flash fire, and he proudly asks himself if he should
desist and withdraw his words. Then imperiously he declares that God's
threats are vain and urges his angels to take up their weapons and raise their
battle standards. Like an epic adversary, he dispatches the messenger back to
the tyrant God to report his reaction. Or there is Lucifer in *Daemonomachiae*,
who passionately resists God's decree of the Son's supremacy:

> O superans pia vota, Dei largissima dextra,
> Quid dignum tanto referam pro munere patri?
> Ergo mihi (neque enim mundi praeclarius ullum
> Exemplar statuisse reor) coniugia Verbi
> Decernis?
>
> > > > [p. 15]

> Prevailing over holy vows, over the most bountiful pledges of
> God,
> Why should I exchange my honors for such great duty to the
> Father?
> Wherefore (since I do not believe a more splendid model to have
> been set
> > > up for the world)
> Do you determine for me the yoke of the Word?

Not in words only but in appearance the poets describe Lucifer as an
imperious epic figure. Acevedo shows him at the head of his army, envious
and proud: "angel superbio y invidioso, / Vertiendo por los ojos abrasados /
Y por la boca fuego impetuoso" (p. 249). In two similes, moreover, Acevedo
gives Lucifer the appearance of an epic hero, comparing him first to a bull in
majestic anger pawing the earth and then to a falcon swooping down on his
prey.[16] Homer had, of course, compared Agamemnon to a bull who stood
conspicuous in the herd (2.480–483) and had compared Achilles as he
pursued Hector to the falcon (22.139–142). Lucifer is treated in simile

analogously to these classical warriors. Also, as Agamemnon is described as kingly in appearance, with eyes and head like those of Zeus who delights in thunder, girth like Ares', and chest like Poseidon's, so Lucifer is kingly. Taubmann compares him, striding among his soldiers, to Orion plunging into the ocean waves, then arising head and shoulders above the ocean. Moreover, the kind of princely anger Lucifer indulges in is both like the classical anger of Agamemnon or Achilles and like the anger of Tasso's Soliman or Ariosto's pagan kings. In book 10 of *Gerusalemme liberata*, for example, Soliman strides forth from the mist to repudiate the pagans for suggesting compromise; or in canto 38 of *Orlando Furioso* the pagan kings contend whether to advance a new assault on the Christians. Accordingly, when Taubmann and Valmarana show Lucifer passionately denouncing his adversaries, they have models in both classical and chivalric literature.

For the Renaissance poets who write wars in Heaven, Lucifer is primarily a kind of "pagan" general or prince. To give him proper ceremony, many poets create "council" scenes before the war in which he can demonstrate his princely qualities. These council scenes are peculiar to Renaissance literature, which found its precedents for them in the classical tradition. Medieval literature rarely showed Lucifer in consult with his angels before the war. It is also interesting that these prelapsarian councils often have as direct analogues or sources "hellish" councils, which some poets of the Renaissance had granted to the fallen Lucifer. A very definite correspondence exists between the behavior of the princely Lucifer who calls together his allies in Heaven and urges them to revolt against God and the prince of Hell who calls together his allies and urges them to a new enterprise. Poets writing councils in Heaven could model their Lucifers not only on King Agamemnon or King Agramant in consult, but also on Vida's Prince Satan or Tasso's kingly devil. The Renaissance permitted its pagan kings and its Satans to be imposing figures who speak with persuasive logic. Assuredly, of course, Vida and Tasso first make Satan in Hell a monster attended, as we have seen in Valvasone's *Angeleida*, with harpies, chimeras, and so forth. The moment he begins to speak, however, his grotesqueness is forgotten. Like an epic hero, he speaks passionately and persuasively. First, Vida's Lucifer pricks the resentment of his followers by reminding them how God hurled them from Heaven and imprisoned them in Hell. At the same time he compliments their valiant resistance to God's tyranny. On the one hand he insinuates that God intends to impose new chains on them in Hell, and on the other he appeals to their courage and resourcefulness to prevent further enslavement to God by swiftly arming against him.[17] Tasso's Satan (some fifty years later) similarly plays on the vanity and fear of his auditors. He praises their angelic origins, reminding them of their glory in Heaven and the boldness of their war against God. He pricks resentment by recalling at the same time how God usurped their rights in Heaven and committed outrage against them. And, to persuade them to a new cause, he threatens that God will encroach upon their rights in Hell if they do not rouse themselves and once more fight courageously (*GL* 4.1–19).

These two council scenes, which present a Lucifer exhorting his followers, influence *Paradise Lost* in that they provide, directly or indirectly, the models for Satan's speeches from the throne both to Hell and in Heaven. In Hell Satan glances at lost glory, guilefully encouraging his angels to think of regaining their seats in Heaven, while in truth encouraging them to new enterprises on earth. In Heaven he attempts to prick the angels' resentment of the yoke imposed upon them by the kingship of the Son and make them fear that still heavier yokes will be imposed. In both these scenes Milton looks back to Vida and Tasso themselves and to later poems influenced by them.

Council scenes (in Heaven, rather than in Hell) come to dominate the poems that describe the war in Heaven. Renaissance poets, after they have shown Lucifer himself moved to revolt, are eager to show how he moved others. They frequently demonstrate how Lucifer appeals, as he did in Vida's *Christiad*, to the twin emotions of vanity and fear. Mollerus's Lucifer invokes pride of place to urge the angels that they deserve greater rights and recognition than they have been given. Then he uses the spurs of virtue, honor, and praise to stir them.

> Ingens consilium latitat sub mente repostum,
> Vnde manet virtus, laus, honor, unde decus.
> Scitis ut in nostra sit magna potentia gente,
> Quòd nullus nostros aequet honore gradus.
>
> > [n.p.]

> Mighty counsel lies hidden, remote in the mind,
> Whence abides virtue, praise, honor, hence glory.
> You know that there is in our race great power,
> Because no one compares with us in degree of honor.

Taubmann's Lucifer also intimates that the angels have been badly treated by God, who puts servile yokes upon them; he appeals to them that in the name of liberty they cast off these yokes. Honor also he invokes, telling them to be heroes and fight for fame without shrinking.[18] Naogeorgus's Lucifer, in like vein, tells the angels that they suffer an unworthy servitude. He has discerned in them willing hearts, faith, and virtue, and in obedience to these qualities they should throw off the yoke they bear and aspire to a rank equal to God's. Valvasone's Lucifer becomes rhapsodic when he speaks of glory. He too has pled the cause of lost honor and place, and he now presents his angels with the grim necessity of war. Invoking justice, reverence, faith, he promises that they will conquer gloriously:

> Che dirò de la gloria? O quanta pompa,
> O che trionfo conduremo in Cielo:
> O frati, o frati, homai nulla interrompa
> Lenta dimora il vostro innato zelo:
>
> [Valvasone, 1.99]

> What should I say of glory? Of such pomp?
> Oh, what a triumph I shall lead in Heaven!
> Oh, brothers, brothers, let no slow delay
> Impede your inborn fervor.

In light, then, not only of Vida and Tasso but of Mollerus, Taubmann, Valmarana, Naogeorgus, and Valvasone, it seems apparent that Milton was following a well-established tradition when he had his Satan appeal to the angels' pride of title: "If these magnific Titles yet remain / Not merely titular" (5.773–774). Lucifers before Milton's had inveighed against the "knee-tribute," "prostration vile," and the yoke imposed in Heaven. Of angelic virtues, Milton's Satan chooses to extol liberty and in its name to suggest that angels band together to "govern, not to serve" (5.802). Thus in book 5, when Satan rises before the multitude, readers familiar with the traditions knew what to expect. English readers could look back to the Satan of Phineas Fletcher, who had called upon the name of honor that the fallen angels throw off their yokes in Hell, or the Satan in Cowley's *Davideis*, who had likewise argued.[19] Milton in *Paradise Lost* does not disappoint his readers. But the effects he produces as Satan prepares to speak are necessarily different. For in book 5 it is not the first time we have seen Satan address a council like an epic hero. We have the experience of books 1 and 2 behind us. We have already heard Satan speak of equality and liberty, honor and degree (cf. 2.18–36). We will not be startled at the epic nobility of this figure. In book 5, however, Satan's epic speech, noble though it is, has lost something of its eloquence. The fact is, almost everything we hear him speak in book 5 we have heard before. And the echoes are hollow. For example, in book 1 Satan provokes his followers' resentment by suggesting that God had "tempted our attempt, and wrought our fall" (1.642); in book 5 he provokes resentment by suggesting that God has selfishly engrossed all power to himself and eclipsed the angels. In Hell he asks, "who can think subjection?" (1.661); in Heaven, "Will ye submit your necks, and choose to bend / The supple knee?" (5.787–788); and still further he states that God demands from them "Knee-tribute, yet unpaid, prostration vile" (5.782). In Hell he encourages aspiring minds to "reascend / Self-rais'd" (1.633–634); in Heaven he described the angels as "self-begot, self-rais'd / By [their] own quick'ning power" (5.860–861). The effect of these words is curious. Sounding the first time in Hell, they possess a vigorous heroic ring. They grant to Satan, as they had to the Lucifers in the Renaissance poems, the status of an epic hero. But repeated in book 5 they are tired and empty. They are clearly the words of a figure who only sounds heroic, whose assurances we have heard before and now no longer believe. In rendering the heroic Satan in book 5, Milton has reduced him.

In Renaissance literature, Lucifer the epic hero and Lucifer the general are one. Not only soldier and hero is he—an Achilles or a Hector—but also a leader of multitudes—an Agamemnon, a Soliman. So, early in the Renaissance epics and dramas, he stands out to issue a call to arms. His supreme trust is in the ethic of force. In assembling his army, therefore, he urges that all he and his angels require to cast off the yoke of the tyrant is unfailing courage in the exercise of arms. Mollerus's Lucifer proposes giving God a choice; either he abdicate in their favor or they chase him from his seat by force. Naogeorgus's Lucifer is likewise direct. If God refuses to divide his empire and concede equal honor to the angels (and Lucifer admits such concession is unlikely), then force must be prepared and used. An encomium on arms follows. Lucifer urges that the enterprise is in itself worth the peril it entails. If the angels will join their might with his and accept him as their leader, they will conquer. But if they refuse such an opportunity, they can only repent in vain. Following this tradition, in book 5 Milton glances, if only briefly, at Satan the general. (He had given us a full-length portrait in books 1 and 2.) Near the end of book 5 Satan the general flexes his muscles and threatens military reprisal against the single angel Abdiel, who has risen as an opponent.

> Our puissance is our own, our own right hand
> Shall teach us highest deeds, by proof to try
> Who is our equal; then thou shalt behold
> Whether by supplication we intend
> Address, and to begirt th' Almighty Throne
> Beseeching or besieging.
>
> [5.864–869]

The scene is necessarily quite different, however, from what we have observed in the Renaissance poems, where Lucifer delivers his military vaunts to his angels alone, to be received, we presume, by their enthusiastic applause. Satan, in raising his vaunts to Abdiel, loses much of his heroic stature. We do not see the experienced general of book 1, who has made his angels rise from off the burning lake to form perfect ranks before him; we do not see the leader of book 2 who proposes to visit Chaos alone and take full upon himself the heroic responsibilities. Instead we see Satan bullying Abdiel with threats and making absurd claims to besiege God. Again Milton has limited Satan.

Most of the Renaissance Lucifers depicted in poems describing the war in Heaven are active leaders who challenge God directly. Few combine demonic cunning with demonic bravura. Thus Vondel's Lucifer, who does so, is an important forerunner of Milton's Satan. He is, first of all, a splendid epic figure; lamenting God's unjust decree and determining to resist it with the full power of his own arm, he equals, indeed surpasses, the rhetoric of the Lucifers before him. But he delivers his speeches to *his own* coterie of angels—Beelzebub, joined by Belial and Apollyon. Here is no Lucifer who openly vaunts his intentions. Not until the very outbreak of war does he take command of that rebellion that he fostered from the outset. There is no doubt in our minds, however, that Lucifer is the natural leader, even though his plots remain unacknowledged in name. It is he who first determines to resist God's decree. (Beelzebub or Apollyon or Belial may dislike it, but none shows any sign of holding forth against it.) It is also he first who suggests that they challenge Michael, the commander-in-chief of God's armies and the possessor of the key to God's armories. (Apollyon lags back, fearing war with the Omnipotent.) Lucifer in private speaks boldly and adventurously as he sets forth his schemes; in public, however, he retains the demeanor of the circumspect and prudent leader. Neither Gabriel nor Michael realizes till late in the poem that he is the author of rebellion.

Both Milton and Vondel stress Lucifer's political cunning. Both dramatize for us—after the archangel has himself determined to revolt—his seduction of his comrade Beelzebub and his subsequent employment of this angel to forward his plot. In *Paradise Lost* Satan directs Beelzebub to move his powers by night, telling "the suggested cause" and casting between "ambiguous words and jealousies, to sound / Or taint integrity" (5.702–704). In *Lucifer* the archangel dispatches his subordinates Apollyon and Belial to stir up the crowd by insinuation and directs Beelzebub to pretend dismay while all the time pressing for insurrection. (Only in Peri's *La guerra angelica* do we find Lucifer using subordinates to do his work for him, and since the subordinates are the allegorical vices Superbia and Invidia, the intention and effect are not the same as in Vondel's drama.) In *Lucifer* the masses of angels, the so-called Luciferists, fully stirred to revolt, drive away their commander Michael, who has attempted to quell them and make them lay down their arms. Now Lucifer at last appears before them. He does not immediately assume command. Indeed, the baton of leadership must be thrust upon him as he pretends hesitancy and caution. Then only does he become the general and then only deliver the words of challenge.

Milton's Satan is similarly indirect. For rather than using exhortation of commands (like Taubmann's or Naogeorgus's archangel), he employs as his basic method the inflammatory question. Are the titles merely titular? Are you now eclipsed in power by God? What new honor and knee-tribute will you pay to God and the Son? Will you submit? Will monarchy be imposed over equals? Will law and edict? Are you not ordained to govern rather than serve? (Of course, the inflammatory question serves Satan well throughout his career in *Paradise Lost*, from the first one he directs to Beelzebub in book 1 to the last he directs to Eve, not to mention the series of inflammatory questions he uses in book 1 to stir his newly wakened angels to action.) Vondel's thrust in *Lucifer* was to illustrate how Lucifer deceived the angels through skillful and deliberate manipulation. Milton also wishes to show this, and he does so first by showing that the crowd that stands before Satan in book 5 has been manipulated by Beelzebub to suspicion and distrust of God. (Unlike Vondel, Milton does not show us the manipulation as it takes place.) Milton's Satan seems at first a straightforward "hero," advocating revolt. But not so. Instead he is the manipulator who undermines the angels' confidence in God's kingdom and leads them to believe they have before them no alternative besides revolt. He is in demeanor like Agamemnon, in tactics like Odysseus. Beneath the appearance of courageous fighter and noble leader is the wily politician. And, outside of Vondel, Milton is the poet who most clearly gives us this impression of Satan.

In book 6 of *Paradise Lost* Satan has his best chance to behave like an epic hero, and at two points in the action he clearly does. The first occurs when, appearing upon the field of battle, brilliantly attired, he issues a general challenge to combat. The second takes place when, preparing to fight Michael alone, he defends "the strife of glory" in which he engages his strength. In so depicting the warring archangel, even momentarily, Milton may be glancing back at those Renaissance poets who granted Lucifer glory in battle. Vondel was certainly one who gives us a splendid description of Lucifer's entry on the field, ringed by troops in sapphire and green:

> Dress'd in a golden coat of mail that shone
> Above his purple tunic, mounted now

His chariot, with gold wheels, ruby-studded.
The Lion and fell Dragon were in his team
In harness all bepearl'd, ready for flight,
Sprinkled with myriad stars upon their backs,
And burning for the wild destructive strife,
He bore a battle-axe; his shimmering shield,
In which the morning star was wrought with art,
Hung of his left arm, ready for all hazard.

[Kirkconnell, p. 410]

In 't gouden panser, dat, op zijnen wapenrock
Van gloeiend purper blonck, en uitscheen, steegh te wagen,
Met goude wielen, van robijnen dicht beslagen.
De Leeuw, en selle Dracck, ter vlucht gereet, en vlugh,
Met starren overal bezaeit op hunnen rugh,
In 't parrele gareel, gespannen voor de wielen,
Verlangden naer den strijt, en vlamden op vernielen.
De heirbijl in de vuist, de scheemrende rondas,
Waer in de morgenstar met kunst gedreven was,
Hing aen den slincken arm, gereet de kans te wagen.

[Vondel, pp. 55–56]

Taubmann similarly presents Lucifer as a formidable epic opponent, armed from head to foot, his terrible helmet on, his cuirass huge and triple-twilled, rigid with scales (p. 87). Murtola tells us how sparkling the arrogant angel appears at the head of his dark and grim troops. Peri first presents the scene in which Lucifer dons his armor for battle and bestows insignia and weapons on the allegorical lieutenants who serve him. Then he shows him as he enters battle, still the splendid epic figure, though captain over a monstrous horde: Discordia, Rabbia, Ingratitudine, and so forth. When he speaks to his soldiers, moreover, he is a proud, bold, and resolute, but nonetheless heroic figure. He spurs them on, telling them not to be afraid of the enemy and disparaging the threat Michael and his soldiers offer. Assuring them of victory, he orders them to the assault.

It is surprising how many poets give Lucifer the opportunity of making a major battle speech, sometimes several, before he actually engages in arms. Of course they are following epic convention in so doing. But in following convention they permit Lucifer a good deal of rather impressive heroic flourish. For Lucifer addressing his soldiers does not speak meanly and despicably. In fact, he sounds little different from any general of epic, who before the battle acknowledges to his soldiers the danger of their course but urges them to be brave. Acevedo, for example, gives Lucifer a brief but stirring speech.

> ¡De mi opinion espíritus secuaces!
> Aunque mas peligroso sea el alarde,
> No entre en vuestros ánimos audaces
> Sombra ni rastro de temor cobarde;
> Estad en el propósito tenaces,
> Por mas que el premio que se os debe, tarde;
> Que yo en mi pensamiento voy tan firme,
> Que no puedo, aunque quiera, arrepentirme.
>
> [p. 249]

> O, spirits, followers of my convictions,
> Although my vaunts may be very dangerous,
> Do not let a shade or trace of cowardly fear enter
> Into your hearts. Be tenacious in your purpose,
> However late in coming be the prize due you.
> I in my intent am so firm that I cannot repent,
> Even though I might wish to do so.

Even though Acevedo has told us before the speech that this is the rebel speaking (thus we should be outraged by his defiance rather than stirred by his valor), it is the valor that impresses us.

Valvasone similarly gives us a curious mixture of the monster and the hero. In outer appearance, of course, Lucifer is a monster: a hideous giant with a hundred arms, seven heads, and seven mouths. And, with his angels likewise transformed, his camp more closely resembles the pit of hell than the glorious fields of Heaven. Moreover, since the fury Megara is his chief companion, this association further emphasizes Lucifer's monstrous qualities. But, despite all, once Lucifer opens his mouth we hear the voice of the hero general. Boldly and extravagantly, he promises the faithful that they will win honor and reward in the coming fight, for the end of their struggle is the conquest not only of Heaven but of earth. Crowns and kingdoms upon earth he promises, the conquest of sea and land, the sun and the moon. All those of earth will come to worship them. Therefore, he urges, take up your arms and do not yield. The opposing side, he insists, is "soft" and unprepared, too unambitious to be equal, too weak, and willing merely to continue to serve God and pray for his favor. Face to face, he vaunts, we will overcome them.

Taubmann's Lucifer also excels in the battle speech. Not once, but repeatedly, do we hear him exhort his angels. On the first occasion he has just received the messenger he had dispatched to God. Hearing that God has refused his terms, he sends the messenger back defiantly and turns to his army. He tells them that the time has come when they must take up their arms.

> Venit summa dies; geritur res maxima, frates.
> Concurrent hodie Rex coeli & Lucifer armis.
> Ingenteis praestate animos, praeclara manebunt
> Praemia victorem.
>
> [p. 85]

> The final day is come; the greatest deed is accomplished,
>   brothers.
> Today, the king of Heaven and Lucifer clash with their armies,
> Exhibit prodigious spirit. The
> Most splendid rewards await the victor.

He next assembles them and drives them forth, and when they stand in arms before him he once more offers encouragement. Go forth, he says, go forth with the hope of future kingdom.

> I decus i nostrum, regni spes una futuri!
> Sentiat has vires belli rudis incola coeli,
> Quidque Draco possit, hodie experiatur in armis.
>
> [p. 88]

> Go forth with my glorious ones, go with a single hope for
>   empire-to-be!
> Let the churlish inhabitant of Heaven feel this strength of battle.
> Whatever the dragon can accomplish, today let him try in arms.

Yet, these are not all. Taubmann twice more gives his Lucifer opportunity to encourage his soldiers-in-arms: once at the end of book 1, after Lucifer has dispatched Satanas to carry out the strategem against the loyal army, once again at the end of book 2, when Lucifer prepares for the final battle with Michael. Having met Michael first and having exchanged challenges, Lucifer turns to his soldiers to assure them of the justice of their cause and to encourage them in the fight now imminent.

> Rerum spes & fortuna mearum,
> O domitor caeli, miles: quod saepè vocasti

Tempus adest: toties quaesitae copia pugnae
In manibus vestris. haec lux praestabit honores
Haec libertatem sceptrumque: haec, judice ferro,
Pandet, uter melior sit bello; uter arma parârit
Iustiùs, heic medio posuit Mars omnia campo.

[p. 104]

Hope and fortune of my affairs,
O Lord of Heaven, soldier, because often you have challenged
The time is now; the occasion of the battle, so often
Sought out, is in your hands.
This glory shall win honor;
This liberty and rule; this with the sword as arbiter
Shall manifest whichever is better in war,
Whichever shall have wielded arms more justly.
At this point war has placed all in the midst of battle.

It is interesting that Milton makes little of the general Satan on the verge of battle. It is perhaps understandable that he has given him no battle speech in book 5; but the omission in book 6 is highly significant. We know from books 1 and 2 that Satan thinks of himself as the superlative leader—not only the great persuader, but the great general. Our first glimpse of him in book 1 was as the general who even in defeat was able to rouse his army. Hearing his voice, his soldiers rise from the burning lake and form perfect ranks before him. The speech he offers them, even in defeat, has kinship with those battle speeches that the aspiring Lucifer of the Renaissance poems offered in heaven in expectation of victory. For Satan is intent not to yield or to be overcome; he even relishes the thought of future conquest on earth, intent on eternal war, open or understood. In book 6 there is neither a comparable scene nor comparable words. Therefore I think it is quite clear that Milton intends by book 6 to limit severely the kind of heroic expansiveness he had earlier permitted Satan. What he allows in the delusive half-light of Hell he will not allow in the clear sun of Heaven. Satan's heroic moments are notably few, and even those are cut very short. First there is the dramatic entrance, "High in the midst exalted as a God / Th' Apostate in his Sun-bright Chariot sat" (6.99–100), and then the brief magnificence as he strides forth, "tow'ring, arm'd in Adamant and Gold" (6.110). But these descriptions do not herald a scene in which Satan appears to advantage before his army or even delivers an effective challenge to the enemy. Instead, Milton has his brilliant hero advance to be met and repulsed (first verbally, then in arms) by the plain soldier Abdiel. Even his speech to Abdiel lacks a heroic ring; it is grumbling and condescending. He promises to repulse Abdiel and of course fails to do so. He mocks the minstrelsy of Heaven and is met with immediate proof that the disparaged minstrelsy is not to be despised. Thus at the first moment that Milton has lifted up the aspiring warrior-hero he very quickly casts him down.

A similar reversal occurs at two other moments when Renaissance poets have permitted Lucifer to sound and act heroic; at his single combat with Michael and at his defeat. Now poets are by no means unanimous in permitting Lucifer to combat Michael fiercely and heroically before his inevitable defeat. Acevedo and Murtola, for example, render Lucifer instant defeat. The sword of Michael cuts through him and he is overcome. Equally instantaneous is the defeat that poets like Naogeorgus and Mollerus describe, though it is not the surrogate, Michael, but God himself who hurls Lucifer from Heaven. Other poets, however, seem less eager to end their epic battles with the instant capitulation of Lucifer. Therefore they grant him the latitude to behave like an epic hero. Taubmann's Lucifer, as we have seen, is particularly impressive in arms. Taubmann permits him to meet Michael before the battle and engage in an extended sequence of flyting, where he defends the heroic ethic of strength as the highest code.

> An armis
> Venisti, an linquâ mecum certare magistrâ?
> Nequidquam increpitas, aufer terrere minaci
> Garrulitate meos;
>
> > [p. 103]
>
> Have you come in arms,
> Do you debate with me what remains of my sovranty?
> To no purpose do you challenge me;
> Cease from threatening my soldiers with menace and prattle.

It seems clear that Taubmann, although he has not finished his epic, intended to conclude it with a heroic single combat between Michael and Lucifer, where the latter is only with difficulty defeated. Both the flying sequence and the description of open battle in book 3 seem to lead to this. Even Valmarana's Lucifer, though he does not meet Michael in single combat, behaves heroically in defeat. With the help of the *Verbum Dei*, Michael has shattered the resistance of Lucifer's legions, but Lucifer still stands resistant, bearing the full brunt of lightning and still defying God. Although his resistance is vain, although it is swiftly followed by degradation and fall, it is still impressive. Left alone on the field he attains some dignity as a single adversary. Davis Harding has argued that Milton's Satan in his defeat resembles the Virgilian Turnus, who desperately and single-handedly defends his cause even against "Heaven's" will, I argue that the Renaissance Lucifer—Satan's ancestor, so to speak—still more closely resembles Turnus.[20] This is particularly so in *Lucifer* and *Angeleida*, where he chooses to stand when others have fled. In *Angeleida*, he scorns the angels who have faltered:

> Ite, cedete, o fiacchi animi, i'voglio
> Restrar qui fermo, & quando il Ciel saetti
> Tutto in me sol, ne vincitor, nè vinto
> Dal mio proposto mai verrò sospinto.
> [2.105]

> Go, yield, sluggish spirits. I wish
> To remain here resolute, and although I shall see the Heavens
>   with arrows
> All on me alone, neither conqueror, nor conquered,
> Never will I be pushed from my purpose.

Valvasone makes Lucifer not only a valiant but a terrible adversary, ranging the field and upsetting those angels who oppose him, holding fifty shields and fifty weapons before him. Not till he meets Michael is he defeated. In *Lucifer* he is a resourceful captain. When the bow of his half-moon formation breaks, he keeps up his courage and swoops here and there, showing himself "brave and great-hearted still to save the day." By his courage in his chariot, as Vondel tells us, he "give[s] courage to the fainting." He wards off blows and arrows and drives fiercely on in the face of imminent defeat. In his chariot he is a fearsome adversary for it is drawn by a lion and a dragon. As Lucifer fights with all his might, the lion roars and bites and tears, and the dragon shoots poison from his cleft tongue. In his final assault he attempts to cut down God's banner and to shatter with his battle-ax Michael's adamantine shield. Only in the face of Michael's superior lightnings is he defeated (Act 5).

In *La guerra angelica* as well, Lucifer is a formidable foe who meets defeat only after a sturdy resistance. Having been metamorphosed into a dragon during the battle with Michael, he breathes fire and smoke and lashes his spiked tail. He is a dangerous as well as a persistent adversary, who is with difficulty defeated.

Milton's treatment of Satan is instructive. Milton *does* permit Satan an epic fight, but it is a fight with the angel Michael, not with the hero Son.

Moreover, the fight occupies a central rather than a climactic position. Nevertheless, we can clearly see that he has been influenced in his depiction of this fight by the epic battle accorded Michael by Renaissance poets. His description of both adversaries is heroic. As Satan approaches Michael to duel with him, he is the prototype of the epic hero, opposing the loyal archangel with his "rocky Orb / Of tenfold Adamant, his ample Shield" (6.254–255). In his speech to Michael, moreover, he sounds, as Taubmann's and Valvasone's Lucifer had sounded before him, like the epic hero defending the ethic of heroic battle. He turns aside what he calls Michael's threats and calls for deeds to answer words. He exalts war as a strife of glory. Finally he dares Michael to expend his utmost force and vows to stand firm against him. It is his most plainly heroic moment during books 5 and 6, the moment when he most resembles the warrior he claimed to be in recalling the war in books 1 and 2. It is also the moment when he most resembles the Lucifer of the Renaissance tradition. Of course he is defeated, slashed through with Michael's sword, but he has at least stood briefly with "next to Almighty Arm." Milton in granting him this much plainly glances back at the Renaissance tradition. After this brief and splendid moment of angelic duel the war swiftly deteriorates and, what is more significant, Satan never again rises to be an epic opponent. Milton, having briefly highlighted Satan the hero, who in the center of the war meets Michael in an inconclusive duel, denies Satan the heroics of a last stand.

Milton differs from the Renaissance poets in another way as well. At the conclusion of the war, Milton's attention is on the Son rather than on Satan. We taste the Son's victory rather than Satan's defeat. In the Renaissance poems, however, there is a good deal of emphasis, negative though it may be, on the horrors of Satan's defeat and fall. He is allowed to retain central focus, however much poets also accord Michael a glamorous victory. This is particularly the case in that many poets make Satan's fall the occasion of his monstrous metamorphosis.[21] In Valmarana's poem, in Acevedo's, in Vondel's, we see Lucifer and his angels suffer a terrible transformation as they rain from Heaven in the form of sphinxes, chimeras, and geryons. Vondel records the very moment that Lucifer's beauty begins to fade. When he is hurled backward from his chariot, as the frontispiece of Vondel's 1654 edition of the play also shows, his transformation begins. The morning star of his banner fades and his countenance becomes brutish.

Valmarana also records Lucifer's transformation: his beauty is marred, horns spring from his head, and he spontaneously falls as the poet laments his loss. In Valmarana's account Isaiah's influence is particularly strong; Valmarana echoes the words from Isaiah as Lucifer falls, "quomodo de Coeli cecedisti, Lucifer, astris." Even though Valmarana makes us aware that

Lucifer deserves his fate, he plays upon our almost inadvertent sympathy for the formerly beautiful angel. He shows us what a humiliating experience his metamorphosis is, how bitterly he reacts to his loss of beauty and honor:

>   omnes
>   Exuit infelix formosae mentis honores
>   Lucifer, & quiquid coelestibus hauserat oris,
>   Angelicumque decus furiales vertit in artus;
>
>   [pp. 28–29]

>   Lucifer, wretched, put off all honor from his glorious being,
>   And whatsoever he gathered from the celestial borders.
>   His angelic glory he transformed into frenzied power.

Moreover, though Lucifer is expelled from Heaven, it is not without the "last word." Looking about him and shedding vain tears, he exclaims that he will never give up his fight, even though now he must leave the skies and relinquish the scepter to the tyrant. While strength remains and virtue, he swears to continue his resistance. Of course Valmarana discredits his "heroics." Speaking directly to Lucifer, he tells him to seek Tartarus and his realm there and upbraids him for too little concern for true glory.

>   pete tartara, pestis,
>   lnnocuumque absolue solum, te digna tyranno
>   Regna manent.....
>
>   [p. 31]

>   Seek Tartarus, you plague,
>   Set free the harmless earth,
>   For a kingdom, worthy a
>   Tyrant, awaits you.

But, despite this speech, the poet has accorded the retreating Lucifer some grudging glory. He leaves Heaven humiliated but still the central figure in our interest.

The "Draco" of *La guerra angelica* also proves an interesting figure in defeat. Though finally driven from Heaven by Michael and the force of his vindicating sword, the dragon yet has power to breathe defiance. He flees, but not through fear of Michael. Fate wills it. Yet he will return stronger and be reborn with a hundred heads. Once more he will fight, now directing his anger against God and man. Acevedo's Lucifer also vaunts at the moment of his fall. And he too speaks heroic words. Though the victory may be God's, he says, the glory is theirs.

For many poets, Lucifer's departure from Heaven is not the end of the account. They are intent to show two things: how Heaven reacted to victory and how Hell reacted to defeat. What is significant for our study of Satan is that the poets continue to show Satan as a heroic figure even after his fall to Hell. We must, of course, discount his appearance, for Renaissance poets apparently relished describing the traditional crude devil with horns, multiple heads, scaly feet, and tail. They delighted in showing blood dripping from his mouth and fire issuing from his nostrils. In physical aspect their Satans are worlds removed from Milton's, who in his late metamorphosis becomes ugly and monstrous, but never crude. The Satan of Renaissance epic (while looking monstrous), however, continues to sound heroic in Hell.

Many poets dramatize the woefulness of his circumstances and show him, as Mollerus does, lamenting his eternal damnation.

> Proh tempus miserum, proh lachrymosa dies,
> Proh facinus, quae nos tam caeca superbia coepit,
> Quod summo intulimus tristia bella Deo?
>
> > [n.p.]

> Alas, the wretched time! Alas the day, causing tears!
> Alas, the wickedness all of which blind pride began,
> Because we undertook this sad war against the highest God.

Yet Lucifer is, as the poets show him, capable of more than lament. Naogeorgus's Lucifer begins by regretting the unlucky fight; he and his soldiers were worthy of better fortune and did not deserve to be so conquered. He swiftly rallies and tells his angels to summon up courage and hope for better fortune on earth. Similarly, in *Angeleida* we have a Lucifer who, though defeated, is not without resources and is eagerly looking forward to recouping his fortunes on earth. Turning his attention to the human seed who will in future inhabit this kingdom, he proposes to bend his enterprise in ordering things below. Valvasone's attitude toward his Lucifer is obviously dual. On the one hand he shows us a resilient leader who, speaking nobly to his soldiers, resembles the Satan of book 1 of *Paradise Lost*. He is a leader who, as in Heaven, still speaks of honor and glory and who is intent on consoling his allies for their loss.

> Perduto habbiamo, o già celesti genti
> Nobili, & belle, hor basso vulgo oscuro:

Perduto habbiam le vaghe stelle ardenti,
Che nostra Patria da principio foro:
Hora qui ci convien non esser lenti
A fondar nouo regno ampio, & securo:
Perdemmo il ciel, faccia hor lo sdegno nostro
Tremendo a par del Ciel l'internal chiostro.

[3–9]

We have lost, O formerly celestial race,
Noble and beautiful, now low, obscure commons:
We have lost the beautiful, burning stars,
That was our native land from the beginning;
Now here we come not slowly together,
To found a new empire, ample and secure,
I have lost Heaven; now our
Disdain makes the infernal cloister tremble, equal to Heaven.

But, while permitting him to voice heroic sentiments, Valvasone reminds his readers that Lucifer is less than heroic in appearance and intent. He describes the former prince of Heaven now as a monster who bellows forth words from his seven mouths. Addressing Lucifer directly, he condemns as base the would-be heroic ambitions and assures him that he will gain nothing for his reward but further damnation, eternal pain and fire. These sentiments are not unlike those voiced by the narrator of *Paradise Lost* who, commenting on Satan's resolutions, remarks that they serve "but to bring forth / Infinite goodness ... but on himself / Treble confusion, wrath and vengeance poured" (1.217–220). But the narrator of *Paradise Lost*, unlike Valvasone, is not dismissing Lucifer from the scene; he is preparing for action to come, action that will include a demonstration of the futility of Satan's previous machinations in Heaven. He is at the beginning, not the end, of his narration. Hence, in his remarks about Lucifer and in his depiction of the newly fallen angel, he resembles the poet-narrators of the *Adam* dramas of the sixteenth and seventeenth centuries as much as he does the poets of celestial battle epics like Valvasone. The situation in which he places his Satan is like that depicted in the *Adam exul* of Grotius, the *Adamo* of Andreini, the *Adamo caduto* of Salandra, or the *Adam in Ballingschap* of Vondel. Milton's Satan, like theirs, first appears on the scene in Hell, newly fallen and still smarting from his defeat. A vigorous leader, resolved to rally his soldiers to new enterprises, he speaks heroically, defending the "glorious" attempt made in Heaven and encouraging a new attempt on earth. Like Valvasone's Lucifer, the Satan of the *Adam* drama recalls, sometimes poignantly, sometimes boastfully, his former attempt on Heaven. Andreini's and Salandra's devils glorify their great feats in arms, which "caused the pale face of Heaven to twitch in fear" (*L'Adamo*, 1.3) or boast how by sheer will they "could have blotted out Michael and all his host and Heaven too" (*Adamo caduto*, 2.1).[22] Milton's Satan speaks in a similar vein. He is more reserved, more ironic, more indirect than his predecessors, more prone to speak of a fight not inglorious than to glorify directly past exploits. But his intent is similar—to raise his allies to new enterprises by recalling the glory of the old ones.

> O Myriads of immortal Spirits, O powers
> Matchless, but with the Almighty, and that strife
> Was not inglorious, though th' event was dire....
>
> [1.622–624]

Milton's Satan in book 1 is a conventional general in defeat that the Renaissance both reviled and glorified. For the Renaissance in making Satan an epic figure perforce made readers grant him grudging admiration. In book 1 at least, Milton is content to grant him that same grudging admiration, to permit him glory-mongering speeches, to show him splendid even in defeat. But Milton has looked not once, but twice, at Satan's fall and defeat. In book 1 Satan falls with flaming glory and Milton raises the Isaiahan lament. In book 1 we are indulged (by Satan at least) in the pathos of lost glory, and we hear Satan boast never to yield and not to be overcome. We are in the world that Renaissance epic had bequeathed to Milton. And we hear the poet-narrator, like other poet-narrators before him, repudiate Satan and his empty vaunting while permitting him to sound the cause of glory.

In book 6 we look at Satan's defeat from another perspective, and there we see clearly that the glory of battle was a Satanic illusion. For Satan did not stand heroically against the loyal sons of Heaven. In truth, even in the so-called heroic warfare of the first day, he suffered repulse by Abdiel and check by Michael in a single crushing blow. On the second day his heroics degenerated to "gamesome mood." The last words we hear him utter in book 6 are not rousing encouragements to his army, not stirring promises to return despite defeat, but the devilish derision he directs to the loyal angels who stand before him offering traditional epic war. As Milton looks at Satan in book 6, hunts him not one scrap of honor either as a soldier or as a general. Instead, Milton strips him of the traditional "honors" that poets before him had allowed. Satan does not even attempt a last duel against the Son (surrogate in *Paradise Lost* for the conqueror Michael); he does not stand resistant while his soldiers flee; he offers no heroic words before he is forced to quit Heaven. And his fall to Hell is not glorious. He is driven with his angels in mass, like a herd of goats and timorous flocks. How far is this from the military defeat Vondel and Valmarana granted him. How far from his flaming retreat as a dragon in Peri's drama. Only in Hell does Milton permit Satan to seem heroic. In Heaven he is defeated unheroically and falls, unnamed and unnoted, in the rout driven before the Son.

NOTES

1. Taubmann, *Bellum angelicum*: "ante alios Genius pulcherrimus omneis" (p. 78); Acevedo, "Dia Primero," in *De la creacion del mundo*: "Del olimpo crió la inmortal gente, / Resplandeciendo con ardor glorioso, / Y entre ellas la mas bella criatura / Se deslumbró de ver su hermosura" (P. 249); Valvasone, *Angeleida*: "Di questi il più diletto, il più gagliardo, / Et di tutte le gratie il più splendente, / Ne la bellezza sua rivolse il guardo, / E s'alzò ne la sua superba mente" (1. 26); Alfano, *La battaglia celeste tra Michele e Lucifero*: "L'Angel piu bel che ne le sedie eccelse / Si godea, egli altri di beltade adorni / A l'ira hai persuaso, astringer, l'else, / Onde la pace for turbi, e i soggiorni" (p. 25); Vondel, *Lucifer*: "Belz. Daer hoor ick Lucifer, en zie hem, die den nacht / Van's hemels aengezicht verdrijven kan, en jaegen. / Waer hy vershijnt, begint het heerlijck op te daegen. / Zijn wassend licht, het eerste en allernaeste aen Godt, / Vermindert nemmermeer" (pp. 13–19). ("There I hear Lucifer, and see the star / That drives away the night from Heaven's face! / For where he shines, day gloriously begins. / His crescent radiance, brightest next to God, / Shall never wane" [Kirkconnell, *Celestial Cycle*, p. 373].) Thomas Heywood, *The Hierarchie of the blessed Angells* (London, 1635): "Amongst which *Lucifer* was chiefe; and hee, / As he might challenge a prioritie / In his Creation, so aboue the rest / A supereminence, as first and best: / For he was chiefe of all the Principalities, / And had in him the stupendious qualities / Of the most holy Trinitie, which include / First, Greatnesse, Wisedome, next, then Pulchritude" (p. 336).

2. Gasparo Murtola, *Della creatione del mondo* (Venice, 1608), canto primo, stanza 56.

3. Odoricus Valmarana, *Daemonomachiae*, "Liber Primus" (1623), pp. 10–11.

4. *Ludus Coventriae*, ed. K.S. Block (London: Early English Text Society, 1922), P. 17.

5. See *York Plays*, ed. Lucy Toulmin Smith, p. 4; *Towneley Plays*, re-ed. George England, p. 5; *Ludus Coventriae*, p. 18; *The Chester Plays*, re-ed. Herman Deimling, p. 17. Several poems of the thirteenth and fourteenth centuries treat Lucifer's rebellion in a similar manner. They tell how Lucifer boasted that he would ascend the throne of God, exactly quoting Lucifer's words from Isaiah. They do not, however, picture the event. Lucifer falls immediately after his boast is made. See *The Story of Genesis and Exodus*, ed. Richard Morris (London, 1865), and "Clannesse," in *Early English Alliterative Poems*, ed. Richard Morris (London, 1864). For a full account of the fall of Lucifer in medieval literature, see P. E. Dustoor, "Legends of Lucifer in Early English and in Milton," *Anglia* 54 (1930); 213–268.

6. Jacob Ruff, *Adam and Heva*, in *Band der Bibliothek der Deutschen National-Literatur* (Quedlinburg and Leipzig, 1848).

7. Fridericus Mollerus, *De creatione et angelorum lapsu carmen*, n.p.

8. See chapter 2, notes 2, 3, and 4.

9. "Canticum de Creatione," MS Trinity College, Oxford, and MS Auchinleck,

Edinburgh, in *Sammlung Altengischer Legenden*, ed. C. Horstmann (Heilbronn, 1878), pp. 124–138, pp. 139 ff.

10. The popularity of this motif is further attested by the Adam plays of the seventeenth century. In *Adamo caduto* (2.1), for example, Lucifer recounts that he was hurled to Hell because he refused to worship man. Similarly, in *L'Adamo* Lucifer tells him he prevented the angels from bowing down before man as the Word incarnate and thus provoked war with God (Kirkconnell, *Celestial Cycle*, pp. 307, 237–238).

11. Giouandomenico Peri, *La guerra angelica* (MS Florence), 1.1; 2.2. Lucifer in Alfano's *La battaglia celeste tra Michele e Lucifero* is also angered at the announcement of the Son's coming Incarnation.

> Lucifero piu d'altri il cor trafitto,
> Di quel parlar, di quella spoglia hauea,
> E d'ira & d'odio, e di superbia abbonda,
> Qual mar che per gran vento gonfia l'onda.
>
> Non potea senza orgoglio, e senza affanni
> Di cor, veder quell' honorata spoglia.
> Era tutto di frodi pieno e 'nganni.
> Di peruersa, maluaggia, e fiera voglia;
> Dona principio à suoi, e d' ali' altrui danni
> Mentre s'attrista dentro l'alma, e addoglia.
> Mentre pensa di far quel tanto ond' egli
> Sia à Dio nemico, egli altri al male suegli.
>   [p. 23]

12. Vondel, *Lucifer*, p. 12. (Kirkconnell, *Celestial Cycle*, pp. 371–372).

13. Milton echoes a traditional sentiment in his lines in book 1. Not only Vondel, but also Salandra in *Adamo caduto* had made his Lucifer express preference for kingship in Hell over mere princehood in Heaven (Kirkconnell, *Celestial Cycle*, p. 309). The phrasing for the line "Better to reign in Hell than serve in Heaven" Milton probably owes to Phineas Fletcher. In the *Apollyonists*, 1.18, Fletcher had exclaimed, "O, let him serve in hell, who scorns in heaven to reign"; in the *Purple Island*, 7.10, he had stated, "In heav'n they scorn'd to serve, so now in hell they reigne" (Kirkconnell, *Celestial Cycle*, pp. 275, 282). Milton has achieved his stunning success with Fletcher's line by transposing the "reign" and "serve" of the *Apollyonists* line and by placing it (as in Vondel and Salandra) not in the mouth of the poet, but in Satan's own mouth.

14. See C.S. Lewis, *A Preface to "Paradise Lost"* (London: Oxford University Press, 1942), pp. 93–95.

15. Helen Gardner, *A Reading of "Paradise Lost"* (Oxford: Clarendon Press, 1965), pp. 99–120.

16. Acevedo, *Angeleida*, pp. 249–250. The pagan Argantes in book 6 of *Gerusalemme Liberata* is also compared to a bull, as he readies himself for battle.

> Like as a bull, when prick'd with jealousy
>   He spies the rival of his hot desire,
> Through all the fields doth bellow, roar, and cry,
>   And with his thund'ring voice augments his ire,
> And threat'ning battle to the empty sky,

Tears with his horn each tree, plant, bush and briar,
And with his foot casts up the sand on height,
Defying his strong foe to deadly fight:
> [Godfrey of Bulloigne (trans. Edward Fairfax), 7.55]

17. For discussion of Vida's council in Hell, see Olin H. Moore, "The Infernal Council," *Modern Philology* 16 (1918): 169–193. Also see Gertrude C. Drake, "Satan's Councils in the *Christiad, Paradise Lost*, and *Paradise Regained*," in the Third *Acta Conventus Neo-Latini Turonensis*, forthcoming.

18. In *Daemonomachiae*, as well, Lucifer heaps praises on his angels, naming them eternal spirits, lit by light and virtue, eager for the good. Considering their excellence, he next demands, should they suffer the *Verbum Dei* to impose his yoke on them and permit man to appear superior? Finally, he exhorts them to hinder this imminent evil, strengthened by the very power God gave them (pp. 15–16).

19. See Kirkconnell, *Celestial Cycle*, pp. 276, 421–422.

20. Harding, *Club of Hercules*, pp. 41–51, 100.

21. For a fuller account of the background of Satan's metamorphosis see John M. Steadman, "Archangel to Devil: The Background of Satan's Metamorphosis," *Modern Language Quarterly* 21 (1960): 321–335.

22. Other Renaissance Satans are also boasters. Cowley describes in *Davideis* how Satan boasted that he took noble arms against God's tyranny and fought so valiantly that he deserved triumph rather than defeat:

There was a *Day*! oh might I see't again
Though he had fierce Flames to thrust us in!
> [Kirkconnell, *Celestial Cycle*, p. 422]

Fletcher's Satan also glorifies his military past:

But me, O never let me, spirits, forget
That glorious day when I your standard bore....
> [Kirkconnell, *Celestial Cycle*, p. 276]

JEFFREY BURTON RUSSELL

Lucifer in
High Medieval Art
and Literature

Art and literature followed, rather than led, the theology of the Devil, yet they dramatically enlarged and fixed certain points in the tradition. The effort to create artistic unity, to make the story a good one and the development of the plot convincing, led to a scenario in some ways more coherent than that of theologians. The Devil went through several movements of decline and revival in the central and late Middle Ages. The fading of Lucifer in the theology of the twelfth and thirteenth centuries was matched by the growth of a literature based on secular concerns such as feudalism and courtly love, and later by the growth of humanism, which attributed evil to human motivations more than to the machinations of demons. Thus many of the greatest writers and works—Chrétien de Troyes, Wolfram von Eschenbach, Hartmann von Aue, and Chaucer; the *Chanson de Roland*, the *Nibelungenlied*, and *El Cid*—usually treated the Devil in a perfunctory manner or as a metaphor for the vices or evil in general. On the other hand the colorful and concrete Devil of the desert fathers, Gregory, and Aelfric remained alive in homiletic literature and in the poetry and drama that drew upon homiletics, liturgy, and theology. The triumph of free-will nominalism in the fourteenth and fifteenth centuries and the terrifying famines and plagues of the same period made the Devil an intensely threatening figure in much of later medieval art and literature.[1]

From *Lucifer: The Devil in the Middle Ages*. © 1984 by Cornell University Press.

125

The pictorial arts followed theology less closely than did literature. Pictorial artists tend to think less in conceptual terms than poets or philosophers, and the Devil's shape depends in part upon the materials used: in sculpture, a human or quasi-human form is easier to portray than a little, black imp; in the cramped confines of an illuminated manuscript the imp is easier; no ivory shows a black devil. Theology and literature permit a careful distinction to be made between the Devil and demons; in art, where precise theological distinctions are difficult to make, the amalgamation of the two is common.[2]

Efforts to trace the development of artistic representations of the Devil yield no clear results. Trends are mostly local in time and place and often reverse themselves. Until the eleventh century the Devil was generally portrayed either as a human or as an imp, and this tendency persisted in Byzantine art. In the West, beginning in England about 1000 and spreading to Germany about 1020 and then beyond, the Devil tends to be a monstrous composite of human and animal. The grotesque was brought to artistic heights in the fifteenth and sixteenth centuries by Derek Bouts, the Van Eycks, Hans Memling, Hieronymous Bosch, Pieter Brueghel, Jan Mandyn, and Peter Huys. As has long been understood, the grotesque work of Bosch and others is no perversity but an exploration of the psychology of the unconscious in more or less traditional religious terms, set forth in terms of monsters and demons. It is also a moral statement of the problem of evil: Bosch portrays this world as a mirror of hell, in which sin, stupidity, and futility rule.[3] Bosch remained in the medieval didactic tradition of art. And this raises the question of the demonic in art. "Demonic" art can have two meanings: the portrayal of the demonic by artists such as Bosch, concerned to set a moral example to their viewers;[4] and art in which the artists themselves are consciously or unconsciously serving the demonic. In the latter, disharmony, meaninglessness, and distortion mirror the evil that obstructs God's plan for the cosmos, and the art is used not to satirize or repel but to allure and entrap.[5] The purpose of this chapter is to indicate the iconographic tendencies of the former.

Lucifer is sometimes closely associated with other threatening figures such as Hell or Death (after the eleventh century Death and the Devil are usually portrayed separately, though on occasion they still accompany one another, or the Devil's head is shown as a skull to suggest the association). Into the eleventh century Satan is usually human or humanoid; from the eleventh century onward he is more likely to be animal or a human/animal monster; from the fourteenth century he becomes increasingly grotesque. The monstrous Devil, with horns on knees, calves, or ankles and with faces on chest, belly, or buttocks reflects Lucifer's inner moral monstrosity. The small, black imp common in the earlier Middle Ages persists but gradually yields to the grotesque.[6]

The Devil is usually black or dark, but the opposite is also common: he is livid or pallid, a hue associated with death, heretics, schismatics, and magicians.[7] He is usually naked or wears only a loincloth, the nakedness symbolizing sexuality, wildness, and animality. His body is often muscular, often, too, very thin, but seldom fat; before the twelfth century he is occasionally handsome or pleasant looking. He is very seldom female, but he can disguise himself in any form he pleases.[8] As an animal, he is most frequently an ape, dragon, or serpent. The serpent with a human face appears in the art of many cultures; such representation seems to have become common in Christian art in the thirteenth century. The serpent's human head related it to Adam and Eve more convincingly; the artistic tradition may have drawn upon the theater, where the serpent had to be able to talk. It also symbolized the complicity in sin between human and Devil. In addition, misogynistic tradition emphasized Eve's guilt more than her husband's, so the serpent more often looked like Eve than like Adam.[9] His most common animal characteristic after the eleventh century was horns, which also still carried the ancient connotation of power.[10] The second commonest animal characteristic was a tail; the third was wings, divided about equally between the feathery wings appropriate to an angel and the sinister bat wings more fitting to the caverns of hell. The Devil's hair is often swept upward into spikey points, whether to represent the flames of hell or to refer to the practice of the barbarians, who swept their hair up into greased points in order to intimidate their enemies.[11] Demons have long, hooked noses, a characteristic transferred to Jews in the process of demonization. Other characteristics are hooves or paws, claws, hairiness, and goat legs (though demons' skin can also be leathery). The Devil rarely has an aura or halo (originally a mark of power, not necessarily of holiness). He can breathe fire and shoot arrows (like Death or elves) to kill the soul. Demons carry tridents, pitchforks, hooks, and other instruments of torture; their fearsome employment in hell as executioners of the damned was one of the commonest scenes in which they appear. Other frequent scenes were the exorcism of the possessed (though this became less common in the later Middle Ages, as interest shifted from biblical scenes to the immediate, current presence of the Devil in everyday life); the fall of the angels into hell, where they were transformed into twisted and scorched demons as they pelted down; Christ or Saint Michael spearing or trampling the Devil; the contest at the scales of justice between a demon and an angel over the soul of a dying person (an ancient motif in Egypt, where Anubis weighed the soul in the scale against justice [*ma'at*]). The most dramatic scene was the harrowing of hell, where Christ casts down the gates of hell; this scene transposed readily into that of the Last Judgment, where Lucifer is finally defeated and the souls of the blessed are led to heaven.[12]

From the eleventh century, medieval literature became increasingly diverse and sophisticated. Lyric, romance, epic, history, beast fables, and other genres now complemented, and to an extent supplanted, sermons and saints' lives. The variety is reflected in *The Canterbury Tales*, where Chaucer displayed a virtuoso control of numerous styles, genres, and levels of sophistication. In the eleventh century, Old English had been the only Western European language other than Latin with a substantial amount of serious literature, but by the next century French, Provençal, German, Italian, Spanish, and other vernacular literatures were emerging. This shift, celebrated in Dante's "De vulgari eloquentia," meant that writers such as Chaucer, Langland, Wolfram, and Chrétien composed in languages more natural to them than Latin and more readily available to a wide audience. Much was still being written in Latin—theology, history, philosophy, lyric poetry, hymns, liturgical drama, and homiletic literature (sermons and exempla)—but Latin was understood only by the clergy and a few other educated individuals. Therefore vernacular versions of saints' lives began to appear in the eleventh century, vernacular sermons were composed, and liturgical plays were performed in the vernacular as well as Latin.

Homiletic, liturgical, and hagiographic literature was the hinge between traditional Latin genres and the new vernacular and between the theology of the elite and the beliefs of the uneducated public. Homiletic literature was popular, not in the sense that it derived from the uneducated, but in the sense that it was written to be understood by the people and took their experience into account. Theological ideas were blended with legendary materials and dramatic stories in order to make an impression upon the audience. Homiletic literature thus drew deeply from hagiography (saints' lives), which affected the idea of the Devil, for saints' lives were still much what they had been in the days of the desert fathers, when Satan was at large in the world and snuffling at every door. Ancient and medieval world views tended to perceive things as static rather than developing through time. All times were one in the mind of God, and all things and individuals on earth manifestations of his eternal ideas. A saint is a saint is a saint, just as a king is a king is a king. A king of one country in one period is just like a king of another country in another period, because essentially a king *really* is a representation of God's eternal idea of king. What saints did, therefore, remained the same through the centuries. The form of the saint's life had been set first by lives of the desert fathers such as Athanasius' *Life of Anthony* and then by medieval lives imitating them, such as Gregory the Great's *Life of Benedict*. Consequently the Devil played a lively role in medieval hagiography as the challenger and opponent of the saints and the chief of all evil forces, the power behind all sins, vices, and worldly concerns. While the Devil was paling among the theologians, he remained vivid in the saints' lives, and though he was always defeated, he retained his ability to terrify. Saints' lives, always popular, had long been a part of the liturgy on appropriate feast days. Preachers found in these colorful and dramatic stories an infinite number of moral exempla, and they realized that ghastly stories of hellfire were effective deterrents to sin. Far from playing down Lucifer's role as the theologians were doing, homilists played it up for dramatic and didactic purposes. But any notion that they were exploiting the idea to "control the poor" misses the point that the clergy were at least as terrified of the Devil as their flocks were. The influence of saints' lives on sermons and liturgy and upon the numerous genres, such as theater, that sprang from them, was one of the chief reasons for the Devil's continued grip on the mind of the later Middle Ages and Renaissance.

The literature includes exempla, sermons, and spiritual anecdotes for the instruction of novices. Alan Bernstein cautions that we must distinguish manuals of preaching and exempla from sermons actually given, for few sermons survive as actually presented. These genres included a wide range of topics. Caesarius of Heisterbach, for example, recounted stories dealing with the origins of the evil angels, their free will, their fall, their knowledge and powers, their temptations and corruption of souls, possession, means of protection against demons, the battle between demon and angel for custody of the soul of a deceased person, and punishment by demons of sinners in hell.[13]

The literature of visions of the other world, which goes back at least to the third century, produced in the eleventh a masterpiece, *The Vision of Tundale*, which influenced Dante and subsequent artistic and literary portraits of Lucifer. *Tundale* gives a thorough description of the torments of the damned in the fiery, sulphurous pit of hell, and offers two striking pictures of demons and one of Lucifer himself. Tundale saw "a beast of unbelievable size and inexpressible horror. This beast exceeded in size every mountain that he had ever seen. His eyes were shining like burning coals, his mouth yawned wide, and an unquenchable flame beamed from his face." He saw another demon having two feet and two wings, with a long neck, an iron beak, and iron talons. This beast sat atop a frozen pool of ice, devouring as many souls as he could seize. These souls, as soon as they were reduced to nothing in his belly, were excreted onto the frozen ice, where they were revived to face new torments. And at last Tundale saw the prince of darkness, the enemy of the human race, who was bigger even than any of the beasts he had seen in hell before.... For this beast was black as a crow, having the shape of a human body from head to toe except that it had a tail and many hands. Indeed, the horrible monster had thousands of hands, each one of which was a hundred cubits long and ten cubits thick. Each hand had twenty fingers, which were each a hundred palms long and ten palms wide, with fingernails longer than knights' lances, and toenails much the same. The beast also had a long, thick beak, and a long, sharp tail fitted with spikes to hurt the damned souls. This horrible being lay prone on an iron grate over burning coals fanned by a great throng of demons.... This enemy of the human race was bound in all his members and joints with iron and bronze chains burning and thick.... Whenever he breathed, he blew out and scattered the souls of the damned throughout all the regions of hell.... And when he breathed back in, he sucked all the souls back and, when they had fallen into the sulphurous smoke of his maw, he chewed them up.... This beast is called Lucifer and is the first creature that God made.[14]

The most important development of the Devil in literary art occurred in the vernacular poetry of the later Middle Ages. The outpouring of such poetry was so vast that only a few of the most influential writers can be treated. Many of the great writers of epic and romance, such as Chrétien de Troyes, Wolfram von Eschenbach, and Hartmann von Aue treated the Devil only tangentially or metaphorically. But he was a negative center in the work of both Dante Alighieri and William Langland.[15]

Dante (1265–1321) is by common consent the greatest medieval poet and lay theologian. His *Comedy*, written in the last fifteen years of his life and called by later admirers the *Divine Comedy*, is a complex mystical poem in which the Devil, though seldom "on stage," is a powerful force operating throughout both hell and earth. Dante's diabology drew upon Christian tradition, scholasticism, vision literature, and Greco-Roman and Muslim thought.

The inner meaning of the *Divine Comedy* appears in its most striking feature: the structure of its cosmos. Dante's arrangement drew upon Aristotelian, Ptolemaic, and Neoplatonic philosophy and science, but the poet did not intend to write an astronomical, a geographical, or in any modern sense a physical or scientific treatise on the universe. Rather he wished to portray the cosmos according to its moral design. For Dante and his contemporaries the ultimate meaning of the cosmos is ethical, not physical, although as a careful artist he wished his ethical world to be as closely analogous to the physical universe as possible. In the *Comedy*, the physical cosmos is a metaphor of the real, ethical cosmos, rather than the other way round. Dante would not have been surprised or troubled to learn that no mountain of purgatory existed on the face of the physical globe, no cavernous hell in its depths. His intention was to describe the inner moral reality of the cosmos, not its external manifestations.

Dante's cosmos, like Ptolemy's, was arranged in a series of concentric spheres, the earth being the sphere at the center of the universe. Above the earth was the sphere of the moon and then in order those of Mercury, Venus, the sun, Mars, Jupiter, Saturn, the fixed stars, and the *primum mobile*, the sphere that moves the whole universe. Beyond that was heaven, the dwelling place of God, the angels, and the blessed. In the center of the earth is hell, and at the very center of hell, imprisoned in the darkness and the ice, is Lucifer.

With this cosmos Dante worked out a mystical vision not unlike that of Dionysius. Every being in the cosmos moves either toward God or toward the Devil. God is ultimately far up and out; the Devil is ultimately far down and in. When we are filled with our true human nature, which is made in the image of God and buoyed by the action of the Holy Spirit within us, we rise naturally up toward God, we spread out, widen our vision, open ourselves to light, truth, and love, with wide vistas in fresh air, clean, beautiful, and true (Paradise 1.135–138). The mystic rose at the threshold of heaven opens out infinitely and eternally. But when we are diverted by illusion and false pleasure, we are weighed down by sin and stupidity, and we sink downward and inward away from God, ever more narrowly confined and stuffy, our eyes gummed shut and our vision turned within ourselves, drawn down, heavy, closed off from reality, bound by ourselves to ourselves, shut in and shut off, shrouded in darkness and sightlessness, angry, hating, and isolated (Parad. 1.134). Each circle of hell as we descend is narrower and darker. There is nothing in that direction, literally nothing: silence, lack, privation, emptiness. God is expansion, being, light; Satan, drawn in upon himself, is nothingness, hatred, darkness, and despair. His isolation stands in utter contrast with the community of love in which God joins our minds with the first star (Parad. 2.29–30).

Dante's journey from the dark forest on the surface of the earth into the center of hell is a moral journey downward, in which he sees represented all the sins that draw the world, each individual, and Dante himself, downward toward ruin. Theologically one cannot go to hell and return, but one can understand and experience hell by grasping the nature of sin and its consequences. Understanding, one can change and transform one's life.

When Dante at last reaches the horrible center, he turns. The poet vividly describes that painful turning on the grotesque flanks of Satan, a turning that heads him upward out of hell and toward the light, where at last he sees the stars again (Inferno 34.139: "uscimmo a riveder le stelle"). Dante's descent into hell is the story of everyman, drawn down by sin and then offered the chance of a metanoia, a conversion, a turning back to the light; it is also an allegory of Christ's descent into hell and his resurrection. Dante's central insight was that the cosmos is a moral as well as a physical entity, that it is in a state of tension between good and evil, as opposed to the modern, strangely anthropomorphic view that it is neutral and that evil is entirely limited to the individual human consciousness. For Dante, ethics rules the sciences as the primum mobile rules the heavens, and all knowledge is morally relevant (*Convivio* 3.15: "la moralitade è bellezza de la filosofia").

This cosmology, morally powerful as it is, nonetheless suffers from difficulties. The Neoplatonic scheme from which Christian cosmology largely derived was in origin a vertical, linear one with the One at the top, emanating the cosmos down rank by rank; at the bottom was *hyle*, pure matter, farthest away from the One and least real. By bending (as it were) this cosmos downward at the ends and making a circle or sphere out of it, this conception could be wedded to Ptolemy's cosmology. Here the earth was at the center, with the planetary spheres in orbit around it, then the sphere of the fixed stars, also in orbit, and outmost the primum mobile, the slowly moving sphere within which the whole cosmos turns. This scheme was adopted by most early Christian writers, who placed God out beyond the primum mobile, the earth at the center, and, usually, hell under the surface of the earth. It was logical (and original) of Dante to complete the vision by putting hell at the very center of the earth and Satan at the very center of hell.

The difficulty posed by this system is that it seems to place the Devil rather than God at the center of the cosmos. Dante addressed the difficulty in two ways. First and most important, he meant God to be placed at the real, moral center of the cosmos, but he could not represent this spatially and indeed went to pains to deny that the moral center can be located in space or time. It is not in space and has no pole (Parad. 22.67); heaven has no other "where" than in the mind of God (Parad. 27. 106–110); it is the point at which all times are present (Parad. 17.17–18: "il punto a cui tutti li tempi son presenti"); the point at which every "where" and every "when" converge (Parad. 29.11–12: "là 've s'appunta ogne *ubi* e ogne *quando*"). As Freccero put it, Satan is the "center of the physical world and beyond the outermost circumference of the spiritual world," but God is "at the center of the spiritual world and is the circumference of the physical."[16] And of course

Dante accepted the idea of Gregory the Great that God was deep inside every individual soul as well.

Each individual has the choice of opening himself or herself to the light or of closing himself off from it. Those who open themselves to the light have all their pretenses and defenses melted away like snow under sun, and then God fills them with such living light as seems to dance when you behold it (Parad. 2.109–111: "voglio informar di luce sì vivace, che ti tremolerà nel suo aspetto"). People also have the choice of aligning themselves along straight lines that look right up to God or of twisting across the lines. It is as if the cosmos that God extends from himself is a sphere with radii running straight and true out from the divine center to the surface. God draws everyone and everything toward him, and everything when seen and used rightly bears toward him (Parad. 28.19: "tutti tirati sono e tutti tirano"; cf. Parad. 5.5–6). But individuals sometimes fail to see the point or recognize the goal. Then, following a false path, they swerve from the course in some other direction. The impulse that God implants in every one of us to seek him is thus diverted and misses its goal (Parad. 1.120–135). Wherever we are in the cosmos we can look straight along the radii toward the truth at its center; whenever we see straight, we see God. When we cut across the lines and force the pattern, our lives become more difficult, since we are going against the grain and trying to wrench the cosmos around to fit our own view of what it ought to be. The direction of such motion leads us inevitably away from God, for only motion toward the center can reach him; the trajectory of any other movement takes us sooner or later right out of the cosmos, out of community, love, and light, to the outer darkness from which no reentry is possible. For the light at the center is the only light; it is the light with which all other lights shine. "I believe, from the keenness that I felt from the living light, that I would have been ruined had I turned my eyes away from it" (Parad. 33.76–78). One whose eyes are open to that light could never consent to leave it for anything else, for it is the very life and wholeness of every thing (Parad. 33.100–105); it is the love that moves the sun and other stars (Parad. 33.145: "l'amore che move il sole e l'altre stelle"). The pathos and horror of Satan is that he is isolated forever from that love.

The second and more concrete resolution to the problem was to use Aristotelian physics, in which everything seeks its natural place in the universe, a view that Saint Augustine had approved.[17] From the sphere of the moon upward, natural movement is curvilinear, orbital; below the moon, and on and inside the earth, movement is rectilinear. Fire moves naturally upward, water naturally downward. When this view of physical locomotion is translated into ethical terms, virtue is seen as rising naturally upward, sin as sinking naturally downward. The love that rules the cosmos raises us with its light (Parad. 1.74–75: "amor che'l ciel governi ... che col tuo lume mi levasti"). The center of the cosmos is the point toward which all heavy, sinful things sink; it is the point farthest away from God (Inf. 14.118: "là dove più non si dismonta"; Inf. 34.110–111: "'l punto al qual si traggon d'ogne parte i pesi"; cf. Inf. 34.93) It is the logical place for the Devil to dwell.

Another difficulty is that this system not only places the Devil at the center of the world but can be misunderstood to thrust God out beyond the boundaries of the cosmos and make him remote—exactly the contrary of what Dante wished to convey. Another system was theoretically possible. If the original Neoplatonic scheme is turned upward at the edges, forming a circle, then it is God who stands at the center of the cosmos. Such a scheme would in many ways have fit Christian tradition better. Augustine and Gregory frequently spoke of interiority, the need to seek God within, the reality of the interior man as opposed to the exterior man. The Neoplatonist conception may be expressed by a series of spheres emanating outward from the One, and such a modification underlay the thought of Dionysius and Eriugena. The overall ethical conception that God is at the center of all things, drawing them toward him, is more congenial to a mystical—or indeed any Christian—conception, and it was fundamental to Dante's thought. But this scheme was virtually impossible to represent in art or in literary description. Moreover it could not be expressed in scientific analogy, for it contradicted Aristotelian physics and Ptolemaic cosmology. If God is at the center, radiating the cosmos out from him, then the material earth must be out beyond all the spheres of fixed stars and planets. It must be represented as an entity of indeterminate shape and locality, or as a globe in an orbit impossible to reconcile astronomically with the other heavenly orbits. These problems made it too difficult for Dante to describe the physical universe theocentrically. The view that came to be called Copernican, with the sun and light at the center, would have made a better metaphor for Dante's system, but it was a view favored by few medieval cosmologists.

God had created the cosmos good, but Lucifer spoiled its perfection by introducing sin. His pride caused him to try to attain beatitude immediately and by his own efforts rather than waiting for God (Parad. 19.48: "per principio del cader fu il maledetto superbir di colui che tu vedasti"; cf. Parad. 27.26–27.) The angels underwent a supernatural test soon after their creation, a test that lasted only a moment (Parad. 29.49–51). Some of the angels chose to remain loyal; others chose sin; still others refused to choose at all.[18] The angels that fell are intelligences exiled from their true native land above; they rained down from heaven, a despised crew driven down from bliss. One tenth of the angels joined in their ruin, a number that God

makes up by the creation of humanity and the salvation of the saints.[19]
Lucifer had been the highest of the angels (Parad. 19.47: "che fu la somma
d'ogne creatura"; Inf. 34.46: his six wings identify him as a seraph). But he
fell like lightning from heaven, plunging through the spheres and hurtling
toward earth. The point at which he fell was in the southern hemisphere at
the polar opposite of Jerusalem, where the earth would be healed by the
Passion of the Savior. The dry land shrank back from his approach in fear
and disgust, pulled away from the impact, and retreated into the Northern
Hemisphere, leaving the southern half of the globe almost entirely covered
with water. "Almost," because when Satan actually struck the earth, the
impact opened a huge crevasse into which he hurtled all the way to the center
of the globe. The land, created by God and governed by God's love, retreats
from God's antithesis as if by inverse magnetism. The heaviness of Satan's sin
was so ponderous that he sank into creation like a plumb into pudding. A
cave or "tomb" was hollowed out by his fall, a "tomb" that became hell.[20]
The earth from this giant excavation was thrust up to the surface, where it
formed the mountain of purgatory.

After one has (like Dante) sunk to the very depths of hell, one "turns"
at that center and ascends up the mount of purgatory to heaven. In physical
reality one descending from the surface of the earth at Jerusalem would not
turn in order to ascend to the opposite point on the globe but rather would
keep going straight ahead. Apparently Dante imagined Vergil (with Dante on
his back) descending feet first as one would a ladder and then when he
reached the center of gravity turning around to climb up the ladder.[21] Since
Dante's journey is a descent toward evil, which now must be reversed into an
ascent toward good, the reversal is dramatically symbolized in a turning
unforgettable in its grotesque drama. Satan is at the very center of the
cosmos, his head sticking up toward Jerusalem and the north, his buttocks
frozen in the ice, his huge, hairy legs rearing up toward purgatory and the
south. Vergil is obliged to turn himself laboriously with Dante on his back
while clinging to the Devil's furry hide, so that they may direct their journey
upward toward purgatory and the clear stars above.

When the Devil makes his rare appearances onstage, notably in the last
canto of Inferno, he is more pathetic and repulsive than terrifying. Some
critics have suggested that Dante simply failed to produce as impressive a
Devil as Milton later did, but this explanation misses his point.[22] Dante
specifically intended Lucifer to be empty, foolish, and contemptible, a futile
contrast to God's energy. Dante viewed evil as negation and would have
thought Milton's Devil much too active and effective. Lucifer's formal
absence from wide tracts of the *Comedy* and from the Inferno itself indicates
Dante's agreement with scholastic theology in limiting the Devil's role. One

of Lucifer's most dramatic parts in medieval literature is at the harrowing of hell, but Dante's reference to the harrowing (Inf. 4.52–63) mentions him not at all. Neither does the poet's discussion of soteriology in canto 7 of Paradise refer to the Dark Lord. Dante distanced himself from ransom theory, and rejection of ransom meant relegating the Devil to a peripheral role in the economy of salvation. The lack of dramatic action on the part of Dante's Lucifer is a deliberate statement about his essential lack of being.

Satan's true being is his lack of being, his futility and nothingness. There he is in the dark at the very dead center of the earth, where sins have sunk to their proper place. As one descends into hell, each circle is filled with graver, heavier sins, until in the lowest circle, the circle of treason, Satan is at the dead center with his buttocks stuck in the ice at the dead point of the turning world, where all the heaviest weights converge. At that point there can be no motion more; the heaviest weights have found their true place and press together in an eternally immobile mass, where Satan is compressed by all the weight of the world (Parad. 29.57: "da tutti i pesi del mundo costretto"). This stalemate is the sign of the futility, meaninglessness, darkness, and nonbeing of this lifeless point.[23] If all things are drawn to God, what can be drawn to Lucifer? Only the nothingness and meaninglessness of sin. As we close upon ourselves when we turn away from God toward unreality, so the center of hell is a dark mass turned infinitely in upon itself, cut completely and forever off from reality. Satan, the symbol of this nothingness, can have no real character except negation, and so his futile immobility is precisely what Dante wished to portray.

Satan's nothingness permeates everywhere, a cold counterpart to the warm presence of the Dove. Cold and dark, it emanates up from the dead center, seeping up through all the cracks of hell onto the sinful earth. Satan's force acts like gravity throughout the earth, pulling men and women down toward its glamour and weighting them down toward hell. This gravity is the exact opposite of the force exerted by God, who draws things toward him to the extent that they are light, spirit, and good. Lucifer's blind, empty idiocy, like a vacuum, sucks and drains the life and color from the earth. While still wandering in the dark wood before his first descent into the underworld, Dante encountered three beasts—the *lonza* (leopardess), *leone* (lion), and *lupa* (she wolf)—a triune symbol of sin, ferocity, and Lucifer (like him, their names begin with "l"), whose triune face they prefigure. In every circle of hell the influence of his idiocy is felt, even in the circle of the good pagans, who would not be in limbo if it were not for the fall of Adam and Eve, which Lucifer engineered. Throughout the circles of hell, other sinister demons are his avatars: Charon (Inf. 3), Minos (5), Cerberus (6), Pluto (7), Phlegyas (8), the Furies and Medusa (9), the Minotaur and Centaurs (12), Geryon (17), the giants (31), and others.[24] The assimilation of these figures to the Devil is clearest in the figure of Pluto, in Inferno 7.1. Over the gate of hell leading to Pluto's realm is the phrase "pape Satàn, pape Satàn, aleppe," words of uncertain meaning that nevertheless make the association of Pluto and Satan explicit. It is an unusual feature of Dante's hell that more traditional Christian demons, like Satan himself, seldom appear on stage. Where medieval art and drama loved to portray demons tormenting the damned with cruel tools, Dante's condemned suffer well-defined torture appropriate to their sins, torture usually inflicted without the visible presence of demons. In this Dante held closer to theological than to artistic and literary trends.[25]

The figure of Lucifer down at the motionless center of hell is a contrast with that of God in every way. The lowest three circles of hell, Cocytus, or the City of Dis, are ruled by Lucifer directly rather than through his surrogates. Here dwell the violent, fraudulent, and malicious. The ninth and lowest circle, Giudecca, the place of Judas, is occupied by traitors to kindred, country, and guests. Lowest of all are traitors to benefactors. Treason is in the lowest pit of hell because of all sins it most twists the just order of the cosmos. Treason against God is the ultimate sin and absurdity: betraying for one's own dark and limited ends the principle of light and justice upon which the whole cosmos, and therefore one's self, depends. As Judas betrayed God the Son, so at the beginning of time Lucifer betrayed God the Father. And such treason is futile. God's light and God's justice still and always inform the cosmos, but Satan and Judas will never see them: they are wrapped up in their own dark terror and pain forever. Traitors and all sinners deceive and betray themselves with their own blind idiocy. Deception and self-deception, blocking out God's light, are the key to all sin.

The nothingness of the Devil is underscored by his absurdity. He is imprisoned and entombed in the lightless cavern of Giudecca with his legs protruding into the air.[26] The narrowness and darkness of this prison, contrasted with the infinite light and space of God's world, symbolize his deliberate blindness and self-imposed ignorance. The darkness of Lucifer contrasts with the light that floods heaven (Parad. 1.79–81; 2.109–111; 5.118: "lume che per tutto il ciel si spazia"; 29.136–138: "la prima luce, che tutta la raia, per tanti modi in essa si recepe, quanti son li splendori a chi s'appaia"). The icy lake that holds him immobile is frozen too hard to creak, a sign of death and absolute cold, a symbol of the spirit closed off from God and an allegorical antinomy of the life-giving waters of baptism.[27] The immobility of Satan is the opposite of the mobility of the angels and the blessed spirits, his frozen hatred the opposite of God's love, which moves the world (Parad. 1.1–3; 14.23–24; 21.80–81; 23.103; 24.16–17; 24.130–133: "io credo in uno Dio solo ed etterno, che tutto 'l ciel move, non moto, con amore e con disio"). Satan's forced motionlessness is also contrasted to God's voluntary serenity, which moves without moving (Parad. 19.64–65: "dal sereno che non si turba mai"). As Jesus was immersed up to his waist in the life-giving Jordan, so Satan is stuck up to his waist in the mortal ice, water that is dead and buried, unlike the warm and living waters of God's love (Parad 33.10–12: "meridiana face di caritate, e ... fontana vivace").

Below each of his three faces Lucifer has a pair of huge wings, six in all, like the six wings of the Seraphim (Parad. 9.78). But these are not the feathery wings of angels, burning with living gold (Parad. 30.13–15) but leathery bat wings, a symbol of his darkness and blindness.[28] The heavy wings beat the frozen air vainly, unable to take off, stirring up winds that freeze the streams of hell as they sink into Cocytus and, seeping up through the earth, stir mortal minds to sin, just as God's light shines out to touch all earthly hearts.[29] The frozen wind of Satan is in direct contrast to the fire of love that blows in the breath of the Holy Spirit (Parad. 22.32: "la carità che tra noi orde") and to the kindling of joy (Parad. 21.88: "l'allegrezza ond'io fammeggio").

The nonbeing of Satan is further manifest in his giant size: he is a towering mass of moribund matter. Theology held that angels remained angels after their fall, though some said that the fallen angels took on the heavy, lower air, as opposed to the good angels, who were made of the rarer ether. But Dante extrapolated a shape that was a gross incarnation mocking the true Incarnation of Christ and the absolute opposite of the spirit of God. Since Platonic/Christian tradition considered pure matter to be that which is farthest from God and closest to nonbeing, Satan is almost pure matter, barely informed with life, and composed of all the densest weights in the cosmos; his shaggy, bestial body emphasizes that he is the polar opposite of reason, truth, and spirit. He is a worm, a monster (Inf. 34.107–108). The feeble, giant Devil, for which numerous literary precedents existed, perfectly symbolized the inner impotence of this being who on earth can seem so powerful and clever.[30] He is the emperor of his wretched kingdom (Inf. 34.28: "lo 'mperador del doloroso regno"), as God is the emperor who rules forever (Parad. 12.40: "lo 'mperador che sempre regna").

The ugliness of this hulking, pathetic creature who had once been an angel of light is in complete contrast to the beauty of God (Parad. 7.64–66). Through pride he dared defy his maker, and his plunge from heaven transformed all his beauty into ugliness.[31] The doomed Devil is grossest in his hideous, eternal mastication of the three traitors, Judas, Cassius, and Brutus. The blind, futile hatred of this act had been prefigured by the fate of the traitor Ugolino, who, himself betrayed by Ruggiero, is trapped in the ice gnawing in eternal rage on the head of the man who betrayed him (Inf. 33).

The *Vision of Tundale* and other literary or artistic sources depicted Satan, Hell, or other demons devouring sinners and (often) excreting them into the fiery pit. Dante avoided the crudities of the tradition and thus better brought out the horror. As Satan chews on his human prey, he weeps, and his tears mingle with their blood and drool down his chin. It is a horrible contrast to Beatrice, who is always smiling for joy (Parad. 18.19; 30.42). Unlike the one tear of repentance that redeemed the sinner Buonconte di Montefeltro (Purg. 5), Satan's tears of frustrated rage serve not to save. Like the gory tears of the cyclops Polyphemus blinded by Odysseus, the bloody weeping of the hideous giant only repels. It repels, and it parodies the blood, water, and tears shed by the heavenly Lord upon his cross.

As Dante descended with Vergil into Giudecca, he distinguished through the murk a huge figure looming before him, shaped like a monstrous windmill or suggesting a distorted outline of the Savior's cross. Lucifer's three faces and three outstretched pairs of wings were like the three points of the cross, the triune Devil an infernal parody of the Holy Trinity. The ironic line "the standard of the hellish king advances" ("vexilla regis prodeunt inferni" [Inf. 34.1]), is a parody of a famous hymn by Fortunatus and also a parody of the cross, for Fortunatus' *vexilla regis*, "royal standard," refers to the cross of Christ.[32] John Freccero linked this parody of the cross with the color of Satan's three faces. Though Dante elsewhere refers to the blackness of the fallen angels (Inf. 21.29; 23.131; 27.113), he gives Satan's three faces three different colors: yellowish white, red, and black. Numerous theories have been coined over the years to explain these colors, but Freccero's is based on careful analysis of the literary background.[33] He begins his explanation with Luke 17.6, in which Christ says that with faith deep enough one could tell a mulberry tree to move and it would move. Saint Ambrose used the mulberry tree as a symbol of the Devil, for just as its fruit begins as white, matures as red, and then turns black, so the Devil begins glorious and white, shines red in his power, and then turns black with sin. But Augustine used the tricolored mulberry as a symbol of the cross, and Ubertino da Casale described the vexilla of Christ as colored in the same way. What Dante did is to draw the cross, the Devil, and the three colors together. Freccero clinches the argument by observing that Dante must have had the actual image of the mulberry in mind, for although the sources used the colors white, red, and black, the mulberry fruit first appears as a waxen, yellowish white, and that is just how Dante describes the color, "tra bianca e gialla" (between white and yellow). Freccero's explanation leaves room for further interpretation of the colors. Given sources such as Ambrose and Dante's own ability to pack every detail with meaning, it is plausible that the red face may indicate sin or shame, the black face ignorance or corruption, the whitish face impotence. But what Dante seems to have had chiefly in mind was to extend and deepen the sense of the moral polarization of the cosmos between Christ and Satan.

Another masterwork of medieval literature in which the Devil's influence is felt throughout the moral cosmos is William Langland's *Piers Plowman*. Langland, a clerk in minor orders, had a grasp of nominalist theology, a mystical conception of the world, and a keen, satirical voice. He wrote at least four versions of the poem between 1360 and his death in 1400. The third, the B version is admired for its poetry, the C version for its reflection of the author's more mature thought.[34]

Different in style, conception, and viewpoint as *Piers Plowman* is from the *Divine Comedy*, it is, like the *Comedy*, a work of vision literature, and it has at its heart a similar mystical view of reality. Langland, like Dante, believed that the way to salvation was through love more than intellect, a view that he derived from, and shared with, both nominalists and mystics. *Piers* differs from the *Comedy* in that its mystical view is centered in this world more than in the other. *Piers* presents plowmen, priests, brewers, lawyers, merchants, street cleaners, and friars at their daily labors, as wide a view of society as Dante's but set in the daily life of street and field. Langland was a poor man, and his down-to-earth mysticism was similar in spirit to that of the Brethren of the Common Life and Thomas à Kempis on the Continent. The central character, Piers Plowman, may be understood as Christ, Saint Peter, Everyman, or as the type of the good Christian, the good ruler, or the honest laborer. The vision is that true priests, monks, plowmen, and kings keep their attention upon God at the center of things and so journey in a world of reality and light toward unity with God, while their false counterparts blind themselves with illusion and wander off toward nowhere. We can look at things straightly and clearly and see God through them, or we can muddy them with the dirt of our own desires until no light can shine through. The Devil squats stupidly behind the scenes, pulling our vision awry, twisting our view, drawing us down into darkness until we see and understand nothing.

The choice is ours. Influenced by the nominalism and voluntarism common in late fourteenth-century theology, Langland asserted the freedom of the human will. When the Devil attacks the Tree of Charity (C.16), which represents Christ, the just person, or the individual Christian, Piers defends the tree by summoning "Liberum Arbitrium," the personification of free will, which, when it obeys Piers (here Christ or justice), defeats the Devil. When it fails to obey Piers, it has no power against Satan. The will is really free only when it chooses the good; otherwise it sinks in bondage to sin. The analysis resembles that of the anonymous mystical treatise *Theologia germanica* (c. 1350), where the will's natural purpose is seen as serving God, but it can be wrenched by sin from its true course. Langland's emphasis upon human freedom and his concern for this world meant that humanity, rather than angels and demons, has center stage. Yet although the Devil seldom appears in person in the poem, he manifests himself constantly in the affairs of this world, and allegorical personifications such as Wrong, Falsehood, and Deceit are his avatars. Lucifer is ever watchful and active, but his works can take shape only when summoned or welcomed by individual human beings. It is ours to decide whether we prefer the freedom of seeing things as they are or the heavy task of maintaining the illusion that they are as our desires would have them be. We can align ourselves with truth or with idolatry. Idolatry is to choose a limited good in preference to the ultimate good. For Langland, money and profit are the chief idolatry, but any lie, falsehood, or evasion, any preference of fame, fortune, or pleasure over God, even the setting of church or theology over the simple, clean truth, is service to the Dark Lord.[35]

Langland emphasized the Devil's works in the unjust activities of the humans who follow him. Justice is the state of affairs that prevails when the affairs of this world are conducted straightforwardly in accord with God's will and plan. Injustice is the state of affairs that usually prevails and that arises from human perversity and stupidity getting in the way of right order. Langland is contemptuous and furious at injustice; he hates its unshakeable stupidity and treats those who perpetrate it harshly. The chief idolatry is the pursuit of gain, whose personification is Lady Meed (13.24 and C.24). Meed can be seen as representing the nascent capitalist economic system, and had Langland thought in such terms he would probably have agreed, but closer to his own world view was the identification of Lady Meed with *cupiditas* or *avaritia*, the ancient cardinal sin of avarice. Langland's belief that avarice is the most deadly of the sins was common in the later Middle Ages, when commercial development enabled a true money economy to develop, making money the measure of all things. Langland's contempt for money appears in his satire of the greedy friars as well as in the passages on Lady Meed, and the venal friars are associated with Antichrist (C.21–22). Like the other six vices, Meed is the daughter of the Devil, or of his avatars Fraud or Deceit.[36]

The marriage of Meed with Fals (Falsehood) is a satire of bureaucracy and law as well as of money. Favel (Deceit) has arranged the marriage, and Fals draws up a legal contract stating that Falsehood, Guile, and Deceit are all pleased at Meed's cupidity and grant her formal license to backbite, boast, bear false witness, despise poverty, and rejoice in avarice, usury, idleness, and all the vices. They give her leave "after her death to dwell day without end in lordship with Lucifer, as this document shows, with all the appurtenances of purgatory and the pain of hell (C.2.106–108)." The charter is given and sealed in the "date of the Devil" instead of in the year of our Lord.[37] Those who choose to follow Meed live false lives and abet injustice, such as the brewer who cries out, "Bah, by Jesus, I won't be ruled, in spite of your jabbering, by the spirit of justice, or by conscience, by Christ, when I can sell dregs and lees and draw either thick ale or thin from the tap as I please. I am the kind of person who doesn't grub after holiness, so hold your tongue, conscience, it isn't doing you any good to talk about the spirit of justice" (C.21.296–402).

The fall of Lucifer is set in the context of the struggle between Wrong and Truth. Though Lucifer is not merely a metaphor, he is chiefly that. It is not so much that Lucifer introduced sin and evil into the world as that his behavior violated eternal principles of truth and justice. God created ten orders of angels; one of those orders fell. Lucifer, who had been "archangel of hevene, on of goddes knyghtes" (C.1.107), sinned, drawing down the many angels of the tenth order with him. As they fell they took on hideous form, "lepen out in lothly forme" (C.1.109). They fell for nine days, some into the dense air, some to the earth, and some underground, depending upon the gravity of their sin, and Lucifer fell lowest of all. The essence of his sin was that he and those who fell with him "helden nat with treuthe" (C.1.108), the result being that he is bound in hell.[38]

The Devil's great scene in *Piers* is at the harrowing of hell, but Langland uses it quite differently from his contemporaries. The liberation of the souls in limbo by the Passion of Christ was originally based upon the ransom theory that the Devil held them by right because of original sin. Even before Langland's time, the idea of Jesus as a ransom paid by God to the Devil yielded gradually to the military metaphor of Christ as a knight come to rescue the oppressed. Langland was thus freed to use the harrowing scene without any assumption of ransom theory. For him the drama of the harrowing is subsumed in a statement about the nature of justice. He has prepared for the harrowing in a number of passages that explain that the Devil eagerly watches to snatch up every apple that falls (every soul that dies) from the tree of life. As a result of original sin, he claims power over mankind and carries sinners to hell. He has even obtained power over the patriarchs, holding them prisoner in limbo.[39] Lucifer claims that he holds just title to these souls, but Langland assumes that Lucifer is a liar, and even Satan finds the claim questionable. Since we got these souls by trickery, Satan observes, we may have no real right to them. Satan's doubts presage the debate between justice and Mercy and that between Christ and Lucifer. Satan, Mercy, and Christ all maintain against Lucifer that the Devil has no rights over humanity. Lucifer claims justice, but the weight of justice is against him.

Immediately before the harrowing, which occurs in passus 18 of the B version and 20 of the C version, the four daughters of God—Truth, Righteousness, Mercy, and Peace—conduct a debate on the nature of justice.[40] Truth and Righteousness defend the notion of strict justice, according to which mankind ought by right to be in Satan's power, for we broke our contract with God of our own free will, and he is in no way obliged to save us. But Peace and Mercy respond with an argument from equity: justice is not always best served by its strict application; though we have doomed ourselves to die, God's mercy will save us. Equity—justice tempered by mercy—is far from being a violation of justice; rather, it is its highest expression. It is the way the real world is constructed. The Old Law, good in itself, was not the truest expression of justice, for it lacked equity and mercy. The New Testament proclaims this perfect reality. The debate among the four daughters of God prefigures the debate between Christ and the Devil at the gates of hell.[41]

Now it is Holy Saturday, and Christ draws near. From the outset Christ is no lawyer come to pay the Devil his due, but a warrior come to tear down the infernal city: "For Jesus comes yonder like a giant to break and beat down all who stand against him and to have out of hell all that he chooses."[42] Jesus is a knight, a jouster with helmet and mail riding up on his warhorse to challenge the Devil in combat and, having defeated him, to bring the prophets up out of hell. As Jesus the Jouster approaches, the demons hold a frantic colloquy that is an inversion of that of the daughters of God. The number of the demons present varies between the B and C texts. In the B there are two—Lucifer and Satoun (also called Gobelyn), and a third semidemon, the personified Helle.[43] In the C text a number of other demons are added to the council: Mahond, Ragamoffyn, Belial, and Astarot. Langland seems to have cared little which was the chief Devil. Lucifer fills that role most frequently, but it is Satoun who in the C text barks orders to Ragamoffyn, Belial, and Astarot to bar the doors and prepare to repulse the advancing army of Christ (Satoun seems to imagine that Jesus has marshaled a great host, including cavalry, against him). And it is Lucifer, rather than Satan, who has gone up to Eden to tempt Adam and Eve. The division of speeches among the demons is purely a literary device to permit lively debate.

As a great light pierces the darkness of hell, a voice thunders, "Open up the gates!" Satoun, recoiling, mutters to Hell that this is just the kind of light that came to wrest Lazarus away from them; now it is come to save all of humanity. Lucifer is outraged, for he believes that God has promised him rights over the human race and that Christ has come to deprive him of his just due, "for by right and by reason the ranks that are here belong to me body and soul, both the good and the bad." Satan rounds on him: "Yes, well, you got us into this, didn't you? It was your fault that you went up to tempt Adam and Eve in the first place. We would be much better off if you hadn't gone. Now all our prey is lost to us because of your lies."[44] But Lucifer stands up to challenge Christ at the gates. "What lord are you?" he demands, but then the light rushes in and strikes him blind.[45] A debate between Christ and Lucifer ensues, Lucifer arguing that he has the right to humanity for two reasons. First, God gave humanity to him at the time of original sin, and God must not go back on his word. It is a nice irony that the Devil should argue from the justice of the Lord whom he hates and daily betrays, and it is an argument from the strict justice of the Old Law, a law of retaliation untempered by mercy. The second reason is derived from English common law, and Langland wants his audience to note how Lucifer, like unjust landholders on earth, tries to turn the common law to his advantage. According to law, he says, I hold humanity by just custom, for I have had possession of them for 7,000 years. In effect, Lucifer is bringing a suit of novel disseisin against Christ.[46]

Christ rebuts Lucifer's arguments with the argument that he is come to fetch out the souls in fulfillment of justice, not in violation of justice: I ransom my servants through both right and reason.[47] But Langland uses the term *ransom* loosely: Christ is not come to pay the Devil, but rather to wrest humanity away from him with a force that springs from justice itself. Christ puts forward three arguments. First, even under the strictness of the Old Law he is justified in taking the souls because of Lucifer's use of trickery in Eden, and "the Old Law teaches that cheaters may be cheated and brought down by their fraud."[48] Second, the New Law provides for equity as well as justice, grace and mercy as well as punishment. Thus mercy wins back what was lost by guile, and fraud is defrauded by grace.[49] Third, Christ observes that as king he has the royal power simply to pardon the damned and release them from hell, but the use of this power is unnecessary because of the effectiveness of the two arguments from justice. The Devil must yield to justice, and Christ binds him in iron bonds (C.20.55–56). In Langland's vision, as in Dante's, God's world is one of simple light and justice; it is blocked and blurred by the sin and folly of humans and angels; but sin eventually perishes and love prevails.

Langland's rejection of ransom theory, his emphasis upon free will, his focus upon love, and his nominalist and mystical assumptions combined to reduce, but not eliminate, the importance of the Devil in his view of the world. It was the impediment to love caused by the sins of the world, especially avarice, that concerned him most. We cannot, Langland says, solve the problem of evil. Following Augustine's admonition, "Do not seek to know more than is appropriate," and the nominalist distrust of intellectual constructions, the poet warns, "Do not wish to know why God permits Satan to cheat his children, but hold to the teachings of the church and ask for God's forgiveness.... If you want to know why God allowed the Devil to lead us astray, or if you wish to fathom the purposes of God Almighty, then your eyes ought to be in your arse. Everything happens as God chooses, and thank God it will continue to, worry over it though we may" (B.10.120–130).

Geoffrey Chaucer (1344–1400), Langland's almost exact contemporary, was a friend of the nobility and a man of the world. Like Shakespeare later, he was the master of a variety of genres and styles and felt his way into a diversity of characters. Chaucer's underlying theology or philosophy, like Shakespeare's, is difficult to define. That he was a believing Christian is clear from the ending of Sir Thopas' tale, and there is every reason to assume that he believed in the Devil. Yet his emphasis is upon the human, not the cosmic, and his devel, feend, or Sathanas is less often a metaphor of the follies of humanity.[50]

In *The Canterbury Tales* the Devil seldom plays an important role other than as metaphor. "The Monk's Tale" offers a vignette of Lucifer among other great figures who have fallen from high station, such as Adam, Hercules, and Nebuchadnezzar: "O Lucifer, brightest of angels alle, / Now artow Satanas, that maist not twinne [depart] / Out of miserye, in which that thou art falle" (lines 14–16). In "The Friar's Tale" he serves to sharpen the satire of the summoners. A summoner meets the Devil in human shape, and the fiend explains in quite orthodox terms how demons have no fixed shape of their own but can change their shapes, either by creating illusions, or by making temporary bodies out of the elements, or even by animating dead bodies.[51] But they can do these things only with the permission of God. God allows them to tempt only because he turns the temptations to his own purpose of fortifying the just. When a Christian resists a temptation, the result of the Devil's efforts is the opposite of what he intends (lines 169–203). Chaucer might have used the Devil's speech to get inside his character and mock the inverted values of the infernal world, as the dramatist Arnoul Gréban did (Chapter 9 below), but the poet's attention is fixed as usual on human greed and folly. The Devil and the summoner ride off in company for a while with the understanding that each will show the other how he works. They encounter a man cursing his horse and consigning it to the Devil, and the summoner wonders why the Devil does not carry off the animal. The Devil replies that it is clear that the man did not mean what he said. Disgusted with Satan's faintheartedness, the summoner shows him how to work without any such scruple. Going to the house of an old widow of impeccable character, he tries to extort a shilling from her. Angrily she curses him: "The Devil, quod she, so fecche him er he deye," unless he repents. The summoner refuses to repent, "and with that word this foule feend hym hente; body and soule he with the devel wente" (lines 328–340).[52]

The summoner replies in his own tale by satirizing the friars. Satan, he observes in the prologue, keeps 20,000 friars up his arse in hell:

> Right so as bees out swarmen from an hyve,
> out of the Develes ers ther gonne dryve
> twenty thousand freres on a route [in a mob],
> and thurghout helle swarmed al aboute,
> and comen agayn as fast as they may gon,
> and in his ers they crepten everychon. (Prologue 30–35)

But the poet's attention is on the friars, not the demons: the tale is broadly scatological, with more to say about farts than about fiends. The Devil's farts upon the stage, his ingestion and excretion of souls, his tendency to thrust out his backside toward audiences or, in the dark of night, to expose his private parts for the veneration of witches, his emission of sulphurous odors, all combine the disgusting with the comic. The Devil is funny, but he is also repulsive, and he is funny in a way that makes us despise and shun him rather than empathize with him. The scatological has certain apotropaic qualities as well, especially in folklore, where the Devil can be driven off by pungent or evil-smelling herbs such as garlic (which can be chewed or hung round the neck) or asafoetida (known in Germany as *Teufelsdreck*).[53]

In "The Pardoner's Tale" a group of young people in Flanders hold drunken orgies "though which they doon the devel sacrisise withinne that develes temple, in cursed wise, by superfluytee abhomnyable" (lines 7–9), but the reference is not to the witches' sabbat but merely to their drunkenness, lechery, and other vices. This was the very eve of the great witch craze, when stories of sabbats were already in circulation, but the poet, if indeed he means to refer to the sabbat at all, does so very much with tongue in cheek.[54]

Of all the tales, that of the Prioress shows the most intense religious feeling, though it is the character of the Prioress, not necessarily Chaucer himself, who is speaking. It is a fiercely anti-Semitic tale, and though the Devil does not appear in person, the audience could have had no doubt that his sinister presence is personified in the Jews. The fate of the pious little lad caught in the street as he sang his antiphon "Alma redemptoris mater"—"the cursed Jew him hente [seized], and heeld hym faste, and kitte his throte, and in a pit hym caste" (lines 82–83)—is the fate of the Christian soul waylaid by the Devil as he passes through the narrow streets of life. The Jew, like the "pagan" Muslim and the heretic "witch," was a servant of the Devil, demonized by his close association with the Dark Lord.[55]

Chaucer shifted the center of moral action away from the cosmic struggle between God and Devil toward the struggle between good and evil in the human soul. At least some of Shakespeare's villains—Iago, Lady Macbeth, Edmund—draw upon a deep well of evil, whose waters seep in from we know not where. The Devil is not named as the source. Yet at the same time that this movement toward humanism was reducing the Devil's stature, the sermons and the theater of the fourteenth, fifteenth, and sixteenth centuries made him more colorful and real to the population at large than he ever had been. The great witch craze, which built upon this wide popular belief, was a phenomenon of the Renaissance, and the witch craze was at its height in England at precisely the time that Shakespeare was at his.

NOTES

1. Far too much material exists to allow more than a survey of the Devil in the art and literature of the period 1100–1500. One can only take representative samples and keep in mind that this is a history of the personification of evil, not a study of art, poetry, and theater in themselves. There is no room for excursions into the jungles of related topics such as the art of Bosch, the development of hell, limbo, or purgatory, the Antichrist, or the tradition of vision literature. On the Antichrist, see R. Emmerson, *The Antichrist in the Middle Ages* (Seattle, 1981), chap. 4, "Antichrist in Medieval Art," and chap. 5, "Antichrist in Medieval Literature." On the vision literature see D.D.R. Owen, *The Vision of Hell* (Edinburgh, 1970); on purgatory see J. LeGoff, *The Birth of Purgatory* (Chicago, 1982).

2. I follow writers better trained in art history than I, with special thanks to Joyce Galpern, Kris Haney, Ellen Schiferl, and others. See B. Brenk, *Tradition und Neuerung in der christlichen Kunst des ersten Jahrtausends* (Vienna, 1966); B. Brenk, "Teufel," *Lexikon der christlichen Ikonographie*, 4 (1972), 295–300; F. Klingender, *Animals in Art and Thought to the End of the Middle Ages* (Cambridge, Mass., 1971); J. M. Galpern, "The Shape of Hell in Anglo-Saxon England" (Ph.D. diss., University of California, Berkeley, 1977); G. Schiller, *Iconography of Christian Art*, 2 vols. (Greenwich, Conn., 1971–1972); H. Seidlmayr, "Art du démoniaque et démonie de l'art," in E. Castelli, *Filosofia dell'arte* (Rome, 1953), pp. 99–114; A. Wienand, "Heils-Symbole and Dämonen-Symbole im Leben der Cistercienser-Mönche," in A. Schneider, ed., *Die Cistercienser* (Cologne, 1974), pp. 509–554. I have also surveyed more than 450 representations of the Devil in Christian art from 1050 to 1500 in the Princeton Index of Christian Art, including illuminated manuscripts, paintings, frescoes, murals, ivories, glass, and sculpture.

3. See M. Lazar, "Caro, mundus, et demonia dans les premières oeuvres de Bosch," *Studies in Art*, 24 (1972), 106–137.

4. See Galpern, pp. 29–31. Medieval artists, like monastic and mendicant homilists, often used scenes of horror to frighten viewers into leading a good life; Augustine had early recommended dwelling on scenes of hell in order to instruct the rustics.

5. See R. Hammerstein, *Diabolus in musica* (Bern and Munich, 1974), pp. 16–19; Seidlmayr, pp. 105–113.

6. The monstrous does not always indicate the demonic. The monstrous Devil blurs into the "monstrous races" of humanity (see above, Chapter 4), gargoyles, and simply comic grotesques. When the Devil has seven heads, crowned or uncrowned, or ten horns,

the representation draws directly upon Rev. 12.3. Occasionally he will have three heads or faces, like Hekate (see DEVIL, p. 130) and in mockery of the Holy Trinity.

7. See above, Chapters 4 and 6. For literary analogies, see Caesarius of Heisterbach, *Dialogus miraculorum*, ed. J. Strange (Cologne, 1851), 5.2 (pallor), and 5.5, 5.8 (shadowy).

8. Brenk, *Tradition*, pp. 178–179.

9. J.K. Bonnell, "The Serpent with a Human Head in Art and in Mystery Play," *American Journal of Archeology*, 21 (1917), 255–291. See Bonnell and J. M. Evans, *Paradise Lost and the Genesis Tradition* (Oxford, 1968), p. 170, for Peter Comestor's statement that the Devil chose the shape of a serpent with a maiden's face ("elegit etiam quoddam genus serpentis virgineum vultum habens"). Peter seems to have been the first to use this idea in his *Historica scholastica: Liber Genesis*, 21. See Chapter 9 below for the serpent on the stage.

10. See R. Mellinkoff, *The Horned Moses in Medieval Art and Thought* (Berkeley, 1970), for the continuation of the iconography of the horns of power into the Middle Ages; unfortunately the symbol was widely misunderstood, for the horns of Moses were thought to represent the evil of the Jews, and the Jews themselves then came to be depicted as horned.

11. The possessed in early Christian art sometimes are shown with hair sticking up into points. See Brenk, *Tradition*, pp. 132, 176. The motif goes beyond Europe: Japanese demons have similar upswept hair. See DEVIL, p. 100.

12. Brenk, *Tradition*, p. 177.

13. I am grateful to Professor A. Bernstein for letting me read his unpublished paper "Theology and Popular Belief: Confession in the Later Thirteenth Century" and for numerous suggestions and ideas, which form the basis of this paragraph. See also G. R. Owst, *Literature and Pulpit in Medieval England* (Oxford, 1961); J.–P. Perrot, "Le diable dans les légendiers français du XIIIe siècle," in *Le diable au moyen âge* (Paris, 1979), pp. 429–442; J. Poly, "Le diable, Jacques le Coupe, et Jean des Portes, ou les avatars de Santiago," in *Le diable au moyen âge*, pp. 443–460; J. Schneyer, *Repertorium der lateinischen Sermones des Mittelalters für die Zeit von 1150–1350, Beiträge zur Philosophie und Theologie des Mittelalters*, 8 vols. (Münster, 1969–1978); G. de Tervarent and B. de Gaiffier, "Le diable voleur d'enfants," in *Homenage a Antoni Rubio I Lluch*, vol. 2 (Barcelona, 1936), pp. 35–38; T. Wolpers, *Die englische Heiligenlegende des Mittelalters* (Tübingen, 1964); J.-T. Welter, *L'exemplum dans la littérature religieuse et didactique du moyen âge* (Paris, 1927); J.-T. Welter, *La tabula exemplorum secundum ordinem alphabeti* (Paris, 1926). Exempla are brief statements of themes that can be incorporated into sermons. See also A.V. Murray, "Religion among the Poor in Thirteenth-Century France," *Traditio*, 30 (1974), 285–324. The most important of these didactic works were the Dominican Stephen of Bourbon's *De diversis materiis praedicabilibus*, partially edited by Lecoy de la Marche, *Anecdotes historiques* (Paris, 1877); J.-C. Schmitt is editing the version in Paris, Bibliothèque Nationale, Lat. 15970. The Cistercian Caesarius of Heisterbach's *Dialogus miraculorum* was edited by J. Strange in 2 volumes (Cologne, 1851). Richalm of Schöntal, another Cistercian, was edited by B. Pez in his *Thesaurus anecdotorum novissimus*, 6 vols. (Augsburg, 1721–1729), vol. 1:2, Col. 324ff. The "Legends of the Saints" of Jacques de Vitry became so popular all over Europe that they gained the name of "The Golden Legend." The edition is by T. Graesse, *Jacobi a Voragine Legenda aurea*, 2d ed. (Leipzig, 1850); see J. Greven, *Die Exempla aus den sermonen feriales et communes des Jakob von Vitry* (Heidelberg, 1914); G. Franklin, ed., *Die Exempla des Jacob von Vitry* (Munich, 1914).

14. On the vision literature, see M. Dods, *Forerunners of Dante* (Edinburgh, 1903); H.R. Patch, *The Other World* (Cambridge, Mass., 1950), esp. pp. 89–120. The most influential of these visions were *The Vision of Saint Paul*, originally third-century Greek and

translated into Latin in the sixth century; the Irish version of Adamnán, ninth to eleventh century; the *Vision of Tundale* (Tnugdal), written in Germany by an Irishman in the twelfth century, and the *Purgatory of Saint Patrick*, twelfth century. The Latin and German versions of the *Vision of Tundale* are edited by A. Wagner, *Visio Tgndali: Lateinisch und Altdeutsch* (Erlangen, 1882). See also V. H. Friedel and K. Meyer, eds., *La vision de Tondale: français, anglo-normand, et irlandais* (Paris, 1907); E. Gardiner, "The Vision of Tundale: A Critical Edition of the Middle English Text" (Ph.D. diss., Fordham University, 1980); P. Dinzelbacher, *Vision und Visionsliteratur* (Stuttgart, 1981); D.D.R. Owen, *The Vision of Hell* (Edinburgh, 1970); H. Spilling, *Die Visio Tngdali* (Munich, 1975); J.C.D. Marshall, "Three Problems in the Vision of Tundal," *Medium Aevum*, 44 (1975), 14–22. For quotations, see Wagner, pp. 16, 27, 35. Compare A. di Paolo Healey, ed., *The Old English Vision of St. Paul* (Cambridge, Mass., 1978).

15. On medieval literature in general and on Dante and Langland in particular see the Essay on the Sources. On the influence of courtly love and lyric on Dante see T. Bergin, *Dante* (New York, 1965); on that of the scholastics see E. Gilson, *Dante et la philosophie* (Paris, 1939); on Muslim influence see M. Asín Palacios, *Islam and the "Divine Comedy"* (New York, 1926). On possible Indian influence see A. de Gubernaitis, "Le type indien du Lucifer chez le Dante," *Giornale Dantesco*, 3 (1895). 49–58.

16. J. Freccero, "Satan's Fall and the *Quaestio de aqua et terra*," *Italica*, 38 (1961), 112–113.

17. Augustine, *Confessions*, 13.9.

18. On the neutral or trimmer angels, "quel cattivo coro de li angeli che non furon ribelli nè furon fedeli a Dio" (that wicked choir of angels who were neither rebels nor faithful to God, Inf. 3.37–39), see M. Dando, "Les anges neutres," *Cahiers d'études cathares*, 27, no. 69 (1976), 3–28; J. Freccero, "Dante and the Neutral Angels," *Romanic Review*, 51 (1960), 3–14; M. Rossi, "Sur un passage de la *Chanson d'Esclarmonde* (vs. 2648–2826)," *Le diable au moyen âge* (Paris, 1979), p. 465. Rossi shows that the idea had precedents in Christian literature and cites the *Chanson d'Esclarmonde* as an example. This third group of angels must wander the world (*Esclarmonde*) or else dwell in the circle of trimmers (Dante). Possibly the idea drew strength from the growing belief in purgatory; the third state of the angels could be seen as paralleling the third state of human souls after death.

19. *Conv.* 3.13: "intelligenze che sono in esilio de la superna patria" (intelligences exiled from their heavenly home); *Conv.* 2.5: "di tutti questi ordini si perderono aliquanti tosto che furono creati, forse in numero de la decima parte; a la quale restaurare fu l'umana natura poi creata" (Some from each of these orders fell almost as soon as they were created—about a tenth of them—and human nature was then created to make up the lost number). Dante does not speak of a tenth order of angels, but rather of one tenth of angels of all ranks. Inf. 7.11–12: Michael throws them out; Inf. 8.83: "da ciel piovuti" (rained down out of heaven); Inf. 9.91: "cacciati del ciel, gente dispetta" (a despised race driven out of heaven). Cf. Parad. 29.50–54. The fallen angels become the demons guarding the battlements of the infernal city of Dis (Inf. 9.91–97).

20. Inf. 34.122–126: "e la terra, che pria di qua si sporse, per paura di lui fé del mar velo, e venne all emisperio nostro; e forse per fuggir lui lasciò qui il loco vòto quella ch'appar di qua, e sù ricorse" (and the land that was here made a veil of itself for fear of Satan and withdrew to the northern hemisphere; and to flee him, the land that was in the midst of the earth left a hollow space for hell and moved up onto the surface). Cf. Purgatory 12.25–27; Parad. 29.55–57 See Freccero, "Satan's Fall." Dante implies that God created the whole cosmos before the fall of Satan; if Satan had fallen earlier, the earth would not have been there to receive him.

21. Singleton's edition (See the Essay on the Sources) vol. 1:2, p. 634.

22. For the relationship between Dante and Milton, see I. Samuel, *Dante and Milton* (Ithaca, n.d.).

23. F. Fergusson, *Dante* (New York, 1966), p. 119: "stalemate."

24. Since the time of the early fathers it had been conventional to portray the pagan gods as demons, but Dante's love of classical civilization made him replace the gods with mythological figures that had been sinister to the classical mind itself. Other medieval writers did the same. Arnoul Gréban's Passion play has a demon named Cerberus, for example, and *Eneas*, a French adaptation of the *Aeneid*, assimilated a number of classical mythological figures such as Charon and Cerberus to demons. See Owen, pp. 142–143.

25. Demons do appear in the fifth of the evil ditches (*malebolge*) of the eighth circle of hell, where the fraudulent are imprisoned. Here they have some elements of the comic stage demons. Though the idiocy of the Devil is so cold as to freeze any sense of laughter, the stupidity of minor demons can have elements of humor. Dante used the term *demonio* for "demon" most frequently, but *diavolo* is an occasional equivalent, as in Inf. 28.37. Dante's usual name for the Devil is Lucifer, e.g., Inf. 31.143, 3489, but he also calls him Satan (Inf. 7.1) and Beelzebub (Belzebù; Inf. 24.127). When Vergil, who was naturally unaware of the Judeo-Christian tradition, speaks, he uses the classical name Dis (Dite) for the lord of the underworld (Inf. 11.65, 12.39, 34.20).

26. Lucifer's tomb is a parody of Holy Sepulchre, the tomb of Christ. See A. Cassell, "The Tomb, the Tower, and the Pit: Dante's Satan," *Italica*, 56 (1979), 331–351.

27. Also the lake, *lago* (Inf. 32.23) harks back to the Latin *lacus*, which means "pit" as well as "lake," and was used as such by Jerome in the Vulgate (Is. 14.15) to designate the place to which Satan fell.

28. Inf. 34–46: "sotto ciascuna uscivan due grand'ali"; Inf. 34.49–50: "non aveari penne, ma di vispistrello era lor modo."

29. He can even (Inf. 33.139–148) animate the bodies of the dead. Dante had believed that Branca Doria and Michel Zanche were alive on earth, but he hears that they are actually dead and are being used like puppets by Satan.

30. Among the precedents: the Titans of Greco-Roman religion; the giant children of the Watcher angels in apocalyptic literature; Vergil's Polyphemus, the cannibal giant from whom Odysseus escaped by clinging onto the woolly bellies of sheep, an image Dante must have had in mind when he wrote of Vergil and Dante clinging to Satan's shaggy sides. Just above the Giudecca, Dante encountered the well of giants, themselves raging, vain, and purposeless. In the twelfth-century *Vision of Tundale*, Tundale saw a huge, black demon, larger than any beast, with a hundred heads and mouths in which he gulped down a thousand sinners at once; he lay bound on a gridiron, thrashing his huge tail, vomiting the sinners up and swallowing them again. Another of Tundale's hideous demons, with great black wings and fiery eyes, sat up to his waist in a frozen lake. On *Tundale* see Chapter 6 above; on the Devil's shape see Chapter 7 above. See also S. Cosmos, "Old English 'Limwaestm' ('Christ and Satan,' 129)," *Notes and Queries*, (1975), 196–198; S. Frascino, "La 'terra' dei giganti ed il Lucifero dantesco," *La cultura*, 12 (1933), 767–783.

31. Inf. 34.28, 35; Parad. 19.46–48. Other references to the Devil: Parad. 9.127–128; Purg. 8.98–99, 32.32; Inf. 6.96, 23.143–144.

32. *Vexilla*, like the Greek *tropaia*, has the root meaning of battle standard(s), but in Christian literature its meaning commonly shifted to connote the cross.

33. J. Freccero, "The Sign of Satan," *Modern Language Notes*, 80 (1965), 11–26. Compare G. Busnelli, *I tre colori di Lucifero Dantesco* (Rome, 1910).

34. For editions of and works on *Piers Plowman* see the Essay on the Sources. I am

grateful to my graduate student Cassandra Potts, whose seminar work did much to advance this section on *Piers Plowman*.

35. B.1.128–129: "Alle that werchen with wrong wende thei shulle after hir dethday and dwelle with that sherewe [the Devil]." Compare B.2.102–104; B.7.117–118. See B. Harwood, "Liberum-Arbitrium in the C-Text of *Piers Plowman*," *Philogical Quarterly*, 52 (1973), 680–695.

36. T.P. Dunning, *Piers Plowman*, 2d ed. (Oxford, 1980), pp. 54, 126. Compare C.6.330, where Robbery is "Luciferes aunte." See L.K. Little, "Pride Goes before Avarice," *American Historical Review*, 76 (1971), 16–49.

37. B.2.69–114; C.2.69–115. D.J. Burton, "The Compact with the Devil in the Middle English *Vision of Piers the Plowman* B. II," *California Folklore Quarterly*, 5 (1946), 179–184, misunderstands this as a pact with the Devil; in fact it is a parody of greed and the law.

38. C.1.120. See B.1.111–129; C.1.103–128; C.16.210–211. See also A. Kellogg, "Satan, Langland, and the North," *Speculum*, 24 (1949), 413–414; R. Risse, Jr., "The Augustinian Paraphrase of Isaiah 14.13–14 in *Piers Plowman* and the Commentary on the *Fables* of Avianus," *Philological Quarterly*, 45 (1966), 712–717. In C.1.111 and B.1.119 Langland changed Augustine's paraphrase in *Ennaratio in Ps.* 47 from "ponam sedem meam in aquilone" (I shall place my throne in the north) to "ponam *pedem* meam," a shift from "seat" or "throne" to "foot." Kellogg and Risse explain *pedem* as meaning pride and self-love. The fall of the angels to various levels: "Wonder wyse holy wryt telleth how thei fallen, summe in erthe, summe in ayr, summe in heele depe as Lucifer lowest lith of hem all; for pruyde" (C.1.125–128). This notion goes as far back as Origen: See SATAN, pp. 125–126. For the idea that ten orders of angels existed, of which one order fell, see Chapter 6, n. 57, above. Earlier writers agreed that only nine orders proper of angels existed and that those who fell constitute a tenth group, but not a tenth order. Duns states the point in his *Commentary on the Sentences*, 2.9: "Sed cum non sint nisi novem ordines, nec plures fuissent, etiamsi illi qui ceciderunt perstitissent, moventur lectores quomodo Scriptura dicat decimum ordinem compleri ex hominibus" (Since only nine orders existed, and only nine would have existed even if the angels who fell had actually remained loyal, the reader may ask how Scripture can say that the tenth order will be filled up by humans). Duns observes that people have loosely used the term *tenth order* for the fallen angels and for the humans who allegedly replace them. But this is not accurate, he argues: "Ex quo apparent non esse de hominibus formandum decimum ordinem, tanquam novem sint angelorum, et decimus hominum: sed homines pro qualitate meritorum statuendos in ordinibus angelorum. Quod veto legitur decimus ordo complendus de hominibus, ex tali sensu dictum fore accipi potest, quia de hominibus restaurabitur, quod in angelis lapsum est: de quibus tot corruerunt, ut possit fieri decimus ordo" (It is clear that a tenth order was not formed out of humans, as if there were nine ranks of angels and a tenth of humans; rather, humans are brought up into all the ranks of angels according to their merits. When we read that a tenth order was to be filled up with humans, we ought to understand it to mean that what had been lost among the angels was restored among humans and that as many angels fell as *could have* made up a tenth order). The "tenth order" is thus a loose manner of speaking into which Langland fell, perhaps inadvertently. The nine days that the angels fell correspond to the nine spheres of the cosmos and to the nine orders of angels, numerologically three times a triad. The giants of Hesiod's *Theogony* took nine days to fall to earth (*Theog.* 722). See above, Chapter 4, for the north as evil.

39. C.16.79–85; C.18.111–117. C.18.115: "and made of holy men his hoerd *in limbo inferni*." Cf. B.10.423–425: Adam, the prophets, and Isaiah held by Satan.

40. The idea of the daughters of God is an old device based on Ps. 84.11. It was frequently used by late medieval poets and dramatists; see for example *The Castle of Perseverence*, below, Chapter 9.

41. J.A. Alford, "Literature and Law in Medieval England," *Publications of the Modern Language Association*, 92 (1977), 941–951; W. J. Birnes, "Christ as Advocate: The Legal Metaphor of *Piers Plowman*," *Annuale medievale*, 16 (1975), 71–93.

42. C.20.261–263: "For Iesus as a geaunt with a gyn cometh zende to breke and to bete adoun all that ben agayne hym and to haue out of helle alle of hem that hym liketh."

43. This reading is preferable to one making Gobelyn different from Satoun or one making "the deuel" yet another demon. In B.18.286ff. a speech is split between Satoun and Gobelyn, and both are equated with "the deuel and "the fend"; as one being they address Lucifer in B.18.311. The C text implies the same identity. That "the deuel" is a common noun here is further clear from C.20.340, where "deueles" appears in the plural.

44. "For bi riht and by resoun the renkes that ben here body and soule beth myne, bothe gode and ille" (C.20.300–301). Satan blames Lucifer: C.20.312–321; Cf. B.18–311. Lucifer had taken a snake's form in Eden: "not in fourme of a fende bore in fourme of an addre" (C.20.315). Gobelyn/Satoun reports that he had been tempting Jesus in vain for over thirty years and has yet to find out whether he is the Son of God: "and som tyme ich askede where we were god or godes sone? He gaf me short answere" (C.20.330–331). Suspecting the worst, Gobelyn/Satoun tried to stop the crucifixion: "Y wolde haue lenghed [lengthened] his lyf, for y leved [believed], if he deyede, that if his soul hider cam, it sholde shende [ruin] vs all" (C.20.335–336).

45. What lord: C.29.360. Blinding light: C.20.368 ("Lucifer loke ne myhte, so liht hym ablende"); cf. B.5.494: "The liz that lepe out of thee, Lucifer it blente"; B.18.325; C.20.141.

46. "Sethen we haen ben sesed seuene thousand wynter," we have possession by right (C.20.309–311). Satan doubts it: C.20.312–313, and Gobelyn adds that God cannot be cheated or mocked: "And God wol not be gylde ... ne byiaped. We haen no trewe title to hem, for thy tresoun hit maketh" (C.20.323–324). For the Devil's lawsuits against Christ see Chapter 9 below.

47. C.20.443–444: Christ has at this time come to take from hell only those who believed in him before his coming, but he promises to save all at the Last Judgment. C.20.413–414: "And thenne shal y come as kynge, with croune and with angeles, and haue out of helle alle mennes soules." C.20.395: "thorw riht and throw resoun [I] ransoun here my lege [security, pledge]."

48. C.20.377–386; C.20.382: "the olde lawe techeth that gylours be begiled, and yn here gyle falle."

49. C.20.396; C.20.392: "So that with gyle was gete, thorw grace is now ywonne.... and Gyle be bigyled thorw grace at the laste." Cf. C.20.163–166: "And riht as the gylour thorw gyle begiled man formost, so shal grace, that bigan al, maken a goed ende and begile be gilour, and that is a goed sleythe: ars ut artem falleret." The last phrase is derived from Fortunatus' famous hymn "Pange lingua," but Langland shifted the original meaning. Fortunatus was using the ransom theory that God tricked Satan into seizing Christ so that he could deprive him of his booty. In Langland this idea is submerged in the more edifying principle that since Satan's original temptation of Adam and Eve was by fraud, he was never legally entitled to anything at all. God's justice replaces God's trickery. Traces of the old idea remain in "beguiling the guileful," but when Langland says that grace "tricks the trickster," he is using an older vocabulary to cloak a newer viewpoint. That grace and mercy and justice prevail over the Devil is no trickery but a straightforward expression of

God's order. But the deluded Devil, who never sees anything straight, thinks of them as trickery. With this viewpoint, Langland can stage the dramatic harrowing of hell without subscribing to the discarded ransom theory that underlay it.

50. The bibliography on Chaucer is enormous. See especially F.N. Robinson, *The Works of Geoffrey Chaucer*, 2d ed. (Oxford, 1957); E.T. Donaldson, *Chaucer's Poetry*, 2d ed. (New York, 1975). On the Devil in Chaucer see J. de Caluwe-Dor, "Le diable dans les Contes de Cantorbéry: Contribution à l'étude sémantique du terme *Devil*," in *Le diable au moyen âge*, pp. 97–116. Caluwe-Dor assembles 106 references to the Devil. R. Kaeuper has a useful article forthcoming in *Studies in the Age of Chaucer*.

51. Lines 161–168, 204–216; see discussion of Dante, above.

52. The Devil wears a green jacket (*courtepy*) in this tale. See Chapter 4 above (see Chapter 4 also for the motif of the fulfilled curse in folklore) and D.W. Robertson, Jr., "Why the Devil Wears Green," *Modern Language Notes*, 69 (1954), 470–472.

53. R.P. Clark, "Squeamishness and Exorcism in Chaucer's *Miller's Tale*," *Thoth* 14 (1973/1974), 37–43; though weighting his case down with leaden Freudianism, Clark makes a valid point in drawing attention to the association of the Devil with the scatological.

54. On "The Man of Lawes Tale" with its misogynistic association of women with the Devil, see Roddy, "Mythic Sequence." On "The Merchant's Tale," where Pluto and Proserpine are figures of the Devil and his wife, see M.A. Dalbey, "The Devil in the Garden," *Neuphilologische Mitteilungen*, 75 (1974), 408–415. Dalbey shows the origin of the identification in the fourteenth-century "Ovide moralisée," which says that "Pluto denote le dyable," and in Petrus Berchorius ("allegorice ... per Plutonem intelligitur dyabolus"). Pluto's rape of Proserpine symbolizes Lucifer's rape of souls. Compare Dante's use of classical figures, including Pluto, to represent the Devil.

55. See Chapter 5 above.

JEFFREY BURTON RUSSELL

The Romantic Devil

T he Revolutions of 1789–1848 shattered the ancient symbiosis of Christianity and the state that had begun a millennium and a half earlier with Constantine the Great. As the old political and legal systems were swept away in the wake of Napoleon's reorganization of Europe, the political powers of the monarchy and the aristocracy, on which the churches had often relied, were drastically reduced. Commercial and industrial elites gradually replaced the aristocracy as political and cultural leaders. The capitalist values of the new elite, with their emphasis on competition and profit, had little ground in common with Christianity.

Although the leaders of capitalist society still found it politically useful to embrace Christianity or at least to appear to do so, two underlying effects were increasingly felt: the religion of the leaders of society tended to become more nominal and superficial; and the intellectual leaders tended to become more openly skeptical of religious values. Further, with the industrialization that proceeded rapidly in much of western Europe during the nineteenth century, a large population shift occurred from the countryside, with its traditional religious customs, to the ugly cities with their anonymity and often cruel working conditions. The industrial proletariat, cut off from access to traditional values, tended to develop a sense of despair and meaninglessness that was eventually alleviated only by such new ideologies as

From *Mephistopheles: The Devil in the Modern World.* © 1986 by Cornell University.

Marxism. In such a society, belief in the transcendent waned, and Christian theology seemed to lose much of its relevance.

Attitudes toward these changes varied radically, and as the Revolution of 1789 came to symbolize the transformation of society, attitudes toward the Revolution often paralleled attitudes toward the Devil. Monarchists and traditional Catholics tended to view the Revolution as the work of the Devil and the restoration of the monarchy as the triumph of Christ the King over Satan. As political reactionaries made common cause with Catholics against the Revolution, republicans and revolutionaries attacked Christianity and rallied to the standard of its opponents—the greatest of whom was Satan. Christ is King, but kings are evil, and the greatest king is the greatest evil. Revolutionaries tended to perceive Satan as a symbol of rebellion against the unjust order and tyranny of the *ancien régime* and its institutions: church, government, and family. Not only radicals but also the bourgeois, who saw individualism and aggressive competition as virtues, were prepared for a shift in symbols. The traditional feudal Devil had been condemned as a rebel against his liege lord; the individualist Devil, struggling against hypocrisy, could be praised as a saint and martyr.

Such positive views of Satan were symbolic rather than literal. The depersonalization of Satan, his reduction to a symbol, and the unmooring of the symbol from Bible and tradition meant that the idea of the Devil could float free of its traditional meanings. The nineteenth-century Devil was good as well as evil, urbane as well as brutal, a proponent of love as well as a lord of strife. Since the history of the Devil in this period from the end of the eighteenth century to about 1860 is more symbolic than theological, the emphasis of this chapter is more literary than philosophical.[1]

The Devil and radical evil were not subjects that preoccupied the leading philosophers and theologians of the period. Materialism, pragmatism, and skepticism of religion dominated. Auguste Comte (1798–1857) formulated the theory of positivism, in which human society was assumed to have advanced through three stages: theological (the effort to understand by revelation), metaphysical (the effort to understand by logic), and positive (the effort to understand by empirical science). The positive stage, the modern period, was characterized by rejection of belief in anything that could not be demonstrated empirically and scientifically. Even though positivism rested upon empirically unverifiable acts of faith that overall human progress exists, that reality is ultimately material, and that the human mind can grasp this material reality, it was pressed with vigor; its influence became enormous.

Ludwig Andreas Feuerbach (1804–1872) used positivism to attack Christianity. Nothing exists except matter, said Feuerbach; anything else is mere speculation having no foundation. All the attributes we assign to God are actually human conceptions projected upon the deity. The same, naturally, is true of the Devil. Ethical philosophers such as Jeremy Bentham (1748–1832) and John Stuart Mill (1806–1872) constructed their systems without reference to a transcendent power of evil. Theologians avoided the question, and the most original theologian of the century, Sören Kierkegaard (1813–1855)—though he had much to say about alienation, anxiety, and despair—held that the concept of the Devil had become so trivial that it actually weakened our sense of the problem of evil.

The Catholic revival after 1815 did little to convince society at large of the Devil's existence. Still, the church continued to affirm its traditional teachings. Gregory XVI (1831–1846), fearing the identification of the church with fading royalism, tried briefly to free Catholic theology from scholasticism but soon restrained his liberalism; Pius IX (1846–1878) flirted briefly with liberalism but, shocked by the revolutions of 1848, returned to a rigidly traditionalist view. Joseph de Maistre (1753–1821) had already identified the Devil with revolution, disorder, disunity, moral degeneracy, and disrespect for proper authority, notably pope and king. Pius IX condemned liberalism in his *Syllabus errorum* (1864) and defended the return to scholasticism against those who, like John Henry Newman (1801–1890), favored a historical and developmental approach. The triumph of the scholastics was assured by the encyclical *Aeterni patris* of Leo XIII (1879), which declared Thomist theology eternally valid. In such an atmosphere, the objective reality of the Devil was widely assumed.[2] Until the 1960s, when Catholicism began to retreat from its own epistemological foundations in scripture and tradition, the existence of the Devil as a personal entity was included in the official line of the Catholic Church.

In Protestantism, growing disregard for church unity and for apostolic succession had long undermined the authority of tradition; the increasing acceptance of higher biblical criticism undermined the authority of scripture as well. With the weakening of these twin pillars of Christian epistemology, first theologians, then preachers, and finally the laity questioned nearly every aspect of Christian belief: heaven, the soul, immortality, sin, redemption, and certainly hell and the Devil. By 1898 the English statesman and churchman William Ewart Gladstone could speak of hell as a shadowy thing relegated to the dusty corners of the Christian mind.[3] Unmoored from its epistemological anchor, liberal Protestantism drifted with secular trends and fashions, tending to reject the Devil (and eventually God) as old-fashioned and outdated. One growing trend of nineteenth-century theology was universalism, the belief that in the end everyone, including Satan, will be saved. Two groups may be distinguished: "soft" universalists holding to a weak, progressive optimism derived from the progressivism of liberal secularists, and "hard" universalists affirming the reality of evil but also the merciful plan of God to transform it into good.[4] In any form, universalism ran the risk of promoting relativism, undermining free will and moral choice, and denying radical evil.

Against liberal Protestantism a counterforce gradually asserted itself, exerted by those who continued loyal to the Reformation faith in scripture and who affirmed the incarnation, the resurrection, and other Christian doctrines on the authority of the Bible. Rejecting compromise with secularism and denying the validity of the higher criticism, these "conservatives," along with traditional Roman Catholics and Eastern Orthodox, tended also to affirm the reality of the Devil. However, the emphasis of conservative Protestants upon the Bible to the exclusion of tradition produced its own inconsistencies, for, like Luther, its exponents tended to ignore the fact that the Christian doctrine of Satan is more traditional than biblical. The kernel of the idea of Satan is certainly present in the New Testament, but the full doctrine developed only gradually. This poses no problem for one who perceives the essential historical and developmental nature of all Christian doctrine; however, for one who believes that the truth lies only in the earliest statements of Christian doctrine, the theology of the Devil is precarious—along with other historically developed ideas such as the identification of Christ with the second person of the Trinity. Each in its own way, both "liberal" and "conservative" sides tended to cut themselves off from the historical development of Christianity which alone gives it form and definition. Cut off from a sound epistemological basis, Christianity as a whole continued to retreat in the face of the intellectually more consistent forces of positivism and materialism.

Even more than by positivism, the early nineteenth century was dominated by Romanticism, a fuzzy-bordered concept that developed in the second half of the eighteenth century. Less an intellectual movement than a literary and artistic reaction against the neoclassicism that had dominated the arts since the seventeenth century, Romanticism in various forms flavored Western thought through the 1860s and even down to 1914.

The elements of this vaguely defined movement included an emphasis upon the esthetic and the emotional as against the rational and the intellectual. Whether a thing was powerfully affecting was more important than whether it was true; the emotions were a surer guide to life than the intellect. This belief encouraged a psychological penetration that prepared for the birth of depth psychology later in the nineteenth century. Romanticism exalted the virtues of love, pity, and mercy against rational and scientific calculation, but the tendency to dismiss reason led to wishful thinking, individualism and selfishness, and a self-satisfied, elitist contempt for those considered less fine, noble, or sensitive. The focus upon the subjective and the interior life pitted the Romantics against both traditional Christianity and emerging science. The search for the emotionally and psychologically stimulating encouraged a taste for the miraculous, the supernatural, the weird, and the grotesque—witness the penchant for oriental tales such as the *Thousand and One Nights* early in the nineteenth century and for medievalism after 1815.

The late eighteenth-century concept of the "sublime" lay close to the heart of Romanticism. As expressed by its most articulate exponent, Edmund Burke (1729–1797), the sublime was to be contrasted with the merely beautiful.[5] The sublime in nature consisted of grandeur, obscurity, vastness, privation, and magnificence and was often accompanied by the experience of terror in the beholder. In humanity it consisted of the individual quest for honor and glory against all odds. Terror, suffering, danger, and heroism were thought to tap the most profound and powerful human emotions and call forth the highest manifestations of the human spirit. God and the Devil were the ultimate symbols of the sublime, but Burke and the Romantics traced the sense of sublimity to inspirations in nature and humanity rather than to God.

Intensely concerned with the conflict of good and evil within the human breast, the Romantics used Christian symbols for esthetic and mythopoeic purposes, usually without much regard for their theological content, thus encouraging the unmooring of such symbols from their basic meanings. In a world view that eschewed logic in favor of emotion there were bound to be many contradictions. The Romantics' concern with good and evil led them to an intense ambivalence about the world. On the one hand they affirmed the optimistic faith that human progress would destroy tyranny and lead to a new world of freedom; on the other they saw humanity at the mercy of selfishness and viciousness. This ambivalence led some of the more thoughtful Romantics toward the coincidence of opposites: the eventual reunion of God and Satan, and the integration and transcendence of the opposing elements of the human psyche. The views of Carl G. Jung at the beginning of the next century were prepared for and anticipated by Romanticism.

The Romantics also expressed dissatisfaction with the bourgeois domination of ideas after the Revolution. Their esthetic bent encouraged them to adopt behavior, dress, manners, and views designed to *épater les bourgeois* and confound the philistines. Later in the century, when Romanticism transposed into decadence and dandyism, Oscar Wilde would flout convention with his green carnation, his velveteen suits, his poppy, his epigrams, and his scandalous sex life.

The Romantic distaste for the church was reciprocated, and clerical attacks on the Romantics only intensified their view that Christianity was evil and its opponents good. It followed that if the greatest enemy of traditional Christianity was Satan, then Satan must be good. This was a philosophically incoherent statement contradicting the core meaning of the Devil, and indeed the Romantics intended such a statement not as a theological proposition but rather as an imaginative challenge and a political program. In his rebellion against unjust and repressive authority, the Devil was a hero. The Romantic idea of the hero, derived from the concept of the sublime, stands in contradiction to the classical epic notion of the hero as one devoted to the welfare of his family and people. The Romantic hero is individual, alone against the world, self-assertive, ambitious, powerful, and liberator in rebellion against the society that blocks the way of progress toward liberty, beauty, and love; the Romantics read these qualities into Milton's Satan. Their admiration for Satan was not Satanism, however—not the worship of evil—for they made the Devil the symbol of what they regarded as good.

Four different aspects of the demonic in art exist. The first is a popular misreading of the artist's intention, as when an audience misunderstands the composer's use of musical dissonance as demonic. The second is a deliberate portrayal of the demonic—as in Moussorgsky's *Night on Bald Mountain* or Shostakovitch's *War and Peace* quartet—but with the intent of condemning the evil. The third is the actual exaltation of evil, as in the performance of certain rock music groups of the late twentieth century. The fourth, characteristic of the Romantics, is the deliberate shift of demonic symbols away from evil toward good. Since the Romantics' view of good was not radically different from the Christian view of good, and since the Romantics themselves were inconsistent in the degree to which they shifted the symbols, their symbolism was incoherent. Their tendency was to transpose the Christian God into a symbol of evil, the Christian idea of humanity into God (in the sense that humanity became the ultimate concern), and the Christian Satan into a hero.

Because of the difficulty inherent in shifting symbols so radically, some of the Romantics chose mythological figures other than Satan to represent the rebellious hero. The eighteenth century had transformed Brutus from traitor to revolutionary hero in its political symbolism; the Romantics in their moral and psychological symbolism would praise Prometheus and Cain (though not Judas). The merging of Prometheus and Satan was one of the crucial symbolic transformations. The traditional Prometheus and Satan had much in common: their rebellion against divine authority, their inevitable defeat and doom, and their sentence to be bound in eternal chains. But there was also a powerful difference: Prometheus did not challenge the gods from selfishness or hatred but from a desire to help humanity. The melding of the two heroes enabled the positive elements of Prometheus to be transferred to Satan, so that the Devil might also appear as a noble liberator of humanity.

The Romantic Satan was not always positive; he could also be evil, symbolizing isolation, unhappiness, hardness of heart, lack of love, insensitivity, ugliness, and sarcasm. The growth of medievalism helped to restore some of the medieval sense of the evil Devil, whom the Romantics saw as impeding the progress of the human spirit and as the representation of destructive forces within the soul. There was, then, no one Romantic Satan or even two, but virtually as many Satans as there were Romantics. Their use of Satan was seldom designed as serious intellectual comment on the principle of evil, and even when it was, it lacked any epistemological basis in logic, science, revelation, tradition, the Bible, or any other specific source. Whether one is a Christian, an idealist, a materialist, or a scientist, one finds such views incoherent and inconsistent.

The Romantic ideas of the Devil had little ultimate impact upon the concept of the Devil. Today one takes either the traditional view or the Enlightenment view, but rarely the Romantic view. Nonetheless, Romanticism did leave some traces: by dramatizing the real conflict of good and evil within the human spirit and by shaking Christian thought violently out of its complacency about the problem of evil, it laid the foundation for a twentieth-century revival of serious theological concern with the problem of evil.

One reflection of the Romantic treatment of evil was the Gothic novel or *roman noir*, popular first in Britain and then on the continent in the late eighteenth and early nineteenth centuries. By 1834, when the *roman noir* was already past its peak, Théophile Gautier wrote in *Le Figaro* that one could now scarcely read a novel, hear a play, or listen to a story without being beset by mystical, angelic, diabological, or kabbalistic concepts.[6] Like a twentieth-century horror film, the Gothic novel used—or degraded—the "sublime" to produce thrills. Its favorite theme was the decay underlying the veneer of the apparently good, rational, and familiar. It was rich in the wild aspects of nature and the world—crags, caves, and castles—as well as the grotesque and decadent in human nature. Physical and moral deformity, sadism, sexual frenzy, distant lands, and medieval times were typical elements. The macabre aspects of the supernatural, including witches, ghosts, phantoms, vampires, and demons, were especially favored. The Devil often made an appearance but less as a serious symbol of evil than as one among many evil monsters designed to entertain and thrill the reader.

One of the most demonic Gothic novels was Matthew Lewis' *The Monk* (1796), which had enormous influence on English, French, and German literature.[7] Written when Lewis was only nineteen, it contains ghosts, incest, poisons, visions, rape, drugs, and whatever else a sex-crazed adolescent mind of the time could conjure up. Ambrosio, a monk who outwardly appears ascetic, is actually boiling with sexual passions. Dominated by spiritual pride, this cleric of that notoriously degenerate and sensual body, the Catholic Church, is easily corrupted by Satan. Abetted by the Devil, he plunges into ever deeper and more grotesque vices, finally ravishing the virgin Antonia in a dark vault upon the brittle bones of long-deceased monks. For Antonia, "to linger out a life of misery in a narrow loathsome cell, known to exist by no human Being save her Ravisher, surrounded by mouldering Corses, breathing the pestilential air of corruption, never more to behold the light, or drink the pure gale of heaven, the idea was more terrible than She could support." She need not have fretted, for Ambrosio proceeds to murder her. English readers could enjoy the moral sense of being instructed about the evils of Catholicism while being entertained by Lewis's lurid prose. But Ambrosio's evil was limited to the narrow purviews of his author's adolescent lust; it fails to plumb the depths, as Sade had done and Lautréamont would do later. Further, such excesses were grist to the mills of satirists, who produced a number of parodies of the Gothic tale that served to trivialize the Devil further. Along with the specters and ghouls with which he was associated, Satan became more than ever a comic figure.

Perhaps the most original artist and writer of the period was William Blake (1757–1827), whose mythology and symbolism showed some Romantic characteristics but were so individual as to defy categories. Rejecting Christian orthodoxy and avoiding Christian worship, Blake nonetheless affirmed that "Man must and will have Some Religion: if he has not the Religion of Jesus, he will have the Religion of Satan."[8] Blake constructed his own religion; whether or not he believed in a spiritual reality beyond the human mind, he found the resources and symbols of his religion in his own imagination.

Since his symbols lacked explicit consistency, it is difficult to define what he meant by the Devil. For Blake, as for the Romantics, both the Devil and God were morally ambivalent. Consequently, when Blake spoke of the Devil, he was only sometimes using the symbol in its conventional negative sense; and when he spoke of God, he was often using that symbol in an unconventional negative sense to mean something like what Christians meant by the term Devil. For Blake, what was good was the poetic imagination, artistic inspiration, creativity; and this could be called either God or Devil. The moment of poetic inspiration, he held, was always free from evil. Divinity for Blake was everywhere, a pulsing reality ever ready to express itself in music, art, or literature. Emotions, sensitivity, love, and commitment were all manifestations of the divine spirit, while "every obstruction to Art and to intuitive Genius is Satanic (evil)."[9] But this evil was manifest, Blake believed, in the traditional view of God, whom Blake called, among other unflattering epithets, Nobodaddy (no one's daddy); in this sense, God was an evil tyrant, like Shelley's Jupiter or Swinburne's "supreme evil, God."[10] A God who is the supreme evil is clearly the traditional Devil; by "God," therefore, Blake and the Romantics often meant "the Devil."

In other words, one must often look for the Romantics' idea of the Evil One under the name of "God." Their point in reversing the symbols was that the traditional Christian view had created a God who was really an evil tyrant. Blake believed that Jesus had understood the true religion of love, sensitivity, and spirituality but that Christians had forgotten that religion and created in its place a tyrannical system of reason and external morality. Blake viewed abstract reasoning as the heart of evil and despised Enlightenment rationalism at least as much as he did traditional Christianity. For him, the philosophes had been right in criticizing Christianity but entirely wrong in the direction they took. Reason was to be rejected in favor of feeling and love, just as feeling and love were to take the place of all external authority, whether of priests, kings, teachers, or parents. Like Rousseau, Blake believed that human nature was essentially good and needed only to be freed from false external restraints to allow loving creativity to spring forth. Yet Blake also attacked the easy optimism of the Enlightenment. "Man," he said, "is born a Spectre or Satan, and is altogether Evil, and requires a New Selfhood continually."[11]

Blake's "Devil" therefore carried two opposite meanings. In his poem *Milton* (1804), Satan's self-righteousness makes him evil, yet his rebellion against the divine tyrant makes him good. And for Blake, Milton's God is at least as evil as Milton's Satan.

Blake was naturally attracted by the idea of the coincidence of opposites, which appears most clearly in his *Marriage of Heaven and Hell* (1790), written in part to elucidate Emanuel Swedenborg's *Heaven and Hell*, which had influenced Blake earlier in his life. In the *Marriage*, Satan is the symbol of creativity. He is activity, energy struggling to be free. Milton, Blake believed, unconsciously realized that active "evil" is better than passive "good." "The reason Milton wrote in fetters when he wrote of Angels and God, and at liberty when of Devils and Hell, is because he was a true Poet and of the Devil's party without knowing it."[12] Jesus himself was really Satanic in that he acted from impulse, not from rules, and cheerfully "broke all the commandments."[13] The loving Jesus is contrasted with Jehovah, God the Father, Milton's judgmental God, who is really evil.

No goods or evils were absolute for Blake. "All Deities reside in the

Human breast," and no element of the psyche is wholly good or evil.[14] True evil arises from the lack of integration of psychic elements; true good from the balance, union, and integration of the opposites. For the original title page of the *Marriage*, Blake drew an angel and a demon embracing. Reason and energy, love and hatred, the passive and the active, apparent good and apparent evil, must all merge in a transcendent, integrated whole of which creativity will be the leading spirit. The true God is poetic creativity, that spirit, poet, maker, who makes not only art but in a real sense the entire world, for the whole cosmos is a creation of the poetic spirit. Whether Blake ultimately believed that the external cosmos is a poem of a Great Creator or that humans create their own cosmos is unclear. Disdaining reason as a guide to ultimate truth, Blake made no effort at philosophical or cosmological consistency. The true God expressed itself in human creativity: that was all he needed to know.

The First Book of Urizen (1794) again shows the interchangeability of the terms "God" and "Devil." Urizen is the old creator God, the Ancient of Days, the blind tyrant; he represents Jehovah, the Old Testament God of laws, the principle of reason. His act of creation is evil because it sets rules and limits (Greek *horizein*: to limit) in the cosmos, which otherwise would be free to express its creativity. Against Urizen stands Orc, representing revolution and the force of liberation from blind tyranny, yet the violence and hostility of Orc make him Satanic in the evil as well as in the good sense. All of Blake's mythical supernatural beings, the Zoas, have Satanic qualities of one kind or another—nature itself is an ambivalence of good and evil— but in all this confused struggle there is a groping toward brotherhood and love. Blake was Christian enough to see this ideal best expressed in Jesus, and he considered it a cruel irony that the followers of Jesus had remade him into a version of his tyrant Father: "Thinking as I do that the Creator of this World is a very Cruel Being, and being a worshiper of Christ, I cannot help saying: 'The Son, O how unlike the Father!'"[15]

No one familiar with Blake can fail to sense his deep empathetic understanding of evil, most poignantly stated in "The Sick Rose":

O Rose, thou art sick!
The invisible worm
That flies in the night,
In the howling storm,
Hath found out thy bed
Of crimson joy:
And his dark secret love
Does thy life destroy.[16]

Blake and the Romantics opened the doors of perception into the depths of the psyche to a degree unprecedented except by the mystics, and in this sense they advanced the understanding of the true nature of evil. It is in such understanding, rather than in their idiosyncratic and incoherent use of symbols, that their contribution to the concept of the Devil is to be sought.

Blake was followed in England by the poets of high Romanticism, such as George Gordon, Lord Byron (1788–1824). Byron revolted as a youth against his Calvinist upbringing and remained throughout his life an opponent of traditional Christian views of evil. Of original sin and redemption he asked: "What have we / Done that we must be victims for a deed / Before our birth, or need have victims to / Atone for this mysterious, nameless sin?" Still, like Blake, Byron was sharply aware of the problem of evil; indeed, it was the degree of evil in the world that convinced him that the Creator could not be good. His Cain demands, "And yet my sire [Adam] says he's [God's] omnipotent. / Then why is evil, he being good?" Later, Lucifer asks Cain, "What does thy God love?" And Cain can only reply, "All things, my father says, but I confess / I see it not in their allotment here." When Lucifer claims to be eternal himself, Cain quickly counters by asking whether he can do humanity any good and, if so, why he has not done it already. Lucifer's riposte is just as quick: Why hasn't Jehovah?[17]

In such a world, Byron was torn between the Romantic optimism that human liberty would eventually triumph and a pessimism derived from his observation of reality. Lucifer speaks from cruel knowledge of the fate awaiting us, the descendants of Cain: "The sixty-thousandth generation shall be / In its dull damp degeneracy, to Thee and thy son" (*Cain*, 2.276–278; cf. 2.424–432). Human dignity lies in eternal striving toward freedom, even though we must not expect to succeed. Metaphorically speaking, we once lived in an age of innocence from which we have fallen owing to our self-consciousness. This self-consciousness has bound us to a set of tyrannical laws, rules, and rational postulates that imprison and starve the life of the soul. Through knowledge of love and liberty we can rebel against the tyranny of government, church, philosophy, science, and morality, all of which repress our divine creativity. The act of artistic creation is the best rebellion against this stifling conformity, a thrust toward freedom and intensity of experience. For Byron, the natural harmony of seals and sparrows was not enough for humans, who require a balance of harmony and intensity. The poet, rebelling against the forces of convention and tyranny, is linked with the great figures of rebellion in the Christian and classical traditions: Satan, Cain, and Prometheus.

Byron's Devil appears in a number of forms.[18] The poetic drama *Cain: A Mystery* (1821) best expresses Byron's views of evil and rebellion. The poet reconstructs the character of Cain, adding to the original figure in Genesis the Promethean elements of benevolence toward humanity and the Satanic (Miltonic) elements of the sublime. The character Lucifer is himself ambivalent, good in his support of Cain's rebellion against tyranny, yet evil in his ironic distance from human suffering. His essential flaw is that he lacks the love needed for redemption.

Early in the poem Lucifer instructs Cain that God rules the world with rigid, unjust laws. Cain's wife/sister Adah expresses the traditional line that God is both good and omnipotent (1.387–388), but for Byron, Jehovah is ambivalent, both evil and good (1.137–163). Jehovah is a pathetic symbol of human striving, creating world after world in an effort to alleviate his loneliness and isolation, and one after another finding them defective and destroying them. Cain is enraged at such apparent wantonness, but it is Jehovah's nature. Like humanity in general and the poet in particular, Jehovah is both maker and destroyer (1.147–163, 264, 529–530). Lucifer is ready to announce the double truth that Jehovah is both good and evil and that the cosmos he has created is both beautiful and cruel. In this he speaks for Byron: any understanding of the world that sees only the beauty or only the cruelty is false. In the light of Jehovah's ambivalence, it is unclear whether he puts the tree of the knowledge of good and evil in the garden to help or hinder us, and whether Adam and Eve were justified in taking its fruit for themselves. The conflict between the demands of Jehovah and those of Lucifer represent a conflict within the human soul, not between good and evil but between various ambivalences that should be transcended and integrated but may perhaps never be.

Lucifer sneeringly asks Cain who the real Devil is: Lucifer, who wanted Adam and Eve to have knowledge and prompted the serpent to tell them the truth about the tree, or Jehovah, who drove them out of the garden into exile and death (1.204–207, 220–230). But though Jehovah is lawbound, insensitive, and sometimes cruel, the rebellious Lucifer is at least as evil as his counterpart—really more so, because Jehovah, for all his faults, feels the pull of creative love, which Lucifer cannot grasp (2.515–531). Though he promotes intellectual freedom and progress, Lucifer is deliberately blind, self-absorbed, and selfish. He argues for creativity but ultimately creates nothing. While inveighing against God's cold rationality, he himself uses reason and dialectic cynically in order to make his argument. He lies to Cain, suppressing the truth that he shares in the world's cruelty. Cain, already dissatisfied and bitter, listens to him readily when he appears, whereas to Adah, Lucifer is scarcely visible.[19] Worst of all, Lucifer rejects the only road to a good cosmos, the integration of himself with Jehovah, preferring instead to blame everything on God and demanding that humans replace their servitude to God with servitude to himself. His vindictiveness and hatred of God's cosmos is limitless:

> All, all will I dispute. And world by world
> And star by star and universe by universe
> Shall tremble in the balance, till the great
> Conflict shall cease, if ever it shall cease,
> Which it ne'er shall, till he or I be quenched....
> He as a conqueror will call the conquered
> Evil, but what will be the good he gives?
> Were I the victor, his works would be decreed
> The only evil ones. [2.641–651]

Lucifer has the Miltonic/Satanic virtues of grandeur and sublimity and the Romantic heroic virtue of rebellion and persistence against odds. He speaks for Byron when he praises

> Souls who dare us their immortality,
> Souls who dare look the omnipotent tyrant in
> His everlasting face and tell him that
> His evil is not good! [1.137–140]

Lucifer's lack of love, however, means that the strife in the cosmos will continue until the cosmos is destroyed. Ultimately, Lucifer's evil lies in his desire to live forever independently of God (1.116). His claim to be everlasting (1.121) is true only in the sense that he is everlastingly alienated by his failure to embrace the love that would be death to selfishness.

Both Jehovah and Lucifer are within Cain and know his thoughts (1.100–104). Cain, representing humanity in general, resolves the conflict between the two forces in the wrong way. Instead of integrating them, he follows Lucifer's suggestions and attacks the Jehovah side of himself. Prompted by Lucifer, he kills his brother Abel under the delusion that he is striking a blow against the tyranny of Jehovah. His desire for vengeance blots out love; his search for abstract justice blinds him to the flesh-and-blood reality of his brother. His act reinforces humanity's failure to open itself to the love that would knit us together. Byron believed that however unlikely the chances of success, we must keep struggling to reverse that failure and to integrate good and evil. Both God and Devil partake of the Satanic, but neither is truly evil. The truly Satanic is the unresolved tension between them. True evil lies in the opposition of the two psychic principles, true good in their reconciliation.

Percy Bysshe Shelley (1792–1822) was interested from his youth in the demonic and the occult for their esthetic effects of terror and sublimity. Shelley was expelled from Oxford in 1811 for publishing a pamphlet called "The Necessity of Atheism," and throughout his life he continued to reject traditional Christianity and all "organized religion." He gradually adopted a personal religion of the spirit of love in nature and in humanity but refused to call his spirit God because of the cruelty associated with the Christian deity. Jesus himself, he argued, had taught the gospel of love in rebellion against organized religion. Shelley's religion was evolutionary, almost vitalistic, influenced by Erasmus Darwin and similar to the idealistic progressivism of Hegel: the spirit of love is moving humanity and the cosmos toward a better, freer, more loving future. Shelley was deeply aware that evil is continually blocking this benign progress, but he rejected the Christian Devil on the basis that all we can know is the product of the human mind. Shelley perceived Satan as the symbol of the obstructive and regressive tendencies within humanity.

On the Devil and Devils (1820–1821) reveals Shelley's intense preoccupation with the problem of evil. Manicheism, he believed, was no more true than Christianity, but it fit the psychic facts better. The Manichean view that there are two spirits of balanced power and opposite dispositions represented an insight into the divided state of the human soul. The Christian view of a Devil subject to the divine will, especially the diluted Satan of Christian liberalism, seemed to Shelley to evade psychic reality. Yet Shelley was as ambivalent about the figure of Satan as Blake or Byron. On the one hand he insisted that a truly Satanic figure was needed to express the reality of human evil; on the other he took Satan as the symbol of the progressive spirit rebelling against the established forces of repression. Like Blake, he admired Milton's Satan as the greatest literary example of the spirit of sublime rebellion, the archetypal Romantic hero pledging his very essence to the struggle against tyranny.

> Nothing can exceed the energy and magnificence of the character of Satan as expressed in "Paradise Lost." It is a mistake to suppose that he could ever have been intended for the popular personification of evil.... Milton's Devil as a moral being is as far superior to his God as One who perseveres in some purpose which he has conceived to be excellent in spite of adversity and torture, is to One who in the cold security of his undoubted triumph inflicts the most horrible revenge upon his enemy.... Milton ... alleged no superiority of moral virture to his God over his Devil. And this bold neglect of a direct moral purpose is the most decisive proof of the supremacy of Milton's genius.[20]

Chagrined as Milton would have been at this interpretation of his epic, it epitomized the Romantics' reading of it, and in this sense Milton's Satan became the greatest of the Romantic Devils, the archetype of the Romantic hero.

For Shelley, evil was better represented by the demonic in humanity than by Satan, whose moral character he saw as good or at least ambivalent. In *The Cenci* (1810), a play in the Gothic vein, Francesco Cenci is a totally evil character who callously seduces his daughter and rejoices at the death of his sons. Francesco represents the extension of the process, visible in Shakespeare's Iago, of transferring evil from an external power to the human soul. What need have we of a Devil, Shelley seems to ask, when we have humanity? The Devil is a figure that we invent in order to project our own vices upon something external. It is we who are the source and center of evil, not he.

In *Prometheus Unbound* (1820) Shelley used Prometheus (as Byron used Cain) as the symbol of rebellion. In the preface Shelley claimed similarities between his work and *Paradise Lost*: he meant Prometheus to resemble Milton's Satan in courage, majesty, and opposition to omnipotent tyranny; however, like Byron, he saw the drawbacks in making Satan the hero of a poem. Even the Romantic Satan was too ambivalent, for Shelley needed his hero to be the incarnation of love, whereas Satan was ambitious, envious, aggressive, and vengeful as well as a rebel. Prometheus was a better symbol; his rebellion, defeat, and bondage were the result not of his faults but of his love for humanity. Prometheus symbolizes Christ, who sacrifices himself for the good of his people; humanity, which struggles toward freedom under the guidance of the spirit of love; and the poet, whose love and creative word are weapons against the darkness. Thus the symbolic cluster around Prometheus comprises Christ, humanity, the poet, Shelley, and Satan (in his good aspects). Prometheus' antagonist is Jupiter, a wholly evil tyrant; the symbolic cluster around Jupiter includes Jehovah and Satan (in his evil aspects).

Prometheus is a Titan, a member of the race that classical mythology represents as impious rebels against the Olympian gods. But Shelley's Prometheus loves humanity and is distressed to see it kept in bondage and ignorance by the Olympians. The poem begins with a reproach to Olympian Jupiter, whose haughty arrogance sets him forever apart from the reality that is love. Prometheus' gift of knowledge to humanity is rewarded by Jupiter with a terrible punishment: the noble Titan is chained to a rock for eternity, while a bird of prey, "heaven's winged hound," plucks at his liver—which is eternally regenerated in order to prolong his torment. Prometheus' self-sacrifice parallels that of Christ, but his predicament is also that of humanity, for we too are bound by the tyrant's chains. Still, we place these chains upon ourselves, for we know the truth and refuse to act by it. Jupiter is only a projection of the tyranny that lies within: our own willful ignorance, selfishness, and vengefulness. Prometheus will not be freed until his understanding of himself and reality allows him to cease cursing his fate, the cosmos, and the gods. He must cease hating Jupiter and learn to pity him for his choice of coldness and isolation.

Shelley's optimism exceeded Byron's: to Shelley, the world of freedom and love seemed really obtainable. Evil proceeds from the human mind, from our own choice of selfishness and hatred. To eliminate the evil in the world, we have only to decide to do so. Since we have created Jupiter in our own minds, we can also dismantle him and create a better god. This new god would emerge not from hatred and rebellion, even rebellion against tyranny, but from love for everyone, including ourselves and the Jupiter we have created. Jupiter's chief evil is his refusal to abandon his own arrogant isolation, which makes him inferior to Prometheus, who can learn to love. If we can integrate and transcend the opposition of Prometheus and Jupiter within ourselves, we shall be ready to proceed on the road that winds upward in peace through the green country of understanding, freedom, and love.

Shelley's wife Mary (1797–1851) had a darker view. Mary Shelley's *Frankenstein, or the Modern Prometheus* (1818) has enjoyed an enduring popularity as entertainment, though the author's philosophical message has generally been ignored. Mary Shelley drew upon the Gothic love of monsters and horrors to entertain, and *Frankenstein* was a bridge between the Gothic and the modern horror tale. It is also one of the original sources for science fiction, for she made some important changes in the Gothic plot: the creator of the monster, Dr. Frankenstein, is no longer a sorcerer or a magician but a scientist; the monster is no medieval demon or specter but a material being of flesh and blood manufactured in a laboratory. *Frankenstein* replaces the old supernatural horror with modern positivist horror.

The author hardly meant this break to be a clean one; indeed, Frankenstein and other human characters in the novel repeatedly call the monster "daemon," "fiend," "devil." But here Mary Shelley's intent was ironic, for the evil lies not so much in the monster as in the humans who create him. The monster becomes evil only because he has been taught evil by humanity. In this lies another shift of symbols, for here humanity symbolizes the creator whose own pride and selfishness spill out to spoil creation; yet the monster (who has no name) also represents the innocent, open aspect of humanity corrupted by its experience of evil. The individual human, Mary Shelley implied, is born innocent and debased; he is destroyed by the viciousness of the world around him. The monster cries out, "I was benevolent and good; misery made me a fiend. Make me happy, and I shall again be virtuous."[21] The monster teaches himself to read from *Paradise Lost* and other books; he compares himself with Adam, who was created good but became miserable, and to Satan, who was wretched in his isolation. Yet even Satan, he exclaims, had his "fellow-devils" (p. 136). As the people whom the monster encounters shun, fear, and despise him, his character is steadily more deformed until he becomes the murdering fiend that people assume him to be.[22]

The monster's last hope of reform lies in Frankenstein's promise to construct a female companion for him, but in the midst of the new experiment the scientist is shaken by revulsion and destroys both the half-formed woman and the equipment. Now the monster pursues his creator with unremitting vengeance, while the latter in turn seeks out his creature to destroy him. Like Byron's God, Frankenstein has made a world that he regrets and wishes to destroy. As each seeks the other, it becomes clear that Frankenstein and his monster are one and the same; they represent two warring aspects of human character. If only we could transcend the conflict within us, Mary agreed with her husband, we could enter a world of peace— but Mary seems closer to Byron in her pessimistic conclusion. After a weird, extended chase through the limitless Arctic night, the two finally meet. But Frankenstein dies of the exhaustion of his long pursuit, and the monster, feeling both frustrated revenge and frustrated love for his creator, vanishes forever into the icy darkness. No reconciliation or integration occurs: both aspects of Frankenstein, both aspects of humanity, perish.

The Gothic, medieval, and marvelous had broad appeal in Germany and France, as well as in England. Nevertheless, François-René de Chateaubriand (1768–1848), virtually the founder of French Romanticism, was an opponent of revolutionary change and therefore saw Milton's Satan differently from Byron or Shelley. His long essay on *Paradise Lost* in *Le génie du christianisme* (1802) expressed admiration for the grandeur of Milton's Satan as the finest product of the Christian imagination but concluded that Satan's rebellion against legitimate authority made him less hero than villain.

By reintroducing the Devil as a serious symbol at the very outset of French Romanticism, Chateaubriand set a tone that was followed throughout the century by other leading authors. In the prose epic *Les Natchez* (1826), Satan appears as a hazy, ill-defined spirit of evil who exhorts the pagan American Indians against Christianity. The Satan of *Les Natchez* wavers on the border between personality and symbol, for the most chilling, evil figure is not Satan but René, the model for a long line of villains in French literature. In *Le génie du christianisme*, Chateaubriand praised the poetic symbolism, ritual, ceremony, symbolism, and morality of Christianity while showing little interest in its traditional theology. His immensely influential prose epic *Les martyrs* (1809) is set during the persecution of the early Christians by the emperor Diocletian, to which the royalist Chateaubriand parallels the persecutions under the Revolution and the Terror. Imitating Milton in a scene where Satan addresses a council of his demonic followers in hell, Chateaubriand painted the Devil as promising fair treatment of humanity while secretly plotting its ruin. As Satan encouraged the Roman persecution of the Christians and did his evil work through Diocletian, so he prompted the Terror and worked his will through Robespierre. To drive his point home, Chateaubriand even had Satan quote the "Marseillaise."[23]

Unlike Chateaubriand, most French writers who followed him in reviving interest in the Devil treated Satan with ironical skepticism or else used him—along with demons, ghosts, and specters—to produce *frissons* of Gothic horror. Many serious writers felt that the Devil had become too trivialized to use effectively in treating evil and preferred to portray evil in such human characters as Chateaubriand's René. Stendhal (1783–1842), famous for his gibe that "God's only excuse is that he does not exist," painted the demonic human figure of Julien Sorel in *Le rouge et le noir* (1830), and Honoré de Balzac (1799–1850) addressed real evil not in his Gothic novels but in his *Comédie humaine*, in which he laid open the cruelty, stupidity, and vice natural to humanity without the intervention of the Devil.[24]

A few writers followed Chateaubriand in taking Christian symbols more seriously. As a child, Alfred de Vigny (1797–1863) had been fascinated by Raphael's painting of Michael slaying the dragon, and Satan remained a powerful symbol throughout his life. Byron's *Cain* reinforced the young poet's interest in the Devil, but his use of Christian mythology was entirely esthetic, for he regarded the Christian notion of a good, omnipotent deity as absurd. Since human life is wretched and miserable, the Christian Deity must be either perverted or powerless, and Vigny preferred to think that he did not exist at all. Vigny's works are a cry against the complacency of Christian optimism, a demand that we face the problem of evil with eyes open and without illusion. *Le jugement dernier* and *Satan*, two unfinished poems written between 1819 and 1823, preceded his masterpiece, *Eloa, ou la soeur des anges*.[25] Eloa is a female angel born from the tear that Jesus shed at the death of Lazarus (John 11:35). Her heart is full of compassion for her fellow creatures, and because she finds everyone happy in heaven, she sets out to wander the cosmos in search of someone who needs her help. She hears of an outcast angel who is alone and sad, in need of love and companionship. Unaware that this is Satan and that Satan has committed real evils, she sheds a tear of pity for him as Jesus had wept for Lazarus. Satan, of course, chooses to conceal the truth about himself; he convinces her instead that he is misunderstood:

He whom they call wicked is really a Consoler
Who weeps for the slave and frees him from his master,
Who saves him with his love and with his own suffering.
Since he is enshrouded in the same common misery,
He can give the wretched a little sympathy and sometimes
blessed forgetfulness. [*Eloa*, 2.212–216]

Vigny's Satan, a pale, voluptuous youth, is the archetype of the
languishing beauty that the Romantics idealized. He is torn by Eloa's presence.
He knows that he has sinned from pride and arrogance, and he is racked by
remorse and grief that he is cut off from the beauty of heaven. Yet he cannot
overcome his hatred of God. He uses his beauty, his feigned innocence, and his
assumed compassion to impress Eloa, shedding tears as false as those of Jesus
and Eloa had been sincere. His response to Eloa's love is as idiotic as
Mephistopheles' response to the young angels in *Faust*: he determines to
seduce her. Eloa resists, worried about his hostility to God: "How can you love
me, if you do not love God?" (3.116). At last she yields, but just at the moment
when he shows for an instant a sincere wish to repent, she is distracted and fails
to understand him. The moment missed, he returns to his hatred. Under such
conditions, Eloa's love cannot relieve his misery, and he drags her with him
down to hell. Only in the last line of the poem does she begin to grasp the
truth: "Who are you then?" she cries; the response is, "Satan" (3.268).

The poem expresses a deep pessimism about the ability of love to
overcome the bitter barriers of hatred and despair. In this, Vigny's vision was
like Byron's. Although he planned a sequel, *Satan sauvé*, in which the dark
lord would at last be redeemed,[26] the optimistic poem was never finished,
and we are left with a vision that is bleak. Nonetheless, in spite of his
religious skepticism, Vigny achieved a more empathetic and psychologically
convincing portrait of Satan than had anyone else since Milton himself. It
remained for Victor Hugo to deepen the character of the sad, isolated Devil
and to render it even more poetically sympathetic.

The Satan of Victor Hugo (1802–1885) is, with that of Byron, among
the most effective of the Romantic Devils. Beginning as a rationalist, Hugo
as a young man experienced an esthetic conversion to Catholicism but soon
abandoned it. Hugo's ideas were never fixed; throughout his life he pursued
a wide variety of views—mysticism, gnosticism, occultism, pantheism,
materialism, dualism. In true Romantic fashion, Hugo made his judgments
less on intellectual than on esthetic and emotional grounds. He insisted upon
a God of pity and mercy, hating the traditional doctrines of original sin,
salvation through crucifixion, and hell. Humanity was intrinsically good, he
believed, and God intrinsically benevolent. He saw the Christian idea of God

as false but Jesus himself as a noble, loving teacher of a beautiful ethic, a model for the pursuit of real truth, which is love.

The alleged tension between Jesus and Christianity that characterized so many Enlightenment and Romantic thinkers, and found intellectual roots in the biblical criticism attempting to discover the "historical" Jesus behind the "Christ" of tradition, raises fundamental questions. It has recently been argued that the philosophes and Romantics were revolting not against Christianity but against a false Christianity that perverted the true teaching of Jesus, and that therefore they were "true" Christians as against traditional Christians. This view, which has found many adherents among those who reject "organized religion" in favor of an ethical, esthetic, or sentimental attachment to Jesus, contains a number of incoherences and inconsistencies. The "historical Jesus" has not been found and almost certainly cannot be found; we have no way of knowing, historically, what Jesus "really" said or did. What history can do, and with great security and accuracy, is show the development of Christianity and of the view of Christ within Christianity; that is, what we can know historically of Christ is the traditional view of Christ as it developed through the ages. The only way of defining Christianity objectively is to define it as what it is historically. Other definitions all rest upon unproven assumptions. The statement, therefore, that "Christianity is really something other than what it has historically been" is not a meaningful statement, because it rests upon unverifiable and unvalidatable faith assumptions. Hugo and the Romantics *felt* that they had got to the real Jesus behind Christianity. That is possible, but it is not capable of verification.

That Hugo had no rational defense of his view was less important to him than the evidence of his feelings; nonetheless, he could use reason when he liked. He was intensely aware of the problem of evil, and his own kindness and generosity led him to repudiate a God who was able to prevent evil yet chose not to do so. He also rejected the traditional Devil, adapting to his purpose the traditional Platonist/Christian argument of privation: evil is a negation, and no negation can truly exist; only the positive exists. If evil were God, nothing would exist; but we observe that something is. The principle of being must therefore be good.[27]

Though he denied the existence of an absolute evil, Hugo was acutely concerned with the effects of evil in the world. Humanity, basically good, was moving gradually toward perfect love and liberty, he believed, but its progress was blocked by cruelty and by a selfishness attracted to the glamor of evil. Yet we did not create the world, nor did we create the shadow within us, so we are to be pitied for our misfortune rather than blamed for our sin.

With Hugo's ever-changing interests, his use of the Devil was diverse and inconsistent. Since he shared the Gothic love for the medieval and the macabre, his Devil was a fantastic figure, fiend, or monster used to excite terror or thrills; he was a prop in dramas about the Middle Ages such as *Notre-Dame de Paris* (1831), used along with grotesques, witches, and hunchbacks to convey a sense of weird medieval darkness. Medieval settings allowed Hugo to indulge himself in fantastic scenes on the excuse of offering an ironic comment on the supposed medieval mind. They also permitted him to satirize the Catholic church by satirizing the alleged medieval expression of its views. That Hugo's Middle Ages bore little resemblance to historical reality blunted neither their popularity nor their effectiveness.

Satan was also the symbol of the Revolution. In Hugo's early days, under Chateaubriand's influence, this meant that Satan was a symbol of evil; later, when Hugo came to see the Revolution as advancing human progress, the Satan of the Revolution came to symbolize good. Satan could represent oppressive societies and governments, or he could mean the opposite: rebellion against oppression in the name of freedom. He could be used as one side of an ambivalent duality Satan/God, good/evil, which represented the alienation of humanity from its own inherent goodness. Hugo felt deeply that alienation, defeat, sadness, and regret are as inherent in evil as cruelty and selfishness, and he painted a dimension of evil that hitherto had been neglected: the poignant sadness and isolation of the sinner. Satan was a metaphor of the longing of creation and humanity to be reintegrated into that loving spirit of life from which they had exiled themselves by their own foolishness and selfishness.

Hugo had an optimistic faith that reintegration would occur. A passionate universalist, he believed that the spirit of light is infinite in its mercy and would eventually restore all its lost creatures to the union of love. Until that happy moment, evil would remain a stark reality. "Satan is gluttony; he is a pig that devours thought; he is drunkenness, the dark depths of the drained cup; he is pride lacking knees on which to kneel; egoism, rejoicing in the blood in which his hands are soaked; he is the belly, the hideous cave wherein rage all the monsters that dwell in us."[28]

In his preface to *Cromwell* (1827), a historical drama in verse, Hugo declared the grotesque—in which he included the Devil—a necessary element in modern literature; his *Odes et ballades* (1826) portrayed the demonic in folkloric and medieval style. In his *Pitié suprême* (1879), he demanded the abolition of hell and the merciful pardon of all creatures. In "Les mages" (in *Contemplations*, 1856), he saw evil as the opposite of good: "Humans call it barbarism and crime, the sky calls it night, and God calls it Satan" (ll. 578–580). He could also see the Devil as Mephistopheles—mocking, ironic, supercilious, and world-weary in the mode favored by the French:

The fellow had troubled eyes,
And on his furrowed forehead
The distortion of two horns
Were quite visible.
His forked foot was bursting his stockings.
Enjoying his leave from hell, he breathed the fresh air;
Though his teeth were not false
His glances were not true.
He came to earth poised for prey.
In his hands with their iron talons
He clutched a hunting permit
Signed by God and countersigned by Lucifer.
He was that worthy Devil Beelzebub.
I recognized him right away:
His undisguisable grimace
Gave him the air of a wicked deity.[29]

The deepest portrait of Satan since Milton is in Hugo's unfinished trilogy of long narrative poems: *La légende des siècles* (in which God and Eblis, the Devil, make a wager on their respective creative powers), *Dieu*, and *La fin de Satan*.[30] The plan of the whole was to portray the destruction of evil by Liberty, opening humanity to light, freedom, and love. In *Dieu*, published posthumously (1891) in extended fragments, Hugo speaks of the Devil as the shadow of God, having no real or even possible existence. "God," he said, "has no Devil hidden in the folds of his robe." In *La fin de Satan*, begun in 1854 but also published posthumously (1886), the Devil is a vivid and convincing personality; he has truly sinned, truly distorted himself and the world through his blindness and selfishness, yet the pain and suffering of his own alienation render him sympathetic. He represents the lack of equilibrium, peace, and balance in the cosmos and the alienation of humanity from its proper repose in love and liberty. Like Satan, we are so wrapped up in our interior world that we cannot see the reality around us; we isolate ourselves from it, though it speaks to us in every tree, bird, and human voice. Miserable as we are, the spirit of love nonetheless draws us toward it, and in the end all will be saved. How could it be otherwise? The spirit of the world is infinitely loving and merciful, desiring all to return to him; against that love who could prevail forever? Further, evil is nothing in itself; it can exist temporarily as privation, but the end of time will refine out such imperfections; the opposites will be reconciled, and the cosmos will be reintegrated in liberty and love.

The poem begins with the fall of Satan. As he falls, his angelic nature is transformed: "Suddenly he sees himself growing bat wings; he sees himself becoming a monster; as the angel in him died, the rebel felt a pang of regret." His prideful envy of God turns into the more bitter envy of regret: "God shall have the blue heavens, but I a dark and empty sky." A fearful voice retorts, "Accursed one, around you the stars shall all fade away." He falls, year after year, for millennia, and as he falls, the stars gradually disappear, leaving the sky darker, emptier, more silent, until only three faint points of light remain—then only one. On this last, dimming star he concentrates all the efforts of his depleted being.

> Toward the star trembling pale on the horizon
> He pressed, leaping from one dark foothold to another....
> He ran, he flew, he cried out: Golden star!
> Brother! Wait for me! I am coming! Do not die yet!
> Do not leave me alone....
> The star was now only a spark....
> The spark
> Was now only a red point in the depths of the dark gulf....
> Hoping to make the star glow more brightly,
> He set himself to blowing on it as one would on coals.
> And anguish flared his fierce nostrils.
> He flew toward it for ten thousand years. Ten thousand years,
> Stretching out his pale neck and his mad fingers,
> He flew without finding a single place of rest.
> From time to time the star seemed to darken and die,
> And the horror of the tomb made the dark angel tremble.
> As he approached the star,
> Satan, like a swimmer making a supreme effort,
> Stretched his bald and taloned wings forward; a wan specter;
> Gasping, broken, exhausted, smoking with sweat,
> He collapsed at the edge of the steep bank of darkness....
> The star was almost gone. The dark angel was so weary
> That no voice, no breath was left to him.
> And the star was dying beneath his anguished stare ...
> And the star went out.[31]

The struggle between Satan and God occupies three sections: "The Sword" (*Le glaive*), dealing with the Old Testament period: "The Gibbet" (*Le gibet*), representing the New Testament; and "The Prison" (*La prison*), representing the modern world. In the Old Testament, Satan struggles to negate or at least minimize God's influence upon humanity. God succeeds in purifying humanity only temporarily and only by destroying the entire world in the flood—a strange manifestation (Hugo observed) of divine love. A feather falls from the wing of the ruined angel, and that feather takes the form of a beautiful angel (like Vigny's Eloa), whose name is Liberty. Thus Satan's evil rebellion contains within it the angelic sign of future return to liberty and love.

In modern times, God allows Liberty to descend to the pit and visit Satan. God also gives her permission to go to the earth and free humanity, but she must have the permission of Satan as well. At first, still brooding selfishly on his own wrongs, he refuses to grant it, but moved by her pleas at last, he grudgingly pronounces the necessary word: Go! Liberty encourages humanity to rebel against evil and to destroy the prison—symbolized by the Bastille—that keeps us from our freedom. The Revolution, then, fulfills the mission of the angel of Liberty under the permission of both God and Devil. The work of reconciliation begins.

Satan feels the pain of knowing that the entire cosmos rejects him:

Throughout the universe I hear the words: Go away!
Even the pig sneers to the dungheap: "I despise Satan."
I feel the night thinking that I dishonor her....
Once, that pure white light, the dawn,
Was I. I! I was the splendid-browed archangel....
But I was envious. There was
My crime. The word was spoken; the divine lips
Pronounced me evil! And God spat me out into the pit.
Ah, I love him! That is the horror, that is the flame!
What will become of me, abyss? I love God!
Hell is his eternal absence,
Hell is to love, to cry, "Alas, where is my light,
Where is my life and my illumination?
[When first I fell, I boasted:]
This God, world's heart, this bright Father
Whom angel, star, man and beast bear within,
This center round which his flock of creature nestles,
This being, source of life, alone true, alone necessary,
I can do without him, I the punished giant....
Yet I love him! ...
I know the truth! God is no spirit, but a heart.
God, loving center of the world, connects with his divine fibers
The filaments and roots of all living things.
[God loves every creature]

But Satan, forever rejected, sad, condemned.
God leaves me out; he stops with me; I am his boundary.
God would be infinite if I did not exist....
A hundred hundred times I repeat my vow,
I love! God tortures me, yet my only blasphemy,
My only frenzy, my only cry, is that I love!
I love enough to make the sky tremble! But in vain!

Now God responds in what Hugo planned as the denouement of the poem.
Satan cries out: "Love hates me!" But God replies:

No, I do not hate you! ...
O Satan, you need only say, I shall live!
Come; your prison will be pulled down and hell abolished!
Come, the angel Liberty is your daughter and mine:
This sublime parentage unites us.
The archangel is reborn and the demon dies;
I efface the baleful darkness, and none of it is left.
Satan is dead; be born again, heavenly Lucifer!
Come, rise up from the shadows with dawn on your brow.[32]

This poignant portrait of the Devil expresses a poetic moral view: our selfishness and stupidity alienate us from the reality of the cosmos, which is love, but love is unlimited, patient, merciful. It waits until we understand that selfishness, anger, and pride are nothing in themselves, nothing but a blind refusal to see, nothing but negation of reality. Once we open our eyes a chink, love's illumination floods in, and with horror and shame we see that we have been standing, alone, staring down into our own darkness. But the first glimmer of love in our dim eyes brings an immediate response. When we are ready, love will fill our darkness to bursting, until there is nothing left but light.

The Romantic reversal of symbols sometimes went to extremes.[33] The abbé Alphonse Louis Constant (1810–1875), who began by believing in the Romantic goal of integrating God and Satan, was led by George Sand to believe that Satan lay unjustly condemned under the curse of an arbitrary God. Plunging into the occult, Constant changed his name to Eliphas Lévi and wrote a number of books portraying Satan as a positive spiritual force. The French Satan was often political, and Lévi's was no exception, though his development was the opposite of Hugo's: in the 1840s, Lévi's Satan was the symbol of revolution and liberty, but after Lévi came to admire Napoleon III, Satan became the hieratic support of law and order.[34] The occult, positive interpretation of Satan laid the foundation for the Satanism of the end of the century, an occasionally serious if tiny movement attracting the naive and foolish as well as literary poseurs.

Apart from the solemnity of Hugo and the pompous Satanism of Lévi, irony, parody, and whimsy were the dominant treatments of the Devil throughout the nineteenth century. The greatest master of irony was Théophile Gautier (1811–1872), who wrote a comic version of *Faust* called *Albertus* (1832) and a satire on Hugo and Vigny, *Une larme du diable*, "A Tear of the Devil" (1839). In Gautier's work the prince of darkness appears as a witty dandy, elegant and soigné, masking his malevolence behind his refined appearance.[35]

Gautier's short story "Onuphrius" (1832) shows his ironic Devil most clearly. Onuphrius, a young dandy poet and painter obsessed by medievalism and the marvelous, begins to see the hand of the Devil in everything; finally the Devil really does appear, smearing his paints and poems, ruining his strategy at checkers, and spoiling his love affair. At a literary soirée where Onuphrius is to read his verse, the Devil sits behind him, catches all his words in a little net, and transforms them into pompous and ridiculous phrases. Gautier's description of the Devil is so perfect a picture of the ironic Mephistopheles that it has become a stock figure in art, opera, literature, and cartoons: a young, handsome man with regular, sardonic features; a red imperial and mustache; green eyes; thin, pale, ironic lips; and a knowing look. The perfect dandy, he wears a black coat, red waistcoat, white gloves, and golden spectacles; on one long, delicate finger he sports a large ruby.[36] He instills not fear or hatred but ironic laughter. He is, in effect, cynical, valueless modern man looking at himself in a mirror.

In portraying Satan as a dandy, Gautier and his imitators, themselves dandies, ironically linked themselves to the Devil, and it is a deliberate coincidence that the favorite victims of Gautier's Evil One were poets and painters, artists like the author himself. The dandy was esthetic and elegant, disdaining convention, dressing and speaking so as to draw attention to himself and to shock the philistines, using exotic and bizarre words and images, spurning morality in favor of the pursuit of the delicate, arrogantly sensitive, self-absorbed, affecting the air of living on a higher plane of being, witty and charming rather than truthful or sincere. Many levels of irony exist in a story such as "Onuphrius." The poet mocks the traditional Devil, whose existence he assumes is absurd. He also ironically argues that belief in the Devil is as reasonable as belief in God: "The existence of the Devil is proved by the most respectable authors, exactly as is that of God; it is even an article of faith."[37]

On another level, Gautier satirizes himself and his fellow artists in the gullible, emotional, naive Onuphrius, so easily frightened and made such a fool of by the insolent dandy demon. And the dandy demon is also an ironic portrait of the other side of the contemporary artist. All these clever ironies lie beneath an overt satire of the contemporary taste for the magical and the miraculous. The story is a glittering mockery of everything it touches: God, Devil, cosmos, humanity, art, and the artist himself.

By midcentury, a number of attitudes were fixed in the artistic imagination: the moral ambiguity of both Devil and God; their possible integration; psychological empathy for Satan as representing the human mind lost in ignorance and selfishness yet yearning for the good; the use of Satan as an ironically distant voice with which to satirize the human condition. With the newer poets, Romanticism began to shade off in two directions: naturalism, which spurned the supernatural and the internal in favor of realistic descriptions of everyday life; and Decadence, which combined some elements of dandyism with exploration of the depths of human corruption, especially sexual depravity.

As early as 1828, long before the emergence of the Decadents, a group devoted to the occult and macabre began to meet at Victor Hugo's house to read works featuring skeletons, daggers, fiends, graveyards, corpses, ghosts, incantations, pacts, and demons. Beginning in February of 1846 another circle of young poets, dedicated to shocking the philistines, collaborated in a session celebrating the seven cardinal sins and dedicated their work to Satan in words that might better have been left unspoken, even for dramatic effect:

To thee, Satan, fair fallen angel,
To whom fell the perilous honor
To struggle against an unjust rule,
I offer myself wholly and forever,
My mind, my senses, my heart, my love,
And my dark verses in their corrupted beauty.[38]

Satan, a theatrical prop for the dandies, was a serious symbol for the anarchist Pierre Joseph Proudhon (1809–1865). "Come, Satan," he prayed, "you who have been defamed by priests and kings, that I may kiss you and hold you against my breast."[39] Such ideas, which became fashionable with Baudelaire and his associates, have led some modern critics to speak of the Satanism of the nineteenth century. A few real Satanists certainly existed, but the term needs to be more carefully delineated.

The poseurs who feigned Satanism for esthetic effect cannot be considered real Satanists; nor can those such as Proudhon, who used a Satan in whom they did not personally believe as a symbol of political or social rebellion. The tendency of some nineteenth-century Christians to term Satanists those who denied the existence of both God and Satan is even less logical. The few eccentrics who took the view that only Satan exists and not God, or that both exist but that Satan is good and God evil, are not real Satanists, either, for they were merely reversing terms emptily. If one calls Satan the good, loving, merciful creator of the cosmos, one is simply applying an unconventional name to God.

The term Satanist is properly applied only to the tiny number who believe that Satan is a personal principle to true evil, selfishness, and suffering, and who worship him as such. It is not helpful to apply the term to Baudelaire and his colleagues, for true Satanism was extremely limited and had little cultural influence.

Charles Baudelaire (1821–1867), an important figure in the transition from Romanticism to naturalism and decadence, renounced the church as a young man. Skeptical by nature, he extended his doubts to scientism as well as religion; he regarded the facile material progressivism of his day as pathetically absurd, and atheism seemed to him incapable of dealing with alienation and evil, the deepest realities of human existence. Like Hugo and the Romantics, Baudelaire was an esthete; he had no systematic theology or philosophy, though he enjoyed speculation more than most of the Romantics and was intensely concerned with moral issues. In later life he considered himself a Catholic, and though he was never close to orthodoxy, his work was permeated with Catholicism and his preoccupation with sin as intense as that of a Jansenist.

Baudelaire's concern with evil in no way made him its advocate. He detested hypocrisy, stinginess, and cruelty; he felt it as a grievance that God had not filled up the world with beauty, love, and justice. He honestly acknowledged that evil is attractive as well as destructive: "In each person two tendencies exist at every moment, one toward God and the other toward Satan. Spirituality, the call to God, is a desire to mount higher; animality, the call to Satan, takes joy in falling lower."[40] Evil destroys by drawing us down into blind selfishness, isolation, and alienation, but this darkness has its attractions, which everyone feels and only hypocrites deny. Baudelaire was pitiless in his determination to remove the blindfold of hypocrisy from his own eyes and from those of others. Observing that George Sand denied the existence of the Devil, he caustically observed that it was to her personal interest that the Devil and hell should not exist.[41] Baudelaire well understood the power of sensual pleasures, particularly over the young, but Satan's most powerful weapon was *ennui* (the esthetic equivalent of theological *acedia* and of materialist boredom), a sense of lassitude in the face of the utter futility of life.

Baudelaire felt the pull of the positive Satan, who appears in his verse as the Romantic champion of liberty as well as the incarnation of hypocrisy, and the poet perceived in the rebel angel the most perfect type of masculine beauty. But more often, Baudelaire took Satan as the symbol of human evil and perhaps even as a personal entity. In a letter to Flaubert, he wrote, "I have always been obsessed by the impossibility of accounting for certain sudden human actions or thoughts without the hypothesis of an evil external force."[42] Like all Christian writers with intense introspective powers, Baudelaire was well aware of the sudden and unannounced irruption into the mind of intensely destructive images, desires, and feelings, which can be explained only by reference to a power beyond the conscious mind—whether it comes from outside, as in traditional Christianity, or from the unconscious, as in depth psychology. Baudelaire was skeptical of the skeptics. "My dear brothers," he wrote, "never forget, when you hear the progress of the Enlightenment praised, that the Devil's cleverest ploy is to persuade you that he doesn't exist."[43]

Baudelaire's masterpiece was his collection *Les Fleurs du Mal* ("The Flowers of Evil"), to which should be added his prose poems entitled *Le Spleen de Paris*.[44] In both collections, the struggle between good and evil, sensuality and spirituality, *spleen* and *idéal*, was central. Though the censors and some of Baudelaire's own followers seem to have mistakenly read his intent as destructive, his message seems clear from the very outset of the *Fleurs*, which commences with a famous address "To the Reader":

> Stupidity, error, sin and stinginess
> Garrison our minds and enslave our bodies....
> On evil's pillow, Hermes Trismegistus
> Slowly rocks our enthralled minds,
> And the rich metal of our wills
> Is vaporized by this learned alchemist....
> It is the Devil who pulls the strings that move us:
> We find charm in the most disgusting things;
> Each day we take another step down into hell,
> Deadened to horror, through stinking shadows....
> Reader, you recognize this delicate monster,
> Hypocrite reader, my likeness, my brother![45]

Such words may be taken as a rejection of evil, as a pessimistic statement of its inherence in humanity, or as ironic acceptance of evil on the part of the poet and artist, who alone in society has the vision and honesty to recognize it within himself.

Baudelaire seems to have meant all three. His work contains examples of the reversal in which the Christian God becomes evil and Satan the center of a symbol cluster that includes art, the poet, humanity, beauty, sentiment, revulsion against injustice, and even Jesus, who defends such values against the tyrannical Father.[46] Toward the cruel Jehovah one can feel only revulsion, combined with sympathy for his great foe. "There is no fiber in my trembling body," the poet exclaimed, "that does not cry, 'Dear Beelzebub, I adore you!'"[47] The lines come from "The Possessed," a poem whose persona is either mad or inspired, possessed by a demon whose moral value is ambivalent. "Hymn to Beauty" (*Hymne à la beauté*) is also ambivalent: beauty may come from God or from Satan; to the poet it does not matter which, for beauty itself is the supreme esthetic ideal. That this beauty serves both kindness and crime is no surprise in a universe that is itself wholly ambivalent.

The poet's "Litanies to Satan" (*Les litanies de Satan*) have often been cited as a sign of his Satanism, a view that neglects the fact that they arise from a literary tradition and that they are to be read, like all of Baudelaire's poems, with an awareness of irony and on several levels. The Satan whom Baudelaire praises is on one level the traditional Christian Satan; on another, Jesus; on another, the ambivalence of the human heart; and on yet another, the artist and the terrible double-edged sword of creativity:

> Prince of the exile, you have been wronged,
> Defeated, you rise up ever stronger....
> You who, even to lepers and accursed outcasts
> Teach through love a longing for Paradise....
> You who know in what corners of envious nations
> God hoards his precious gems....
> You who teach us to console the frail and suffering
> By mixing saltpeter and sulfur....
> Glory and praise to you, lord Satan, in the highest,
> Where once you reigned, and in the depths
> Of hell, where you lie defeated and dreaming.
> Let my soul one day, in the shadow of the tree of knowledge,
> Rest next to you.

Baudelaire, who would die reconciled to the church, dedicated the *Fleurs* to that great mocker Théophile Gautier. He did not know quite how to take the demon that troubled him, but he realized that it would never leave him alone:

> The Devil is active at my side;
> He swims around me like the impalpable air;
> I swallow him and feel him burning my lungs,

Filling them with an eternal, guilty desire.
Sometimes, knowing my great love of art,
He takes the shape of a seductive woman,
And under the false pretenses of cafard
Accustoms my lips to the taste of forbidden potions.
He leads me far from the face of God,
Panting and broken with weariness, into the midst
Of the deep and deserted plains of ennui
And thrusts into my confused sight
Dirty clothing, open wounds,
And the bloody costume of Destruction.[48]

Paul Verlaine (1844–1896) read Baudelaire's *Fleurs* at the age of fourteen and became his most devoted disciple and a leader of the Decadent movement. Verlaine coined the name "accursed poets" (*poétes maudits*) for the group who imitated Baudelaire's Satanic symbolism without his serious concern for the problem of evil.[49]

Arthur Rimbaud (1854–1891) died a Catholic after having spent his early career attacking authority, including church, education, and parents. For Rimbaud, who burned out young and abandoned the artistic life, the Devil was the symbol of the dull authority that suppresses and crushes artistic freedom, the only true good. His collection of prose poems *Une saison en enfer* ("A Season in Hell") was dedicated to the Devil with the words, "Dear Satan ... you who love the absence of descriptive and didactic faculties in the poet, I dash off for you these few hideous leaves from the notebook of a damned soul."[50] Full of pretension, self-absorption, and despair, the poet sees himself as the battleground between the forces of God and Satan, sin and innocence, good and evil, past and present. The poet is at one and the same time intensely involved in the struggle and, like the Devil, coolly detached from it. Unlike Hugo, Rimbaud calls less for integration and transcendence of the conflicting sides of the personality than for simply accepting them and regressing with them to a preconscious state of the soul where good and evil are undifferentiated.

The most truly Satanic of the Decadents was Isidore Ducasse (1846–1870), who wrote under the name Lautréamont. He argued that we must renounce all evasions and face evil in its most intense and shocking forms; he then made the transition from facing evil to reveling in it. A follower of Sade, Lautréamont argued that creative cruelty was a mark of genius and of honesty; he took Baudelaire's contemptuous attack upon hypocrisy as an excuse to explore the most loathsome recesses of his own soul. Maldoror, the persona of his dark masterpiece *Les chants de Maldoror*, is a combination of Sade, Satan, and Ducasse himself; he contemplates or commits an endless series of perverted outrages.[51]

It is unclear whether Lautréamont was mad; he clearly did not practice, or seriously advocate practicing, everything that came to his mind. Yet the ironic dandy posing as a Satanist and mocking his own secret vices found himself excited by his fantasies, and the distance between ironic evil and true evil foreshortened and attenuated. Maldoror sees a child sitting on a park bench and immediately imagines a hog gnawing away her genitals and burrowing through her body. He dreams of torturing young boys and drinking their blood and tears. When he kisses a baby, he fantasizes about slashing its cheeks with a razor. Vampirism, necrophilia, blasphemy, bestiality, incest, bondage, pederasty, mutilation, murder, and cannibalism obsess him.

In *Maldoror* the poet intended to paint a true picture of the human soul free from all hypocrisy: "Maldoror was born evil. He admitted the truth and said that he was cruel" (1.3). But Lautréamont, reacting against the bland Enlightenment-Romantic assumption that human nature was essentially good, plunged to the other untenable extreme. Just as the belief that humans are good raises the question where evil comes from, Lautréamont's dark universe leaves the presence of good unexplained. To a degree he meant Maldoror as an evil joke, a pose pointing the way to surrealism and dadaism. It is true that Maldoror's excesses are so bizarre as to be ridiculous as well as horrible, yet the author seems to have opened himself up to dark forces beyond his conscious control. Maldoror begins by boasting that he causes his "genius" to "paint the delights of cruelty" (1.4) and ends by killing an angel who has been sent to save him, thus symbolizing his rejection of redemption (5.8).

In America the tendency was even stronger than in Europe to detach serious studies of evil from works dealing with the Devil and to relegate the latter to tales of whimsy or horror. Neither Nathaniel Hawthorne (1804–1864) nor Herman Melville (1819–1891), both of whom made the study of human evil their central concern, had much use for the Devil even as symbol. Hawthorne's only serious use of Satan is in his story "Young Goodman Brown." The Devil appears when Brown yields to despair. "My faith is gone," Brown exclaims. "There is no good on earth; and sin is but a name. Come, devil; for to thee is this world given." Satan appears, takes him to a witches' sabbat in his fantasy, and persuades him of the Calvinistic (and, as Hawthorne sees it, Satanic) view that human nature is essentially corrupt. For Hawthorne, Brown is doomed because he despairs of humanity and fails to trust in God's goodness.[52] Melville's Moby Dick is one of the most polysymbolic figures in literature, but one of the symbols is demonic. Moby Dick is determined to destroy humanity body and soul; when at the end he bears down upon the *Pequod* to annihilate it, he does so with "retribution, swift vengeance, eternal malice."[53] In Melville's *The Confidence Man* (1857), the Devil appears as a cosmic trickster on a Mississippi steamer, the *Fidèle*, which begins its voyage on All Fools' Day. It is a ship of fools blinded by dreams of naive greed, ready to betray one another for profit, and all ultimately tricked by the Confidence Man, the eternal Cheater, the shapeshifter who appears in a variety of personalities and forms. It is the story of simple Christlike love overwhelmed and effaced by Satanic confusion and cynicism, symbolized by the motto that one of the characters tacks up in his shop: "No Trust." Melville's pessimism would be taken further by Mark Twain, as Hawthorne's deep probing of secret evil would be taken further by Dostoevsky, but Twain and Dostoevsky represent a dark view more attuned to the modern than to the Romantic era.

The horror story, an American adaptation from the Gothic novel or *roman noir*, had its first great expression in Edgar Allan Poe (1809–1849).[54] Like the Gothic writers, Poe wrote to entertain and to thrill, not to investigate evil seriously, though he was well aware of its power. It is indicative of the Devil's decline that when Poe wrote of real evil, as in "The Pit and the Pendulum," "The Cask of Amontillado," and "The Facts in the Case of Monsieur Valdemar," the Devil plays little part; he is a presence only in Poe's comic tales. In "The Devil in the Belfry," for example, the Devil causes the bells of a Dutch church to toll thirteen. In "Never Bet the Devil Your Head," a reprobate named Toby incautiously enters into a wager with Satan, and "a little lame old gentleman of venerable aspect" supernaturally causes an accident in which Toby loses his head; the doctors fail to replace it properly, and eventually Toby notices its loss and dies. This sort of whimsical tale, loosely derived from folklore, is typical of American Devil stories. The favorite theme among American (and other Anglophone) writers has been the bargain with the Devil, which affords opportunity for everything from broad humor through satire to wit. It also permits virtuosity in devising new ways for the protagonist to outwit the Devil or to be outwitted by him.[55]

The development of music in the nineteenth century produced a change that some writers have associated with the demonic. The idealist view is that some music is more inherently harmonious with the cosmos than other music—that is, it reflects divine or cosmic order more closely. In this view, Bach or Mozart, for example, wrote "truer" or "better" music than Chopin or Stravinsky. Harmonious composers might introduce discords in order to make a musical point, sometimes explicitly to portray evil itself, but disharmonious music is less good, less true, less real—perhaps even demonic. The discordant reflects the chaotic, the disruption of the cosmos and of God's orderly plan.

Beginning with Beethoven, however (or even Mozart in his late quartets), composers deliberately introduced disharmony, mainly to give both the music and their emotions freer rein. Many composers of the Romantic period wanted their music to integrate all human experience—emotional as well as rational, evil as well as good—and used disharmony for this purpose. A few, such as Paganini, and François Boieldieu in his "Valse Infernale," ironically claimed to have been inspired by the Devil. Modern composers such as Stravinsky have employed disharmony to discredit and supplant the idealist view. But whether one can call some kinds of music better or more real than others depends upon whether one believes that music can reflect the cosmos and whether one ultimately believes that the universe is cosmos or chaos.[56]

The literary imagination dominated the concept of the Devil in the nineteenth century, but by midcentury literary and artistic interest in the Devil had began to diminish. He had been milked dry of much of his horror and even of his comedy. The growth of realism and naturalism, with their shift away from the metaphysical, and the gradual but continual rise of positivism returned the literary focus on evil to the human personality. Still, the inconsistencies and vagaries of the Romantic uses of the symbol had tended to dissipate and blur its meaning, and with secularism and materialism slowly replacing Christianity as the dominant world view of Western society, belief in a personal Satan dwindled rapidly even among professed Christians. At the same time, the decline of Romanticism and of the literary Devil eventually led to the return of the symbol to the theologians. When the figure of Satan eventually regained some of its power in the twentieth century, it was in the traditional rather than in the Romantic mode. Meanwhile, powerful statements about evil would be made by Nietzsche, Twain, and above all Dostoevsky, who understood evil better than anyone in his century and whose dark vision became a model for the modern age.

NOTES

1. The Devil took on a variety of forms in art as well, often in satires combining skepticism of the traditional Devil with insight into human evil. The most notable is the long series of paintings by Goya (Francisco Goya y Lucientes, 1746–1828). See also the *Walpurgisnacht* of Ferdinand Delacroix (1798–1863), William Blake's numerous illustrations of the subject, and the famous engravings illustrating Dante and Milton by Gustave Doré (1832–1883).

2. The First Vatican Council (1869–1870), in renewing the decree *Firmiter* of the Fourth Lateran Council (see LUCIFER, pp. 189–190), did not include the specific affirmation of the Devil's existence, though no contradiction of *Firmiter* on this point was implied. See First Vatican, *Constitutio dogmatica* no. 1: *De fide, caput primum, De Deo rerum*

omnium creatore. For the First Vatican, see J. Mansi, *Sacrorum conciliorum nova et amplissima collectio*, vols. 49–53 (Graz, 1961).

3. Quoted in G. Rowell, *Hell and the Victorians: A Study of the Nineteenth-Century Theological Controversies concerning Eternal Punishment and the Future Life* (Oxford, 1974), p. 212.

4. Rowell, pp. 217–218.

5. E. Burke, *A Philosophical Enquiry of the Origin of the Sublime and the Beautiful* (1757), ed. J.T. Boulton (New York, 1958). The term "sublime" ceased to be fashionable by 1800.

6. M. Milner, *Le Diable dans la littérature française*, 2 vols. (Paris, 1960), vol. 1, p. 520, citing *Le Figaro* of May 3, 1834.

7. Other influential Gothic novels included Horace Walpole, *The Castle of Otranto* (1764); Ann Radcliffe, *The Mysteries of Udolpho* (1794); Walter Scott, *The Black Dwarf* (1816); Charles Robert Maturin, *Melmoth the Wanderer* (1820); Matthew G. Lewis, *The Isle of Devils* (1827). See also C.O. Parsons, *Witchcraft and Demonology in Scott's Fiction* (Edinburgh, 1964); and for other Romantic works dealing with the Devil, see the bibliographies in Milner and in H. Vatter, *The Devil in English Literature* (Bern, 1978).

8. W. Blake, *Jerusalem*, Pt. 52. A recent edition of Blake's works is G. Keynes, ed., *The Complete Writings of William Blake* (London, 1966).

9. Quoted in T.A. Birrell, "The Figure of Satan in Milton and Blake," in Bruno de Jésus-Marie, ed., *Satan* (New York, 1952), p. 391. See also R.D. Stock, *The Holy and the Daemonic from Sir Thomas Browne to William Blake* (Princeton, 1982).

10. A.C. Swinburne, "Choruses from Atalanta in Calydon."

11. *Jerusalem*, pt. 52.

12. W. Blake, *The Marriage of Heaven and Hell*, "The Voice of the Devil."

13. *Marriage of Heaven and Hell*, conclusion.

14. *Marriage of Heaven and Hell*, "Proverbs of Hell."

15. Quoted in K. Raine, *William Blake* (London, 1970), p. 86. See also K. Raine, *Blake and Tradition*, 2 vols. (Princeton, 1968), vol. 2, pp. 214–238, for the figure of Satan in Blake. Blake was as creative in the pictorial arts as in poetry. Among his artistic works dealing with Satan are *The Marriage of Heaven and Hell* (1790); *The Good and Evil Angels* (1795); *Satan Watching Adam and Eve* (1808); *Satan Tempting Christ to Turn the Stone into Bread* (1816–1818); *Christian and Apollyon* (from Bunyan; 1824); *Michael Binding Satan* (c. 1805); *Satan Killing the Children of Job* (1825); *Satan Smiting Job with Sore Boils* (c. 1826–1827); *Satan, Sin, and Death* (c. 1808).

16. *Complete Writings*, p. 213.

17. Byron, *Cain*, in *The Poetical Works of Lord Byron* (London, 1960), 3.88–91; 1.144–147; 2.490, 515–517.

18. In *The Deformed Transformed* (1824), an unfinished drama modeled on *Faust*, the Devil is "a stranger" later named "Caesar"; in *The Vision of Judgment* (1822), Satan appears as a haughty dignitary; in the dramatic poem *Manfred* (1817), the hero Satanically (in the good sense) defies the evil lord Arimanes (Ahriman), who is Satanic in the evil, tyrannical sense.

19. God is always invisible: *Cain* 1.500–505.

20. *Shelley, Defence of Poetry* (Indianapolis, 1965), p. 60.

21. Mary Shelley, *Frankenstein* (London, 1818), p. 101.

22. A factual antidote to this pessimism is the life of the historical Elephant Man, who was treated with equal horror and contempt yet maintained a generous heart.

23. Chateaubriand, *Les martyrs*, ed. V. Giraud (Paris, n.d.), p. 141: "Le jour de gloire est arrivé."

24. One writer who made much of demonology was Collin de Plancy (1794–1881) in books such as *Le diable peint par lui-même* (1819), *Démonomanie* (1820), and *Dictionnaire infernale* (1818); see *Dictionnaire infernale: Edition princeps intégrale* (Verviers, 1973). Charles Nodier (1780–1844) used the Devil with ghouls and ghosts to enhance his tales of Gothic horror; Nodier and other French writers of the *roman noir* were following the lead of Jacques Cazotte (1719–1772), whose *Le diable amoureux* (1772), a demonic horror story, influenced both French and German writers. Irony and the excitement of horror surround the figure of Satan in the works of E.T.A. Hoffmann (1776–1822), Jean Paul Richter (1763–1825), and Christian Friedrich Hebbel (1813–1863); see Hoffmann, *Die Elixiere des Teufels*, 2 vols. (Berlin, 1815–1816), and Richter, *Auswahl aus den Teufels Papieren* (n.p., 1789). Jules Michelet (1798–1874) transferred these literary attitudes to pseudohistory in his book on the witch craze, *La sorcière* (1862). Eugène Sue (1804–1875) and Balzac preferred to satirize the evil that exists within humanity. In addition to his "human comedy," Balzac also produced a *Comédie du diable* (1830), in which he uses a banquet of demons to satirize human folly. See also J.P. Houston, *The Demonic Imagination: Style and Theme in French Romantic Poetry* (Baton Rouge, La., 1969).

25. Vigny, *Eloa*, published in his *Poèmes antiques et modernes* (Paris, 1826).

26. Portions were posthumously preserved in *Vigny's journal d'un poète* (Paris, 1867).

27. *Postscriptum de ma vie* (Paris, 1901), August 25, 1844. On Hugo, see C. Villiers, *L'univers métaphysique de Victor Hugo* (Paris, 1970).

28. *Postscriptum*, 1852–1854.

29. "Les bonnes intentions de Rosa" in "L'éternel petit roman," from Hugo's *Chansons des rues et des bois* (Paris, 1865).

30. V. Hugo, *Poésie*, 3 vols., ed. B. Leuilliot (Paris, 1972). *La fin de Satan* appears in vol. 3, pp. 216–301. Since Hugo never finished the poem, its text and organization are unsettled; thus the following references are to general sections rather than specific line numbers.

31. Section "Nox facta est."

32. These passages are from sections "Hors de la terre" III and IV, concluding: "L'archange ressuscite et le démon finit; / Et j'efface la nuit sinistre, et rien n'en reste. / Satan est mort; renais ô Lucifer céleste! / Viens, monte hors de l'ombre avec l'aurore au front."

33. Gérard de Nerval (the pen name of Gérard Labrunie, 1808–1855) used a phrase in his revision of *Le diable amoureux* that Baudelaire would later make his own: "Mon cher Belzébuth, je t'adore." On Nerval, see R.E. Jones, *Gérard de Nerval* (New York, 1974).

34. Milner, vol. 2, pp. 246–256.

35. *Albertus ou l'âme et le péché* (Paris, 1832), in *Poésies complètes de Théophile Gautier* (Paris, 1970), vol. 1, pp. 127–188. Strophe 114: "Ce n'était pas un diable / Empoisonnant le soufre et d'aspect effroyable, / Un diable rococo.—C'était un élégant / Portant l'impériale et la fine moustache, / Faisant sonner sa botte et siffler sa cravache." *Une larme du diable* appears in Gautier's *Oeuvres complètes*, vol. 8: *Théâtre, mystère, comédies et ballets* (Geneva, 1978), pp. 1–52. Also note his "Deux acteurs pour un rôle," in Gautier, *Contes fantastiques* (Paris, 1974), pp. 165–178, in which an actor playing the Devil is replaced on stage by the Devil himself.

36. "Onuphrius," in *Contes fantastiques*, pp. 23–62; the description appears on pp. 53–56.

37. Onuphrius, p. 34.

38. Quoted in Milner, vol. 2, p. 243. "A toi, Satan, bel archange déchu, / A qui le périlleux honneur échut / De guerroyer contre un pouvoir injuste, / Je m'offre tout entier

et sans retour, / Mon esprit, mes sens, mon coeur, mon amour, / Et mes sombres vers dans leur beauté fruste."

39. Quoted in Milner, vol. 2, p. 260, from Proudhon's *De la justice dans la révolution et dans l'église* (1858). In Italy, Giacomo Leopardi (1798–1837) wrote a Satanic revolutionary hymn, "Ad Arimane," in 1833; see his *Opere* (Milan, 1937), vol. 2, pp. 391–396. Giosuè Carducci (1835–1907) composed a liturgy to Satan, "Inno a Satana," in *Inni civili* (1869), *Edizione nazionale delle opere di Giosuè Carducci*, 16 vols. (Bologna, 1935–1957) vol. 2, pp. 377–385. See also Carducci, *Satana e polemiche satanistiche* (Bologna, 1879).

40. Baudelaire, *Journaux intimes*, ed. J. Crépet and G. Blin (Paris, 1949) no. 11. See also G. Bataille, *Literature and Evil* (London, 1973).

41. *Journaux intimes*, no. 17.

42. Letter of June 26, 1860, in Baudelaire, *Correspondance*, 6 vols., ed. J. Crépet (Paris, 1947–1953), vol. 3, p. 125.

43. "Le joueur généreux," in *Le Spleen de Paris*, ed. Y. Florenne (Paris, 1972): "Mes chers frères, n'oubliez jamais, quand vous entendrez vanter le progrès des lumières, que la plus belle ruse du diable est de vous persuader qu'il n'existe pas."

44. The first edition of the *Fleurs* appeared in 1857; a second in 1861; a third posthumously in 1868. Owing to deletions by the censor and to additions, the three differ significantly. See the critical edition by J. Crépet and G. Blin (Paris, 1942), and *Les fleurs du mal: Texte de la deuxième édition*, cd. J. Crépet and G. Blin (Paris, 1968). *Le Spleen* first appeared in 1860.

45. "Tu le connais, lecteur, ce monstre délicat, / —Hypocrite lecteur—mon semblable—mon frère!"

46. *Fleurs*, "Le reniement de Saint Pierre": "What does God make of this flood of curses that daily rises toward his angels? Like a tyrant gorged with flesh and wine, he drifts off to sleep on the sound of horrible blasphemies.... Ah, Jesus, do you remember Gethsemane, where in your simplicity you knelt and prayed?"

47. *Fleurs*, "Le possédé"; "O mon cher Belzébuth, je t'adore" is the line from Nerval.

48. *Fleurs*, "La déstruction." Some of Baudelaire's contemporaries shared his serious concern with the Devil: for example, Jules Amédée Barbey d'Aurevilly (1808–1869), a Catholic dandy who held that Satan was an essential element in Christian theology. See Barbey's *Les Diaboliques* (Paris, 1874). Others were Leconte de Lisle (1818–1894), who wrote a poem entitled "Tristesse du diable," and Gustave Flaubert, author of *La Tentation de Saint Antoine* (Paris, 1968), esp. pp. 241–243.

49. See P. Verlaine, *Poèmes saturniens* (Paris, 1866); *Jadis et naguère* (Paris, 1884), which contains "Crimen amoris," a poem on the salvation of Satan; and *Les poétes maudits* (Paris, 1884).

50. Rimbaud, *Une saison en enfer*, in *Oeuvres de Jean-Arthur Rimbaud* (Paris, 1904), pp. 215–259.

51. Lautréamont, *Les chants de Maldoror* (Paris, 1868).

52. "Young Goodman Brown" appears, with other tales dealing with evil, in Hawthorne's *Mosses from an Old Manse* (1846). On Hawthorne, Poe, and Melville, see H. Levin, *The Power of Blackness* (New York, 1958).

53. H. Melville, *Moby-Dick; or, The Whale* (Berkeley, 1981; originally published 1851), esp. chs. 41, 51, 135. H.R. Trimpi, "Melville's Use of Demonology and Witchcraft in *Moby-Dick*," *Journal of the History of Ideas*, 30 (1969), 543–562, provides full demonstration of the diabolical theme.

54. See *The Complete Works of Edgar Allan Poe* (Boston, 1856). "The Devil in the Belfry" is in vol. 3, pp. 252–264; "Never Bet the Devil Your Head," vol. 4, pp. 342–356.

The most influential of Poe's followers was Howard Phillips Lovecraft (1890–1937). See also Washington Irving's "The Devil and Tom Walker" (1824).

55. Examples include I. Azimov, "The Brazen Locked Room," *Magazine of Fantasy and Science Fiction* (November 1956); M. Beerbohm, "Enoch Soames," in M. Beerbohm, *Seven Men* (New York, 1920); S. V. Benét, "The Devil and Daniel Webster," in *Selected Works of Stephen Vincent Benét* (New York, 1937); T. Cogswell, "Impact with the Devil," *Magazine of Fantasy and Science Fiction* (November 1956); M.A. DeFord, "Time Trammel," *Magazine of Fantasy and Science Fiction* (November 1956); H. Ellison, "The Beast That Shouted Love at the Heart of the World," in I. Azimov, ed., *The Hugo Winners* (New York, 1971); U. K. LeGuin, "The Ones Who Walk Away from Omelas," in LeGuin, *The Wind's Twelve Quarters* (New York, 1975); J. Masefield, "The Devil and the Old Man," in Masefield, *A Mainsail Haul* (London, 1941). A good collection is B. Davenport, ed., *Deals with the Devil* (New York, 1958).

56. For the Devil in music, see S. Leppe, "The Devil's Music: A Literary Study of Evil and Music," Ph.D. diss., University of California, Riverside, 1978; R. Hammerstein, *Diabolus in musica: Studien zur Ikonographie der Musik im Mittelalter* (Bern, 1974). The Devil appeared frequently in nineteenth-century and early twentieth-century music, especially in opera: Daniel Auber, *Fra Diavolo* (1830); Michael Balfe, *Satanella* (1858); Arthur Benjamin, *The Devil Take Her* (1932); Hector Berlioz, *La damnation de Faust* (1846); Arrigo Boito, *Mefistofele* (1868); Ferruccio Busoni, *Doktor Faust* (1920); Anton Dvorák, *The Devil and Kate* (1899); Charles Gounod, *Faust* (1859); Douglas Moore, *The Devil and Daniel Webster* (1938); Vincenzio Tommasini, *Le diable s'amuse* (ballet, 1950).

ELAINE PAGELS

The Social History of Satan:
From the Hebrew Bible to the Gospels

T he conflict between Jesus' followers and their fellow Jews is not, of
course, the first sectarian movement that divided the Jewish world, a world
whose early history we know primarily from the Hebrew Bible, a collection
of authoritative law, prophets, psalms, and other writings assembled
centuries before the four gospels and other Christian writings were brought
together in the New Testament. Who assembled this collection we do not
know, but we may infer from its contents that it was compiled to constitute
the religious history of the Jewish people, and so to create the basis for a
unified society.[1]

Excluded from the Hebrew Bible were writings of Jewish sectarians,
apparently because such authors tended to identify with one group of Jews
against another, rather than with Israel as a whole. Christians later came to
call the writings of such dissidents from the main group the *apocrypha*
(literally, "hidden things") and *pseudepigrapha* ("false writings").[2]

But the writings collected to form the Hebrew Bible encourage
identification with Israel itself. According to the foundation story recounted
in Genesis 12, Israel first received its identity through election, when "the
Lord" suddenly revealed himself to Abraham, ordering him to leave his
home country, his family, and his ancestral gods, and promising him, in
exchange for exclusive loyalty, a new national heritage, with a new identity:

From *The Origin of Satan*. © 1995 by Elaine Pagels.

"I will make you a great nation, and I will make your name great
... and whoever blesses you I will bless; and whoever curses you I
will curse." (Gen. 12:3)

So when God promises to make Abraham the father of a new, great, and
blessed nation, he simultaneously defines and constitutes its enemies as
inferior and potentially accursed.

From the beginning, then, Israelite tradition defines "us" in ethnic,
political, and religious terms as "the people of Israel," or "the people of
God," as against "them"—the (other) nations (in Hebrew, *ha goyim*), the alien
enemies of Israel, often characterized as inferior, morally depraved, even
potentially accursed. In Genesis 16:12, an angel predicts that Ishmael,
although he was Abraham's son, the progenitor of the Arab people, would be
a "wild ass of a man, with his hand against everyone, and everyone's hand
against him; and he shall live at odds with all his kin." The story implies that
his descendants, too, are hostile, no better than animals. Genesis 19:37–38
adds that the Moabite and Ammonite nations are descended from Lot's
daughters, which means that they are the illegitimate offspring of a drunken
and incestuous union. The people of Sodom, although they are Abraham's
allies, not his enemies, are said to be criminally depraved, "young and old,
down to the last man," collectively guilty of attempting to commit
homosexual rape against a party of angels, seen by the townspeople as
defenseless Hebrew travelers (Gen. 19:4). These accounts do not idealize
Abraham or his progeny—in fact, the biblical narrator twice tells how the
self-serving lies of Abraham and Isaac endangered their allies (Gen. 20:1–18;
26:6–10). Nevertheless, God ensures that everything turns out well for the
Israelites and badly for their enemies.

The second great foundation story is that of Moses and the Exodus,
which also confronts "us" (that is, "Israel") with "them" (that is, "the
nations") as Moses urges Pharaoh to let the Hebrews leave Egypt. Yet the
narrator insists that it was God himself who increasingly hardened Pharaoh's
heart, lest he relent and relieve the suffering of Moses and his own people—
and why? God, speaking through Moses, threatens Pharaoh with devastating
slaughter and concludes by declaring, "but against any of the Israelites, not a
dog shall growl—*so that you may know that the Lord makes a distinction between
the Egyptians and Israel*." (Exod. 11:7; my emphasis).

Many anthropologists have pointed out that the worldview of most
peoples consists essentially of two pairs of binary oppositions: human/not
human and we/they.[3] Apart from anthropology, we know from experience
how people dehumanize enemies, especially in wartime.

That Israel's traditions deprecate the nations, then, is no surprise.

What is surprising is that there are exceptions. Hebrew tradition sometimes reveals a sense of universalism where one might least expect it. Even God's election of Abraham and his progeny includes the promise of a blessing to extend through them to all people, for that famous passage concludes with the words, "in you all the families of the earth shall be blessed" (Gen. 12:3). Furthermore, when a stranger appears alone, the Israelites typically accord him protection, precisely because they identify with the solitary and defenseless stranger. Biblical law identifies with the solitary alien: "You shall not wrong or oppress a stranger; for you were strangers in the land of Egypt" (Exod. 22:21). One of the earliest creeds of Israel recalls that Abraham himself, obeying God's command, became a solitary alien: "A wandering Aramean was my father ..." (Deut. 26:5). Moses, too, was the quintessential alien, having been adopted as an infant by Pharaoh's daughter. Although a Hebrew, he was raised as an Egyptian; the family of his future in-laws, in fact, mistook him for an Egyptian when they first met him. He even named his first son Gershom ("a wanderer there"), saying, "I have been a wanderer in a foreign land" (Exod. 2:16–22).

Nevertheless, the Israelites are often aggressively hostile to the nations. The prophet Isaiah, writing in wartime, predicts that the Lord will drive the nations out "like locusts" before the Israelite armies (Isa. 40:22). This hostility to the alien enemy seems to have prevailed relatively unchallenged as long as Israel's empire was expanding and the Israelites were winning their wars against the nations. Psalms 18 and 41, attributed to King David, builder of Israel's greatest empire, declare, "God gave me vengeance and subdued the nations under me" (Ps. 18:47), and "By this I know that God is pleased with me—in that my enemy has not triumphed over me" (Ps. 41:11).

Yet at certain points in Israel's history, especially in times of crisis, war, and danger, a vociferous minority spoke out, not against the alien tribes and foreign armies ranged against Israel, but to blame Israel's misfortunes upon members of its own people. Such critics, sometimes accusing Israel as a whole, and sometimes accusing certain rulers, claimed that Israel's disobedience to God had brought down divine punishment.

The party that called for Israel's allegiance to "the Lord alone," including such prophets as Amos (c. 750 B.C.E.), Isaiah (c. 730 B.C.E.), and Jeremiah (c. 600 B.C.E.), indicted especially those Israelites who adopted foreign ways, particularly the worship of foreign gods.[4] Such prophets, along with their supporters, thought of Israel as a truly separate people, "holy to the Lord." The more radical prophets denounced those Israelites who tended toward assimilation as if they were as bad as the nations; only a remnant, they said, remained faithful to God.

Certain of these prophets, too, had called forth the monsters of

Canaanite mythology to symbolize Israel's enemies.[5] Later (sixth century) material now included in the first part of the book of the prophet Isaiah proclaims that "the Lord is coming *to punish the inhabitants of the earth*; and the earth will disclose the blood shed upon her, and will no more cover the slain" (Isa. 26:21; emphasis added). The same author goes on, apparently in parallel imagery, to warn that "in that day, the Lord with his great hand will *punish the Leviathan, the twisting serpent, and he will slay the dragon that is in the sea*" (Isa. 27:1; emphasis added). The author of the second part of Isaiah also celebrates God's triumph over traditional mythological figures—over Rahab, "the dragon," and "the sea"—as he proclaims God's imminent triumph over Israel's enemies. Thereby, as the biblical scholar Jon Levenson observes, "the enemies cease to be merely earthly powers ... and become, instead or in addition, cosmic forces of the utmost malignancy."[6]

Certain writers of the sixth century B.C.E. took a bold step further. They used mythological imagery to characterize their struggle against some of their fellow Israelites. But when Israelite writers excoriated their fellow Jews in mythological terms, the images they chose were usually not the animalistic or monstrous ones they regularly applied to their foreign enemies. Instead of Rahab, Leviathan, or "the dragon," most often they identified their Jewish enemies with an exalted, if treacherous, member of the divine court whom they called the *satan*. The *satan* is not an animal or monster but one of God's angels, a being of superior intelligence and status; apparently the Israelites saw their intimate enemies not as beasts and monsters but as *superhuman* beings whose superior qualities and insider status could make them more dangerous than the alien enemy.

In the Hebrew Bible, as in mainstream Judaism to this day, Satan never appears as Western Christendom has come to know him, as the leader of an "evil empire," an army of hostile spirits who make war on God and humankind alike.[7] As he first appears in the Hebrew Bible, Satan is not necessarily evil, much less opposed to God. On the contrary, he appears in the book of Numbers and in Job as one of God's obedient servants—a messenger, or angel, a word that translates the Hebrew term for messenger (*mal'ak*) into Greek (*angelos*). In Hebrew, the angels were often called "sons of God" (*bene 'elohim*), and were envisioned as the hierarchical ranks of a great army, or the staff of a royal court.

In biblical sources the Hebrew term the *satan* describes an adversarial role. It is not the name of a particular character.[8] Although Hebrew storytellers as early as the sixth century B.C.E. occasionally introduced a supernatural character whom they called the *satan*, what they meant was any one of the angels sent by God for the specific purpose of blocking or obstructing human activity. The root *śṭn* means "one who opposes, obstructs, or acts as adversary." (The Greek term *diabolos*, later translated "devil," literally means "one who throws something across one's path.")

The *satan*'s presence in a story could help account for unexpected obstacles or reversals of fortune. Hebrew storytellers often attribute misfortunes to human sin. Some, however, also invoke this supernatural character, the *satan*, who, by God's own order or permission, blocks or opposes human plans and desires. But this messenger is not necessarily malevolent. God sends him, like the angel of death, to perform a specific task, although one that human beings may not appreciate; as the literary scholar Neil Forsyth says of the *satan*, "If the path is bad, an obstruction is good."[9] Thus the *satan* may simply have been sent by the Lord to protect a person from worse harm. The story of Balaam in the biblical book of Numbers, for example, tells of a man who decided to go where God had ordered him not to go. Balaam saddled his ass and set off, "but God's anger was kindled because he went; and the angel of the Lord took his stand in the road as his *satan*" [*le-śāṭān-lō*]—that is, as his adversary, or his obstructor. This supernatural messenger remained invisible to Balaam, but the ass saw him and stopped in her tracks:

> And the ass saw the angel of the Lord standing in the road, with a drawn sword in his hand; and the ass turned aside out of the road, and went into the field; and Balaam struck the ass, to turn her onto the road. Then the angel of the Lord stood in a narrow path between the vineyards, with a wall on each side. And when the ass saw the angel of the Lord, she pushed against the wall, so he struck her again. (22:23–25)

The third time the ass saw the obstructing angel, she stopped and lay down under Balaam, "and Balaam's anger was kindled, and he struck the ass with his staff." Then, the story continues,

> the Lord opened the mouth of the ass, and she said to Balaam, "What have I done to you, that you have struck me three times?" And Balaam said to the ass, "Because you have made a fool of me. I wish I had a sword in my hand, for then I would kill you." And the ass said to Balaam, "Am I not your ass, that you have ridden all your life to this very day? Did I ever do such things to you?" And he said, "No." (22:28–30)

Then "the Lord opened the eyes of Balaam, and he saw the angel of the Lord standing in the way, with his drawn sword in his hand, and he bowed his head, and fell on his face." Then the *satan* rebukes Balaam, and speaks for his master, the Lord:

> "Why have you struck your ass three times? Behold, I came here to oppose you, because your way is evil in my eyes; and the ass saw me.... If she had not turned away from me, I would surely have killed you right then, and let her live." (22:31–33)

Chastened by this terrifying vision, Balaam agrees to do what God, speaking through his *satan*, commands.

The book of Job, too, describes the *satan* as a supernatural messenger, a member of God's royal court.[10] But while Balaam's *satan* protects him from harm, Job's *satan* takes a more adversarial role. Here the Lord himself admits that the *satan* incited him to act *against* Job (2:3). The story begins when the *satan* appears as an angel, a "son of God" (*ben 'elohim*), a term that, in Hebrew idiom, often means "one of the divine beings." Here this angel, the *satan*, comes with the rest of the heavenly host on the day appointed for them to "present themselves before the Lord." When the Lord asks whence he comes, the *satan* answers, "From roaming on the earth, and walking up and down on it." Here the storyteller plays on the similarity between the sound of the Hebrew *satan* and *shût*, the Hebrew word "to roam," suggesting that the *satan's* special role in the heavenly court is that of a kind of roving intelligence agent, like those whom many Jews of the time would have known—and detested—from the king of Persia's elaborate system of secret police and intelligence officers. Known as "the king's eye" or "the king's ear," these agents roamed the empire looking for signs of disloyalty among the people.[11]

God boasts to the *satan* about one of his most loyal subjects: "Have you considered my servant Job, that there is no one like him on earth, a blessed and upright man, who fears God and turns away from evil?" The *satan* then challenges the Lord to put Job to the test:

> "Does Job fear God for nothing? ... You have blessed the work of his hands, and his possessions have increased. But put forth your hand now, and touch all that he has, and he will curse you to your face." (1:9–11)

The Lord agrees to test Job, authorizing the *satan* to afflict Job with devastating loss, but defining precisely how far he may go: "Behold, all that belongs to him is in your power; only do not touch the man himself." Job withstands the first deadly onslaught, the sudden loss of his sons and daughters in a single accident, the slaughter of his cattle, sheep, and camels, and the loss of all his wealth and property. When the *satan* appears again among the sons of God on the appointed day, the Lord points out that "Job still holds fast to his integrity, although you incited me against him, to harm him without cause." Then the *satan* asks that he increase the pressure:

> "Skin for skin. All that a man has he will give for his life. But put forth your hand now, and touch his flesh and his bone, and he will curse you to your face." And the Lord said to the satan, "Behold, he is in your power; only spare his life." (2:4–6)

According to the folktale, Job withstands the test, the *satan* retreats, and "the Lord restored the fortunes of Job ... and he gave him twice as much as he had before" (42:10). Here the *satan* terrifies and harms a person but, like the angel of death, remains an angel, a member of the heavenly court, God's obedient servant.

Around the time Job was written (c. 550 B.C.E.), however, other biblical writers invoked the *satan* to account for division within Israel.[12] One court historian slips the *satan* into an account concerning the origin of census taking, which King David introduced into Israel c. 1000 B.C.E. for the purpose of instituting taxation. David's introduction of taxation aroused vehement and immediate opposition—opposition that began among the very army commanders ordered to carry it out. Joab, David's chief officer, objected, and warned the king that what he was proposing to do was evil. The other army commanders at first refused to obey, nearly precipitating a revolt; but finding the king adamant, the officers finally obeyed and "numbered the people."

Why had David committed what one chronicler who recalls the story regards as an evil, aggressive act "against Israel"? Unable to deny that the offending order came from the king himself, but intent on condemning David's action without condemning the king directly, the author of 1 Chronicles suggests that a supernatural adversary within the divine court had managed to infiltrate the royal house and lead the king himself into sin: "The *satan* stood up against Israel, and incited David to number the people" (1 Chron. 21:1). But although an angelic power incited David to commit this otherwise inexplicable act, the chronicler insists that the king was nevertheless personally responsible—and guilty. "God was displeased with this thing, and he smote Israel." Even after David abased himself and confessed his sin, the angry Lord punished him by sending an avenging angel to destroy seventy thousand Israelites with a plague; and the Lord was barely restrained from destroying the city of Jerusalem itself.

Here the *satan* is invoked to account for the division and destruction that King David's order aroused within Israel.[13] Not long before the chronicler wrote, the prophet Zechariah had depicted the *satan* inciting factions among the people. Zechariah's account reflects conflicts that arose within Israel after thousands of Jews—many of them influential and educated—whom the Babylonians had captured in war (c. 687 B.C.E.) and exiled to Babylon, returned to Palestine from exile. Cyrus, king of Persia, having recently conquered Babylon, not only allowed these Jewish exiles to go home but intended to make them his allies. Thus he offered them funds to reconstruct Jerusalem's defensive city walls, and to rebuild the great Temple, which the Babylonians had destroyed. Those returning were eager to reestablish the worship of "the Lord alone" in their land, and they naturally expected to reestablish themselves as rulers of their people.

They were not warmly welcomed by those whom they had left behind. Many of those who had remained saw the former exiles not only as agents of the Persian king but as determined to retrieve the power and land they had been forced to relinquish when they were deported. Many resented the returnees' plan to take charge of the priestly offices and to "purify" the Lord's worship.

As the biblical scholar Paul Hanson notes, the line that had once divided the Israelites from their enemies had separated them from foreigners. Now the line separated two groups *within Israel*:

> Now, according to the people who remained, their beloved land was controlled by the enemy, and although that enemy in fact comprised fellow Israelites, yet they regarded these brethren as essentially no different from Canaanites.[14]

The prophet Zechariah sides with the returning exiles in this heated conflict and recounts a vision in which the *satan* speaks for the rural inhabitants who accuse the returning high priest of being a worthless candidate:

> The Lord showed me Joshua, the high priest, standing before the angel of the Lord, and the *satan* standing at his right hand to accuse him. The Lord said to the *satan*, "The Lord rebuke you, O *satan*! The Lord who has chosen Jerusalem rebuke you." (Zech. 3:1–2)

Here the *satan* speaks for a disaffected—and unsuccessful—party against another party of fellow Israelites. In Zechariah's account of factions within Israel, the *satan* takes on a sinister quality, as he had done in the story of

David's census, and his role begins to change from that of God's agent to that of his opponent. Although these biblical stories reflect divisions within Israel, they are not yet sectarian, for their authors still identify with Israel as a whole.

Some four centuries later in 168 B.C.E., when Jews regained their independence from their Seleucid rulers, descendants of Alexander the Great, internal conflicts became even more acute.[15] For centuries, Jews had been pressured to assimilate to the ways of the foreign nations that successively had ruled their land—the Babylonians, then the Persians, and, after 323 B.C.E., the Hellenistic dynasty established by Alexander. As the first book of Maccabees tells the story, these pressures reached a breaking point in 168 B.C.E., when the Seleucid ruler, the Syrian king Antiochus Epiphanes, suspecting resistance to his rule, decided to eradicate every trace of the Jews' peculiar and "barbaric" culture. First he outlawed circumcision, along with study and observance of Torah. Then he stormed the Jerusalem Temple and desecrated it by rededicating it to the Greek god Olympian Zeus. To enforce submission to his new regime, the king built and garrisoned a massive new fortress overlooking the Jerusalem Temple itself.

Jewish resistance to these harsh decrees soon flared into a widespread revolt, which began, according to tradition, when a company of the king's troops descended upon the village of Modein to force the inhabitants to bow down to foreign gods. The old village priest Mattathias rose up and killed a Jew who was about to obey the Syrian king's command. Then he killed the king's commissioner and fled with his sons to the hills—an act of defiance that precipitated the revolt led by Mattathias's son Judas Maccabeus.[16]

As told in 1 Maccabees, this famous story shows how those Israelites determined to resist the foreign king's orders and retain their ancestral traditions battled on two fronts at once—not only against the foreign occupiers, but against those Jews who inclined toward accommodation with the foreigners, and toward assimilation. Recently the historian Victor Tcherikover and others have told a more complex version of that history. According to Tcherikover, many Jews, especially among the upper classes, actually favored Antiochus's "reform" and wanted to participate fully in the privileges of Hellenistic society available only to Greek citizens.[17] By giving up their tribal ways and gaining for Jerusalem the prerogatives of a Greek city, they would win the right to govern the city themselves, to strike their own coins, and to increase commerce with a worldwide network of other Greek cities. They could participate in such cultural projects as the Olympic games with allied cities and gain the advantages of mutual defense treaties. Many wanted their sons to have a Greek education. Besides reading Greek literature, from the *Iliad* and the *Odyssey* to Sophocles, Plato, and Aristotle, and participating in public athletic competitions, as Greeks did, they could advance themselves in the wider cosmopolitan world.

But many other Jews, perhaps the majority of the population of Jerusalem and the countryside—tradespeople, artisans, and farmers— detested these "Hellenizing Jews" as traitors to God and Israel alike. The revolt ignited by old Mattathias encouraged people to resist Antiochus's orders, even at the risk of death, and oust the foreign rulers. After intense fighting, the Jewish armies finally won a decisive victory. They celebrated by purifying and rededicating the Temple in a ceremony commemorated, ever since, at the annual festival of Hanukkah.

Jews resumed control of the Temple, the priesthood, and the government; but after the foreigners had retreated, internal conflicts remained, especially over who would control these institutions. These divisions now intensified, as the more rigorously separatist party dominated by the Maccabees opposed the Hellenizing party. The former, having won the war, had the upper hand.

Ten to twenty years after the revolt began, the influential Hasmonean family gained control of the high priesthood in what was now essentially a theocratic state. Although originally identified with their Maccabean ancestors, successive generations of the family abandoned the austere habits of their predecessors. Two generations after the Maccabean victory, the party of Pharisees, advocating increased religious rigor, challenged the Hasmoneans. According to Tcherikover's analysis, the Pharisees, backed by tradespeople and farmers, despised the Hasmoneans as having become essentially secular rulers who had abandoned Israel's ancestral ways. The Pharisees demanded that the Hasmoneans relinquish the high priesthood to those who deserved it—people like themselves, who strove to live according to religious law.[18]

During the following decades, other, more radical dissident groups joined the Pharisees in denouncing the great high priestly family and its allies. Such groups were anything but uniform: they were fractious and diverse, and with the passage of time included various groups of Essenes, the monastic community at Kirbet Qûmran, as well as their allies in the towns, and the followers of Jesus of Nazareth. What these groups shared was their opposition to the high priest and his allies and to the Temple, which they controlled.

The majority of Jews, including the Pharisees, still defined themselves in traditional terms, as "Israel against 'the nations.'" But those who joined marginal or more extreme groups like the Essenes, bent on separating Israel radically from foreign influence, came to treat that traditional identification as a matter of secondary importance. What mattered primarily, these rigorists claimed, was not whether one was Jewish—this they took for granted—but rather "which of us [Jews] really are on God's side" and which had "walked in the ways of the nations," that is, adopted foreign cultural and commercial practices. The separatists found ammunition in biblical passages that invoke terrifying curses upon people who violate God's covenant, and in prophetic passages that warn that only a "righteous remnant" in Israel will remain faithful to God.

More radical than their predecessors, these dissidents began increasingly to invoke the *satan* to characterize their Jewish opponents; in the process they turned this rather unpleasant angel into a far grander—and far more malevolent—figure. No longer one of God's faithful servants, he begins to become what he is for Mark and for later Christianity—God's antagonist, his enemy, even his rival.[19] Such sectarians, contending less against "the nations" than against other Jews, denounce their opponents as apostate and accuse them of having been seduced by the power of evil, whom they call by many names—Satan, Beelzebub, Semihazah, Azazel, Belial, Prince of Darkness. These dissidents also borrowed stories, and wrote their own, telling how such angelic powers, swollen with lust or arrogance, fell from heaven into sin. Those who first elaborated such stories, as we shall see, most often used them to characterize what they charged was the "fall into sin" of human beings—which usually meant the dominant majority of their Jewish contemporaries.

As Satan became an increasingly important and personified figure, stories about his origin proliferated. One group tells how one of the angels, himself high in the heavenly hierarchy, proved insubordinate to his commander in chief and so was thrown out of heaven, demoted, and disgraced, an echo of Isaiah's account of the fall of a great prince:

> How are you fallen from heaven, day star, son of the dawn! How are you fallen to earth, conqueror of the nations! You said in your heart, "I will ascend to heaven, above the stars of God; I will set my throne on high ... I will ascend upon the high clouds...." But you are brought down to darkness [or: the underworld, *sheol*], to the depths of the pit. (Isa. 14:12–15)

Nearly two and a half thousand years after Isaiah wrote, this luminous falling star, his name translated into Latin as Lucifer ("light-bearer") was transformed by Milton into the protagonist of *Paradise Lost*.

Far more influential in first-century Jewish and Christian circles, however, was a second group of apocryphal and pseudepigraphic stories, which tell how lust drew the angelic "sons of God" down to earth. These stories derive from a cryptic account in Genesis 6, which says:

> When men began to multiply on the earth, and daughters were
> born to them, the sons of God saw the daughters of men, that
> they were fair.

Some of these angels, transgressing the boundaries that the Lord had
established between heaven and earth, mated with human women, and
produced offspring who were half angel, half human. According to Genesis,
these hybrids became "giants in the earth ... the mighty men of renown"
(Gen. 6:4). Other storytellers, probably writing later,[20] as we shall see, say
that these monstrous offspring became demons, who took over the earth and
polluted it.

Finally, an apocryphal version of the life of Adam and Eve gives a third
account of angelic rebellion. In the beginning, God, having created Adam,
called the angels together to admire his work and ordered them to bow down
to their younger human sibling. Michael obeyed, but Satan refused, saying,

> "Why do you press me? I will not worship one who is younger
> than I am, and inferior. I am older than he is; he ought to worship
> me!" (*Vita Adae et Evae* 14:3)

Thus the problem of evil begins in sibling rivalry.[21]

At first glance these stories of Satan may seem to have little in
common. Yet they all agree on one thing: that this greatest and most
dangerous enemy did not originate, as one might expect, as an outsider, an
alien, or a stranger. Satan is not the distant enemy but the intimate enemy—
one's trusted colleague, close associate, brother. He is the kind of person on
whose loyalty and goodwill the well-being of family and society depend—but
one who turns unexpectedly jealous and hostile. Whichever version of his
origin one chooses, then, and there are many, all depict Satan as an *intimate*
enemy—the attribute that qualifies him so well to express conflict among
Jewish groups. Those who asked, "How could God's own angel become his
enemy?" were thus asking, in effect, "How could one of *us* become one of
them?" Stories of Satan and other fallen angels proliferated in these troubled
times, especially within those radical groups that had turned against the rest
of the Jewish community and, consequently, concluded that others had
turned against them—or (as they put it) against *God*.

One anonymous author who collected and elaborated stories about
fallen angels during the Maccabean war was troubled by wartime divisions
among Jewish communities. He addressed this divisiveness indirectly in the
Book of the Watchers, one of the apocryphal books that would become famous
and influential, especially among Christians, by introducing the idea of a

division in heaven. The *Book of the Watchers*, a collection of visionary stories, is set, in turn, into a larger collection called the *First Book of Enoch*. It tells how the "watcher" angels, whom God appointed to supervise ("watch over") the universe, fell from heaven. Starting from the story of Genesis 6, in which the "sons of God" lusted for human women, this author combines two different accounts of how the watchers lost their heavenly glory.[22] The first describes how Semihazah, leader of the watchers, coerced two hundred other angels to join him in a pact to violate divine order by mating with human women. These mismatches produced "a race of bastards, the giants known as the *nephilim* ["fallen ones"], from whom there were to proceed demonic spirits," who brought violence upon earth and devoured its people. Interwoven with this story is an alternate version, which tells how the archangel Azazel sinned by disclosing to human beings the secrets of metallurgy, a pernicious revelation that inspired men to make weapons and women to adorn themselves with gold, silver, and cosmetics. Thus the fallen angels and their demon offspring incited in both sexes violence, greed, and lust.

Because these stories involve sociopolitical satire laced with religious polemic, some historians have recently asked to what specific historical situations they refer. Are Jews who thus embellish the story of angels that mate with human beings covertly ridiculing the pretensions of their Hellenistic rulers? George Nickelsburg points out that from the time of Alexander the Great, Greek kings had claimed to be descended from gods as well as from human women; the Greeks called such hybrid beings heroes. But their Jewish subjects, with their derisive tale of Semihazah, may have turned such claims of divine descent against the foreign usurpers.[23] The *Book of the Watchers* says pointedly that these greedy monsters "consumed the produce of all the people until the people hated feeding them"; the monsters then turned directly to "devour the people."

Or does the story express instead a pious people's contempt for a specific group of Jewish enemies—namely, certain members of the Jerusalem priesthood? David Suter suggests that the story aims instead at certain priests who, like the "sons of God" in the story, violate their divinely given status and responsibility by allowing lust to draw them into impurity—especially marriages with outsiders, Gentile women.[24]

Either interpretation is possible. As John Collins points out, the author of the *Book of the Watchers*, by choosing to tell the story of the watchers instead of that of the actual Greek rulers or corrupt priests, offers "a paradigm which is not restricted to one historical situation, but which can be applied whenever an analogous situation arises."[25] The same is true of all apocalyptic literature, and accounts for much of its power. Even today, readers puzzle over books that claim the authority of angelic revelation, from the biblical book of Daniel to the New Testament book of Revelation, finding in their own circumstances new applications for these evocative, enigmatic texts.

The primary apocalyptic question is this: Who are God's people?[26] To most readers of the *Book of the Watchers*, the answer would have been obvious—Israel. But the author of *Watchers*, without discarding ethnic identity, insists on moral identity. It is not enough to be a few. One must also be a Jew who acts morally. Here we see evidence of a historical shift—one that Christians will adopt and extend and which, ever after, will divide them from other Jewish groups.

The author of the *Book of the Watchers* intended nothing so radical as the followers of Jesus undertook when they finally abandoned Israel to form their own distinct religious tradition. He takes for granted Israel's priority over the rest of the nations, always mentioning Israel first. But this author takes a decisive step by separating ethnic from moral identity and suggesting a contrast between them. He takes his beginning from the opening chapters of Genesis, choosing as his spokesman the holy man Enoch, who far antedates Abraham and Israel's election and, according to Genesis, belongs not to Israel but to the primordial history of the human race. This author omits any mention of the law given to Moses at Sinai, and praises instead the universal law that God wrote into the fabric of the universe and gave to all humankind alike—the law that governs the seas, the earth, and the stars. Addressing his message to "the elect and the righteous" among all humankind, he demonstrates not only, as George Nickelsburg observes, an "unusual openness to the Gentiles," but also an unusually negative view of Israel, or, more precisely, many—perhaps a majority—of Israel's people.[27]

The *Book of the Watchers* tells the stories of Semihazah and Azazel as a moral warning: if even archangels, "sons of heaven," can sin and be cast down, how much more susceptible to sin and damnation are mere human beings, even those who belong to God's chosen people. In the *Book of the Watchers*, when Enoch, moved with compassion for the fallen watchers, tries to intervene with God on their behalf, one of God's angels orders him instead to deliver to them God's judgment: "You used to be holy, spirits possessing eternal life; but now you have defiled yourselves." Such passages suggest that the *Book of the Watchers* articulates the judgment of certain Jews upon others, and specifically upon some who hold positions that ordinarily convey great authority.

In 160 B.C.E., after the Maccabees' victory, a group who regarded themselves as moderates regained control of the Temple priesthood and temporarily ousted the Maccabean party. Recalling this event, one of the

Maccabeans adds to the collection called the *First Book of Enoch* another version of the story of the watcher angels, a version aimed against those who had usurped control of the Temple. This author says that the watchers, falling like stars from heaven, themselves spawned Israel's foreign enemies, depicted as bloody predators—lions, leopards, wolves, and snakes intent on destroying Israel, here depicted as a herd of sheep. But, he continues, God's chosen nation is itself divided; some are "blind sheep," and others have their eyes open. When the day of judgment comes, he warns, God will destroy the errant Jews, these "blind sheep," along with Israel's traditional enemies. Furthermore, God will finally gather into his eternal home not only Israel's righteous but also the righteous from the nations (although these will remain forever secondary to Israel).

A third anonymous writer whose work is included in the *First Book of Enoch* is so preoccupied with internal division that he virtually ignores Israel's alien enemies. This author has Enoch predict the rise of "a perverse generation," warning that "all its deeds shall be apostate" (*1 Enoch* 93:9). Castigating many of his contemporaries, this author, as George Nickelsburg points out, like several biblical prophets, speaks for the poor, and denounces the rich and powerful, predicting their destruction.[28] He even insists that slavery, along with other social and economic inequities, is not divinely ordained, as others argue, but "arose from oppression" (*1 Enoch* 98:5b)—that is, human sin.[29]

The story of the watchers, then, in some of its many transformations, suggested a change in the traditional lines separating Jew from Gentile. The latest section of the *First Book of Enoch*, the "Similitudes," written about the time of Jesus, simply contrasts those who are righteous, who stand on the side of the angels, with those, both Jews and Gentiles, seduced by the *satans*. Accounts like this would open the way for Christians eventually to leave ethnic identity aside, and to redefine the human community instead in terms of the moral quality, or membership in the elect community, of each individual.

Another devout patriot, writing around 160 B.C.E., also siding with the early Maccabean party, wrote an extraordinary apocryphal book called *Jubilees* to urge his people to maintain their separateness from Gentile ways. What troubles this author is this: How can so many Israelites, God's own people, have become apostates? How can so many Jews be "walking in the ways of the Gentiles" (*Jub.* 1:9)? While the author takes for granted the traditional antithesis between the Israelites and "their enemies, the Gentiles" (*Jub.* 1:19), here again this conflict recedes into the background. The author of *Jubilees* is concerned instead with the conflicts over assimilation that divide Jewish communities internally, and he attributes these conflicts to that most intimate of enemies, whom he calls by many names, but most often calls Mastema ("hatred"), Satan, or Belial.

The story of the angels' fall in *Jubilees*, like that in the *First Book of Enoch*, gives a moral warning: if even angels, when they sin, bring God's wrath and destruction upon themselves, how can mere human beings expect to be spared? *Jubilees* insists that every creature, whether angel or human, Israelite or Gentile, shall be judged according to deeds, that is, ethically.

According to *Jubilees*, the angels' fall spawned the giants, who sow violence and evil, and evil spirits, "who are cruel, and created to destroy" (*Jub.* 10:6). Ever since, their presence has dominated this world like a dark shadow, and suggests the moral ambivalence and vulnerability of every human being. Like certain of the prophets, this author warns that election offers no safety, certainly no immunity; Israel's destiny depends not simply on election but on moral action or, failing this, on repentance and divine forgiveness.

Yet Jews and Gentiles do not confront demonic malevolence on equal footing. *Jubilees* says that God assigned to each of the nations a ruling angel or spirit "so that they might lead them astray" (*Jub.* 15:31); hence the nations worship demons (whom *Jubilees* identifies with foreign gods).[30] But God himself rules over Israel, together with a phalanx of angels and spirits assigned to guard and bless them.

What, then, does God's election of his people mean? The author of *Jubilees*, echoing the warnings of Isaiah and other prophets, suggests that belonging to the people of Israel does not guarantee deliverance from evil. It conveys a legacy of moral struggle, but ensures divine help in that struggle.

Jubilees depicts Mastema testing Abraham himself to the breaking point. For according to this revisionist writer, it is Mastema—not the Lord—who commands Abraham to kill his son, Isaac. Later Abraham expresses anxiety lest he be enslaved by evil spirits, "who have dominion over the thoughts of human hearts"; he pleads with God, "Deliver me from the hands of evil spirits, and do not let them lead me astray from my God" (*Jub.* 12:20). Moses, too, knows that he and his people are vulnerable. When he prays that God deliver Israel from their external enemies, "the Gentiles" (*Jub.* 1:19), he also prays that God may deliver them from the intimate enemy that threatens to take over his people internally and destroy them: "Do not let the spirit of Belial rule over them" (*Jub.* 1:20). This sense of ominous and omnipresent danger in *Jubilees* shows the extent to which the author regards his people as corruptible and, to a considerable extent, already corrupted. Like the *Book of the Watchers*, *Jubilees* warns that those who neglect God's covenant are being seduced by the powers of evil, fallen angels.

Despite these warnings, the majority of Jews, from the second century

B.C.E. to the present, reject sectarianism, as well as the universalism that, among most Christians, would finally supersede ethnic distinction. The Jewish majority, including those who sided with the Maccabees against the assimilationists, has always identified with Israel as a whole.

The author of the biblical book of Daniel, for example, who wrote during the crisis surrounding the Maccabean war, also sides with the Maccabees, and wants Jews to shun contamination incurred by eating with Gentiles, marrying them, or worshiping their gods. To encourage Jews to maintain their loyalty to Israel, the book opens with the famous story of the prophet Daniel, sentenced to death by the Babylonian king for faithfully praying to his God. Thrown into a den of lions to be torn apart, Daniel is divinely delivered; "the Lord sent an angel to shut the lions' mouths," so that the courageous prophet emerges unharmed.

Like the authors of *Jubilees* and *Watchers*, the author of Daniel, too, sees moral division within Israel, and warns that some people "violate the covenant; but the people who know their God shall stand firm and take action" (Dan. 11:32). Though concerned with moral issues, he never forgets ethnic identity: what concerns him above all is Israel's moral destiny as a whole. Unlike the writers of the *Book of the Watchers* and *Jubilees*, the author of Daniel envisions no sectarian enemy, either human or divine. Grieved as he is at Israel's sins, he never condemns many, much less the majority, of his people as apostate; consequently, he never speaks of Satan, Semihazah, Azazel, Mastema, Belial, or fallen angels of any kind.

Although there are no devils in Daniel's world, there *are* angels, and there are enemies. The author presents the alien enemies, rulers of the Persian, Medean, and Hellenistic empires, in traditional visionary imagery, as monstrous beasts. In one vision, the first beast is "like a lion with eagles' wings"; the second "like a bear," ferociously devouring its prey; the third like a leopard "with four wings of a bird on its back and four heads"; and "a fourth beast [is] terrible and dreadful and exceedingly strong; and it had great iron teeth: it devoured and broke in pieces, and stamped the residue with its feet." In another vision, Daniel sees a horned ram that the angel Gabriel explains to him "is the king of Greece." Throughout the visions of Daniel, such monstrous animals represent foreign rulers and nations who threaten Israel. When Daniel, trembling with awe and terror, prays for his people, he is rewarded with divine assurance that all Israelites who remain true to God will survive (12:1–3). Thus the book of Daniel powerfully reaffirms the integrity of Israel's moral and ethnic identity. It is for this reason, I suggest, that Daniel, unlike such other apocalyptic books as the *Book of the Watchers* and *Jubilees*, is included in the canonical collection that we call the Hebrew Bible and not relegated to the apocrypha.

The majority of Jews, at any rate those who assembled and drew upon the Hebrew Bible, apparently endorsed Daniel's reaffirmation of Israel's traditional identity, while those who valued such books as *1 Enoch* and *Jubilees* probably included a significant minority more inclined to identify with one group of Jews against another, as Daniel had refused to do. Most of those who *did* take sides within the community stopped far short of proclaiming an all-out civil war between one Jewish group and another, but there were notable exceptions. Starting at the time of the Maccabean war, the more radical sectarian groups we have mentioned—above all, those called Essenes—placed this cosmic battle between angels and demons, God and Satan, at the very center of their cosmology and their politics. In so doing, they expressed the importance to their lives of the conflict between themselves and the majority of their fellow Jews, whom the Essenes consigned to damnation.

Many scholars believe that the Essenes are known to us from such first-century contemporaries as Josephus, Philo, and the Roman geographer and naturalist Pliny the Elder, as well as from the discovery in 1947 of the ruins of their community, including its sacred library, the Dead Sea Scrolls. Josephus, at the age of sixteen, was fascinated by this austere and secretive community: he says that they "practiced great holiness" within an extraordinarily close-knit group ("they love one another very much").[31] Josephus and Philo both note, with some astonishment, that these sectarians practiced strict celibacy, probably because they chose to live according to the biblical rules for holy war, which prohibit sexual intercourse during wartime. But the war in which they saw themselves engaged was God's war against the power of evil—a cosmic war that they expected would result in God's vindication of their fidelity. The Essenes also turned over all their money and property to their leaders in order to live "without money," as Pliny says, in a monastic community.[32]

These devout and passionate sectarians saw the foreign occupation of Palestine—and the accommodation of the majority of Jews to that occupation—as evidence that the forces of evil had taken over the world and—in the form of Satan, Mastema, or the Prince of Darkness—infiltrated and taken over God's own people, turning most of them into allies of the Evil One.

Arising from controversies over purity and assimilation that followed the Maccabean war, the Essene movement grew during the Roman occupation of the first century to include over four thousand men. Women, never mentioned in the community rule, apparently were not eligible for admission. Although the remains of a few women and children have been found among the hundreds of men buried in the outer cemetery at Qûmran, they probably were not community members.[33] (Since the whole cemetery has not yet been excavated, these conclusions remain inconclusive.) Many adjunct members of the sect, apparently including many who were married, lived in towns all over Palestine, pursuing ordinary occupations while striving to devote themselves to God; but the most dedicated withdrew in protest from ordinary Jewish life to form their own "new Israel," the monastic community in desert caves overlooking the Dead Sea.[34] There, following the rigorous community rule, they dressed only in white and regulated every detail of their lives according to strict interpretations of the law set forth by their priestly leaders.

In their sacred books, such as the great *Scroll of the War of the Sons of Light Against the Sons of Darkness*, the brethren could read how God had given them the Prince of Light as their supernatural ally to help them contend against Satan, and against his human allies.

> The Prince of Light thou has appointed to come to our support:
> but Satan, the angel Mastema, thou hast created for the pit; he
> rules in darkness, and his purpose is to bring about evil and sin.
> (1 QM 19:10–12)

The Essenes called themselves the "sons of light" and indicted the majority as "sons of darkness," the "congregation of traitors," as people who "depart from the way, having transgressed the law, and violated the precept" (CD 1:13–20). The Essenes retell the whole history of Israel in terms of this cosmic war. Even in earliest times, they say, "the Prince of Light raised up Moses" (CD 5:18), but the Evil One, here called Beliar, aroused opposition to Moses among his own people. Ever since then, and especially now, Beliar has set traps in which he intends to "catch Israel," for God himself has "unleashed Beliar against Israel" (CD 4:13). Now the "sons of light" eagerly await the day of judgment, when they expect God will come with all the armies of heaven to annihilate the corrupt majority along with Israel's foreign enemies.

Had Satan not already existed in Jewish tradition, the Essenes would have invented him. In the *Book of the Watchers* fallen angels incite the activities of those who violate God's covenant, but the Essenes go much further and place at the center of their religious understanding the cosmic war between God and his allies, both angelic and human, against Satan, or Beliar, along with his demonic and human allies. The Essenes place themselves at the very center of this battle between heaven and hell. While they detest Israel's traditional enemies, whom they call the *kittim* (probably a coded epithet for the Romans),[35] they struggle far more bitterly against their fellow Israelites, who belong to the "congregation of Beliar." David Sperling, scholar of the ancient Near East, suggests that substitution of Beliar for earlier Belial may be a pun on *belî 'ôr*, "without light."[36] They invoke Satan—or Beliar—to characterize the irreconcilable opposition between themselves and the "sons of darkness" in the war taking place simultaneously in heaven and on earth. They expect that soon God will come in power, with his holy angels, and finally overthrow the forces of evil and inaugurate the Kingdom of God.

The Essenes agree with *Jubilees* that being Jewish is no longer enough to ensure God's blessing. But they are much more radical: the sins of the people have virtually canceled God's covenant with Abraham, on which Israel's election depends. Now, they insist, whoever wants to belong to the true Israel must join in a *new* covenant—the covenant of their own congregation.[37] Whoever applies to enter the desert community must first confess himself guilty of sin—guilty, apparently, of participating in Israel's collective apostasy against God. Then the candidate begins several years of probation, during which he turns over his property to the community leaders and swears to practice sexual abstinence, along with ritual purity in everything he eats, drinks, utters, or touches. During the probationary period he must not touch the pots, plates, or utensils in which the members prepare the community's food. Swearing can earn him instant expulsion, and so can complaining against the group's leaders; spitting or talking out of turn incurs strict penalties.

A candidate who finally does gain admission is required, at his initiation ritual, to join together with the whole community to bless all who belong to the new covenant and ritually curse all who are not initiates, who belong to the "men of Beliar." The leaders now reveal to the initiate the secrets of angelology, and according to Josephus, he must solemnly swear to "keep secret the names of the angels" (*War* 2.8). Through practices of purity, prayer, and worship, the initiate strives to unite himself with the company of the angels. As the historian Carol Newsome has shown, Essene community worship—like the Christian liturgy to this day—reaches its climax as the community on earth joins with angels in singing the hymn of praise that the angels sing in heaven ("Holy, holy, holy, Lord God of hosts; heaven and earth are filled with thy glory").[38] Sacred Essene texts like the *Scroll of the War of the Sons of Light Against the Sons of Darkness* reveal secrets of angelology, which the sectarians regarded as valuable and necessary information, for recognizing and understanding the interrelationship of supernatural forces, both good and evil, is essential for their sense of their own identity—and the way they identify others.[39]

The Essenes, then, offer the closest parallel to Mark's account of Jesus' followers, as they invoke images of cosmic war to divide the universe at large—and the Jewish community in particular—between God's people and Satan's. Yet the two movements differ significantly, especially in relation to outsiders. The Essene covenant, as we have seen, was extremely exclusive, restricted not only to Jews, who must be freeborn and male, but to those devout few who willingly joined the "new covenant." Although Mark and Matthew saw the beginning of Jesus' movement primarily within the context of the Jewish community, its future would increasingly involve the Gentile world outside.

Nonetheless, the Essenes, though rigorously exclusive, were led by their objections to the assimilationist tendencies of their fellow Jews to move, paradoxically, in the universalist direction indicated by the *Book of the Watchers* and *Jubilees*. (The Essenes treasured both of these writings in their monastic library; *Jubilees*, wrote an anonymous Essene, is a book that reveals divine secrets "to which Israel has turned a blind eye" [CD 16.2].) The Essenes outdid their predecessors in setting ethnic identity aside, not as wrong, but as inadequate, and emphasized moral over ethnic identification. When they depict the struggle of the Prince of Light against the Prince of Darkness, they do not identify the Prince of Light with the archangel Michael, the angelic patron of Israel.[40] Instead, they envision the Prince of Light as a universal energy contending against an opposing cosmic force, the Prince of Darkness. For the Essenes these two energies represent not only their own conflicts with their opponents but a conflict within every person, within the human heart itself.

> The spirits of truth and falsehood struggle within the human heart.... According to his share in truth and right, thus a man hates lies; and according to his share in the lot of deceit, thus he hates truth. (1 QS 4:12–14)

The Essenes, of course, took their own identification with Israel for granted. Since they required every initiate to their covenant to be Jewish, male, and freeborn, "every person" meant in practice only Jews who met these qualifications. But certain followers of Jesus, especially after 100 C.E., having met with disappointing responses to their message within the Jewish communities, would draw upon such universalist themes as they moved to open their movement to Gentiles.

As we saw in the previous chapter, Jesus' followers, according to Mark, also invoke images of cosmic war to divide the universe at large—and the Jewish community in particular—between God's people and Satan's. Mark, like the Essenes, sees this struggle essentially in terms of intra-Jewish conflict. So does the follower of Jesus we call Matthew, who, as we shall see in the next chapter, took up and revised Mark's gospel some ten to twenty years later. Taking Mark's basic framework, Matthew embellished it and in effect updated it, placing the story of Jesus in a context more relevant to the Jewish world of Matthew's own time, Palestine c. 80–90 C.E. By the time Matthew was writing, Jesus' followers were a marginal group opposed by the ruling party of Pharisees, which had gained ascendancy in Jerusalem in the decades following the Roman war. In the central part of Matthew's version of the gospel, the "intimate enemies" had become primarily Pharisees.

About the same time, another follower of Jesus, whom tradition calls Luke, also took up Mark's account and extended it to fit his own perspective—apparently that of a Gentile convert. Yet Luke, as fervently as any Essene, depicts his own sect as representing Israel at its best; according to Luke, as we shall see, Jesus' followers are virtually the only true Israelites left.

Near the end of the century, c. 90–100 C.E., the writer called John offers a bold interpretation of these events. Many scholars agree that the gospel of John presents the viewpoint of a radically sectarian group alienated from the Jewish community because they have been turned out of their home synagogues for claiming that Jesus is the Messiah. Like the Essenes, John speaks eloquently of the love among those who belong to God (John 10:14); and yet John's fierce polemic against those he sometimes calls simply "the Jews" at times matches in bitterness that of the Essenes.

NOTES

1. For a more detailed scholarly treatment of the material in this chapter, see E. Pagels, "The Social History of Satan, the 'Intimate Enemy': A Preliminary Sketch," *Harvard Theological Review* 84:2 (1991): 105–28.

2. See M. Hengel, *Judaism and Hellenism* (London, 1974), 209, which argues that apocalyptic writings are the work of a pious minority who segregated themselves from the official cult. See also M. Barker, "Some Reflections on the Enoch Myth," *Journal for the Study of the Old Testament* 15 (1980): 7–29; her article interprets *1 Enoch* as the work of a group protesting against Jerusalem cult practices, and suggests a link between such works as *Enoch* and the later development of Christian tradition.

3. See, in particular, the incisive essays by Jonathan Z. Smith, "What a Difference a Difference Makes," and William S. Green, "Otherness Within: Towards a Theory of Difference in Rabbinic Judaism," in Jacob Neusner and Ernest S. Frerichs, eds., *To See Ourselves as Others See Us: Christians, Jews, "Others" in Late Antiquity* (Chico, Calif: Scholars Press, 1985), 3–48 and 49–69.

4. See Morton Smith, *Palestinian Parties and Politics That Shaped the Old Testament* (New York: Columbia University Press, 1971), especially 62–146; also Paul Hanson, *The Dawn of Apocalyptic* (Philadelphia: Fortress Press, 1975).

5. Jon D. Levenson, *Creation and the Persistence of Evil: The Jewish Drama of Divine*

Omnipotence (San Francisco: Harper and Row, 1988). I am grateful to John Collins for referring me to this work.

6. *Ibid.*, 44.

7. Many scholars have made this observation; for a recent discussion see Neil Forsyth, *The Old Enemy: Satan and the Combat Myth* (Princeton: Princeton University Press, 1987), 107: "In the collection of documents ... known to Christians as the Old Testament, the word [Satan] never appears ... as the name of the adversary.... rather, when the satan appears in the Old Testament, he is a member of the heavenly court, albeit with unusual tasks." See also the article on *démon*, in *La Dictionnaire de Spiritualité* 3 (Paris: Beauschesne, 1957), 142–46; H.A. Kelly, "Demonology and Diabolical Temptation," *Thought* 46 (1965): 165–70.

8. M. Delcor, "Le Mythe de la chute des anges et l'origine des géants comme explication du mal dans le monde dans l'apocalyptique juive: Histoire des traditions, *Revue de l'histoire des religions* 190:5–12; P. Day, *An Adversary in Heaven: Satan in the Hebrew Bible* (Atlanta, Ga.: Scholars Press, 1988).

9. Forsyth, *The Old Enemy*, 113.

10. See discussion in Day, *An Adversary*, 69–106.

11. Forsyth, *The Old Enemy*, 114.

12. Note that 2 Samuel 24:1–17 tells a different version of the story, in which the Lord himself, not "the *satan*," incites David to take the census. For discussion, see Morton Smith, *Palestinian Parties and Politics That Shaped the Old Testament* (New York: Columbia University Press, 1971), 62–146; Forsyth, *The Old Enemy*, 119–20.

13. Pagels, "The Social History of Satan, the 'Intimate Enemy': A Preliminary Sketch," *Harvard Theological Review* 84:2 (1991): 112–14.

14. Paul D. Hanson, *The Dawn of Apocalyptic* (Philadelphia: Fortress Press, 1975), 125.

15. An excellent account of these events is to be found in Victor Tcherikover's *Hellenistic Civilization and the Jews* (New York: Atheneum, 1970).

16. 1 Maccabees, 2.

17. Tcherikover, *Hellenistic Civilization*, 132–74.

18. *Ibid.*, 253–65.

19. Such scholars as Knut Schäferdick, in his article "Satan in the Post Apostolic Fathers," s.v. "satanas," *Theological Dictionary of the New Testament* 7 (1971): 163–65, attributes this development to Christians. Others, including Harold Kuhn, "The Angelology of the Non-Canonical Jewish Apocalypses," *Journal of Biblical Literature* 67 (1948: 217; Claude Montefiore, *Lectures on the Origin and Growth of Religion as Illustrated by the Religion of the Ancient Hebrews* (London: Williams and Norgate, 1892), 429; and George Foote Moore, *Judaism in the First Centuries of the Christian Era*, vol. 1, *The Age of the Tannaim* (Cambridge, Mass.: Harvard University Press, 1927), rightly locate the development of angelology and demonology in pre-Christian Jewish sources, and offer different interpretations of this, as noted in Pagels, "The Social History of Satan, the 'Intimate Enemy,'" 107.

20. Which account is earlier—that in Genesis 6 or in *1 Enoch* 6–11—remains a debatable issue. See, for example, J.T. Milik, *The Books of Enoch: Aramaic Fragments of Qûmran Caves* (Oxford: Clarendon, 1976); George W. E. Nickelsburg, "Apocalyptic and Myth in *1 Enoch* 6–11," *Journal of Biblical Literature* 96 (1977): 383–405; Margaret Barker, "Some Reflections on the Enoch Myth," *JSOT* 15 (1980): 7–29; Philip S. Alexander, "The Targumim and Early Exegesis of the 'Sons of God' in Genesis 6," *Journal of Jewish Studies* 23 (1972): 60–71.

21. For a survey of this theme of rivalry between angels and humans, see Peter

Schäfer's fine work *Rivalität Zwischen Engeln und Menschen: Untersuchungen zur rabbinischen Engelvorstellung* (Berlin and New York: de Gruyter, 1975). For a discussion of one strand of Muslim tradition, see Peter Awn, *Satan's Tragedy and Redemption: Iblis in Sufi Psychology* (Leiden: E.J. Brill, 1983).

22. Note scholarly debate cited in note 20 concerning the priority of Genesis 6. I am following those scholars who see *1 Enoch* 6–11 as amplifications of Gen. 6:1–4, including Philip S. Alexander and Paul Hanson, "Rebellion in Heaven, Azazel, and Euhemenistic Heroes in *1 Enoch* 6–11," *Journal of Biblical Literature* 96 (1977): 195–233.

23. George W.E. Nickelsburg, "Apocalyptic and Myth in *1 Enoch* 6–11," *Journal of Biblical Literature* 96 (1977): 383–405.

24. David Suter, "Fallen Angel, Fallen Priest: The Problem of Family Purity in *1 Enoch* 6–16," *Hebrew Union College Annual* 50 (1979): 115–35. Cf. George W. E. Nickelsburg, "The Book of Enoch in Recent Research," *Religious Studies Review* 7 (1981): 210–17.

25. John Collins, *The Apocalyptic Imagination: An Introduction to the Jewish Matrix of Christianity* (New York: Crossroad, 1984), 127.

26. This question dominated the concerns of many others as well; for discussion, see the forthcoming book by Howard C. Kee, *Who Are the People of God?*

27. George W.E. Nickelsburg, "Revealed Wisdom as a Criterion for Inclusion and Exclusion," in Neusner and Frerichs, eds., *To See Ourselves As Others See Us*, 76.

28. See the article by George W.E. Nickelsburg, "Riches, the Rich, and God's Judgment in *1 Enoch* 92–105 and the Gospel According to Luke," *New Testament Studies* 25 (1979), 324–49.

29. On the basis of the Watcher story in *1 Enoch* 6–16, Forsyth (*The Old Enemy*, 167–70) comments that it implies "a radically different theology" from that of the Genesis primordial history, in that "in Enoch we have heard nothing about a wicked humanity. Instead, all human suffering is attributed to the angelic revolt and the sins of their giant brood." Yet as I read the Enoch literature, its authors demonstrate awareness of the tension between—and correlation of—human and angelic guilt, or at least of the possibility of contradiction. The passage may be included as a corrective to any who exempt humans from responsibility by blaming the angels' transgressions. For a discussion, see Martha Himmelfarb, *Tours of Hell: An Apocalyptic Form in Jewish and Christian Literature* (Philadelphia: University of Pennsylvania Press, 1983).

30. This identification occurs commonly in later Jewish sources, often traced to the Septuagint translation of 1 Chronicles 16:26: οἱ τῶν ἐθνῶν θεοί δαίμονες εἰσιν.

31. Josephus, *Life*, 10.

32. Pliny the Elder, *Natural History*, Loch edition, vol. 2, 5.15, 73. For discussion of Pliny's description of the Essenes, see J. P. Audet, "Qûmran et la notice de Pline sur les Esséniers," *Revue Biblique* 68 (1961): 346–87; D.F. Graf, "Pagan Witness to the Essenes," *Biblical Archaeologist* 40 (1977): 125–29.

33. L.H. Schiffman, *Archaeology and History in the Dead Sea Scrolls* (Sheffield: JSOT Press, 1989).

34. G. Vermes, *The Dead Sea Scrolls: Qûmran in Perspective* (Atlanta, Ga.: Scholars Press, 1989).

35. See F.F. Bruce, "The Romans Through Jewish Eyes," in M. Simon, ed., *Paganisme, Judaïsme, Christianisme* (Paris: E. de Boccard, 1978), 3–12; G. Vermes, *Post Biblical Jewish Studies* (Leiden: E.J. Brill, 1975), 215–24.

36. S. David Sperling, "Belial," forthcoming in Karel van der Toorn, *Dictionary of Deities and Demons* (Leiden: E.J. Brill).

37. See, for example, Matthew Black, *The Scrolls and Christian Origins* (New York: Scribner, 1961), 91–117.

38. Carol Newsome, *Songs of Sabbath Sacrifice: A Critical Edition* (Atlanta, Ga.: Scholars Press, 1985).

39. Yigael Yadin, who edited the *War Scroll*, commented that this text, like others from Qûmran, "considerably extends our knowledge of Jewish angelology—a subject of utmost importance in the Judaism of that time" (*Scroll*, 229). But Yadin did not tell us what constitutes its importance: Discernment of spirits, the capacity to recognize and understand the interrelationship of supernatural forces, both good and evil, is essential to the Essenes' sense of their own identity and the way they identify others. Having set aside, not so much as wrong but as inadequate, more traditional forms of Jewish identity, the Essenes articulate, through their accounts of the battle between angelic and demonic forces, on which side of the cosmic battle each person and each group of Jews stands.

40. Yigael Yadin assumes that the Prince of Light "is Michael, Prince of Israel": *The Scroll of the War of the Sons of Light Against the Sons of Darkness* (Oxford: Oxford University Press, 1962), 236. But this identification ignores the sectarianism that dominates the Qûmran texts. Instead, as John Collins observes, "In 1 QM Michael is no longer simply the Prince of Israel but leader of the Sons of Light. This designation may have been correlated in practice with members of the congregation, but in principle it was open to broader interpretations and freed from ethnic associations. Belial, too, is no longer the prince of a specific nation.... Rather, he represents evil at large, like Satan or Mastema in the book of *Jubilees*.... The adoption of this terminology in preference to the traditional, national, and social affiliations opens up considerably the range of application of the eschatological language. Specifically, it invites the correlation of the eschatological drama with the ... moral conflict of good and evil within every individual" (*The Apocalyptic Imagination*, 128–31).

LAURA LUNGER KNOPPERS

Satan and the Papacy in Paradise Regained

T raveling in Rome in 1644, John Evelyn toured Saint Peter's, "that most stupendious & incomparable Basilicam," and noticed "amongst all the Chappells one most glorious, having for Altar-piece a Madona bearing a Cristo mortuo in White marble, on her knees, the worke of Mich: Angelo."[1] In Michelangelo's *Pieta*, Mary—youthful, lovely, and serene though sorrowful—holds the lifeless but graceful body of Christ, marked on the hands, side, and feet with the wounds of the Crucifixion. With one hand, Mary frames Christ's wounded side; with the other, palm upward, she offers her dead son to the worshipper in a gesture recalling the elevation of the host at the Eucharist. The observer comes face-to-face with the reality of suffering for the human Christ and his grieving mother; yet, as altarpiece, the *Pieta* is poised at the moment of transformation, as the body and blood of Christ are literally renewed in the sacrifice of the mass.[2]

If John Milton, visiting Rome five years earlier in 1638–1639, viewed the Michelangelo *Pieta* in Saint Peter's, he left no record. Indeed, one looks in vain for Milton's impression of any sculpture, painting, or work of architecture observed during his time in Italy.[3] Some influential Milton scholars have assumed that the artistic masterpieces that Milton saw during his grand tour must have had a distinct and profound impact on his visual and poetic imagination.[4] Yet, as Michael O'Connell has recently observed, the art

From *Milton Studies XLII*: Paradise Regained *in Context: Genre, Politics, Religion.* © 2003 by the University of Pittsburgh Press.

that Milton—and Evelyn—viewed was not culturally neutral, but part of the sacramental complex of Catholic worship and belief.[5] As altarpiece, the Michelangelo *Pieta* pointed to mysteries of life and death, spirituality and materiality in the mass, which Milton and his contemporaries regarded as idolatrous. Indeed, a wide array of Renaissance and baroque artwork—the wall frescoes of the Sistine Chapel, Michelangelo's ceiling, the Raphael tapestries, the new Saint Peter's, the Julius tomb, and the Vatican *stanze*—variously celebrated and forwarded the temporal and ecclesiastical power of the papacy.[6] I want to argue, then, that art and learning of papal Rome did have a distinct impact on Milton's late poetry, albeit in a different sense than previously understood. Much of the alleged asceticism of *Paradise Regained* is the Son's renunciation of the culture of papal Rome: the wealth, power, learning, military might, and arts that reached an apogee in the Renaissance and were reclaimed for the Counter-Reformation in Milton's own time. But the Son rejects false (papal) appropriations of the visual arts, architecture, classical learning, and the heroic, only to reappropriate the arts and learning in service of a radical Protestant inwardness and spiritual discipline.

The papacy reached its golden age under Julius II (1503–1513) and, especially, Leo X (1513–1521).[7] A patron of Michelangelo, Raphael, and Bramante, Julius II commissioned plans for the new Saint Peter's Basilica, to be funded by the sale of indulgences. Julius also had vast military and imperial ambitions and directed much of his energies toward restoring and enlarging the papal states. Leo X was acclaimed as bringing a time of peace after the warmongering Julius. A highly cultured Renaissance prince, born Giovanni de Medici, Leo presided over a rich florescence of art and learning; among the artists he patronized were Raphael, Michelangelo, and Leonardo da Vinci. But in his support of indulgences and his flagrant sale of ecclesiastical offices to support his own opulent lifestyle and lavish church-building programs, Leo embodied, for Martin Luther and the reformers who came to oppose him, the worst excesses of the Catholic Church.

Within a broader Reformation tradition of anti-Catholic polemic, *Paradise Regained* directs an attack on papal Rome.[8] While considerable attention has been given to *Paradise Regained* in a Restoration context, analysis of the work in relation to the papacy helps to explain some of the still puzzling features of the poem, including the choice of the temptation in the wilderness, the "coldness" of its hero Jesus, the inclusion of the lavish banquet, the depiction of Rome, and the harsh rejection of learning.[9] Milton's choice of topic in *Paradise Regained* eschews both the Crucifixion and the Virgin Mary upon which so much attention had been lavished in Catholic art. The poem reflects a broad and uncompromising "Protestant" vision of inwardness and self-discipline in contrast to the material splendors of the papacy.[10] The false models of the church, in particular the temptations to wealth, glory, learning, and temporal power that Satan offers, reflect Milton's lifetime opposition to the corrupting conjunction of spiritual and temporal power evinced in the papacy. *Paradise Regained*, then, continues the anti-Catholic impetus that recent scholars have explored in *Comus*, *Lycidas*, *Paradise Lost*, and in Milton's prose.[11]

Exploring the anti-Catholic resonance of the temptations and the alignment of Satan with the papacy in *Paradise Regained* adds a new dimension to recent studies showing how the poem—seemingly quietist and pacifist—in fact polemically engages its political and religious Restoration context.[12] Popery—long a concern of Milton's and of many of his contemporaries—was perhaps an obvious target in 1671, with the looming threat of an absolutist and Catholic France under Louis XIV and Charles II's perceived pro-French and pro-Catholic sympathies.[13] Although the secret provisions in the 1670 Treaty of Dover, in which Charles had agreed to profess Catholicism and impose it upon England in return for French subsidies, were not yet known, suspicions ran high.[14] Two years after the publication of *Paradise Regained*, Milton's final prose work, *Of True Religion*, addressed the specific religious/political situation in England, arguing in part that in not tolerating their fellow Protestants the prelates were themselves behaving like papists.[15] Adumbrating the concerns of this last prose tract, *Paradise Regained* evokes both popery and prelacy in their shared abuses of temporal and ecclesiastical power to impinge upon the conscience of the true believer.

Yet I would also argue that the critique of Catholicism in *Paradise Regained* is deeper and broader than a topical response to the immediate political situation in England. Aligned with Reformation polemic, Milton targets the history of the Roman Catholic Church and points his attack in part at the golden age of the papacy, marked by the rebirth of art and learning. The painting, sculpture, and architecture of Renaissance Rome, along with the rediscovery of Greek and Latin learning, helped to shape and promulgate the imperial and ecclesiastical mission of the papacy. The poverty and humility of the Son of God in the wilderness and his rejection of satanic offers of wealth, power, glory, and learning boldly redefine spirituality as the inner discipline of hearing and obeying the word of God.

The seeming avoidance of the Crucifixion and the treatment of Mary as fully human and struggling for patience make *Paradise Regained* a sharp contrast to Catholic art. Travelers to Italy in Milton's time routinely noticed the Madonna altarpieces, the *Pietas*, and the numerous depictions of Mary as mother of the infant Christ.[16] In addition to the Michelangelo *Pieta* in Saint Peter's, John Evelyn observes at Santa Maria della Vitoria "the high Altar ...

infinitely frequented for an Image of the Vergine." Of Santa Maria Maggiore, he writes "Here they affirme that the B: Virgine appearing, shewed where it should be built, 300 yeares since."[17]

Like other travelers to Rome, Evelyn also notes the relics—and their accompanying miracles—associated with Mary and with Christ. Hence, at the Cathedral of Saint John de Laterana, relics include "a robe of the B: virgins which she gave to Christ, and the towell with which he dried the Disciples feete: the reed, sponge, some of the blood & water of his precious side: some of the Virgins haire, the Table on which the Passover was celebrated, the rods of Aron & Moses, and many such bagatells" (275). In a chapel dedicated to Saint Helena, Evelyn views with equal skepticism "a world of Reliques, expos'd at our request, with a Phial of our B: Saviours blood, two thornes of the Crowne, three Chips of the real Crosse, one of the Nailes, wanting a point, St. Thomas's doubting finger, and a fragment of the Title, being part of a thin board, some of Judas's pieces of silver, and innumerable more, if one had faith to believe it" (380). The relics of Rome— the robe or hair of the blessed Virgin, the Veronica or handkerchief showing the imprint of Christ's face at the time of his Passion, chips of the cross, thorns of the crown, and, above all, drops or vials of Christ's blood—gave tangible contact with the humanity and suffering of Christ.

In sharp contrast, the more radical and iconoclastic Milton seems to avoid the Crucifixion and any focus on the body of Christ. The Son in *Paradise Regained* knows that his "way must lie / Through many a bard assay even to the death" (1.263–64), and Satan himself foresees that ahead of the Son lie "scorns, reproaches, injuries, / Violence and stripes, and lastly cruel death" (4387–88).[18] But the poem itself depicts temptation and testing, martyrdom as witness to the truth rather than physical suffering. In a redefinition of martyrdom countering both the Catholic relics and the more recent English example of martyrdom with Charles I, Milton's Son of God waits, abstains, resists, declines, perseveres: he seems intent on doing nothing.[19] Similarly, Mary, mother of Jesus, is presented not as intercessor or miracle worker but as a humble, historical figure who waits with patience for news of her Son, aligned with the "plain Fishermen" (2.27) who likewise lament the loss of their Lord.

The language used by and about Satan in *Paradise Regained* recalls the language in which Milton—from his earliest antiprelatical tracts to his final prose work, *Of True Religion*—critiqued and attacked the pope and popery as fraudulent, carnal and idolatrous. The brief epic opens with a "gloomy Consistory" (1.42) in midair, a "Council" (1.40) in which Satan consults his troops, reminiscent of the papal conclave in which the new pope is elected. Satan's initial disguise as "an aged man in Rural weeds" (1.314) evokes

Spenser's Archimago as a figure of Catholic deception. Christ himself is described in the opening of *Paradise Regained* as "this glorious Eremite" (1.8)—perhaps a true eremite or friar in comparison to the false Satan. Satan's "vain importunity" (4.24), "ostentation vain" (3.387), and "vain batt'ry" (4.20) recall the explicitly antipapal Limbo of Vanity in *Paradise Lost*, in which are blown about "Cowls, Hoods and Habits with thir wearers tost / And flutter'd into Rags, then Reliques, Beads, / Indulgences, Dispenses, Pardons, Bulls, / The sport of Winds" (3.490–93).

Most strikingly, Milton employs with Satan language of pretense, fraud, and usurpation that is elsewhere part of his anti-Catholic arsenal. Satan in *Paradise Regained* is, above all, a fraud: he lies, feigns, dissembles, changes shape, and claims miracles. As such, he recalls the "shifts and evasions" and the "wiles and fallacies" of papists as depicted in *Of True Religion* (YP 8.432–33). As the title of that tract indicates, Milton highlights, above all, the *true* worship and service of God in contrast to the pretenses of popery. As *Paradise Regained* opens, Satan recreating the world in his own image, labels John the Baptist an imposter who "pretends to wash off sin (1.73) and prepare the way for Christ's kingdom. But Satan himself is the great pretender. His weapons in the battle with the Son are "not force, but well couch't fraud, well woven snares" (1.97); he seeks "temptation and all guile on him to try" (1.123). Satan brings with him "a chosen band / Of Spirits likest to himself in guile" (2.236–37). The narrator describes Satan's "gray dissimulation" (1.498) and "the persuasive Rhetoric / That sleek't his tongue" (4.4–5). As such, Satan is linked with what Milton and his contemporaries saw as the deceit and pretense of the Roman Catholic Church.

The relics of Rome were one obvious example, for Protestant Englishmen, of popish fraud. Francis Mortoft, traveling in Rome in 1659, observes in the Church of Saint Sebastian a stone "on which, they say, remaines the representation of the print of our Saviour Christ's foote, which he left when he appeared to St. Peter."[20] After recounting the alleged dialogue between Christ and Peter and the genesis of the miraculous footprint, Mortoft adds tellingly: "whether this is true I know not, onely it must be taken as a narration of the Papists, who wil not spare sometymes to tel bouncers, especially if it may advance their Romish Church" (95). Mortoft elsewhere implies that other claims put forward for relics are equally "bouncers." He describes, for instance, the statue of Saint Helena, "holding 3 great nailes in her hand to represent that three of the nailes that naild our Saviour to the Crosse are kept in a place just over the statue, but I leave it to the pleasure of whoe will to beleeve"; nonetheless, he notes the widespread credulity of the people, so that "whether they be the true nailes or noe, they are shewed, with a great piece of the Crosse also on the Easter weeke to thousands of People that for that purpose comes to see them" (82).

The first temptation in *Paradise Regained* employs the fraud and false dependence on materiality associated by Milton and his contemporaries with Rome and the Catholic Church. Satan's words—"But if thou be the Son of God, Command / That out of these hard stones be made thee bread; / So shalt thou save thyself and us relieve / With Food, whereof we wretched seldom taste" (1.342–45)—tempt the Son to perform a miracle to save himself by material means, rather than trusting in God. In response, the Son rebuffs the temptation of "distrust," but he also exposes Satan as a liar and establishes his own role as true oracle. His ploy rejected, Satan endures an additional reproof: "Deservedly thou griev'st, compos'd of lies / From the beginning, and in lies wilt end" (1.407–8). Indeed the Son goes onto charge that "lying is thy sustenance, thy food. / Yet thou pretend'st to truth" (1.429–30).

While Satan's ensuing reference to the "Hypocrite or Atheous Priest" (1.487) may have an immediate referent in the Restoration church, the anti-Catholic language also places the current situation in England in the context of a long history of alleged papal abuses. The specific point at issue here—Satan's claim to speak oracular truth—may in itself aim at the oracular infallibility of Rome; more broadly, "pretense" is one crucial element of Milton's explicit prose attacks on popery, linked with fraud, usurpation, and carnality. Hence, Milton refers in *Animadversions* (1641) to "our pretended Father the Pope" (YP 1:728) and writes in *Of True Religion* (1673) that "of all known Sects or pretended Religions at this day in Christendom, Popery is the only or the greatest Heresie" (YP 8:421). In *Paradise Regained*, Christ's role as "living Oracle" (1.460) and the spirit of truth dwelling "In pious Hearts, an inward Oracle / To all truth requisite for men to know" (1.463–64) replaces the external corrupt church with the true, spiritual, and invisible church not aligned with temporal power.

If the first temptation in *Paradise Regained* is based on the false claim to truth, the second and longest temptation of the kingdoms evokes the dangerous commingling of temporal and ecclesiastical power that for Milton characterized the papacy. For Milton, popery was always marked not simply in doctrinal or ecclesiastical terms, but as a political threat. Hence, Milton explains in *Of True Religion* that most dangerous is the papal pretense to temporal power: "Ecclesiastical is ever pretended to Political. The Pope by this mixt faculty, pretends rights to Kingdoms and States, and especially to this of England, Thrones and Unthrones Kings, and absolves the people from their obedience to them" (YP 8:429). For Milton, this dangerous conjunction of temporal and spiritual power leads to corruption and carnality, as he writes in *Of Reformation* (1641): "But when through *Constantines* lavish Superstition they forsook their *first love*, and set themselvs up two Gods instead, *Mammon* and their Belly, then taking advantage of the spiritual power which they had on mens consciences, they began to cast a longing eye to get the body also, and bodily things into their command ... and supporting their inward rottenes by a carnal, and outward strength" (YP 1:576–77).

Appearing in the second temptation of *Paradise Regained* as "one in City, or Court, or Palace bred" (2.300), Satan offers the Son luxury, wealth, military power, learning, and arts characteristic of the papacy. Having apparently rejected Belial's advice to "set women in his eye and in his walk" (2.153), Satan nonetheless begins the kingdoms temptation with a sensual offering: an elaborate banquet in the wilderness. The culinary delights of the banquet are designed to appeal to the fasting Son:

> A Table richly spread, in regal mode,
> With dishes pil'd, and meats of noblest sort
> And savor, Beasts of chase, or Fowl of game,
> In pastry built, or from the spit, or boil'd,
> Grisamber steam'd; all Fish from Sea or Shore,
> Freshet, or purling Brook, of shell or fin,
> And exquisitest name, for which was drain'd
> *Pontus* and *Lucrine Bay*, and *Afric* Coast.   (2.340–47)

The stately sideboard and lavish display contrast with the simple temptation of the fruit in *Paradise Lost*, which the narrator explicitly recalls: "Alas how simple, to these Cates compar'd, / Was the crude Apple that diverted *Eve*!" (2348–49). Intensifying the appeal to the senses, the culinary display is accompanied by "Harmonious airs" (2.362) and heightened by evocative odors, including "wine / That fragrant smell diffus'd" (2.350–51) and winds bringing "*Arabian* odors" (2.364) and "*Flora's* earliest smells" (2.365).

Set in "regal mode," the table may recall Milton's animus in *The Readie and Easie Way* (1659) against the "sumptuous courts" and "vast expence and luxurie" of monarchy, including the "eating and drinking of excessive dainties" in the court of Louis XIV (YP 7:425–26). But the "stately sideboard" and the lavish display also recall the purported corruption and carnality of the papacy—intertwined with temporal power. Satan's pastoral grove with its sensuous banquet might well have recalled a papal history of luxurious feasting such as that under Leo X, well recorded by his admirers and detractors alike.[21] English histories of the papacy reiterated the accusations of carnality against Leo. John Bale includes in his *Pageant of Popes* the charges that Leo, "addicting him selfe to nicenesse, and takinge ease did pamper his fleshe in diverse vanities and carnal pleasures: At banqueting he delighted greatly in wine and musike: but had no care of preaching the Gospell."[22] *A Looking-Glasse for Papists* (1621) similarly asserts that Leo X "gave himself to pleasures, and lusts of the flesh: he had singers, and Musitians at his Table."[23]

Detailed accounts of Leo's banquets—such as those given upon his accession to the papal throne and on the occasion of Roman citizenship being granted to his brother and nephew—survive.[24] A contemporary account of the courses at one such banquet lists peacocks, a calf, a boar, a deer, and an eagle with a rabbit in its talons, served *rivestiti* or "redressed" in their own skins so that they appeared almost alive, and such other delicacies as kids stuffed with roast birds, testicles of roosters, gilded calves' heads with lemons in their mouths, and big pastry balls that contained live rabbits. The banquets also featured lavish wine, music, and entertainment by buffoons. Skits and plays that followed included young men playing both nymphs and male characters.[25]

While Satan had earlier argued—against Belial—that the Son would be impervious to "beauty and her lures" (2.194), carnality nonetheless returns in a distinctly antipapal guise in the youths and maidens, as well as the lavish food and drinks, of the banquet. The banquet also appeals to sexual intemperance, as it features "tall stripling youths rich clad, of fairer hue / Than *Ganymede* or *Hylas*" (2.352–53) as well as "Nymphs of *Diana*'s train, and *Naiades*" (2.355) and "Ladies of th' *Hesperides*" (2.357). As Claude Summers writes, "Ganymede, the beautiful Trojan boy abducted by Jupiter and made cupbearer to the gods and Hylas, the young companion beloved of Hercules, were in the Renaissance not only archetypes of male adolescent beauty but also bywords for male homosexuality."[26] Summers adduces these youths as evidence of Milton's "sophisticated recognition of the range of fully human sexual possibilities," while Gregory Bredbeck has similarly argued that Milton has deliberately added a new and original homoerotic component to the exegetical tradition of the temptation in order to interrogate the strong masculinist stance and the language of patriarchy adopted by Belial and Satan.[27] Yet it is more likely that the stripling lads are part of a stereotypical if oblique attack on alleged homosexuality and sodomy in the Roman Catholic Church.

Again, specific instances could be adduced from the history of the Renaissance papacy. Among the "carnalities" he was said to enjoy, Pope Leo was alleged to favor banquets and entertainments that featured young boys. Antipapal writings seized upon an obscure passage in Leo's biographer, Paolo Giovio, to charge the pope with sexual intemperance and pederasty. Such accusations were reiterated in seventeenth-century England. Hence, *Two*

Treatises: The First, of the Lives of the Popes (London, 1600), states that "Leo had also an evill report, because it appeared that he affected unhonestly some of his chamberlains.... It is not Luther his enemie, that saith this against him: but his friend, an Italian, and Bishop, Paulus Iovius."[28] Accordingly, in *Paradise Regained*, the Son's sharp rebuke—"Thy pompous Delicacies I contemn, / And count thy specious gifts no gifts but guiles" (2.390–91)—not only evinces temperance as a model for the individual Christian but recalls the church to its earlier purity in the aftermath of papal corruption.

Satan's ensuing offers of wealth, glory, and empire, based on Alexander the Great, Julius Caesar, Scipio Africanus, and Pompey, similarly have antipapal resonance. Under the Renaissance papacy, and in particular Julius II as the "warrior pope," triumph, glory, and imperial dominion replaced martyrdom and holiness as subjects for praise and worthy ideals. The Roman pontiffs seized upon the legacy of the Caesars to bolster their own imperial ambitions: the ambitious and warmongering Julius II found suitable forms in imperial Rome for expression of his military and triumphal aims. Julius identified himself as the second Julius Caesar, while his successor, Leo X, was lauded as an Augustus fully ushering in a golden age of peace and prosperity, art and learning.[29] Classicized triumphal motifs were applied to Christ himself in such works as Marcus Hieronymus Vida's *Christiad*, commissioned by Pope Leo.[30] In Milton's own time, the Rome of Pope Urban VIII (1623–1644) boasted of producing a second Roman renaissance modeled on the golden age of Julius and Leo X.[31]

Hence, in response to Satan's offers of wealth, the Son points to self-rule and spiritual kingship which sharply contrast with the luxury and power-mongering of the Renaissance papacy. Rejecting the model of the Caesars, the Son argues that military conquerors "rob and spoil, burn, slaughter, and enslave / Peaceable Nations" (3.75–76). While Satan offers glory and empire, the Son sees his kingdom as invisible and spiritual. Further, to the offer of Parthian military power—by conquest or by league—as the means to gain the throne of Israel and deliver the ten lost tribes, the Son again reiterates the spiritual nature of his kingdom and refuses to free the self-enslaved and idolatrous. The true church does not need "fleshly arm, / And fragile arms" (3387–88). In the Son's rejections of military power, *Paradise Regained* defines the true church as not allied with worldly wealth or state power.

Satan's offer of the wealth, dominion, glory, and opulence of Rome incorporates all of the earlier worldly temptations and most centrally evokes the splendor of the papacy. Rebuffed in his offer of Parthian military power, Satan turns to "great and glorious *Rome*, Queen of the Earth / So far renown'd, and with the spoils enrich / Of Nations" (4.45–47). Satan's description recalls the traditional Protestant linkage of Rome with the

Roman Catholic Church and the whore of Babylon, who in Revelation, chapter 17, sits resplendent upon a scarlet, seven-headed beast with ten horns and in Revelation, chapter 18, "saith in her heart, I sit a queen and am no widow and shal see no sorrow" (Rev. 18:7).[32]

Satan's depiction of the "Imperial City" recalls the spectacle and stately magnificence of not only classical but also papal Rome:

> With Towers and Temples proudly elevate
> On seven small Hills, with Palaces adorn'd
> Porches and Theaters, Baths, Aqueducts,
> Statues and Trophies, and Triumphal Arcs,
> Gardens and Groves.   (4.34–38)

The Rome depicted in the poem, with its conflux of "Praetors, Proconsuls to thir Provinces, / Hasting or on return, in robes of State; / Lictors and rods, the ensigns of thir power" (4.63–65), recalls the frequent arrivals and departures of legations to papal Rome as a hub of international politics during the late Renaissance.

The "Houses of Gods" (4.56) that Satan reveals with his "Airy Microscope" (4.57) and Rome's "ample Territory, wealth, and power, / Civility of Manners, Arts, and Arms, / And long Renown" (4.82–84) point toward the spectacle that reached new heights in Julius's classicized triumphs and Leo's coronation and the festivities conferring citizenship on Leo's brother, Giuliano, and nephew, Lorenzo De Medici.[33] Rome's imperial palace, with its "compass huge, and high / The Structure, skill of noblest Architects, / With gilded battlements, conspicuous far / Turrets and Terraces and glittering Spires" (4.51–54), may also suggest that central sanctuary, Saint Peter's Basilica, the rebuilding of which began under Julius and Leo.[34]

While Satan urges the Son to expel the aging and much-hated Tiberius from his throne and free his vassal subjects, Jesus again refuses to free a people "deservedly made vassal" (4.133), whether enslaved to pope or monarch. The Son also points to the carnality that characterizes worldly Rome, also marking, for Milton, the Roman Catholic Church:

> Nor doth this grandeur and majestic show
> Of luxury, though call'd magnificence,
> More than of arms before, allure mine eye,
> Much less my mind; though thou should'st add to tell
> Thir sumptuous gluttonies, and gorgeous feasts
> On *Citron* tables or *Atlantic* stone.   (4.110–15)

In rejecting the luxury and carnality of Rome, the Son returns the true church to the chaste and humble poverty of its origins, underscored by his own humble origins, in Satan's words, "unknown, unfriended, low of birth, / A Carpenter thy Father known, thyself / Bred up in poverty and straits at home" (2.413–15).

The historical source of that carnality emerges in the aftermath of the temptation of Rome, as Satan suddenly, almost petulantly, reveals the "abominable terms, impious condition" of idolatry, prompting the Son's rebuke: "It is written / The first of all Commandments, Thou shalt worship / The Lord thy God, and only him shalt serve" (4.175–77). But the Son goes on to challenge Satan in language evocative of the pretended dominion of the papacy: "The Kingdoms of the world to thee were giv'n, / Permitted rather, and by thee usurp't, / Other donation none thou canst produce" (4.182–84). Elsewhere, Milton repeatedly links both usurpation and "donation" with popery. In *The Readie and Easie Way*, he writes that for a Christian man to claim his kingship is from Christ is "wors usurpation then the Pope his headship over the church" (YP 7:429). He represents the pope himself as a usurper in *Of True Religion*, writing that "Popery is a double thing to deal with, and claims a twofold Power, Ecclesiastical and Political, both usurpt, and the one supporting the other" (YP 8:429). Similarly, Milton uses the term "donation" elsewhere almost exclusively in connection with the (spurious) donation of Constantine, the first Christian emperor (c. 285–337), who built stately churches and encouraged "a Deluge of Ceremonies" (*Of Reformation*, in YP 1:556–57). Papal claims for temporal authority were based on this document, by which Emperor Constantine, miraculously cured of leprosy through baptism by Pope Sylvester, donated the City of Rome, the Western empire, and the imperial regalia to the pope. Although as early as 1440 Lorenzo Valla had shown the document to be an eighth-century forgery, Constantine was prominently featured in the art and architecture of Renaissance and baroque Rome, undergirding papal claims to imperial power.[35] For later critics, however, including Dante, Wyclif, Hus, and Martin Luther, the donation was the source of the church's corruption.

Milton too saw Constantine's gift of temporal power as setting the church on a long and sharp decline. In more than a dozen references in his prose, Milton decries the deleterious influence of the donation of Constantine on the church. In *The Likeliest Means to Remove Hirelings* (1659), for instance, Milton writes that "the church fell off and turnd whore sitting on that beast in the Revelations, when under Pope *Silvester* she receivd those temporal donations" (YP 7:306). Milton at times seems to acknowledge that the alleged donation endowing Pope Sylvester and his successors with supremacy in religion and temporal dominion over Rome was a forgery, writing in *Of Reformation*: "Mark Sir how the Pope came by *S. Peters* Patrymony, as he feigns it, not the donation of *Constantine*, but idolatry and rebellion got it him" (YP 1:578). But most often, for polemical purposes, Milton takes the donation at face value, observing in *Eikonoklastes*, for instance, that "those [true] Churches in *Piemont* have held the same Doctrin and Government since the time that *Constantine* with his mischievous donations poyson'd *Silvester* and the whole church" (YP 3:514).

The Son's rebuke of Satan's idolatrous terms thus takes on historically specific connotations in Restoration England. In his rejection of the dangerously commingled powers of church and state, the Son both condemns current practices and places the bishops in a papal tradition. The Son reveals that underlying this dangerous conjunction is the danger of idolatry, and he definitively rejects the offer of the kingdoms: "Get thee behind me; plain thou now appear'st / That Evil one, Satan for ever damn'd" (4.193–94).

The temptation of learning is both unique to Milton and, for many commentators, the most puzzling of the earthly temptations. Coming after the apparent end of the kingdoms temptation—Satan avows, "Therefore let pass, as they are transitory, / The Kingdoms of this world; I shall no more / Advise thee, gain them as thou canst, or not" (4.209–11)—the temptation nonetheless continues the commingling of temporal and ecclesiastical power that marks Satan's earlier offers. In turning to Athens and Plato's Academy, Satan once again evokes the learning and arts revived under Popes Julius and Leo as part of their claim to temporal and spiritual power and reclaimed again by Pope Urban in Milton's own time. Hence, he offers these arts as a means of power and glory—"Be famous then / By wisdom; as thy Empire must extend, / So let extend thy mind o'er all the world" (4.221–23). In keeping with the claim of the papacy to incorporate the best of classical learning, Satan eschews a strict biblicism:

> All knowledge is not couch't in *Moses'* Law,
> The *Pentateuch* or what the Prophets wrote;
> The *Gentiles* also know, and write, and teach
> To admiration, led by Nature's light.   (4.225–28)

The description of "*Athens*, the eye of *Greece*, Mother of Arts / And Eloquence" (4.240–41) recalls the arts and rhetoric that Milton himself had studied and admired. But those arts were also part of the intellectual and artistic revival of Renaissance Italy, nurtured by and contributing to the enhanced power of the papacy. Although in the end the revival of Latin, not Greek, mattered more to Renaissance Rome, the theme of Rome as the new

Athens developed under both Julius and Leo, in particular with the acquisition of Greek manuscripts in the Vatican library.³⁶ Further, Satan's presentation of Plato's enchanting grove summons up the sensuous appeal of the earlier banquet scene: "See there the Olive Grove of *Academe*, / *Plato's* retirement, where the *Attic* Bird / Trills her thick-warbl'd notes the summer long" (4.244–46). The revival of ancient Greek eloquence and Ciceronian rhetoric also marked Renaissance Rome, recalled in Satan's evocation of the "famous Orators" (4.267) whose "resistless eloquence / Wielded at will that fierce Democraty" (4.268–69).

And thus while Milton himself followed the example of Cicero and used classical oratory for republican ends in his *Defenses*, the Son must reject the arts and learning of Rome as they serve temporal power and pretend to divine wisdom. As Satan pretends to truth, evoking the fraudulence of popery, so classical learning has been misappropriated as the false twin of divine wisdom: "Who therefore seeks in these / True wisdom, finds her not, or by delusion / Far worse, her false resemblance only meets, / An empty cloud" (4.318–21).

The Son's rejection of arts and rhetoric defines true faith and the true church in terms sharply opposed to the flourishing of learning and humanistic knowledge that marked the corrupt papacy. Much of what Satan offers Christ in the kingdoms temptation—wealth, power, military power, learning and the arts—was central to the exultant vision of the Renaissance papacy. To the pursuit of temporal power, territorial consolidation, and military expenditure marking the papacy, *Paradise Regained* opposes the contrasting values of humility, obedience, poverty, and chastity.

Following the kingdoms temptation, the third and final temptation of the tower in *Paradise Regained* again shows antipapal sentiment. But while Milton had earlier seemed to avoid the Crucifixion, attention to physical suffering—and the rhetoric, arts, banquet, and heroic mode earlier rejected when offered in the service of temporal power—are returned in spiritualized form to the triumphant Son. The storm preceding and Satan's placing of the Son on the tower threaten violence and foreshadow the Passion and death.³⁷ Satan himself now professes to read in the stars the suffering and death that the Son must endure: "Sorrows, and labors, opposition, hate, / Attends thee, scorns, reproaches, injuries, / Violence and stripes, and lastly cruel death" (4386–88). The tower temptation suggests the violence of the scourging and Crucifixion. Having placed the Son on a precarious, perhaps impossible, perch on the pinnacle—"There stand, if thou wilt stand; to stand upright / Will ask thee skill" (4.551–52)—Satan further challenges him to show his divinity:

> if not to stand,
> Cast thyself down; safely if Son of God:
> For it is written, He will give command
> Concerning thee to his Angels, in thir hands
> They shall up lift thee, lest at any time
> Thou chance to dash thy foot against a stone.   (4.554–59)

While Satan tauntingly paraphrases the Psalms, his words also evoke the reviling of Christ upon the cross: "If thou be the Son of God, come down from the cross.... He saved others; himself he cannot save. If he be the King of Israel, let him now come down from the cross, and we will believe him" (Matt. 27:40–42). Hence, if much of *Paradise Regained* has seemed to avoid the suffering and the Crucifixion, the body of Christ so prominent in Catholic art and sacrament, this final scene boldly reinscribes and revises that climactic moment.

The Son's patient refusal to save himself by miracle—or to call upon God miraculously to save him—points ahead to and on one level enacts the temporary submission to satanic power evinced in the Crucifixion. But that very submission brings about revelation of divinity and victory over the forces of evil: "To whom thus Jesus. Also it is written, / Tempt not the Lord thy God; he said and stood" (4.560–61). If, at the cross, the centurions acknowledge, "Truly this was the Son of God" (Matt 27:54), Satan is likewise amazed and at the same time defeated in the only real action of the poem:

> But Satan smitten with amazement fell
> As when Earth's *Antaeus* (to compare
> Small things with greatest) in *Irassa* strove
> With *Jove's Alcides*, and oft foil'd still rose,
> Receiving from his mother Earth new strength,
> Fresh from his fall, and fiercer grapple join'd,
> Throttl'd at length in th' Air, expir'd and fell:
> So after many a foil the Tempter proud,
> Renewing fresh assaults, amidst his pride
> Fell whence he stood to see his Victor fall.   (4.562–71)

In this and the simile of the "*Theban* Monster" that follows, Milton brings back in the classical myth and learning refused in the temptations of Athens—Oedipus overthrowing the Sphinx, the story of Hercules and Antaeus—not to further the worldly, imperial church but to reveal the achievement and true identity of the obedient, disciplined Son. The comparison to Hercules assigns to the Son the heroic qualities and conquest eschewed in the temptation of Parthia, now revised as appropriate to his spiritual conquest over Satan. If the Son has earlier rejected false, worldly models of imperial conquest, he is nonetheless now praised as a conqueror in a spiritual triumph that outgoes the physical, as "Angelic Choirs / Sung Heavenly Anthems of his victory / Over temptation and the Tempter proud" (4.593–95). While the Son has rejected satanic offers of fame on earth, "where glory is false glory" like the glittering display of papal Rome, he now attains true renown in heaven.

Similarly, for the false, luxurious banquets that he has rejected, the Son is now given a heavenly banquet, with Eucharistic overtones that replace and defeat the earlier parodic banquets in the wilderness and of Rome offered by Satan. Rescued by angels from his precarious perch, the Son receives "A table of Celestial Food, Divine, / Ambrosial, Fruits fetcht from the tree of life, / And from the fount of life Ambrosial drink" (4.588–90). The "Heavenly Feast" with which the Son is refreshed at the end of *Paradise Regained* recaptures for the steadfast believer the true sacrament of Christ's sacrifice: the song of victory replaces the lavish displays of imperial power as the heavenly feast replaces papal extravagance and luxury.

While *Paradise Regained* rejects what Milton views as the beautiful, opulent, but ultimately decadent and even idolatrous culture of papal Rome, it is not in the end a wholly ascetic work. The obedient and patient Son ultimately gains—albeit in revised and spiritualized form—both renown and the riches of human culture, not to promulgate the false temporal power of the papacy, but to nurture the internal discipline that marked the true believer in an age of persecution. From an external, worldly perspective, nothing has changed for the Son. But he now has within him the faith, knowledge, and discipline by which worldly powers can ultimately be overturned. "Sung Victor, and from Heavenly Feast refresht" (4.636), the Son returns privately, quietly to "his Mother's house" (4.638). As the Son of God begins "to save mankind" (4.635), the agony—and triumph—of Michelangelo's *Pieta* lie just ahead.

NOTES

An earlier version of my essay was presented in the general Milton session of the December 2000 Modern Language Association meeting, chaired by John Mulryan. I am grateful for the valuable responses I received at that session, as well as for the useful insights and suggestions of David Loewenstein and Al Labriola, the editors of this volume.

1. John Evelyn, *The Diary of John Evelyn*, ed. E.S. de Beer, 6 vols. (Oxford, 1955), 2:255, 264.

2. See Loren Partridge, *The Art of Renaissance Rome, 1400–1600* (New York, 1996), 101–4.

3. Milton does not allude to the art and architecture in his description, some years later, of his travels in *Defensio Secunda* (1654). All quotations from Milton's prose are taken from *Complete Prose Works of John Milton*, 8 vols., ed. Don. M. Wolfe et al. (New Haven, 1953–82), 4:614–19; hereafter designated as YP and cited parenthetically by volume and page number in the text.

4. Roland Frye, *Milton's Imagery and the Visual Arts: Iconographic Tradition in the Epic Poems* (Princeton, 1978), argues that the corporeal forms that Milton delineates in *Paradise Lost* and *Paradise Regained* derive from the traditions of sacred art.

5. Michael O'Connell, "Milton and the Art of Italy: A Revisionist View," in *Milton in Italy: Contexts, Images, Contradictions*, ed. Mario Di Cesare (Binghamton, N.Y., 1991), 221. O'Connell goes on to argue for a "strong disapprobation" of such visual arts in *Paradise Regained* (235).

6. For a broad overview, see John T. Paoletti and Gary M. Radke, *Art in Renaissance Italy* (New York, 1997); and Partridge, *The Art of Renaissance Rome*.

7. On Julius and Leo, see Ludwig Pastor, *The History of the Popes*, trans. and ed. Ralph Francis Kerr (London, 1923), vols. 6 and 7; and on Leo X, Thomas Roscoe, *The Life and Pontificate of Leo X*, 2 vols., 5th ed. (London, 1846). For an influential contemporary life of Leo, see Paolo Giovio, *Pauli Iovii Novocomensis episcopi Nucerini de Vita Leonis Decimi Pont. Max. libri quatuor* (Florence, 1549).

8. On anti-Catholicism in seventeenth-century England, see Caroline Hibbard, *Charles I and the Popish Plot* (Chapel Hill, N.C., 1983); Anthony Milton, *Catholic and Reformed: The Roman and Protestant Churches in English Protestant Thought, 1600–1640* (Cambridge, 1995); Robin Clifton, "Fear of Popery" in *The Origins of the English Civil War*, ed. Conrad Russell (London, 1973), 144–67; John Miller, *Popery and Politics in England, 1660–1688* (Cambridge, 1973); Peter Lake, "Anti-Popery: The Structure of a Prejudice," in *Conflict in Early Stuart England: Studies in Religion and Politics, 1603–1642*, ed. Richard Cust and Ann Hughes (London, 1989); and Frances Dolan, *Whores of Babylon: Catholicism, Gender, and Seventeenth-Century Print Culture* (New York, 1999).

9. Barbara Lewalski, *Milton's Brief Epic: The Genre, Meaning, and Art of "Paradise Regained"* (Providence, R.I., 1966), notes that "precedents for a brief epic on the subject of the temptation of Christ are almost nonexistent" (104). Much of the dissatisfaction centers on the character of the Son. John Carey, *Milton* (London, 1969), terms Christ a "celibate detective" (137), while for Alan Fisher, "Why Is *Paradise Regained* So Cold?" in *Milton Studies* 14, ed. James D. Simmonds (Pittsburgh, 1980), the Son is "heartless, prissy, or downright cold" (206); Northrop Frye, "The Typology of *Paradise Regained*," in *Milton: Modern Essays in Criticism*, ed. Arthur E. Barker (New York, 1965), sees an "inhuman snob" (439). Of the particular temptations, the temptation of learning has most puzzled commentators. In early studies, Douglas Bush, *The Renaissance and English Humanism* (Toronto, 1939), termed "the violent denunciation of Greek culture" a "painful shock," going on to observe that "it is painful to watch Milton turn and rend some main roots of his being" (124–25); and George Sensabaugh, "Milton on Learning," *Studies in Philology* 43 (1946): 258–72, likewise found it "distinctly surprising" to "hear Christ, in *Paradise Regained*, belittle the whole heritage of Greece and Rome" (258), positing that "not so much the march of events as the force of theological dogma compelled Milton to speak against his earlier convictions and his deepest experience" (272). In my view, these concerns have not been fully answered in subsequent criticism. A helpful perspective is given by David Loewenstein, *Representing Revolution in Milton and His Contemporaries: Religion, Politics, and Polemics in Radical Puritanism* (Cambridge, 2001), who notes that Jesus "dramatizes that fierce Miltonic stance of polemical

engagement and vehement response ... countering rhetorical extreme with rhetorical extreme" (266).

10. On the politics of interiority and radical religious culture, albeit not in the context of Catholicism, see Loewenstein, *Representing Revolution*, 254–59.

11. Particularly instructive on Milton and Catholicism are recent studies by Achsah Guibbory *Ceremony and Community from Herbert to Milton* (Cambridge, 1998), and John King, *Milton and Religious Controversy* (Cambridge, 2000). Both focus more on *Paradise Lost* than on Milton's later poems, but see the helpful brief comments on *Paradise Regained* in Guibbory, 219–27, and King, 189–90. Also useful is John Shawcross, "'Connivers and the Worst of Superstitions': Milton on Popery and Toleration," *Literature and History*, 3d ser, 7, no. 2 (1990): 51–69. The most sustained treatment of *Paradise Regained* and Catholicism, however, remains the early work of Howard Schultz which, while useful, tends to overallegorize the Son as a figure for the true church versus the Catholic Antichrist. See Schultz, "Christ and Antichrist in *Paradise Regained*," *PMLA* 43 (1952): 790–808, and his *Milton and Forbidden Knowledge* (London, 1955)

12. Christopher Mill, *Milton and the English Revolution* (New York, 1978), 413–27, views the Son as rejecting those things that led the revolutionaries astray. Andrew Milner, *John Milton and the English Revolution: A Study in the Sociology of Literature* (Totowa, N.J., 1981), 167–79, and Michael Wilding, *Dragons Teeth: Literature in the English Revolution* (Oxford, 1987), 249–53, find quietism and withdrawal in the poem. Among recent studies, David Loewenstein, "The Kingdom Within: Radical Religious Culture and the Politics of *Paradise Regained*," *Literature and History* 3, no. 2 (1994): 63–89, sees the poem as more radically resistant, linked with the Quakers. Loewenstein places even greater emphasis on the polemical dimensions of *Paradise Regained*, including the subversiveness of the Son's obscurity and "mighty weakness," in *Representing Revolution*, 242–68. David Quint traces the poem's ongoing challenge to Stuart monarchy in "David's Census: Milton's Politics and *Paradise Regained*," in *Re-membering Milton: Essays on the Texts and Traditions*, ed. Mary Nyquist and Margaret Ferguson (New York, 1988), 128–47. My own book, *Historicizing Milton: Spectacle, Power, and Poetry in Restoration England* (Athens, Ga., 1994), 13–41, discusses *Paradise Regained* as challenging Stuart claims to Christie martyrdom.

13. On anti-Catholicism in seventeenth-century England, see Caroline Hibbard, *Charles I and the Popish Plot* (Chapel Hill, N.C., 1983); Anthony Milton, *Catholic and Reformed: The Roman and Protestant Churches in English Protestant Thought, 1600–1640* (Cambridge, 1995); Robin Clifton, "Fear of Popery" in *The Origins of the English Civil War*, ed. Conrad Russell (London, 1973), 144–67; John Miller, *Popery and Politics in England, 1660–1688* (Cambridge, 1973); Peter Lake, "Anti-Popery: The Structure of a Prejudice," in *Conflict in Early Stuart England: Studies in Religion and Politics, 1603–1642*, ed. Richard Cust and Ann Hughes (London, 1989); and Frances Dolan, *Whores of Babylon: Catholicism, Gender, and Seventeenth-Century Print Culture* (Ithaca, N.Y., 1999).

14. On anti-popery in the 1670s, see especially Miller, *Popery and Politics*.

15. On *Of True Religion*, see Reuben Sanchez, *Persona and Decorum in Milton's Prose* (Madison, N.J., 1997), 180–94; Raymond Tumbleson, *Catholicism in the English Protestant Imagination: Nationalism, Religion, and Literature, 1660–1745* (Cambridge, 1998), 41–68; Shawcross; "'Connivers and the Worst of Superstitions'"; and, most recently, Hong Won Suh, "Belial, Popery, and True Religion: Milton's *Of True Religion* and Antipapist Sentiment," in *Living Texts: Interpreting Milton*, ed. Kristin Pruitt and Charles Durham (Selinsgrove, Pa., 2000), 283–302.

16. In addition to Evelyn's account, see Fynes Moryson, *An Itinerary Containing His Ten Yeeres Travell*, vol. 1 (Glasgow, 1907), 258–304; *Francis Mortoft, his Book: Being His*

Travels through France and Italy, 1658–59, ed. Malcolm Letts (London, 1925). See also John Raymond, *An Itinerary Contayning a Voyage Made Through Italy* (London, 1648); Richard Lassels, *The Voyage of Italy* (Paris, 1670).

17. *The Diary of John Evelyn*, 2:240, 242.

18. All quotations from *Paradise Regained* and *Paradise Lost* are taken from *John Milton: Complete Poems and Major Prose*, ed. Merritt Y. Hughes (Indianapolis, 1957).

19. On *Paradise Regained* as a rebuttal of Stuart claims of martyrdom, see Knoppers, *Historicizing Milton*, 13–41; on the poem in alliance with Quaker martyrdom, see Loewenstein, "The Kingdom Within," and *Representing Revolution*, 242–68.

20. *Francis Mortoft, his Book*, 94.

21. I am indebted to Stella Revard for suggesting a link between the banquet scene and Leo X.

22. John Bale, *The Pageant of Popes Contayning the lyves of all the Bishops of Rome, from the beginninge of them to the yeare of Grace 1555* (London, 1555), fol. 179v.

23. *A Looking-Glasse for Papists ... with a briefe History of Popes lives* (London, 1621), 67.

24. Bonner Mitchell, *Italian Civic Pageantry in the High Renaissance: A Descriptive Bibliography* (Firenze, 1979), 117–24. Primary sources are collected in Fabrizio Cruciani, *Il Teatro del Campidoglio e le Feste Romane del 1513* (Milano, 1968); see especially the account of Paolo Palliolo (21–67), including a detailed listing of the banquet courses (39–44).

25. See the description in Bonner Mitchell, *Rome in the High Renaissance: The Age of Leo X* (Norman, Okla., 1973), 68–70, and the primary sources in Cruciani, *Il Teatro del Campidoglio*.

26. Claude J. Summers, "The (Homo)Sexual Temptation in Milton's *Paradise Regained*," in *Reclaiming the Sacred: The Bible in Gay and Lesbian Culture*, ed. Raymond-Jean Frontain (New York, 1997), 53.

27. Ibid., 65; Gregory Bredbeck, "Milton's Ganymede: Negotiations of Homoerotic Tradition in *Paradise Regained*," *PMLA* 106 (1991): 262–76.

28. *Two Treatises: The First, of the Lives of the Popes* (London, 1600), 150; see similar charges in *A True History of the Lives of the Popes of Rome* (London, 1679), 12, and *A Satirical Account of the Lives of the Popes* (London, 1702), 177.

29. Charles L. Stinger, *The Renaissance in Rome* (Bloomington, 1985), 10–12.

30. Lewalski, *Milton's Brief Epic*, 53–67, points to Vida's *Christiad* as well as other humanist biblical epics as part of the literary tradition of Milton's brief epic; she does not, however, explore Milton's epic as a *challenge* to the triumphal epics produced as part of an overarching papal cultural program.

31. John D'Amico, *Renaissance Humanism in Papal Rome: Humanists and Churchmen on the Eve of the Reformation* (Baltimore, 1983), 142.

32. For other commentators on this point, see Schultz, "Christ and Antichrist," 803; Barbara K. Lewalski, *The Life of John Milton* (Oxford, 2000), 519; and Lewalski, *Milton's Brief Epic*, 275–77.

33. See sources cited in Bonner Mitchell, *Italian Civic Pageantry*, esp. 15–25 (on Julius II) and 117–24 (on Leo X). Such ceremonies continued in the mid-seventeenth century. Evelyn, *The Diary of John Evelyn*, for instance, observes the people busy "in erecting temporary Triumphs & arches, with statues, and flattering Inscriptions" in preparation for a papal installation (2.228).

34. Lewalski, *The Life of John Milton*, also makes this point (519). For an important (and neglected) early linkage of Stunt Peters and Milton's Pandemonium, see Rebecca W. Smith, "The Sources of Milton's Pandemonium," *Modern Philology* 29 (1931–1932): 187–98.

35. On Constantine, see Partridge, *The Art of Renaissance Rome*, 14–15. On Constantine's arch, the various churches said to be founded by Constantine, and the relies linked with Constantine and his mother, Helena, see the travel accounts of Evelyn, *The Diary of John Evelyn*; *Francis Mortoft, his Book*; Lassels, *The Voyage of Italy*; and Raymond, *An Itinerary Contayning a Voyage*.

36. Stinger, *The Renaissance in Rome*, 286–87.

37. On this point regarding the third temptation, and on literary precedents, see Lewalski, *Milton's Brief Epic*, 308–15.

Character Profile

Satan in the popular imagination generally moves between three primary conceptions. He is either a lobster-red, cloven-hoofed, pointy-tailed, horned half-man-half-beast Prince of Hell, or he is the suave, seductive, powerful, serpentine tempter who caused the Fall of Man and took the souls of Faust and Robert Johnson (among others), or he is the archangel, beautiful, arrogant and inspiring, who brought about the only war in heaven.

Yet, when the term "satan" originated in the text of the Hebrew Bible, it did not connote the red, horned beast with which it has been associated for the past few centuries. Instead, according to religion scholar Elaine Pagels, "satan" referenced an enemy of the Israelites, one who was quite powerful, a member of God's court. With these superior supernatural powers and the backing of God, the enemy might prove overwhelming. The "satan" might also be one of many angels; it did not specifically reference one, only a specific activity, that of obstructing the path of a human, whether for good or for evil. In the book of Job, Satan acts in collusion with God, as one of His court. This changed with the schism of the Israelites. The more extreme groups pitted Satan as an opponent of God and a malevolent doer of evil as they believed their enemies to be. All those who went against the faction became Satan, rendering the character larger than life, yet still accessible, as the enemy had once been a part of the family, as Satan had been one of God's family.

As Christianity progressed, the role of Satan changed as well. He made his way from the strictly religious into the secular, stringing behind him a series of stories in every country. In the mystery plays and cycles of the

Middle Ages, Satan is silly, posturing and ambitious, eager to take the place of God and be worshipped accordingly. He appears as the archangel destined to Fall; and as the tempter, the serpent slithering through the Garden of Eden; and finally, the comic fool who tries to tempt Christ. It is his failure that so amused audiences. Satan was a dramatic figure of fun; he was hairy and grotesque, a kind of joke as Satan could easily be outsmarted. In the book of Isaiah, Satan is given more motivation. He is jealous, disgusted that both man and the Son are currying more favor with God, even though he feels himself to be the superior being. These new upstarts threaten his position, giving him no choice but to gather an army in opposition. While he is not precisely a sympathetic character, he is beginning to at least be an evil rendered reasonable by these attempts at motivation.

Satan began in literature in the Middle Ages as something comic, then later evolved into something both pathetic and horrifying. For Dante, Satan had been exiled from heaven, thrown so forcibly to the ground that a hole was made in the earth, wherein the many levels of Hell were built, with Satan residing in the lowest level, struck dumb, a character chewing and gnawing at sinners, insensible to the two poets who climb over his body. He had three faces: a black one (left) containing Brutus; a yellow one (right) containing Cassius; and a red one (middle) containing Judas Iscariot. His body is gigantic, hairy and grotesque. Clearly, certain trends in Italy affected those contained within the mouths of Satan, solidifying a trend wherein Satan assumes the mores of a particular culture. In *The Inferno*, Satan takes one of his most important positions as Prince of Hell.

For Edmund Spenser, Satan was a fire-breathing dragon. Martin Luther claimed that Satan was part of God's plan, that he was fated to fall from grace. Christopher Marlowe's Satan was something else altogether, the beginning of what we recognize today as the devil. He was charming, eloquent, haunted by his fall, a figure with which many sympathized. His hubris was human, begun in a kind of sibling rivalry and ending in exile. He became the tempter of man, strengthening his small kingdom and frustrating the efforts of God and his angels by using His creatures against Him. Shakespeare never overtly wrote of Satan, though both Iago and Macbeth compare themselves to devils. Ultimately, it is Milton who made the character of Satan into the one we know today.

In *Paradise Lost*, Satan speaks with both authority and eloquence. He possesses a sly sense of humor and an infernal logic. He is the proprietor of knowledge, a beautiful and powerful fallen angel, still possessing much of the charm that brought him followers in heaven. He has the ability to rally people, angels, and demons to his cause. Unfortunately for Satan, as the epic progresses, his character declines until readers and followers alike can see that his rhetoric is hollow, that his promises cannot be kept. Laura Lunger Knoppers suggests that Satan's double speech and immoral character was Milton's indictment of Roman Catholic dogma and particular figures within the papacy.

After *Paradise Lost*, it is hard to find a version of the devil that is not in someway beholden to Milton's Satan, though some tried. William Blake gave the devil a positive spin, claiming that the demonic was representative of the genius of poetry. Lord Byron played with the idea of Satan too, amplifying the mystique of the devil as sexual and attractive, although one suspects that Byron had an ulterior motive in spinning the press about those possessing a clubfoot. Baudelaire suggested that Satan was the most learned of the angels, the possessor of great knowledge. He also wrote one of the most quoted lines regarding the devil and his power: "the loveliest trick of the devil is to persuade you that he does not exist!" Such a feat is in keeping with the Satan that Baudelaire describes as "…inexhaustible in his irrefutable jests, and he expressed himself with a splendor of diction and with a magnificence in drollery such as I have never found in any of the most famous conversationalists of our age."

This amiable Satan returns in Mark Twain's *Letters from the Earth*, where Satan writes back to the archangels to tell them of earth and all of its hypocrisy. In this version, Satan speaks rationally if incredulously of man. Twain makes it clear that Satan is yet to be impressed by this poor-relation creation of both his and God's.

In the twentieth century, Satan still finds himself in literature as well as song, television, and movies. In an apocryphal tale of the blues, Robert Johnson, famed blues guitarist, sold his soul to the devil in order to play his guitar like no one else. Satan also had a notable run in "Damn Yankees," "The Devil's Advocate," and even a cameo in "The Passion of the Christ." In literature, he still makes his way into international bestsellers like Salman Rushdie's *Satanic Verses*. He even graces the pages of endless literary magazines in poems and short stories.

Of course, both C.S. Lewis and Mark Twain understood the appeal of Satan. He is quantifiable. Regardless of his trappings at any particular moment, he has definite characteristics and he lives in a definite place. While people may have trouble picturing paradise, few have trouble picturing hell. It is perfection that boggles the mind, not sin, destruction, and folly. Those have always had a figure whether he was red and carrying a pitchfork or picture-perfect and purchasing a soul. As Jacques Madaule said of Satan in Gogol, "The devil would not be so dangerous if he were not crouching in the inner core of our very selves."

Contributors

HAROLD BLOOM is Sterling Professor of the Humanities at Yale University. He is the author of over 20 books, including *Shelley's Mythmaking* (1959), *The Visionary Company* (1961), *Blake's Apocalypse* (1963), *Yeats* (1970), *A Map of Misreading* (1975), *Kabbalah and Criticism* (1975), *Agon: Toward a Theory of Revisionism* (1982), *The American Religion* (1992), *The Western Canon* (1994), and *Omens of Millennium: The Gnosis of Angels, Dreams, and Resurrection* (1996). *The Anxiety of Influence* (1973) sets forth Professor Bloom's provocative theory of the literary relationships between the great writers and their predecessors. His most recent books include *Shakespeare: The Invention of the Human* (1998), a 1998 National Book Award finalist, *How to Read and Why* (2000), *Genius: A Mosaic of One Hundred Exemplary Creative Minds* (2002), and *Hamlet: Poem Unlimited* (2003). In 1999, Professor Bloom received the prestigious American Academy of Arts and Letters Gold Medal for Criticism, and in 2002 he received the Catalonia International Prize.

WILLIAM BYSSHE STEIN is the author of *The Poetry of Melville's Late Years: Time, History, Myth, and Religion, Two Brahman Sources of Emerson and Thoreau* and *Hawthorne's Faust: A Study of the Devil Archetype*.

C.S. LEWIS was the Chair of Medieval and Renaissance Literature at Cambridge, an Honorary Fellow of Magdalen College, Oxford, and an elected Fellow of the British Academy. He is the author of many works of fiction and criticism with religious themes, *The Screwtape Letters* and *The Chronicles of Narnia* among them.

STANLEY BRODWIN is the author and editor of a number of books, including *The Old and New World Romanticism of Washington Irving* and *William Cullen Bryant and His America: Centennial Conference Proceedings, 1878–1978*.

FRANK S. KASTOR, Professor Emeritus at Wichita State University, is the author of *Milton and the Literary Satan, Giles and Phineas Fletcher (Twayne's English Author Series)*, and *C.S. Lewis's* The Chronicles of Narnia*: A Study Guide and Workbook*.

J.W. SMEED is the author of *German Song and its Poetry 1740–1900, The Theophrastan Character: The History of a Literary Genre*, and *Faust in Literature*.

STELLA PURCE REVARD is a Professor Emerita at Southern Illinois University. She is the author of *The War in Heaven: Paradise Lost and the Tradition of Satan's Rebellion* and *Pindar and the Renaissance Hymn-Ode: 1450–1700*.

JEFFREY BURTON RUSSELL is Professor of History, Emeritus, at the University of California, Santa Barbara. He is the author of seventeen books, *A History of Heaven: The Singing Silence* and *Inventing the Flat Earth*, among them.

ELAINE PAGELS is the Harrington Spear Paine Professor of Religion at Princeton, and a recipient of the Rockefeller, Guggenheim and MacArthur Fellowships. She is the author of *The Gnostic Gospels, The Origin of Satan, Adam, Eve and the Serpent*, and *Beyond Belief: The Secret Gospel of Thomas*, as well as numerous scholarly articles and book reviews.

LAURA LUNGER KNOPPERS is a Professor of English at Penn State University. She is the author of *Historicizing Milton: Spectacle, Power, and Poetry in Restoration England* and *Constructing Cromwell: Ceremony, Portrait, and Print, 1645–1661*.

Bibliography

Aers, David, Bob Hodge, and Gunther Kress. *Literature, Language and Society in England 1580–1680*. Totowa: Barnes and Noble Books, 1981.

Anshen, Ruth Nanda. *The Reality of the Devil: Evil in Man*. New York: Harper & Row, 1972.

Anstice, Sir Robert H. *The "Satan" of Milton*. Aberdeen: G. Cornwall & Sons, 1910.

Bidney, Martin. *Blake and Goethe: Psychology, Ontology, Imagination*. Columbia: University of Missouri Press, 1988.

Biletzky, I. Ch. *God, Jew, Satan in the Works of Isaac Bashevis Singer*. Lanham: University Press of America, Inc., 1995.

Birrell, T.A. "The Figure of Satan in Milton and Blake." *Satan*. Pére Bruno de Jésus-Marie, O.C.D., ed. London: Sheed and Ward, 1951, pp. 379–393.

Buxton, Charles Roden. *Prophets of Heaven & Hell: Virgil, Dante, Milton, Goethe*. New York: Russell & Russell, 1945.

Cigman, Gloria. *Exploring Evil through the Landscape of Literature*. Bern: Peter Lang, 2002.

Connolly, Julian W. *The Intimate Stranger: The Devil in Nineteenth-Century Russian Literature*. New York: Peter Lang Publishing, Inc., 2001.

Davidson, Pamela, ed. *Russian Literature and Its Demons*. New York, NY : Berghahn, 2000.

Defoe, Daniel. *The Political History of the Devil.* Irving N. Rothman and R. Michael Bowerman, eds. New York, AMS Press, 2003.

Fleissner, Robert F. *The Prince and the Professor: The Wittenberg Connection in Marlowe, Shakespeare, Goethe and Frost.* Heidelberg: Carl Winter, 1986.

Friedman, Hershey H., Steve Lipman. "Satan the Accuser: Trickster in Talmudic and Midrashic Literature." *Thalia: studies in literary humor (Univ. of Ottawa)* (18:1–2) [1998:1–2], p.31–41.

Frye, Roland Mushat. *God, Man, and Satan: Patterns of Christian Thought and Life in* Paradise Lost, Pilgrim's Progress, *and the Great Theologians.* Port Washington, N.Y.: Kennikat Press, 1960.

Hamilton, G. Rostrevor. *Hero or Fool? A Study of Milton's Satan.* New York: Haskell House Publishers, 1969.

Howard, John. *Infernal Poetics: Poetic Structures in Blake's Lambeth Prophecies.* Rutherfurd: Farleigh Dickinson University Press, 1984.

de Jésus-Marie, O.C.D., Pére Bruno, ed. *Satan.* Malachy Carroll, et al., trans. London: Sheed and Ward, 1951.

Kellogg, Alfred L. "Langland and Two Scriptural Texts." *Chaucer, Langland, Arthur: Essays in Middle English Literature.* New Brunswick, New Jersey: Rutgers University Press, 1972, pp. 32–50.

Knoppers, Laura Lunger. "Satan and the Papacy in *Paradise Regained.*" *Milton Studies* (42): 2003, pp. 68–85.

Langton, Edward. "In Post-Reformation Literature." *Satan, A Portrait.* London: Suffington& Son, Ltd., 1945.

Larrimore, Mark, ed. *The Problem of Evil.* Oxford: Blackwell Publishers, 2001.

Lépée, Marcel. *Satan.* Pére Bruno de Jésus-Marie, O.C.D., ed. London: Sheed and Ward, 1951, pp. 97–102.

Lewis, C.S. *A Preface to* Paradise Lost. New York: Oxford University Press, 1961.

Madaule, Jacques. "The Devil in Gogol and Dostoievski." *Satan.* Pére Bruno de Jésus-Marie, O.C.D., ed. London: Sheed and Ward, 1951, pp. 414–431.

Malin, Irving, ed. *Critical Views of Isaac Bashevis Singer.* New York: New York University Press, 1969.

Miller, Chris. "Diamants élus: the Romantic agony and the politics of The Waste Land." *PN Review (Manchester)* (25:2) [November-December 1998], p. 50–56.

Muchembled, Robert. *A History of the Devil: From the Middle Ages to the Present.* Jean Birrell, trans. Cambridge: Polity Press, 2003.

Pagels, Elaine. *The Origin of Satan.* New York: Random House, 1995.

Redner, Harry. *In the Beginning was the Deed: Reflection on the Passage of Faust.* Berkeley: University of California Press, 1982.

Revard, Stella Purce. "Satan as Epic Hero." *The War in Heaven:* Paradise Lost *and the Tradition of Satan's Rebellion.* Ithaca: Cornell University Press, 1980, pp. 198–234.

Russell, Jeffrey Burton. *The Devil: Perceptions of Evil From Antiquity to Primitive Christianity.* Ithaca: Cornell University Press, 1977.

⊬ Russell, Jeffrey Burton. *Lucifer: The Devil in the Middle Ages.* Ithaca: Cornell University Press, 1986.

Russell, Jeffrey Burton. *Mephistopheles: The Devil in the Modern World.* Ithaca: Cornell University Press, 1984.

Russell, Jeffrey Burton. *Satan: The Early Christian Tradition.* Ithaca: Cornell University Press, 1981.

Sabri-Tabrizi, G.R. *The Heaven and Hell of William Blake.* New York: International Publishers, 1973.

de Saint-Joseph, O.C.D., P. Lucien-Marie. *Satan.* Pére Bruno de Jésus-Marie, O.C.D., ed. London: Sheed and Ward, 1951, pp. 84-96.

Samuel, Irene. *Dante and Milton: The* Comedia *and* Paradise Lost. Ithaca: Cornell University Press, 1966, pp. 94–116.

Sawhney, Simona. "Satanic Choices: Poetry and Prophecy in Rushdie's Novel." *Twentieth Century Literature: a scholarly and critical journal* (45:3) [Fall 1999], p. 253–277.

Sheed, F.J., ed. *Soundings in Satanism.* New York: Sheed and Ward, 1972.

Sloan, Gary. "Twain's The Man That Corrupted Hadleyburg." *Explicator* (58:2) [Winter 2000], p. 83–85.

Smeed, J. W. *Faust in Literature.* London: Oxford University Press, 1975.

Stein, William Bysshe. *Hawthorne's Faust: A Study in the Devil Archetype.* Gainesville: University of Florida Press, 1953.

Tuckey, John S. *Mark Twain and the Little Satan: The Writing of* The Mysterious Stranger. Westport, Connecticut: Greenwood Press Publishers, 1963.

Twain, Mark. *Letters from the Earth.* Bernard DeVoto, ed. New York: Harper & Row, 1938.

Urbanczyk, Aaron. "Melville's Debt to Milton: Inverted Satanic Morphology and Rhetoric in The Confidence-Man," *Papers on Language and Literature: A Journal for Scholars and Critics of Language and Literature.* [2003 Summer] 39(3): 281–306.

Wehlau, Ruth. "The power of knowledge and the location of the reader in

Christ and Satan." *JEGP. Journal of English and Germanic Philology*: (97:1) Urbana: January 1998, pp. 1–12.

Ziolkowski, Theodore. *The Sin of Knowledge: Ancient Themes and Modern Variations.* Princeton: Princeton University Press, 2000.

Acknowledgements

"The Devils of Hawthorne's Faust Myth," by William Bysshe Stein. From *Hawthorne's Faust: A Study of the Devil Archetype*. © 1953 by the University of Florida. Reprinted by permission.

"Satan," by C.S. Lewis. From *A Preface to Paradise Lost*. © 1961 by Oxford University Press. Reprinted by permission.

"Mark Twain's Masks of Satan: The Final Phase," by Stanley Brodwin. From *American Literature* 45, no. 2 (May 1973): 206–227. © 1973 Duke University Press. Reprinted by permission.

"The Satanic Pattern," by Frank S. Kastor. From *Milton and the Literary Satan*. © 1974 by Editions Rodopi N.V. Reprinted by permission.

"The Devil," by J.W. Smeed. From *Faust in Literature*. © 1975 University of Durham. Reprinted by permission of Oxford University Press.

"Satan as Epic Hero," by Stella Purce Revard. From *The War in Heaven:* Paradise Lost *and the Tradition of Satan's Rebellion*. © 1980 by Cornell University. Used by permission of the publisher, Cornell University Press.

"Lucifer in High Medieval Art and Literature," by Jeffrey Burton Russell. From *Lucifer: The Devil in the Middle Ages*. © 1984 by Cornell University Press. Used by permission of the publisher, Cornell University Press.

"The Romantic Devil," by Jeffrey Burton Russell. From *Mephistopheles: The Devil in the Modern World.* © 1986 by Cornell University. Used by permission of the publisher, Cornell University Press.

"The Social History of Satan: From the Hebrew Bible to the Gospels," by Elaine Pagels. From *The Origin of Satan.* © 1995 by Elaine Pagels. Used by permission of Random House, Inc.

"Satan and the Papacy in *Paradise Regained,*" by Laura Lunger Knoppers. From *Milton Studies XLII:* Paradise Regained *in Context: Genre, Politics, Religion,* Albert C. Labriola and David Loewenstein, eds. © 2003 by University of Pittsburgh Press. Reprinted by permission of the University of Pittsburgh Press.

Index

809.9338235 S253

Satan
Park Place ADU CIRC
07/05

Friends of the
Houston Public Library

D0022889

ALICE WALKER

GARLAND REFERENCE LIBRARY
OF THE HUMANITIES
(Vol. 889)

ALICE WALKER
An Annotated Bibliography
1968–1986

Erma Davis Banks
Keith Byerman

GARLAND PUBLISHING, INC. • NEW YORK & LONDON
1989

016.813
W17b

© 1989 Erma Davis Banks and Keith Byerman
All rights reserved

Library of Congress Cataloging-in-Publication Data

Banks, Erma Davis
    Alice Walker, an annotated bibliography, 1968–1986 / Erma Davis Banks,
Keith Byerman.
      p. cm. — (Garland reference library of the humanities ;
vol. 889)
    Includes index.
    ISBN 0–8240–5734–1 (alk. paper)
    1. Walker, Alice, 1944– —Bibliography. I. Byerman, Keith
Eldon, 1948– . II. Title. III. Series.
Z8947.42.B36 1989
[PS3573.A425]
016.813'54—dc19   89–1251
                                                      CIP

Printed on acid-free, 250-year-life paper
Manufactured in the United States of America

CONTENTS

University Libraries
Carnegie Mellon University
Pittsburgh, Pennsylvania 15213

Hende Libraries
Carnegie Mellon University
Pittsburgh, Pennsylvania 15213

PREFACE

In 1984, while teaching LIS 105 (library research techniques), I required my students to prepare pathfinders. As examples, I prepared two pathfinders; one on acid rain and one on Alice Walker. My selection of Alice Walker came from a growing number of requests at the reference desk from students experiencing difficulty locating critical material on black writers, particularly Walker. It occurred to me that the pathfinder could be expanded into a journal article. Some months later I sent the expanded pathfinder to various journal publishers who might be interested, but most felt that the research was too extensive for a journal article. Merryll Penson, Director of the Library, encouraged me to expand the idea to book length.

Using the standard traditional research tools, such as *Humanities Index, Social Science Index, Reader's Guide to Periodical Literature, Contemporary Literary Criticism* and databases on Dialog, in addition to various other reference sources and personal contacts, I compiled the basic bibliography. I then began to work with non-traditional or standard research aids such as *Alternative Press Index, Newsbank, Index to Little Magazines* and initiated correspondence with other researchers in the field for the more obscure items.

In 1986, I met Dr. Keith Byerman, an English Professor specializing in Afro-American literature, then at Columbus College, and we decided to collaborate on the book. Garland Publishing Company expressed an interest in the project, and we felt committed to producing a thorough bibliography. In working on the project I have often thought of something that Alice Walker said in a 1972 speech delivered to students at Sarah Lawrence: "But please remember, especially in these times of group-think and the right-on chorus, that no person is your friend (or kin) who demands your silence, or denies your right to grow and be perceived as fully blossomed as you were intended. Or who belittles in any fashion the gifts you labor so to bring into the world."

This statement and the encouragement of many individuals have made this project possible. The bibliography now consists of 1000 citations by and about Alice Walker from a wide variety of sources.

Many thanks to my family who survived for the last three years, sometimes without my full attention; my sons Christopher and Justin; my parents, Mr. and Mrs. John G. Davis, for their loving support and understanding; my sister Elaine Davis for her proofreading initially and her understanding; Columbus College Library Staffs of Cataloging, Inter-Library Loan, Circulation and Acquisition Departments; Columbus College Library Faculty Merryll Penson, Callie McGinnis, Merne Posey, Trisha Simonds, Sandra Stratford, and Kimberly Sangster; the Reference Department at Georgia State University Library; Helene Watson and staff at Mildred L. Terry Library; Auburn University Library Staff; Bradley Library Reference Department; Georgia Southern Library Staff; David Johnson for his interest and encouragement; Mary Margaret Byerman for her supportive attitude; Vicky Adkins, my assistant who performed most of the clerical support and listens to me daily about the project; Dr. John Lupold for his computer assistance and guidance; and my co-author, colleague and friend Keith Byerman who believed in this project and spent many hours of his time in support of that belief.

Erma Davis Banks
Columbus College

ARRANGEMENT OF THE BIBLIOGRAPHY

The bibliography is divided into eight parts as follows:

I.   **Introduction**

II.   **Primary Sources** - Books, essays, poetry, short stories and miscellaneous writings arranged by genre. The book section arranged chronologically; essays, poetry and short stories alphabetically by the title with those appearing in more than one source listed chronologically; miscellaneous writings arranged alphabetically by titles.

III. **General Books and Reference Sources** - Arranged alphabetically by author or title.

IV.   **General Periodicals** - Arranged alphabetically by author, title of the articles or by name of periodicals.

V.   **Interviews** - Arranged by interviewer, title or publication.

VI.   **Criticism of Individual Works** - Divided into book criticisms and short story criticisms. The citations arranged by three categories, books, journal articles and book reviews.

VII. **Bibliographies** - Listed alphabetically.

VIII. **Unverified** - Sources are known to exist, which could not be located for annotation.

INTRODUCTION

I

BIOGRAPHY

Before the publication of *The Color Purple*, Alice Walker was one of a number of contemporary black writers who had established solid but not stellar reputations, especially among those interested in Afro-American literature. When the novel came out in 1982, however, she quickly became a literary and popular celebrity. The book was a bestseller, became a successful movie, and stirred considerable controversy. Its winning of both the Pulitizer Prize and the American Book Award only enhanced the notoriety of it and its author. It also became the focal point for intense debate over the nature and meaning of her work. Strong defenses of and attacks on her artistic skills and especially her attitudes toward black women and men became commonplace in both popular and academic publications.

It is somewhat surprising that for many readers she seemed to come suddenly on the scene. After all, by 1982, she had been publishing poetry, fiction, and essays for fifteen years. She had by this time two novels, three books of poetry, and two collections of short stories in print, in addition to numerous stories and essays in *Ms.*, *Black Scholar*, and other periodicals. Her work had been the subject of several scholarly articles as well as book reviews. She was one of a group of black writers, including Toni Morrison, Ernest Gaines, and Ishmael Reed, who had emerged in the late sixties and early seventies as artists whose work lacked the ideological stridency found in much of the Black Arts Movement, but which nonetheless expressed a strong sense of black heritage and pride. Each of these writers came to be taken seriously and the works of each received attention, but nothing to match what happened with *The Color Purple*.

Part of the reason for its success may well be that, at a certain level, the story of Celie is Walker's story. Similar violence, she has said, happened to her great-grandmother. But, in a more general sense, the experiences of a girl in the rural South who came to feel that she was ugly and worthless, who felt oppressed by her environment, and who eventually triumphed over it, is Walker's own story. She was born 9 February 1944, the youngest child of Willie Lee and Minnie Grant Walker, sharecroppers in Eatonton, Georgia. Eatonton was a small, poor town, known primarily for being the home of Joel Chandler Harris. Alice's parents made only about three hundred dollars a year in the cotton fields and on this tried to raise eight children. To this poverty was added the threat of racial violence and white economic domination, realities which found their way into Walker's writing.

At the age of eight, Alice was disfigured and partially blinded when she was accidentally struck in the eye by pellets from her brother's BB gun. The scar tissue, which was removed six years later in a relatively simple operation, made her feel ugly and unwanted; it changed her from a vivacious child to one much more reclusive. She has commented that the injury had the effect of making her more attentive to other people and their relationships. It also led her to extensive reading and to writing her first poetry. Even after the surgery removed the most obvious damage and she became class valedictorian and high school prom queen, the pattern of observation and writing continued.

The injury also made her eligible for a scholarship to Spelman College, a black women's school in Atlanta. It was at this time that her mother gave her three gifts--a suitcase, a typewriter, and a sewing machine--that she has commented had important symbolic as well as practical value. The three signified the encouragement of a creative, independent, and self-sufficient life, something that was difficult to imagine or attain in the rural South. Spelman had a paradoxical effect on her life. On the one hand, members of its faculty like Staughton Lynd, and Howard Zinn enlarged her perspective on the world. Similarly, her two years at the college (1961-63) were years of intense civil rights activity, much of it in and around Atlanta. She became involved in the demonstrations at a time when participation meant real physical danger. At the same time, Spelman saw its mission in part as the training of "proper" young women and to this end maintained strict standards of behavior and discouraged political activity. Many of the attitudes of the institution are represented by Meridian Hill's experiences at Saxon College in the novel *Meridian* (1976).

Both of these elements--a desire to experience a larger world and frustration at restrictions--were probably involved in Walker's decision to accept a scholarship to Sarah Lawrence College, an exclusive and prestigious women's school in Bronxville, New York. It was here that she began her public writing career. This occurred again as the result of traumatic experiences which had positive effects. Between her junior and senior years, she had an opportunity to travel to Africa; she also learned that she had become pregnant. Her anguish over her condition manifested itself in serious thought of suicide, an action she had contemplated since her childhood accident. She kept a razor blade under her pillow and even practiced slitting her wrists. One of her friends found an abortionist for her, and during the period of recovery, she wrote poetry incessantly. She showed her work to Muriel Ruykeyser, a teacher and well-known poet. Ruykeyser arranged to have them read by an editor at Harcourt, Brace, and Jovanovich, which published them in 1968 in a collection entitled *Once*.

Following her graduation from Sarah Lawrence in 1965, she worked in voter registration projects in Georgia and in the welfare department in New York City. Upon receiving a writing fellowship in 1966, she spent the summer working in civil rights programs in Mississippi. It was here that she met Melvyn Rosenman Leventhal, a white civil rights lawyer. They lived together in New York for a year, during which time her first essay, "The Civil Rights Movement: What Good Was It?" and her first story, "To Hell with Dying," were published. They were married on 17 March 1967, and later that year moved to Jackson, Mississippi. During seven years in the Deep South, Walker worked with Head Start programs and served as writer in residence at Jackson State University and Tougaloo College. Their daughter, Rebecca Grant, was born at this time and *The Third Life of Grange Copeland* was written. This first novel was published by Harcourt, Brace, and Jovanovich in 1970.

In 1972, she accepted temporary teaching positions at Wellesley College and the University of Massachusetts-Boston, while her husband remained in Mississippi. The year 1973 saw the publication of three books: *Revolutionary Petunias*, her second collection of poems; *In Love and Trouble*, a book of short stories; and *Langston Hughes*, a children's biography of the famous black poet. The book of stories won the Rosenthal Award of the National Institute of Arts and Letters in 1974; two of the pieces, "Everyday Use" and "The Revenge of Hannah Kemhuff," were published in *Best American Short Stories*.

In 1974, the Leventhals moved back to New York, where Alice took a position as contributing editor of *Ms.* magazine. They were divorced in 1976, the same year that *Meridian*, another novel, was published. She was also working on her third book of poetry, *Good Night, Willie Lee, I'll See You in the Morning* and editing an anthology of writing by Zora Neale Hurston, *I Love Myself When I'm Laughing...and Then Again When I Am Mean and Impressive*; both were published in 1979.

After the divorce, she moved first to San Francisco and then to a farm outside the city. She was living here in 1981 when her second collection of stories, *You Can't Keep a Good Woman Down*, was published by Harcourt. The second move was prompted in part by difficulties she was having with the writing of her third novel. She has said that the characters simply could not emerge in the environment of the city, but that when she moved to a place much like her home in rural Georgia, then their stories could be told. Those characters came to populate *The Color Purple* (1982), the work which has won its author fame, wealth, and a number of literary prizes. It was on the *New York Times* best-seller list for six months and was made into a very popular movie by Steven Spielberg. The movie was nominated for several Academy Awards and itself aroused controversy both by its failure to win awards and by its presentation of black characters.

She followed this success a year later with *In Search of Our Mothers' Gardens*, a collection of essays concerning her own life, the civil rights movement, literature, and black women. In 1984, Harcourt published *Horses Make a Landscape Look More Beautiful*, her fourth book of poetry. She continues to live outside San Francisco with her daughter and Robert Allen, former editor of *Black Scholar*, and is actively involved in women's rights and anti-nuclear activities. As this bibliography goes to press, she has issued a new book of essays, *Living With the Word*.

II

WORKS AND RESPONSES

Walker has worked in a variety of literary forms: poetry, essays, and long and short fiction. One of the dominant patterns that cuts across these genres is her blending of the personal and the political. She has consistently shown how the concerns of herself or her characters are involved in more general issues; this is especially true in terms of the lives of black women, including her own. From the publication of *Once* to the present, this dialectic of the individual and society has been at work.

The first book of poems focuses on four subjects: Africa, the South, love, and suicide. The ways in which these subjects are involved with her own life should be evident from the previous section. However, it would be a mistake to view her work as narrowly autobiographical or confessional. For one thing, the succinct, almost haiku form of the poems of *Once* militates against sentimentality or self-indulgence. The lines of the poems are usually very short, the poems themselves brief, and the images very precise and direct. The African poems present the concrete realities of that continent's people and nature. The pieces on the South and the Civil Rights movement are imbued with an irony that requires an emotional distance, even as the poems clearly express sympathy with the cause. "Once," for example, explores the complex relationships among Southern racists, white sympathizers with the movement, and blacks themselves. "Hymn," on the other hand, recreates traditional black religious experience.

The verses on love examine its complications, including desire, loneliness, uncertainty, and forgiveness. "Johann" talks about the fear and hope involved in mixed-race relationships, while "To the Man in the Yellow Terry" combines desire with a sense of melancholy. The poems on suicide move from despair to transcendence. "Ballad of the Brown Girl" describes a self-destroying response to racial and sexual violence, while "Suicide" examines the subject from a philosophical perspective, consistent with Walker's reading of Albert Camus. "Exercises on Themes from Life" establishes the bases on which one chooses life over death.

While *Once* attracted little attention among reviewers, the comments it did receive were consistently positive. Estelle Benedict called it "a lovely book of poems," while Lisle Mueller took note of its private concerns and simplicity of style.

Walker's second book, *The Third Life of Grange Copeland*, covered some of the same ground as *Once*, but, as is common with novels, received considerably more comment than the poetry. It is the story of three generations of a black sharecropping family whose brutal experience leads to abandonment, promiscuity, self-hatred, abuse, and even murder. But, as in the poems, love enables at least some of them to save themselves. The Southern landscape, with its harsh working conditions, racism, economic oppression, and frustration of black dreams, offers little hope for the characters. Yet, ironically, out of this same environment come possibilities; these emerge in two elements consistently important to Walker: Afro-American folk culture and the civil rights movement.

The plot of the novel is straightforward. The title character, Grange Copeland, begins his married life with high expectations; he believes that work as a sharecropper is only a starting point for a successful life. But constant indebtedness, white exploitation of his labor, and the need to suppress his frustration lead to feelings of rage and self-hatred. He abuses his wife Margaret, neglects his son, and finds a sexual outlet in the prosititute Josie. Margaret, from motives of revenge and self-degradation, begins liaisons with white men. When she has a light-skinned baby, Grange abandons her and the children. She kills her baby and then herself, leaving their son Brownfield alone in the world.

The story then shifts to this young man as he begins replication of his father's life. He unknowingly becomes the sexual partner of his father's mistress. Despite his near-illiteracy, he marries Josie's educated niece, Mem, who desires a middle-class life for them. Brownfield believes, like his parents, that he can begin as a sharecropper on the way to such a life. The inevitable frustration leads him, not to the escapes of his father, but to abusive treatment of his family. He foils Mem's every effort to improve their situation and works to degrade her in the belief that she ought to be the broken-down wife a man such as himself deserves. When even this mistreatment does not destroy her dream, he murders her.

During this time, Grange returns and tries to change his son. When Mem dies and Brownfield is imprisoned, he takes custody of his youngest granddaughter. He marries Josie and buys a farm. We learn that he has lived in New York, where life was little better for him than it had been in the South. The turning point in his life comes when a white woman he tries to save from drowning prefers dying to being saved by a black man. He understands from that moment the importance of individual responsibility and thus stops seeing himself as the victim of some overpowering force called whiteness. When he ceases to be a victim, he begins to have power in his own life. He uses that power to avoid contact with whites and to raise his granddaughter who must learn to nurture rather than abuse her own humanity. He does this by training her in the folk wisdom of the race and educating her in the ways of the white world.

He succeeds almost too well, as she comes to believe in the possibility of social even more than individual change. She welcomes civil rights workers, including whites, to the farm; Grange contends that such people are brave but foolish. He would defend their lives but not join their cause; his efforts remain individual. When Brownfield is released and given custody of Ruth by an indifferent white judge, Grange kills his son rather than let him destroy the child. He accepts the fact that he himself must die for this act of violence, but his death is not so much an abandonment of Ruth as a surrendering to her of the future.

Thus, a novel of harsh naturalistic detail eventuates in a message of moral responsibility, of hope through love, and of secular redemption. Crucial to Walker's perspective is the fact that her black characters find such a way out by themselves. Like a number of contemporary writers, she is more interested in the inner lives of black people and communities than she is in relationships between blacks and whites. Moreover, within such communities, it is black women who are most interesting and valuable to her as a writer. Even in this novel of fathers and sons, our judgments of them are based on their treatment of women. These concerns will develop as Walker's career continues.

The reviews of the novel were generally positive, with some qualifications. Loyle Hairston compared it to the work of Russian writers, especially Maxim Gorky. Several reviewers praised the concrete detail of Southern rural life, including the violence. Some saw it essentially as the story of a family, and others as the story of black women. A consistent criticism was the weakness of plot structure, with Laura Marcus adding that it occasionally becomes polemical.

Revolutionary Petunias returns to some of the poetic concerns of *Once* while developing some of the themes of *Grange Copeland*. It is divided into five sections of poems which move from assertions of the value of the past through the difficulties of the present to hope for the future. "In These Dissenting Times" offers various images of black life in the poet's childhood. Emphasis is placed on the ceremonies of that life, including church and funerals. "Revolutionary Petunias" combines introspection and activism. The title poem tells the story of Sammy Lou, who is found guilty of killing the man who murdered her husband. Her last words to her children are a reminder to take care of her petunias. The poem thus restates a persistent idea: the love of life often requires sacrifice and even violence. Other pieces in this section explore the idea of being an outcast and accepting loneliness as necessary to a certain kind of life. The third section, "Crucifixions," presents the obstacles in the way of life and love. These include power, ideology, exploitation, and demands for perfection. Walker here explores another of the ironies that recur in her work: the relentless pursuit of change and justice itself can become a life-denying activity. "Mysteries" opposes the impulses toward perfection and control of the previous section with images of the irrationality and disorderliness of love. Desire can be confusing, troubling, and mysterious; it is almost never "correct." This perception leads then to the final section, "The Nature of This Flower Is to Bloom." Here the values of the old people presented at the beginning are affirmed as life giving and sustaining. Diversity is given preference over unity and perfection. And finally, in a crucial observation, living and loving are themselves seen as the finest acts of rebellion.

Reviewers consistently commented on the economy and precision of the language and on the importance of cultural traditions to the poetry. Several also noted the theme of the individual in history, who is valued over ideology. On this last point, the *Black World* reviewer saw the book as an indictment of black activism in the 1960's.

In Love and Trouble collected a number of short stories that had already been published as well as some that were new. The title phrase suggests the classic blues situation: life is full of both love and trouble, and often love *is* trouble. The subtitle, "Stories of Black Women," clearly indicates the focus of the book. These are narratives of women who must deal with the complexities of life, including violence, injustice, oppression, false ideals, and death, while trying to retain some sense of dignity.

The first four stories depict women who are in some way victimized by men. Roselily, for example, sees the marriage ceremony she is going through as the beginning of imprisonment, even though it is the only way out of a life of deprivation. "The Child Who Favored Daughter" tells of double victimization: a sister named Daughter cast out of her family because she desires sexual freedom and a girl-child of her brother, whose ambivalent feelings about his sister are transferred to this child of his own. As a result, when he discovers that his daughter has a lover, he cuts off her breasts, an act that both affirms and denies his own confusion by assaulting womanhood. This is only the most graphic of a set of stories in which women are punished for wanting their own identities.

The next group of stories suggests that black folk culture can provide nurture for such women. "The Revenge of Hannah Kemhuff" tells of an old black woman who years before suffered the loss of her family through the negligence of a condescending white woman. Now near death, she seeks justice through the aid of a conjurer. "The Welcome Table" concerns another old woman whose religious faith helps her maintain her dignity even when she is thrown out of a white church service. "Strong Horse Tea" describes the education of a poor woman who must learn to put her faith in "those who will come," including the black woman healer, rather than in a white world that does not care if her child dies. Finally, "Everyday Use" demonstrates that the skills and traditions of the black family are more valuable and humane than black liberation ideology.

The last group of stories involves the complex rituals of black life. "Diary of an African Nun" describes a black missionary who finds herself torn between her Eurocentric religion and her African heritage. "The Flowers" sets up an ironic contrast between the springtime ritual of flower-gathering and the racist "ceremony" of lynching. "To Hell With Dying," the last story, tells of the rituals of love, life, and death. Mr. Sweet, a man with a troubled life, repeatedly takes to his death bed, only to be revived by the loving attention of his neighbor's children. The daughter-narrator believes this to be somehow magical. But when she is older and returns one last time, he dies, leaving her his treasured guitar. What she learns then is not that love conquers death, but that it transcends it.

Reviewers consistently praised the book for its detailed depictions of the lives of black women. Mary Helen Washington noted that Walker's fiction emerges from her sense of the historical experiences of such women. Some commentators also pointed out the rejection of ideology implicit in several of the pieces. Criticisms of the book included an occasional lack of substance and a tendency toward contrivance.

Meridian, Walker's second novel, is, in a sense, a continuation of the story of *Grange Copeland*. Meridian Hill can be seen as Ruth Copeland grown up and involved with that civil rights movement that so fascinated her. Meridian, however, has her own set of difficulties to overcome as a young woman. In fact, womanhood itself is problematic in this novel. As it opens, we learn the story of a woman who was killed by her husband because she refused to simply "lay back and be pleasured." Her body is now on display as part of a freak show. We hear the tale of Louvinie, who had her tongue cut out for telling stories so well that a white child died of fright. And we learn of Fast Mary of the Tower, who was so afraid of losing respectability that she murdered her new-born, illegitimate child and later killed herself.

For Meridian herself, life seems to be setting traps for her. Men want her body, but care nothing for her soul. She marries a highschool friend, but quickly realizes that he will never truly mature or try to understand her. Even when she has his son, she alternates between loving the baby and wanting to kill it. Only when she discovers the civil rights movement does she feel any possibility for liberation. It gives meaning to her life by defining a purpose for her. It opens up new vistas, embodied by Truman Held, who speaks French and seems part of a much larger world. When the opportunity arises, she accepts a scholarship to Saxon College. To do this she decides to give up her child, an act which creates guilt for several years. In all these stories, we are made to see that womanhood and motherhood are difficult conditions; in fact, Walker appears to be saying that motherhood is a form of psychological suicide.

In conjunction with this study of women, the novel explores the complex experience of the civil rights movement. The author is much more interested in the inner dynamics of the movement than in its effect on history. She presents the personal stories of men and women, black and white, while developing the political implications of such stories. She studies the fascination black men and white women had for each other. Truman tells Meridian that he admires such women because "They read the *New York Times*." But such fascination can turn to hostility, as when Tommy Odds rapes Lynne as revenge for what he has suffered from white men. For these same men, black women serve alternately as something to escape and as some essence of the race to be returned to. Thus, Truman repeatedly abandons Meridian and then searches for her.

Walker also addresses the morality of radicalism. As some in the movement give up on nonviolence, they turn to revolutionary ideology. A key question in the novel is "Would you kill for the revolution?" When this is asked of Meridian, she affirms that she would gladly die, but that killing is another matter. When she finally realizes that she cannot do it, she leaves her friends and goes back to the people to help them in life-affirming ways. She works in voter registration drives, and she leads protests against acts of discrimination which seem trivial, but which in fact define the possibility of dignity in ordinary life. In her travels, she gradually gives up all possessions, choosing to share what is available to those whom she serves.

In this way, Walker suggests sanctity in such a life. And in the process of self-sacrifice, Meridian heals herself of all the guilt and anxiety of her earlier life. At the end, Truman returns to begin a similar life. Thus, as in the poetry and the earlier fiction, the author contends that love and sacrifice make redemption possible.

Several reviewers noted that the book reads more like a history of the civil rights movement than a novel; they see the book as effective even with this qualification. Other commentators note weaknesses: in the revelation of Meridian's past, in the sections treating experiences of ecstasy, and in the conclusion, which tells rather than shows Meridian's transformation. Some also assert that the best writing occurs in passages which are somewhat self-contained because these most effectively reveal Walker's story-telling skills. Positive comments are also made about the economy of language and the psychological accuracy of the characterizations.

Good Night, Willie Lee, I'll See You in the Morning returns to the concerns of the earlier books of poetry, though with more emphasis on feminist ideas and less on sense of place. The collection is divided into five parts. "Confession" contains poems of love and self-examination. These focus most often on disappointments in relationships and ways of dealing with them. "Never Offer Your Heart to Someone Who Eats Hearts" is typical of the section in its warning that love can be all-consuming. "On Stripping Bark from Myself," the second part, concerns the life of the artist. In it, "Now that the Book is Finished" describes the psychology of writing, while "Light Baggage" talks about some writers who have influenced Walker: Zora Neale Hurston, Jean Toomer, and Nella Larsen. Part three, "Early Losses: A Requiem," comprises mostly poems about strong men, such as Martin Luther King, Jr., and Malcolm X, and also about the relationships of male power to the lives of women. "Malcolm," for example, indicates a preference for a nationalist leader who laughs and aids in the liberation of women. "Facing the Way", the penultimate section, looks at history from a variety of angles. "Women of Color" describes the discrimination suffered by Shirley Graham because she wanted to talk about her romantic life with her famous husband W.E.B. Du Bois. The title poem of this section discusses the eternal tension, especially for black writers, between art and political action, while "Talking to My Grandmother" explores changing dreams. The final section, "Forgiveness", as its title implies, involves Walker's persistent quest for transcendence. Each of the four poems considers what lasts in loving relationships which must change. Lovers may go, but the beauty of love remains. In "Good Night, Willie Lee, I'll See You in the Morning", even death itself is only a temporary obstacle to the unifying power of love.

The book was praised for the effectiveness of its language and for Walker's ability, as Sean Williamson put it, to capture "the luminous image which makes the entire poem coalesce around it". At the same time, Williamson criticizes the collection as self-important, while Robert Fleming expresses disappointment in the overabundance of poems about love's failures. He believes that the author's best work lies in her portraits of everyday life.

Walker's second collection of short stories, *You Can't Keep a Good Woman Down* (1981), represents in some ways a departure from her earlier fiction. While some pieces, such as "Nineteen Fifty-Five" and "A Sudden Trip Home in the Spring", could fit into *In Love and Trouble*, several others are quite clearly designed as ideological statements in fictional form. These pieces make arguments about "womanist" issues; that is, matters that have both feminist and racial connotations. "Nineteen Fifty-Five" comes close to such writing as it dramatizes the exploitation of women blues singers by white record companies and musicians. The principal characters are thinly-veiled versions of Big Mama Thornton and Elvis Presley, who turned Thornton's "Hound Dog" into a commercial success for himself. The story is clearly sympathetic to the woman, who, though she does not attain wealth and fame, maintains her dignity. "A Sudden Trip Home in the Spring" tells the story of a young black woman who leaves the exclusive Northern college in which she is enrolled to attend the funeral of her father. As an artist learning her craft, she has been unable to depict black men, because she has always considered such men as her father as failures because they did not strike out against discrimination. What she comes to understand on her "sudden trip home" is that there is a certain dignity in the quiet, constant struggle to make life better for one's children.

Several pieces are much more overtly political in their messages. "Coming Apart" and "Porn," for example, examine the effects of pornography on personal relationships. In both cases, the author-narrator takes the side of women, often through the inclusion of anti-pornography statements by other writers. "The Abortion" similarly describes the insensitivity of men to the emotional needs of women. "Advancing Luna--and Ida B. Wells" is an experimental work which presents a narrator trying to construct a story about interracial rape that will satisfy her beliefs about both blacks and women.

The reviews of the collection have been mixed. Nearly all have noted the departure from story-telling tradition into confrontation with social issues. Several critics contend that such an approach weakens the fiction. *Kirkus Review* even describes the work as didactic and thin, while Katha Pollitt finds the political pieces innovative but not as effective as the other stories. She and others, however, praise Walker for raising issues, such as pornography and rape, which are seldom addressed in mainstream fiction. Others note that the author's sense of humor saves some of the pieces. In contrast, C.L.R. James, who had praised earlier works, is troubled by the collection because he cannot identify in it a valid fictional purpose; he finds the focus on the problems of the black middle class to be inherently uninteresting.

The Color Purple (1982), her third novel, is the work that made Alice Walker a celebrity. Some of its reputation can be explained by interpreting it as a classic American success story. Its protagonist begins in a world of deprivation, violence, and family problems, but through determination and love achieves financial success, self-confidence, and a reunited family. Moreover, it sets this tale in the exotic (for most Americans) spaces of the black rural South and Africa. In addition, the fact that the protagonist is a woman who struggles against the cruelty of a male-dominated world and achieves her goals through the aid of strong sympathetic women makes an effective appeal to female readers. Finally, the narrative voice of Celie, nearly illiterate yet also by turns pathetic, angry, wise, and funny, is an effective device for all readers.

The story is told primarily through letters that Celie writes to God. This technique is explained by the warning of her stepfather, who sexually abuses her, that she should tell "nobody but God" what he has done. The form is used not only to tell of rape, but also of physical violence, of the birth and loss of her two children, of marriage to and mistreatment by Mr._____ (whose name Celie is afraid to speak), and of her fears of her sister Nettie, who soon leaves to go with a missionary family to Africa. We also learn of the day-to-day lives of rural blacks, as they farm, fight, love, hate, entertain themselves, and try to deal with white racism.

Celie's life is one of drudgery and self-denial until the appearance of Shug Avery, a blues singer and Mr.____'s former lover. She has reputation as an independent woman and therefore as one who is "evil". After she enters Celie's life, they slowly develop a friendship and even for a time become lovers. It is through Shug's encouragement that Celie comes to see herself as a worthwhile human being who did not deserve the abuse she suffered. When they discover letters from Nettie that Mr.____ has been concealing for years, a new world--Africa--is opened to them. Celie learns from these letters that the man who first raped her was not her father and that her children have been raised by the missionaries. The effect of Shug's affection and Nettie's information is to free Celie psychologically from the oppression of men. Her economic independence comes as she begins making and selling pants for both men and women. The novel concludes with forgiveness for past wrongs, with restoration of rightful property, and with the reunion of scattered family members.

Reviewers have been consistent in their opinions about the strengths and weaknesses of the novel. Celie's voice, with its folk speech patterns and its precision, pathos, and humor, has been regularly praised. Several approved of the characterizations, especially of the female characters, as well as the religious element in the book, which offered a sense of hope. Weaknesses were found in Nettie's letters from Africa, both because of their relatively colorless standard English and because these sections imposed an ideology not apparent in Celie's correspondence.

In Search of Our Mothers' Gardens (1983) brings together essays on various topics written from 1968 to 1982. The collection includes pieces on writers important to Walker, on the activity of writing, on various political issues, especially feminism and civil rights, and on key personal experiences. She describes her often complex responses to Flannery O'Connor, Jean Toomer, and Zora Neale Hurston. She notes, for example, that though she and O'Connor grew up within a few miles of each other, that the white writer's home has become a tourist attraction and literary shrine, while her own has virtually disappeared. Hurston she identifies as a kind of literary mother figure, both for her writing and her independence. She also discusses the writer's role in social activism; she expresses the view that the demands of art and those of activism are very different, but that both can contribute to change.

The title essay of the book establishes the historical ground for her womanist beliefs. In it she points out that black women consistently have been frustrated in their creativity. The oppression they have suffered by being both black and female has kept them from writing the stories and poems that would tell of their experiences. Their creative impulse emerge in their gardening and their quilting, activities traditionally derided as ephemeral "women's work". Walker argues that it is the responsibility of the daughters, like herself, to speak the stories for mothers denied their voices.

Commentators have seen the book as something of an autobiography, with the author's personal experiences providing the basis for her social, political, and literary views. While some concern is expressed for occasional stridency, the consensus is that the essays effectively present the concerns of black women and the relationship of Walker's own life to her beliefs and her writing. Typical is Lynn Munro's comment: "This volume demonstrates the versatility of Walker's style and her capacity for intellectual and personal growth".

Horses Make a Landscape Look More Beautiful is a collection of poems about the success and failure of various kinds of love. The successes come in personal relationships based on respect, in social and political action which has liberation as its goal, and in appreciation for nature. Failure here is in personal dishonesty, in greed and violence, and in cultural exploitation and condescension. In poems such as "The Diamonds on Liz's Bosom" and "When Golda Meir Was in Africa", the writer contends that a Eurocentric worldview blinds people to both the suffering and achievement of non-whites. "No One Can Watch the Wasichu" describes the pervasiveness of greed and violence in contemporary society, while "If 'Those People' Like You" examines the tendency to refuse respect for difference. "She Said", "Walker", and "I'm, Really Very Fond" all discuss problems encountered by lovers.

On the other hand, "Poem at Thirty-Nine" is Walker's act of reconciliation with her dead father, who she felt did not do enough for his family. "Listen", "Attentiveness", and "My Daughter is Coming!" demonstrate a belief in love's affirmation of life. "Songless" praises Nicaragua as creative and free, while "Mississippi Winter IV" commends women who choose to go their own way. In a pattern followed in all the books of poetry, the final piece offers hope for renewal. "These Days" lists the speaker's friends who have in some way made her life, or the lives of women, or nature, or life in general better by their presence and concern.

As with the other poetry collections, *Horses Make a Landscape Look More Beautiful* has received much less comment than the fiction. Moreover, the comments that have been made tend to be more negative than those on earlier books. The work is said to be flat, artistically immature, irritating, preachy, and stereotypical. The title of Michael Weaver's review summarizes the negative response: "A Great Novelist Doesn't Always Make a Great Poet". Nonetheless, some positive statements have been made. L.M. Rosenberg, who says that the pieces are "Almost never poetry", also acknowledged that many of them have a musical quality. Both Gail Gilliland and Sonia Gernes express the view that the best poems are those based on personal experience. Gernes, in fact, places Walker in the self-singing tradition of Walt Whitman.

III

LITERARY CRITICISM

The literary criticism on Walker's work has generally focused on influences; literary forms; the use of folklore; and the themes of religion, race, and, most commonly, women (and their relationships with men). Influences have been identified in two categories: personal/cultural and literary. In the former, Mary Helen Washington and Barbara Christian have devoted considerable commentary to the role black women, especially those of earlier generations, have played in Walker's thinking and writing. These are the women that she talks about in "In Search of Our Mothers' Gardens", and the critics have noted the effects on characterization and on the kinds of stories which are told.

In the literary category, Walker herself has identified certain influences--Zora Neale Hurston, Jean Toomer, and nineteenth-century Russian novelists--but others have been noted by critics. Martha J. McGowan points out the connection of *Meridian* to Albert Camus' *The Rebel* on the crucial question of killing in the name of revolution. Chester Fontenot has commented on the relevance of W.E.B. Du Bois's concept of double-consciousness to the psychological conflict of "Diary of an African Nun". The complexity of Walker's relationship to Hurston has been explored by Alma S. Freeman and Diane Sadoff.

Relatively few studies have been done of formal aspects of Walker's work. Most that have concentrate on the use of letters in *The Color Purple*. Elizabeth Fifer and Margaret McFadden have pointed out that the form creates an intimacy between narrator and reader, with Fifer showing how the letters reveal Celie's growing sophistication. Valerie Babb suggests that Walker achieves a sense of orality through the character's writing that counteracts cultural domination. A different approach to form is taken by Deborah McDowell, who describes *Meridian* as a *bildungsroman* in which the title character comes to self-awareness through mystical experience.

Folk elements have been examined by Mary Jane Lupton, Trudier Harris, and Keith Byerman. Lupton argues that the Cinderella tale is important in understanding *The Color Purple*. She sees clothing as a means and symbol of a transformation that undermines gender distinctions. The happy ending then marks a return to the fairy tale tradition which neutralizes the radical implications of the work. Harris points out several of the sources and uses of folk material in Walker's early fiction. She asserts that the material is used for psychological and political purposes rather than for local color. Byerman contends that Walker, in line with other contemporary fictionists, develops a dialectical tension between ideology and folk values. Folklore functions both thematically and structurally to question and subvert ideological claims to truth and control.

Although several reviewers and critics have mentioned the idea of redemption in Walker's work, Viralene J. Coleman and Ruth El Saffar have focused specifically on the theme of religion in *The Color Purple*. Coleman believes that Shug's religious views are crucial to Celie's transformation. The perception of God in everything makes it possible to forgive even those who have done great evil. El Saffar traces the changes in the image of God through the work and relates them to the shift in the text from history to romance.

The theme of race has drawn critical commentary about two of the novels, *The Third Life of Grange Copeland* and *Meridian*. The analyses can be divided into those which focus on the civil rights movement and those which treat oppression and violence. Joan S. Griffin has explained how the movement was the vehicle for the change in Meridian from passive, guilt-ridden victim to committed activist. Martha McGowan examines the philosophical implications of such activism, especially when it potentially involves violence. Vernessa C. White continues this line of thought by arguing that the novel makes the point that revolutionary action must be life-affirming. Karen F. Stein moves in a different direction when she contends that Walker uses the work to criticize the movement for failing to value women.

White and Harold Hellenbrand see the exploitation and oppression of blacks as central to *Grange Copeland*. White traces the various responses of characters to their victimization, while Hellenbrand connects it to silence and speech, both of which he sees as growing out of suffering. In two essays, Trudier Harris interprets the male characters as victims and victimizers. In one instance she places them in a literary tradition of emasculated black men; in the other, she shows how they turn their frustration and anger against other blacks.

The most controversial aspect of Walker's work has been her presentation of women, especially black women. This area includes not only the characterizations and fates of such figures, but also the treatment of families and black male characters in relationship to them and the advocacy of a black feminist (Womanist) perspective. Some critics have examined the works to explain various aspects of the representation of female and male characters, while others have concentrated on the implications of womanism for Walker's art. The latter group includes those who offer negative evaluations of writing influenced by such a perspective.

Peter Erickson views family as a central theme in both the poetry and the fiction; he sees it as the source of both conflict and identity. Mary Helen Washington, Gloria Wade-Gayles, and Susan Willis examine the motif of motherhood, though they differ on its implications. Washington notes the importance of mother figures in both Walker's life and her writing. In the fiction, daughters learn to speak for their silenced mothers. In contrast, Wade-Gayles indicates that mother-child relationships are often complex in the writing and that, in *Meridian* at least, motherhood does not necessarily mean nurture. Willis goes even further by suggesting that mothering is often associated with death.

Critics have pointed out various aspects of the treatment of female characters. Barbara Christian sees Walker working through themes of contrariness and waywardness in such characters generally and artist characters in particular. In this view, the role of the outsider is a positive one. Bettye J. Parker-Smith traces a progression in the three novels from women as victims in the first two to women as royalty in *The Color Purple*. Karen C. Gaston argues that in *Grange Copeland*, female characters serve as the moral centers of the work, even though the males are the central characters. Christine Froula uses Freudian seduction theory to suggest motivation for the silencing of Celie in *The Color Purple* and then contends that patriarchal oppression is broken when Celie tells her story to Shug.

Womanism as an ideological stance and as the basis for literature has stimulated considerable comment. W. Lawrence Hogue reads *The Third Life of Grange Copeland* as an example of feminist discourse which makes the argument that the social order dehumanizes black men who then abuse their families. Hogue also asserts that Walker sacrifices character development when necessary to prove her point. Chikwenge Okonjo Ogunyemi defines womanism as the focus on women's issues in the context of black culture. While he considers several writers, he presents Walker as one who is optimistic on such issues, especially in *The Color Purple*. Barbara Smith offers the most laudatory reading by showing how the emphasis on women enables Walker to see through the myths surrounding the lives of black women and to reveal the unpleasantries of married life.

In sharp contrast are a number of critics who see womanism as problematic both as a concept and as a basis for literature. Two of the more complex of these responses have been written by Philip M. Royster and Trudier Harris. Royster uses essays, poems, and fiction to work through the argument that, while Walker likes to represent herself as an outcast of white patriarchal culture, she often castigates those outsiders--blacks and women--with whom she appears to identify in terms similar to those of the dominant culture. He finds her more of a "darling" than a true outcast. Harris examines *The Color Purple* as a text which is very troubling both in its content and its reception. She sees it as presenting a distorted picture of black life. This has been especially important since it is becoming a "sacred text", one to be adored rather than evaluated. The effect is to make Walker *the* spokesperson for the experience of black women rather than one voice among many.

The negative effects of ideology are pointed out by three critics. Edward Twum Akwaboah contends that the womanist thesis gets in the way of story-telling in several pieces in *You Can't Keep a Good Woman Down*. Similarly, George Stade argues that womanism is different from feminism in that it implies the superiority rather than the equality of women. One result in *The Color Purple* is that masculinity itself becomes the evil, making it impossible to render male characters effectively. Gerald Early develops a similar argument by asserting that the same novel defeats its own ideological purpose by using the conventions of the Victorian novel rather than working through the literary implications of radical feminism.

IV

CONCLUSION

Alice Walker is likely to continue to stir interest and controversy as her career continues. She has aroused strong support and deep antagonism, even among other writers. For every Marge Piercy defending her, there is an Ishmael Reed talking about the ways she and other women writers reinforce the negative sterotypes of black men. Moreover, many aspects of her work remain to be explored in more traditional critical terms. Her poetry, for example, has received virtually no explication or analysis. One purpose of a bibliography such as this is to facilitate such further study by making available to readers the record of both her writings and the commentaries on her and her work.

Keith Byerman
Indiana State University

ALICE WALKER

PRIMARY SOURCES

BOOKS

PS 3573. A425 O5

1. *Once: Poems*. New York: Harcourt, Brace and Jovanovich, 1968.

    African Images, Glimpses from a Tiger's Back
    Love
    Karamojans
    Once
    Chic Freedom's Reflection
    South: The Name of Home
    Hymn
    The Democratic Order: Such Things in Twenty Years I
        Understood
    They Who Feel Death
    On Being Asked to Leave a Place of Honor for One of
        Comfort
    The Enemy
    Compulsory Chapel
    To the Man in the Yellow Terry
    The Kiss
    What Ovid Taught Me
    Mornings
    So We've Come at Last to Freud
    Johann
    The Smell of Lebanon
    Warning
    The Black Prince
    Medicine
    Ballad of the Brown Girl
    Suicide
    Excuse
    To Die Before One Wakes Must Be Glad
    Exercises On Themes From Life

ALICE WALKER

PS3573.A425 T5

2. *The Third Life of Grange Copeland.* New York: Harcourt, Brace and Jovanovich, 1970.

PS3573 A425 R4

3. *Revolutionary Petunias and Other Poems.* New York: Harcourt, Brace and Jovanovich, 1971.

> In These Dissenting Times
> The Old Men Used to Sing
> Winking at a Funeral
> Women
> Three Dollars Cash
> You Had To Go To Funerals
> Uncles
> They Take a Little Nip
> Sunday School, Circa 1950
> Burial
> For My Sister Molly Who in the 50's
> Eagle Rock
> Baptism
> J, My Good Friend (Another Foolish Innocent)
> View From Rosehill Cemetery: Vicksburg
> Revolutionary Petunias
> Expect Nothing
> Be Nobody's Darling
> Reassurance
> Nothing Is Right
> Black Mail
> Lonely Particular
> Perfection
> The Girl Who Died #1
> Ending
> Lost My Voice? Of Course./For Beanie
> The Girl Who Died #2/for d.p.
> The Old Warrior Terror
> Judge Every One With Perfect Calm
> The QPP
> He Said Come

Mysteries
Gift
Clutter-Up People
Thief
Will
Rage
Storm
What the Finger Writes
Forbidden Things
No Fixed Place
New Face
When Love is Unfashionable/for Mel
Beyond What
The Nature of This Flower is to Bloom

4. *Five Poems.* Detroit: Broadside Press, 1972.

Revolutionary Petunias
J, My Good Friend
Lost My Voice? Of Course./For Beanie
He Said Come
The Girl Who Died #1

5. *In Love and Trouble: Stories of Black Women.* New York: Harcourt, Brace and Jovanovich, 1973.

Roselily
Really, Doesn't Crime Pay?
Her Sweet Jerome
The Child Who Favored Daughter
Everyday Use
The Revenge of Hannah Kemhuff
The Welcome Table
Strong Horse Tea
Entertaining God
The Diary of an African Nun
The Flowers

ALICE WALKER

> We Drink the Wine in France
> To Hell With Dying

818.5 W151

6. *Langston Hughes, American Poet*. New York: Crowell, 1974.

7. *Meridian*. New York: Harcourt, Brace and Jovanovich, 1976.

PS3573. A 425 N 4

8. *Meridian* (Excerpt). *Essence*, July 1976, 35-70, 73-78.

9. *I Love Myself When I Am Laughing ...And Then Again When I Am Looking Mean and Impressive: A Zora Neale Hurston Reader*. Edited by Alice Walker. Old Westbury, New York: Feminist Press, 1979.

PS3573.A 425 G6

10. *Good Night, Willie Lee, I'll See You In The Morning: Poems*. New York: Dial, 1979.

> Did This Happen to Your Mother?
> Did Your Sister Throw Up a Lot?
> More Love to His Life
> Gift
> Never Offer Your Heart to Someone Who Eats Hearts
> Threatened
> My Husband Says
> Confession
> The Instant of Our Parting
> He Said:
> The Last Time
> After the Shrink
> At First
> Janie Crawford
> Moody
> Now That the Book is Finished
> Having Eaten Two Pillows (for Bessie Head)
> Light Baggage (for Zora, Nella, Jean)
> On Stripping Bark from Myself (for Jane, who said trees die
>   from it)

Early Losses: a Requiem
In Uganda an Early King
Forgive Me If My Praises
The Abduction of Saints
Malcolm
(In Answer to Your Silly Question) (for Algernon)
Streaking (a phenomenon following the sixties)
"'Women of Color' Have Rarely Had the Opportunity to Write About Their Love Affairs"
Facing The Way
Talking to My Grandmother Who Died Poor (While Hearing Richard Nixon Declare "I am not a crook.")
January 10, 1973
Your Soul Shines
Forgiveness
Even As I Hold You
Good Night, Willie Lee, I'll See You in the Morning

PS3573 . A425 Y6

11. *You Can't Keep a Good Woman Down: Stories.* New York: Harcourt, Brace and Jovanovich, 1981. London: Women's Press, 1982.

Nineteen Fifty-five.
How Did I Get Away With Killing One of the Biggest Lawyers in the State? It Was Easy.
Elethia
The Lover
Petunias
Coming Apart
Fame
The Abortion
Porn
Advancing Luna--and Ida B. Wells
Laurel
A Letter of the Times, or Should This Sado-Masochism Be Saved?
A Sudden Trip Home In the Spring

5

ALICE WALKER

12. ✕ *The Color Purple*. New York: Harcourt, Brace and Jovanovich, 1982. London: Women's Press, 1983.

13. *In Search of Our Mothers' Gardens: Womanist Prose*. New York: Harcourt, Brace and Jovanovich, 1983.

Breaking Chains and Encouraging Life.
If the Present Looks Like the Past, What Does the Future Look Like?
Looking to the Side, and Back.
To the Black Scholar.
Brothers and Sisters.
Silver Writes.
Only Justice Can Stop A Curse.
Nuclear Madness: What You Can Do.
To the Editors of *Ms*. Magazine.
Writing the Color Purple.
One Child of One's Own: A Meaningful Digression Within the Work(s).
Beauty: When the Other Dancer is the Self.

14. *Horses Make a Landscape Look More Beautiful: Poems.*   New York: Harcourt, Brace and Jovanovich, 1984.

Remember?
These Mornings of Rain
First, They Said
Listen
S M
The Diamonds On Liz's Bosom
We Alone
Attentiveness
1971
Every Morning
How Poems Are Made/A Discredited View
Mississippi Winter I
Mississippi Winter II
Mississippi Winter III
Mississippi Winter IV
Love Is Not Concerned
She Said
Walker
Killers

ALICE WALKER

Songless
A Few Sirens
Poem at Thirty-nine
I Said to Poetry
Gray
Overnights
My Daughter Is Coming
When Golda Meir Was In Africa
If "Those People" Like You
On Sight
I'm Really Very Fond
Representing the Universe
Family Of
Each One, Pull One
Who?
Without Commercials
No One Can Watch the Wasichu
The Thing Itself
Torture
Well
Song
These Days

ESSAYS

15. "The Almost Year." In *In Search of Our Mothers' Gardens: Womanist Prose*. New York: Harcourt, Brace and Jovanovich, 1983.

16. "Am I Blue?" *Ms.*, July 1986, 29-30.

17. "Anais Nin: 1930-1977." *Ms.*, April 1977, 46.

18.   "Beauty: When the Other Dancer is the Self." In *In Search of Our Mothers' Gardens: Womanist Prose*. New York: Harcourt, Brace and Jovanovich, 1983.

19.   "Beyond the Peacock: The Reconstruction of Flannery O'Connor." *Ms.*, Dec. 1975, 77-79, 102, 104-106.

20.   "Beyond the Peacock: The Reconstruction of Flannery O'Connor." In *In Search of Our Mothers' Gardens: Womanist Prose*. New York: Harcourt, Brace and Jovanovich, 1983.

21.   "The Black Writer and the Southern Experience." *New South*, Fall 1970, 23-26.

22.   "The Black Writer and The Southern Experience." In *In Search of Our Mothers' Gardens: Womanist Prose*. New York: Harcourt, Brace and Jovanovich, 1983.

23.   "Breaking Chains and Encouraging Life." In *In Search of Our Mothers' Gardens: Womanist Prose*. New York: Harcourt, Brace and Jovanovich, 1983.

24.   "Brothers and Sisters." In *In Search of Our Mothers' Gardens: Womanist Prose*. New York: Harcourt, Brace and Jovanovich, 1983.

25.   "But Yet and Still the Cotton Gin Kept On Working." *Black Scholar*, January - February 1970, 17-21.

26.   "But Yet and Still the Cotton Gin Kept On Working." In *In Search of Our Mothers' Gardens: Womanist Prose*. New York: Harcourt, Brace and Jovanovich, 1983.

27.   "Can I Be My Brothers' Sister? (Brothers and Sisters)." *Ms.*, October 1975, 64-65.

28.   "China." *Ms.*, March 1985, 51-54, 106-107.

29.   "Choice: A Tribute to Dr. Martin Luther King, Jr." In *In Search of Our* Mothers' Gardens: Womanist Prose. New York: Harcourt, Brace and Jovanovich, 1983.

30.   "Choosing to Stay at Home: Ten Years After the March on Washington." In *In Search of Our Mothers' Gardens: Womanist Prose*. New York: Harcourt, Brace and Jovanovich, 1983.

31.   "The Civil Rights Movement: What Good Was It?" *American Scholar* 36 (1967): 550-54.

32.   "The Civil Rights Movement: What Good Was It?" In *In Search of Our Mother's Gardens: Womanist Prose.* New York: Harcourt, Brace and Jovanovich, 1983.

33.   "The Color Purple Didn't Come Easy; (Writing the Color Purple)." *San Francisco Chronicle Book Review*, 10 October 1982.

34.   "Coretta King: Revisited." In *In Search of Our Mothers' Gardens: Womanist Prose*. New York: Harcourt, Brace and Jovanovich, 1983.

35.   "The Divided Life of Jean Toomer." In *In Search of Our Mother's Gardens: Womanist Prose*. New York: Harcourt, Brace and Jovanovich, 1984.

36.   "Embracing the Dark and Light." *Essence*, July 1982, 67, 114, 117-118, 121.

37.   "Father: For What You Were." *Essence*, May 1985, 93-94, 96.

38.   "Finding Celie's Voice." (adaptation of an address, 1984) *Ms.*, Dec. 1985, 71-72, 96.

39.   "Finding Celie's Voice." *Spare Rib*, April 1986, 37.

40. "From an Interview." In *In Search of Our Mothers' Gardens: Womanist Prose*. New York: Harcourt, Brace and Jovanovich, 1983.

41. "Gifts of Power: The Writings of Rebecca Jackson." In *In Search of Our Mothers' Gardens: Womanist Prose*. New York: Harcourt, Brace and Jovanovich, 1983.

42. "Good Morning, Revolution: Uncollected Writings of Social Protest." In *In Search of Our Mothers' Gardens: Womanist Prose*. New York: Harcourt, Brace and Jovanovich, 1983.

43. "The Growing Strength of Coretta King." *Redbook*, September 1971, 96-97, 184.

44. "Hum Inside the Skull" (interview). *New York Times Book Review*, 13 May 1984.

45. "If the Present Looks Like the Past, What Does the Future Look Like?" In *In Search of Our Mothers' Gardens: Womanist Prose*. New York: Harcourt, Brace and Jovanovich, 1983.

46. "In Search of Our Mothers' Gardens: The Creativity of Black Women in the South." *Ms.*, May 1974, 64-70, 105.

47. "In Search of Our Mothers' Gardens." In *In Search of Our Mothers' Gardens: Womanist Prose*. New York: Harcourt, Brace and Jovanovich, 1983.

48. "In Search of Our Mothers' Gardens." In *The Norton Anthology of Literature by Women: The Tradition in English*. Edited by Sandra M. Gilbert and Susan Gubar, 2374-82. New York: W. W. Norton and Company, 1985.

49. "In Search of Zora Neale Hurston." *Ms.*, March 1975, 74-79.

50. "In The Closet of The Soul: A Letter to an African-American

Friend." *Ms.*, November 1986, 32-33.

51.   "A Letter to the Editor of *Ms.*" In *In Search of Our Mothers' Gardens: Womanist Prose*. New York: Harcourt, Brace and Jovanovich, 1983.

52.   "Looking for Zora." In *In Search of Our Mothers' Gardens: Womanist Prose*. New York: Harcourt, Brace and Jovanovich, 1983.

53.   "Looking to the Side, and Back." In *In Search of Our Mothers' Gardens: Womanist Prose*. New York: Harcourt, Brace and Jovanovich, 1983.

54.   "Lulls." *Black Scholar*, May 1976, 2-12.

55.   "Lulls: A Native Daughter Returns to the Black South." *Ms.*, January 1977, 58-6, 89-90.

56.   "Lulls." In *In Search of Our Mothers' Gardens: Womanist Prose*. New York: Harcourt, Brace and Jovanovich, 1983.

57.   "Making the Moves and the Movies We Want." In *In Search of Our Mothers' Gardens: Womanist Prose*. New York: Harcourt, Brace and Jovanovich, 1983.

58.   "My Father's Country Is The Poor." *New York Times*, 21 March 1977, 27.

59.   "My Father's Country is the Poor." *Black Scholar*, Summer 1977, 41-43.

60.   "My Father's Country is the Poor." In *In Search of Our Mother's Gardens: Womanist Prose*. New York: Harcourt, Brace and Jovanovich, 1983.

61.   "Nuclear Exorcism: Beyond Cursing The Day We Were Born."

Mother Jones, September - October 1982, 20-21.

62. "Nuclear Madness: What You Can Do." In *In Search of Our Mothers' Gardens: Womanist Prose*. New York: Harcourt, Brace and Jovanovich, 1983.

63. "One Child Of One's Own." *Ms.*, August 1979, 47-50, 72-75.

64. "One Child of One's Own: A Meaningful Digression Within the Work(s)." In *In Search of Our Mothers' Gardens: Womanist Prose*. New York: Harcourt, Brace and Jovanovich, 1983.

65. "Only Justice Can Stop a Curse." In *In Search of Our Mothers' Gardens: Womanist Prose*. New York: Harcourt, Brace and Jovanovich, 1983.

66. "Other Voices, Other Moods." *Ms.*, February 1979, 50-51, 70.

67. "Porn At Home." *Ms.* February 1980, 67-70, 75-76.

68. "Recording the Seasons." In *In Search of Our Mothers' Gardens: Womanist Prose*. New York: Harcourt, Brace and Jovanovich, 1983.

69. "Redemption Day." *Mother Jones*, December 1986, 43-45.

70. "Saving the Life That is Your Own: The Importance of Models in the Artist's Life." In *The Third Woman: Minority Women Writers of the United States*. Edited by Dexter Fisher. Boston: Houghton Mifflin Company, 1980.

71. "Saving the Life That is Your Own: The Importance of Models in the Artist's Life". In *In Search of Our Mothers' Gardens: Womanist Prose*. New York: Harcourt, Brace and Jovanovich, 1983.

72. "Silver Writes." In *In Search of Our Mothers' Gardens: Womanist*

Prose. New York: Harcourt, Brace and Jovanovich, 1983.

73. "Staying Home In Mississippi." *New York Times Magazine*, 26 August 1973, 9, 49, 52-53, 58.

74. "A Talk: Convocation 1972." In *In Search of Our Mother's Gardens: Womanist Prose*. New York: Harcourt, Brace and Jovanovich, 1983.

75. "To the Black Scholar." In *In Search of Our Mothers' Gardens: Womanist Prose*. New York: Harcourt, Brace and Jovanovich, 1983.

76. "To the Editors of *Ms*. Magazine." In *In Search of Our Mothers' Gardens: Womanist Prose*. New York: Harcourt, Brace and Jovanovich, 1983.

77. "The Unglamorous but Worthwhile Duties of the Black Revolutionary Artist, or of the Black Writer Who Simply Works and Writes." *Black Collegian*, September - October 1971, 5, 43, 46.

78. "The Unglamorous but Worthwhile Duties of the Black Revolutionary Artist, or of the Black Writer Who Simply Works and Writes." In *In Search of Our Mothers' Gardens: Womanist Prose*. New York: Harcourt, Brace and Jovanovich, 1983.

79. "View from Rosehill Cemetery: A Tribute to Dr. Martin Luther King, Jr." *South Today* 4 (1973): 11.

80. "When a Tree Falls." *Ms.*, January 1984, 48-49.

81. "When the Other Dancer Is the Self." *Ms.*, May 1983, 70, 72, 142-43.

82. "A Writer Because of, Not in Spite of, Her Children." In *In Search*

of Our Mothers' Gardens: Womanist Prose. New York: Harcourt, Brace and Jovanovich, 1983.

83. "Writing the Color Purple." In *In Search of Our Mothers' Gardens: Womanist Prose.* New York: Harcourt, Brace and Jovanovich, 1983.

84. "Zora Neale Hurston--a cautionary tale." *Moving On*, 2 November 1978, 12-15.

85. "Zora Neale Hurston: A Cautionary Tale and a Partisan View." In *In Search of Our Mothers' Gardens: Womanist Prose.* New York: Harcourt, Brace and Jovanovich, 1983.

POETRY

86. Abduction of Saints. *Freedomways*, Fall 1975, 266-67.

87. Abduction of Saints. In *Good Night, Willie Lee, I'll See You in the Morning.* New York: Dial Press, 1979.

88. African Images, Glimpses from a Tiger's Back. In *Once: Poems.* New York: Harcourt, Brace and Jovanovich, 1968.

89. After the Shrink. In *Good Night, Willie Lee, I'll See You in the Morning.* New York: Dial Press, 1979.

90. At First. In *Good Night, Willie Lee, I'll See You in the Morning.* New York: Dial Press, 1979.

91. Attentiveness. In *Horses Make a Landscape Look More Beautiful: Poems.* New York: Harcourt, Brace and Jovanovich, 1984.

ALICE WALKER

92. Ballad of the Brown Girl. In *Once: Poems*. New York: Harcourt, Brace, Jovanovich, 1968.

93. The Black Prince. In *Once: Poems*. New York: Harcourt, Brace and Jovanovich, 1968.

94. Burial. *Harper*, March 1972, 72-3.

95. Chic Freedom's Reflection. In *Once: Poems*. New York: Harcourt, Brace and Jovanovich, 1968.

96. Compulsory Chapel. In *Once: Poems*. New York: Harcourt, Brace, and Jovanovich, 1968.

97. Confession. In *Good Night, Willie Lee, I'll See You in the Morning*. New York: Dial Press, 1979.

98. Crucifixions. In *Revolutionary Petunias and Other Poems*. New York: Harcourt, Brace and Jovanovich, 1971.

99. The Democratic Order: Such Things in Twenty Years I Understood. In *Once: Poems*. New York: Harcourt, Brace and Jovanovich, 1968.

100. The Diamonds On Liz's Bosom. In *Horses Make a Landscape Look More Beautiful: Poems*. New York: Harcourt, Brace and Jovanovich, 1984.

101. Did This Happen to Your Mother? Did Your Sister Throw Up a Lot? In *Good Night, Willie Lee, I'll See You In The Morning*. New York: Dial Press, 1979.

102. Each One, Pull One. In *Horses Make a Landscape Look More Beautiful: Poems*. New York: Harcourt, Brace and Jovanovich, 1984.

103. Early Losses: a Requiem. In *Good Night, Willie Lee, I'll See You In the Morning*. New York: Dial Press, 1979.

104. Early Losses: A Requiem. In *Black Sister: Poetry by Black American Women, 1746-1980*. Edited by Erlene Stetson, 223. Bloomington: Indiana University Press, 1981.

105. The Enemy. In *Once: Poems*. New York: Harcourt, Brace and Jovanovich, 1968.

106. Even As I Hold You. In *Good Night, Willie Lee, I'll See You in the Morning*. New York: Dial Press, 1979.

107. Every Morning. In *Horses Make a Landscape Look More Beautiful: Poems*. New York: Harcourt, Brace and Jovanovich, 1984.

108. Every Morning. *Ladies Home Journal*, May 1985, 103.

109. Excuse. In *Once: Poems*. New York: Harcourt, Brace and Jovanovich, 1968.

110. Exercises On Themes From Life. In *Once: Poems*. New York: Harcourt, Brace and Jovanovich, 1968.

111. Facing the way. *Freedomways*, Fall 1975, 265-66.

112. Facing the Way. In *Good Night, Willie Lee, I'll See You in the Morning*. New York: Dial Press, 1979.

113. Family of. *Freedomways*, Winter 1981, 46.

114. Family of. In *Horses Make a Landscape Look More Beautiful: Poems*. New York: Harcourt, Brace and Jovanovich, 1984.

115. A Few Sirens. In *Horses Make a Landscape Look More Beautiful: Poems*. New York: Harcourt, Brace and Jovanovich, 1984.

ALICE WALKER

116. First, They Said. In *Horses Make a Landscape Look More Beautiful: Poems*. New York: Harcourt, Brace and Jovanovich, 1984.

117. For My Sister Molly. *Harper*, March 1972, 72-3.

118. Forgive Me If My Praises. *Black Scholar*, November-December 1978, 46.

119. Forgive Me If My Praises. In *Good Night, Willie Lee, I'll See You in the Morning*. New York: Dial Press, 1979.

120. Forgiveness. In *Good Night, Willie Lee, I'll See You in the Morning*. New York: Dial Press, 1979.

121. Gift. *Essence*, July 1972, 6.

122. Gift. In *Good Night, Willie Lee, I'll See You in the Morning*. New York: Dial Press, 1979.

123. The Girl Who Died #1. In *Five Poems*. Detroit: Broadside Press, 1972.

124. Good Night, Willie Lee, I'll See You in the Morning. In *Good Night, Willie Lee, I'll See You in the Morning*. New York: Dial Press, 1979.

125. Gray. In *Horses Make a Landscape Look More Beautiful: Poems*. New York: Harcourt, Brace and Jovanovich, 1984.

126. Having Eaten Two Pillows. (for Bessie Head). In *Good Night, Willie Lee, I'll See You in the Morning*. New York: Dial Press, 1979.

127. He Said:. In *Good Night, Willie Lee, I'll See You in the Morning*. New York: Dial Press, 1979.

128. He Said Come. In *Five Poems*. Detroit: Broadside Press, 1972.

129. How does it feel to watch your neighbor. In *In These Times*, 17 December 1986, 14.

130. How Poems are Made/A Discredited View. In *Horses Make a Landscape Look More Beautiful: Poems*. New York: Harcourt, Brace and Jovanovich, 1984.

131. Hymn. In *Once: Poems*. New York: Harcourt, Brace and Jovanovich, 1968.

132. Hymn. Hayden, Robert, David Burrows, and Frederick R. Lapides. *Afro-American Literature: An Introduction*. New York: Harcourt, Brace and Jovanovich, Inc., 1971.

133. I Must Whistle Like a Woman Undaunted. *Essence*, October 1984, 90-91.

134. I Said to Poetry. In *Horses Make a Landscape Look More Beautiful: Poems*. New York: Harcourt, Brace and Jovanovich, 1984.

135. I'm Really Very Fond. In *Horses Make a Landscape Look More Beautiful: Poems*. New York: Harcourt, Brace and Jovanovich, 1984.

136. If "Those People" Like You. In *Horses Make a Landscape Look More Beautiful: Poems*. New York: Harcourt, Brace and Jovanovich, 1984.

137. (In Answer to Your Silly Question) (for Algernon). In *Good Night, Willie Lee, I'll See You in the Morning*. New York: Dial Press, 1979.

138. In These Dissenting Times. *Black World*, November 1970, 60-63.

139. In These Dissenting Times. In *Revolutionary Petunias and Other Poems*. New York: Harcourt, Brace and Jovanovich, 1971.

140. In Uganda an Early King. In *Good Night, Willie Lee, I'll See You in the Morning*. New York: Dial Press, 1979.

141. The Instant of Our Parting. In *Good Night, Willie Lee, I'll See You In the Morning*. New York: Dial Press, 1979.

142. J, My Good Friend. In *Five Poems*. Detroit: Broadside Press, 1972.

143. Janie Crawford. *Aphra*, Fall 1974, 52.

144. Janie Crawford. In *Good Night, Willie Lee, I'll See You in the Morning*. New York: Dial Press, 1979.

145. Janie Crawford. *Black Collegian*, May-June 1979, 93.

146. January 10, 1973. In *Good Night, Willie Lee, I'll See You in the Morning*. New York: Dial Press, 1979.

147. Johann. In *Once: Poems*. New York: Harcourt, Brace and Jovanovich, 1968.

148. Karamojans. In *Once: Poems*. New York: Harcourt, Brace and Jovanovich, 1968.

149. Killers. In *Horses Make a Landscape Look More Beautiful: Poems*. New York: Harcourt, Brace and Jovanovich, 1984.

150. The Kiss. In *Once: Poems*. New York: Harcourt, Brace and Jovanovich, 1968.

151. The Last Time. In *Good Night, Willie Lee, I'll See You in the Morning*. New York: Dial Press, 1979.

152. Light Baggage (for Zora, Nella, Jean). In *Good Night, Willie Lee, I'll See You In the Morning.* New York: Dial Press, 1979.

153. Listen. In *Horses Make a Landscape Look More Beautiful: Poems.* New York: Harcourt, Brace and Jovanovich, 1984.

154. Lost My Voice? Of Course./For Beanie. In *Five Poems.* Detroit: Broadside Press, 1972.

155. Love. In *Once: Poems.* New York: Harcourt, Brace and Jovanovich, 1968.

156. Love is Not Concerned. In *Horses Make a Landscape Look More Beautiful: Poems.* New York: Harcourt, Brace and Jovanovich, 1984.

157. Malcolm. *Black Collegian,* May-June 1979, 93.

158. Malcolm. In *Good Night, Willie Lee, I'll See You in the Morning.* New York: Dial Press, 1979.

159. Medicine. In *Once: Poems.* New York: Harcourt, Brace and Jovanovich, 1968.

160. Mississippi I. In *Horses Make a Landscape Look More Beautiful: Poems.* New York: Harcourt, Brace and Jovanovich, 1984.

161. Mississippi II. In *Horses Make a Landscape Look More Beautiful: Poems.* New York: Harcourt, Brace and Jovanovich, 1984.

162. Mississippi III. In *Horses Make a Landscape Look More Beautiful: Poems.* New York: Harcourt, Brace and Jovanovich, 1984.

163. Mississippi IV. In *Horses Make a Landscape Look More Beautiful: Poems.* New York: Harcourt, Brace and Jovanovich, 1984.

164. Moody. In *Good Night, Willie Lee, I'll See You in the Morning.*

New York: Dial Press, 1979.

165. More Love to His Life. In *Good Night, Willie Lee, I'll See You in the Morning: Poems*. New York: Dial Press, 1979.

166. Mornings. In *Once: Poems*. New York: Harcourt, Brace and Jovanovich, 1968.

167. My Daughter Is Coming. In *Horses Make a Landscape Look More Beautiful: Poems*. New York: Harcourt, Brace and Jovanovich, 1984.

168. My Husband Says. In *Good Night, Willie Lee, I'll See You in the Morning*. New York: Dial Press, 1979.

169. Mysteries...the Living Beyond. In *Revolutionary Petunias and Other Poems*. New York: Harcourt, Brace and Jovanovich, 1971.

170. The Nature of This Flower Is To Bloom. In *Revolutionary Petunias and Other Poems*. New York: Harcourt, Brace and Jovanovich, 1971.

171. Never Offer Your Heart to Someone Who Eats Hearts. In *Good Night, Willie Lee, I'll See You in the Morning*. New York: Dial Press, 1979.

172. New Face. *Essence*, November 1983, 122.

173. New Poems. *Freedomways*, Spring 1984, 95-99.

174. 1971. In *Horses Make a Landscape Look More Beautiful: Poems*. New York: Harcourt, Brace and Jovanovich, 1984.

175. No One Can Watch the Wasichu. In *Horses Make a Landscape Look More Beautiful: Poems*. New York: Harcourt, Brace and Jovanovich, 1984.

176. Now That the Book is Finished. In *Good Night, Willie Lee, I'll See You in the Morning*. New York: Dial Press, 1979.

177. The Old Men Used to Sing. In *Revolutionary Petunias and Other Poems*. New York: Harcourt, Brace and Jovanovich, 1971.

178. On Being Asked to Leave a Place of Honor For One of Comfort. In *Once: Poems*. New York: Harcourt, Brace and Jovanovich, 1968.

179. On Sight. In *Horses Make a Landscape Look More Beautiful: Poems*. New York: Harcourt, Brace and Jovanovich, 1984.

180. On Stripping Bark From Myself (for Jane, who said trees die from it). In *Good Night, Willie Lee, I'll See You in the Morning*. New York: Dial Press, 1979.

181. Once. In *Once: Poems*. New York: Harcourt, Brace and Jovanovich, 1968.

182. Once. In *Black Sister: Poetry by Black American Women, 1746-1980*. Edited by Erlene Stetson, 213. Bloomington: Indiana University Press, 1981.

183. Overnights. In *Horses Make a Landscape Look More Beautiful: Poems*. New York: Harcourt, Brace and Jovanovich, 1984.

184. Poem at Thirty-nine. *Ms.*, June 1971, 101.

185. Poem at Thirty-nine. In *Horses Make a Landscape Look More Beautiful: Poems*. New York: Harcourt, Brace and Jovanovich, 1984.

186. Remember? In *Horses Make a Landscape Look More Beautiful: Poems*. New York: Harcourt, Brace and Jovanovich.

187. Representing the Universe. In *Horses Make a Landscape Look*

ALICE WALKER

      More Beautiful: Poems. New York: Harcourt, Brace and Jovanovich, 1984.

188.   Revolutionary Petunias...the Living Through. In *Revolutionary Petunias and Other Poems.* New York: Harcourt, Brace and Jovanovich, 1971.

189.   Revolutionary Petunias. In *Five Poems.* Detroit: Broadside Press, 1972.

190.   Revolutionary Petunias. In *Black Sister: Poetry by Black American Women, 1746-1980.* Edited by Erlene Stetson, 212. Bloomington: Indiana University Press, 1981.

191.   Rock Eagle. *Freedomways,* Fall 1971, 368.

192.   S M . In *Horses Make a Landscape Look More Beautiful: Poems.* New York: Harcourt, Brace and Jovanovich, 1984.

193.   She Said. In *Horses Make a Landscape Look More Beautiful: Poems.* New York: Harcourt, Brace and Jovanovich, 1984.

194.   The Smell of Lebanon. In *Once: Poems.* New York: Harcourt, Brace and Jovanovich, 1968.

195.   So We've Come at Last to Freud. In *Once: Poems.* New York: Harcourt, Brace and Jovanovich, 1968.

196.   Song. In *Horses Make a Landscape Look More Beautiful: Poems.* New York: Harcourt, Brace and Jovanovich, 1984.

197.   Songless. In *Horses Make a Landscape Look More Beautiful: Poems.* New York: Harcourt, Brace and Jovanovich, 1984.

198.   South. *Freedomways,* Fall 1971, 368.

199.   South: The Name of Home. In *Once: Poems.* New York:

Harcourt, Brace and Jovanovich, 1968.

200. Streaking (a phenomenon following the sixties). In *Good Night, Willie Lee, I'll See You in the Morning*. New York: Dial Press, 1979.

201. Suicide. In *Once: Poems*. New York: Harcourt, Brace and Jovanovich, 1968.

202. Talking To My Grandmother Who Died Poor Some Years Ago. (While Listening to Richard Nixon Declare I Am Not a Crook!). *Black Scholar*, June 1975, 62.

203. Talking To My Grandmother Who Died Poor Some Years Ago. (While Hearing Richard Nixon Declare I Am Not a Crook.) In *Good Night, Willie Lee, I'll See You in the Morning*. New York: Dial Press, 1979.

204. These Days. In *Horses Make a Landscape Look More Beautiful: Poems*. New York: Harcourt, Brace and Jovanovich, 1984.

205. These Mornings of Rain. In *Horses Make a Landscape Look More Beautiful: Poems*. New York: Harcourt, Brace and Jovanovich, 1984.

206. They Who Feel Death. In *Once: Poems*. New York: Harcourt, Brace and Jovanovich, 1968.

207. Thief. *Essence*, July 1972, 6.

208. The Thing Itself. In *Horses Make a Landscape Look More Beautiful: Poems*. New York: Harcourt, Brace and Jovanovich, 1984.

209. Threatened. In *Good Night, Willie Lee, I'll See You in the Morning*. New York: Dial Press, 1979.

ALICE WALKER

210. Three Dollars Cash. In *Revolutionary Petunias and Other Poems*. New York: Harcourt, Brace and Jovanovich, 1971.

211. To Die Before One Wakes Be Glad. In *Once: Poems*. New York: Harcourt, Brace and Jovanovich, 1968.

212. To the Man in the Yellow Terry. In *Once: Poems*. New York: Harcourt, Brace and Jovanovich, 1968.

213. Torture. In *Horses Make a Landscape Look More Beautiful: Poems*. New York: Harcourt, Brace and Jovanovich, 1984.

214. Walker. In *Horses Make a Landscape Look More Beautiful: Poems*. New York: Harcourt, Brace and Jovanovich, 1984.

215. Warning. In *Once: Poems*. New York: Harcourt, Brace and Jovanovich, 1968.

216. What Ovid Taught Me. In *Once: Poems*. New York: Harcourt, Brace and Jovanovich, 1968.

217. When Golda Meir Was In Africa. *Black Scholar*, March-April 1979, 8.

218. When Golda Meir Was In Africa. In *Horses Make a Landscape Look More Beautiful: Poem*. New York: Harcourt, Brace and Jovanovich, 1984.

219. Who? In *Horses Make a Landscape Look More Beautiful: Poems*. New York: Harcourt, Brace and Jovanovich, 1984.

220. Winking at a Funeral. In *Revolutionary Petunias and Other Poems*. New York: Harcourt, Brace and Jovanovich, 1971.

221. Without Commercials. In *Horses Make a Landscape Look More Beautiful: Poems*. New York: Harcourt, Brace and Jovanovich, 1984.

222. Women. *Essence*, May 1980, 102.

223. Women. In *Women Working: An Anthology of Stories and Poems*.
      Edited by Nancy Hoffman and Florence Howe. Old Westbury,
      New York: Feminist Press, 1979.

224. 'Women of Color' Have Rarely Had the Opportunity to Write
      About Their Love Affairs. In *Good Night, Willie Lee, I'll See
      You in the Morning*. New York: Dial Press, 1979.

225. Your Soul Shines. In *Good Night, Willie Lee, I'll See You in the
      Morning*. New York: Dial Press, 1979.

SHORT STORIES

226. The Abortion. *Mother Jones*, August 1980, 30.

227. The Abortion. In *You Can't Keep a Good Woman Down*. New
      York: Harcourt, Brace and Jovanovich, 1981.

228. The Abortion. In *Prize Stories, 1981: The O. Henry Awards*. Edited
      by William Abrahams, 127-37. Garden City, New York:
      Doubleday Inc., 1981.

229. The Abortion. In *Buying Time; an Anthology Celebrating 20 Years
      of the Literature Program of the National Endowment for the
      Arts*. Edited by Scott Walker, 280-290. St. Paul, Minnesota:
      Graywolf Press, 1985.

230. Advancing Luna--and Ida B. Wells. *Ms.*, July 1977, 75-79.

231. Advancing Luna--and Ida B. Wells. In *Midnight Birds: Stories of*

ALICE WALKER

Contemporary Black Women Writers. Edited by Mary Helen Washington, 63-81. Garden City, New York: Anchor/Doubleday, 1980.

232. Advancing Luna--and Ida B. Wells. In *Fine Lives: the Best of Ms. Fiction*. Edited by Ruth Sullivan, 85-105. New York: Scribner, 1981.

233. Advancing Luna--and Ida B. Wells. In *You Can't Keep a Good Woman Down*. New York: Harcourt, Brace and Jovanovich, 1981.

234. "America Should Have Closed Down on the First Day a Black Woman Observed That Supermarket Collard Greens Tasted Like Water." *Ms.*, January 1985, 53, 68.

235. The Child Who Favored Daughter. In *In Love and Trouble: Stories of Black Women*. New York: Harcourt, Brace and Jovanovich, 1973.

236. Coming Apart. In *Take Back the Night: Women on Pornography*. Edited by Laura Lederer, 95-104. New York: William Morrow, 1980.

237. Coming Apart. In *You Can't Keep a Good Woman Down*. New York: Harcourt, Brace and Jovanovich, 1981.

238. Coming Apart. In *The Other Woman: Stories of Two Women and a Man*. Edited by Susan Koppelman, 323-34. New York: Feminist Press, 1984.

239. Cuddling. *Essence*, July 1985, 74-76, 110, 114.

240. The Diary of an African Nun. *Freedomways*, Summer 1968, 6-29.

241. The Diary of an African Nun. In *In Love and Trouble: Stories of Black Women*. New York: Harcourt, Brace and Jovanovich,

1973.

242. Elethia. In *You Can't Keep a Good Woman Down*. New York: Harcourt, Brace and Jovanovich, 1981.

243. Entertaining God. In *In Love and Trouble: Stories of Black Women*. New York: Harcourt, Brace and Jovanovich, 1973.

244. Everyday Use. In *In Love and Trouble: Stories of Black Women*. New York: Harcourt, Brace and Jovanovich, 1973.

245. Everyday Use: a story. *Harpers*, April 1973, 74-76.

246. Everyday Use. In *Women and Fiction: Short Stories by and About Women*. Edited by Susan Cahill, 363-364. New York: New American Library, 1978.

247. Everyday Use. In *Black-eyed Susans: Classic Stories by and About Black Women*. Edited by Mary Helen Washington, 78-88. Garden City, New York: Anchor/ Doubleday, 1975.

248. Everyday Use. In *The Ethnic American Woman: Problems, Protests, Lifestyle*. Edited by Edith Blicksilver, 267-72. Dubuque, Iowa: Kendall/Hunt Publishing Company, 1978.

249. Everyday Use. In *Woman as Writer*. Edited by Jeannette L. Webber and Joan Grumman, 432-438. Boston: Houghton Mifflin Company, 1978.

250. Everyday Use. In *Woman: An Affirmation*. Edited by Alice Fannin, Rebecca Lukens and Catherine Hoyser Mann, 2366-73. Lexington, Mass.: D. C. Heath, 1979.

251. Everyday Use. In *Between Mothers and Daughters; Stories Across a Generation*. Edited by Susan Koppelman, 229-39. New York: Feminist Press, 1985.

252. Everyday Use. In *The Norton Anthology of Literature by Women: The Tradition in English*. Edited by Sandra M. Gilbert and Susan Gubar, 2365-73. New York: W. W. Norton and Company, 1985.

253. Fame. In *You Can't Keep a Good Woman Down*. New York: Harcourt, Brace and Jovanovich, 1981.

254. First Day (a fable after Brown). *Freedomways*, Fall 1974, 314-16.

255. The Flowers. In *In Love and Trouble: Stories of Black Women*. New York: Harcourt, Brace and Jovanovich, 1973.

256. Her Sweet Jerome. In *In Love and Trouble: Stories of Black Women*. New York: Harcourt, Brace and Jovanovich, 1973.

257. Her Sweet Jerome. In *We Be Word Sorcerers: 25 Stories by Black Americans*. Edited by Sonia Sanchez, 216-24. New York: Bantam Books, 1973.

258. How Did I Get Away With Killing One of the Biggest Lawyers in the State? *Ms.*, November 1980, 72.

259. How Did I Get Away with Killing One of the Biggest Lawyers in the State? It Was Easy. In *You Can't Keep a Good Woman Down*. New York: Harcourt, Brace and Jovanovich, 1981.

260. Kindred spirits. *Esquire*, August 1985, 106-7, 109-111.

261. Kindred Spirits. In *Prize Stories, 1986: The O. Henry Awards*. Edited by Williams Abrahams, 1-11. New York: Doubleday, 1986.

262. Laurel. *Ms.*, November 1978, 64-66.

263. Laurel. In *Midnight Birds: Stories by Contemporary Black Women*

Writers. Edited by Mary Helen Washington, 48-59. Garden City, New York: Anchor Books, 1980.

264. Laurel. In *You Can't Keep a Good Woman Down*. New York: Harcourt, Brace and Jovanovich, 1981.

265. Letter of the Times. *Ms.*, October 1981, 62-64.

266. A Letter of the Times or Should This Sado-Masochism Be Saved? In *You Can't Keep a Good Woman Down*. New York: Harcourt, Brace and Jovanovich, 1981.

267. The Lover. In *You Can't Keep a Good Woman Down*. New York: Harcourt, Brace and Jovanovich, 1981.

268. The Lover. *Essence*, April 1981, 87, 132, 135, 137.

269. Nineteen Fifty-five. In *You Can't Keep a Good Woman Down*. New York: Harcourt, Brace and Jovanovich, 1981.

270. 1955 or, You Can't Keep a Good Woman Down. *Ms.*, March 1981, 54-57, 86-87.

271. "Nineteen Fifty-five. Alice Walker Reads 'Nineteen Fifty-five'." Sound Recording. Columbia, Missouri: American Audio Prose Library, 1981. 36 minutes.

272. Olive Oil. *Ms.*, August 1985: 34-36, 78.

273. Petunias. *Conditions*, Spring 1978, 41.

274. Petunias. In *You Can't Keep a Good Woman Down*. New York: Harcourt, Brace and Jovanovich, 1981.

275. Porn. In *You Can't Keep a Good Woman Down*. New York: Harcourt, Brace and Jovanovich, 1981.

276. Really, Doesn't Crime Pay? In *In Love and Trouble: Stories of Black Women.* New York: Harcourt, Brace and Jovanovich, 1973.

277. The Revenge of Hannah Kemhuff. In *In Love and Trouble: Stories of Black Women.* New York: Harcourt, Brace and Jovanovich, 1973.

278. The Revenge of Hannah Kemhuff. In *The Best American Short Stories, 1974.* Edited by Martha Foley, 318-32. Boston: Houghton Mifflin, 1974.

279. Roselily. In *In Love and Trouble: Stories of Black Women.* New York: Harcourt, Brace and Jovanovich, 1973.

280. Sojourner. *Ms.,* May 1976, 67-70.

281. Something You Done Wrong. *Mother Jones,* June 1982, 33-35, 50, 54.

282. Source. In *You Can't Keep a Good Woman Down.* New York: Harcourt, Brace and Jovanovich, 1981.

283. Strong Horse Tea. *Negro Digest,* June 1968, 53-60.

284. Strong Horse Tea. In *Black Short Story Anthology.* Edited by Woodie King, 133-40. New York: Columbia University Press, 1972.

285. Strong Horse Tea. In *In Love and Trouble: Stories of Black Women.* New York: Harcourt, Brace and Jovanovich, 1973.

286. Strong Horse Tea. In *Stories of the Modern South.* Edited by Ben Forkner and Patrick Samway, S.J., 371-378. New York: Penguin Books, 1986.

287. A Sudden Trip Home. *Essence,* September 1971, 58-59.

288. A Sudden Trip Home in the Spring. In *Black-Eyed Susans: Classic Stories by and About Black Women*. Edited by Mary Helen Washington, 141-54. Garden City, New York: Anchor Press/Doubleday, 1975.

289. A Sudden Trip Home in the Spring. In *Woman: An Affirmation*. Edited by Alice Fannin, Rebecca Lukens and Catherine Hoyer Mann, 163-72. Lexington, Mass.: D. C. Heath, 1979.

290. A Sudden Trip Home in the Spring. In *You Can't Keep a Good Woman Down*. New York: Harcourt, Brace and Jovanovich, 1981.

291. To Hell With Dying. In *Best Short Stories by Negro Writers: An Anthology From 1899 to the Present*. Edited by Langston Hughes, 490-96. Boston: Little, Browm and Company, 1967.

292. To Hell With Dying. In *Out of Our Lives: a Selection of Contemporary Black Fiction*. Edited by Quandra Prettyman Stadler, 263-73. Washington, D. C.: Howard University Press, 1975.

293. To Hell With Dying. In *Tales and Stories For Black Folks*. Edited by Toni Cade Bambara, 52-59. Garden City, New York: Doubleday and Company, 1971.

294. To Hell With Dying. In *In Love and Trouble: Stories of Black Women*. New York: Harcourt, Brace and Jovanovich, 1973.

295. To Hell With Dying. *Reader's Digest*, October 1983, 110-14.

296. To Hell With Dying. In *Afro-American Writing: An Anthology of Prose and Poetry*. Edited by Richard Long and Eugenia W. Collier, 713-19. University Park, Pa.: Pennsylvania State University Press, 1985.

ALICE WALKER

297. We Drink the Wine in France. In *In Love and Trouble: Stories of Black Women*. New York: Harcourt, Brace and Jovanovich, 1973.

298. The Welcome Table. In *In Love and Trouble: Stories of Black Women*. New York: Harcourt, Brace and Jovanovich, 1973.

299. The Welcome Table. In *Keeping the Faith: Writings by Contemporary Black Women*. Edited by Pat Crutchfield Exum, 234-39. Greenwich, Conn.: Fawcett Publications, Inc., 1974.

MISCELLANEOUS

300. *Alice Walker Calendar*. New York: Harcourt, Brace and Jovanvich, 1985.

301. Review of *Black Anima*, by N. J. Loftis. *Parnassus*, Spring 1974, 5-14.

302. "Breaking Chains and Encouraging Life." Review of *The Black Women's Issue, Conditions*, Volume 2, no. 2 (Autumn 1979). Edited by Lorraine Bethel and Barbara Smith, 35-36, 38, 40-41. Brooklyn, New York: Conditions, 1979.

303. Review of *Good Morning Revolution: Uncollected Writings of Social Protest*, by Langston Hughes. Edited by Faith Berry, 53-55. *Black Scholar*, July/August 1976.

304. Review of *Ruby*, by Rosa Guy. *Black Scholar*, December 1976, 51-52.

305. Review of *Gifts of Power: The Writings of Rebecca Jackson, (1795*

- *1871), Black Visionary, Shaker Eldress.* Edited by Jean McMahon Humez. *Black Scholar,* September/October 1981, 64-67.

306. Review of *Gifts of Power: The Writings of Rebecca Jackson,* (1795 - 1871), *Black Visionary,* Shaker Eldress. Edited by Jean McMahon Humez. Correction *Black Scholar,* November / December 1981, 80.

307. Review of *Nuclear Madness: What You Can Do*, by Helen Caldicott. *Black Scholar,* Spring 1982, 81.

308. "Black Sorority Bankrolls Action Film." Review of *Countdown at Kusini*, film produced by Delta Sigma Theta. *Ms.*, July 1976, 45.

309. "Black Women's Private Writings: Diaries and Journals." *Sage: A Scholarly Journal on Black Women* 2 (Spring 1985): 53.

310. "Can't Hate Anybody and See God's Face." Review of *Fannie Lou Hamer*, by June Jordan. *New York Times Book Review*, 29 April 1973, 8.

311. "Children's Fall Book Review." *The Friends* by Rosa Guy. *New York Times Book Review*, 4 November 1973, 26.

312. "A Daring Subject Boldly Shared." Review of *Loving Her*, by Ann Allen Shockley. *Ms.*, April 1975, 120, 124.

313. "The Divided Life of Jean Toomer." Review of *The Wayward and the Seeking: A Collection of Writings by Jean Toomer*, edited by Darwin T. Turner. *New York Times Book Review*, 13 July 1980, 7:11,16.

314. "For Young Readers." Review of *The Almost Year*, by Florence Engel Randall. *New York Times*, 11 April 1971, 7:22.

ALICE WALKER

315. "Jane Didn't Stay in a Corner.", Review of *The Autobiography of Miss Jane Pittman*, by Ernest J. Gaines. *New York Times Book Review*, 23 May 1971, 6:7.

316. "Judith Jamison." Review of *Dance - 'Cry'*. *Ms.*, March 1973, 66-67.

317. "Learning in Literature: Alice Walker, *The Color Purple* (excerpt)." *Language Arts* 62 (January 1985):11-14.

318. Letter (On the *Founding of the National Black Feminist Organization*). *Ms.*, August 1974, 4-6.

319. *A Library of Literary Criticism: Modern Black Writers*. Edited by Michael Popkin, 199-200, 441. New York: Frederick Ungar Publishing Company, 1978.

320. "Like the Eye of a Horse." Review of *Cruelty* by Ai (Florence Anthony). *Ms.*, June 1974, 41, 42.

321. "The Negro College Dead-End, (The Experience)." *Moderator*, March 1966, 13-14.

322. "On Anais Nin: 1903- 1977." (a reply to letter by Lani M. Nolan). *Ms.*, August 1977, 8.

323. Review of *Another Life*, by Derek Walcott. *Village Voice*, 11 April 1974, 26.

324. "The Silver Writes Movement." *The Civil Rights Quarterly*, Summer 1982, 22-23.

325. "Something To Do With The Real Life; Eudora Welty: An Interview." *Harvard Advocate*, Winter 1973, 68-72.

326. "The Strangest Dinner Party I Ever Went To." Review of *Fireless Cookery: A Traditional Energy-Efficient Method of Slow*

Cooking, by Heidi Kirschner. *Ms.*, July-August 1982,58,63.

327. A Talk By Alice Walker '65: Convocation 1972. *Sarah Lawrence Alumni Magazine*, Summer 1972, 6-8.

328. "A Walk Through 20th Century Black America." Review of *A Short Walk* by Alice Childress. *Ms.*, December 1979, 46,48.

329. "Who's Reading What: 45 Books That Changed 16 Minds." Review of *One Hundred Years of Solitude*, by Gabriel Garcia Marquez. *Ms.*, July 1977, 6, 33.

330. "A Writer Because of, Not in Spite of, Her Children." Review of *Second Class Citizen*, by Buchi Emecheta. *Ms.*, January 1976, 40, 106.

331. Zora Neale Hurston - *A Cautionary Tale and a Partisan View*. Foreword to *Zora Neale Hurston: A Literary Biography*, by Robert E. Hemenway. Chicago: University of Illinois Press, 1977.

GENERAL BOOK CRITICISM AND REFERENCE SOURCES

332. Adams, Timothy Dow. *Critical Survey of Long Fiction*. Edited by Frank Magill, Volume 7, 2746-57. Englewood, N. J.: Salem Press, 1983.

A general overview of literary forms,achievements and biography of Alice Walker. The analysis section provides key themes and patterns in *The Third Life of Grange Copeland*, *Meridian*, and *The Color Purple*.

333. *All the Women Are White, All the Blacks Are Men, But Some of Us Are Brave: Black Women's Studies*. Edited by Gloria T. Hull, Patricia Bell Scott, and Barbara Smith. Old Westbury, New York: The Feminist Press, 1982.

Discusses generally Alice Walker's relationship to black women's studies and black feminist movement. Also includes Walker's essay "One Child of One's Own" and general critical analysis of her works.

334. Byerman, Keith E. "Women's Blues: The Fiction of Toni Cade Bambara and Alice Walker." In *Fingering the Jagged Grain: Tradition and Form in Recent Black Fiction*, 129-70. Athens: University of Georgia Press, 1985.

Covers the novels and selected short stories. Examines the effects of folk material, especially that of black women, on the structure and themes of the fiction. Argues that folklore and history create open-ended narratives, and that Walker's ideological concerns, especially feminism, become problematic in this context.

335. Christian, Barbara. "Alice Walker: The Black Woman Artist as Wayward." In *Black Women Writers (1950-1980): A Critical Evaluation*. Edited by Mari Evans, 457-77. Garden City: Anchor, 1984. Also collected in Barbara Christian, *Black*

Feminist Criticism: Perspectives On Black Woman Writers, 81-101. New York: Pergamon Press, 1985.

Describes the major motifs of Walker's work as struggle, change, and the black woman as creator. A central theme is contrariness, the willingness to pursue the "forbidden" as a path to truth. Sees Walker's early work as challenging ideas of cultural nationalism, including the idea that racism was the only problem. But there is also resistance to the position of white feminists that gender makes race irrelevant. Sees the stories of *You Can't Keep a Good Woman Down* as developing an aesthetic of process rather than product.

336.   Christian, Barbara. *Black Woman Novelists: The Development of a Tradition, 1892-1976*, 180-238. Westport: Greenwood Press, 1980.

Examines *The Third Life of Grange Copeland* and *Meridian*. Sees Walker continuing a pattern in black women's writing of moving from private experience to community over the course of her career. The shift is marked in Grange's attention to the lives of himself and his granddaughter Ruth in contrast to Meridian's discovery of selfhood through concentration on the needs of the black community.

337.   Christian, Barbara. *Dictionary of Literary Biography*. Volume 33. *Afro-American Fiction Writers After 1955*. Edited by Thadious M. Davis and Trudier Harris, 258-71. Detroit: Gale Research Company, 1984.

Deals with Walker's life and works.

338.   *Contemporary Authors: A Bio-Bibliographical Guide to Current Authors and Their Works*. Volume 37-40. Edited by Clare D. Kinsman and Mary Ann Tennenhouse, 524. Detroit: Gale Research Company, 1973.

ALICE WALKER

A brief general overview of Alice Walker's life and writings.

339.   *Contemporary Authors: A Bio-Bibliographical Guide to Current Authors and Their Works*. Volumes 37-40, First Revision. Edited by Ann Evory, 582-83. Detroit: Gale Research Company, 1979.

Brief general overview of Walker's life and writings.

340.   *Contemporary Literary Criticism: Excerpts From Criticism of the Works of Today's Novelists, Poets, Playwrights, and Other Creative Writers*. Volume 5. Edited by Carolyn Riley and Phyllis Carmel Mendelson, 476-77. Detroit: Gale Research Company, 1976.

Brief critical overview of some of Walker's writings.

341.   *Contemporary Literary Criticism: Excerpts From Criticism of the Works of Today's Novelists, Poets, Playwrights and Other Creative Writers*. Volume 6. Edited by Carolyn Riley and Phyllis Carmel Mendelson, 553-54. Detroit: Gale Research Company, 1976.

More brief critical anaylsis of Walker's writings.

342.   *Contemporary Literary Criticism: Excerpts From Criticism of the Works of Today's Novelists, Poets, Playwrights and Other Creative Writers*. Volume 9. Edited by Dedria Bryfonski, 557-58. Detroit: Gale Research Company, 1978.

Brief critical analysis of *Meridian*, *Once* and *Revolutionary Petunias*.

343.   *Contemporary Literary Criticism: Excerpts From Criticism of the Works of Today's Novelists, Poets, Playwrights, Short Story Writers, Filmmakers, Screenwriters, and Other Creative Writers*. Volume 19. Edited by Sharon R. Gunton, 450-54. Detroit:

Gale Research Company, 1981.

Brief critical analysis of "The Diary of an African Nun", *The Third Life of Grange Copeland, Good Night Willie Lee, I'll See You in the Morning*, "The Child Who Favored Daughter" and "A Sudden Trip Home in the Spring".

344. *Contemporary Literary Criticism: Excerpts From Criticism of the Works of Today's Novelists, Poets, Playwrights, Short Story Writers, Scriptwriters, and Other Creative Writers.* Volume 27. Edited by Jean C. Stine, 448-54. Detroit: Gale Research Company, 1984.

Brief critical analysis of *You Can't Keep a Good Woman Down*, "Nineteen Fifty-Five", *Meridian, The Color Purple*, and *The Third Life of Grange Copeland*.

345. *Contributions of Black Women to America: The Arts, Media, Business, Law, and Sports.* Volume 1. Edited by Marianna W. Davis, 182, 185-87. Columbia, South Carolina: Kenday Press, 1982.

Included in the Arts volume of this two volume set Alice Walker is listed along with her contributions.

346. Cooke, Michael G. *Afro-American Literature in the Twentieth Century: The Achievement of Intimacy*, 133-76. New Haven: Yale University Press, 1984.

See annotation #781.

347. *Current Biography Yearbook*. Edited by Charles Moritz, 430-33. New York: H. W. Wilson, 198
A biographical sketch of Alice Walker.

348. Davis, Thadious M. "Alice Walker." *Dictionary of Literary Biography*. Volume 6. Edited by James E. Kibler, Jr., 350-58.

41

Detroit: Gale Research Company, 1980.

A discussion of Walker's life and works.

349. Davis, Thadious M. "Alice Walker's Celebration of Self in Southern Generations." In *Women Writers of the Contemporary South*. Edited by Peggy Whitman Prenshaw, 39-53. Oxford University Press of Mississippi, 1984.

Argues that Walker uses generational patterns to structure her writing. Sees her uniqueness in her joining of intellectual concerns to the experiences of rural poor Southern blacks. Traces the development of this linkage from the early poetry through The Color Purple.

350. *A Directory of American Poets and Fiction Writers*, 30. New York: Poets and Writers, Inc., 1980.

Published contemporary poets and fiction writers of the United States. Alice Walker is listed.

351. *Georgia Women: A Celebration*. Edited by Barbara B. Reitt, 65-66. Atlanta: American Association of University Women, 1976.

This publication was a project of the Atlanta Branch of The American Association of University Women. Alice Walker was included as a writer of the new generation.

352. Harris, Trudier. "Three Black Women Writers and Humanism: a Folk Perspective." In *Black American Literature and Humanism*. Edited by R. Baxter Miller, 50-74. Lexington, Kentucky: University Press of Kentucky, 1981.

Discusses *The Third Life of Grange Copeland* as it relates to the concept of Black folk tradition. The humanistic element exhibited in Walker's *Third Life* is explored and analyzed.

353. Harris, Trudier. *From Mammies to Militants: Domestics in Black American Literature, 6.* Philadelphia: Temple University Press, 1982.

Briefly discusses Meridian's job as a maid for a college professor.

354. Howard, Lillie P. "Alice Walker." *American Women Writers: A Critical Reference Guide From Colonial Times to the Present.* Edited by Lina Mainiero, 313-315. New York: Frederick Ungar Publishing Company, 1982.

Brief background and achievements of Alice Walker.

355. Kirkpatrick, D. L. editor. *Contemporary Novelists.* 4th Edition, 844-46. Chicago: St. James Press, 1986.

General background on Walker's life and achievements. Briefly analyzes *The Third Life of Grange Copeland, Meridian* and *The Color Purple.*

356. Matney, William C. *Who's Who Among Black Americans, 1980-1981.* 3rd Edition, 814. Northbrook, Illinois: Who's Who Among Black Americans, Inc., 1981.

Brief background with honors listed.

357. Mickelson, Anne Z. *Reaching Out: Sensitivity and Order in Recent American Fiction by Women*, 112-74. Metuchen, N. J.: Scarecrow Press, 1978.

Provides brief discussions of the way Walker presents female characters in *Meridian* and several stories from *In Love and Trouble*. Sees the stories as tales of the problems of marriage and the failures of love, while viewing the novel as a process of purification through which Meridian achieves her independence.

358.   Noble, Jeanne. *Beautiful Also Are the Souls of My Black Sisters: A History of the Black Women in America*, 188-90. Englewood Cliffs, New Jersey: Prentice-Hall, 1978.

Examines in the section "Black Women Writers of the New Renaissance" Alice Walker's contribution to the growing movement and thought in literature. The thought of the "responsibility for putting the black male/female problem/question/partnership out of the closet." Also dissects *The Third Life of Grange Copeland*.

359.   Parker-Smith, Bettye J. "Alice Walker's Women: In Search of Some Peace of Mind." In *Black Women Writers (1950-1980): A Critical Evaluation*. Edited by Mari Evans, 478-93. Garden City, New York: Anchor, 1984.

Argues for the importance of the South to Alice Walker and her writing. Emphasizes the focus in her fiction on black women, and specifically, on the relationship of their alleged weaknesses to their social and economic condition. Women in the first two novels feel the need to accept the rage of black men, in contrast to *The Color Purple*, where women become royalty rather than victims. In the earlier works death and religion seem the only options for women, whereas the more recent work shows them making a place for themselves in the world.

360.   Petry, Alice Hall. *Beacham's Popular Fiction in America*. Volume 4. Edited by Walton Beacham, 1433-43. Washington: Beacham Publishing Company, 1986.

Examines publishing history, honors, themes of selected titles, characters, social concerns, and techniques of Alice Walker. Also gives sources of information in the form of a short bibliography.

361.   Ploski, Harry, and James Williams. *Negro Almanac: A Reference Work on the Afro-American*, 740. New York: Wiley, 1983.

A brief account of Walker's life and a listing of her major works.

362.   Popkin, Michael, editor. *Modern Black Writers*, 443-46. New York: Ungar Publishing Co, 1978.

Summary of six articles written about Walker from different magazines and journals.

363.   Pryse, Marjorie and Hortense J. Spillers. *Conjuring: Black Women, Fiction, and Literary Tradition*, 1-24. Bloomington: Indiana University Press, 1985.

Develops a metaphor of conjuring to explore the tradition of black women writers. Gives special attention to *The Color Purple* and the author's insistence that she was simply a medium for the voices of her characters. Uses this idea to place Walker in the context of women storytellers.

364.   Redmond, Eugene B. *Drumvoices: The Mission of Afro-American Poetry: A Critical History*, 376-77. Garden City, New York: Anchor Press/Doubleday, 1976.

Brief discussion of *Once* and *Revolutionary Petunias*. Emphasizes satiric element and use of Southern materials for poetry.

365.   Salzman, Jack. *The Cambridge Handbook of American Literature*, 251. London: Cambridge University Press, 1986.

Briefly gives her educational background, and work experience. Last selected publications of Walker up to 1983.

366. *Screen World*. Edited by John Willis, 94-95. New York: Crown Publishers, Inc., 1986.

Gives complete movie credits: technical staff, producer and cast, plus still shots from the film.

367. Shockley, Ann A. *Living Black American Authors*, 163. New York: Bowker, 1973.

A very brief inclusion of background, professional experience, awards and mailing address.

368. *Something About the Author*. Volume 31. Edited by Anne Commire, 177-79. Detroit: Gale Research Company, 1983.

Gives personal and career information of Alice Walker. List writings and work in progress. In an area called "Sidelights" she tells of her childhood experiences and her marriage to Mel Levanthal.

369. Steinem, Gloria. *Outrageous Acts and Everyday Rebellions*, 259-75. New York: Holt, Rinehart and Winston, 1983.

"Alice Walker: Do You Know This Woman? She Knows You" appeared as an article in *Ms.* Magazine, June 1982. Steinem discusses Walker's life as it relates to her work.

370. Uglow, Jennifer S. and Frances Hinton. *The International Dictionary of Women's Biography*, 485. New York: Continuum, 1982.

A brief sketch of Walker's life and chronology of some of her works.

371. Wade-Gayles, Gloria. *No Crystal Stair: Visions of Race and Sex in Black Women's Fiction*, 102-03, 111-14. New York: The Pilgrim Press, 1984.

Explores character development in *The Third Life of Grange Copeland* and *Meridian*. Contends that characters fail in the first novel because "racism and sexism work together as deterrents to joy and wholeness." In the second novel, points out that Walker provides a catalogue of the abuses suffered by women.

372. Walters, Marian. *Contemporary Authors: A Bio-Bibliographical Guide to Current Writers in Fiction, General Nonfiction, Poetry, Journalism, Drama, Motion Pictures, Television, and Other Fields*. New Revision Series, Volume 9. Edited by Ann Evory and Linda Metzger, 514-17. Detroit: Gale Research Company, 1983.

Brief account of Alice Walker, her life and writings.

373. Washington, Mary Helen. "An Essay on Alice Walker." In *Sturdy Black Bridges: Visions of Black Women in Literature.* Edited by Roseann P. Bell, Betty J. Parker and Beverly Guy-Sheftall, 133-56. Garden City, New York: Anchor Press/Doubleday, 1979.

Argues that a basic belief for Walker is that black women suffer the greatest oppression. Says that in this writing this suffering often emerges as psychological distortion. Traces an evolution in the fiction from pure victimization to control for women.

374. Willis, Susan. "Black Woman Writers: Taking a Critical Perspective." In *Making a Difference: Feminist Literary Criticism*. Edited by Gayle Greene and Coppelia Kahn, 211-31. London: Methuen, 1985.

Identifies three issues in fiction by black women: community, journey, and sensuality/sexuality. Focuses on work by Walker, Toni Morrison, Paule Marshall, and Zora Neale Hurston.

ALICE WALKER

Sees in this writing an impulse to involve a community rather than an isolated individual; but believes that the idea of community is consistently problematic, as in the case of Walker's rural South, which has been deformed by racist domination. Emphasizes the interrelationship of history and economics in *The Third Life of Grange Copeland* and *The Color Purple*. Points out the ambivalence toward both sexuality and motherhood in much of the fiction, including *Meridian*.

375.   Abron, Jo Nina M. "Movie Review of *The Color Purple*." *Black Scholar*, March/April 1986, 54.

   Asks the question of the film not only as a story of Celie's growth but also a statement to the status of the black American family. Also raises the question of stereotyping.

376.   Adams, J.W. "Goldberg Wants To Be Who She Is: A Character Actor." *(Manchester, New Hampshire) Union Leader*, 15 December 1985, G11-12.

   Goldberg discusses with Adams her feelings and thoughts about her performance. Briefly talks about the beginnings and about the *Color Purple*. (Newsbank)

377.   "Alice Walker." *Ebony*, March 1974, 102+.

   Mentions Alice Walker's affiliations with the McDowell Colony and Radcliffe Institute, plus works and honors.

378.   "Alice Walker Addresses Students Via TV Hookup." *Jet*, 15 December 1986, 60.

   Discusses "A Private Conversation With Alice Walker," a program sponsored by KQED public television station at San Francisco via TV hookup.

379.   "Alice Walker, Coretta King Most Outstanding: Poll (World Almanac Poll)." *Jet*, 19 January 1987, 17.

   Alice Walker listed as one of "America's 25 Most Outstanding Women in 1986". The World Almanac poll of newspaper editors from newspapers around the country named the women.

ALICE WALKER

380.   "Alice Walker Goes Home to Eatonton, Ga. for 'Color Purple' Premiere." *Jet*, 10 February 1986, 28-30.

Gives an account of events during "Alice Walker Day" in Eatonton, Georgia, surrounding gala "Color Purple" movie premiere.

381.   "Alice Walker Going Her Own Way." *Vanity Fair*, April 1983, 90.

Addresses the elements found in Walker's writings as being her ability to "retrieve discarded bits of black culture as they fall from fashion."

382.   "Alice Walker Was Recently Awarded the Townsend Prize for Fiction During Ceremonies in Atlanta, Ga." *Jet*, 16 April 1984, 21.

A brief announcement of the Townsend Prize for Fiction given to Alice Walker for "The Color Purple."

383.   "Alice Walker Wins Townsend Award." *Atlanta Journal*, 20 March 1984, B:2.

Announces Alice Walker as the winner of Townsend Prize for Fiction, for "The Color Purple." The late Jim Townsend was founding editor of the *Atlanta Magazine*. Award given every two years to a Georgia author.

384.   Allen, Robert. "Best Books of the 70's." *Black Scholar*, March-April 1981, 80.

Lists "Meridian" as one of the best books of the 1970's. Robert Allen, editor of *The Black Scholar*, compiled this list.

385.   "American Scholar Forum: Women on Women." *American Scholar* 41 (Fall 1972): 599-622.

This discussion on the women's movement was moderated by Lillian Hellman with Ann Birstein, Nancy Wilson Ross, Norma Rosen, Renata Adler, Carolyn Heilbrun, Alice Walker and Elizabeth Janeway.

386. Ansen, David. "We Shall Overcome." *Newsweek*, 30 December 1985, 59-60.

Discusses Spielberg's and Meyjes' interpretation of Walker's novel *The Color Purple*. Criticizes some of the interpretation as being a "Disney movie about incest". States that strong cast and characters redeemed the movie.

387. Armstrong, Douglas D. "'Color Purple' Proves Some Points About Book Movies." *Milwaukee (Wisconsin) Journal*, 2 March 1986, C11-13.

Armstrong considers the consequences of making movies from books. Gives four points where the film was "filtered" through the visions of Meyjes and Spielberg. (Newsbank)

388. Armstrong, Douglas D. "Director Shows His Versatility in 'Color'." *Milwaukee (Wisconsin) Journal*, 20 December 1985, B3.

Another review by Armstrong with a different slant. He summarizes the plot of the film while evaluating the principal actors. (Newsbank)

389. Attanasio, Paul. "The Odds and the Oscars: Figuring the Favorites for Tomorrow Nights Awards." *Washington Post*, 23 March 1986, H:1, 5.

Gives odds on movie "The Color Purple" and cast winning an Oscar. Attanasio does not feel strongly the "Purple" has much of a chance. (Newsbank)

390.   Atwood, Margaret. "The Certain Thing Called the Girlfriend."
        The New York Times Book Review, 11 May 1986, 1, 38-39.

        Briefly mentions *The Color Purple* in connection with other
        novels concerning female relationships and friendships.

391.   "Author Alice Walker Wins Pulitzer Prize." *Atlanta Constitution*,
        19 April 1983, A:1.

        Announces Walker's winning of the 1983 Pulitzer Prize for
        fiction for her novel *The Color Purple*. States that she is the
        first black woman to win award for fiction.

392.   Barrington, Judith. "A Hazy Shade of Purple." *San Francisco
        Chronicle*, 23 March 1986, E4-5.

        Barrington criticizes Spielberg's interpretation of Walker's
        Color Purple. Accuses him of having limited vision when
        compared to Walker's. Contends that the lack of vision in
        terms of characters and plot affected the creditability of the
        film.

393.   Beasley, David. "Hometown Rolls Out Red Carpet for Pulitzer
        Prize-Winning Author." *Atlanta Constitution and Journal*, 19
        January 1986, D:3.

        Beasley relates the event of local premiere of "The Color
        Purple" in Eatonton. Planned by Ruth Walker Hood, sister
        of Alice Walker, the event raised $10,000 for scholarships in
        author's name.

394.   Benson, Sheila. "'The Color Purple'." *Los Angeles (California)
        Times*, 18 December 1985, D14, E1.

        Film critic Benson describes the film as having "three
        memorable performances." Relates that the transforming of
        the book to film was done so with the cost of sacrificing the

"tone" and "theme" of Walker's work.

395. "The Black Books Roundup #7 Spring 1981." (Photos of Robert Chrisman, Andrew Salkey, Charles Rowell, Alice Walker, and Ernest Gaines). *Black Scholar*, March-April 1981, 31.

Photos of participants of the Black Scholar Press Book Party: Robert Chrisman, Andrew Salkey, Charles Rowell, Alice Walker, and Ernest Gaines.

396. "Black Women Novelists: New Generation Raises Provocative Issues." *Ebony*, November 1984, 59-60, 62, 64-65.

Discusses the emerging black women novelists onto the literary scene. Alice Walker is briefly discussed as one of these novelists, along with Toni Morrison, Margaret Walker, Ntozake Shange, Gayl Jones, Toni Cade Bambara, Paule Marshall, Gloria Naylor and Ann Petry.

397. "Black Writer's Views on Literary Lions and Values: A Survey." *Negro Digest* 17 (January 1968): 13.

The results of a 1968 survey of approximately 38 black writers some well established, others unknown. Alice Walker is included and asked to respond to specific questions.

398. Blake, Richard A. "Survivors." *America*, 1 February 1986, 75.

Criticizes Spielberg's direction as manipulative and Jones' music as "overwhelming and saccharine". Feels that Walker's story is lost in the over-dramatization.

399. Blank, Ed. "'Color Purple' Radiates." *Pittsburgh (Pennsylvania) Press*, 19 December 1985, A4, 5.

Blank praises the film and thus the director and cast for "supreme screen achievements, a life-affirming experience about the dividends of perseverence." (Newsbank)

400. Bowles, Billy. "Town's Party for 'Purple' Author Has No Color Bars." *Detroit (Michigan) Free Press*, 19 January 1986, G1, 2.

Gives an account of the premiere of film "Color Purple" held in Eatonton and attended by Alice Walker and her relatives. (Newsbank)

401. Boyd, Melba Joyce. "The Ten Books for the Seventies." *Black Scholar*, March-April 1981, 81.

Boyd gives title of ten books that have impressed her. *Meridian* is on the list.

402. Bradley, David. "Telling the Black Woman's Story." *New York Times Magazine*, 8 January 1984, 24-37.

Bradley recalls conversation with Alice Walker. Gives his thoughts on some of her works.

403. Brittenum, Lonnie. "Alice Walker Shares Her Theology of Worship From Within." *Oakland (California) Tribune*, 31 January 1986, B7.

Reports on 85th annual E. T. Earl Lectures at Pacific School of Religion where Alice Walker spoke to a standing room only audience of 1,800. (Newsbank)

404. Brown, Cecil. "Brown's Ten." *Black Scholar*, March-April 1981, 82.

What Cecil Brown, novelist, considers books that impressed him from the 1970's. Included in this list is *I Like Myself When I'm Laughing, Then Again When I'm Looking Mean and Impressive: A Zora Neale Hurston Reader*, edited by Alice Walker.

405.   Bruning, Fred.   "An American View: When E.T. Goes to Georgia". *Maclean's*, 24 March 1986, 9.

Argues that "Color Purple" is "one-dimensional and contains phony emotions". Questioned the use of Spielberg as the director over a black director and Walker's reasons for allowing this "surrender". Relates how some blacks have spoken negatively about the film.

406.   Bunke, Joan.   "Talented Cast Portrays Triumphs of Black Women." *Des Moines (Iowa) Register*, 22 December 1985, E14.

This reviewer had all good things to say about Spielberg and company concerning "Color Purple" film. A refreshing departure from most critics. (Newsbank)

407.   Cain, Scott.   "Spielberg's 'Purple' Makes Play for Prestige." *Atlanta (Georgia) Journal*, 20 December 1985, E12, 13.

Reviewer states, that Spielberg's project is a departure from his usual presentations, i.e. "E.T." Commends him for his attempt at "something arty." (Newsbank)

408.   Caldecott, Leonie. "Alice Walker's Vision of Renewal." *New Age Journal*, May 1985, 44-52.

Discusses impressions formed while interviewing Alice Walker.

409.   Caldecott, Leonie. "The Voices and Visions of Alice Walker." *UTNE Reader* 12 (October 1985): 152-57.

Appeared in *New Age Journal*, May 1985. Gives impressions formed while interviewing Alice Walker.

410.   Callahan, John. "The Higher Ground of Alice Walker." *The New*

Republic, September 14, 1974, 21-22.

Discusses the themes and techniques in Walker's works. Relates a poem written for Alice Walker by Michael Harper.

411. Campbell, Genie. "'The Color Purple' is a Winner You Don't Want to Miss." *Madison, (Wisconsin) Capital Times*, 22 December 1985, B1,2.

Another positive review of the film "The Color Purple." Compliments Spielberg for creating on film the true essence of what Walker intended in the book. (Newsbank)

412. Canby, Vincent. "From a Palette of Cliches Comes 'The Color Purple.'" *The New York Times*, 5 January 1986, 17.

Criticizes the film "The Color Purple" for being too "Hollywood." Gives several points where scenes and set were not realistic for the South.

413. Carmody, Deirdre. "'Night, Mother' Wins Pulitzer Drama Prize." *New York Times*, 19 April 1983, A1, B4.

Announces *"Color Purple"* as winner of Pulitzer Prize for fiction.

414. Carroll, Kathleen. "See It and Weep." *New York Daily News*, 18 December 1985, G3.

Discusses the visual aspects of the film "Color Purple." "The colors used in the film somehow soften the harsh reality of the subject matter." Compliments Spielberg on the project. (Newsbank)

415. Champlin, Charles. "Critic At Large: Spielberg's Primary 'Colors.'" *Los Angeles Times*, 28 December 1985, E2.

Accuses Spielberg of being a "mass-audience director." Reviewer feels that Spielberg knows and uses techniques to get "tears and gasps." (Newsbank)

416.   "'Color Purple' a Disturbing Film." *St. Paul (Minnesota) Pioneer Press*, 22 December 1985, F7, 8.

Reviewer feels that the film "Color Purple" has great chances for Oscar nomination. Also states film solidified black male stereotypes. (Newsbank)

417.   "'Color Purple' Cause for Joy." *New York Post*, 18 December 1985, G4, 5.

Reviewer refers to the film as "Spielberg's finest film." Relates points of the plot and gives credit to cast. (Newsbank)

418.   Connelly, Sherryl. "Celie's Story." *New York Daily News*, 15 December 1985, C2, 3.

Announces opening of the film "The Color Purple" directed by Steven Spielberg. Discusses the theme of the film. (Newsbank)

419.   Conyus. "Looking Over My Shoulder at the 70's (24 of the Best in the Field)." *The Black Scholar*, March-April 1981, 83.

Cites *In Love and Trouble* as one of the 24 best books in his opinion of the 70's.

420.   Corliss, Richard. "The Three Faces of Steve." *Time*, 23 December 1985, 78.

Criticizes Spielberg, the cast and the movie. Contends the director "softened Walker's messages."

ALICE WALKER

421.   "Creative Woman: Success Requires Talent and Drive." *Ebony*, August 1977, 135.

A brief mention of Alice Walker and some of her achievements. Announces her "latest" novel, *Meridian*.

422.   Crumpler, David. "'Color Purple' Fans Should Be Delighted With Movie Adaptation." *(Jacksonville) Florida Times Union*, 19 December 1985, E10.

Discusses the movie, director and cast. Compares the story to the "black experience" in American history. (Newsbank)

423.   Curtright, Bob. "'Color Purple' Could Be Best Film of Year." *Wichita (Kansas) Eagle-Beacon*, 20 December 1985, Fl.

Discusses the movie and its cast and recommends the movie highly. Praises Goldberg's performance. (Newsbank)

424.   Davis, Bridgette. "Spielberg to Direct 'Color Purple' Film." *Atlanta (Ga.) Journal*, 30 May 1985, F7.

Discusses the imminent filming of the movie "The Color Purple". Possible casting choices are also discussed. (Newsbank)

425.   Davis, Bridgette. "Spielberg Will Direct Film of 'Color Purple.'" *Atlanta Constitution*, 30 May 1985, C:1.

Announces the filming schedule of "The Color Purple" and the films director, Steven Spielberg. Discusses possible casting choices. (Newsbank)

426.   DeBrossee, Jim. "Review: A Powerful Movie." *Cincinnati (Ohio) Enquirer*, 19 December 1985, G10, 11.

Deals with the emotion in movie and the relationships of the characters. Praises the director for his delivery of the message of the novel. (Newsbank)

427. Douglas, John. "'Color Purple' is Acting Treasure." *Grand Rapids (Michigan) Press*, 22 December 1985, F6.

Reviewer declares Spielberg "courageous" for tackling "The Color Purple" and characterizes the movie as "something a little different, a treasure." (Newsbank)

428. Elliott, David. "It's a Fine Time for Heroines." *San Diego (California) Union*, 20 December 1985, E3, 4.

Contends that the "Color Purple" is a movie of "heroines." Praises Spielberg for interpretation of the novel. (Newsbank)

429. Erickson, Peter. "Cast Out Alone/To Heal/ and Re-create/ Ourselves: Family-Based Identity in the Work of Alice Walker." *CLA Journal*, 23 (Spring 1979): 71-94.

Sees the family in Walker's fiction and poetry as the connection between the character and his/her past. In *The Third Life of Grange Copeland*, family is the means of registering both despair and hope. The relationship between Grange and Ruth is the center of the book. In "A Sudden Trip Home in the Spring", return to the family is a way of finding identity. *Revolutionary Petunias* is noteworthy for its absence of father figures. In *Meridian* the mother-daughter conflict and the whole question of family is crucial to our understanding of the book.

430. Finn, James. "Alice Walker and Flight 007." *Christianity and Crisis* 43 (31 October 1983): 397-98.

Discusses the writer's impressions of Alice Walker's analysis of Flannery O'Connor, in her essay "Beyond the Peacock: The Reconstruction of Flannery O'Connor." Relates this to his impressions of the downing by the Soviets of the Korean KAL 007 airline.

431.   Foil, David. "Spielberg's 'Color' Smooth, Well Done But Story Softened." *Baton Rouge (Louisiana) Morning Advocate*, 20 December 1985, F2, 3.

Criticizes the director for softening the story written by Walker. (Newsbank)

432.   Foley, Ellen. "Writer Walker Says We Can Learn By 'Listening' to Trees." *Minneapolis (Minnesota) Star and Tribune*, 3 March 1983, F1-2.

Speaks of Walker's views of nature and environment. Gives brief overview of her life and *The Color Purple*. Mentions her appearance at the College of St. Catherine and the Walker Art Center in St. Paul. (Newsbank)

433.   Freedman, Richard. "Spielberg Comes of Age With 'The Color Purple.'" *(Springfield, Massachusetts) Morning Union*, 20 December 1985, F5.

Commends Spielberg and cast on "making a movie by, for and about grownups." Relates that director did not have much to work with considering the content of the novel. (Newsbank)

434.   Freeman, Alma S. "Zora Neale Hurston and Alice Walker: A Spiritual Kinship." *Sage: A Scholarly Journal on Black Women* 2 (Spring 1985): 37-40.

Discusses the similarities of style of Walker and Hurston. Their use of folklore and or folkways are but one example of their sameness.

435.   Gable, Mona. "Author Alice Walker Discusses 'The Color Purple'." *The Wall Street Journal*, 19 December 1985, 26.

Walker discusses her decision to release "The Color Purple" for filming, the meeting of Spielberg and Jones. Also her visit to the movie set.

436. "Georgia Native Alice Walker Wins National Award in Fiction." *Atlanta Consititution* 15 April 1983, C:21.

Announces Walker as the winner of the 1983 American Book Award for fiction for *The Color Purple*. The Association of American Publishers choose as judges authors, critics, librarians, booksellers and editors to arrive at this award.

437. "Georgian's Novel Gets Top Award." *Atlanta Journal*, 15 April 1983, A:3.

Announces *The Color Purple* as receiving the 1983 American Book Award for fiction.

438. Goldstein, William. "The Story Behind the Movie: Alice Walker on the Set of The Color Purple." *Publishers Weekly*, 6 September 1985, 46-48.

Discusses Walker's impressions of the casting and filming of The Color Purple. Menno Meyjes and Steven Spielberg give their thoughts on technical and creative production.

439. Graham, Keith. "2nd Townsend Prize to be Awarded Tues." *Atlanta Constitution*, 19 March 1984, B:3.

Announces nominees for the Second Townsend Award. Walker's "The Color Purple" is one of six books being considered.

440. Graham, Keith. "Townsend Lives on for State Writers." *Atlanta Constitution*, 21 March 1984, B:1.

61

Walker as winner of Townsend Award for "The Color Purple" "despite strong field of nominees." Award was presented at luncheon honoring Georgia's authors.

441.   Graham, Keith. "Three to Get Lillian Smith Writing Awards." *Atlanta Constitiution*, 14 November 1984, B:8.

The awarding of the 1984 Lillian Smith awards to regional writers, Alice Walker, John Egerton and Eudora Welty.

442.   Griffin, Ada Gay. "Have You Read This Movie Somewhere Before?" *Womanews*, 7 February 1986, 5, 15.

Criticizes the film for not being "historically, economically, or politically" accurate. Accuses Walker of selling out and Spielberg of manipulation.

443.   Grimm, Fred. "'Color Purple' Author Receives Joyous Welcome." *Miami* (Florida) *Herald*, 19 January 1986, D5, D6.

Tells of the opening of the movie "Color Purple" in Eatonton, Georgia with Alice Walker attending. (Newsbank)

444.   Grossberg, Michael. "'Color Purple' Spielberg's Royal Triumph." *Columbus (Ohio) Dispatch*, 19 December 1985, G12.

Contends that "Purple" is "one of the best movies of this or any other year". Praises Spielberg and cast for the adaptation of Walker's novel. (Newsbank)

445.   "Guggenheim Prizes Are Awarded to 313; Fellowships Totaling $4.6 Million Given to Scholars, Scientists and Artists in Competition." *New York Times*, 10 April 1977, 25.

Announces Walker as a winner of Guggenheim Memorial Foundation Award.

446.   Halprin, Sara. "The Color Purple/Community of Women."
        Jump Cut, March 1986, 1, 28.

        Points out certain aspects where the movie differs from
        Walker's novel. Praises the work for bringing images of black
        women into public awareness.

447.   Hanscom, Leslie. "A Homage in 'Purple': Alice Walker Has Put
        Her Sharecropper Childhood Into a Prize-Winning Novel."
        Long Island, New York Newsday, 5 May 1983, 3.

        Relates some of the feeling of Walker about her work and her
        background. (Newsbank)

448.   Harper, Michael S. "Alice" (Poem for Alice Walker). *Black
        World*, April 1975, 94.

        Michael Harper wrote this poem for Alice Walker and her
        quest for Zora Neale Hurston.

449.   Harris, Trudier. "Folklore in the Fiction of Alice Walker: A
        Perpetuation of Historical and Literary Traditions." *Black
        American Literature Forum* 11 (Spring 1977): 3-8.

        Describes the uses to which Walker puts folk material.
        Examines "The Revenge of Hannah Kemhuff" in terms of the
        conjure woman tradition. Compares Walker's use to that of
        Charles Chestnutt. Shows that Walker modifies the tradition
        to develop political and psychological themes. In "Strong
        Horse Tea," folklore shows the value of retaining connection
        with one's heritage. In *The Third of Grange Copeland*, folk
        material defines the relationship between Ruth and Grange.

450.   Harti, John. "'Purple' Perfection." *Seattle (Washington) Times*,
        20 December 1985, A12, 13.

        Commends Spielberg for his direction of "serious, realistic film

ALICE WALKER

'The Color Purple'". (Newsbank)

451.   Hernton, Calvin. "The Sexual Mountain and Black Women Writers." *Black Scholar*, July/August 1985, 2-11.

Alice Walker is discussed as one of the black women writers included in the article. Discussion of *Third Life of Grange Copeland*, and *Color Purple*.

452.   Hey, Kenneth R. "Films: The Color Purple." *U.S.A. Today*, March 1986, 92-93.

Criticizes Spielberg's direction of the film. Relates the thought that the film has "confused intentions", also creates an expression of unreality.

453.   Hill, Alma. "Alice Walker: She Dares to Write What Others Shudder to Think." *(Portland) Oregonian*, 10 October 1986, D1-2.

An interview given in Portland, Oregon where she was speaking for the Portland Arts and Lecture Series. She talks of the themes of the writings. (Newsbank)

454.   Hollyday, Joyce. "The Color of Pain, The Color of Triumph". *Sojourners: An Independent Christian Monthly*, April 1986, 47-49.

Characterizes the film as a story "pain and triumph". Compliments Goldberg for her debut performance and Spielberg for his direction. The successful direction is attributed to Spielberg's willingness to "counsel" with Walker during the filming.

455.   Hunter, Stephen. "Extraordinary Cast Makes Film Powerful." *Baltimore (Maryland) Sun*, 20 December 1985, F4.

Reviewer gives the film praises but also criticism. States that Spielberg made the film too glossy while Walker's style in book was "harsh and spare". (Newsbank)

456.   "In Perspective: About Writers and Writing." *First World*, May-June 1977, 37.

Brief announcement of Walker's participation in Ascension (no. 25) Series at Howard University.

457.   Janusonis, Michael. "Purple Haze: In Spielberg's Self-Conscious New Movie, the Characters Don't Stay in Focus." *Providence (Rhode Island) Journal*, 20 December 1985, A6.

Contends that Spielberg has painted pretty pictures of rural South which are unrealistic. Also feels that characters are in and out of focus. (Newsbank)

458.   Janusonis, Michael. "Whoopi Tickled Purple." *Providence (Rhode Island) Journal*, 15 December 1985, A1-2.

Whoopi Goldberg gives reactions to doing "The Color Purple". (Newsbank)

459.   Jarrell, Frank. "Movie May Spark Some Arguments." *(Charleston, South Carolina) News and Courier*. 20 December 1985, A7.

Jarrell felt after seeing movie "The Color Purple" that he was "used". Spielberg's play with the emotions is questioned. (Newsbank)

460.   "Jet Celebrates Black Pulitzer Recipients." *Jet*, 17 November 1986, 35.

Discusses the blacks who have received the Pulitzer Prize. Alice Walker listed.

461. Johnson, Malcolm L. "A Vivid Tableau of Life, Love in the Rural South." *Hartford (Connecticut) Courant*, 20 December 1985, E8, 9.

Praises the movie for its interpretation of Walkers' novel. Reviewer compliments the cast on their performances. (Newsbank)

462. Johnson, Paul. "Color It Powerful." *(Little Rock) Arkansas Gazette*, 20 December 1985, D12, 13.

Reviewer praises Goldberg's performance but contends that Spielberg's direction did not do the story justice, although he compliments Spielberg's attempt.

463. Kauffman, Stanley. "Signs of the Times." *The New Republic*, 27 January 1986, 24-25.

Commends Spielberg for the switch to a more adult type of movie, and the actors for the performances.

464. Keal, Pauline. "Sacred Monsters." *The New Yorker*, 30 December 1985, 67-71.

Criticizes movie, director, actors, alike as not having substance.

465. Kelley, Ernece B. "Most Dangerous Film Since 'Birth of a Nation'." *Guardian*, 19 February 1986, 19.

Reacts to the Jill Nelson article concerning the distortions in "Color Purple."

466. Ketcham, Diane. "Alice Walker Back on Scene as Poet and Publisher." *(Oakland, California) Tribune*, 11 November 1984, B9.

Announces Walker's latest book *Horses Make a Landscape Look More Beautiful* and informs the public of Walker and Allen's publishing company Wild Tree Press. (Newsbank)

467.	Ketcham, Diane. "Authors Alice Walker, J.S. Holliday Honored." *Oakland (California) Tribune*, 28 April 1982, C2.

Reports the awarding of the 1981 BABRA award to Alice Walker for *You Can't Keep a Good Woman Down*. The award was sponsored by the Northern California Book Publicists Association.

468.	Kilman, Lawrence. "Black Woman Wins Pulitzer Fiction Prize." *Staten Island, New York Advance*, 19 April 1983.

Announces Walker as the first Black woman to win Pulitzer Prize for fiction.

469.	LaBadie, Donald. "Magic Touch Smears 'The Color Purple'." *(Memphis, Tennessee) Commercial Appeal*, 20 December 1985, A8.

Review of the movie The Color Purple expressing critic's thoughts that Spielberg's attempt has "uneasy reverence." (Newsbank)

470.	Ladd, Susan. "'The Color Purple'." *Greensboro (North Carolina) News and Record*, 19 December 1985, G8.

Praises the film as the "best American film of 1985." Compliments the cast, on their performances and Spielberg's direction. (Newsbank)

471.	"Letters; Black Women Writers." Letter to the editor, written by Gayle R. Pemberton. *New York Times Book Review*, 27 July 1986, 7:21.

Gayle Pemberton responds to Mel Watkin's article "Sexism, Racism and Black Women Writers." Mentions Walker's *Color Purple* as an example of an author airing dirty laundry which emphasizes ideas of stereotypes.

472. "Letters to God Are Postmarked With a Pulitzer." *People Weekly*, 26 December 1983 - 2 January 1984, 85, 87.

Relates the story of Alice Walker and the winning of the Pulitzer Prize.

473. Leven, Carol. "Purple Prose Still Flows." *Guardian*, 5 March 1986, 19-21.

Responds to the reactions of negative images in the film of black males. Reveals the feelings of some, that this portrayal of black males "offer aid and comfort to white racist ideas".

474. Lewis, Richard Gregory. "Culture: Depicting Struggle, Survival is the Task for Alice Walker." *The National Leader*, 7 October 1982, 19-20, 22.

Relates Walker's philosophy of the struggle women have to survive. Discusses her thoughts on critics of her work and her writing *The Color Purple*.

475. Lipper, Hal. "'Color Purple' Paints Vivid Portrait." *St. Petersburg (Florida) Times*, 20 December 1985, E11.

Describes the film as "remarkably faithful", despite its shortcomings. Lipper is very specific in his critical appraisal. (Newsbank)

476. Lovell, Glenn. "Movies: The Biggies Are Here." *San Jose (California) Mercury News*, 20 December 1985, E7.

Praises Spielberg for his attempt at the project but criticizes him for the "flaws". However the cast and their performance lauded. (Newsbank)

477. Lyman, Rick. "Spielberg Gets Serious With 'Color Purple'." *Philadelphia (Pennsylvania) Inquirer*, 22 December 1985, A1-3.

Relates Spielberg's feelings about why he made"The Color Purple"film and the selection of the cast. Members of the cast tells of certain improvisation they contributed to the film. (Newsbank)

478. McCreadie, Marsha. "'Purple' Taps Struggles from Rural South." *(Phoenix) Arizona Republic*, 20 December 1985, D11.

Focuses on the Goldberg's performance in the film. That performance characterized as "extraordinary" and at least should get an academy award nomination. Other members of the cast are briefly mentioned. (Newsbank)

479. McDowell, Edwin. "American Book Awards Given in 27 Categories." *New York Times*, 14 April 1983, 24.

Announces the American Book Award for fiction, Alice Walker's *The Color Purple*.

480. McDowell, Edwin. "American Book Awards Announced." *New York Times*, 14 April 1983, 30.

Announces *The Color Purple* as winner.

481. McDowell, Edwin. "About Books and Authors." *New York Times Book Review*, 15 May 1983, 38.

Reports that *The Color Purple* is on Best Sellers list soon after winning the Pulitzer and American Book Award.

ALICE WALKER

482. McGrady, Mike. "Spielberg Goes Serious in 'Color Purple'." *(Long Island, New York) Newsday*, 18 December 1985, G2.

   Criticizes the selection of Spielberg as director of the film "The Color Purple." (Newsbank)

483. McGuigan, Cathleen. "Whoopee for Whoopi." *Newsweek*, 30 December 1985, 60.

   Gives Goldberg's impressions of her career before and after Color Purple. Also relates some of the feelings about her performances.

484. Mahar, Ted. "Shades of Black Realities Paint 'The Color Purple'." *(Portland) Oregonian*, 21 December 1985, G13-14.

   Discusses the cast and the directors' techniques in interpreting Walker's work. (Newsbank)

485. Makowski, Elizabeth. "Familiar Matters: Women and Role Models." *North American Review* 270 (June 1985): 60-61.

   Discusses Alice Walker's thoughts, expressed in *In Search of Our Mothers' Gardens*, relating to preserving the memory and writings of Zora Neale Hurston. Relates other women writers feelings on the importance of role models and the need to write more about women.

486. Mars-Jones, Adam. "Mauve." *New Statesman* 11 July 1986, 27-28.

   Critical of Steven Spielberg's visual interpretation of Walker's novel.

487. Millburg, Steve. "'Color Purple' is Done 'Superbly Well'." *Omaha (Nebraska) World Herald*, 27 December 1985, F12.

Praises Spielberg and cast for a job well done. Quincy Jones is applauded for creating "authenic" sounding songs and music for the movie. (Newsbank)

488. Minudri, Regina U. "Books For Young Adults." *Library Journal*, 15 December 1973, 3692.

Walker's *In Love and Trouble* included in a recommended list for young adults by San Francisco Bay Area Committee of Public and School Library YA Specialists.

489. Mitgang, H. "Alice Walker Recalls the Civil Rights Battle." *New York Times Biography Service*, April 1983, 500.

Discusses her experiences of the civil rights era in Mississippi. Mentions that *The Color Purple* has also won the American Book Award.

490. Morrison, Bill. "Steven Spielberg's 'Purple' Mystery." (Raleigh, N.C.) *News and Observer*, 28 July 1985, G12-14.

Reports the measures taken to preserve the privacy of the set and shooting of the film. (Newsbank)

491. Morrison, Bill. "Shades of Oscar in 'Color Purple'." *(Raleigh, North Carolina) News and Observer*, 20 December 1985, G9.

Recounts the plot with comments on the director's interpretation. Both praises and criticizes Spielberg for techniques used and compromises made of Walker's work. (Newsbank)

492. Moynihan, Martin. "The Color Purple." *(Albany, New York) Times Union*, 22 December 1985, F14, G1.

Reports Spielberg's direction as "radical departure and a synthesis of his styles." Praises the cast for excellent performances.   (Newsbank)

493.   Muwakkil, Salim. "Bad Image Blues." *In These Times*, 9 April 1986, 24.

Examines the negative images in *The Color Purple* of black males. Discusses groups that are concerned with the images today.

494.   Myers, Leslie R. "Goldberg Looks Great in 'Purple'." *(Jackson, Mississippi) Clarion-Ledger*, 27 December 1985, F9, 10.

Examines the cast and their performances, particularly Goldberg's "excellent" one. Introduces the thought of two unneccessary details in the film: 1. two Celie's and 2. the "pat-a-cake game" play by Celie and Nettie played over and over again during the film and at the end. Other interesting points are made by reviewer. (Newsbank)

495.   Nelson, Jill. "Spielberg's Purple is Still Black." *Guardian*, 29 January 1986, 1, 17.

Challenges critics of *The Color Purple*, both film and novel, to look beyond certain aspects of the work to the real theme of what Walker is really portraying. Contends that Walker has depicted truth, and sometimes the truth hurts. Cites certain statistics on black poverty, divorce and women supporting children alone.

496.   Norment, Lynn. "The Color Purple." *Ebony*, February 1986, 146-51.

Describes the movie techniques, cast, direction.   Discusses some of the criticism the novel and movie received.

497.   O'Brien, Tom. "Tenuous Places: Out of Africa and The Color Purple." *Commonweal*, 31 January 1986, 52-54.

Views the film as "creditable and worthwhile," yet criticizes Spielberg for manipulation and overstatement via photography.

498. Peden, William. "The Black Explosion." *Studies in Short Fiction* 7 (1975): 231-41.

Puts *In Love and Trouble*, the collection of stories in the context of short fiction by other black writers. Sees Walker as creating a variety of stories in terms of subject matter and technique and praises her discipline and honesty.

499. Perry, Claudia. "Novelist's Visit to Jacksonville to Precede Time Out for Living." *(Jacksonville) Florida Times-Union*, 5 February 1984, B12.

Reports brief and general information about Walker's life writing and interests. Announces her coming appearance and reading at Kent Campus of Florida Junior College before taking off a period of time for herself just for living. (Newsbank)

500. Persico, Joyce J. "The Color Purple." *Trenton, (New Jersey) Times*, 22 December 1985, F13.

Discusses the feelings Director Spielberg has for Walker's novel. Relates how he felt his attitude would have to be different in directing this film. (Newsbank)

501. "Pride in the Pulitzers." (editorial) *Atlanta Constitution*, 20 April 1983, A: 14.

An editorial praising Walker as one of two Georgians winning Pulitzer Prize.

502. Randall, Dudley. "The Most Important Books of the 1970s."

ALICE WALKER

Black Scholar, March/April 1981, 86-87.

A list of eleven books Randall considers important to the 1970s. Walker's *The Third Life of Grange Copeland* is included.

503.   "Readers' Response: Seeing Art and Life in *The Color Purple*." *Christian Century*, 14 May 1986, 495-97.

Readers response to William H. Williamon's review of *The Color Purple* in *Christian Century*, April 2, 1986.

504.   "Real to Reel." *Savoy*, December 1984, 22.

Discusses plans to begin filming on a documentary on Alice Walker. Eleana Featherston, founder and executive director of Reel Directions was awarded a $5,000 grant to do the project.

505.   Reed, J.D. "Post Feminism Playing for Keeps." *Time*, 10 January 1983, 60-61.

Briefly mentions Alice Walker in connection with other emerging women writers and the attention their work is receiving.

506.   Rhetts, JoAnn. "Take the Family and Lots of Tissue." *Charlotte (North Carolina) Observer*, 20 December 1985, G6, 7.

Announces the opening of the movie in theaters across the country. Contends that the film can be enjoyed by elementary school children as well as adults--even with the scene between Celie and Shug. (Newsbank)

507.   "A Rich 'Color Purple'--Politics Aside." *The Washington (District of Columbia) Times*, 20 December 1985, A14.

Reviewer believes you must put aside political thoughts to look at this movie and the "richness of the story." Concerns regarding an unrealistic plot, stereotypes, racism, and abuse will hamper appreciation of the efforts put forth by Walker and Spielberg. (Newsbank)

508. Robertson, Nan. "Actresses' varied roads to 'The Color Purple'." *The New York Times*, 13 February 1986, C21.

Relates feelings of Whoopi Goldberg, Akosua Busia, Margaret Avery, and Oprah Winfrey about getting the roles in 'The Color Purple'.

509. Rosenfeld, Megan. "Alice Walker and Her Purple Muse." *New York Herald Tribune*, 1 November 1982.

This article appeared in the *Washington Post*, October 15, 1982.

510. Rosenfeld, Megan. "Profiles in Purple and Black." *Washington Post*, 15 October 1982, E-1, E-3.

Expresses Alice Walker's feelings and thoughts about writing *The Color Purple*. Her philosophy of black male/female relationships are explored.

511. Ross, Michelle. "Georgia Writer Alice Walker Didn't Know They Had Pulitzer for Fiction." *Atlanta Journal*, 19 April 1983, A:3.

Gives an account of Walker learning of her winning the Pulitzer Prize for *The Color Purple*.

512. Ross, Michelle. "Complete List of 1983 Pulitizer Winners." *Atlanta Journal*, 19 April 1983, A:3.

Among the winners is Alice Walker for her novel *The Color Purple*.

513. Ross, Michelle. "Alice Walker Stunned Over Pulitzer Prize." *Atlanta Constitution*, 19 April 1983, B:1.

Announces Walker's *The Color Purple* as winner of Pulitzer Prize for fiction category. Gives the winners of all categories for Pulitzer Prize. Walker surprised at announcement of "The Color Purple" winning prize. Gives account of early life in Eatonton, Ga.

514. Rothenstein, Richard. "The Color, Film." *Saturday Review*, May/June 1986, 79.

Examines the colors in movie titles recently. "The Color Purple" is one of the movies mentioned. Color experts relate that purple represents "spiritual."

515. Sadoff, Dianne F. "Black Matrilineage: The Case of Alice Walker and Zora Neale Hurston". *Signs: Journal of Women in Culture and Society* 11 (Autumn 1985): 4-26.

Applies the notions of anxiety of influence and anxiety of authorship to Walker's relationship to Hurston. Argues that, despite Walker's enthusiasm for her predecessor, she reveals a need for a foremother who will validate her own creative activity. Suggests that one element revealed in Walker's fiction is ambivalence about returning to the South, an attitude she shares with Hurston; they both see it as a source of inspiration but also as a place from which they have escaped. Points out that they similarly undermine while appearing to idealize matriarchy.

516. Sague, Maria. "Alice Walker: A Writer With a Cause." *(Baltimore, Maryland) Sun*, 5 July 1987, A7, 8.

Reports on an appearance Alice Walker made at the Women's Cultural festival "Sisterfire 87" in Upper Marlboro.

Walker read poems and passages from *The Color Purple*.

517.   Salamon, Julie.   "...As Spielberg's Film Version Is Released." *The Wall Street Journal*, 19 December 1985, 26.

Criticizes the movie, "The Color Purple", as not an accurate intrepretation of Walker's novel. Believes the musical scenes are sterotypical and unnecessary.

518.   Shorey, Kenneth. "This Is a Movie To Cherish and Be Grateful For....." *The Birmingham News*, 19 December 1985, 8G.

See the movie, *The Color Puple*, as an expression and invitation for compassion, sympathy and understanding.

519.   Silverman, Stephen. "'Purple': A Long Way From 'E.T.'." *New York (New York) Post*, 16 December 1985, C1.

Quincy Jones gives background on the creative and technical aspects of movie "The Color Purple".   Discusses casting selections. (Newsbank)

520.   Simon, John. "Black and White in Purple." *National Review*, 14 February 1986, 56-59.

Very critical of the novel and the movie, *The Color Purple*. Points out what he considers weaknesses in the novel and movie.

521.   Siskel, Gene. "Wunderkind, with 'The Color Purple', Spielberg Takes His Greatest Risk since 'E. T'." *The Birmingham News*, 19 December 1985, 9G.

Discussed Spielberg's reactions to the making of *The Color Purple* in comparison to the other movies in his career.

522.   Smith, Barbara. "'Color Purple' Distorts Class, Lesbian Issues."

ALICE WALKER

Guardian, 19 February 1986.

Smith expresses her concerns for the distortions of the "Color Purple". This was written in response to Jill Nelson's article.

523.   "Southern Accent Garnishes the Pulitzer Prizes." *New York Times Book Review*, 24 April 1983, 8.

Announces the Pulitzer winners Alice Walker and Marsha Norman.

524.   Steinem, Gloria. "Do You Know This Woman? She Knows You: A Profile of Alice Walker." *Ms.*, June 1982, 35, 37, 89-94.

Discusses Walker's life as it compares to and influences her work.

525.   Stone, Judy.   "Keeping 'Purple's' Spirit." *San Francisco (California) Chronicle*, 18 December 1985, B4, 5.

Walkers' impressions of the movie the 'Color Purple' are explored. Discusses her apprehensions about releasing the work for film and her concerns about casting. (Newsbank)

526.   Stone, Judy.   "Many Shades of 'Purple'." *San Francisco (California) Chronicle*, 20 December 1985, E5, 6.

Compliments Spielberg on his interpretation of Walker's work. Praises cast for performances. (Newsbank)

527.   Struthers, Ann.   "Of Love and Politics." *Des Moines (Iowa) Register*, 26 May 1985, G10, 11.

Discusses subjects and techniques of Walker's poetry in *Good Night, Willie Lee, I'll See You in the Morning* and *Horses Make a Landscape Look More Beautiful*. (Newsbank)

528.   Sulter, Maud. "Alice Walker at the Poetry Society." *Spare Rib*, July 1985, 41.

An account of Alice Walker's appearance at the Africa Centre in London. At this session she read from *The Color Purple* and *Horses Make a Landscape Look More Beautiful*.

529.   Thomas, Joyce Carol. "Literary Fruits of the 1970's." *Black Scholar*, March-April 1981, 87.

A list which includes *In Love and Trouble* as one of eleven books recommend by Joyce Thomas to read.

530.   Toppman, Lawrence. "In Search of Spielberg: Quiet On the Set." *Charlotte (N.C.) Observer*, 2 July 1985, A4.

Report of tight security on the set of the movie 'The Color Purple'. (Newsbank)

531.   Trescott, Jacqueline. "Past and Present Reflections." (Jamaica, New York) *Long Island Press*, 25 October 1976.

Discusses a conversation with Alice Walker about her life as it influences her work. Points out that two of Walker's key themes are finding beauty in the depths of poverty and degradation and finding strength in generational ties. Traces Walker's background and expecially her feelings about the South. Article appeared in *Washington Post* earlier.

532.   Vincent, Mal. "Spielberg's Dazzling 'Color Purple' Overflows With Talent; Don't Miss It." *(Norfolk) Virginian-Pilot*, 24 December 1985, A10, 11.

Advances opinions on the film and what its success will be for Oscar nominations. (Newsbank)

533.   "Walker." *Spelman Messenger*, Spring 1980, 13.

Reports on her visit to the Spelman College to read her poetry and works of Zora Neale Hurston.

534.   Wall, James M. "Current Cinema: The Color Purple." *Christian Century*, 29 January 1986, 99.

Compares the direction of the movie to John Ford-style direction. Expresses the opinion that Spielberg's attempt "works very well up to a point."

535.   Washington, Mary Helen. "Ten Into the Seventies." *Black Scholar*, March-April 1981, 89.

Walker's Hurston Reader is included on a list of books Mary Washington recommends.

536.   Washington, Mary Helen. "Alice Walker: Her Mother's Gifts." *Ms.*, June 1982, 38.

Discusses Walker's relationship with her mother and its effect on her philosophy and writings.

537.   Washington, Mary Helen. "Black Women Myth and Image Makers." *Black World* 23 (August 1974): 10-18.

Examines images of black women in literature. Briefly discusses "Roselily" and "Everyday Use".

538.   Watkins, Mel. "Sexism, Racism and Black Women Writers." *New York Times Book Review*, 15 June 1986, 7: 4, 35-37.

Deals with the issue of black women writers addressing black male/female relationships in their works.

539.   Wilkinson, Jack. "'Purple' Gets Varied Reactions at Spelman Forum." *Atlanta Constitution*, 7 February 1986, 12: 1.

Staff writer Wilkinson relates the concerns students, staff and faculty of Atlanta's Spellman and Morehouse expressed during a forum on the book and film--*The Color Purple*. (Newsbank)

540. Williams, Stephen. "Whoopi Goldberg's 'Purple' Passion." *(Long Island, New York) Newsday*, 15 December 1985, G13, 14.

Describes Goldberg's feelings about playing the role of Celie in the movie version of *The Color Purple*. Includes background of her career and attitudes toward celebrity. (Newsbank)

541. Willimon, William. "Seeing Red over The Color Purple." *Christian Century*, 2 April 1986, 319.

Reviewer feels that the movie is full of "stereo-types and images" rather than reality.

542. Wilson, Barbara. "Zora Neale Hurston Sought and Found." *In These Times*, 23-29 January 1980, 15.

Briefly mentions some of Hurston's works as it interprets black culture in the 1930's. States the connection with Walker and *I Love Myself When I'm Laughing....*

543. Wilson, Sharon. "A Conversation with Alice Walker." *Kalliope: Journal of Women's Art* 6 (1984): 37-45.

Alice Walker appeared on the television program "Worth Quoting", in Jacksonville, Florida with an audience and editor of Kalliope, Sharon Wilson.

544. Wolgamott, L. Kent. "Steven Spielberg Excels with Adult Drama; Acting Superb." *(Lincoln, Nebraska) Journal and Star*, 26 December 1985, F11.

Recounts the movie's plot, praises the cast for excellent performances and Spielberg for his direction. (Newsbank)

545. Woolner, Ann and Michele Ross. "Two Georgia Natives Win '83 Pulitzer Prizes." *Atlanta Journal*, 19 April 1983, A:1.

Announces Alice Walker winning Pulitzer Prize for fiction with *The Color Purple* and newsman Claude Sitton for commentary as editor of *The News and Observer* in Raleigh, North Carolina.

546. Wuntch, Philip. "'The Color Purple' a Masterful Tearjerker." *Dallas (Texas) Morning News*, 20 December 1985, A9.

Discusses Spielberg's ability to "manipulate emotions" without a "sense of subtlety". (Newsbank)

INTERVIEWS

547. Bannon, Barbara A. "Authors and Editors." *Publishers Weekly*, 31 August 1970, 195-97.

An interview with Alice Walker in 1970 when she was in Mississippi working with NAACP Legal Defense Fund.

548. Bannon, Barbara A. "Author Speaks: Selected PW Interviews, 1967-1976," 167-8. New York: Bowker, 1977.

An interview with Alice Walker in 1970 when she was in Mississippi working with NAACP Legal Defense Fund.

549. Bonetti, Kay. "Interviews." Sound Cassette. Columbia, Missouri: American Audio Prose Library, 1981. 47 minutes.

An interview conducted by Kay Bonetti with Alice Walker.

550.   Friedman, Mickey. "The Voices of Black Southern Women." *San Francisco (California) Examiner*, 28 January 1980, E6-7.

Discusses Walker's poetry writing. *Good Night, Willie Lee, I'll See You in the Morning*, her third volume of poems recently published was discussed. Tells of her investigation of Zora Neale Hurston. (Newsbank)

551.   Gagnon, Ronald A. "Alice Walker Reading 'Nineteen fifty-five' and interview. (recordings) *Library Journal*, June 15, 1982, 1207.

A Review of Walker's reading of her short story "Nineteen Fifty-five," with an interview expressing her views on the story.

552.   Harris, Jessica. "An Interview With Alice Walker." *Essence*, July 1976, 33.

Jessica Harris interviews Alice Walker after *Meridian* is published.

553.   Jacques, Hylah. "Alice Walker." *Northwest Passage*, 19 September 1978, 6-7.

An interview with Alice Walker conducted by Hylah Jacques, sharing her thoughts on the South, racism and her philosophy. Walker had appeared at Bumbershoot in Seattle, Washington.

554.   O'Brien, John. *Interviews With Black Writers*, 184-211. New York: Liveright, 1975.

This interview was conducted during the period of time Alice Walker lived in Jackson, Mississippi. Her answers are lengthy and give great insight into her philosophy.

555.   "A Survey: Black Writers' Views on Literary Lions and Values."
        Negro Digest 17 (January 1968): 13.

        Brief comment by Walker in which she identifies John A.
        Williams and Mari Evans as important recent writers and then
        says that black writers do not necessarily need to limit
        themselves to a black audience.

556.   Tally, Justine.   "Black Women's Studies in the 1980's: An
        Interview with Beverly Guy-Sheftall". *Revista Canaria de
        Esterdios Ingleses* 10 (April 1985): 195-204.

        An interview conducted by Justine Tally with Beverly Guy-
        Sheftall on black women's studies.

557.   Tate, Claudia. *Black Women Writers at Work*, 175-87. New York:
        Continuum, 1983.

        An interview conducted by Claudia Tate with Alice Walker.

558.   Trescott, Jacqueline. "Alice Walker: A Child of the South, a
        Writer of the Heart." *Washington Post*, 8 August 1976, G:1.

        Discusses a conversation with Alice Walker about her life as
        it influences her work.

CRITICISM OF INDIVIDUAL WORKS

THE COLOR PURPLE

BOOKS

559.   Christian, Barbara. "No More Buried Lives: The Theme of Lesbianism in Audre Lorde's *Zami*, Gloria Naylor's, *The Women in Brewster Place*, Ntozake Shange's *Sassafras, Cypress and Indigo*, and Alice Walker's *The Color Purple*". In *Black Feminist Criticism: Perspectives on Black Women Writers*, 187-203. New York: Pergamon Press, 1985.

Describes lesbian relationships in four contemporary novels. Sees Walker's work as distinct from Lorde's and Shange's in that it does not create a lesbian subculture; instead the love between Shug and Celie helps to create a truly human community for both men and women. Celie's affection for Shug is in part a reaction to her mistreatment by men. The emphasis is on female bonding rather than sexuality.

560.   Davis, Lisa. "An Invitation to Understanding Among Poor Women of the Americas: *The Color Purple* and *Hasta No Verte Jesus Mio*." In *Reinventing the Americas: Comparative Studies of Literature of the United States and Spanish America*. Edited by Bell Gale Chevigny and Gari Laguardia, 224-41. New York: Cambridge University Press, 1986.

Sees the two books as portraits of women in poverty. Argues that Walker's work is the more radical of the two in challenging patriarchal authority and also the more hopeful in suggesting possibilities for change.

561.   Fifer, Elizabeth. "The Dialect and Letters of *The Color Purple*." In *Contemporary American Women Writers: Narrative Strategies*. Edited by Catherine Rainwater and William J. Scheick, 155-71. Lexington: University of Kentucky Press, 1985.

Discusses the relationships between the letters and diction of Celie and Nettie. The letter form itself allows for both narrative intimacy and authorial distance. Celie's language gives very precise shape to her experience, while Nettie's standard usage is a foreign form in Celie's world. Celie's letters progress from a simple reporting to insight and humor. The dialect gives us both the positive qualities of Celie's world and the sinister aspects. The principal value of Nettie's letters is in establishing that Celie's values have validity in the macrocosm. Includes a bibliography of primary materials.

562.   McFadden, Margaret. "The Color Purple." In *Magill's Literary Annual, 1983: Essay--Reviews of 200 Outstanding Books Published in the United States During 1982*, Volume 1. Edited by Frank Magill, 139-43. Englewood Cliffs, New Jersey: Salem Press, 1983.

Argues that the epistolary form makes the story more intimate, since no authorial voice stands between Celie and the reader. Suggests that while Nettie's letters are important in making cultural connections between Africa and America and in providing plot information, they nonetheless are weaker than Celie's. Sees the main themes as redemptive love and female bonding. Finds the language of black folk English to be crucial to our appreciation of the novel. "Alice Walker's triumph here is in creating a unique set of people who speak to the human condition."

563.   Miller, Jane. *Women Writing About Men*, 241-49. London: Virago Press, Limited, 1986.

Suggests that the novel turns the tables on men by showing

resistance to their brutality. Notes the centrality of sex to the meaning of the story. Points out that Walker indicates the possibility of redemption for men.

564. Taylor, Daniel. *Masterplots II: American Fiction Series*, Volume I. Edited by Frank N. Magill, 311-14. Englewood Cliffs, New Jersey: Salem Press, 1986.

Examines the novel critically in addition to summarizing the plot. Provides themes, meanings and character analysis.

565. Williams, Delores S. "Black Women's Literature and the Task of Feminist Theology." In *Immaculate and Powerful: The Female in Sacred Image and Social Reality*. Edited by Clarissa W. Atkinson, Constance H. Buchanan and Margaret R. Miles, 88, 96-102, 105. Boston: Beacon, 1985.

Sees *The Color Purple* as a means for feminist theologians to begin to understand the lives of black women. Suggests that the implications of this model, one of moral agency, are that personal and family improvement can produce communal vitality.

PERIODICAL ARTICLES

566. Abramson, Pam. "Alice Walker Makes the Big Time With Black Folk Talk." *San Francisco Sunday Examiner and Chronicle's Image Magazine*, 15 August 1982, 16-20.

Mentions the positive reception the book has received. Uses comments from Walker to suggest the meaning of the novel. Talks about the book's connection to the author's own hard-won happiness. Describes Walker's present life.

567.   Babb, Valerie. "The Color Purple: Writing to Undo What Writing Has Done." *Phylon* 47 (Summer 1986): 107-16.

Argues that Walker uses the epistolary mode as a means of injecting the oral into the written and thus diminishing the role of writing in cultural domination. Reveals in Celie's writing several characteristics Walter Ong associates with oral traditions. Shows that Nettie's letters serve to preserve oral cultures that might otherwise be lost.

568.   Barksdale, Richard K. "Castration Symbolism in Recent Black American Fiction." *College Language Association Journal* 29 (June 1986): 400-13.

In the context of an essay of imagery of castration in recent black fiction, examines the abuse suffered by women in Walker's novel. Shows that the male characters, themselves economic victims, victimize the women in their lives. Points out, however, that eventually these men either die or are converted to a less violent way of living.

569.   Bass, Carole, and Paul Bass. "Censorship American-Style." *Index on Censorship* 14 (June 1985): 6-7.

Reports on a conference on censorship and culture in New York. Alice Walker spoke the first night of the conference concerning her work "The Color Purple" and efforts to ban it in the public schools of California.

570.   Berry, Faith. "A Question of Publishers and a Question of Audience." *Black Scholar* 17 (March/April 1986): 41-49.

Examines the publishing business and its attitudes toward and treatment of black women writers. Places the success of *The Color Purple* in this context, claiming that the reaction says more about cultural attitudes, including negative stereotypes of black men, than it does about the book's quality.

571. Cliff, Michelle. "I Found God in Myself and I Loved Her/I Love Her Fiercely: More Thoughts on the Work of Black Women Artists." *Journal of Feminist Studies in Religion* 2 (1986): 7-39.

Discusses the idea of the divine in the individual black woman as it is articulated in the novel. Gives special emphasis to the scene in which Celie and Shug discuss God.

572. Coleman, Viralene J. "Miss Celie's Song." *Publications of the Arkansas Philological Association* 11 (Spring 1985): 27-34.

Sees *The Color Purple* as a story of redemptive love and forgiveness. Shows the importance of Shug's religious perspective in changing Celie's life. The protagonist's forgiveness of Albert is the measure of her maturity.

573. Davis, Thadious M. "Alice Walker's Celebration of Self in Southern Generations." *Southern Quarterly* 21 (April 1983): 39-53.

Argues that Walker uses generational patterns to structure her writing. Sees her uniqueness in her joining of intellectual concerns to the experiences of rural poor Southern blacks. Traces the development of this linkage from the early poetry through *The Color Purple*.

574. Duckworth, Victoria. "The Redemptive Impulse: Wise Blood and *The Color Purple*." *The Flannery O'Connor Bulletin* 15 (Fall 1986): 51-56.

Contrasts Walker's *The Color Purple* with O'Connor's *Wise Blood*. Explores the theme of redemption in each novel.

575. Dworkin, Susan. "The Strange and Wonderful Story of Making

ALICE WALKER

of 'The Color Purple'." *Ms.*, December 1985, 66-70, 94-99.

Tells the story of how Walker came to be involved with the filming of the novel. Describes how various people became involved in the project: Quincy Jones, Steven Spielberg, Menno Meyjes, and the various actors.

576.   Early, Gerald. "The Color Purple as Everybody's Protest Art." *The Antioch Review* 44 (Summer 1986): 261-75.

Argues that both the novel and the film are of poor quality. Attacks first the film as cliched, sanitized, and historical nonsense. Says of the book, *"The Color Purple* is a poor novel because it ultimately fails the ideology it purports to serve." Sees Walker using the conventions of women's Victorian literature rather than a truly contemporary and radical feminism. Views the novel as espousing a liberal theology that denies the reality of evil. "Not surprisingly, the book lacks any real intellectual or theological rigor or coherence, and the fusing of social protest and utopia is really nothing more than confounding and blundering."

577.   El Saffar, Ruth.   "Alice Walker's *The Color Purple*." *International Fiction Review* 12 (Winter 1985): 11-17.

The novel "is about the magical recovery of truth that a world caught in lies has all but obscured." Writing is important to Celie's sense of self-worth. Writing is a form of survival. Naming is a means of humanizing that which is brutalizing and brutalized. Also, the image of God changes as the novel progresses. Spirit is both troubling and redeeming, as God becomes immanent in Celie's world. In this sense the novel moves from history to romance and ends with a return to the Garden.

578.   Fannin, Alice. "A Sense of Wonder: The Pattern for Psychic Survival in *Their Eyes Were Watching God* and *The Color*

Purple." The Zora Neale Hurston Forum 1 (Fall 1986): 1-11.

Discusses the similarities of Hurston's *Their Eyes Were Watching God* and Walker's *The Color Purple*. Both Celie and Janie progress through "trials" and arrive at "self". The ultimate overriding idea in each of these authors' writings are described as a sense of self through the struggle survived.

579. Froula, Christine. "The Daughter's Seduction: Sexual Violence and Literary History." *Signs* 11 (Summer 1986): 621-44.

Combines Freud's notions on family romance and hysteria with Virginia Woolf's discussions of the silencing of women to produce a theory of cultural repression of women's stories that is broken in part by Maya Angelou's *I Know Why the Caged Bird Sings* and Walker's *The Color Purple*. Uses the homeric narrative of Helen and Freud's seduction theory to establish the cultural basis for denying women their voices. Argues that Celie's telling of her story of violence to Shug breaks the cultural and individual authority of men; but rather than engage in counter-violence she uses language to deconstruct patriarchy. Also points out that Celie's creativity becomes a means of economic independence from male domination.

580. Harris, Trudier. "On *The Color Purple*, Sterotypes, and Silence." *Black American Literature Forum* 18 (Winter 1984): 155-161.

Points out that *The Color Purple* has in some ways become a sacred text. Suggests detrimental effects of this phenomenon: creation of spectator readers, who do not identify black women critics, to engage in careful analysis of the novel. Discusses her own problems with the work: passivity of female characters, African sections, voice of Nettie. Acknowledges the power of Celie's voice, but says that very power has tended to silence critics. Sees fundamental problem as the book's reinforcement of negative stereotypes of black life in depictions of promiscuity, failed family life, and violence. A key problem is that the great success of her book has made Walker *the* spokeswoman for the black female experience rather than one voice among many. Also points out the fairy tale quality of the story, which strengthens negative qualities.

581. Harris, Trudier. "From Victimization to Free Enterprise: Alice Walker's *The Color Purple*." *Studies in American Fiction* 14 (Spring 1986): 1-17.

Establishes a background of Walker's earlier versions of victimized women, and then argues that Celie seems to overcome her mistreatment, but only by being presented in an unrealistic manner. Notes her similarity to these other figures and questions how such a character can be transformed into one so dynamic.

582. Henderson, Mae G. "*The Color Purple*: Revisions and Redefinitions." *Sage: A Scholarly Journal on Black Women* 2 (Spring 1985):14-18.

Indicates that the novel blends harsh realism with comic elements. It is a fable of the failure of domination. Men are culturally trained to dominate; women prevail because they do have this training and are therefore more humane. The primary virtues of the book are the versatility and effectiveness of its Black English; its weakness is in the representation of Africa.

583. Jackson, James E. "The Destructive Design of The Color Purple." *Political Affairs* 65 (March 1986): 26-30.

Argues that both the book and the movie distort the reality of black men and the history of blacks in America. Traces the history of black women in terms of their oppression under slavery and capitalism. Cites a number of commentaries on the novel which criticize its portrayal of black life. Sees the work as an ideological challenge to progressive activities.

Compares the film to *Birth of a Nation* as an insult to black people.

584.   Krauth, Leland. "Mark Twain, Alice Walker, and the Aesthetics of Joy." *Proteus* 2 (Fall 1984): 9-14.

Compares *The Color Purple* to *Huckleberry Finn* in terms of ideas of joy. Argues that both novels make a connection between pain and joy. The self emerges from a world of dehumanization. Both books emphasize the power of evil and insist on moral good. Good triumphs in both cases.

585.   Lupton, Mary Jane. "Clothes and Closure in Three Novels by Black Women." *Black American Literature Forum* 20 (Winter 1986): 409-21.

Compares *The Color Purple* to works by Jessie Faucet and Toni Morrison in terms of the Cinderella myth and specifically in terms of the semiotics of clothing. In Walker's novel, clothing and its manufacture becomes a means of bonding for women. Argues that the making of pants becomes Celie's means of independence and identity; moreover, this particular article of clothing undermines gender distinctions. Criticizes the film version for ignoring this aspect of the story. Sees the happy ending as returning to the Cinderella myth and thereby neutralizing the radical implications of the narrative.

586.   McDowell, Deborah E. "The Changing Same: Generational Connections and Black Women Novelists." *New Literary History: A Journal of Theory and Interpretation* 18 (Winter 1987): 281-302.

Establishes a plot of paradigms--public and private narrative to explain the history of black women's writing. Places *The Color Purple* in the second category because it is addressed primarily to an audience within black culture rather than to a "universal" audience. Interprets the novel as a revision of the uplift model operative in early black women writers. Sees it as exploring the inner reality of character rather than defending a social image. Notes that the epistolary form reinforces Walker's views about the writing and voices of black women. Contends that, within the literary history of black women writers, there is respect rather than the anxiety apparent in male writers.

587. McKenzie, Tammie. "The Color Purple's Celie: A Journey of Selfhood." *Conference of College Teachers of English Studies* 51 (September 1986): 50-58.

Sees the source of Celie's personal growth in the strength of other female characters. Also suggests that men are brutal out of inner fear rather than strength.

588. Nadelhaft, Ruth. "Domestic Violence in Literature: A Preliminary Study." *Mosaic* 17 (Spring 1984): 242-59.

Mosiac places *The Color Purple* in the context of a tradition of representing domestic violence in literature, a tradition which goes back as far as *Othello*. Contends that the tradition allows women only loss of self, breakdown of relationships, or destruction of the husband. Sees Walker as breaking new ground by creating alternatives in female bonding and the healing power of love.

589. Nowik, Nan. "Mixing Art and Politics: The Writings of Adrienne Rich, Marge Piercy, and Alice Walker." *The Centennial Review* 30 (Spring 1986): 208-218.

Describes Walker's life in terms of her increasing awareness of politics.

590. Ogunyemi, Chikwenye Okonjo. "Womanism: The Dynamics of the Contemporary Black Female Novel in English." *Signs: Journal of Women in Culture and Society* 11 (1985): 63-80.

Examines a number of novels by African and Afro-American writers to establish the principles of womanist writing. Defines womanism as the placement of the issues of women in the context of black culture. Sees the Afro-American womanist novel as consistently optimistic, as female characters find a way to play a role in their cultures. Notes that the epistolary form gives a strong sense of authenticity, while simultaneously subverting the mechanisms of expression by being a record of suffering.

591. Robinson, Daniel. "Problem in Form: Alice Walker's *The Color Purple.*" *Notes on Contemporary Literature* 16 (January 1986): 2.

Explores the problem of writing in two voices. Expresses the concern that Nettie does not show personality. Rates the novel even with its problems as "outstanding."

592. Royster, Philip M. "In Search of Our Fathers' Arms: Alice Walker's Persona of the Alienated Darling." *Black American Literature Forum* 20 (Winter 1986): 347-70.

Takes the polarized responses to *The Color Purple* as the starting point for a discussion of Walker's attitudes toward black men and women. Sees her commitment to social change as complicated by her conflicting desires to be both an outcast and a darling. Asserts that this conflict is responsible for her attitude toward her potential black audience and the attitudes of her personal and her female characters toward black men. On the first point, observes that she repeatedly has expressed an alienation from the very folk for whom she has said she is writing. On the second point, states that she is often very critical of black women for not identifying more fully with the women's movement. Associates her ambivalence with her childhood experience of alienation from her father.

593.   Shelton, Frank W. "Alienation and Integration in Alice Walker's *The Color Purple*." *College Language Association Journal* 28 (June 1985): 382-92.

Contends that possibility for change is the central theme in Walker's work. Sees *The Color Purple* as her most optimistic novel in these terms. Its movement is from alienation and separation to integration. Identifies four categories of separation: men from women, women from women, people from nature, and people from God. Women are brought together through bonding: men are made to see the falsehood of their viewpoint, and God is made personal by being identified with nature.

594.   Stade, George. "Womanist Fiction and Male Characters." *Partisan Review* 52 (1985): 265-70.

Distinguishes among womanism, feminism, and women's liberation. Argues that *The Color Purple* is not feminist, since it does not favor equality of the sexes. Rather it is womanist in proclaiming the superiority of women. The source of the male evil in the text is not explained. Masculinity is unredeemable; only by becoming feminized can the men be saved. Identifies a tradition of womanist writing, especially in nineteenth-century popular writing, which consistently revealed hatred of the masculine realm. Sees *Uncle Tom's Cabin* as prominent precursor of Walker's novel.

595.   Tavormina, M. Teresa. "Dressing the Spirit: Clothworking and Language in *The Color Purple*." *Journal of Narrative Technique* 16 (Fall 1986): 220-230.

Talks about the connections between language and clothing in the book. Notes that the clothes Celie comes to make give a feeling of freedom to the wearer. Argues that clothwork generally in the novel creates community and preserves history as in quilt making. Says that language in the novel gives the same purposes.

596. Taylor, Clyde. "Black Writing as Immanent Humanism." *The Southern Review* 21 (July 1985): 790-800.

Argues that a humanist sensibility has emerged in recent black fiction, especially that of black women. Notes that the novel combines the story of the individual with a strong statement of womanist ideology. Sees the work as a humanist utopia, in which happiness and fulfillment are not gained at the expense of others.

597. Wesley, Richard. "Can Men Have It All? 'The Color Purple' Debate: Reading Between the Lines." *Ms.*, September 1986, 62, 90-92.

Examines the controversy over both the film and the novel, especially as it concerns the representation of black men. Objects to "tribunals" which attack Walker and other women writers for portraying black life as they see it. Criticizes the film and publishing industries for having few blacks in positions of authority, which means that few images of black experience are brought to the public.

598. Williams, Delores S. "Women's Oppression and Lifeline Politics in Black Women's Religious Narratives." *Journal of Feminist Studies in Religion* 1 (1985): 59-71.

Argues that the book is a religious narrative which views the oppression of black women as multidimensional, involving assaults on their nurturing functions, their self-esteem, and their choice of relationships. Designates as lifeline politics, which are religious in nature, the responses of black women to these attacks. Uses as examples Sofia's mistreatment by the mayor and his wife, Celie's willingness to accept verbal abuse, and the same character's forced marriage to Albert.

Points to a number of responses to this treatment, the most important being a redefinition of God.

599. Willis, Susan. "Alice Walker's Women." *New Orleans Review* 12 (Spring 1985): 33-41.

Argues that the condition of the "wile chile" in the novel is a paradigm of the situation of women in Walker's fiction. A key issue is the problem of mothering, which is often associated with death in the novel. Women search for a language through which to create a sense of community. Meridian must give up mothering in order to achieve status as a communal mother. Her regained health at the end of the book affirms the black community. Novel compared to *Grange Copeland*, which shifts from a male to a female line, and to the *The Color Purple*, which shows both sexual and economic changes.

600. Worthington, Pepper. "Writing a Rationale for a Controversial Common Reading Book: Alice Walker's *The Color Purple*." *English Journal* 74 (January 1985): 48-52.

Treats the question of censorship in the teaching of literature and uses *The Color Purple* as an example of the problem and a possible solution. Categorizes problem areas as violent subject matter, indelicate language, ungrammatical narrative, and a mode of telling--letters--usually considered outdated. Suggests that the violence represented is not atypical of modern reality and that, moreover, the novel emphasizes survival and hope. Argues that the language and grammar patterns create the authenticity of the work.

601.   Addison, Laura. "Letters to God Help Her Give, Not Give In."
        Wichita (Kansas) Eagle, August 1982, B9.

        Discusses the letters of Celie's character and what the reader
        learns about her existence. (Newsbank)

602.   Ahrens, Ronald. "A 'Poor Colored Woman' Grows in 'Color
        Purple'." *Fairbanks (Alaska) Daily News-Miner,* 7 May 1983,
        E6-7.

        Discusses the growth process of Celie, reconciliation of Celie
        and Albert, and some concerns which are included in Walker's
        other works. (Newsbank)

603.   Anello, Ray. "Characters in Search of a Book." *Newsweek,* 21
        June 1982, 67.

        Cites Walker's comments that the novel is happy book and
        that the characters are very much alive for her. Discusses the
        relevance of her background to the book.

604.   Bannon, Barbara A. "P W Forecasts--Fiction." *Publishers Weekly,*
        14 May 1982, 205.

        Brief summary of the novel. "Spanning some 3 years, this is a
        saga filled with joy and pain, humor and bitterness, and an
        array of characters who live, breath [sic] and illuminate the
        world of these black women."

605.   Bardacke, Francis L. "The Novels of the Summer: A Literary
        Mix for Your Hammock." *San Diego Magazine,* August 1983,
        68-72.

        Views the novel as a mixture of "fantasy" and "realism," united to make something special happen. The reviewer questions the ability of Celie to write these letters. But feels that Walker exhibits in this novel a special outlook of life.

606. Bartelme, Elizabeth. "Victory Over Bitterness." *Commonweal* 11 (February 1983): 93-94.

The female characters come alive through dealing with suffering. Bitterness, for both men and women, turns gradually to love.

607. Baumgaertner, Jill. "The Color Purple." *Cresset*, May 1983, 28.

Sees book in a twentieth century tradition of autobiographical forms used by women writers. Novel is centrally about a writer writing. Women are artist figures, creating while men are merely enduring.

608. Begley, Jane. "The Color Purple." *Peace Newsletter*, March 1983, 11.

Summarizes the novel and discusses the roles played by various female characters.

609. Birtha, Becky. "From Alice Walker with Love." *New Women's Times Feminist Review* 9 (July 1983): 54.

Praises Walker's portrayal of black women characters and the colloquial language used in telling the story. Points to the importance of letter-writing as a form of bonding. Sees the lesbian element as unrelated to any sense of a homosexual community or identity. Lists the principal themes as bonding, family, and faith.

610. Blount, Marcellus. "A Woman Speaks." *Callaloo: A Black South Journal of Arts and Letters* 16 (Spring-Summer 1983): 118-22.

Shows the importance of "God's sense of beauty" to understanding the characters. The novel focuses on a variety of relationships between women. *The Color Purple* is a "womanly text": it presents the acquisition of the female voice and identity. The epistolary form reinforces womanist content since letters are a traditional means of expression for women. A flaw is the stiffness of the letters from Nettie.

611.   Bovoso, Carole. "Ntozake Shange and Alice Walker Celebrate the Magic and Power of Black Women in Two Exciting, Insightful and Stylish New Novels." *Essence*, October 1982, 20.

Calls the novel a tour de force in its use of epistolary form. "*The Color Purple* is one of the great books of our time."

612.   "Briefly Noted: *The Color Purple*." *New Yorker*, 6 September 1982, 106.

Describes Celie as "a woman of marvellous sense and sensibility." "This is fiction of the highest order."

613.   Brosnahan, John. "*The Color Purple*." *Booklist*, 15 April 1982, 1042.

The novel's success is based on Walker's "exceptionally eloquent writing".

614.   Brown, Rita Mae. "Learning to Escape the Emotional Tower of Babel." *San Francisco (California) Examiner*, 4 July 1982, C2.

Views the language used by Walker as a great technique. One must know or understand the language used by Celie to understand everything else that happens in the novel. Reviewer hopes that *The Color Purple* will not be categorized as a black novel or a feminist novel. (Newsbank)

615.   Buckley, Reid. *"The Color Purple."* *American Spectator* 16
        (November 1983): 38-39.

Calls the novel "undeniably a work of human understanding,
a work of the heart, a deeply felt exploration of goodness in
adversity, and a hymn to the power of love." Argues that the
work shows the dehumanizing effects of oppression and
deprivation. Praises the economy of language. Justifies the
intimate relationship between Celie and Shug as a
demonstration of the power of love. Criticizes the
"theologizing" treatment of white and black male characters.
Questions whether the homosexuality might be corrupting for
immature readers.

616.   Carr, Anne. "Religious Book Week: Critics' Choices."
        Commonweal, 24 February 1984, 120.

Emphasizes the connection between theology and self-
awareness in the novel. "If one wonders how the experience
of women, or the poor, is significant for theological reflection,
The Color Purple is a good place to begin."

617.   Clifton, Lucille. "'The Color Purple' Tells Its Story in Letters."
        (Baltimore, Maryland) Sun, 18 July 1982, C4.

Contends that the technique of letters Walker uses in *The
Color Purple* causes problems for the reader. Concludes that
even with problems the novel establishes Walker as a "serious
American author of major intent." (Newsbank)

618.   Cornish, Sam. "Alice Walker: Her Own Woman." *Christian
        Science Monitor*, 3 February 1984, B1.

Begins with a discussion of *In Search of Our Mothers' Gardens*,
which he sees as dominated by Zora Neale Hurston. Notes
also the role of Walker's family and literary influences in the
essays. Views the poetry as less polemical than that of other

writers of the Sixties and early Seventies. Sees the short stories as depicting a variety of experiences of black women, with *You Can't Keep a Good Woman Down* as more clearly about the problems of male-female relationships. Argues that the three novels form a trilogy about "people living in the South but outside history." Says that *The Color Purple* resolves both the racial and sexual conflicts of the earlier works. Claims Walker is "a generous and intellectual writer, and her accounts and memories of friends and family are honest and engaging."

619.   Derman, Lisa. "The Color Purple." *Boston Review*, October 1982, 29.

The novel is inspiring in showing the triumph of its female characters. A weakness is the ideological character of Nettie's letters.

620.   "Ebony Book Shelf: The Color Purple." *Ebony*, October 1982, 26.

Novel continues Walker's concern with relationships among black women. Questions the "extreme bleakness of her view of Black male/Black female relationships."

621.   Ford, Andrea. "Pain, Postmarked by Poetry." *Detroit (Michigan) Free Press*, 8 August 1982, D7.

Sees *The Color Purple* not as letters but as "sheer poetry disguised as the broken prose of an uneducated girl-woman." The work presents a feminist point of view wrapped in a texture of blackness. (Newsbank)

622.   Fox-Alston, Jeanne. "The Color Purple". *Chicago (Illinois) Tribune*, August 1982, B8.

Recounts the plot of the novel. Regards Walker as

noteworthy among today's talented black women writers. (Newsbank)

623.　Graham, Maryemma. "Skillful But Disturbing Novel." *Freedomways* 23 (1983): 278-80.

Notes that with this novel, Walker finally receives the attention she deserves. "Regardless of whether or not the earlier fiction has been correctly assessed, *The Color Purple* is an outstanding novel whose themes and dominant motifs combine with stylistic innovations and an authentic folk voice in perfect harmony." Nonetheless, finds disturbing elements in the story, including Walker's view that men are the only source of suffering for women. Believes this to be a distortion of the systematic economic as well as racial and sexual oppression that black women have endured.

624.　Grutzmacher, Harold M.　"Their Poetry Sings With Simple Beauty." *Milwaukee (Wisconsin) Journal*, 6 January 1985, G2.

Grutzmacher contends that Walker has the ability in her poetry to write what she means. The poetry is characterized as simple, direct and comprehensible.

625.　Gussow, Adam. "Review of *The Color Purple*." *Chicago Review* 34 (Summer 1983): 124-26.

Describes the book as the tale of five black women who triumph against a world trying to destroy them. Compares Celie's language to that of Huck Finn in that it is the expression of an innocent trying to understand the horrors of life. Notes that the black world depicted is degraded and violent. Criticizes Nettie's letters as "decorous travelogue." Argues that these letters debunk the Afro-American myth of an African paradise.

626.　Guy, David. "A Correspondence of Hearts." *Washington Post's*

Book World, 25 July 1982, 1.

The novel is not really epistolary, since the writers never correspond with each other. Celie's dialect is poetic. The men in the book, though in positions of power, are weaker than the women. The intellectual center of the book is redefinition of God. "Alice Walker has...written a fable for the modern world."

627. Heyward, Carter. "The Color Purple." *Religious Studies Review* 10 (April 1984): 162.

Suggests that one basis for the novel is relational theology, advocated by some feminist theologians.

628. Higgins, Chester A. "Pulitzer Beginning to Do Something Right." *Crisis* 90 (June/July 1983): 49.

Discusses the past racism of Pulitzer committees, then praises them for recognizing Walker's novel. The book provides a realistic portrait of the rural South.

629. Hitz, Henry. "Strictly San Francisco." *San Francisco Review of Books*, Summer 1982, 5.

Sees the novel as a translation into literature of the blues tradition. The "discovery of the creative spirit" enables the characters to overcome their environment. Walker's third novel "is a transcendent synthesis of the dramatic simplicity of *The Third Life of Grange Copeland* and the metaphysical complexity of *Meridian*."

630. Jefferson, Margo. "The Color Purple." *Nation*, 25 December 1982, 696.

Expresses her preference for the second part of the novel, "where we see Africa, London, Memphis, all manner of sexual choice."

631. Kelley, Ernece B. "The Color Purple." *College Language Association Journal* 27 (September 1983): 91-96.

Views the novel as a subversion of male domination of the epistolary form in its creation of a female voice and its valorizing of female bonding. It becomes a way of transposing the black female oral tradition into a western narrative form. Consistent with structure, the theme of the novel is Celie's entrapment in the "scheme of patriarchy." Escape from this pattern is through female bonding and redefinition of gender roles.

632. Ketcham, Diane. "Alice Walker's Daring Reach." *Oakland (California) Tribune,* 11 July 1982, B14-C1.

Discusses Walker's courage in her use of language, Black folk English, humor and subjects covered in this novel. Relates her philosophy of the black woman's experience during the time of the novel. Gives some background into names of the characters, Celie and Nettie.

633. *Kirkus Review*, 15 April 1982, 518.

Emphasizes the beauty of Celie's letters. "A lovely, painful book: Walker's finest work yet."

634. Leckey, Dolores. "The Color Purple." *Commonweal*, 24 February 1984, 125.

The novel is richly religious, without theological cliches.

635. Lodge, Sally A. "P W Forecasts--Fiction Reprints." *Publishers Weekly*, 29 April 1983, 50.

Summarizes earlier review on occasion of paperback

publication. Notes that book won American Book Award.

636.   *London Review of Books*, 2 June 1983, 20.

Notes that Walker is widely recognized as a major figure in black writing, but insists that the novel is a "one-sided view of woman's lot."

637.   Marcus, Laura. "Feminism Into Fiction: The Women's Press." *Times Literary Supplement*, 27 September 1985, 1070.

Discusses several works published by Britain's Women's Press, including *The Third Life of Grange Copeland*, *In Love and Trouble*, and *The Color Purple*. Interprets the latter as a fable whose unrealistic elements are therefore not jarring. Compliments the author for the technical versatility apparent in the collection of stories. Sees *Grange Copeland* as establishing key themes--individual responsibility, the power of love--to which Walker will consistently return. "Powerfully and lucidly written, only occasionally slipping into polemic, the novel has a compelling directness."

638.   Marshment, Margaret. "The Color Purple." *Race and Class* 25 (Fall 1983): 91-94.

Takes the story "Advancing Luna," with its dilemma for the writer-narrator, as representative of Walker's approach to racial and sexual issues. Sees several pieces in *You Can't Keep a Good Woman Down* as violating traditional forms in order to explore social problems. Argues that the happiness that Celie achieves in *The Color Purple* is earned and not imposed as a happy ending. The novel then "can be read less as a realist novel than as an allegory of the black woman's learning to speak."

639.   Merritt, Robert. "Novel Traces 2 Black Southern Sisters." *Richmond (Virginia) Times-Dispatch*, 4 July 1982, C5.

Extols Walker for the successful efforts to deliver philosophical thought to her readers. Cites as her basic themes, "pain of inner life, the bonds and the strengths of women, and thoughts of her characters regardless of their temperment." (Newsbank)

640. Mootry-Ikerionwu, Maria K. "The Color Purple." *College Language Association Journal* 27 (March 1984): 345-48.

Summarizes the novel. Weaknesses are unconvincing nature of Celie's passivity and her devotion to writing to God. Use of Black English is the chief virtue.

641. Morris, Deb. "Good Women and God's Color." *Off Our Backs* 13 (April 1983): 16.

Summarizes several stories from *You Can't Keep a Good Woman Down*. Describes *The Color Purple* as "a wondrous book interviewing characters' lives in surprising ways."

642. Mort, Mary-Ellen. "Bleak Birthright, Sustaining Joy." *Library Journal*, 1 June 1982, 1115.

States that the letter form shows Celie's gradual growth into independence. "Walker's use of language, especially black idiom, is masterful."

643. Muller, Carol Doup. "'Color Purple' Weaves a Rich Texture." *San Jose (California) Mercury*, 4 July 1982, C3.

Characterizes novel as "a book good for the soul," delivering uncompromising sermons on sexism, bigotry, love and human dignity. (Newsbank)

644. Olson, Clarence E. "Lives of Different Shades." *St. Louis (Missouri) Post-Dispatch*, 2 January 1983, G6.

Contends that Alice Walker's past experiences enable her to bring to her writing characters like Celie and others. However, feels that *The Color Purple* message is "too sweet and too sour." (Newsbank)

645.   "Paperbacks: News and Noteworthy. The Color Purple." *New York Times Book Review*, 29 May 1983, 19.

Brief summary. Cites Mel Watkins' earlier review of the hardcover edition.

646.   Osborne, Karen Lee. "The Color Purple: Reflects Lives of Black Women." *Big Mama Rag*, January 1983, 13, 17.

Sees Walker as "one of America's finest fiction writers" and this novel as her best work. Views the lesbian relationship between Shug and Celie as one of the most positive in literature. Argues that joy rather than suffering dominates the novel. "It's a book that makes you want to cry--and sing."

647.   Petrie, Phil W. "Visiting Good Friends During the Holidays." *Black Enterprise*, December 1982, 30.

Brief summary of novel, with comment that he is troubled by the message of the book.

648.   Prescott, Peter S. "A Long Road to Liberation." *Newsweek*, 21 June 1982, 67-67a.

Calls it a novel of "permanent importance." Finds a significant feature of the book the fact that the letters Celie and Nettie write are never directly answered, which means that each of them must find her own salvation. Sees it as a novel of redemptive love premised on female bonding.

649.   Ramsay, Heather. "Writing from the Heart With a Dose of

Rage." *Body Politic,* June 1984, 38-39.

Praises Walker's use of epistolary mode, a difficult form in which to present the action of a novel. Believes that *The Color Purple* should not be criticized for a lack of homoerotic focus, since lesbianism is not really central to Walker's message of female bonding. Also points out the importance of faith, though not in the traditional religious sense. Sees black women as the real subject of *In Search of Our Mothers' Gardens*, regardless of the ostensible topic. Criticizes Walker's lack of clarity on lesbianism.

650. Randall-Tsuruta, Dorothy. "The Black Scholar Book Reviews." *Black Scholar*, Summer 1983, 54-55.

Sees the characters coming alive. Sofia is most effective character. This story of separation and reconciliation is told sucessfully through letters. "While narration through letters can be a risky approach to writing a novel, Walker's handling, particularly her ear for dialect which results in nothing less than poetry, stages away from undo awareness of technique to fix on the beauty of expression."

651. Schaefer, Jay. "The Color Purple." *San Francisco Review of Books*, January-February 1983, 23.

Brief summary of the novel, "an unusual, absorbing account."

652. See, Carolyn. "As All the Oppressed Women Close Ranks, a Whole New Complicated Cosmos is Created." *Los Angeles (California) Times*, 8 August 1982, D4.

Recounts the plot of the novel. Viewed the work as a possibility of a new day for women. (Newsbank)

653. Singer, Davida. "The Power a Woman Can Own." *The Feminist Renaissance*, May/June 1983, 6.

Describes the transformation of Celie, primarily through Shug Avery, in this novel of "political and spiritual quest." Notes that the book successfully combines the themes of black power, feminism, and spiritual growth.

654.　　Smith, Dinitia. "Celie, You a Tree." *Nation*, September 1982, 181-83.

Points out that Walker introduces readers to the lives of rural Black women. "No writer has made the intimate hurt of racism more palpable." Contends that the weakness of the novel is that the ideology often interferes with the story-telling.

655.　　Sparks, Mary Kahl. "Missives Serves as Bonds Between God, Sisters." *Kansas City (Missouri) Star*, 22 August 1982, D8.

Focuses on what is felt the central theme of the novel, that of women helping women. Also the bonding process which happens in relation to some of the characters.

656.　　Towers, Robert. "Good Men Are Hard to Find." *New York Review of Books*, 12 August 1982, 35-36.

Points out that the focus of the novel--poor black Southern women--has not drawn the attention of writers. Identifies the key weaknesses of the novel in plot structure and Nettie's voice. Sees these balanced by the power of Celie"s language.

657.　　Walker, Robbie Jean. "Sister Becomes Confident for Woman's Fettered Secrets." *Montgomery (Alabama) Advertiser*, 18 December 1983, B1.

Ventures the thesis that Walker wants the reader to realize the importance of female bonding. Characterized as Walker's "fullest development to date", reviewer feels she sometimes "sacrifices plausibility." (Newsbank)

658. Wallace, Gail Smith. "Uncommon Story of Black Woman." *The News and Observer, (Raleigh, North Carolina)*, 8 August 1982, 6D.

Points out that Celie and Nettie remain sisters in spirit despite the vast differences in their experience. In addition, "part of the power of Celie's words is in the use of black folk dialect and part is in the beauty of the way the words are put together by the author." (Newsbank)

659. Watkins, Mel. "Some Letters Went to God." *New York Times Book Review*, 25 July 1982, 7.

Major theme is estrangement between black men and women. Sees weakness in characterization of male figures and flatness of Nettie's letters. "These are only quibbles, however, about a striking and consummately well-written novel."

660. Weil, Lise. "In Review: The Color Purple." *Trivia*, Spring 1983, 91-94.

Sees the novel as giving voice to generations of silenced black women. Points out the importance of women in developing Celie's sense of self. Argues that the novel's very form shows Walker's indebtedness to previous generations of women. "Their creativity lives on in the very texture of the novel: scenes are stitched together with a quiltmaker's delicacy and eye for color; the power of rhythm and pattern to give shape to experience is felt on every page." Contends that the book both follows the *bildungsroman* tradition and reverses it by having characters use the wisdom they gain to move from experience to innocence.

661. Wells, Robert W. "A Winner from Walker." *Milwaukee (Wisconsin) Journal*, 24 April 1983, G1.

Characterizes Walker's novel as "vital and fascinating." Although glooming on the surface the novel gives experiences of women coping with life's trials. (Newsbank)

662.   *West Coast Review of Books*, September 1982, 22.

Argues that Walker has an intensely personal vision which immerses the reader in the characters' experiences. " A remarkable, unforgettable work."

663.   Williams, Delores S. "What Was Missed--*The Color Purple*." *Christianity and Crisis*, 14 July 1986, 230-32.

Relationship between Celie and God. God in the novel is male and authoritarian. The change in this definition corresponds to change in Celie.

664.   Williams, Lynora. "To Be Black and Female in a White, Male Land." *Guardian Book Review Supplement*, 29 June 1983, 57.

Describes the oppression Celie suffers as an experience with which gay men can identify. Sees a key theme in the community's need to accept Celie's homosexuality. "Study the tapestry long enough and you'll find yourself woven into it, not to be released until you put down the book."

665.   Yeoman, Barry. "The Color Purple." *RFD*, Summer 1984, 39.

Views the novel's central character, Celie, as a "poor black lesbian." Asserts that gay men will identify with the experiences and the feelings expressed in the *Color Purple*.

ALICE WALKER

GOOD NIGHT WILLIE LEE,
I'LL SEE YOU IN THE MORNING

REVIEWS

666.   Braham, Juanita. "Touches All Women." *New Directions for Women*, July 1980, 10.

    Quotes extensively from poems that highlight Walker's feminist views. Asserts that while much of the poetry emphasizes the experiences of black women, it also articulates the reality of life for all women.

667.   Fleming, Robert. "Good Night, Willie Lee, I'll See You in the Morning." *Encore*, 2 April 1979, 50.

    Argues that emphasis is on self-exploration, which produces an overabundance of poems on love's disappointments. Much of the best writing focuses on descriptions of everyday life. Walker's contribution to Black literature is that rather than focus on racial ideology, she considers "the vast area between the cradle and the grave."

668.   "Good Night, Willie Lee, I'll See You in the Morning." *Booklist*, 1 April 1980, 1103.

    Compares this collection with the earlier volumes of poetry. Sees her new work as remaining alienated, but freer of southern elements.

669.   "In Praise of Poetry." *Book World*, 9 December 1979, 11.

Emphasizes allegorical element in the collection combined with "clean, clear language and syntax."

670.   Ratner, Rochelle. "Review of *Good Night, Willie Lee, I'll See You in the Morning*". *Library Journal* 104 (July 1979): 1464.

Praises the poetry as "valuable reading. Views the work as a combination of feminist anger, with a black viewpoint."

671.   Struthers, Ann. "Of Love and Politics". *Des Moines (Iowa) Register*, 26 May 1985, G10-11.

Discusses a few poems included in Walker's *Good Night, Willie Lee, I'll See You in the Morning* and *Horses Make a Landscape Look More Beautiful*. Struthers feels that Walker's message sometimes overpowers the poetry. (Newsbank)

672.   Stuttaford, Genevieve. "PW Forecasts" Review of *Good Night, Willie Lee, I'll See You in the Morning*. *Publishers Weekly*, 30 July 1979, 61.

Contends that poetry is "forthright, spare, antithetical, and eloquent of spirit." Reviewer feels the poet is a part of a new order poets and women.

673.   Williamson, Alan. "In a Middle Style." *Poetry*, March 1980, 348-54.

Contends that much of the collection is self-important and preachy. Nevertheless, "at her best, Walker has a gift for the luminous image which makes the entire poem coalesce around it."

674.   Wilson, Judith. "Recollections." *Essence*, December 1979, 16.

Praises the poems as "written with the magic simplicity and

spine-chilling directness that are hallmarks of Walker's style."

HORSES MAKE A LANDSCAPE LOOK MORE BEAUTIFUL

BOOK REVIEWS

675. Bach, Julian. "Poetry--Horses Make a Landscape Look More Beautiful." *Publishers Weekly*, 24 August 1984, 71.

Notes the themes of love and friends. Hers is "not the work of a mature poet."

676. Disch, Tom. "The Perils of Poesy." *Book World*, 30 December 1984, 6.

Walker is part of a trend in poetry which offers the poet's persona as an idealized figure for the reader.

677. Gernes, Sonia. "Horses Make a Landscape Look More Beautiful." *America*, 2 February 1985, 93-94.

Sees the primary theme as the legacy of racism. The best poems are those which bring together the political and personal implications of the heritage. "In the tradition of Whitman, Walker sings, celebrates and agonizes over vicissitudes that link and separate all of humankind."

678. Gilliland, Gail. "Walker's Poetic Voice." *New Directions for Women*, May 1985, 21.

Expresses frustration with Walker's tendency to reduce to stereotype women who are not black. Believes the best poems are those which emerge from the author's private experience. These selections have "the wonderful magnanimity that is in *The Color Purple*, a magnanimity that seems a bit too rare in this group of poems, and which, I am afraid, no matter what she produces from now on, will be the quality that for me constitutes her voice."

679. Grutzmacher, Harold M. "Their Poetry Sings With Simple Beauty." *Milwaukee (Wisconsin) Journal*, 6 January 1985, G2.

Grutzmacher contends that Walker has the ability in her poetry to write what she means. The poetry is characterized as simple, direct and comprehensable. (Newsbank)

680. Keefe, J. T. "Horses Make a Landscape Look More Beautiful." *World Literature Today* 60 (Winter 1986): 118.

Brief review of *Horses Make a Landscape Look More Beautiful*. Keefe refers to the work as eloquent and filled with her personal statements on love and justice.

681. Low, Denise. "'Horses' Hits Canter for Poet". *Kansas City (Missouri) Star*, 18 November 1984, B10.

Views the poetry as an illustration of simplicity. Contends that not all of the poetry accomplishes the same simplicity but the author's sincerity is obvious.

682. Nower, Joyce. "*Horses Make a Landscape More Beautiful.*" *Library Journal* 101 (15 October 1984): 1949.

Notes that despite occasional flatness of language and imagery, several poems are very good. "Here is a variety of themes spoken in humor, anger, and love."

683. Rosenberg, L. M. "Largesse, Erudition, Wit and Sweetness." *New York Times Book Review*, 7 April 1985, 12.

"Whatever else the book may be--often touching, sometimes irritating; a little stiff, a touch preacherly, with gems of wisdom inserted parenthetically--it is almost never poetry." Acknowledges, however, that the work does have a musical quality.

684.   Struthers, Ann. "Of Love and Politics." *Des Moines (Iowa) Register*, 26 May 1985, G10-11.

Discusses subjects and techniques of Walker's poetry in *Good Night, Willie Lee, I'll See You in the Morning* and *Horses Make a Landscape Look More Beautiful*. (Newsbank)

685.   Weaver, Michael S. "A Great Novelist Doesn't Always Make a Great Poet." *(Baltimore, Maryland) Sun*, 21 October 1984, G7.

Criticizes Walker's poetry as not approaching the brilliant of her fiction. (Newsbank)

I LOVE MYSELF WHEN I AM LAUGHING ... AND THEN AGAIN WHEN I AM LOOKING MEAN AND IMPRESSIVE: A ZORA NEALE HURSTON READER

BOOK REVIEWS

686.   Blundell, Janet Boyarin. "Review of *I Love Myself When I am Laughing...and Then Again When I Am Looking Mean and Impressive*." *Library Journal* 104 (15 November 1979): 2463.

Discusses briefly Hurston's life and the nature of her work. Says that Walker's comments "help restore Hurston to her

118

proper place as a seminal woman writer."

687.　*Choice* 17 (June 1980): 538.

Walker is praised for creating an anthology of selections of Zora Neale Hurston's works. The anthology contains writings that for the most part have not been available.

688.　"Ebony Book Shelf: *I Love Myself When I Am Laughing.*" *Ebony*, January 1980, 24.

Brief mention of book, with an indication of contents.

689.　Kennedy, Randall. "Looking for Zora." *New York Times Book Review*, 30 December 1979, 8, 17.

Sees the reader as signifying the emergence of feminism and of more sophisticated approaches to Black literature. Traces Hurston's life and career, noting that her quest for independence created difficulties. Calls Walker's introduction "extraordinary," especially for its emphasis on the importance of taking Hurston seriously as a writer and not merely a personality. Praises Walker for making selections that allow the full range of Hurston's talents to be seen.

690.　Wilson, Barbara. "*I Love Myself When I Am Laughing... And Then Again When I Am Looking Impressive: A Zora Neale Hurston Reader.*" *In These Times*, 23-29 January 1980, 15.

Discusses the importance of Walker's role in the selection of material by Hurston. Praises the publication for bringing attention to an important black woman writer.

691.　Wilson, Judith. "Filled With Surprises." *Essence*, February 1980, 17.

Says that Walker has performed a valuable editorial service

by making available several out-of-print and hard-to-find pieces by Zora Neale Hurston in this collection.

IN LOVE AND TROUBLE

BOOKS

692. *Black Fiction: New Studies in the Afro-American Novel Since 1945*. Edited by A. Robert Lee, 181-89. New York: Barnes and Noble, 1980.

   Provides analysis of selected Walker's short stories from *In Love and Trouble* and the novel *Meridian*.

693. Christian, Barbara. "Contrary Women of Alice Walker: A Study of Female Protagonists in *In Love and Trouble* (1980)." In *Black Feminist Criticism: Perspectives on Black Women Writers*, 31-46. New York: Pergamon Press, 1985.

   Argues that the book as a whole focuses on black women and the black community and the special significance of the southern black female. The characters in the stories try to be their true selves within the limiting conventions of their world. They tend to resist specific restrictions rather than generalized oppression. Most often these restrictions are created and maintained by men. Resistance expresses a desire for wholeness.

694. Mickelson, Anne Z. *Reaching Out: Sensitivity and Order in Recent American Fiction by Women*, 154-74. Metuchen, New Jersey: Scarecrow Press, 1979.

CRITICISM OF INDIVIDUAL WORKS

Includes brief analysis of several stories from *In Love and Trouble*. Explores the ways in which Alice Walker depicts black women experiencing life in their search for dignity and in doing so resist victimization. The short stories involve problems in love and marriage.

PERIODICAL ARTICLES

695.   Christian, Barbara. "Contrary Women of Alice Walker." *Black Scholar*, March/April 1981, 21-30, 70-71.

   See annotation #693.

696.   Smith, Barbara. "The Souls of Black Women." *Ms.*, February 1974, 42-43, 78.

   Says that Walker penetrates the myths surrounding the lives of black women and shows the lack of love between men and women. The stories are realistic in portraying the unpleasantness and bitterness of marriage. Racism has subverted the natural relationships among black men, women, and children. This is Walker's real insight.

BOOK REVIEWS

697.   Bannon, Barbara A. "PW Forecasts." *Publishers Weekly*, 2 July 1973, 78.

   Calls the stories "heartbreaking and beautiful." Praises Walker's ability to reveal both the joy and madness of the lives of black women.

698.   *Booklist*, 1 January 1974, 473.

Says that the stories "capture the quintessence of being black and being a woman."

699.   *Booklist*, 15 January 1974, 538.

Recommends the collection for mature teenagers on the basis of its superior style and characterizations.

700.   Bouise, Oscar A. "*In Love and Trouble*." *Best Sellers*, 15 October 1973, 335.

Praises Walker for a "magic touch" which gives the characters, narrative, and language of her fictions a sense of life. Notes that she uses this skill to depict the universality of the experiences of black women.

701.   Bryant, Jerry H. "Books and the Arts: The Outskirts of a New City." *Nation*, 12 November 1973, 501.

Compares Walker's technique and style to Ed Bullins. Bryant contends that both writers have unusual powers of observation and command of language and image. Views *In Love and Trouble* as political and sociological.

702.   *Choice*, January 1974, 1723.

Notes the power of Walker's portraits of black women. "With super-subtle skill, Walker probes the psyches of women who are sometimes unlovely, seldom unloved, and nearly always loving."

703.   Collier, Betty. "*In Love and Trouble*." *Journal of Social and Behavioral Sciences* 21 (Winter 1975): 136-42.

Suggests that Walker in these stories sought a new direction for black writing, rejecting the black nationalist agenda. She also rejects the image of black women as victims, showing a variety of experiences of women.

704. Cornish, Sam. "Alice Walker: Her Own Woman." *Christian Science Monitor*, 3 February 1984, B 1.

See annotation #618.

705. Didion, Joan. "*In Love and Trouble.*" *London Review of Books*, 4 October 1984, 16.

Discusses *In Love and Trouble* and introduction to the London Reading audience. Relates one liners to each story in the collection.

706. *Encore*, January 1974, 57.

Brief evaluation that emphasizes that the stories constitute one tale: the response of black women to their world.

707. Fowler, Carolyn. "Solid at the Core." *Freedomways* 14 (First Quarter 1974): 57-62.

Argues that Walker is concerned with the "unfulfilled heart" of black women. She offers "insight into the quiet dramas enacted in the inner lives of those who are anonymous and ineffable." Book contains an anti-nationalist bias and is flawed by occasional cynicism and contrivance. Nonetheless it gives a strong sense of the authentic experience of black women.

708. Giovanni, Nikki. "So Black and Blue." *Book World*, 18 November 1973, 1.

Makes personal comments on relationships between black

women and between women and men. Uses these as the basis for praising Walker for writing painful but true stories.

709.   Goodwin, June. "Book Briefings." *Christian Science Monitor*, 19 September 1973, 11.

Contends that the stories are about much more than black women. They are about relationships, poverty, hope, and frustration. "Somewhere in growing up she learned to watch people, to put in words what must have been their wordless hopes and agonies."

710.   Grumbach, Doris. "Fine Print." *New Republic*, 21 December 1974, 24.

Agrees with comments by John Callahan about the virtues of the book.

711.   Ingoldby, Grace. "Fall Out." *New Statesman*, 14 September 1984, 32.

Sees the stories as effective recreations of the South in which Walker grew up. "Miss Walker gets right to the quick of the character and situation, funny and sad and remarkably unsentimental in her tribute to her roots."

712.   *Kirkus Review*, 1 July 1973 712-13.

Criticizes the stories as somewhat thin, but says that the author is best at letting the significance of the material slowly reveal itself. "They've basically got the light touch of her poems and the same slow fondling description as her novel, *The Third Life of Grange Copeland*."

713.   McLellan, Joseph. "Paperbacks." *Book World*, 5 May 1974, 4.

Sees the collection as a series of searches for "love, revenge, and respect."

714.   Maginnis, Ruth. *"In Love of Trouble."* *Library Journal*, 15
        November 1973, 3476.

        Calls the book a "magnificent" collection which reveals the
        essence of womanhood and a universality of human
        experience. Warns, however, that "readers might be offended
        by man's inhumanity, especially to those he loves, rather than
        by language or the inclusion of sex as a natural part of life."

715.   Manna, Tony and Jan Yoder. "Focus on Black Literature:
        Conversation With Darwin Turner." *English Journal* 64
        (December 1975): 78-81.

        Cites the central theme as liberation. "Walker's prose
        effectively evokes the reader's pathos as she looks deeply into
        the lives of her characters."

716.   Nyabongo, V. S. "In Love and Trouble." *Books Abroad*, Autumn
        1974, 787.

        Calls the stories "realistic, poignant, very readable." Praises
        the skillful depiction of male characters.

717.   Pfeffer, Susan Beth. "In Love and Trouble." *Library Journal* 98
        (August 1973): 2338.

        Describes the stories as concerned with the changes occurring
        in the lives of black women. Sees the women as fighting to
        protect that which is valuable to them. Notes that the quality
        is uneven but that the book is worthwhile nonetheless.

718.   Rosenfelt, Debby. Review of *In Love and Trouble. Radical
        Teacher* 15 (March 1980): 59.

        This column "Teaching Notes", which appears in *Radical*

Teacher, consist of brief descriptions of works and how they are taught or utilized in the classroom. Rosenfelt uses *In Love and Trouble: Stories of Black Women* in her upper-division classes in Women and Literature and Literature and Social Change. Relates student's reactions to the stories read.

719.   Washington, Mary Helen. "Books Noted." *Black World*, October 1974, 51.

Argues that Walker's fiction is based on her understanding of the history of black women. That history is one of suppression, frustrated creativity, and suffering.

720.   Watkins, Mel. "In Love and Trouble." *New York Times Book Review*, 17 March 1974, 40.

Shows connections between the stories and traditional women's blues as well as the work of Zora Neale Hurston. Finds the writing efficient and economical and the short pieces much like prose poems.

721.   Wright, Mercedes A. "Black Woman's Lament." *Crisis*, January 1974, 31.

Recommends the book as a group of portraits of the painful lives of black women. Insists that the troubled relationships depicted represent a common reality for such women. Sees the stories as helping to create the possibility of sexual liberation.

IN SEARCH OF OUR MOTHER'S GARDENS

BOOKS

722.   Bell, Carolyn Wilkerson. "In Search of Our Mothers' Gardens: Womanist Prose." In *Magill's Literary Annual, 1984: Essay--Reviews of 200 Outstanding Books Published in the United States During 1983*, Vol. 1. Edited by Frank Magill, 368-73. Englewood Cliffs, New Jersey: Salem Press, 1984.

Notes that Walker's perspective--award-winning author, scholar, and activist--lends authority to her commentary on various subjects. Argues that there is unity in the diversity of the essays. Shows how the experiences of women, especially black women, determine Walker's sense of a literary tradition and her connection between mothering and artistic creation. Criticizes those who have attacked Walker's commitment to her race by pointing out her activities in and comment on the civil rights movement.

723.   Washington, Mary Helen. "I Sign My Mother's Name: Alice Walker, Dorothy West, Paule Marshall." In *Mothering the Mind: Twelve Studies of Writers and Their Silent Partners*. Edited by Ruth Perry and Martine Watson Brownley, 142-63. New York: Holmes and Meier, 1984.

Describes the importance of Walker's mother to the writer's creative potential. Her mother created a permissive space of trust and books, even though this was a world of sharecroppers. Three gifts from the mother--a sewing machine, a suitcase, and a typewriter--signified the creativity and independence that she wanted for her daughter. In Walker's fiction, the mothers are often inarticulate; the daughters find ways to speak for them. In addition, the mother can provide evidence of the past. "The Revenge of Hannah Kemhuff," for example, is a variation of a true story told by Walker's mother.

PERIODICAL ARTICLES

724. Byrd, Rudolph P. "Sound Advice from a Friend: Words and Thoughts from the Higher Ground of Alice Walker." *Callaloo* 16 (Spring-Summer 1983): 123-29.

Points out the four-part structure of the collection: models for all artists, responsibilities of black artists, struggles of the artist, and reassurance that the struggles are worthwhile. Generally finds it a "splendid collection." Devotes considerable space to refuting Walker's argument that Jean Toomer "passed" for white.

725. Payne, James Robert. "Review of *In Search of Our Mothers' Gardens*." *World Literature Today* 59 (Winter 1985): 101.

Discusses the scope of the Walker's work. Relates the central thoughts running through most of her writing.

726.   Albright, Susan. "Walker Essays Reflect Strength of Character."
        (Tucson) *Arizona Daily Star*, 11 December 1983, B3.

        Considers *In Search of Our Mothers' Gardens* as informative,
        moving, insightful and reflecting character that has strength.
        Characterizes Walker as a woman to some degree by her own
        definition. Contends that Walker appreciates heritage and
        gives voice to it in her essays.

727.   Allen, Bruce. "*In Search of Our Mother's Gardens: Womanist
        Prose.*" *Smithsonian* 14 (January 1984): 133-34.

        Describes the book as concerned with racial justice, women's
        rights, and literature. Criticizes the author for occasional
        stridency. Nevertheless, "in this fervent, moving book --which
        adds up, really, to Alice Walker's autobiography--it *is* written,
        on the whole, wisely and well."

728.   Bach, Julian. "In Search of Our Mother's Gardens: Womanist
        Prose." *Publishers Weekly*, 2 September 1983, 62.

        Finds the collection in some ways more rewarding than *The
        Color Purple*. "This womanist of intelligence, memory, will,
        humor and energy encourages us to speak out against offenses
        to human dignity as she reminds us of what is essential to
        survival."

729.   Benet, Mary Kathleen. "Life-Saving Models." *Times Literary
        Supplement*, 20 July 1984, 818.

        States that Walker's purpose is finding a past. Sees her as
        transcending regional, racial, and sexual categories. Asserts
        that the desire for accessibility sometimes leads to banality.

730. Block, A. G. "'Mothers' Gardens' Nurtures Black Women of Rural South." *San Jose (California) Mercury*, 6 November 1983, E4.

   Discusses Walker's work *In Search of Our Mothers' Gardens*, a collection of memoirs, essays, lectures, interviews based on experiences of black women with each other and their families and society. Block has problem with Walker's "absolutes" which he states are prevalent in her writings. (Newsbank)

731. *Booklist*, 1 September 1983, 22.

   Lists the various subjects covered by the essays; "all of these selections detail the wealth of experience and the richness of vision that Walker has molded into an indelible art."

732. "Books About the South." *Southern Living*, January 1984, 84.

   Sees Walker as a passionate writer very much concerned with the South. States that, though she is angry, she is always fair.

733. Bradley, David. "On the Need For Mentors and Heritage to a Writer." *Birmingham (Alabama) News*, 5 February 1984, A3.

   Bradley again criticizes the book for being poorly organized. Stating that it loses some of its effectiveness to the reader. *In Search of Our Mothers' Gardens* is a collection of Walker's essays, speeches and reviews from 1967 to 1983. He asserts the organization should have shown a progression of thought for her writings. (Newsbank)

734. Bradley, David. "A Writer Who Raises Polemics to an Art." *Philadelphia* (Pennsylvania) *Inquirer*, 25 December 1983, B4-5.

   Views *In Search of Our Mothers' Gardens* as not very good, because of organization. Bradley expresses concerns for the content not being understood because of this rambling disorganization. He refers to Walker as a genius and her writing thoughtful and philosophical. (Newsbank)

735.   Brown, Beth. "In Search Our Mother's Gardens: Womanist Prose." *College Language Association Journal* 27 (March 1984): 348-52.

Reflects on the personal experiences of herself and her associates to show the relevance of Walker's work. Focuses on the interrelated topics of motherhood and childhood, as well as the essays on feminism and writing.

736.   Bunkers, Suzanne. *"In Search of Our Mother's Gardens: Womanist Prose."* *Feminist Connection* 5 (December 1984): 9.

Discusses Walker's definition of womanism. Emphasizes the role of creativity in the lives of black women, especially that of the author's mother. *"In Search of Our Mothers' Gardens* represents her attempt to pass on to the readers what she, as a black American woman writer, feels has been passed on to her."

737.   *Choice*, May 1984, 1311.

Says that the collection "will prove invaluable to those interested in tracing the evolution of the talented writer who produced...*The Third Life of Grange Copeland* and ...*The Color Purple*." Sees it as an appropriate companion to June Jordan's *Civil Wars*.

738.   Clark, Beverly Lyon. *"In Search of Our Mother's Gardens."* *Modern Fiction Studies* 30 (Summer 1984): 334.

Expresses attachment to Walker as a writer who is honest, sensitive, and courageous. "In her best essays she makes a pilgrimage in quest of the past, to redeem the past for the present." Shows how the essays use personal experience to illuminate universal experience.

739.   Cornish, Sam. "Alice Walker: Her Own Woman." *Christian Science Monitor*, 3 February 1984, B 1.

See annotation #618.

740.   Daniels, Gabrielle.   "Reflections of a 'Womanist'."   *San Francisco (California) Examiner*, 16 October 1983, F3-4.

Affirms that *In Search of Our Mothers' Gardens* is a collection of Alice Walker's best essays, articles and reviews. Examines the essays, "Beauty: When the Other Dancer is the Self" and "One Child of One's Own." Explores "womanist" as used by Walker in her works.

741.   Davidon, Ann Morrissett. "Beacons." *Progressive*, February 1984, 42-43.

Compares the book to Gloria Steinem's *Outrageous Acts and Everyday Rebellions*. Sees the books related as "beacons" of feminism that join life experiences with political perspectives.

742.   DeCosta-Willis, Miriam. "The Spirit of 'exquisite butterflies.'" *(Memphis, Tennessee) Commercial Appeal*, 18 March 1984, G13.

Discusses the spirit within Walker's collection of prose, *In Search of Our Mothers' Gardens*. Describes her works as in the best tradition of black women writers celebration of life.

743.   Eder, Richard. *Los Angles Times Book Reviews*, 4 December 1983, 1.

Calls the book "a battle and a party," in that Walker attacks repression wherever she finds it and yet is often sardonic in expressing her views.

744. Eder, Richard. "In Search of Our Mothers' Gardens." *(Phoenix) Arizona Republic*, 11 December 1983, B2.

Eder's exploring of Walker's *In Search of Our Mothers' Gardens*, characterizes the work as a battle and party and Walker as uncompromising and a black patriot. With mixed signals he lauds the work and Walker, on one hand and critiques her on the other for the fierceness of expression. He feels that the work is filled with contradiction.

745. Golden, Marita. "Alice Walker: Odyssey of Spirit and Intellect." *(Baltimore, Maryland) Sun*, 6 November 1983, F6.

Contends that Alice Walker has great vision of her self and the world. Explores the different issues covered in *In Search of Our Mothers' Gardens* from Walker's point of view. Refers to the venture of the reader through her points of view as an odyssey.

746. Hairston, Loyle. "Alice in the Mainstream." *Freedomways* 24 (Summer 1984): 182-90.

Criticizes Walker for not offering a penetrating analysis of the social order. Contends that Walker prefers subjective (individualistic) rather than social critique. This often leads her to despair. Despite the central importance of the condition of women in her work, Walker is ultimately not radical. Black fiction ought to be written out of the historical/social/economic reality of black Americans. Walker writes only as a talented individualist.

747. Hill, Frances. *"In Search of Our Mother's Gardens."* *Times Education Supplement*, 30 November 1984, 27.

Briefly praises the author's talent. "Alice Walker's energy, sense, wit and passion are startling and she writes like an angel."

748. *Kirkus Review*, 15 August 1983, 957-8.

Notes the importance of patience in Walker's life and work, as well as her sense of the past. "Thoughtful, intelligent, resonant musings."

749. Liebrum, Martha. "Enriching Collection.", *Houston (Texas) Post*, 30 October 1983, F7.

Discusses Walker's *In Search of Our Mothers' Gardens* as giving the reader insight into the force that inspires her fiction. This collection draws upon her personal views and philosophy of politics, love, black women and men, and heritage. The writing of *The Color Purple* and "One Child of One's Own" are two essays discussed.

750. McDowell, Deborah. "Black Literature: The World in the Artist's Seeing Eyes." *In These Times*, 18 April 1984, 19.

Praises Walker for prose that is "crisp, confident, elegant and moving." Points out in the essays the strong connection between the personal undeveloped sketches. In sum, sees Walker as affirming the creativity of the oppressed.

751. Milan, Karen. "Alice Walker's Pulitzer Encore." *Dallas (Texas) Morning News*, 15 January 1984, A4-5.

Discusses Walker's collection of essays, speeches, articles and reviews on a different level. Examines the humor, warmth poignant moods, separatism found in this work. Describes her as a role model for black artists. (Newsbank)

752. Mort, Jo-Ann. "A Prose of Her Own." *Commonweal*, 1 June

1984, 345.

Argues that the essays are important for writers and especially women writers. Gives particular attention to Walker's defense of her civil rights activities and her balanced view of the Arab world.

753.   Mort, Mary-Ellen.   "In Search of Our Mothers' Gardens: Womanist Prose-Reviews." *Library Journal* 108 (1 November 1983): 2086.

Discusses briefly the contents of work.   Recommends *In Search of Our Mothers' Gardens* for library purchase.

754.   Munro, C. Lynn.   "In Search of Our Mothers' Gardens." *Black American Literature Forum* 18 (Winter 1984): 161.

Stresses the importance to Walker of differing points of view. Admires the range of subject matter in the collection. "In addition to making the essays more accessible, this volume demonstrates the versatility of Walker's style and her capacity for intellectual and personal growth."

755.   *New York Times Book Review*, 16 October 1983, 28.

756.   *New Yorker*, 7 November 1983, 184.

Summarizes the principal themes and subjects of the collection. "Occasionally--in a piece on Cuba, for instance-- Miss Walker's style fails, but most of the time it is eloquent."

757.   Okri, Ben. "Colouring Book." *New Statesman*, 22 June 1984, 24.

Contends that "the volume is firstly and always concerned with the infernal oppression of colour and the double oppression of black women."   Shows how personal history becomes a means of recovering a heritage.

758. Parini, Jay. "Blowing Through the Ram's Horn: Berry, Ozick, and Others." *New England Review* (Summer 1984): 630-38.

Points out the centrality of black feminism to the essays. A moral point of view is important to such writing, and Walker has that.

759. Pate, Nancy. "Works of Pulitzer Authors Show Knack's Still There, Bring Thoughts and Smiles." *Wichita (Kansas) Eagle*, 13 November 1983, B2.

Examines *In Search of Our Mothers' Gardens* by Walker and *The Rescue of Miss Yaskell and Other Pipe Dreams* by Russell Baker in this review.

760. Pennington, Dorothy. "Review of In Search of Our Mothers' Gardens." *Quarterly Journal of Speech* 72 (August 1986): 341-44.

Notes that Walker's term "womanist" implies differences between black and white feminists. Believes that for Walker home and roots are central concerns and the sources of creativity. Says that the personal style of the writing makes it especially effective.

761. Porter, Veneita. "Each Petal in the Garden." *Gay Community News*, 21 April 1984, 5-6.

Develops the metaphor of the garden in describing the importance of writers and of Afro-American culture in the growth of Walker's era. Devotes considerable space to the author's views on lesbianism. "This woman checks out the details on the petals in her garden; each dew drop and withered leaf is seen."

762. Ragsdale, Rose. "Alice Walker's Latest is Painful in its

Honesty." (Jackson, Mississippi) *Clarion Ledger*, 9 October 1983, C3.

Analyzes *In Search of Our Mothers' Gardens*, and characterzies it as "brutally honest prose." Recommends that reader take "small helpings and chew thoroughly the wisdom, pain and honesty between its covers." (Newsbank)

763.   Ramsay, Heather. "Writing from the Heart with a Dose of Rage." *Body Politic*, June 1984, 38.

See annotation #649.

764.   Rhodes, Jewell Parker. "For There is No Friend Like a Sister in Calm or Stormy Weather." *America*, 25 February 1984, 137-38.

Praises Walker for both autobiographical essays and social and historical comments, which are said to demonstrate that "all life is interconnected." "Black women, in particular, will be uplifted, since Walker's art and life demonstrate that she loves us all so very much."

765.   Schwartz, Karen. "*In Search of Our Mother's Gardens*." *Women and Therapy* 4 (Summer 1985): 71-75.

Suggests that Walker's concerns are very similar to those of professional therapists, especially in pointing out the complex connections of all aspects of life. Notes the importance of process in the writer's thinking and writing. Criticizes her for assuming that the writer's need for nurture is unique.

766.   Smith, Valerie. "Creating Connections." Review of *In Search of Our Mothers' Gardens*. *Sewanee Review* 93 (Spring 1985): xxxi-xxxiv.

"These pieces offer a subtle and compelling portrait of the

author's mind and display the versatility of her talent." Emphasizes the importance of continuity as a theme for the book. Finds the style vivid and precise.

767. Vigderman, Patricia. "From Rags to Rage to Art." *Nation*, 17 December 1983, 635, 637-38.

Indicates that the book focuses on what it means to be a "black Southern woman writer," with the full implications of the modifiers of that phrase. Points out the connections for Walker between art and survival. Discusses the centrality of the essay on Flannery O'Connor in the writer's effort to balance her rage and her art and of the comments on Zora Neale Hurston in her search for a tradition for herself. Criticizes Walker for avoiding "the larger and more difficult issues in favor of much smaller, flashing assertions."

768. Ward, Lucretia B. "In Search of Our Mothers' Gardens." *(Louisville, Kentucky) Courier-Journal*, 23 October 1983, F6.

Examines *In Search of Our Mothers' Gardens*, as it relates the philosophical thought characterized in Walker's writings. Praises Walker as "tough, enchanted and a wise writer", delivering a work that sings. Offers that Walker not only sings of contradictions and cruelties, hypocrisy, racism but of revelation and transformation.

LANGSTON HUGHES: AMERICAN POET

BOOKS

769.   Rollock, Barbara. *The Black Experience in Children's Books.* New York: New York Public Library, 1974.

Brief annotation in a listing of books on black subjects for children. "A lively biography of the poet is presented by one whom he inspired."

BOOK REVIEWS

770.   "Notable Children's Trade Book in the Field of Social Studies." *Social Education*, March 1975, 172-73.

Brief annotation in bibliography of children's books. Says that it does a "perceptive job of analyzing for beginning readers the life and work of the poet." Books on the list were published in the years 1973 and 1974.

771.   Dreyfuss, Joel. "Beyond Booker T." *Book World*, 19 May 1974, 4.

Very brief comment on the biography. "This is the story of one poet told by another master of words and the slim volume seems all too brief."

772.   Jenkins, Betty L. "Langston Hughes." *Library Journal*, 15 October

1974, 2743.

Sees the work as "adulatory" and focused on the poet's youth. "Unfortunately, Walker provides only cursory treatment of Hughes' adult years and creative accomplishments."

773.   "Review of Langston Hughes: American Poet." *Wilson Library Bulletin*, June 1974, 789.

Reviewer wished for the inclusion of more of Hughes's poetry in the work. Suggests that the Crowell series of biographies for children may make the subjects too heroic.

774.   "Review of Langston Hughes: American Poet." *Kirkus Review*, 15 March 1974, 307.

Attributes the effectiveness of the writing to Walker's careful selection of aspects of Hughes's life. Emphasizes the importance to the interpretation of the negative influence of the father.

775.   "Books in the Classroom." *Elementary English*, January 1975, 147.

Calls the book a "sketchy account." "Complex concepts of prejudice, racial pride, non-relevant education and family problems are introduced that seem to be inconsistent with the simple language in which the book is written."

776.   "Review of Langston Hughes: American Poet." *Bulletin of the Center for Children Books*, December 1974, 71.

Calls the biography "sympathetic but not adulatory." Notes that Walker's evaluation of the poet's father is more negative than that of other biographers.

777.   "Where Have the Good Children's Biographies Gone." *Christian Science Monitor*, 13 May 1983, B 7.

Praises the style of the book. Recommends it for grades 2-4.

MERIDIAN

BOOKS

778. *Black Fiction: New Studies in the Afro-American Novel Since 1945.* Edited by A. Robert Lee, 169-71, 198-200. New York: Barnes and Noble, 1980.

   Discusses the themes found in *Meridian* and the characters within that novel. The Character Meridian is examined as leader and saint in relation to persons in the story. Lee characterizes Walker as "an accurate and skillful storyteller."

779. Carmean, Karen. *Masterplots II: American Fiction Series*, Volume 3. Edited by Frank N. Magill, 997-1001. Englewood Cliffs, New Jersey: Salem Press, 1986.

   Gives novel summary, character analysis, themes and critical context of Walker's *Meridian*. Characterizes the novel as "Walker's fully, most beautifully crafted novel."

780. Christian, Barbara. "An Angle of Seeing: Motherhood in Buchi Emecheta's *Joys of Motherhood* and Alice Walker's *Meridian*." In *Black Feminist Criticism: Perspectives on Black Women Writers*, 211-52. New York: Pergamon Press, 1985.

   Places fictional uses of motherhood in the cultural contexts of Africa and the United States. Discusses at length the complex status of women and motherhood in traditional African societies and compares them to the situation of black women in the American South, then shows how such material is represented in the two novels. In *Meridian*, racism and male dominance lead to an ideology of motherhood that restricts women and produces violence against children. Even though Meridian's father is more sensitive than her mother, he cannot teach his daughter how to be in the world as a female human being. Since only the mother can pass along that training and Meridian's mother herself feels betrayed by the ideology, the daughter must find her own way. In effect, Walker's argument is that the American idea of motherhood threatens the development of a meaningful female self.

781.   Cooke, Michael G. "Intimacy: The Interpenetration of the One and the Many in Robert Hayden and Alice Walker." In *Afro-American Literature in the Twentieth Century*, 157-176. New Haven: Yale University Press, 1984.

Contends that the idea of intimacy helps to explain the political perspective in *Meridian*. It leads to both self and group realization. Meridian's quest for intimacy produces authentic political action. Walker identifies a complex pattern of spiritual bonding that transcends sexuality, conventional politics, and even grief.

782.   Griffin, Joan S. "*Meridian*." In *Magill's Literary Annual, 1977: Essay - Reviews of 200 Outstanding Books Published in the United States During 1976*, Volume 2. Edited by Frank Magill, 501-4. Englewood Cliffs, New Jersey: Salem Press, 1977.

Contends that the novel is about social and individual change, even to the point of revolution. Says that the civil rights movement becomes Meridian's vehicle of transformation. Argues that Truman is eventually changed but that Lynne remains locked in the fantasy of the superiority of white women. Believes the novel to be ultimately optimistic despite the pain it describes. "Alice Walker gives us a haunting depiction of what it means to create oneself out of time, effort, and pain in order to emerge triumphant in the knowledge of who one is and what it takes to truly live."

783.   White, Vernessa C. "*The Third Life of Grange Copeland* and *Meridian*: The Southern Experience and the Evolution of Black American Consciousness." In *Afro-American and East German Fiction: A Comparative Study of Alienation, Identity and the Development of Self*, 91-115. New York: Peter Lang, 1983.

Discusses the importance of the South in Walker's fiction and especially the development of black political consciousness. In *Grange Copeland* the focus is on agricultural life. Walker insists that choice is possible even for the exploited black peasant. Grange remains a failure until, late in his life, he recognizes the systematic nature of oppression. Margaret chooses suicide, while Brownfield willingly gives up the quest for a better life. Individual liberation is possible in this novel, but it has little connection to social consciousness. In *Meridian*, Walker returns to the question. Mrs. Hill's sense of loss and her subsequent assault on her family make her comparable to Brownfield. Meridian, burdened by guilt, initially turns to social action as a form of self-flagellation. Eventually, she transcends both her guilt and her pseudo-revolutionary friends by insisting that revolution must be life-affirming.

DISSERTATIONS

784.   Harris, Norman. *Understanding the Sixties: A Study of Character Development and Theme in Seven Recent Afro-American*

ALICE WALKER

Novels. Bloomington: Indiana University, 1980, 207pp.

Discusses the novel in the context of several fictions about the Afro-American experience in the 1960's. Establishes Meridian's early character as directionless, a fact which changes when she becomes aware of the civil rights movement. Notes that her initial involvement is not based on conscious thought about the nature of the cause. Distinguishes differing types of personalities associated with the movement. Connects the attitudes and actions of the novel with their historical counterparts.

PERIODICAL ARTICLES

785.   Fisher, Berenice. "Guilt and Shame In the Women's Movement: The Radical Ideal of Action and Its Meaning For Feminist Intellectuals." *Feminist Studies* 10 (Summer 1984): 185-212.

Examines the concept of shame as it applies to racial attitudes among feminists. Compares the characters of Meridian and Lynne in these terms. Argues that Meridian becomes truly radical while Lynne plays a traditional woman's role.

786.   Fishman, Charles. "Naming Names: Three Recent Novels by Women Writers." *Names: Journal of the American Name Society* 32 (March 1984): 33-44.

Delineates the various ways names and naming are used in the novel. Examines symbolic uses, as in the different meanings of "meridian"; social status, as in adult blacks being called by their first names; or rejection, as in the insulting terms Lynne and Truman use for each other.

787.   Homans, Margaret. "Her Very Own Howl: The Ambiguities of Representation in Recent Women's Fiction." *Signs: Journal of Women in Culture and Society* 9 (Winter 1983): 186-205.

Delineates the differences in American and French-based feminism in terms of attitudes toward language. In several contemporary novels, including *Meridian*, examines the ambivalence of women authors to the self-expression of female characters. Discusses specifically the Sojouner tree as an emblem of the female voice. Sees the destruction of the tree as symbolic of the self-silencing of women.

788.   McDowell, Deborah E. "The Self in Bloom: Alice Walker's *Meridian*." *CLA Journal* 24 (March 1981): 262-75.

Sees *Meridian* as a *bildungsroman* that transcends the issues of womanhood. Identifies a pattern of death and rebirth. Meridian faces deadening traditions, especially those associated with womanhood and blackness. She rejects the roles of daughter, wife, and mother, as well as proper woman. Her rebirth into a true self comes through a mysticism related to her return to the black traditions of the South. Her sense of self is established through connection with the folk world.

789.   McGowan, Martha J.   "Atonement and Release in Alice Walker's *Meridian*." *Critique* 23 (1981): 25-36.

Considers the moral and philosophical implications of political awakening. Discusses the relevance of Camus to the novel's theme of responsibility. Meridian's questioning of killing for the sake of revolution is important, but the deeper issue is the relationship of personal guilt to social action. Meridian acts as a form of atonement for her disconnection from the tradition of black motherhood. Includes brief discussions of *The Third Life of Grange Copeland* and "Advancing Luna--and Ida B. Wells" for purposes of comparison. *Meridian* "offers small hope of ordinary human happiness for black womanhood."

790.　　　Stein, Karen F. *"Meridian*: Alice Walker's Critique of Revolution." *Black American Literature Forum* 20 (Spring/Summer 1986): 129-41.

Argues that *Meridian* is about the failure of the civil rights movement to value women. Both the title character and the book itself emphasize transformation rather than revolution. Sees the novel as a "fictionalized political essay" that sacrifices inwardness of the characters to ideological statement. The movement lacked a "sustained sociopolitical critique," symbolized by its objectification of women. This is consistent with the death-in-life of Meridian's parents, her own sterility, and the college's rituals of beauty and propriety. Truman is symbolic of the movement's attitude that women are objects to satisfy the complex needs of men and not self-determining human beings. The insistence by the revolutionaries that it was important to kill for the Movement reveals a similar attitude. Meridian gains proper perspective when she comes to see herself as an artist supporting life-affirming values. True revolution comes in the transformation of the self.

791.　　　Wade-Gayles, Gloria. "The Truths of Our Mothers' Lives: Mother-Daughter Relationships in Black Women's Fiction." *SAGE: A Scholarly Journal on Black Women* 1 (Fall 1984): 8-12.

Discusses the novel in terms of tradition in black women's writing of presenting complex mother-child relationships. Argues that Walker questions the assumption of motherhood as an automatic source of nurturance. Sees Mrs. Hill as a figure who needed some alternative to motherhood in order to live a meaningful life.

792.　　　Willis, Susan. "Alice Walker's Women." *New Orleans Review* 12 (Spring 1985): 33-41.

See annotation #599.

BOOK REVIEWS

793. Adams, Phoebe-Lou. "PLA." *Atlantic Monthly*, June 1976, 106.

Briefly summarizes the main story line of the novel. "The work is angry and moving."

794. Bannon, Barbara. "P W Forecasts - Fiction." *Publishers Weekly*, 29 March 1976, 47.

Praises Walker for telling her story "in terms of people, not issues." Sees it covering a range of racial issues in the process of discussing the civil rights movement.

795. *Booklist*, 15 May 1976, 1320.

Sees Meridian troubled by her heritage until she learns what is essential. "Meridian Hill is a transcendent figure, drawn with psychological acumen and the leavening touch of poetry."

796. Brandmark, Wendy. "You Can't Keep a Good Woman Down." *Africa*, June 1982, 70.

Compares *Meridian* and *You Can't Keep a Good Woman Down* to Toni Cade Bambara's *The Salt Eaters* as texts concerned with racism and sexism. Suggests that the novel affirms sisterhood while the stories confront "the most uncomfortable, the most basic issues facing Americans."

797. Burnside, Gordon. "Books." *Commonweal*, 29 April 1977, 281-85.

Connects the novel to its Southern context and the early civil rights movement. Questions whether the book works as a novel. "But if Meridian is a failure as a novel--and I think it is--it is also an extremely interesting historical document."

798.   *Choice*, September 1976, 829.

Says that the novel sums up the civil rights movement. Notes that the action of book is circular rather than linear. "Mandatory for black literature collections; recommended for general fiction holdings."

799.   Clifford, Gay. "In the Black Light of Noon." *Times Literary Supplement*, 19 August 1977, 1014.

Links the title to the sense of time and place in the novel. Defines the title character in terms of her Southern world and her participation in its history, including but not limited to the civil rights movement. In addition, "the whole story is really about managing to be neither conned nor cynical."

800.   Cooke, Michael G. "Recent Novels: Women Bearing Violence." *Yale Review*, October 1976, 146-55.

Notes that violence in the contemporary world has become evasive in a variety of forms: personal, social, natural, psychological, and physical. Even efforts to control it end by generating new forms. Compares *Meridian* to Ernest Gaines's *The Autobiography of Miss Jane Pittman* in terms of violence in the civil rights movement and contends that Walker's work is more "inward and more socially complex." Interprets *Meridian* as a silent center, who rejuvenates herself and makes possible the rejuvenation of others in "creative self-denial" rather than violence.

801.   Cornish, Sam. "Alice Walker: Her Own Woman." *Christian Science Monitor*, 3 February 1984, B 1.

See annotation #618.

802. Gilbert, Harriett. "Sun, Sand and Something to Read." *New Statesmen*, 30 July 1982, 2.

Brief positive mention of *Meridian* in longer review of *You Can't Keep a Good Woman Down*.

803. James, Cyril Lionel Robert. "Zenith: Alice Walker's Meridian." *Race Today*, August/September 1982, 140-44.

Proclaims his review "propaganda" in favor of the novel. "Since the end of the WWII I had not read a novel superior to this." Suggests that the thematic center is the relationship of the masses to social revolution.

804. Jefferson, Margo. "Across the Barricades." *Newsweek*, 31 May 1976, 71-72.

Calls the novel "ambitious and complicated," as it traces the development of the civil rights movement. Notes in the book the "Southern writer's love for storytelling."

805. *Kirkus Review*, 15 March 1976, 348.

Argues that *Meridian* lacks a center. Questions the effectiveness of various scenes and characters. "Like the resolution (to which they are tangential), they seem mandated by history rather than invoked by the story."

806. Larson, Charles R. "Legacy of the Movement: A Woman Who Cares." *National Observer*, 17 July 1976, 17.

Presents the book as a history of the civil rights movement. Notes that it sometimes reads more like a documentary history than a novel. Its theme is the new consciousness that emerged from the civil rights movement.

807.　　Marcus, Greil. "Limits." *New Yorker*, 7 June 1976, 133-36.

Talks about the influence of Albert Camus on Walker's writing. *Meridian* addresses the questions raised in *The Rebel* concerning the necessity of murder in support of a just cause. The flat, direct style is consistent with the development of this theme. Problems arise in the novel when Walker attempts to go beyond realism and make the novel a parable.

808.　　Marr, Virginia W. *Library Journal* 101 (1 May 1976):1145.

Sees the novel as presenting a positive view of its protagonist and her heritage. She not only makes sacrifices, but also leads others to enlightenment. Says of Walker, "Hers is a major talent whose articulate concern succeeds in erasing racial barriers through the revelation of common humanity."

809.　　Martin, Ruth.　　*Best Sellers*, September 1976, 187.

Expresses impatience with Walker's technique, especially the means of revealing Meridian's past. However, does note that the "characters are psychologically well defined."

810.　　Mellors, John. "Caradock's Caves." *The Listener*, 17 March 1977, 350.

Summarizes the plot.　Finds "powerful and deeply felt passages," but is unconvinced by the sections on ecstasy.

811.　　"Notes on Current Books." *Virginia Quarterly Review* 52 (Autumn 1976): 130.

Finds the character of Meridian less convincing than that of Lynne. Believes that the book is influenced by both Faulkner and the tradition of melodrama. The latter is apparent when "scenes which start out convincingly deteriorate when the situation is over-developed or when contrivances are added on." Says that the best writing is in the shortest sections, indicating that Walker might find stories more appropriate to her skill.

812.   Peacock, Mary. "A Moveable Feast: Paperback Picks." *Ms.*, July 1978, 29.

Brief summary of the novel. "An unforgettable portrait of a woman's coming of age during the Civil Rights Movement."

813.   Piercy, Marge. *New York Times Book Review*, 23 May 1976, 5, 12.

Calls the work a "fine, taut novel" that deals with large issues. Sees the title character as "an attempt to make real in contemporary terms the notion of holiness and commitment." Contends that the only weakness is in the conclusion, in which readers are told rather than shown Meridian's transformation.

814.   Rogers, Norma. "Struggle for Humanity." *Freedomways*, 2nd Quarter 1976, 120-22.

Says that Walker recognizes the dehumanization that comes from oppression. "It is an exceptional piece of literature, beautifully written."

815.   Rumens, Carol. "Heirs to the Dream." *Times Literary Supplement*, 18 June 1982, 676.

Compares *Meridian* to *You Can't Keep a Good Woman Down* and to Toni Cade Bambara's *The Salt Eaters* as books created in the context of Martin Luther King, Jr's dream of a better, more just America. Calls *Meridian* "the most accessible of the books...with a narrative that is solidly constructed and makes powerful use of symbols in a manner reminiscent of Toni

Morrison." The stories in *Good Woman* are "less subtly imagined" than the novel, suggesting that Walker "is happier with a larger canvas."

816.   Sage, Lorna. "From Pregnancy to Rape." *London Observer*, 20 March 1977, 28.

Sees the short, anecdotal sections as the best parts of the novel. Argues that the fundamental tensions in the novel remain unresolved.

817.   Smith, Cynthia J. "Black Fiction by Black Females." *Cross Currents*, Fall 1976, 340-43.

Discusses the history of representations of black female protagonists. Compares *Meridian* to Toni Morrison's *Sula* as novels that place their protagonists in concrete histories. Argues that the character Meridian is a symbol of black willingness to suffer in the civil rights movement, though her motivation is private guilt.

818.   Stuttaford, Geneviene. "P W Forecasts--Paperbacks." *Publishers Weekly*, 2 May 1977, 68.

Summarizes and quotes Bannon's review from an earlier issue.

819.   Walker, Cam.   *Southern Exposure* 5 (Spring 1977): 102-3.

Reviews both *Meridian* and *The Third Life of Grange Copeland*. Views Southern black women as central to Walker's work. Gives biographical information on the author and uses it to show how Walker connects her characters to the South. Sees the novels as continuous in that *Meridian* begins with the movement that ends *Grange Copeland*. Points out that change is not always hopeful, since in *Meridian* all the children either die or disappear. Believes that *Grange Copeland* is the more coherent and successful of the two.

820.   Walters, Ray. "New and Noteworthy." *New York Times Book Review*, 29 May 1977, 23.

Brief summary of the novel. "An unsentimental yet tender novel, fascinating for its revelations, admirable for its deft telling."

ONCE

PERIODICALS

821.   Williams, Mary C. "The Poetic Knife: Poetry by Recent Southern Women Poets." *South Carolina Review* 11, (November 1978): 44-59.

In the context of a discussion of contemporary women poets of the South, in which she considers whether women's poetic voices are distinct from those of men, examines Walker's first two books of poetry. Notes that *Once* focuses on a desire to know her heritage, but also on a recognition that she is isolated from it. Sees *Revolutionary Petunias* as a coming to terms with both her Southern past and her identity as an expressive woman.

BOOK REVIEWS

822.   Benedict, Estelle. *"Once." Library Journal* 93 (15 September 1968):3145.

"When the simplest, most basic feelings of a poetic soul are sensitively transposed on to paper, the result is a lovely book of poems. Such is Alice Walker's". Notes that Walker's work depends more on exposition than imagery.

823.   Cornish, Sam. "Alice Walker: Her Own Woman." *Christian Science Monitor*, 3 February 1984, B1.

See annotation #618.

824.   Mueller, Lisel. "Versions of Reality." *Poetry* 117 (February 1971): 322.

Says that Walker shares with the other poets reviewed the "private nature of their reality," which cannot be explained by either social conditions or biography. Is reminded by the poetry of the extent to which color determines identity for blacks, even when the experience is private. "Her poems are like pencil sketches which are all graven outline: no shaded areas, no embellishments."

825.   "Once." *Booklist*, 1 January 1969, 474.

Brief comment on the poems. "They have a young voice, humanity, and often the bitterness of the black intellectual's record from ego-bruising episodes."

826.   Rodgers, Carolyn M. "Books Noted." *Negro Digest* 17 (September/October 1968): 52, 11-13.

An analysis of the poetry in her collection of poems *Once*. Walker's technique is compared to Emily Dickinson in some ways.

REVOLUTIONARY PETUNIAS

PERIODICALS

827.   Williams, Mary C. "The Poetic Knife: Poetry by Recent Southern Women Poets." *South Carolina Review* 11, (November 1978): 44-59.

See annotation #822.

BOOK REVIEWS

828.   "Books Noted." *Black World*, September 1973, 51-52, 89.

Believes that the poetry is not as effective as the fiction, but is nonetheless useful for understanding Walker. It provides a sense of the Southern past out of which she writes. Contends that the second part of the book is an indictment of black revolutionary activities of the Sixties. Sees the poems' final statement as an affirmation of love and hope.

829.   Cornish, Sam. "Alice Walker: Her Own Woman." *Christian Science Monitor*, 3 February 1984, B 1.

See annotation #618.

830.   Davis, Gwendolyn. "Revolutionary Petunias." *New South*, Winter 1973, 62-63.

Sees the basic theme as the survival of romantic ideals--love, truth, beauty--in a chaotic world. Divides the book into sections dealing with Southern experience, humanity's place in the universe, and a challenge to destructive revolutionaries. Calls the book "a wholly stimulating and distinctive volume of poetry."

831. Dollard, Peter. "Revolutionary Petunias." *Library Journal* 98 (1 January 1973): 73.

Contends that the poems present three stages in the lives of women: childhood, militancy, and love. "Walker's style is terse, direct, sometimes colloquial, often ironic, and always poetic rather than didactic; and since she is readily comprehensible, she should reach a comparatively large audience."

832. Kenworthy, Duncan. "Contemporary Poetry: Six Touchstones." *American Scholar* 2 (Summer 1973): 514.

Says that Walker has a "loving sense of the individual in history." Points out the organic structure of the collection, as well as the pervasive sense of hope. Calls the style uncompromising, "well suited to a simple, yet revolutionary message."

833. "Revolutionary Petunias." *Booklist*, 1 June 1973, 928.

Emphasizes the importance of tradition and roots in this collection in contrast to the theme of travel in *Once*. Calls the poems "sophisticated verses, sometimes gently witty, often cryptic, but always evoking an image and suitable for reading aloud in small or large groups."

834. "Revolutionary Petunias." *Bulletin of the Center for Children's Books*, February 1974, 103.

Describes the writing as "clean, spare, and incisive." Asserts that the poems grow out of Walker's experience and race.

835.   "Revolutionary Petunias." *Choice*, September 1973, 986.

Sees race as largely irrelevant in the poetry, which is narrative in structure. Says Walker is "a fresh, new, unafraid voice that should be listened to."

836.   "Revolutionary Petunias." *Kirkus Review*, 1 December 1972, 1402.

Compares Walker to Nikki Giovanni in her ability to capture an experience in a brief statement. Argues that the poems work by implication rather than commentary. They are "brightly sensate, true to a definite, attractive mind."

837.   "Revolutionary Petunias." *Publishers Weekly*, 18 December 1972, 39.

Believes that Walker establishes her place in literature with this collection. "This is poetry of total purity, lean of line, direct and forceful."

838.   Roberts, Mary M. "Reviews of Teaching/Learning Resources." *Communication Education*, September 1978, 258-69.

Recommends the collection for students because some of the poems explore universal problems, while others provide a sense of life in the South.

839.   Turner, Darwin. "A Spectrum of Blackness." *Parnassus: Poetry in Review* 5 (Spring/Summer 1976): 202-19.

Compares the work of Walker to that of Ishmael Reed. Praises her straight forward diction and presentation of the simple truths of human experience. The world of the poetry is a world broken up. Sees her as an individualist rejecting false militancy.

840.   Ward, Jerry W. *College Language Association Journal* 17
         (September 1973): 127-29.

         Sees the collection as a major poetic achievement, especially
         in its use of Walker's black Southern roots. "The promising
         seeds she planted in *Once* (1968) have blossomed into poems
         of extraordinary grace, wisdom, and strength." They provide
         hopeful strategies for humanity.

841.   Ward, Jerry W. "Five Contemporary Black Poets." *Obsidian* 1
         (Spring 1975): 88-97.

         Emphasizes the virtues of organization, economy, and
         craftsmanship, with simple syntax and short lines. Points out
         themes of individual experience and the value of ancestral
         wisdom in times of loss.

THE THIRD LIFE OF GRANGE COPELAND

BOOKS

842.   Banks, Thomas. *Masterplots II: American Fiction Series*, Volume
         4. Edited by Frank N. Magill, 1629-1634. Englewood Cliffs,
         New Jersey: Salem Press, 1986.

         A summary and analysis of Walker's novel *The Third Life of
         Grange Copeland.*

843.   Ensslen, Klaus. "Collective Experience and Individual
         Responsibility: Alice Walker's *The Third Life of Grange
         Copeland*." In *The Afro-American Novel Since 1960*. Edited
         by Peter Bruck and Wolfgang Karrer, 189-218. Amsterdam: B.

R. Gruner, 1982.

Analyzes the differences between Grange and Brownfield. Emphasizes Brownfield's role as self-hating victim. Sees both men as functions in the novel, one positive and the other negative. Grange demonstrates the dangers of isolation from collective experience. Female characters serve a different programmatic function; they serve as targets of brutalization. Even when folk material is introduced, its use is individual rather than collective. Grange's training of Ruth illustrates this. The focus in the novel is on individual moral regeneration. Points out a didactic deep structure of moral options: self-abandonment, defensive escape, or self-transcendence.

844.   Harris, Trudier. *Exorcising Blackness: Historical and Literary Lynching and Burning Rituals*, 35-37, 192, 193. Bloomington, Indiana: Indiana University Press, 1984.

Places the male characters of the novel in the tradition of characters in black literature who have been emasculated. Argues that Walker uses Grange and Brownfield to show the destructive effects of a system of exploitation which robs black males of any sense of manhood. Notes also that, compared to male writers, Walker is much more concerned with the psychological than the physical effects of mistreatment.

845.   Hogue, W. Lawrence. "History, the Feminist Discourse, and *The Third Life of Grange Copeland*." In *Discourse and the Other: The Production of the Afro-American Text*, 86-106. Durham: Duke University Press, 1986.

Sees this novel as a feminist text which explores how and why women receive certain kinds of treatment. The discursive facts of the text are their conditions and their interrelationships. The novels theme is that the American social structure dehumanizes the black man and makes him violent toward his family. The image of the black woman as victim runs counter to the common image of her as enduring. Grange himself is a transformed discursive fact who solves the problem of how to humanize the victim; he does this by combining roles as nurturer and protector. Nonetheless, the text often violates character in order to make its feminist argument. As an example Brownfield is never given an opportunity to develop, yet he is blamed for not doing so. In this novel, Walker does not allow mature men and women to share the same textual space.

846. Schulz, Elizabeth. "Free in Fact and at Last: The Image of the Black Woman in Black American Literature." *What Manner of Woman: Essays on English and American Life and Literature*. Edited by Marlene Springer, 316-44. New York: New York University Press, 1977.

Reads the novel as the joint coming-of-age of Grange and Ruth, with the message that black women can prosper only when black men stop brutalizing them. When Grange becomes a nurturer, then Ruth can learn from his experience and wisdom to make for herself a self-sufficient life.

847. Southgate, Robert L. *Black Plots and Black Characters: A Handbook for Afro-American Literature*, 167-68. Syracuse, New York: Gaylord Professional Publications, 1979.

Discusses Walker's *The Third Life of Grange Copeland* in reference to plot summary and characters.

848. White, Vernessa C. "*The Third Life of Grange Copeland* and *Meridian*: The Southern Experience and the Evolution of Black American Consciousness." In *Afro-American and East German Fiction: A Comparative Study of Alienation, Identity and the Development of Self*, 91-115. New York: Peter Lang, 1983.

See annotation #782.

DISSERTATION

849.   Hogue, Willie L. "To Saddle Time: Sociocriticism and the Afro-American Text". Dissertation Abstracts International, 41 (February 1981), 3581-A.

An abstract from *Dissertation Abstracts International* on the work of Hogue.

PERIODICAL ARTICLES

850.   Gaston, Karen C. "Women in the Lives of Grange Copeland." *College Language Association Journal* 24 (March 1981): 276-86.

Argues that, though men are the central characters of the novel, it is the female characters who determine the meaning of the novel. They are both foil and impetus to the male characters. Actions directed toward them reveal the relative evil and goodness of the men. Mem, Margaret, and Josie are complex characters in that their love often subverts their strength. Ruth ultimately redeems Grange through her love.

851.   Halio, Jay. "First and Last Things." *Southern Review* 9 (April 1973): 455-67.

Discusses the idea of loss in modern fiction. In Walker's novel this is rendered as the need to accept responsibility even in the context of oppression. Praises her for her "honest treatment of both past and present." Sees the book as controlled and eloquent.

852.   Harris, Trudier. "Violence in *The Third Life of Grange Copeland*." *College Language Association Journal* 19 (December 1975): 238-47.

Discusses Walker's attention to the violence that blacks direct against themselves. Examines the parallel cases of Grange and Brownfield. Shows that Brownfield chooses his condition and brings his family down to it, whereas Grange learns that violence should only be used to resist oppression. For Walker, violence is deliberate, not accidental, and thus her characters are not caught in a deterministic world. Spiritual qualities can overcome dehumanization.

853.   Hellenbrand, Harold. "Speech, After Silence: Alice Walker's *The Third Life*." *Black American Literature Forum* 20 (Spring-Summer 1986): 113-26.

Argues that Walker makes a distinction between works that focus on the black family and those that focus on racial confrontation. *The Third Life* deals with family, but its essential developments have to do with oppression. Silence is very important in the text as basis of fear and violence. Those prevented from speaking express themselves through violence. But violence also can lead to speech, as in Grange's stories to Ruth. The awareness of oppression leads him to prepare her for the world.

854.   Hogue, W. Lawrence. "History, the Feminist Discourse, and Alice Walker's *The Third Life of Grange Copeland*. *MELUS: The Journal of the Society for the Study of the Multi-Ethnic Literature of the United States* 12 (Summer 1985): 45-62.

Examines *The Third Life of Grange Copeland* as it relates in theory to the feminist discourse. Emphasizes his third life as more significant than his previous two life cycles. Explores the control that women have historically been denied over their lives and interpretation of that oppression.

855. McDonnell, Jane. "Contemporary Black Themes: Social, Historical, Hopeful." *Cross Currents* 21 (Fall 1971):469-75.

Gives brief biographical background on Walker. Reads the novel as a blues piece in which title character emerges triumphant. Praises author for letting characters tell the story. Emphasizes that book leads to a Black Power perspective.

856. Wandor, Michelene. "Family Sagas." *Books and Bookmen*, 42. October 1985.

Views Walker's novel as powerful, religious and spiritual. Compares it to a previous work *Meridian* in that its character, Ruth, "carries the burden of hope."

857. Willis, Susan. "Alice Walker's Women." *New Orleans Review* 12 (Spring 1985): 33-41.

See annotation #599.

BOOK REVIEWS

858. Coles, Robert. "To Try Men's Souls." *New Yorker*, 27 February 1971, 104-6.

Places the novel in the context of studies of blacks in the cities, as well as in their Southern rural origins, but feels that the book is not in the protest tradition. Praises Walker for her understanding and appreciation of the Southern environment. Sees her success in characterization rather than analysis of problems. "I suppose it can be said that *The Third Life of Grange Copeland*' is concerned with the directions a suffering people can take." Views the relationship of Grange and Ruth as especially effective.

859.   Cornish, Sam. Alice Walker: Her Own Woman." *Christian Science Monitor*, 3 February 1984, B 1.

See annotation #618.

860.   Cornish, Sam. "Review of *The Third Life of Grange Copeland*." *Essence*, April 1971, 2.

Attacks the tendency among reviewers and critics to ignore black writing if it is naturalistic. Views the novel as a story of family, with its members struggling to deal with their blackness. The focus on the tragedy of the black family "makes *The Third Life of Grange Copeland* one of the most important black novels we have."

861.   Davidon, Ann Morrisett. Review of "Third Life of Grange Copeland." *Win Magazine*, 1 June 1980, 10.

Ann Davidon contends that Walker's novel *The Third Life of Grange Copeland* affected her own life.

862.   Glastonbury, Marion. "Of the Fathers." *The New Statesman*, 4 October 1985, 28-29.

Summarizes the plot, focusing on Brownfield and Grange. Identifies two purposes for which Walker creates an optimistic ending: belief in the wisdom of oppressed ancestors and celebration of the slave narrative theme of triumph over oppression.

863.   Hairston, Loyle.   "Work of Rare Beauty and Power."
         Freedomways, 11 (Second Quarter 1971): 170-77.

         Makes a comparison of Walker with nineteenth-century
         Russian novelists, especially Maxim Gorky. The novel is a
         study of how the economic and social system dehumanizes
         men. Labels the ending optimistic. The flaws are contrived
         scenes and characters who mouth the ideas of the author.

864.   Hendin, Josephine. "Review of *The Third Life*." *Saturday Review*,
         22 August 1970, 55.

         Asserts that it is a novel with real heroes and villains,
         determined by their capacity for love or hate. Notes that
         while Walker makes Brownfield a villain, she never examines
         the inner sources of his evil.

865.   *Kirkus Review*, 1 July 1970, 711.

         Presents the plot as the history of Grange and his
         relationships with his family. "The pressures and responses of
         such beleaguered families are traced step by grim step, with
         stern sympathy and a clean, functional style."

866.   Kramer, Victor A. "Review of *The Third Life*." *Library Journal*
         95 (July 1970): 2522.

         Contends that the novel is about dreams and the ways they
         are crushed and sometimes saved. Identifies the central
         theme as the maintaining of dignity despite degradation. "This
         novel will be strong medicine for some, but it should have a
         cathartic value."

867.   Marcus, Greil. "January White Sale." *Rolling Stone*, 26 January
         1978, 55.

         Focuses on Mem as a heroic figure. Sees Walker's prose as

powerful, especially in scenes of violence. Quotes as unforgettable a scene in which Brownfield's children try to survive the psychological effects of his brutality.

868.   Marcus, Laura. "Feminism into Fiction: The Women's Press." *Times Literary Supplement*, 27 September 1985, 1070.

Discusses several works published by Britain's Women's Press, including *The Third Life of Grange Copeland*, *In Love and Trouble*, and *The Color Purple*. Interprets the latter as a fable whose unrealistic elements are therefore not jarring. Compliments the author for the technical versatility apparent in the collection of stories. Sees *Grange Copeland* as establishing key themes--individual responsibility, the power of love--to which Walker will consistently return. "Powerfully and lucidly written, only occasionally slipping into polemic, the novel has a compelling directness."

869.   Plumpp, Falvia D.   "Review of *The Third Life of Grange Copeland*." *Black Books Bulletin,* Fall 1971, 26-27.

Characterizes the novel as "philosophical or authoritative" and not entertaining. In reading Walker's work one has to *look* for the message which is always there.

870.   *Publishers Weekly*, 25 May 1970, 55.

Brief summary. "Alice Walker's graphic and authentic novel of black family life in the South--three generations of it--is moving, tender, true, and all too tragic."

871.   Schorer, Mark. "Novels and Nothingness." *American Scholar* 40 (Winter 1970-71): 169-70.

Argues the centrality of nothingness in the novel. Compares it to works by Dan Wakefield and Joan Didion. Says that Brownfield is the most fully developed character, though the book rejects what he stands for. Suggests that Walker still has technical weaknesses.

872. Shapiro, Paula Meinetz. "Pygmalion Reversed." *New Leader*, 25 January 1971, 19-20.

Views the book as essentially objective in point of view, presenting characters and situations and allowing readers to judge them. Compares the novel to Athol Fugard's play *Boesman and Lena* as stories of wives tormented by their husbands. Sees the only flaw as the inclusion of the civil rights workers.

873. "Teacher Writes Book, Assails White People." *Jet*, 3 September 1970, 31.

Notes that the novel confirms Walker's view that blacks must not depend on whites to make their lives better.

874. Theroux, Paul. "A Glimpse of Freedom." *Book World*, 13 September 1970, 2.

Summarizes the novel, finding the verbal confrontations more horrifying than the violence. Notes that the setting is carefully established. Sees weakness in the plotting of the book, strength in the characterizations.

875. Walker, Cam. "Review of *The Third Life of Grange Copeland*." *Southern Exposure* 5 (Spring 1977): 102-3.

See annotation #819.

876. Wandor, Michelene. "Family Sagas." Review of *The Third Life of Grange Copeland*. *Books and Bookmen*, October 1985, 42.

See annotation #857.

ALICE WALKER

YOU CAN'T KEEP A GOOD WOMAN DOWN

BOOKS

877.   Twum-Akwaboah, Edward. *"You Can't Keep a Good Woman Down."* In *Magill's Literary Annual, 1982: Essay - Reviews of 200 Outstanding Books Published in the United States During 1981*, Volume 2. Edited by Frank Magill, 976-80. Englewood Cliffs, New Jersey: Salem Press, 1982.

Attacks Walker for allowing her ideology to override coherence in this collection. Summarizes several of the pieces in order to demonstrate their feminist bias. "The book is written in a belligerent, racist language which, coupled with its confused welter of thoughts and actions, hampers the understanding and enjoyment of the reading". Selects "Coming Apart" and "Advancing Luna-and Ida B. Wells" for especially emphatic criticism.

BOOK REVIEWS

878.   Adams, Alice. "All About Women-Heroines and the Uneasy and Vulnerable." *San Francisco (California) Examiner,* 10 May 1981, F6-7.

Examines a few of the stories with the collection, *You Can't Keep a Good Woman Down.* Discusses "Source," "Nineteen Fifty-Five," and "Coming Apart." Refers to Walker as a marvelous writer. (Newsbank)

879.   Brandmark, Wendy. *"You Can't Keep a Good Woman Down."* *Africa,* June 1982, 70.

168

See annotation #796.

880.   Connor, Elizabeth. *"You Can't Keep a Good Woman Down."* *Library Journal* 106 (15 April 1981):905.

Asserts that love unifies the stories, even when they address social and political issues. Finds the characters "endearing and compelling." "Walker's cadent style of writing is irresistible: her words stick to your ribs."

881.   Cornish, Sam. "Alice Walker: Her Own Woman." *Christian Science Monitor*, 3 February 1984, B 1.

See annotation #618.

882.   DeRamus, Betty. "Her Women Are Strong and Joyful." *Detroit (Michigan) Free Press*, 24 May 1981, F8.

Examines this collection of short stories which she characterizes as "stand-up and shout stories." "Nineteen-fifty-five", reviewer believes, is the strongest story in the collection. (Newsbank)

883.   Gilbert, Harriet. *"You Can't Keep a Good Woman Down."* *New Statemen*, 30 July 1982, 21.

Points out that the issues dealt with are concrete in the lives of black women: rape, pornography, passing. Compares the stories with the best *New Yorker* fiction: "tangy with intellectual and imaginative confidence."

884.   James, C. L. R. "Sexual Relations." *Race Today*, May/June 1982, 111-12.

Acknowledges that he is troubled by the collection because he cannot identify its fictional purpose. Sees it as exploring the fictional lives of the black middle class, which he considers an uninteresting topic. Is especially disappointed since he admires Walker's earlier work.

885. Johnson, Bonnie. "Self-determination and Self-affirmation." *New Directions for Women*, September 1981, 15.

Points out that Walker considers this collection "the second cycle," since it is an affirmative response to the theme of self-destructiveness in *In Love and Trouble*. Sees the stories as involved in the author's "deep probing for truth." "Through her fiction, Walker struggles with the contradictions of several moral situations not promulgating answers but leading the discussion."

886. Marshment, Margaret. "You Can't Keep a Good Woman Down." *Race and Class* 25 (Fall 1983): 91.

See annotation #638.

887. Morris, Deb. *"You Can't Keep a Good Woman Down."* *Off Our Backs* 13 (April 1983): 16.

Summarizes several stories from *You Can't Keep a Good Woman Down*. Describes *The Color Purple* as "a wondrous book interweaving characters' lives in surprising ways."

888. Naylor, Carolyn. *"You Can't Keep a Good Woman Down."* *Black Scholar*, Spring 1982, 84-85.

Claims that Walker has reshaped short fiction by blending fiction and history. Identifies "Advancing Luna--and Ida B. Wells," "The Abortion," "Coming Apart," and "Porn" as most characteristic of the experimental mode developed. "It is a powerful, evocative collection which must be read."

889. Piercy, Marge. "Little Nuances of History." *Book World*, 31 May 1981, 11.

Emphasizes humor in several of the stories. Finds "1955" especially good, though some of the more serious pieces are praised as well. "If I had to select one adjective for these stories, I would say sophisticated in the best sense of the word."

890.   Pollitt, Katha. *New York Times Book Review*, 24 May 1981, 9, 15.

Congratulates Walker for addressing some of the major racial and sexual issues in her fiction. The more conventional stories in the collection have authority and effective detail. The political pieces are more innovative in technique but are less effective as fiction.

891.   Postell, Charlene. "Walker's Voyage of Self-Discovery." *Des Moines (Iowa) Register*, 29 August 1982, D6.

Sees *The Color Purple* as work of "self-discovery." Compares Walker's novel to Richard Wright's *The Long Dream*. (Newsbank)

892.   Rumens, Carol. "Heirs to the Dream." *Times Literary Supplement*, 18 June 1982, 676.

See annotation #815.

893.   Seidenbaum, Art. "Make Shelf Room for Alice Walker." *Los Angeles (California) Times,* 29 April 1981, F5.

Reviewer suggest that this collection would be great on any reader's book shelf. Discusses "Nineteen fifty-five," "How Did I Get Away With Killing One of the Biggest Lawyers in the State? It Was Easy," "Laurel," and "Source." (Newsbank)

894.   Wilson, Judith. "Main Events." *Essence*, July 1981, 17.

Views Walker's work as traditional in that it communicates moral and political messages, but revisionist in the content of the messages. Prefers the stories that are less overtly political. *"You Can't Keep a Good Woman Down* is ambitious, frustrating, and often disturbing, but Walker redeems herself by offering sharp insight into the familiar themes we tend to overlook because they are so close to home."

895. *"You Can't Keep a Good Woman Down." ABR*, May 1982, 9.

896. *"You Can't Keep a Good Woman Down."* "New in Paperback." *Book World*, 2 May 1982, 12.

On occasion of paperback publication, cites Marge Piercy's earlier review.

897. *"You Can't Keep a Good Woman Down." Booklist*, 1 April 1981, 1080.

Says that all the stories deal with love and/or self-expression, with a definite black point of view. Notes that anger is apparent, though it never becomes polemic.

898. *"You Can't Keep a Good Woman Down." Kirkus Review*, 1 March 1981, 309.

Criticizes the collection as didactic and thin. Finds the more traditional pieces obvious and the experimental ones largely propaganda and sociological debate. "Ragged, often superficial work, then--with more sociological interest (the black/feminist intersection) than literary."

899. *"You Can't Keep a Good Woman Down." Kliatt*, Fall 1982, 30.

Identifies issues of pornography and oppression as central to the stories. Questions Walker's tendency to be social critic rather than fictionist, but says that her senses of humor often saves the work.

900.   *"You Can't Keep a Good Woman Down."* "Paperbacks: News and Noteworthy." *New York Times Book Review*, 11 April 1982, 27.

Divides the collection into stories that create versions of the "good woman" of the title and others that are focused on issues. Quotes Katha Pollitt's earlier praise of the book.

901.   *"You Can't Keep a Good Woman Down."* *Publishers Weekly*, 20 March 1981, 56.

Says that the stories probe the meaning of being black and female and that such probing leads to universality of meaning. Selects the stories on rape and abortion as especially effective. Misnames the author "Alice Adams."

CRITICISM OF SHORT STORIES

THE CHILD WHO FAVORED DAUGHTER

BOOKS

902.   Mickelson, Anne Z. *Reaching Out: Sensitivity and Order in Recent American Fiction by Women*, 158-59. Metuchen, New Jersey: Scarecrow Press, 1979.

See annotation #693.

ALICE WALKER

PERIODICAL ARTICLES

903. Harris, Trudier. "Tiptoeing Through Taboo: Incest in 'The Child Who Favored Daughter'." *Modern Fiction Studies* 28 (Autumn 1982): 495-505.

Notes that incest has generally not been an acceptable topic for black writers; the few exceptions are in works by Ralph Ellison, James Baldwin, and Toni Morrison. In "The Child Favored Daughter," incestuous sexuality poisons the atmosphere even though it is never enacted. The central character obsessively loves his sister, but this love turns to hatred for all women, including his daughter, for whom he feels latent sexual desire. Walker creates within the story substitutions for incest and evades direct confrontation with the issue.

THE DIARY OF AN AFRICAN NUN

PERIODICAL ARTICLES

904. *Black Fiction: New Studies in the Afro-American Novel Since 1945.* Edited by A. Robert Lee, 188-89. New York: Barnes and Noble, 1980.

Critiques Walker's short story "Diary of an African Nun." Critic feels Walker should have used a different form to tell this story.

905.   Fontenot, Chester J. "'The Diary of an African Nun' and W. E.
         B. Du Bois' double consciousness." *Journal of Afro-American
         Issues* 5 (Spring 1977): 192-96.

         Views contemporary black artists entrapped in a form of
         double consciousness, between literary traditions and black
         nationalist ideology. The story represents the issue by placing
         the nun of the title between African traditions and European
         religion.

906.   O'Leary, Donald J. "On 'The Diary of an African Nun', Rev.
         Donald J. O'Leary's Reaction to the story and Alice Walker's
         Reply to His Reaction." *Freedomways* 9 (Winter 1969): 70-73.

         On the appearance of Walker's short story "The Diary of an
         African Nun," Reverend Donald J. O'Leary gave his reaction
         to the story. Freedomways published his reaction and Alice
         Walker's reply.

EVERYDAY USE

BOOKS

907.   *Black Fiction: New Studies in the Afro-American Novel Since
         1945.* Edited by A. Robert Lee, 184-186. New York: Barnes
         and Noble, 1980.

         Discusses Walker's short story "Everyday Use", as it relates to
         culture and identity.

908.   Mickelson, Anne Z. *Reaching Out: Sensitivity and Order in
         Recent American Fiction by Women*, 159. Metuchen, New

Jersey: Scarecrow Press, 1979.

See annotation #693.

909.   Rosinsky, Natalie M.   "Mothers and Daughters: Another
        Minority Group."   In *The Lost Tradition: Mothers and
        Daughters in Literature*. Edited by Cathy N. Davidson and E.
        M. Broner, 284. New York: F. Ungar Publishing Company,
        1980.

        Explores the characters, Dee, Maggie, and Mrs. Johnson and
        their mother-daughter relationships in "Everyday Use."

910.   Ross, Diane M. *Masterplots II: Short Story Series*, Volume 2.
        Edited by Frank N. Magill, 731-34. Englewood Cliffs, New
        Jersey: Salem Press, 1986.

        Explores the themes and symbols Walker uses in this short
        story "Everyday Use." The use of the quilt is very symbolic to
        the message of confusion of past heritage for Dee, one of the
        characters. This source gives brief summary of plot and
        meanings of the story and techniques used by Walker.

911.   Yancy, Preston. *Afro-American Short Story: A Comprehensive,
        Annotated Index with Commentaries*, 70-71. Westport, Conn.:
        Greenwood Press, 1986.

        Provides a summary of the story's plot and a brief analysis.

PERIODICAL ARTICLES

912.   Baker, Houston A. and Charlotte Pierce-Baker. "Patches: Quilts
        and Community in Alice Walker's 'Everyday Use'." *Southern*

Review 21 (Summer 1985): 706-720.

Discusses the patch as a metaphor for both loss and potential design. Sees the quiltmaker as a figure for the woman novelist who takes bits and pieces of marginal humanity to make her art. Emphasizes the communal nature of quilting and the quilts as an emblem of difference. The story takes on the significance of ritual, with the crafting of quilts as the making of the self. The insight in the story is in the mother's recognition of the value of that which is ignored or rejected, as in her second daughter.

913.   Forrey, Carolyn. "Women's Heritage: The Question of 'Everyday Use.'" *Animia* 1 (Fall 1976): 45-52.

Uses Walker's story "Everyday Use" as the basis for discussion of the theme of heritage in women's fiction of the nineteenth and twentieth centuries.

914.   Kane, Patricia. *Notes on Contemporary Literature* 15 (March 1985): 7.

Views the short story as part of the tradition of prodigal child narratives. Notes Walker's reversal of the tradition in the embrace of the child who stayed instead of the one who left.

HER SWEET JEROME

BOOKS

915.   Mickelson, Anne Z. *Reaching Out: Sensitivity and Order in Recent Fiction by Women*, 156-57. Metuchen, New Jersey: Scarecrow Press, 1979.

ALICE WALKER

See annotation #693.

REALLY, DOESN'T CRIME PAY?

BOOKS

916.   *Black Fiction: New Studies in the Afro-American Novel Since 1945*. Edited by A. Robert Lee, 182-84. New York: Barnes and Noble, 1980.

Discusses some of the strengths of Walker's short story.

917.   Mickelson, Anne Z. *Reaching Out: Sensitivity and Order in Recent American Fiction by Women*, 154-74. Metuchen, New Jersey: Scarecrow Press, 1979.

See annotation #693.

REVENGE OF HANNAH KEMHUFF

918.   *Black Fiction: New Studies in the Afro-American Novel Since 1945*. Edited by A. Robert Lee, 186. New York: Barnes and Noble, 1980.

Analyzes this short story as Walker's interpretation of religion.

CRITICISM OF INDIVIDUAL WORKS

ROSELILY

BOOKS

919.   *Black Fiction: New Studies in the Afro-American Novel Since 1945*. Edited by A. Robert Lee, 181-82. New York: Barnes and Noble, 1980.

A brief analysis of the short story, "Roselily" and the use of simple vocabulary.

920.   Mickelson, Anne Z. *Reaching Out: Sensitivity and Order in Recent American Fiction by Women*, 155. Metuchen, New Jersey: Scarecrow Press, 1979.

See annotation #693.

STRONG HORSE TEA

BOOKS

921.   Forman, Robert J. *Masterplots II: Short Story Series*, Volume 5. Edited by Frank N. Magill, 2259-61. Englewood Cliffs, New Jersey: Salem Press, 1986.

An analysis of Walker's short story "Strong Horse Tea" in addition to a summary.

922.   Mickelson, Anne Z. *Reaching Out: Sensitivity and Order in Recent American Fiction by Women*, 157-58. Metuchen, New Jersey: Scarecrow Press, 1979.

See annotation #693.

TO HELL WITH DYING

BOOKS

923.   Mickelson, Anne Z. *Reaching Out: Sensitivity and Order in Recent American Fiction by Women*, 159-160. Metuchen, New Jersey: Scarecrow Press, 1979.

See annotation #693.

924.   Yancy, Preston. *Afro-American Short Story: A Comprehensive, Annotated Index with Commentaries*, 57-58.   Westport, Connecticutt: Greenwood Press, 1986.

Discusses the short story "To Hell With Dying" and its themes of death and aging.

THE WELCOME TABLE

BOOKS

CRITICISM OF INDIVIDUAL WORKS

925. *Black Fiction: New Studies in the Afro-American Novel Since 1945*. Edited by A. Robert Lee, 187-188. New York: Barnes and Noble, 1980.

Religious aspects are explored in Walker's short story "The Welcome Table."

926. Yancy, Preston. *Afro-American Short Story: A Comprehensive, Annotated Index with Commentaries*, 66. Westport, Connecticut: Greenwood Press, 1986.

Examines Walker's short story "The Welcome Table" as it relates to church segregation during that time.

BIBLIOGRAPHIES

927. *Afro-American Fiction, 1853-1976: a Guide to Information Sources*. Edited by Edward Margolies and David Bakish, Volume 25, 96, 100-1. Detroit: Gale Research Company, 1979.

This bibliography lists two works which has information about Alice Walker.

928. *Afro-American Poetry and Drama,1760-1975: A Guide to Information Sources*. Edited by William P. French, Michel J. and Genevieve Fabre, and Amritjit Singh, 239. Detroit: Gale Research Company.

A brief review of *Meridian* giving summary and contending that novels like *Meridian* keep the memory of this period alive.

ALICE WALKER

929.   "The Afro-American Short Story". Compiled by Preston M. Yancy, 147-51. Westport, Connecticut: Greenwood Press, 1986.

Lists short stories written by Alice Walker with brief summaries in addition to sources where stories can be found.

930.   *Black American Writers Past and Present: A Biographical and Bibliographical Dictionary*. Edited by Theressa Rush, Carol Myers and Esther Arata, Volume 2, 727-29. Metuchen, New Jersey: Scarecrow Press, 1975.

Briefly gives background information on Alice Walker's education, career, awards and honors. The list selected critical sources of her writings in addition to listing some of her writings.

931.   *The Black Family and the Black Women: a Bibliography*. Compiled by Phyllis R. Klotman and Wilmer H. Baatz, 128-9. New York: Arno Press, 1978.

The bibliography contains sources by and about Alice Walker.

932.   Clark, Edward. *Black Writers in New England: A Bibliography with Biographical Notes of Books By and About Afro-American Writers Associated with New England in the Collection of Afro-American Literature*, 65. Boston: National Park Service, 1985.

Walker is included on list of New England writers. A selected bibliography of her works is also included.

933.   Fairbanks, Carol, and Eugene A. Engeldinger. *Black American Fiction: a Bibliography*. 278-80. Metuchen, New. Jersey: Scarecrow Press, 1978.

A short bibliography of Walker's works, with listing of where to find some of her short stories. Also included are a representative number of books and articles about her life and work.

934. Fairbanks, Carol. *More Women in Literature: Criticism of the Seventies*, 380-82. Metuchen, New Jersey: Scarecrow Press, 1979.

Brief bibliography of her works and listing of information sources.

935. Guy, Patricia A. *Women's Poetry Index*, 51. Phoenix, Arizona: Oryx Press, 1985.

Contains a list of eleven poems written by Alice Walker, giving collections or source in which each poem is found.

936. *In Black and White*. Edited by Mary Mace Spalding, 3rd edition, 993. Detroit: Gale Research Company, 1980.

Brief list of sources on Alice Walker.

937. Kirschner, Susan. "Alice Walker's Nonfictional Prose: A Checklist, 1966-1984." *Black American Literature Forum*, 18 (Winter 1984): 18, 162-63.

A compilation of Walker's essays, reviews, interviews, letters and miscellaneous writings.

938. Minudri, Regina U. "Books for Young Adults (*In Love and Trouble*)." *School Library Journal*, 15 December 1973, 34.

Characterizes *In Love and Trouble* as a "magnificent collection" of short stories related to women and especially black women.

939. "Notable Children's Trade Books in the Field of Social Studies." *Social Education*, March 1975, 172-73.

ALICE WALKER

This annotated bibliography of children's books in the field of social studies includes the biography of Langston Hughes by Alice Walker. Books on the list were published in the years 1973 and 1974.

940. Pettus, Eloise S. *Master Index to Summaries of Children's Books, Volume I: A-Z*, 969. Metuchen, New Jersey: Scarecrow Press, Inc., 1985.

Lists Alice Walker's *Langston Hughes, American Poet*.

941. *The Reader's Adviser: A Layman's Guide to Literature*. Edited by Fred Kaplan. *The Best in American And British Fiction, Poetry, Essays, Literary Biography and Bibliography, and Reference*, 13th Edition, volume 1, 632. New York: R.R. Bowker, 1986.

Walker's *In Search of Our Mother's Gardens* is listed in Chapter 16 of Feminist Criticism.

942. *Selected Black American Authors: An Illustrated Bio-Bibliography*, compiled by James A. Page, 276-77. Boston: G. K. Hall, 1977.

A brief biographical sketch in addition to career and professional accomplishments mentioned. A list of sources are also given.

943. *Short Story Index Supplement 1969-1973: An Index to 11,561 Stories in 805 Collections*. Edited by Estelle A. Fidell, 563. New York: H. W. Wilson, 1974.

Lists many of Walker's short stories found in other short story collections.

944. *Short Story Index Supplement 1974-1978: An Index to Stories in Collections and Periodicals*. Edited by Gary L. Bogart, 713. New York: H. W. Wilson, 1979.

Lists many of Walker's short stories and where to find them in short story collections.

945. *Short Story Index Supplement 1979-1983: An Index to Stories in Collections and Periodicals.* Edited by Juliette Yaakov, 813. New York: H.W. Wilson, 1984.

Lists many of Walker's short shories found in other collections of short stories.

946. *Short Story Index Supplement, 1985 Annual: An Index to Stories in Collections and Periodicals.* Edited by Juliette Yaakov, 219. New York: H.W. Wilson, 1986.

Lists Walker's short stories: "Cuddling", "Everyday Use" and "Kindred Spirits" and where to find them in other collections.

947. *Short Story Index Supplement, 1986: An Index to Stories in Collections and Periodicals.* Edited by Juliette Yaakov, 204. New York: H.W. Wilson, 1987.

Lists Walker's short stories: "The Abortion", "Kindred Spirits" and "Strong Horse Tea."

948. Stanford, Barbara Dodds and Karima Amin. *Black Literature for High School Students,* 88-90. Urbana, Illinois: National Council of Teachers of English, 1978.

Published by the National Council of Teachers of English students this source lists Alice Walker's works recommended for high school students.

949. Stetson, Erlene. *Black Sister: Poetry by Black American Women, 1946-1980,* 311. Bloomington: Indiana University Press, 1981.

A selected list of Alice Walker's works.

ALICE WALKER

950. Stevenson, Rosemary. "Black Women in the United States/a Bibliography." *Black Scholar*, March/April 1985, 45, 47-49.

Lists sources which include Alice Walker as author and also sources of information.

951. Walker, Alice. "Who's Reading What: 45 Books That Changed 16 Minds." *Ms.* July 1977, p.33.

Sixteen individuals give the titles of books they have read recently. Alice Walker lists three.

952. Ward, Jerry W. "Selected Bibliography for the Study of Southern Black Literature in the Twentieth Century." *Southern Quarterly* 23, (Winter 1985): 94-115.

This bibliography includes the novels and collections of short stories and poetry of Alice Walker.

UNVERIFIED SOURCES

953. Alladi, Uma Kuppuswami. *Woman and Her Family: Indian and Afro American: A Literary Perspective*. Ph.D. diss., State University of New York at Buffalo,

954. Awkward, Michael. *A Circle of Sisters*. Ph.D. diss., University of Pennsylvania, 1986, 257 pp.

955. Basaninyenz, Gatsinzi. *Ideology and Four Post-1960 Afro-American Novelists*. Ph.D. diss., University of Iowa, 1986, 316 pp.

956. Bogrem, Joy Gould. *Glamour*, March 1986, 235-36.

957. Braun, Ute Kerstin. *The Living Extension of a Tradition: The White Woman in Afro-American Fiction*. Ph.D. diss., State University of New York at Stony Brook, 1984, 355 pp.

958. Campbell, James. "The Color Rosy." *Times Literary Supplement*, 11 July 1986, 762.

959. Collier, Aldore. *Jet*, 10 March 1986, 58-60.

960. Cooper, Barbara Eck. *The Difficult Arts of Family Life: The Creative Force in the Domestic Fictions of Six Contemporary Women Novelists*. Ph.D. diss., University of Missouri-Columbia, 1986, 208 pp.

961. Dirda, Michael. "In Praise of Poetry." *Book World*, 9 November 1979, 11.

962. Dixon, Melvin. *The American Book Review* 4 (May 1982):9-10.

963. Eaglen, Audrey. *Voice of Youth Advocates* 8 (April 1985): 70.

964. Everson, Susan Corey. *Bodyself: Women's Bodily Experience in Recent Feminist Theology and Women's Literature*. Ph.D. diss., University of Minnesota, 1984, 322 pp.

965. Foster, Frances S. *You May Plow Here: The Narrative of Sara Brooks*. Edited by Thordis Simonsen. *New York Times Book Review*, 9 March 1986, 25.

966. Harding, William Harry. *Westways* 76 (January 1984): 68-69.

967. Ingram, Elwanda Deloris. *Black Women: Literary Self-Portraits*. Ph.D. diss., University of Oregon, 1980.

968. Jones, Nancy Baker. *On Solid Ground: The Emergence of the*

Self-Created Woman in Contemporary American Literature. Ph.D. diss., University of Texas at Austin, 1986, 411 pp.

969. Kearns, Katherine Sue. *Some Versions of Violence in Three Contemporary American Novels: John Irving's The World According to Garp, Tim O'Brien's Going After Cacciato, and Alice Walker's The Color Purple.* Ph.D. diss., University of North Carolina at Chapel Hill, 1982, 212 pp.

970. Kehr, Dave. "Call of the Wild." *American Film* 12 (December 1986): 43-46 ff.

971. Kennedy, Harlan. "Amazon Grace." *Film Comment* 22 (September-October 1986): 9-15.

972. Koolish, Lynda Lee. *A Whole New Poetry Beginning Here: Contemporary American Women Poets.* (Volume 1 and 11) Ph.D. diss., Stanford University, 1981, 847 pp.

973. Kopkind, Andrew. "Films." *The Nation*, 1 February 1986, 124-25.

974. "Let Us Now Praise Unsung Writers." *Mother Jones*, January 1986, 27.

975. Lowe, Cynthia. *Black Book Bulletin*, Winter 1976, 60-61.

976. Macaffery, Larry. *Los Angeles Times Book Review*, 20 April 1986, 15.

977. Marcus, Jane. Chicago 30 (April 1981): 107-108.

978. Martin, Odette Ewell. *Curriculum and Response: A Study of the Images of the Black Woman in Black Fiction.* Ph.D. diss., University of Chicago, 1980.

979. Mathews, Jack. "Spielberg Upstages Oscar Race." *Los Angeles*

Times, 7 February 1986, 6:1.

980.   Modleski, Tanya. *The Minnesota Review* 23 (Fall 1984): 194-95.

981.   Moore, Trudy. "Danny Glover: William in Color Purple is a Kind Family Man." *Jet*, 17 March 1986, 28-31.

982.   Murray, G. E. *Fiction International*, June/July 1976, 171-72.

983.   O'Meally, Robert G. "The Cosmic Zora." *Book World*, 30 December 1979, 12.

984.   Page, James and Jae Roh. *Selected American, African, and Caribbean Authors: A Bio-Bibliography*,282-83. Littleton, Colorado: *Libraries Unlimited*, 1985.

985.   Pally, Marcia. "Women in Love." *Film Comment*, April 1986, 35-39.

986.   Pinckney, Darryl. "Black Victims, Black Villains." *New York Review of Books*, 29 January 1987, 17-20.

987.   Review of *Meridian*. *Progressive* 40 (October 1976):60.

988.   Richards, Johnetta. "Zora Neale Hurston: A Literary Biography." *Freedomways* 18 (1978): 170-72.

989.   Rolfe, Rebecca. "Honors for Alice Walker", *Atlanta*, June 1984, 30 ff.

990.   Scruggs-Rodgers, Emma. *Sepia*, May 1982, 18.

991.   Shipley, William M. "History's Phoenix: The Black Woman in Literature," *Journal of Caribbean Studies* 4 (February/March 1984): 15-24.

992.   Sorel, Nancy. "A New Look at Noble Suffering." *New York*

ALICE WALKER

Times Book Review, 26 January 1986, 1 ff.

993. Staples, Brent. "Media-Lashed and Sex-Listed." *New York Times*, 23 March 1986, 11.

994. Toombs, Charles Phillip. *For My People: The Development of Self in Afro-American Fiction--The Example of Alice Walker*. Ph.D. diss., Purdue University, 1986, 283 pp.

995. Varga-Cole, Barbara Jean. *The Novels of Black American Women*. Ph.D. diss., State University of New York at Stony Brook, 1981, 229 pp.

996. Wade-Gayles, Gloria Jean. *The Narrow Space and the Dark Enclosure: Race and Sex in the Lives of Black Women in Selected Novels Written by Black Women*. Ph.D. diss., Emory University, 1981, 359 pp.

997. Walsh, Chad. "A Present Rooted in the Past." *Book World*, 3 November 1968, 20.

998. Whitelaw, Nancy. "Where Have the Good Children's Biographies Gone?" *Christian Science Monitor*, 13 May 1983, B7.

999. Wilentz, Gay Alden. *From Africa to America: Cultural Ties That Bind in the Works of Contemporary African and African-American Women Writers*. Ph.D. diss., University of Texas at Austin, 1986, 330 pp.

1000. "Writers are Picking Up the Pieces and Then Regrouping at the Front Lines: (Afro-American Writers)." *Black Enterprise* 16 (August 1985):130.

INDEX

Numbers represent citations rather than pagination.

A

B

C

389, 392, 393, 394, 398, 399, 400, 405, 406, 407,
411, 412, 414, 415, 416, 417, 418, 420, 422, 423,
424, 425, 426, 427, 428, 431, 433, 435, 438, 442,
443, 444, 446, 452, 454, 455, 457, 458, 461, 462,
463, 464, 465, 469, 470, 473, 475, 476, 477, 478,
482, 483, 484, 486, 487, 490, 491, 492, 493, 494,
495, 496, 497, 500, 506, 507, 508, 514, 517, 518,
519, 520, 521, 522, 525, 526, 530, 532, 534, 539,
540, 541, 544, 546, 602, 608,
"Coming Apart" 11, 236, 237, 238, 877, 878, 888
Commire, Anne 368
Connelly, Sherryl 418
Connor, Elizabeth 880
Conyus 419
Cooke, Michael G. 346, 781, 800
Cooper, Barbara Eck 960
Corliss, Richard 420
Cornish, Sam 618, 704, 739, 801, 823, 829, 859, 860,
881
Crumpler, David 422
Curtright, Bob 423

D

Daniels, Gabrielle 740
Davidon, Ann Morrissett 741, 861
Davidson, Cathy N. 909
Davis, Bridgette 424, 425
Davis, Gwendolyn 830
Davis, Lisa 560
Davis, Marianna W. 345
Davis, Thadious M. 337, 348, 349, 573
DeBrossee, Jim 426
DeCosta-Willis, Miriam 742
DeRamus, Betty 882
Delta Sigma Theta 308
Derman, Lisa 619
"Diary of an African Nun" 5, 240, 241, 343, 904, 905,
906

Didion, Joan 705
Dirda, Michael 961
Disch, Tom 676
Dixon, Melvin 962
Dollard, Peter 831
Douglas, John 427
Dreyfuss, Joel 771
Duckworth, Victoria 574
Dworkin, Susan 575

E

Eaglen, Audrey 963
Early, Gerald 576
Ebory, Ann 339
Eder, Richard 743, 744
El Saffar, Ruth 577
Elliott, David 428
Emecheta, Buchi 330
Engeldinger, Eugene A. 933
Ensslen, Klaus 843
Erickson, Peter 429
Evans, Mari 335, 359
Everson, Susan Corey 964
"Everyday Use" 5, 244, 245, 246, 247, 248, 249, 250,
    251, 252, 537, 907, 908, 909, 910, 911, 912, 913,
    914
Evory, Ann 372
Exum, Pat Crutchfield 299

F

Fabre, Genevieve 928
Fabre, Michel J. 928
Fairbanks, Carol 933, 934
Fannin, Alice 250, 281, 578
Fidell, Estelle A. 943
Fifer, Elizabeth 561
Finn, James 430

Kinsman, Clare D. 338
Kirkpatrick, D. L. 355
Kirschner, Heidi 326
Kirschner, S. 937
Klotman, Phyllis R. 931
Koolish, Lynda Lee 972
Kopkind, Andrew 973
Koppelman, Susan 238, 251
Kramer, Victor A. 866
Krauth, Leland 584

L

LaBadie, Donald 469
Ladd, Susan, 470
Laguardia, Gari 560
Langston Hughes: American Poet 6, 769, 770, 771, 772,
773, 774, 775, 776, 777, 939, 940
Lapides, Frederick R. 132
Larson, Charles R. 806
"Laurel" 893
Leckey, Dolores 634
Lederer, Laura 236
Lee, A. Robert 778, 904, 907, 916, 918, 919,925
Leven, Carol 473
Lewis, Richard Gregory 474
Liebrum, Martha 749
Lipper, Hal 475
Lodge, Sally A. 635
Loftis, N. J. 301
Long, Richard 296
Lovell, Glenn 476
Low, Denise 681
Lowe, Cynthia 975
Lukens, Rebecca 250, 289
Lupton, Mary Jane 585
Lyman, Rick, 477

M

MaCaffery, Larry 976
McCreadie, Marsha 478
McDonnell, Jane 855
McDowell, Deborah E. 586, 750, 788
McDowell, Edwin 479, 480, 481
McFadden, Margaret 562
McGowan, Martha J. 789
McGrady, Mike 482
McGuigan, Cathleen 483
McKenzie, Tammie 587
McLellan, Joseph 713
Magill, Frank N. 332, 562, 564, 722, 779, 782, 842,
    877, 910, 921
Maginnis, Ruth 714
Mahar, Ted 484
Mainiero, Lina 354
Makowski, Elizabeth 485, 977
Mann, Catherine Hoyser 250, 289
Manna, Tony 715
Marcus, Greil 807, 867
Marcus, Laura 637, 868
Margolies, Edward 927
Marquez, Gabriel Garcia 321
Marr, Virginia W. 808
Mars-Jones, Adam 486
Marshment, Margaret 638, 886
Martin, Odette Ewell 978
Martin, Ruth 809
Mathews, Jack 979
Matney, William C. 356
Mellors, John 810
Mendelson, Phyllis Carmel 340, 341
Meridian 7, 8, 332, 336, 342, 344, 346, 353, 355, 357,
    371, 374, 384, 401, 421, 429, 552, 629, 778, 779,
    780, 781, 782, 783, 784, 785, 786, 787, 788, 789,
    790, 791, 792, 793, 794, 795, 796, 797, 798, 799,
    800, 801, 802, 803, 804, 805, 806, 807, 808, 809,
    810, 811, 812, 813, 814, 815, 816, 817, 818, 819,

Nower, Joyce 682
Nowik, Nan 589
Nyabongo, V. S. 716

O

Okri, Ben 757
O'Brien, John 554
O'Brien, Tom 497
Ogunyemi, Chikwenye Okonjo 590
O'Leary, Donald J. 906
Olson, Clarence E. 644
O'Meally, Robert G. 983
Once 1, 342, 364, 821, 822, 823, 824, 825, 826
One Child of One's Own" 13, 63, 64, 333, 740, 749
Osborne, Karen Lee 646

P

Page, James A. 942, 984
Pally, Marcia 985
Parini, Jay 758
Parker, Betty J. 373
Parker-Smith, Bettye J. 359
Pate, Nancy 759
Payne, James Robert 725
Peacock, Mary 812
Peden, William 498
Pemberton, Gayle R. 471
Pennington, Dorothy 760
Perry, Claudia 499
Perry, Ruth 723
Persico, Joyce J. 500
Petrie, Phil W. 647
Petry, Alice Hall 360
Pettus, Eloise S. 940
Pfeffer, Susan Beth 717
Pierce-Baker, Charlotte 912
Piercy, Marge 813, 889

R

Roh, Jae M. 984
Rolfe, Rebecca 989
Rollock, Barbara 769
"Roselily" 5, 279, 537, 919, 920
Rosenberg, L. M. 683
Rosenfelt, Debby 718
Rosenfield, Megan 509, 510
Rosinsky, Natalie M. 909
Ross, Diane M. 910
Ross, Michelle 511, 512, 513, 545
Rothenstein, Richard 514
Royster, Philip M. 592
Rumens, Carol 815, 892
Rush, Theressa 930

S

Sadoff, Dianne F. 515
Sage, Lorna 816
Sague, Maria 516
Salamon, Julie 517
Salzman, Jack 365
Samway, Patrick 286
Sanchez, Sonia 257
Schaefer, Jay 651
Scheick, William J. 561
Schorer, Mark 871
Schulz, Elizabeth 846
Schwartz, Karen 765
Scott, Patricia Bell 333
Scruggs-Rodgers, Emma 990
See, Carolyn 652
Seidenbaum, Art 893
Shapiro, Paula Meinetz 872
Shelton, Frank W. 593
Shipley, William M. 991
Shockley, Ann A. 312, 367
Shorey, Kenneth 518
Silverman, Stephen 519

T

Tavormina, M. Teresa 595
Taylor, Clyde 596
Taylor, Daniel 564
Tennenhouse, Mary Ann 338
Theroux, Paul 874
Third Life of Grange Copeland 2, 332, 336, 343, 344,
352, 355, 371, 374, 429, 449, 451, 453, 502, 629,
637, 783, 789, 819, 842, 843, 844, 845, 846, 847,
848, 849, 850, 851, 852, 853, 854, 855, 856, 857,
858, 859, 860, 861, 862, 863, 864, 865, 866, 867,
868, 869, 870, 871, 872, 873, 874, 875, 876
Thomas, Joyce Carol 529
"To Hell With Dying" 5, 291, 292, 293, 294, 295, 296,
923, 934
Toombs, Charles Phillip 994
Toppman, Lawrence 530
Towers, Robert 656
Trescott, Jacqueline 531, 558
Turner, Darwin T. 313, 839
Twum-Akwaboah, Edward 877

U

Uglow, Jennifer S. 370

V

Varga-Cole, Barbara Jean 995
Vigderman, Patricia 767
Vincent, Mal 532

W

Wade-Gayles, Gloria 371, 791, 996
Walcott, Derek 323
Walker, Cam 819, 875
Walker, Robbie Jean 657
Walker, Scott 229
Wall, James M. 534

Y

Yaakov, Juliette 945, 946, 947
Yancy, Preston M. 911, 924, 926, 929
Yeoman, Barry 665
Yoder, Jan 715
You Can't Keep a Good Woman Down 11, 335, 344,
467, 618, 638, 641, 796, 802, 815, 877, 878, 879,
880, 881, 882, 883, 884, 885, 886, 887, 888, 889,
890, 891, 892, 893, 894, 895, 896, 897, 898, 899,
900, 901